ELEGANT COOKING
FOR PRACTICAL PEOPLE

Ever since *Woman's Day* started to publish the "Collector's Cook Book" as a monthly feature, the magazine has received countless requests for a permanent collection in one volume. Now here it is, attractively packaged and inexpensively priced in this special new Fawcett edition.

Anyone can become a wizard in the kitchen with this fascinating and unusual book. Each of the 1500 recipes has been meticulously tested in the famed *Woman's Day* Kitchens to insure foolproof results. Even the novice will be able to turn out exotic delights; the experienced cook will find new inspiration and challenge in the wide variety of foods offered.

If you want a cookbook that has everything—glamor, ease of preparation, economy, distinction and wonderfully successful results—this is it.

Woman's Day
COLLECTOR'S
COOK BOOK

Introduced by

JAMES BEARD

international authority on fine foods

Illustrated by JOSEPH LOW

A FAWCETT SPECIAL

FAWCETT PUBLICATIONS, INC., GREENWICH, CONN.
MEMBER OF AMERICAN BOOK PUBLISHERS COUNCIL, INC.

CONTENTS

APPETIZERS

Appetizers should tease the eye and taste buds just enough to pique one's interest in the dinner to follow and never be so heavy and filling that they dull the appetite. Here are some helpful rules for the hostess: don't try to prepare your entire repertoire of hors d'oeuvres for one party. If the cocktail hour is to be followed by dinner, serve at most two delicate, tasty appetizers, perhaps one hot and one cold. For the large cocktail party, an assortment of four or five hors d'oeuvres is plenty. Allow six to eight pieces of food per person. Add bowls of good nuts and olives and your guests can nibble as much as they like. Give stuffed eggs a piquant seasoning, cut them in quarters and serve them atop fingers of fried toast. Remember to keep crisp foods crisp (don't spread toast with a mixture which will make it soggy); keep cold foods cold (heap raw vegetables in an ice-filled bowl); and keep hot foods hot (put the hot dunk sauce in a chafing dish). Here are interesting appetizers to help the party hostess with her cocktail-hour menu.

POTATOES MAYONNAISE

You coat the potato cubes with mayonnaise and serve on toothpicks.

Boil 3 medium potatoes in their jackets, being careful not to overcook them, as they must not be mushy. Cool, peel, and cut in small cubes. Mix 2 tablespoons sour cream, ½ cup mayonnaise, dash curry powder, and salt and pepper. Carefully coat potatoes with this mixture. Serve on toothpicks. Makes 4 to 5 dozen.

CURRIED CHEESE

The cheese is blue cheese.

½ pound blue cheese	½ teaspoon Worcestershire
1 teaspoon curry powder	Mayonnaise
	Melba toast rounds

Mash cheese thoroughly. Add curry powder and Worcestershire, and enough mayonnaise to hold all together and form spreading consistency. It should be quite firm. Spread on Melba toast rounds. Makes about 1 cup.

SALMON-STUFFED EGGS

The salmon is blended with anchovies and the egg yolks.

10 hard-cooked eggs	½ cup butter or margarine
½ cup cooked or canned salmon	1 teaspoon Worcestershire
1 anchovy fillet	Salt and pepper

Shell eggs, and cut in half lengthwise. Take out yolks. Rub salmon, anchovy, and egg yolks through a sieve, or whirl in the blender. Cream butter. Add salmon mixture, Worcestershire, and seasonings to taste. Mix well. Stuff whites with the mixture. Makes 20.

BACON ROLLS

Bacon, cheese, and parsley rolled in bread, then broiled.

½ pound bacon	½ cup grated Parmesan cheese
24 thin slices very fresh white bread	¼ cup minced parsley
Butter	Paprika
	Cayenne

Cook bacon until crisp. Drain well on absorbent paper, and crumble well. Remove crusts from bread, and butter it. Down middle of each slice, put a line of crumbled bacon, and sprinkle with cheese and parsley. Sprinkle with paprika and a dash of cayenne. Roll up each slice like a cigarette, as tightly as possible, and fasten with a toothpick. Grill until brown. Makes 24.

CURRY PUFFS

Curried ginger-beef in pastry rounds.

2 garlic cloves, mashed	2 tablespoons butter
1 slice ginger root, mashed	½ pound ground beef
1½ tablespoons minced onion	1 tablespoon lime juice
1½ tablespoons curry powder (or more to taste)	½ teaspoon salt
	1 recipe plain pastry, made with half butter, half lard

Fry garlic, ginger root, onion, and curry powder together in butter 5 minutes. Add meat, and stir constantly until it loses its red color. Add lime juice and salt, and mix well. Roll out pastry, and cut into 2″ rounds. Place a bit of meat mixture on one round, and cover with another, pinching edges well to hold them together. Bake on cookie sheet in very hot oven, 450°F., 15 minutes, or until nicely browned. Makes about 24.

HAM-AND-CHEESE BITES

Boiled-ham and Mozzarella slices sautéed in butter.

Remove crusts from 6 slices white bread. Slice thin 1 package (8 ounces) Mozzarella cheese. On 3 bread slices, place a layer of cheese, a slice of boiled ham, and another layer of cheese. Cover with other 3 slices of bread. Fry gently in butter until golden on both sides. With a sharp knife, cut each into quarters. Serve hot. Makes 12.

EGGPLANT CAVIAR

Eggplant cubes with chopped onion, garlic, and tomato.

1 medium eggplant	1 teaspoon salt
1 large onion	Freshly ground
1 clove garlic	black pepper
2 large tomatoes	½ teaspoon sugar
½ cup olive oil	Crackers or toast

Wash eggplant, and cook over hot coals or in a moderate oven, 375°F., until outside is black and inside soft (about ¾ hour). Run cold water over it, peel carefully, and dice. Peel onion, garlic, and tomatoes, and chop them well. Mix with eggplant. Add olive oil, salt, pepper, and sugar, and mix thoroughly. Chill well before serving with crackers or toast points. Makes 6 to 8 servings.

CHEESE TARTLETS

You can use Swiss or Parmesan cheese.

Make a sauce with 2 tablespoons each butter and flour and 1 cup cream. Stir in 1 cup grated Swiss or Parmesan cheese, dash cayenne. Make 24 Tea Tartlet shells, page 265. Fill shells with cheese mixture. Put under broiler until browned (about 3 minutes). Makes 24.

TARTAR CANAPÉS

Highly seasoned raw beef.

½ pound freshly ground top round	¼ teaspoon Worcestershire
Freshly ground pepper	2″ rounds of pumpernickel, sautéed in butter (about 24)
Dash of cayenne	
1 tablespoon finely minced onion	

Mix meat with seasonings, and heap smoothly on the pumpernickel rounds. Or, if you prefer, serve in a mound with half-slices of pumpernickel for the guests to serve themselves. Makes 24.

SMITHFIELD HAM AND BISCUITS

Serve Dijon mustard on the side.

Make 24 little baking-powder biscuits, or heat beaten biscuits from a package. Split biscuits, and place bits of Smithfield ham, sliced paper-thin, between halves. (You'll need about ¼ pound in all.) Makes 24.

RAW VEGETABLE TRAY

The vegetables can be served with salt, seasoned salt, or a dip.

Choose any vegetables you like to eat raw, in good variety. Carrot sticks, green and sweet red-pepper sticks, cauliflower broken into flowerets, celery stalks, leaves of Belgian endive, radish roses, tiny plum tomatoes are all beautiful and delicious. They should be served crisply cold and prettily arranged, accompanied by a dish of seasoned salt and a dish of plain salt or a dip.

DIP FOR RAW VEGETABLES

Sour cream, seasoned with basil, paprika, chili powder, and salt.

Mix together well: ½ pint sour cream, 1 tablespoon chopped fresh basil, I teaspoon sweet paprika, ½ teaspoon chili powder, and salt to taste. Serve well chilled. Makes 1 cup.

OLIVES IN CHEESE

They are rolled in almonds.

1 package (3 ounces) cream cheese	Cream
	16 large stuffed olives
½ teaspoon Worcestershire	¼ pound salted almonds, chopped

Mix cheese and Worcestershire together with enough cream to make a thick, smooth paste. Roll olives in mixture so that each is well coated, then roll in almonds. Makes 16.

DIP FOR SHRIMP

Highly seasoned mayonnaise for cold or hot fried shrimp.

Mix well: 1 cup mayonnaise, ½ teaspoon each curry powder and chili powder, 1 clove garlic, crushed, and ¼ cup chili sauce. Serve cold with cold boiled shrimp or fried breaded shrimp. Makes about 1 cup.

BAHAMIAN TOMATO CANAPÉS

The mayonnaise topping puffs up and browns under the broiler.

3 or 4 small, ripe tomatoes	Butter
12 or 16 bread rounds	Bahamian mustard
	¾ cup mayonnaise (about)

Slice tomatoes about ¼" thick. Cut the bread rounds as nearly as possible to match size of tomato slices, and sauté in butter until golden. Put a tomato slice on each round, and spread lightly with mustard. Now spread fairly thickly with mayonnaise. Broil about 3" from heat until mayonnaise puffs up (3 to 5 minutes). Makes 12 or 16.

LORENZO À LA FILIPINI

Toast slices spread with crab meat and topped with a cheese ball.

2 tablespoons butter	1 tablespoon milk
1 tablespoon minced onion	2½ tablespoons each grated Parmesan and grated Swiss cheese
2 tablespoons flour	
½ cup chicken stock	
1 cup crab meat	
Dash cayenne	6 slices toast, crust removed
Salt and pepper	

Melt 1 tablespoon butter, and cook onion in it without browning. Mix in well 1 tablespoon flour. Add stock, stirring constantly until smooth. Add crab meat, and simmer gently a few minutes. Season to taste with cayenne and salt and pepper. Melt remaining butter, and stir in remaining flour smoothly. Add milk and cheeses, and cook, stirring constantly, until cheeses are melted and blended. Cool, and form into 6 little balls. Spread crab mixture on toast, and top each slice with a cheese ball. Place in very hot oven, 450°F., 5 minutes. Serve on plates with forks. Makes 6.

SAVORY CANAPÉS

Eggs, pimiento, mustard, cheese, parsley, and ketchup baked on toast.

2 hard-cooked eggs	¼ teaspoon salt
2 tablespoons minced pimiento	1 tablespoon minced parsley
¼ teaspoon dry mustard	¼ cup butter
1 tablespoon grated Parmesan cheese	Ketchup to moisten
	12 to 14 small toast rounds

Shell eggs, and chop fine. Mix with next 7 ingredients, using just enough ketchup to moisten and hold the rest together. Spread on toast rounds, and place in very hot oven, 450°F., 5 minutes. Makes 12 to 14.

BOEUF BOURGUIGNON

Cubes of beef, which guests cook themselves, then dip in sauce.

Put 2 cups peanut oil and 1 cup butter into a deep pot over an alcohol lamp or other heat which will keep them sizzling. Cut beef tenderloin (¼ pound per person) into 1" cubes, and pile on platter. Provide long-handled wooden picks or 2-pronged wooden forks so that guests may spear meat and put it into the hot fat, where it is left until done (for rare, only 2 minutes, if that). Serve as many sauces as you wish, into which guests dip the cooked tidbits. For instance, a garlic sauce, Béarnaise, page 239, Tartar, page 240, or paprika.

CRAB CANAPÉS

Crab meat and chopped cucumber broiled on sautéed toast rounds.

2 cups crab meat	1 large cucumber
¼ cup mayonnaise (about)	Salt and pepper
¼ teaspoon Worcestershire	24 sautéed small toast rounds
	Parsley sprigs

Pick over crab meat carefully, and shred it fine. Mix with enough mayonnaise to hold it together, and season with Worcestershire. Peel cucumber, and chop very fine. Season lightly with salt and pepper. Spread a thin layer of cucumber on each toast round. Cover with a mound of crab meat, well smoothed. Place under the broiler to brown lightly. Decorate with parsley. Makes 24.

SALMON HORSE-RADISH CONES

*Thin cones of smoked salmon filled
with horse-radish whipped cream.*

½ cup heavy cream	1 envelope un-flavored gelatin
2 tablespoons grated horse-radish	1 tablespoon vinegar
½ teaspoon salt	8 thin slices smoked salmon

Whip cream until quite stiff. Fold in
horse-radish (if possible, freshly grated,
otherwise well-drained bottled or dried)
and salt. Mix gelatin with vinegar, and
soften over hot water. Cool, and fold
into first mixture. Form salmon slices
into cones, and fill with mixture. Refrigerate at least 2 hours before serving on
plates with forks. Makes 8.

HAM DIP

*Deviled ground ham
moistened with mayonnaise.*

Mix well: 1 cup ground cooked ham, 3
tablespoons mayonnaise, 2 tablespoons
chili sauce, 1 tablespoon prepared mustard, and ½ teaspoon each chili powder
and brown sugar. Add more mayonnaise
if necessary to make a proper dip consistency. Serve with hot potato chips.
Makes 1 cup.

SPINACH-CHEESE STRIPS

*Puff-paste pastry filled with
spinach, then cheese and olives.*

¼ recipe Puff Paste, page 269	1 tablespoon olive oil
1 pound spinach	½ cup grated Parmesan cheese
2 tablespoons minced onion	6 stuffed olives, sliced

Roll out puff paste to about 18″ by 6″.
Cut 1″-wide slice from both sides and
ends. Put slices on main strip to form
border. Wash spinach, and drain very
well. Tear it coarsely. Fry onion in olive
oil until golden, and mix with spinach.
Place on pastry strip between borders,
and top with grated Parmesan and the
olive slices. Bake in very hot oven,
450°F., 20 minutes, or until pastry is
puffed and brown. Cut into strips to
serve with forks. Makes 6 servings.

BROILED HAM AND CHUTNEY

They're broiled on toast rounds.

2 cups minced cooked ham	⅓ cup Major Grey's chutney
⅓ cup mayonnaise	1″ toast rounds

Mix ham with mayonnaise. Chop chutney fine if some of it is in large pieces.
Add to ham mixture, using some chutney liquid but not enough to make the
mixture runny. Spread on toast rounds
and run under broiler about 5 minutes
before serving. Makes about 25.

GUACAMOLE

Mashed, well-seasoned avocado.

1 large avocado	1 clove garlic, crushed
2 teaspoons lemon juice	2 tablespoons mayonnaise
1 teaspoon chili powder	Salt
	Corn chips

Peel avocado, and remove seed. Mash
pulp completely. (A food mill does this
beautifully.) Add lemon juice, and mix
well. Add chili powder, garlic, and
enough mayonnaise to make the proper
dunking consistency. Season. Serve with
king-size corn chips. Makes 1½ cups.

TARATOR

*A spread made of garlic, crushed
walnuts, and soaked, softened bread.*

½ cup shelled walnuts	1½ tablespoons vinegar
2 cloves garlic, crushed	1 teaspoon olive oil
2 slices bread, crust removed	Salt
	Toast or crackers

Pound the walnuts in a mortar, or whirl
them in the blender. Add garlic, and
mix well. Soak bread in water. Squeeze
out, and mix well with nuts and garlic
until you have formed a paste. Add
vinegar and oil slowly, mixing thoroughly. Salt to taste. Serve with toast or
crackers. Makes about ½ cup.

CHICKEN-LIVER PÂTÉ

*You must refrigerate it
a day and a half before serving.*

½ pound butter or margarine	½ teaspoon salt
1 pound chicken livers	Freshly ground pepper
¼ cup cognac	Dash nutmeg
2 shallots or green onions, chopped	Hot toast

Melt butter, and fry chicken livers in it until done (about 8 to 10 minutes). Put into blender with next 5 ingredients, and whirl until well mixed. Put into a crock, and refrigerate for at least a day and a half before serving on hot toast. Makes 2 cups.

QUAIL EGGS WITH CRAB SALAD

Crab salad tops the chilled eggs.

Chill 8 quail eggs (1 small jar) thoroughly. Mix 2 tablespoons crab meat, ½ teaspoon mayonnaise, ¼ teaspoon paprika, drop of Worcestershire. Put eggs in a serving dish, and put a dab of crab mixture on top of each. Makes 8.

CLAM BITES

They're deep-fried.

1 egg, separated	1 teaspoon melted butter
1 can (10½ ounces) minced clams and liquid	½ cup flour
	Salt and pepper

Beat egg yolk until light. Drain clams, reserving juice. To egg yolk, add butter, flour, ¼ teaspoon salt, and ¼ cup clam liquid (add milk, if necessary, to make ¼ cup). Fold in stiffly beaten egg white. Add clams, and let stand at least 1 hour at room temperature. Drop by teaspoonfuls into hot deep fat (375°F. on a frying thermometer), and fry until golden brown (5 to 6 minutes). Drain on absorbent paper. Sprinkle with salt and pepper; serve hot on toothpicks. Makes about 24.

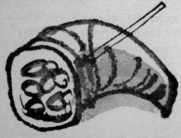

TOMATO CAVIAR

*Tomatoes, onion-cream cheese,
mayonnaise, and dots of red caviar.*

1 can (28 ounces) tomatoes	1 tablespoon onion juice
1 package (3 ounces) cream cheese	12 rounds Melba toast
1 tablespoon cream	¼ cup mayonnaise
	1 small jar red caviar

Drain tomatoes for at least 2 hours, reserving juice for other purposes. Smooth cheese with enough cream to make it spreadable, and mix onion juice into it well. Spread each sautéed Melba toast round with cheese. Mash tomatoes, and spread a little over cheese on each round. Cover with mayonnaise, and top with a few dots of red caviar. Makes 12.

CHICKEN-CLAM SPREAD

You can use leftover or canned chicken.

1 can (7 ounces) minced clams	1 tablespoon finely minced onion
1 cup minced chicken	1 tablespoon mayonnaise
1 package (3 ounces) cream cheese	Salt and pepper
	Toast rounds
	Parsley

Drain clams, reserving liquid. Mix with chicken and cream cheese. Add enough clam liquid to make clam mixture smooth and spreadable. Add onion, mayonnaise, and seasonings to taste. Serve on toast rounds, and decorate with bits of fresh parsley. Makes about 2 cups.

DANISH BEEF CANAPÉS

*Rare roast beef on rye rounds,
topped with crisp fried onions.*

Butter thin slices of tiny rye bread loaves generously. Top with thin slices of cold, rare roast beef, and sprinkle over that onions, sliced paper-thin and fried crisp and dark brown.

PEANUT-ONION CANAPÉS

*Rounds of toast with peanut
butter, onion rings, and ketchup.*

Spread rounds of toast with peanut butter. Put an onion ring on each, and a few drops of ketchup in the middle.

HOT BREADS

Not too many years ago, almost every home was filled at least once a week with the warm yeasty smell of fresh bread and rolls. Baking day, along with the family Christmas and the Fourth of July picnic, was one of America's finest traditions. On that day children did not loiter on the way from school but raced home, headed for the big comfortable kitchen, to watch the tasty morsels come from the oven: round golden loaves of white or wheaten bread, pans of light fluffy rolls, coffee rings studded with nuts and raisins, cinnamon and sweet buns oozing sugar and spices and buttery fillings. What a mouth-watering array. This wonderful custom can be revived easily. Today's modern conveniences, well-regulated stoves and electric mixers, actually make baking a pleasant task. And for the woman who is looking for a hobby, there's no better way to be creative. For good baking is an art and the results have always won a loudly appreciative audience. Why not start today to build a reputation as the woman who sets a good table in the old tradition?

"Here is bread,
which strengthens man's heart."
MATTHEW HENRY

DOUGH FOR NON-SWEET ROLLS

Shape it as you wish,
and bake plain or with seeds.

2 packages active dry yeast	2 teaspoons salt
½ cup lukewarm water	2 cups milk, scalded
½ cup sugar	7 to 8 cups sifted flour
Butter or margarine	2 eggs, well beaten

Soften yeast in water; let stand 5 minutes. In large bowl mix sugar, 6 tablespoons soft butter, salt, and milk; cool to lukewarm, and mix well. Add 1 cup of the flour, and beat until smooth. Add softened yeast; mix well. Add about half of remaining flour; beat until smooth. Beat in eggs. Add enough remaining flour to make soft dough. Turn out on floured board, let stand 5 minutes, and knead 5 minutes, or until smooth and elastic. Put in large greased bowl, turn to bring greased side up. Cover with waxed paper and towel, and let stand in warm place 1½ hours, or until double in bulk. Punch down, cover, and let rise ½ hour as before. Turn out on lightly floured board. Shape dough in desired rolls; put on greased baking sheets or in baking pans. Brush with melted butter; sprinkle with poppy, sesame, or other seed, if desired; cover, and let rise about 15 minutes. Bake in hot oven, 425°F., 15 minutes, or until browned. **Note:** For early-morning baking, or for delayed baking, see notes following Dough for Sweet Rolls, page 16.

CROISSANTS

The French, crescent-shaped roll.

Roll raised non-sweet dough in 12″ circle ¼″ thick; brush with melted butter. Cut in 16 wedges. Roll each wedge separately, beginning at wide edge. Put on baking sheet with wedge point underneath, and shape into crescents. Brush with melted butter, let rise; bake as directed above.

MASHED-POTATO ROLLS

You can use the dough for non-sweet
rolls and bread, or for sweet rolls.

½ envelope instant mashed potato granules	⅔ cup shortening
Water	½ cup sugar
Milk	1½ teaspoons salt
1 package active dry yeast	2 eggs, well beaten
	6 cups sifted flour
	Melted butter

Prepare potato as directed on package, using ¾ cup water, ¼ cup milk. Soften yeast in ½ cup lukewarm water. Scald 1 cup milk; pour over shortening, sugar, salt, and potato. Cool. Add yeast, eggs, and 3 cups flour; beat until smooth and light. Add enough more flour to make a dough firm enough to knead. Knead about 10 minutes. Put in greased bowl; brush with butter. Cover; refrigerate until ready to use. Or, cut in 36 pieces; shape each in a ball; put in 2½″ muffin cups. Brush with butter; let double. Bake in hot oven, 400°F., 20 minutes.

Braided Loaf: Use half of dough. Divide in 3 strips. Braid tightly. Put on greased cookie sheet; brush with egg white, sprinkle with sesame or poppy seed. Let rise until double. Bake in 400°F. oven 30 to 40 minutes.

Cinnamon Rolls: Use half of dough, and roll in a rectangle ¼″ thick. Spread with butter; mix ½ cup sugar, 2 teaspoons cinnamon; spread on dough. Sprinkle with raisins. Roll up; cut in 1″ slices. Put, cut side down, in greased baking dish. Let rise until double; brush with melted butter; bake in 375°F. oven 15 to 20 minutes. Frost. Makes 18.

Sticky Pecan Rolls: Prepare as for Cinnamon Rolls, substituting ½ cup brown sugar for the granulated. Roll up; cut. Arrange pecans in well-greased pan. Sprinkle with ¼ cup brown sugar; dot with butter. Put rolls, cut side down, in pan. Let double. Bake in 400°F. oven 15 minutes. Turn out. Makes 18.

SOUR-CREAM ROLLS

The sour cream is stirred into the softened yeast.

Soften 1 package active dry yeast in ½ cup lukewarm water in large bowl. Stir in ¾ cup soft butter, 2 well-beaten eggs, 1 cup sour cream. Sift 6 cups sifted flour, ½ cup sugar, 1½ teaspoons salt. Beat one-half into first mixture until smooth. Then stir in remainder. Let rise until double. Punch down; shape in balls the size of a large walnut; let rise on greased cookie sheet until light. Bake in hot oven, 400°F., 10 to 15 minutes. Makes 3 dozen.

WHIZZER ROLLS

Luncheon, dinner, or supper rolls.

1 package active	¼ cup shortening
dry yeast	¾ teaspoon salt
¼ cup lukewarm	2 eggs
water	2 cups sifted flour
½ cup milk,	3 tablespoons
scalded	melted butter
1 tablespoon sugar	or margarine

Soften yeast in water. Pour milk over sugar, shortening, salt in large bowl. Vigorously beat in yeast, eggs, flour. Let rise about 1 hour. Spoon into greased 2½″ muffin pans, filling them half-full. Let rise about 30 minutes. Pour ½ teaspoon butter over each. Bake in moderate oven, 375°F., about 20 minutes. Makes 16.

CREAM COFFEE ROLLS

Thin strips of dough rolled pinwheel-fashion, and baked.

Soften 1 package active dry yeast in ¼ cup lukewarm water. Heat ¾ cup heavy cream to lukewarm. Mix with ⅓ cup melted butter or margarine, 2 tablespoons sugar, 1 teaspoon salt. Beat in yeast, 1 beaten egg, 2 cups sifted flour. Then stir in 1½ cups flour. Let rise until double. Punch down, cut off small pieces of dough; roll between hands to about the length and diameter of a pencil. Roll up pinwheel-fashion; dip in ¼ cup melted butter; put in 2″ muffin pans. Let rise until light. Bake in hot oven, 400°F., about 15 minutes. While hot, spread tops with confectioners'-sugar frosting. Makes 2½ dozen.

KENTUCKY ROLLS

Circles of dough dipped in butter, folded in half, and baked.

1 package active	¾ teaspoon salt
dry yeast	1½ tablespoons
¼ cup lukewarm	shortening
water	1 egg, beaten
¾ cup milk,	2½ cups sifted flour
scalded	Melted butter or
1½ tablespoons	margarine
sugar	

Soften yeast in water. Pour milk over sugar, salt, shortening in large bowl; cool. Stir in yeast and egg. Beat in 2 cups of the flour. Pat butter over top. Cover, and let rise until double. Beat in ½ cup flour; pat out to ½″ thickness. Cut with floured 2½″ cutter; dip each in butter; fold in half. Let rise on cookie sheet until very light. Bake in hot oven, 425°F., 10 to 12 minutes. Makes 18.

BUTTERFLY DINNER ROLLS

There's butter in the dough and melted butter on top.

1 package active	Butter or margarine
dry yeast	1 tablespoon sugar
¼ cup lukewarm	1 teaspoon salt
water	2 eggs
½ cup milk	2 cups sifted flour

Soften yeast in water; let stand 5 minutes. Scald milk; stir in ¼ cup butter, sugar, and salt; cool to lukewarm. Add eggs, yeast, and flour. Beat vigorously; cover, and let rise in warm place about 1 hour. Stir well, and spoon into greased muffin pans, filling them about half-full. Let rise in warm place until double in bulk, about 30 minutes. Pour ½ teaspoon melted butter over each roll; bake in moderate oven, 375°F., 20 minutes. Makes sixteen 2½″ rolls.

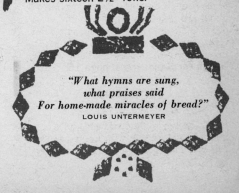

"What hymns are sung, what praises said For home-made miracles of bread?"
LOUIS UNTERMEYER

DOUGH FOR SWEET ROLLS

You can use it for coffeecakes, too.

2 packages active dry yeast	½ cup warm milk
	½ cup sugar
½ cup lukewarm water	1 teaspoon salt
	2 eggs
5 cups sifted flour	½ cup soft butter

Soften yeast in water; let stand 5 minutes. In large bowl, mix 3 cups of the flour and remaining ingredients; beat until smooth. Gradually add enough of remaining flour to make soft dough. Turn out on floured board, and knead 5 minutes, or until smooth and elastic. Put in large greased bowl; turn to bring greased side up. Cover with waxed paper and cloth, and let stand in warm place (80-85°F.) 1½ hours, or until double in bulk. Punch down, cover, and let rise in warm place about ½ hour. Turn out on floured board, and let rest 10 minutes. Follow individual recipe.

To prepare all or part of dough for early-morning baking: Cover shaped coffeecake or rolls, and let stand in refrigerator overnight. Remove from refrigerator about ½ hour before baking time, set in warm place to rise, and bake as directed.

To hold dough for later baking: After first rising, punch down the dough; cover, and set in refrigerator. When ready to bake, remove dough, and set in warm place until double. Punch down again, shape; bake as directed.

STREUSEL COFFEECAKE

It has a crumb topping.

After second rising of dough for sweet rolls, roll ⅓ of sweet dough into circle to fit 9″ layer-cake pan. Sprinkle top with mixture of ⅓ cup flour, ⅓ cup sugar, and 3 tablespoons soft butter. Cover, and let rise until double in bulk. Bake in hot oven, 400° F., about 25 minutes. Serve warm.

"The Muffin reigns in realms beyond his own."
OLD ENGLISH SONG

CURRANT RUM ROLLS

Currants and rum are spiced.

After second rising of dough for sweet rolls, roll ⅓ of sweet dough in rectangle ¼″ thick. Brush with melted butter; sprinkle ¼ cup dried currants, ¼ cup sugar, 1 tablespoon rum, and ¼ teaspoon nutmeg over dough. Roll up, jelly-roll fashion. Cut roll in 1″ slices, and put, cut sides down, in greased 9″ square pan. Flatten to cover bottom of pan. Cover, and let rise about 2 hours. Bake in very hot oven, 450°F., about 20 minutes. Frost with icing made by mixing ½ cup confectioners' sugar, 1 teaspoon melted butter, 1 tablespoon rum. Makes 12.

CINNAMON NUT TWISTS

They bake in butterscotch syrup.

Melt ¼ cup butter; stir in ⅓ cup brown sugar, 1 teaspoon corn syrup. Bring to rolling boil; spread in 13″ x 9″ x 2″ pan. Sprinkle with ⅓ cup chopped nuts. Soften 1 package dry yeast in ¾ cup warm water. Beat in 2½ cups biscuit mix. Knead, and roll in 12″ square. Brush with 2 tablespoons melted butter. Mix ¼ cup brown sugar, 1 teaspoon cinnamon; sprinkle half on center third of dough; fold one-third over center; sprinkle with remaining mixture. Fold remaining third over; cut in 1″ strips; twist each; pinch ends. Put in pan; let double. Bake in hot oven, 400°F., 20 minutes. Makes 14.

BAKED SUGAR RINGS

You start with hot-roll mix.

Prepare 1 box hot-roll mix as directed on label, adding only half the flour. Add ¼ cup sugar, 1 beaten egg, ¼ cup melted butter, 1 teaspoon grated lemon rind; beat until bubbly. Mix ½ teaspoon each cinnamon and nutmeg with remaining flour; stir into first mixture. Beat in ¼ to ½ cup sifted extra flour to make soft dough. Let rest 10 minutes on floured board. Knead, put in greased bowl; grease top. Cover; let rise until double. Pat to ½″ thickness; brush with melted butter; cut with floured 2½″ doughnut cutter. Put 2″ apart on greased sheets. Let double. Bake in 375°F. oven about 10 minutes. Brush with melted butter; roll in sugar. Makes 24.

RAISED DOUGHNUTS

Serve these plain, or dust with sugar.

1 package active dry yeast	¾ cup sugar
½ cup lukewarm water	3 eggs
¼ cup shortening	2½ teaspoons salt
½ cup undiluted evaporated milk	1 teaspoon nutmeg
	About 5 cups sifted flour
	Fat for frying

Soften yeast in water. Melt shortening; add milk; heat just to lukewarm; pour onto yeast. Add sugar and eggs; beat lightly. Add salt and nutmeg; gradually beat in flour to make a soft dough. Cover, let rise until double. Knead 5 minutes. Roll to ½" thickness; cut with 2½" doughnut cutter. Let rise until doubled. Fry in hot deep fat (370°F. on frying thermometer) until browned, turning once. Makes 30.

RAISED SALLY LUNN

Serve this in slices, as it is, or toasted.

Soften 1 package active dry yeast in ¼ cup lukewarm water. Scald 1¾ cups milk, and pour over 2 tablespoons sugar, 1 teaspoon salt, ¼ cup butter in bowl; cool. Stir in yeast and 2 well-beaten eggs. Vigorously beat in about 3 cups sifted flour. Then stir in about 2 cups more, or enough to make a soft dough. Divide into 2 greased 9" x 5" x 3" loaf pans. Let rise until double. Bake in hot oven, 400°F., 15 minutes. Reduce heat to 350°F., and bake about 10 minutes longer. Serve with butter and jam.

KUGELHOPF

A coffee ring with raisins and nuts.

1 package active dry yeast	5 eggs
¼ cup lukewarm water	1 teaspoon salt
¾ cup milk	Grated rind 1 lemon
4 cups sifted flour	1 cup seedless raisins
1 cup butter	½ cup chopped blanched almonds
¾ cup sugar	

Soften the yeast in water. Add milk, scalded and cooled. Beat in 1 cup flour; let rise 1½ hours. Cream butter and sugar. Beat in eggs, one at a time. Add yeast, remaining flour, and salt. Beat well. Stir in lemon rind, raisins, and ¼ cup nuts. Butter a 10" tube pan; sprinkle with ¼ cup nuts. Pour in the batter. Let rise until light. Bake in 350°F. oven 1 hour.

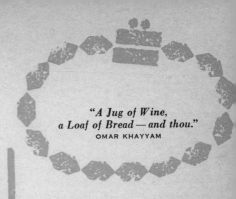

"A Jug of Wine,
a Loaf of Bread — and thou."
OMAR KHAYYAM

GEORGIA RAISED BISCUITS

You bake these in pairs, one on top of the other.

1 package active dry yeast	5 cups sifted flour
1½ cups lukewarm water	2 teaspoons salt
	1 tablespoon sugar
	Butter or margarine

Soften yeast in water; let stand 5 minutes. Sift dry ingredients into large bowl. Cut in ½ cup soft butter. Add yeast, and mix. Roll about ¼" thick on floured board, and brush with melted butter. Cut with floured 2" cutter, and put on baking sheet, placing biscuits in pairs, one on top of another. Let rise in warm place (80-85°F.) 1 hour. Bake in hot oven, 425°F., about 10 minutes. Makes about 3 dozen.

CHEESE-FILLED ROLLS

The cheese is cream cheese.

Soften 1 package dry yeast in 2 tablespoons lukewarm water. Scald ½ cup milk; pour over ⅓ cup sugar, ½ teaspoon salt, ⅓ cup butter; cool. Stir in yeast, 1 whole egg, 1 egg yolk, 1 teaspoon grated lemon rind. Beat in 1½ cups sifted flour; then stir in 1¾ cups. Cover; let double. Punch down; roll in 14" x 10½" rectangle. Cut in twelve 3½" squares. Mix 4 ounces cream cheese and 1½ tablespoons milk. Spread 2 teaspoons on each square; fold in triangles. Let rise until light on greased sheets. Brush with 1 egg white beaten with 2 teaspoons water. Sprinkle with 2 tablespoons sugar and 1 teaspoon cinnamon. Bake in 350°F. oven 10 to 15 minutes. Makes 1 dozen.

"All sorrows are less with bread."
MIGUEL CERVANTES

CINNAMON RAISIN BUNS

They have a cinnamon frosting.

1 package active dry yeast	½ teaspoon salt
2 tablespoons lukewarm water	1 egg, beaten
	3½ to 4 cups sifted flour
1 cup milk, scalded	1 teaspoon cinnamon
¼ cup butter or margarine	¾ cup seedless raisins
⅓ cup sugar	Cinnamon Frosting

Soften yeast in water. Pour milk over butter, sugar, and salt in bowl. Stir in egg and half the flour sifted with cinnamon; beat smooth. Stir in raisins and enough more flour to make a soft dough. Cover; let rise in warm place until double. Punch down; shape in balls the size of a walnut; let rise on baking sheet until double. Bake in hot oven, 425°F., 25 minutes. Spread with Frosting of confectioners' sugar, water, and cinnamon. Makes 24.

YORKSHIRE PUDDING

Traditionally served with roast beef.

Sift 1 cup sifted flour, ½ teaspoon salt. Add 1 cup milk; beat with rotary beater until smooth. Add 2 eggs; beat 2 minutes. Heat 3 tablespoons drippings in 9″ x 9″ x 2″ pan. Pour in batter. Bake in 450°F. oven 12 minutes. Reduce heat to 350°F., bake 10 to 15 minutes.

BOSTON BROWN BREAD

A dark corn-meal, whole-wheat, and molasses bread.

Mix ⅔ cup each sifted all-purpose flour, yellow corn meal, whole-wheat flour, ¾ teaspoon each salt and soda. Add ½ cup molasses, 1 cup buttermilk. Put in greased 1½-quart mold; cover tightly. Put on trivet in deep kettle. Add boiling water to come halfway up sides of mold; cover. Steam about 3 hours.

DOUBLE-CORN STICKS

You use both corn meal and cream-style corn.

1 cup sifted flour	1 teaspoon salt
1 cup yellow corn meal	¼ teaspoon soda
2 tablespoons sugar	2 tablespoons butter
1½ teaspoons baking powder	1 egg
	¾ cup cream-style corn
	⅔ cup buttermilk

Sift dry ingredients together. Cut in butter. Add egg, corn, and buttermilk; mix only enough to dampen dry ingredients. Fill well-greased corn-stick pans two-thirds full. Bake in hot oven, 425°F., about 20 minutes. Makes 1 dozen.

BLUEBERRY PANCAKES

Serve them with melted butter and sprinkle with brown sugar.

Sift 1½ cups sifted flour, 2½ teaspoons baking powder, 3 tablespoons sugar, ¾ teaspoon salt. Beat 2 egg yolks; mix with 1 cup milk and 3 tablespoons melted butter or margarine. Add to dry ingredients; mix until smooth. Stir in 1 cup blueberries. Then fold in 2 egg whites, stiffly beaten. Bake on hot greased griddle. Makes 12.

BUTTERMILK GRIDDLE CAKES

Beat these well to make them light and fluffy.

Sift 1½ cups sifted flour, ¾ teaspoon salt, ½ teaspoon soda, 1 tablespoon sugar. Cut in ¼ cup shortening. Add 1 egg, 1½ cups buttermilk; beat well. Bake on lightly greased griddle over low heat, turning to brown both sides. Makes sixteen 4″ cakes.

BUTTERMILK DOUGHNUTS

They're deliciously spiced with cinnamon, mace, and nutmeg.

Cream 2 tablespoons shortening and ¾ cup sugar; add 2 eggs, one at a time, beating well after each. Sift 4 cups sifted flour, 2 teaspoons baking powder, ½ teaspoon each cinnamon, mace, nutmeg, salt, soda. Add alternately to first mixture with 1 cup buttermilk. Mix well; chill 1 hour or longer. Roll to ½″ thickness. Cut with floured 3″ doughnut cutter. Fry in hot deep fat (370°F. on frying thermometer) until golden brown on both sides, turning once. Drain on absorbent paper. Makes about 2½ dozen.

18

ITALIAN SPINACH SALAD

1 qt. torn spinach
4 crisply cooked
 bacon slices,
 crumbled
1/4 cup (1 oz.) KRAFT
 Grated Parmesan
 Cheese

1/3 cup KRAFT
 "Zesty" Italian
 Dressing
2 hard-cooked eggs,
 chopped

Combine spinach, bacon and Parmesan Cheese. Add KRAFT Dressing; toss lightly. Top with eggs.
    4 servings

NUTRITION TIP*: This delicious salad is a good source of iron and calcium. Plus each serving provides 100% of the recommended allowance of Vitamin A.

CHERRY DREAMS

1 8-oz. pkg.
 PHILADELPHIA
 BRAND Cream
 Cheese,
 softened
1/2 cup sugar
1 teaspoon
 brandy
 extract

1 teaspoon lemon
 juice
1 cup whipping
 cream, whipped
1 21-oz. can cherry
 pie filling
3 tablespoons
 slivered
 almonds,

NUTRITION TIP: SQUEEZE™ PARKAY Margarine has no cholesterol. This Recipe is a good source of five important Vitamins: A, C, E, thiamin and riboflavin.

"CATALINA" CHEF'S SALAD

1 1/2 qts. torn romaine
2 medium
 tomatoes,
 sliced
1 medium green
 pepper, cut
 into strips
2 hard-cooked
 eggs, sliced

1/2 lb. cooked chicken
 or turkey, cut
 into strips
1/4 cup chopped
 cucumber
1/2 cup CATALINA
 Brand Reduced
 Calorie
 Dressing

On lettuce-covered salad plates, arrange tomatoes, peppers, eggs, chicken and cucumbers. Serve with CATALINA Brand Reduced Calorie Dressing
    4 servings

GARDEN-FRESH PASTA SALAD

2 cups mushroom halves
1 cup cherry tomato halves
1 cup (4 ozs.) corkscrew noodles, cooked, drained
½ cup green pepper chunks
1 8-oz. bottle KRAFT "Zesty" Italian Dressing
6 iceberg lettuce wedges

Combine mushrooms, tomatoes, noodles, peppers and ½ cup KRAFT Dressing; mix lightly. Chill. Arrange lettuce on serving platter; surround with vegetable mixture. Serve with remaining KRAFT Dressing.   6 servings

NUTRITION TIP: Try this tempting summer salad, a significant source of Vitamins A, C and riboflavin.

CHEESY STEAK SANDWICHES

1 large onion, sliced
2 tablespoons PARKAY Margarine
1 lb. thin roast beef slices
1 8-oz. jar CHEEZ WHIZ Pasteurized Process Cheese Spread
6 6-inch French bread rolls, partially-split, heated

Saute onions in margarine; remove onions from skillet. Add meat to skillet; heat thoroughly. Heat CHEEZ WHIZ Process Cheese Spread in saucepan over low heat. Fill rolls with meat and onions; top with process cheese spread.
6 sandwiches

MICROWAVE: Omit heating of rolls. Reduce margarine to 1 tablespoon. Microwave margarine and onions in 1-quart bowl on High 1 minute; add meat. Microwave 2 minutes, stirring after 1 minute. Remove lid from CHEEZ WHIZ Process Cheese Spread jar. Microwave 1 to 1½ minutes or until hot, rotating jar one-half turn every 30 seconds. Stir carefully before using. Fill rolls with meat and onions; place on paper towels. Microwave 30 seconds. Top with process cheese spread.

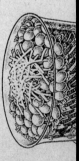

mins, turn to this Recipe. CHEEZ WHIZ Process Cheese Spread is a good source of calcium. The Recipe is not recommended for people on a low sodium diet.

CHEDDAR-FRUIT LAYERED SALAD

½ cup KRAFT Real
   Mayonnaise
½ cup sour cream
1 tablespoon honey
1½ cups (6 ozs.)
   shredded
   J. L. KRAFT
   SELECT Sharp
   Natural
   Cheese

1 qt. shredded
   lettuce
3 cups peach slices
3 cups strawberry
   slices
3 cups grapes

Combine KRAFT Real Mayonnaise, sour cream and honey; mix well. Chill. Combine 1 cup J. L. KRAFT SELECT Cheese and lettuce; toss lightly. In 2½-quart serving bowl, layer half of lettuce mixture, peaches, remaining lettuce mixture, strawberries and grapes; sprinkle with remaining cheese. Serve with mayonnaise mixture.   8 servings

NUTRITION TIP*: This Recipe has 100% of the recommended allowance of Vitamin C in each serving. And with 100% natural J. L. KRAFT SELECT Cheese, it's a good source of calcium, Vitamin A and riboflavin.

TV GUIDE

SAUSAGE KABOBS

1 cup KRAFT
   Thick 'N Spicy
   Original
   Barbecue
   Sauce
1½ lbs. fully-cooked
   bratwurst or
   Polish sausage,
   cut into
   1½-inch pieces

2 medium summer
   squash, cut into
   1-inch pieces
2 green or red
   peppers, cut into
   1-inch pieces
12 whole mushrooms

Pour KRAFT Thick 'N Spicy barbecue sauce over combined remaining ingredients. Cover; marinate in refrigerator several hours or overnight. Remove sausage and vegetables from KRAFT Thick 'N Spicy barbecue sauce; reserve sauce. Arrange sausage and vegetables on skewers; place on greased outdoor grill over low coals (coals will be ash gray). Grill, uncovered, 25 to 30 minutes or until vegetables are tender, brushing frequently with reserved barbecue sauce and turning occasionally.
   6 servings

NUTRITION TIP*: Each serving of this savory Recipe gives you 100% of the recommended allowance of Vitamin C. It's a source of iron, protein, Vitamin A, and several B Vitamins.

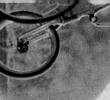

toasted

Combine PHILLY Brand Cream Cheese, sugar, extract and juice, mixing until well blended. Fold in whipped cream. For each serving, spoon approximately ½ cup cream cheese mixture onto wax paper-lined cookie sheet. With back of spoon, spread and shape into shells; freeze until firm. Fill shells with pie filling; sprinkle with almonds.

8 servings

GRILLED CORN ON THE COB

| 4 ears corn on the cob, unhusked | ½ teaspoon dried oregano leaves, crushed |
| ½ cup SQUEEZE™ PARKAY Margarine | ½ teaspoon garlic or onion salt |

Pull back corn husks; remove silk. Drizzle each ear of corn with 1 tablespoon SQUEEZE™ PARKAY Margarine. Sprinkle with seasonings; replace husks. Place on open grill over hot coals (coals will be glowing). Grill 30 minutes or until tender, turning occasionally. Serve with remaining SQUEEZE™ PARKAY Margarine.

4 servings

RIBS RANCHERO

| 6 lbs. pork spareribs | 2 large oranges, sliced |
| 2 cups KRAFT Barbecue Sauce | |

Parboil ribs 10 minutes; drain. Place ribs, bone side down, on greased outdoor grill over low coals (coals will be ash gray). Grill, uncovered, 30 minutes. Brush with KRAFT Barbecue Sauce and continue grilling 30 minutes, turning and brushing with barbecue sauce every 10 minutes. Brush oranges with barbecue sauce; grill with ribs last 10 minutes.

6 servings

TV GUIDE

CHEESE POPOVERS

The cheese is grated cheddar.

2 eggs	¼ teaspoon salt
1 cup milk	¼ cup grated sharp
1 cup sifted flour	cheddar cheese

Beat eggs slightly; add milk. Then add flour and salt; beat vigorously 2 minutes. Pour batter into very hot greased custard cups or iron popover pans, filling two-thirds full. Sprinkle with cheese. Bake in hot oven, 425°F., about 40 minutes. Serve at once. Makes 6.

GINGERBREAD

Spiced with cinnamon, nutmeg, ginger.

Add ½ cup boiling water to ½ cup butter. Stir until butter is melted. Add 1 cup molasses. Sift 2½ cups flour, ½ teaspoon each salt and cinnamon, 1½ teaspoons soda, 1 teaspoon ginger, ¼ teaspoon nutmeg. Stir into first mixture. Bake in greased 9" x 9" x 2" pan in 350°F. oven about 25 minutes.

RAISIN OATMEAL MUFFINS

You use seedless raisins and rolled oats.

Sift 1 cup sifted flour, ¼ cup sugar, 3 teaspoons baking powder, ½ teaspoon salt. Cut in 3 tablespoons soft shortening. Stir in 1 cup rolled oats and ½ cup seedless raisins. Add 1 beaten egg and 1 cup milk, stirring just enough to dampen dry ingredients. Fill greased muffin pans two-thirds full. Bake in hot oven, 425°F., 15 to 25 minutes, depending on size. Makes 8 to 16.

DATE-NUT MUFFINS

Make them with pecans or walnuts.

1 cup milk	¼ cup sugar
1 egg, well beaten	½ cup packaged
2 cups sifted flour	chopped dates
1 teaspoon salt	½ cup chopped
3 teaspoons baking	nuts
powder	¼ cup butter,
	melted

Mix milk and egg in bowl. Add sifted dry ingredients; mix well. Add dates and nuts, then butter, and mix only enough to blend. Half-fill greased muffin pans, and bake in hot oven, 400°F., 20 minutes, or until browned. Makes 9.

Wheat-germ Muffins: Add 1 cup wheat germ to milk and egg, and let stand 5 minutes; omit 1 cup flour; use ¼ cup brown sugar in place of granulated sugar; omit dates and nuts.

RAISIN BRAN MUFFINS

The liquid used is buttermilk.

Cream 3 tablespoons soft butter or margarine and ¼ cup molasses. Add 1 egg; beat well. Add 1 cup shredded bran cereal, ¾ cup buttermilk; let stand 5 minutes. Add 1 cup sifted flour, 1 teaspoon baking powder, ½ teaspoon each soda and salt, sifted together; mix only enough to dampen dry ingredients. Add ⅓ cup seedless raisins. Fill greased 2¾" muffin pans two-thirds full. Bake in hot oven, 400°F., about 25 minutes. Makes 9 large muffins.

PEANUT-BUTTER DATE MUFFINS

You cream the peanut butter with the shortening and sugar, and add the dates before baking.

Cream ¼ cup peanut butter, 1 tablespoon shortening, ¼ cup sugar. Sift 1¾ cups sifted flour, 2 teaspoons baking powder, ½ teaspoon salt. Add alternately to first mixture with 1 beaten egg, 1 cup milk, mixed. Mix only enough to dampen dry ingredients. Fold in ¾ cup chopped dates. Fill greased 2½" muffin pans two-thirds full. Bake in hot oven, 400°F., about 20 minutes. Makes 12 large muffins.

BLUEBERRY MUFFINS

A special treat anytime: for breakfast, lunch, dinner, or tea.

Sift 2 cups sifted flour, 2 teaspoons baking powder, ½ teaspoon salt, ¼ cup sugar. Cut in ¼ cup butter or margarine. Add 1 egg, 1 cup milk; mix only enough to dampen dry ingredients. Fold in 1 cup blueberries. Fill greased 2¾" muffin pans two-thirds full. Bake in hot oven, 400°F., about 25 minutes. Makes 10 large muffins.

"Bring me, I pray thee, a morsel of bread in thine hand."
I KINGS 17:11

HERB BISCUITS

The herb is sage.

To 2 cups biscuit mix, add ¼ teaspoon nutmeg, ½ teaspoon dried sage, 1¼ teaspoons caraway seed. Stir in ⅔ cup milk. Roll, and cut with 2″ cutter. Put on greased sheet; brush with 1 egg, beaten. Bake in 450°F. oven 10 minutes. Makes about 1 dozen.

HERB DUMPLINGS

You use fresh or dried herbs.

Sift 3 cups sifted cake flour, 1¼ teaspoons baking powder, 1 teaspoon salt. Blend in 2 tablespoons shortening. Add 2 tablespoons chopped fresh or 2 teaspoons dried herbs, scant 1 cup milk; mix. Drop from tablespoon onto vegetables or meat in stew. Cover; cook 15 minutes. Serves 6.

APPLE STICKS

They're made with diced apple, cinnamon, and a little grated cheese.

1½ cups sifted cake flour	1 tablespoon grated sharp cheese
¼ cup cornstarch	
3 teaspoons baking powder	1½ cups finely diced apples
¾ teaspoon salt	⅓ cup milk
2 tablespoons butter or margarine	⅓ cup sugar
	¼ teaspoon cinnamon

Sift dry ingredients; cut in butter and cheese; stir in apples and milk. Knead 1 minute on floured board. Roll ¼″ thick; cut in finger lengths 1″ wide. Fry in hot deep fat (375°F. on frying thermometer) 5 minutes. Drain; roll in sugar and cinnamon. Makes 18.

"*Bread is worth all, being the Staffe of life.*"
JOHN PENKETHMAN

FRUIT BUNS

The fruit filling: apricot, prune, peach.

Combine 2 cups biscuit mix, 1 tablespoon sugar, ⅛ teaspoon nutmeg. Stir in ¾ cup milk. Roll to ⅛″ thickness. Spread with ¼ cup soft butter or margarine; fold dough in half; roll out again; spread with ¼ cup more butter. Fold; roll in a rectangle 18″ x 6″; cut in twelve 3″ squares. Put squares in greased large muffin pans; fill with Fruit Filling. Pull corners of dough together; pinch. Bake in moderate oven, 375°F., about 25 minutes. **Fruit Filling:** Beat 1 egg, ½ cup sugar, 1 teaspoon lemon juice, ½ teaspoon cinnamon. Stir in 6 chopped drained cooked dried apricots, 3 chopped pitted cooked prunes, 1 chopped cooked dried peach. (Or use ⅔ cup any drained stewed fruit.)

SESAME-SEED DIPS

They should be eaten hot, right from the oven.

2¼ cups sifted flour	1½ teaspoons salt
1 tablespoon sugar	1 cup milk
3½ teaspoons baking powder	⅓ cup butter or margarine
	Sesame seed

Sift dry ingredients into bowl. Add milk, and mix with fork. Turn out on well-floured board; sprinkle lightly with flour. Knead about 10 times. Roll out, making rectangle about 12″ x 8″. With floured knife, cut strips 4″ x ½″. Meanwhile, melt butter in 13″ x 9″ x 2″ pan in very hot oven, 450°F. Remove pan from oven, and dip strips in butter, covering all sides. Lay in rows in the same pan, sprinkle with sesame seed, and bake about 15 minutes. Makes 48.

PEANUT-HONEY SQUARES

You use both peanuts and peanut butter.

⅓ cup peanut butter	¼ cup honey
	¾ cup milk
2 cups biscuit mix	½ cup salted peanuts, chopped
1 egg, beaten	

Cut peanut butter into biscuit mix with pastry blender. Mix egg, honey, and milk; add to first mixture, and stir just to blend. Fold in peanuts. Pour into greased 9″ square pan. Bake in hot oven, 400°F., about 25 minutes.

QUICK SALLY LUNN

They have a topping of sugar and cinnamon.

½ cup butter or margarine	2 cups sifted flour
Sugar	3 teaspoons baking powder
2 eggs	¾ teaspoon salt
1 cup milk	Cinnamon

Cream butter; add ⅓ cup sugar gradually, creaming until light and fluffy. Beat eggs well; add milk. Add sifted next 3 ingredients and liquid alternately to sugar mixture, beating until smooth. Turn into two greased 8″ x 8″ x 2″ pans. Sprinkle with sugar and cinnamon. Bake in hot oven, 425°F., about 20 minutes. Cut each square in 9 pieces, and serve warm. Makes 18.

PEANUT ORANGE COFFEECAKE

You use peanut butter and orange marmalade.

Sift 2 cups sifted flour, 2 teaspoons baking powder, ½ teaspoon salt. Cut in ¼ cup each soft butter and peanut butter. Add ¾ cup orange marmalade, 1 egg, ⅔ cup milk. Mix only enough to dampen dry ingredients. Bake in greased 9″ x 9″ x 2″ pan in moderate oven, 350°F., about 35 minutes.

BUTTERSCOTCH NUT CRUMBCAKE

There are dates in the cake, too.

1⅓ cups biscuit mix	¾ cup milk
¾ cup granulated sugar	1 cup chopped dates
3 tablespoons soft shortening	3 tablespoons soft butter or margarine
1 egg	⅓ cup brown sugar, packed
1 tablespoon grated orange rind	½ cup chopped nuts

Put first 5 ingredients and ¼ cup milk in bowl. Beat vigorously 1 minute. Add remaining ½ cup milk; beat ½ minute. Add dates. Put in greased and floured deep 9″ layer pan. Bake in moderate oven, 350°F., 35 to 40 minutes. Mix butter and brown sugar until crumbly; add nuts. Spread on hot cake. Put under broiler 2 or 3 minutes, or until bubbly. Cut in squares, and serve warm.

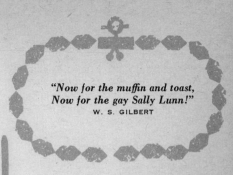

*"Now for the muffin and toast,
Now for the gay Sally Lunn!"*
W. S. GILBERT

ORANGE VELVET CRUMBCAKE

You serve it warm.

1½ cups biscuit mix	2 tablespoons cream
¾ cup granulated sugar	1½ teaspoons orange juice
1 tablespoon soft butter	1½ teaspoons grated orange rind
1 egg	½ cup flaked coconut
¾ cup milk	¼ cup chopped nuts
3 tablespoons melted butter	
⅓ cup light-brown sugar, packed	

Combine biscuit mix and granulated sugar. Add soft butter, egg, and ¼ cup of the milk; beat vigorously 1 minute. Stir in remaining ½ cup milk, and beat ½ minute. Pour into greased and floured 9″ round or 8″ square cake pan. Bake in moderate oven, 350°F., about 35 minutes. Mix remaining ingredients; spread on hot cake as soon as it is done, and set about 3″ under broiler 3 minutes, or until brown and bubbly. Serve warm.

PINEAPPLE COFFEECAKE

Crushed pineapple, brown sugar, and cinnamon form the topping.

Sift 2 cups sifted flour, 2 teaspoons baking powder, ½ teaspoon salt. Cut in 2 tablespoons butter or margarine. Mix ¼ cup light corn syrup, 1 beaten egg, ⅔ cup syrup drained from 1-pound can crushed pineapple. Add to first mixture, and mix only enough to dampen dry ingredients. Spread in greased 8″ x 8″ x 2″ pan; brush with melted butter; cover with ¾ cup drained crushed pineapple; sprinkle with ¼ cup brown sugar and some cinnamon. Bake in hot oven, 400°F., about 30 minutes.

DATE SCONES

*Split, butter, and eat them
while they're warm.*

Sift 2 cups sifted flour, 2 teaspoons baking powder, 2 tablespoons sugar, ½ teaspoon salt. Cut in ¼ cup butter or margarine. Add ½ cup chopped dates, 1 beaten whole egg, 1 egg yolk, ⅓ cup light cream. Mix well; pat in a round ¾" thick. Cut in 8 wedges; brush with unbeaten egg white; sprinkle with sugar. Bake in very hot oven, 450°F., about 15 minutes. Split; butter.

EAST INDIAN PURI

*These are made with whole-wheat
flour and yogurt.*

Mix 2½ cups whole-wheat flour and 1¼ teaspoons salt. Cut in ½ cup soft butter or margarine. Add 1⅓ cups plain yogurt; mix well. Roll to ⅛" thickness; cut with floured 4" cutter. Fry in hot deep fat (385°F. on a frying thermometer) until puffed and golden brown on both sides. Or fry in 1" hot fat in skillet, if preferred. Drain on absorbent paper. Makes about 3 dozen.

CUSTARDY CORN BREAD

You serve it as you do spoonbread.

¾ cup white corn meal	1 teaspoon baking powder
¼ cup sifted flour	1½ cups plus 2 tablespoons milk
1 to 2 tablespoons sugar	1 egg, well beaten
½ teaspoon salt	2 tablespoons butter

Sift dry ingredients; stir in 1 cup plus 2 tablespoons milk and the egg. Melt butter in 8" square pan, and pour mixture into pan. Just before baking, pour remaining ½ cup milk over batter; do not stir. Bake in hot oven, 400°F., about 30 minutes. Makes 4 to 6 servings.

*"When one is hungry,
Hurray! for bread."*
PROVERB FROM THE CAUCASUS

HUSH PUPPIES

*A Southern favorite, made of corn meal,
to serve with fish.*

Mix 2 cups water-ground corn meal, 1½ teaspoons salt, 1 teaspoon sugar, 2 teaspoons baking powder, 1 tablespoon instant minced onion. Add 2 beaten eggs, ½ cup milk; mix well; shape in balls the size of a large walnut. Fry in hot deep fat (375°F. on a frying thermometer) until well browned and done, turning once. Drain on absorbent paper. Makes 4 servings.

BACON WAFFLES

*Crumbled bacon is baked
on top of the waffles.*

Dice 1 pound bacon; fry until crisp; drain on absorbent paper, and reserve ⅓ cup bacon fat. Sift 2 cups sifted flour, 3 teaspoons baking powder, ¼ teaspoon salt, 1 tablespoon sugar. Add 2 cups milk; beat until smooth. Beat in 2 eggs, one at a time. Stir in reserved bacon fat. Pour small amount of batter in waffle iron, sprinkle with bacon; cook. Repeat until all of batter and bacon is used. Serve with butter and honey or maple syrup. Makes 4 to 6.

PINWHEEL ONION ROLLS

*They're baked with a topping of egg
and evaporated milk.*

4 onions, thinly sliced	3 teaspoons baking powder
2 tablespoons butter	¼ cup shortening
2¼ teaspoons salt	⅔ cup milk
Dash cayenne	1 egg, beaten
2 cups sifted flour	⅓ cup evaporated milk

Cook onions in the butter until golden; cool. Add ¾ teaspoon salt and cayenne. Sift flour, baking powder, 1 teaspoon salt. Cut in shortening. Add milk; mix only enough to dampen dry ingredients. Roll in 12" x 8" rectangle. Spread with onions; roll up like jelly roll. Cut in eight 1" slices. Put cut side down in greased 13" x 9" x 2" pan. Mix egg, evaporated milk, ½ teaspoon salt. Pour over rolls. Bake in hot oven, 400°F., 25 minutes.

MAIN
DISH
SOUPS

The soup pot, simmering on the back of the stove, could once be seen in
every kitchen and it never left the fire. There it stood, rich
with meat, bones, herbs, seasonings, and broth, ready for the addition of a
few vegetables to make a hearty meal. Sometimes the contents
were eaten cold. Then the broth would be nicely jellied and
this, with bits of the cold meat and some mustard or horse-radish, made
a most tasty lunch. Near the seacoast, rib-sticking soups, almost
stews, were made of fish: the classic French *bouillabaisse* and
our New England chowders are examples of these fish concoctions. The
soups given here come from all over the world. Each is a meal in itself,
needing only the addition of a salad and perhaps some cheese and
fruit. Try them for the family and also for informal buffet parties.
Besides the chowders and *bouillabaisse*, you will find satisfying
meat soups, such as *petite marmite*, pepper pot, the popular
Italian vegetable soup, *minestrone*, and a host of others.

23

SALMON-TOMATO BISQUE

You use evaporated milk for the creamy texture a bisque should have.

1 can (1 pound) salmon	1 small onion, minced
1 can (10½ ounces) tomato purée	2 tablespoons butter
2 sprigs parsley, minced	2 tablespoons flour
2 cups water	1 can (14½ ounces) evaporated milk
	Salt and pepper
	Cheese popcorn

Put salmon with liquid into large saucepan with tomato purée, parsley, and water. Bring to boil, and simmer 20 minutes. Cook onion in butter in another saucepan until golden brown; blend in flour. Add milk gradually, and cook until thickened, stirring constantly. Add salmon mixture; season to taste. Heat well, and serve with a sprinkling of popcorn. Makes 4 servings.

COCKALEEKIE SOUP

A slow-cooking soup, starring chicken.

Salt	2 dried hot red peppers or dash cayenne
1 fowl, cut up	
2½ quarts water	
3 onions, sliced	1 dozen leeks, white part only, cut in 1-inch pieces
1 clove garlic, minced	
Few sprigs parsley	
1 bay leaf	6 potatoes, peeled and diced
1 teaspoon poultry seasoning	Pepper

Put 1 tablespoon salt and remaining ingredients, except last 3, in large kettle. Bring to boil, and simmer, covered, 4 hours, or until fowl is tender. Remove skin and bones from chicken, and cut meat in good-sized chunks. Skim fat from broth, and add chicken, leeks, and potatoes. Cover, and cook 30 minutes longer. Add salt and pepper to taste. Makes about 3 quarts.

CHICKEN-SHRIMP GUMBO

A New Orléans specialty, with gumbo filé, okra, and shrimp.

1 fowl (about 4 pounds), cut up	2 teaspoons gumbo filé
5 cups water	1 box thawed frozen okra or 1 can (16 ounces) cut okra, drained
1 clove garlic	
Salt	
¼ pound salt pork, diced	
1 sweet red pepper, cut up	1 pound shrimp, peeled and cleaned
1 cup chopped onion	Pepper
⅓ cup flour	Tabasco
1 can (19 ounces) tomatoes	Hot cooked rice

Cook fowl with water, garlic, and 1 tablespoon salt 3 hours, or until tender. Cool; remove meat from bones; cut in pieces. Strain broth, and reserve. Cool, and skim off fat. Cook salt pork until well browned and done. Remove pork from kettle, and pour off most of fat. Cook red pepper and onion in remaining fat 5 minutes. Blend in flour. Add broth and water, if necessary, to make 6 cups. Add pork and tomatoes. Cover, and simmer 30 minutes. Add filé, chicken, okra, and shrimp. Simmer until shrimp turns pink. Season with salt, pepper, and Tabasco. Put a scoop of rice in center of each soup bowl, and fill bowl with soup. Makes 6 servings.

Note: Filé is made of powdered young sassafras leaves. It can be bought wherever herbs are sold.

CURRIED CHICKEN SOUP

You serve this one icy cold, garnished with chopped hard-cooked egg.

2 cans cream-of-chicken soup	1 teaspoon curry powder
2 cups cold milk	Paprika
2 tablespoons finely chopped green onions or chives	Slivered lemon rind
	1 hard-cooked egg, chopped

Mix all ingredients, except last 3. Chill several hours, or overnight. Garnish each serving with a sprinkling of paprika, lemon rind, and a spoonful of chopped egg. Makes 4 servings.

LOBSTER BISQUE

You can serve this hot or cold.

2 tablespoons quick-cooking tapioca	1 can (6½ ounces) lobster, or 1½ cups cooked lobster meat, cut in chunks
1¼ teaspoons salt	
⅛ teaspoon each pepper and paprika	
1 tablespoon minced onion	2 tablespoons butter
3 cups milk	2 tablespoons sherry or brandy
1 cup light cream	

In top part of double boiler mix tapioca, salt, pepper, paprika, onion, milk, and cream. Put over rapidly boiling water, and cook 15 minutes, stirring frequently. Add lobster and butter. Keep over hot water 15 minutes to blend flavors. Add sherry or brandy. Serve at once, or cool, stir, then chill overnight. Makes 4 servings.

Crab-meat Bisque: Substitute 1 can (6½ ounces) crab meat for the lobster in the above recipe.

MINESTRONE

An Italian soup, featuring hot sausage.

¼ pound bacon, chopped	1 can (19 ounces) tomatoes
2 onions, sliced	½ cup canned chick peas
1 clove garlic, minced	½ teaspoon dried basil
½ cup chopped celery and leaves	¼ teaspoon orégano
1 carrot, sliced	Salt
¼ cup chopped parsley	½ cup fancy macaroni
1 cup chopped escarole	Cayenne
1 cup chopped cabbage	1 pound hot Italian sausage, sliced and fried
6 cups water	Grated Parmesan cheese
1½ cups cooked dried beans	

Brown bacon and onion in large kettle. Add remaining raw vegetables; cook 10 minutes, stirring occasionally. Add water, beans, tomatoes, chick peas, herbs, and 2 teaspoons salt. Bring to boil; cover, and simmer 30 minutes. Add macaroni, and cook 10 minutes, or until tender. Add salt and cayenne to taste. Serve topped with sausage and cheese. Makes about 3 quarts.

CRÈME VICHYSSOISE

A rich, smooth blend of leeks, onion, and potatoes.

4 large leeks	1 large bay leaf
1 onion, chopped	4 whole cloves
¼ cup butter or margarine	3 cups milk
	2 cups cream
3 large potatoes, thinly sliced	Salt
	White pepper
4 cups well-seasoned chicken stock	Chopped chives

Wash leeks well, and chop white part fine. Cook with onion in the butter 5 minutes. Do not brown. Add potatoes, stock, bay leaf, and cloves. Bring to boil, cover, and simmer 45 minutes. Force through a fine sieve. Add milk and cream; bring to scalding point. Season to taste. Chill overnight. Serve in chilled bowls with a garnish of chives. Makes about 2 quarts.

MIDWEST CORN CHOWDER

You use cream-style corn blended with evaporated milk.

8 ounces salt pork, diced	3 cups diced potato
2 onions, chopped	1 can (1 pound, 1 ounce) cream-style corn
½ cup chopped celery and tops	2 cups evaporated milk
½ bay leaf, crumbled	Salt and pepper
2 tablespoons flour	Chopped parsley
4 cups water	Paprika

In large kettle, cook salt pork until browned and crisp. Remove pork, and pour off all but 3 tablespoons fat. Add next 3 ingredients, and cook 5 minutes. Blend in flour. Add water and potato; bring to boil, and simmer, covered, 15 minutes. Add corn and milk; heat well. Season. Add pork, and serve with parsley and paprika. Makes about 2 quarts.

"Soup is to a meal what a portico is to a palace."
GRIMMOD DE LA REYNIÈRE

POLISH BORSCH

*Boiled potatoes are served
with this beet and sour-cream soup.*

1½ pounds beef	1 onion, minced
chuck, cut up	Salt and pepper
1½ quarts water	¼ cup sour cream
4 medium beets,	2 tablespoons
cooked and sliced	flour
2 stalks celery,	1 egg
diced	Hot boiled potatoes

Put meat in kettle, and add water. Bring
to boil, and simmer, covered, 2 hours,
or until meat is almost tender. Add
beets, celery, and onion; cook about
30 minutes longer. Season to taste.
Blend sour cream, flour, and egg. Stir
into soup, and bring again to boil.
Serve in hot soup bowls. Pass potatoes.
Makes 4 servings.

CHEDDAR-CHEESE SOUP
WITH FRANKFURTERS

*It contains vegetables, too:
celery and onions and a carrot.*

1 onion, sliced	2 bouillon cubes
1 cup diced celery	2 cups water
¼ cup butter or	1 carrot, diced
margarine	1 quart milk
¼ cup flour	6 ounces sharp
½ teaspoon dry	cheddar cheese,
mustard	shredded
1 teaspoon	Salt and pepper
Worcestershire	2 frankfurters,
½ teaspoon	thinly sliced
garlic salt	
½ teaspoon Accent	

In large saucepan, cook onion and celery in butter about 5 minutes. Blend in
next 5 ingredients. Add bouillon cubes,
water, and carrot. Bring to boil, and
simmer, covered, 15 minutes. Add milk,
and heat almost to boiling. Add cheese;
stir until cheese is melted. Season to
taste. Add frankfurters, and heat. Makes
about 1½ quarts.

RUMANIAN CABBAGE SOUP

*Sugar, vinegar, and dill
give this a sweet-sour flavor.*

2 pounds beef	1 onion
chuck, in one	1 clove garlic
piece	Few sprigs parsley
2 pounds beef	1 bay leaf
soup bones	1 head cabbage
2 quarts water	1 tablespoon sugar
1 tablespoon salt	1 tablespoon
¼ teaspoon pepper	vinegar
1 can (19 ounces)	Minced fresh dill,
tomatoes	or dill seeds

Put all ingredients, except last 4, in
large kettle. Bring to boil, and simmer
covered, 1½ hours. Shred cabbage
coarsely, and add with sugar and vinegar to soup. Continue simmering 1½
hours longer, or until meat is very tender. Skim off fat. Remove meat, and cut
in bite-size pieces. Cut marrow from
bones, and return with meat to soup.
Add more seasoning if necessary. Serve
hot with sprinkling of dill. Makes about
4 quarts.

BOUILLABAISSE

*All kinds of white fish, plus shrimp,
crab or lobster, and oysters or clams.*

1 carrot, chopped	1 box (12 ounces)
2 onions, chopped	frozen shelled
White part of 2	cleaned shrimp,
leeks, chopped	or 1 can (6½
1 clove garlic,	ounces) crab or
crushed	lobster meat
½ cup olive oil	1 dozen oysters
3 pounds boned	or clams in the
assorted white	shells, scrubbed
fish	2 pimientos,
2 large tomatoes,	minced
chopped, or 1	Few grains
cup canned	powdered saffron
tomatoes	½ cup dry
1 bay leaf	white wine
2 cups water	Pepper
Salt	Chopped parsley

In large kettle, cook first 4 ingredients
in olive oil until golden brown. Add fish,
cut in 3″ pieces, tomatoes, bay leaf,
water, and 2 teaspoons salt. Bring to
boil, and simmer 20 minutes. Add shellfish, and simmer 5 minutes longer. Add
pimientos, saffron, wine, and salt and
pepper to taste. Serve with garnish of
parsley. Makes 6 servings.

*"This Bouillabaisse a noble
dish is, A sort of soup, or
broth, or brew."*
WILLIAM MAKEPEACE THACKERAY

ENGLISH MULLIGATAWNY

A hearty, curried chicken soup.

1 fryer, cut up	¼ cup vegetable
1½ quarts water	oil
Salt	⅓ cup flour
3 onions	2 tablespoons
1 stalk celery,	curry powder
chopped	Dash cayenne
3 carrots, sliced	Pepper
1 clove garlic,	Hot cooked rice
minced	Chopped parsley
1 peeled tart	
apple, chopped	

Put chicken in kettle with water, 2 teaspoons salt, 2 quartered onions, celery, and carrots. Bring to boil, and simmer, covered, 30 minutes. Chop the remaining onion, and cook with garlic and apple in the oil 5 minutes. Blend in flour and curry powder. Add 1 cup broth from chicken, and simmer 30 minutes longer. Add cayenne; season. Serve with rice and parsley. Makes about 1½ quarts.

SHRIMP SOUP, SUPREME

Heavy cream and sherry are what make this so supreme.

¾ pound fresh or	½ teaspoon paprika
frozen shrimp	½ teaspoon
Salt	seasoned salt
1 bay leaf	¼ teaspoon white
1 sliced carrot	pepper
1 sliced onion	1 teaspoon
3 cups milk	Worcestershire
2 tablespoons butter	1 cup heavy cream
1 cup minced celery	2 tablespoons
1 onion, minced	sherry
1 tablespoon flour	Minced parsley

Cook shrimp in boiling salted water with bay leaf, carrot, and sliced onion. Drain, remove shells, and clean. Purée in electric blender with 1 cup of the milk, or chop very fine. Melt butter in top part of double boiler. Add celery and onion; cook 5 minutes. Blend in flour, 1 teaspoon salt, remaining seasonings. Add shrimp, 2 cups milk, cream. Cook over boiling water until slightly thickened, stirring occasionally. Add sherry, and serve garnished with parsley. Makes about 1½ quarts.

Crab Soup, Supreme: Substitute 1 box (6 ounces) frozen king crab meat, chopped fine, for the shrimp.

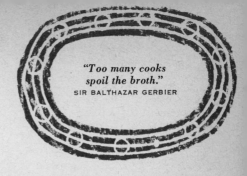

"Too many cooks spoil the broth."
SIR BALTHAZAR GERBIER

CREAM-OF-LENTIL SOUP

This contains several vegetables, plus bologna, salami, or ham.

1 pound dried	¼ teaspoon dry
lentils	mustard
3 quarts water	¼ pound Genoa
2 tablespoons	bologna, hard
instant bouillon	salami, or
1 onion, chopped	boiled ham,
1 clove garlic,	cut in thin strips
minced	Salt and pepper
1 carrot, chopped	1 cup cream
1 stalk celery,	
chopped	

Wash lentils, and soak overnight in the water; do not drain. Add bouillon, vegetables, and mustard. Bring to boil, and simmer, covered, 2 hours, or until lentils are very tender. If desired, force through sieve. Add meat; season to taste; simmer 10 minutes. Add cream just before serving. Makes 2 quarts.

BEAN AND BACON CHOWDER

The beans are dried navy or pea beans.

1 cup dried navy	1 cup diced potato
or pea beans	1 cup diced celery
1 quart water	and leaves
4 slices bacon,	1 can (19 ounces)
diced	tomatoes
1 onion, chopped	2 tablespoons flour
2 teaspoons salt	2 cups hot milk
¼ teaspoon pepper	

Combine beans and water in large kettle. Bring to boil, and boil 2 minutes. Remove from heat. Let stand 1 hour. Cook bacon and onion until lightly browned. Add, with fat, to beans. Simmer, covered, 1 hour. Add all ingredients, except last 2, and simmer 30 minutes. Thicken with flour blended with a little cold water. Add milk. Makes about 2 quarts.

*"Beautiful Soup,
so rich and green,
Waiting in a hot tureen!"*
LEWIS CARROLL

MUSHROOM BISQUE

*The broth is chicken stock,
milk, and sherry.*

1 pound mushrooms	⅛ teaspoon
1 small onion,	pepper
grated	4 cups milk
Butter or margarine	½ cup chicken
¼ cup flour	stock
1 teaspoon salt	¼ cup sherry

Slice, and reserve 6 mushrooms. Chop remainder, including stems. Cook with onion in ¼ cup butter 10 minutes. Blend in flour and seasonings. Add milk and chicken stock, and cook until thickened, stirring constantly. Add sherry. Garnish with sliced mushrooms, cooked in small amount of butter. Makes about 1½ quarts.

CANADIAN SPLIT-PEA SOUP

There's meat in it, too: pork sausage.

1 pound green	Few sprigs
split peas	parsley,
2½ quarts water	chopped
3 onions, chopped	Dash cayenne
2 carrots, diced	Salt and pepper
2 or 3 small	1 pound pork
bay leaves	sausage meat
Few celery tops,	Rye-bread
chopped	croutons

Wash, and drain peas. Put in 6-quart kettle with all ingredients, except last 4. Bring to boil, and simmer, covered, 2 hours, or until peas are mushy. Season to taste. Purée through sieve, food mill, or in blender. (Or serve as is.) Reheat. Shape sausage into 16 small balls, and cook slowly in skillet until browned and done. Drain on absorbent paper, and serve on soup with croutons. Makes about 3 quarts.

CHINESE EGG-DROP SOUP

*The eggs, beaten, are
stirred in just before serving.*

2 tablespoons	½ teaspoon Accent
cornstarch	1 to 1½ cups
6 cups stock	chopped raw
2 tablespoons	vegetables
soy sauce	and cooked
3 tablespoons	shrimp, meat,
vinegar	poultry, or fish
¼ teaspoon pepper	3 eggs, beaten

In large saucepan, mix cornstarch with small amount of cold stock. Add remaining stock and other ingredients, except eggs. Bring to boil, and simmer until clear, stirring occasionally. Gradually stir in eggs, season to taste, and serve at once. Makes about 1½ quarts.

SENATE BEAN SOUP

*The beans can be marrow,
navy, great northern, or pea.*

1 pound dried	3 potatoes, cooked
marrow, navy,	and mashed
great northern,	2 onions, chopped
or pea beans	1 cup diced celery
5 quarts water	2 cloves garlic,
1 large smoked-	minced
ham hock	Salt and pepper

Wash beans, and cover with the water. Bring to boil, and boil 2 minutes. Remove from heat, and let stand 1 hour. Bring again to boil, and simmer, covered, 2 hours, or until beans begin to mush. Add all but salt and pepper, and simmer 1 hour longer. Remove bone, cut up meat, and return to soup. Season to taste. Makes about 4 quarts.

SCALLOP STEW

*The base is milk and cream, the
scallops minced.*

3 cups milk	1½ teaspoons salt
1 cup heavy cream	1 pound sea
2 tablespoons butter	scallops
2 teaspoons sugar	Paprika
1 teaspoon	Chopped parsley
Worcestershire	

In top part of large double boiler over boiling water, heat first 6 ingredients. Mince scallops, and add to milk mixture. Cook 5 minutes. Serve sprinkled with paprika and chopped parsley. Makes 4 servings.

TOMATO-PEANUT BISQUE

*You use both peanut butter
and chopped salted peanuts.*

1 can (1 pint, 2 ounces) tomato juice	½ teaspoon seasoned salt
1 cup peanut butter	⅛ teaspoon pepper
1 cup milk	2 hard-cooked eggs, sliced
½ teaspoon Worcestershire	Chopped parsley
	Coarsely chopped salted peanuts

Put tomato juice, peanut butter, and milk in saucepan. Beat with rotary beater until blended. Add seasonings, and heat. Serve with garnish of last 3 ingredients. Makes about 1 quart.

PARISIAN ONION SOUP

Onions are cooked in milk and cream.

3 onions, minced	Salt and pepper
3 tablespoons butter or margarine	Toasted French-bread slices
1 tablespoon flour	¾ cup grated Gruyère cheese
2 cups each light cream and milk	

In large saucepan, cook onions in the butter 5 minutes. Blend in flour. Add cream and milk, and bring to boil. Simmer 10 minutes. Season to taste. Put toast in a tureen. Pour soup over toast, and sprinkle with cheese. Grate some pepper over top. Makes 4 servings.

SCOTCH BROTH

*A hearty combination of lamb,
barley, and lots of vegetables.*

2 pounds breast of lamb, cut up	1½ cups diced carrot
1 lamb shank	½ cup diced rutabaga
2 quarts water	3 onions, chopped
Salt	1½ cups sliced celery
Whole peppers	Thyme
½ cup pearl barley	Pepper
1 soup bunch, chopped	

Brown breast of lamb in heavy kettle, stirring frequently. Pour off fat. Add shank, water, 1 tablespoon salt, whole peppers, barley, and soup bunch. Bring to boil; cover, and simmer about 2 hours. Remove meat; cool, trim off any excess fat; remove bones, and put meat back in kettle. Add vegetables, bring to boil, and simmer ½ hour. Season to taste. Makes about 2½ quarts.

OYSTER STEW

*During the R-less months, you can
use canned or frozen oysters.*

3 dozen oysters with liquid	½ cup clam juice
½ cup butter or margarine	4 cups hot milk
⅛ teaspoon Worcestershire	4 cups hot light cream
Dash cayenne	Salt and pepper
	Paprika

Cook first 4 ingredients in large skillet just until edges of oysters begin to curl. Add clam juice, milk, and cream; heat, but do not boil. Add salt and pepper to taste. Sprinkle servings with paprika. Makes 4 servings.

Clam Stew: Substitute 3 dozen shucked soft-shell clams with liquid for the oysters. Omit ½ cup clam juice.

Lobster Stew: Substitute 2 cups diced cooked lobster meat for the oysters.

BLACK-BEAN SOUP

*A Southern favorite, garnished
with lemon and hard-cooked egg slices.*

3 cups dried black beans	Pinch thyme
1 ham bone	2 onions, chopped
3 quarts water	1 carrot, diced
2 ounces salt pork, minced	Salt and pepper
1 clove garlic, minced	Sherry
1 bay leaf	Lemon slices
	Hard-cooked egg slices

Soak beans and bone in water overnight. Cook in same water with next 4 ingredients 2 hours. Add onion and carrot; simmer 1 hour longer, remove bone. Put mixture, a small amount at a time, in blender; run until smooth. Return to kettle; heat, and add seasonings and sherry to taste. Serve with garnish of lemon and egg. Makes about 2 quarts.

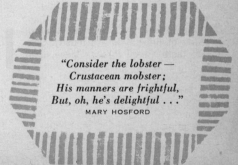

*"Consider the lobster —
Crustacean mobster;
His manners are frightful,
But, oh, he's delightful . . ."*
MARY HOSFORD

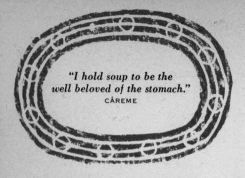

"I hold soup to be the well beloved of the stomach."
CÂREME

TURKISH WEDDING SOUP

Spirals of lemon peel and a sprinkling of paprika give this a festive look.

3 pounds lamb neck, cut up	2½ quarts water
1 medium onion, sliced	¼ cup butter or margarine
1 carrot, peeled	¼ cup flour
Salt	3 egg yolks, beaten
⅛ teaspoon cayenne	Juice 1 large lemon
	Paprika
	Spirals of lemon peel

Put first 3 ingredients in kettle. Add 2 teaspoons salt, the cayenne, and water. Bring to boil, and simmer, covered, 3 hours, or until lamb is tender. Strain broth, and skim off excess fat. Discard bones, and chop meat fine. Melt butter, and blend in flour. Stir in some of the broth. Add to rest of broth in kettle, cook until slightly thickened. Add meat, and season to taste. Mix egg yolks and lemon juice. Stir in about 2 cups of soup, then stir mixture into remaining soup. Serve with paprika and lemon peel. Makes about 3 quarts.

ANCHOVY AND RICE SOUP

The base is beef consommé, and grated cheese is a last-minute touch.

¼ cup butter or margarine	3 cans (10½ ounces each) beef consommé
1 onion, minced	3 cans water
⅓ cup uncooked rice	Grated Parmesan cheese
1 can (2 ounces) anchovy fillets, mashed	

Melt butter. Add onion, and cook 5 minutes. Add remaining ingredients, except cheese. Simmer, covered, 30 minutes. Serve with cheese and a few whole anchovies, if desired. Makes 4 servings.

BONITO CHOWDER

A chowder without salt pork, for those who observe meatless days.

1 tablespoon butter	1 can (7 ounces) bonito
1 onion, minced	3 cups milk
1 cup diced potato	1 teaspoon salt
½ cup diced celery	¼ teaspoon pepper
1 carrot, diced	Dash of thyme
1 cup boiling water	2 tablespoons flour
	Chopped chives

Melt butter in large saucepan, add onion, and cook until onion is golden. Add vegetables and water; cover, and cook 15 minutes, or until vegetables are tender. Add bonito, 2¾ cups of the milk, and the seasonings; heat well. Blend remaining ¼ cup milk with flour, and add slowly to hot mixture, stirring constantly. Cook until slightly thickened, stirring constantly. Serve with a sprinkling of chives. Makes 4 servings.

CRÈME MONGOLE

Cream-of-tomato and pea soups are laced with sherry.

1 can each tomato soup and green-pea soup	1 cup light cream
¾ cup water	2 teaspoons Worcestershire
	¼ cup sherry

Mix all ingredients, except sherry. Heat slowly, stirring frequently. Remove from heat, and add sherry. Makes 1 quart.

PORTUGUESE EGG SOUP

The eggs are poached in simmering seasoned broth.

1 cup sliced onions	½ teaspoon thyme
1 clove garlic, minced	1 teaspoon celery salt
1 tablespoon olive oil	¼ teaspoon pepper
6 cups water	French bread
6 bouillon cubes	4 eggs
	Minced parsley

In large saucepan, cook onion and garlic in the olive oil until golden. Add water, bouillon cubes, and seasonings. Bring to boil, and simmer 5 minutes. Break French bread in bits, and toast lightly in moderate oven. Drop eggs, one at a time, into simmering broth, and poach 5 minutes. Remove, putting 1 in each of 4 hot bowls. Add some toast bits; fill bowls with broth. Garnish with parsley. Makes 4 servings.

CHICKEN SOUP WITH SWEDISH DUMPLINGS

The dumplings contain cardamom seeds and minced almonds.

1½ quarts chicken broth	1 tablespoon sugar
2 cups diced cooked chicken	2 tablespoons butter
¼ cup flour	1 egg, beaten
1 cup milk	8 blanched almonds, minced
¾ teaspoon salt	2 sprigs parsley, minced
2 cardamom seeds, crushed, or ⅛ teaspoon nutmeg	

Bring broth and chicken to boil in kettle. To make dumplings, in saucepan, blend flour and a little milk to a paste. Add remaining milk, salt, cardamom, and sugar. Cook until thickened, stirring constantly. Add butter, and stir until melted. Pour over egg; mix, and cool. Add almonds and parsley. Drop into gently boiling soup. Cook 2 minutes, or until dumplings rise to top. Makes 4 servings.

CREAM-OF-CHICKEN SOUP AUX FINES HERBES

The herbs: thyme, marjoram, and chives.

1 fryer, cut up	½ teaspoon each dried thyme, marjoram, and chives (or fresh herbs to taste)
4 cups water	
2 chicken bouillon cubes	
1 bay leaf	
1 onion	⅛ teaspoon nutmeg
1 stalk celery	½ teaspoon turmeric
1 peeled carrot	¾ cup cooked rice
½ cup butter or margarine	Salt and freshly ground pepper
½ cup flour	Chopped parsley
2 cups each milk and light cream	Toasted sesame seeds

Put first 7 ingredients in kettle, bring to boil, and simmer, covered, 1½ hours, or until chicken is tender. Remove skin and bones from chicken, and cut meat in bite-size pieces. Strain broth, and reserve. In same kettle, melt butter, and blend in flour. Add milk and cream, and cook until thickened, stirring constantly. Add herbs, nutmeg, turmeric, rice, chicken broth, and chicken. Heat well. Season to taste. Serve with a sprinkling of parsley and sesame seeds. Makes about 2½ quarts.

SALMON AND TOMATO SOUP

Thyme, bouillon cubes, tomatoes, and sherry flavor this.

1 onion, chopped	1½ teaspoons salt
½ green pepper, chopped	¼ teaspoon pepper
2 tablespoons butter	2 bouillon cubes
3 cups diced potato	1 can (1 pound) tomatoes
4 cups water	1 can (1 pound) salmon
½ teaspoon crumbled thyme	2 tablespoons sherry

Cook onion and pepper in the butter 5 minutes. Add all ingredients, except last 2, and simmer about 15 minutes. Add salmon, broken in chunks, and the liquid from the can. Add sherry, and heat. Makes 6 servings.

MEAT-BALL SOUP

Well seasoned, in the Italian way.

¾ pound ground beef	Dash of pepper
1 small clove garlic, minced	2 eggs
	Flour
Few sprigs parsley, chopped	2 beef bouillon cubes
¼ teaspoon marjoram	4 cups water
¼ teaspoon dried basil	1 cup canned tomatoes
¼ teaspoon onion salt	1 small bay leaf, crumbled
1½ teaspoons salt	2 tablespoons uncooked rice

Mix first 6 ingredients, ½ teaspoon salt, pepper, and 1 egg. Shape into 32 tiny balls; dredge with flour. Bring bouillon cubes, water, tomatoes, 1 teaspoon salt, and bay leaf to boil in kettle. Add meat balls and rice. Cover, and simmer 45 minutes. Just before serving, stir in remaining egg, beaten slightly with fork. Makes 4 servings.

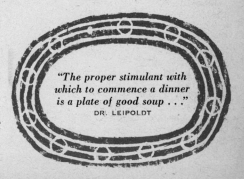

"The proper stimulant with which to commence a dinner is a plate of good soup . . ."
DR. LEIPOLDT

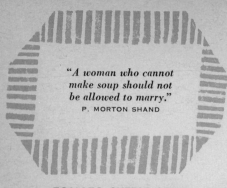

"A woman who cannot make soup should not be allowed to marry."
P. MORTON SHAND

TOMATO-CHEESE SOUP

A smooth, chilled mixture of cream-of-tomato soup and cottage cheese.

1 can cream-of-tomato soup	¼ teaspoon pepper
Juice ½ lemon	½ cup cottage cheese
2 cups milk	2 tablespoons chopped green onion
1 teaspoon prepared horse-radish	4 thin unpeeled cucumber slices
Cayenne	
½ teaspoon salt	

Put soup in bowl. Add remaining ingredients, except last 3. Beat with rotary beater, or put in blender and run until thoroughly mixed. Add cottage cheese and onion. Mix well, and chill several hours. Serve with a garnish of cucumber. Makes 4 servings.

FRENCH ONION SOUP

The onions are cooked in stock and white wine.

6 medium onions	Salt and pepper
Butter or margarine	Small slices crisp toasted French bread
4 cups beef or chicken stock	Grated Parmesan or hard Gruyère cheese
2 cups dry white wine or stock	

Peel onions, and slice thin. Melt 4 tablespoons butter in heavy kettle or Dutch oven. Brown onions in the butter. Add stock and wine; bring to boil, and simmer ½ hour, or until onions are tender. Season to taste. Put in large earthenware casserole or individual casseroles. Top with toast, sprinkle with cheese, and dot with butter. Put in moderate oven, 350°F., about 10 minutes. Serve with more cheese. Makes about 1½ quarts.

FRENCH POTATO SOUP

A bit of butter goes into each bowl.

4 medium potatoes	1½ cups top milk, scalded
3 to 4 leeks, white part only	White pepper
Butter or margarine	2 egg yolks
Salt	Croutons

Peel, and dice potatoes; put in large saucepan. Chop leeks fine, and brown lightly in 2 tablespoons butter. Add to potatoes. Add boiling water to cover and ½ teaspoon salt. Cover, bring to boil, and cook until potatoes are tender. Put entire mixture through food mill, or purée in blender. Add milk, and heat. Season to taste. Beat in egg yolks. Serve with a spoonful of butter and a few croutons in each bowl. Serves 4.

GREEK LEMON SOUP

The base is chicken stock, with eggs and rice to give it body.

4 cups strained well-seasoned chicken stock	3 eggs
	Juice 1 medium lemon
¼ cup uncooked rice	Salt
	White pepper

Heat stock in saucepan. Add rice, cover, and simmer until rice is tender, about 25 minutes. Beat eggs and lemon juice; add ½ cup hot stock, 1 tablespoon at a time, stirring. Then stir into rest of stock. Season; serve. Makes 1 quart.

COTTAGE-CHEESE SOUP

A pale soup, with pimiento and watercress garnish to give it color.

1 teaspoon celery seed	⅛ teaspoon white pepper
4 cups milk	½ teaspoon paprika
1 tablespoon minced onion	Dash nutmeg
¼ cup butter or margarine	2 cups dry cottage cheese
2 tablespoons flour	2 tablespoons minced pimiento
1¾ teaspoons salt	Minced watercress

Put celery seed and milk in top part of double boiler. Heat over boiling water 15 minutes; strain. Cook onion in the butter 5 minutes. Blend in flour and seasonings. Add milk, and cook until thickened, stirring constantly. Force cheese through a sieve, and add to soup. Heat. Serve garnished with pimiento and watercress. Serves 4.

MAINE FISH CHOWDER

The fish is cod or haddock.

4 cups water	¼ pound salt pork,
Salt and pepper	diced
1 bay leaf	2 onions, chopped
4 whole cloves	3 cups diced potato
1 pound frozen cod	4 saltines
or haddock	2½ cups top milk

Bring to boil: water, 1 teaspoon salt, ¼ teaspoon pepper, bay leaf, and cloves. Add fish, and simmer 15 minutes, or until cooked. Drain, reserving liquid. Remove fish, and separate in large pieces. Cook salt pork in kettle until golden brown. Remove pork, and reserve. Pour off all but 1 tablespoon fat. Add onion, and cook until golden brown. Add strained fish liquid and potato. Bring to boil; cover, and simmer 15 minutes. Add fish, crumbled saltines, and milk. Heat well. Season to taste with salt and pepper. Serve garnished with pork. Makes about 1½ quarts.

PETITE MARMITE

There's nothing petite about this beef, chicken, and vegetable soup.

3 medium onions,	Few sprigs parsley
sliced	½ teaspoon thyme
1 tablespoon butter	2 whole cloves
2 pounds beef	1 cup diced celery
chuck in one	4 carrots, diced
piece	3 sliced leeks,
2 pounds beef	white part only
soup bones	¼ small green
1 fowl	cabbage, slivered
3 quarts water	1 box frozen peas
Salt	Pepper
2 bay leaves	Grated cheese
8 whole black	
peppers	

Brown onions in butter in large kettle. Add beef, bones, fowl, water, 1 tablespoon salt, bay leaves, whole peppers, parsley, thyme, and cloves. Bring to boil, and simmer, covered, 4 hours, or until meats are tender. Remove meats, cool, and slice thin. Cook remaining vegetables for garnish until barely tender in a little boiling salted water. Drain. Strain soup mixture, and reheat. Season to taste with salt and pepper. Put some vegetables and meat slices in individual marmites or soup bowls. Cover with broth. Serve with grated cheese. Makes 6 to 8 servings.

PORTUGUESE BEAN SOUP

The beans are dried red kidney beans.

1 cup dried red	6 potatoes, diced
kidney beans	2 bay leaves
2 quarts water	1 teaspoon ground
3 onions, sliced	allspice
2 cloves garlic,	1 can (8 ounces)
minced	tomato paste
¼ cup bacon fat	Salt and pepper

Put beans and water in kettle, and bring to boil. Boil 2 minutes. Remove from heat, and let stand 1 hour. Then bring again to boil, and simmer, covered, 1½ hours, or until beans are tender. Cook onions and garlic in bacon fat until lightly browned. Add with remaining ingredients, except salt and pepper, to beans. Cover, and simmer 1½ hours. Season. Makes 3 quarts.

PEPPER POT SOUP

A traditional Pennsylvania Dutch recipe, featuring veal and tripe.

Veal bone	1½ quarts water
1 pound boneless	2 potatoes, diced
stewing veal,	2 carrots, diced
cut up	¼ cup diced
½ pound tripe,	celery
cubed	½ medium green
½ bay leaf	pepper, chopped
Salt	2 tablespoons
⅛ teaspoon whole	butter
black peppers	Pepper
3 onions, diced	Minced parsley

Put bone, veal, tripe, bay leaf, 2 teaspoons salt, whole peppers, and ⅓ of onion in large kettle. Add water. Bring to boil; cover, and simmer 2 hours; remove bone. Cook remaining onion, potato, carrot, celery, and green pepper in butter 10 minutes. Add to meat mixture, and simmer 30 minutes. Season. Serve with parsley. Makes 2 quarts.

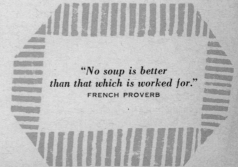

"No soup is better than that which is worked for."
FRENCH PROVERB

NEW ENGLAND CLAM CHOWDER

This clam chowder has a milk base.

18 chowder clams	2 onions, sliced
1 cup water	2 potatoes, diced
1 stalk celery	3 cups milk
¼ pound salt pork, diced	Salt and pepper
	6 pilot crackers, crumbled

Scrub clams, and put in large kettle with water and celery; cover, and simmer 15 minutes, or until shells open. Strain off clam broth, and reserve. Cook salt pork slowly in heavy kettle until browned. Pour off all but 2 tablespoons fat. Cook onions with pork until tender but not browned. Mince hard part of clams; add to onions and pork with potatoes and clam broth; bring to boil, and simmer 20 minutes, or until potatoes are tender. Scald milk; add to soup with soft part of clams; season. Add crackers. Makes 1½ quarts.

CHICK-PEA SOUP

This soup contains ham broth, smoked ham, and Spanish sausage.

1¾ cups dried chick peas	1 potato, diced
4 cups water	⅓ cup diced cooked smoked ham
1 clove garlic, minced	½ pound Spanish sausage, sliced
2 onions, chopped	Salt
1 tablespoon oil	Cayenne
4 cups ham broth	Minced parsley

Put chick peas in kettle, and cover with the water. Bring to boil, and boil 2 minutes. Remove from heat, and let stand 1 hour. Cook garlic and onion in oil 5 minutes; add to soaked chick peas with the ham broth. Bring to boil, and simmer, covered, 1½ hours, or until chick peas are tender. Add potato, ham, and sausage; cook 30 minutes, or until potato is tender. Season to taste. Serve with parsley. Makes about 2 quarts.

MANHATTAN CLAM CHOWDER

The clam chowder that contains tomato and other vegetables.

¼ pound salt pork, diced	3 cups diced potato
1 large onion, sliced	3 cups water
	Salt
½ medium green pepper, chopped	1 pint clams and liquid
½ cup each diced celery, carrot, and turnip	Pinch of thyme
	2 cups tomato juice
	½ cup tomato purée
	Chopped parsley

Brown pork in heavy kettle. Pour off all but 1 tablespoon fat. Add onion, pepper, and celery; brown lightly. Add carrot, turnip, potato, water, and 1 teaspoon salt. Chop hard part of clams, and add to soup with clam liquid; reserve soft part of clams. Simmer about 30 minutes. Add coarsely cut soft part of clams, thyme, tomato juice, and tomato purée; bring to boil, and simmer 5 minutes. Season with salt and pepper to taste. Serve garnished with parsley. Makes about 2 quarts.

PENNSYLVANIA DUTCH CHICKEN-CORN SOUP

The Pennsylvania Dutch touch is rivels, dumpling-like bits of dough.

1 fowl, cut up	2 cans (1 pound, 1 ounce each) whole-kernel corn, drained
1 onion, quartered	
3 quarts water	
½ teaspoon whole mixed pickling spice	2 hard-cooked eggs, chopped
Salt	Pepper
2 stalks celery with leaves, chopped	Rivels

Put fowl in large kettle. Add onion, water, spice, and 2 teaspoons salt. Bring to boil, and simmer, covered, 4 hours, until fowl is tender. Remove from broth, and cool. Cut meat in small pieces. Strain broth, and skim off most of fat. Add chicken, celery, and corn. Bring to boil, and simmer 10 to 15 minutes. Add eggs, and salt and pepper to taste. Add small bits of Rivel dough, cover, and simmer 7 minutes. Makes about 3 quarts of soup.

Rivels: Beat 1 egg and ¼ cup milk. Add to 1 cup sifted flour and ⅛ teaspoon salt; mix well.

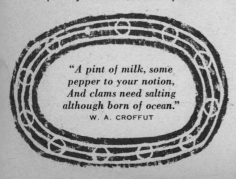

"A pint of milk, some pepper to your notion, And clams need salting although born of ocean."
W. A. CROFFUT

BEEF

Beefsteak is the most popular dinner entree in all sections of the country. It has been estimated that the average American consumes about 100 pounds of beef every year. Our great western range lands, our rich corn and grain belt, our scientific meat packers, and our government inspection and grading give us an abundance of high-quality beef. But our excellent supply of heavy aged beefsteaks and roasts may lead us to forget the many delicious ways of preparing other beef cuts, just as flavorful and sometimes even tastier. Take, for example, the classic dish beef à la môde, fine eating when it's hot and even better cold; the succulent beef and kidney pie, oozing rich juices; shepherd's pie, a subtle blend of vegetable and beef flavors and a meal in itself; boiled beef steeped in seasoned broth, the specialty of Viennese chefs. These and more recipes are here to give a new lift to your menus and help you appreciate one of our basic American foods.

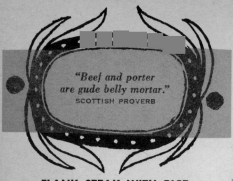

"Beef and porter
are gude belly mortar."
SCOTTISH PROVERB

FLANK STEAK WITH RICE

*You use packaged precooked rice
with onion soup as the liquid.*

½ to ¾ pound flank steak	1 package dry onion-soup mix
1 teaspoon sugar	1½ cups packaged precooked rice
3 cups water	

Cut flank steak into ⅛-inch-thick slivers. Brown sugar in pan, add meat, and cook until meat loses its color. Add water; bring to boil, stir in onion-soup mix, and simmer 15 minutes. Stir in rice; cover, remove from heat, and let stand about 5 minutes. Serves 3 to 4.

CHINESE PEPPER STEAK

Soy sauce flavors the gravy.

½ to ¾ pound flank steak	½ cup celery, cut in chunks
2 tablespoons vegetable oil	½ cup beef bouillon or ½ cup boiling water and 1 beef bouillon cube
½ teaspoon salt	
Dash pepper	
2 tablespoons chopped onion or green onion	1 tablespoon cornstarch
½ clove garlic, minced	2 tablespoons water
2 green peppers, cut in large pieces	1 teaspoon soy sauce
	Hot cooked rice

Cut flank steak slantwise into ⅛-inch-thick slivers, and brown in large, heavy frying pan in oil with salt and pepper. Add onion, garlic, green pepper, and celery. Add beef bouillon; cover, and cook until meat and vegetables are tender but not limp, about 10 minutes. Blend cornstarch, water, and soy sauce; add to meat and vegetables. Cook until thickened, stirring constantly. Serve at once with rice. Makes 2 servings.

STUFFED STEAK, VENEZUELAN

*The stuffing is diced bacon
and dried hot red pepper.*

2 to 3 pounds round steak	¼ cup butter or margarine
Salt and pepper	1 tablespoon brown sugar
2 strips bacon, diced	1 can (19 ounces) tomatoes
1 crumbled dried hot red pepper	1 cup water
	1 bay leaf

Make a gash lengthwise through steak. Sprinkle pocket with salt and pepper; fill with bacon and red pepper. Brown on both sides in butter. Add sugar; heat until bubbly. Add next 3 ingredients, and a little wine, if desired. Cover; simmer 1½ to 2 hours. Remove steak to hot platter. Boil sauce a few minutes; season; serve with the steak. Serves 4 to 6.

BAKED SIRLOIN STEAK

*It's covered with
lemon and onion slices.*

3 pounds sirloin steak, about 1½ inches thick	1 lemon, sliced very thin
2 tablespoons butter or margarine	2 white onions, thinly sliced
1 teaspoon salt	1 cup ketchup
½ teaspoon pepper	1 tablespoon Worcestershire
	¼ cup water

Rub both sides of steak with butter; sprinkle with salt and pepper. Put on greased rack in shallow baking pan. Arrange lemon on steak; cover with onion. Mix ketchup, Worcestershire, water; pour over all. Bake in hot oven, 425°F., 30 to 45 minutes, depending on the degree of rareness desired. Makes 6 to 8 servings.

FILET MIGNON, BÉARNAISE SAUCE

*You dip the filets in melted
butter before broiling them.*

Have filets cut thick and uniform in size. Dip each in melted butter, and broil 10 to 15 minutes under moderate heat. Season with salt and freshly ground pepper; arrange on a bed of Béarnaise Sauce, page 239.

36

SWISS CUBED STEAKS

*They simmer in tomato sauce with
onion, garlic, celery, Worcestershire.*

1½ pounds cubed steaks	1 cup water
2 tablespoons flour	1 teaspoon Worcestershire
½ teaspoon salt	1 stalk celery, diced
⅛ teaspoon pepper	1 onion, chopped
2 tablespoons fat	1 clove garlic, minced
1 can (8 ounces) tomato sauce	

Shake the steaks in a plastic bag with
flour, salt, and pepper until steaks are
well coated. Brown on both sides in hot
fat. Add remaining ingredients; cover,
and simmer 1 hour, or until meat is
tender. Makes 4 servings.

PAN-BROILED ROUND STEAK

*You marinate the steak in
seasoned vinegar and oil.*

2 pounds round steak, 1 inch thick	½ teaspoon salt
	⅛ teaspoon pepper
¼ cup each vinegar and vegetable oil	Flour
	Fat

Put steak in bowl. Mix all ingredients
except last 2, and pour over steak. Let
stand several hours in cool place, turning several times. Drain, and dredge
steak with flour. Pound well with dull
side of knife. Heat small amount of fat
in skillet, and brown steak quickly on
both sides. Makes 6 servings.

DEVILED FLANK STEAK

*Beef is cut in strips and cooked
in a piquant sauce.*

1½ pounds flank steak	¼ teaspoon paprika
Flour	1 teaspoon prepared mustard
1 onion, minced	1 teaspoon vinegar
3 tablespoons fat	½ cup tomato sauce
2 teaspoons salt	1½ cups hot water
¼ teaspoon pepper	

Cut steak in strips across the grain.
Roll in flour; brown meat and onion in
hot fat. Stir in 2 tablespoons flour and
seasonings. Add remaining ingredients;
cover, and simmer 1 hour, or until meat
is tender. Good with rice, noodles, or
mashed potato. Makes 4 servings.

SAVORY BROILED STEAK

*You sprinkle it with
garlic salt and seasoning salt.*

Brush steak with vegetable oil before
broiling. When done as desired, sprinkle with garlic salt and seasoning salt.

LONDON BROIL

*Mushrooms and onions,
which go well with broiled steak,
are an excellent accompaniment.*

Salt both sides of a flank steak well,
and smear generously with French
dressing. Marinate in refrigerator several hours. Broil under high heat 2
inches from unit, allowing 5 to 7 minutes for each side. Carve against the
grain and on a slant in very thin slices.
Use a board containing a gravy well,
tray, or deep platter. (Mushrooms and
onions are an excellent accompaniment
and blend deliciously with the steak
juices, which may be thickened with a
little flour and water, if desired.) Makes
2 servings if using ⅓ of whole steak.

PRESSED BEEF

*Chopped cooked beef is pressed into
a loaf and served in thin slices.*

Put 1 flank steak (about 2 pounds) in
a kettle with 6 cups boiling water, 2
teaspoons salt, ¼ cup vinegar, ½ teaspoon whole black peppers, small bay
leaf. Simmer, covered, 3 hours, or until
meat is very tender. Drain, reserving
liquid. Chop beef fine, and pack into
9" x 5" x 3" loaf pan. Strain liquid;
reduce to ½ cup by boiling uncovered.
Pour over meat, cover with waxed paper,
and press with a heavy weight. Chill
overnight. Turn out, and slice thin.
Serve with horse-radish. Serves 6.

*"Oh, the roast beef
of England,
And old England's roast beef!"*
HENRY FIELDING

MIRACLE ROAST OF BEEF

This is beef cooked to perfection,
rare all the way through.

Roast beef in very slow oven, 200°F., allowing about 1 hour per pound.

RIB ROAST OF BEEF

Use a standing roast (2 or 3 ribs),
or have it boned and rolled.

If possible, have meat at room temperature. Season. If rolled, put on a rack, fat side up. Insert meat thermometer. Roast uncovered in moderate oven, 325°F., to desired doneness (140°F. for rare, 160°F. for medium, and 170°F. for well done). Makes 10 to 12 generous servings of roast beef.

OLD-FASHIONED RIB ROAST OF BEEF

You rub it with seasoned flour
before roasting.

Sprinkle roast with salt and pepper, and rub with flour. Insert meat thermometer. Put in very hot oven, 450°F., 20 minutes. Reduce heat to 300°F., and continue roasting to desired doneness (140°F. for rare, 160°F. for medium, and 170°F. for well done).

ROASTED BEEF TENDERLOIN

The most tender of all beef cuts.

Buy a tenderloin weighing 4 to 6 pounds. Have it trimmed and larded. Put on a rack in a shallow roasting pan, brush with oil, and roast in a very hot oven, 450°F., 30 to 45 minutes for rare, and 45 to 60 minutes for medium. Makes 6 to 8 servings.

"But we hae meat,
and we can eat
Sae let the Lord
be thankit."
ROBERT BURNS

OXTAILS À LA BOURGEOISIE

They're cooked with ham, carrots,
peas, turnips, and seasonings.

2 oxtails	1 clove garlic, minced
2 onions, chopped	Pinch of thyme
1 tablespoon butter	1 bay leaf
½ cup chopped ham	2 bouillon cubes
2 carrots, diced	2 cups water
1 white turnip, diced	1 cup cooked peas
	Salt and pepper

Have oxtails cut up. Brown with onion in butter. Add ham, carrot, and turnip; cook until lightly browned. Add remaining ingredients; simmer about 3 hours. Makes 6 to 8 servings.

BEEF À LA MODE

Delicious hot or cold.

3 pounds beef rump, or round	2 teaspoons mixed pickling spice
2 onions, sliced	1½ cups dry red burgundy
2 carrots, sliced	1 tablespoon fat
Few sprigs parsley	12 each small carrots and white onions, cooked
2 bay leaves	
2 teaspoons salt	
¼ teaspoon pepper	

Have butcher lard the meat. Put in a deep bowl. Mix next 8 ingredients, and pour over meat. Cover, and refrigerate 12 to 24 hours. Strain the liquid, and pat meat dry. Brown the meat on all sides in fat. Slip a rack under meat, and add liquid. Cover, and simmer 2½ to 3 hours. Remove meat, and skim fat from liquid. Do not thicken. Serve with vegetables heated in the liquid. Makes 6 servings.

CHILI POT ROAST

Dill pickle is mixed with chili sauce.

3 pounds beef for pot roast	1 bottle (12 ounces) chili sauce
1 tablespoon fat	2 dill pickles, chopped
Salt and pepper	Hot cooked rice
¼ cup water	
3 onions, sliced	

Brown meat in fat in kettle. Add salt and pepper. Slip a rack under meat; add water and onion. Cover, and simmer 3 to 3½ hours. About 1 hour before meat is tender, add chili sauce and pickles. Simmer until meat is tender. Slice meat; serve with rice. Serves 4.

HUNGARIAN POT ROAST

*It's seasoned with caraway seed
and paprika and served with noodles.*

Salt and pepper	1 teaspoon caraway
4 pounds beef	seed
for pot roast	1 tablespoon
Flour	paprika
2 tablespoons fat	1½ cups tomato
2 onions, quartered	juice
	Hot cooked noodles

Season meat. Dredge with flour. Brown
well on all sides in fat. Add remaining
ingredients, except noodles. Cover, and
simmer 3½ hours, or until tender. If
liquid evaporates, add a little water
during cooking. Remove meat, and
thicken liquid, if desired. Serve with
noodles. Serves 6.

INDIVIDUAL POT ROASTS

*You cut boneless beef into
four serving pieces before cooking it.*

2 pounds beef	½ teaspoon basil,
for pot roast	rosemary, or
Flour	thyme
1 tablespoon fat	1 onion, sliced
Salt and pepper	½ cup water

Cut meat in 4 pieces. Dredge with flour,
and brown in fat. Sprinkle with salt,
pepper, and herb. Add onion and water.
Cover, and simmer 2 hours, or until
meat is tender, adding more water, if
necessary. Remove meat, and thicken
gravy. Season. Makes 4 servings.

CURRIED BEEF AND RICE

*Pimiento is tossed with the beef
and rice, and the garnish is parsley.*

1½ pounds bone-	1 package (5
less beef chuck	ounces)
Salt and pepper	precooked rice
Flour	1 to 2 tablespoons
¾ cup boiling	curry powder
water	2 pimientos, cut
	in strips
	Chopped parsley

Cut meat in 1″ cubes; roll in seasoned
flour. Brown in heavy saucepan, using
a little fat, if necessary. Add boiling
water; bring to boil. Cover tightly, and
simmer about 2 hours. Meanwhile, prepare rice according to package directions. Add curry powder and pimiento.
Toss lightly with meat. Season, and
garnish with parsley. Serves 4.

*"For its merit,
I will knight it
and make it sir-loin."*
CHARLES II

BEEF STROGANOFF

*Beef, mushrooms, and onion in tomato
juice, sherry-and-sour-cream sauce.*

2 pounds sirloin	½ pound mush-
of beef	rooms, sliced
Flour	Salt and pepper
⅓ cup butter or	⅔ cup tomato juice
margarine	½ cup sherry
3 medium onions,	1½ cups water
chopped	⅔ cup sour cream

Cut meat in thin strips; dredge with
flour. Brown quickly in skillet in half
the butter. Remove meat, and add remaining butter. Add onion and mushrooms, and cook 5 minutes. Add meat,
and sprinkle with salt and pepper. Add
tomato juice, sherry, and water. Bring
to boil; cover, and simmer 1 hour, or
until meat is tender. Season with salt
and pepper. Stir in sour cream, and
serve at once. Makes 4 servings.

BEEF STEW WITH HERB DUMPLINGS

The vegetables are onions and beans.

3 pounds boneless	1 tablespoon salt
beef chuck	½ teaspoon pepper
Flour	3 cups water
1 onion, chopped	1 pound green
3 tablespoons fat	beans, cut
1 bay leaf	Herb Dumplings,
1 teaspoon celery	page 20
seed	

Cut meat in 1½″ cubes; roll in flour.
Brown with onion in fat in large, heavy
kettle. Add bay leaf, celery seed, salt,
pepper, water; cover, and simmer 1½
hours. Add beans, and cook 15 minutes
longer, or until meat and beans are
tender. If desired, thicken stew with
flour mixed with a little cold water.
Drop Dumpling batter from tablespoon
into gently boiling stew. Cover; cook
15 minutes. Makes 6 servings.

"After a good dinner, one can forgive anybody, even one's own relations."
OSCAR WILDE

SHORT RIBS, BAYOU STYLE

They're cooked in seasoned tomato sauce.

3 pounds short ribs, cut in 6 pieces	¼ cup chopped celery leaves
Flour	1 tablespoon salt
2 bay leaves	¼ teaspoon pepper
8 whole cloves	1 can (8 ounces) tomato sauce
1 clove garlic, minced	1 cup water
½ green pepper, chopped	½ lemon, sliced

Sprinkle meat lightly with flour. Brown slowly in heavy kettle or Dutch oven without added fat. Pour off any fat which collects. Add remaining ingredients. Cover, and cook very slowly 2 to 3 hours, or until meat is very tender, adding more water if necessary. Makes 6 servings.

BRAISED SHORT RIBS OF BEEF, JARDINIERE

Carrots, rutabaga, onions, and green beans bake with the meat.

3 pounds beef short ribs, cut in 3" pieces	2 carrots, diced
	½ small rutabaga, diced
Flour	4 small onions
Salt and pepper	½ pound green beans, cut up
2 tablespoons fat	Chopped parsley
1 cup meat stock or water	

Dredge meat with flour. Season. Brown on all sides in fat in Dutch oven. Add stock; cover, and bake in slow oven, 300°F., 2 to 3 hours, or until meat is very tender. Baste frequently with liquid in pan. During last hour of cooking, add vegetables. When meat and vegetables are tender, put meat on a hot platter. Arrange vegetables around it; sprinkle with parsley. Serves 4.

GOULASH AND SPAETZLE

Spaetzle are thin strips of dough cooked in boiling water.

3 pounds boneless beef chuck	2 teaspoons salt
3 tablespoons butter or margarine	1 tablespoon paprika
3 cups thinly sliced onion	1 cup water
	Spaetzle

Cut meat in 1½" pieces. Melt butter in a heavy kettle. Add onion, and cook slightly. Season meat with salt and paprika; add to onions, and cook, uncovered, 20 minutes, or until onion and liquid cook down, stirring occasionally. Add water; cover, and cook slowly 1½ hours, or until meat is tender, adding more water, if necessary, to make additional gravy. Serve with Spaetzle. Makes about 6 servings.

Spaetzle: Sift 3 cups sifted flour, 1 teaspoon salt, and dash each nutmeg and paprika. Add 4 eggs and ¾ cup water. Beat well with spoon until thick and smooth. Dampen end of small cutting board; put on ¾ cup of dough. With spatula, smooth a small amount of dough very thin. Cut off small strips of dough into a large kettle of boiling salted water. Dip spatula in water several times during cutting. If dough is too thin to hold together, add a little flour. Cook until tender (about 5 minutes). Lift out; place in dish, and pour a little melted butter over strips. Continue with remaining dough, adding a little fresh boiling water to kettle each time. Serve hot.

BRISKET OF BEEF, VIENNESE STYLE

The beef is cooked with onions, celery, carrots, bay leaves, salt, and pepper.

4 pounds boneless fresh beef brisket	1 stalk celery
2 onions, sliced	2 bay leaves
2 carrots	Salt and pepper
	Chopped parsley

Put meat in heavy kettle. Add onion, carrots, celery, bay leaves, salt, and pepper. Cover with water. Cover, and simmer 3 to 4 hours, or until meat is tender. Remove, slice, and serve with a sprinkling of parsley. Serves 6 to 8.
Note: Also good with Horse-radish Sauce, page 238.

BAKED SPICY CORNED BEEF

Pickling spice, pickle juice, brown sugar, and mustard season the beef.

4 pounds corned brisket of beef	⅓ cup brown sugar, packed
1 tablespoon whole mixed pickling spice	1 tablespoon prepared mustard
1 stalk celery	½ cup sweet-pickle juice or fruit juice
1 onion	
1 carrot	

Wash corned beef, and put in large kettle. Cover with cold water. Add pickling spice, celery, onion, and carrot. Bring to boil; cover, and simmer 4 to 4½ hours, or until tender. Cool beef in the broth; then put in shallow roasting pan, and score fat layer. Mix brown sugar and mustard; pat on beef. Pour pickle juice into pan. Bake in slow oven, 300°F., 1 hour, basting from time to time with some of the drippings in pan. Slice, and serve hot or cold. Makes 8 servings.

BEEF AND ONION PIE

You bake the crust separately and add it just before serving the pie.

Cut 3 pounds boneless beef chuck in 1½″ cubes. Brown meat in a little fat in kettle. Sprinkle with salt and pepper. Add 2 cups water. Bring to boil; cover, and simmer 2 hours, or until tender. Drain, reserving broth. Put meat in shallow baking dish. Measure broth, and add liquid from 16-ounce can onions to make 3 cups. Add ¼ cup cornstarch, blended with a little cold water. Cook until slightly thickened. Season to taste. Add onions and gravy to meat. Bake in hot oven, 425°F., 10 minutes. Reduce heat to 350°F., and bake 20 minutes longer. Put baked pastry on top of meat, and serve. Makes 6 servings.

Beef-pie Pastry: Sift 2 cups sifted flour and 1 teaspoon salt. Cut in ⅔ cup vegetable shortening. Mix 1 egg yolk with 3 tablespoons water. Mix lightly into flour mixture. Roll to ½″ thickness. Cut in diamonds or other desired shapes. Put on ungreased baking sheet. Prick tops with fork, and brush with slightly beaten egg white. Bake at the same time as the pie.

BEEF-ONION BIRDS WITH POTATOES

Onions are rolled up in pieces of steak and cooked in horse-radish tomato sauce.

1 pound round steak	1 can (19 ounces) tomatoes
1 teaspoon salt	2 tablespoons ketchup
⅛ teaspoon pepper	
¼ teaspoon sage	2 tablespoons horse-radish
4 onions	8 small potatoes
¼ cup flour	
2 tablespoons fat	

Cut steak in 4 pieces; pound each piece flat. Sprinkle top and bottom with salt and pepper; sprinkle top with sage. Put one onion on sage-coated side of each piece of steak. Fold ends of meat over onions, and fasten with a skewer. Roll meat in flour, and brown in hot fat in heavy skillet. Add next 3 ingredients; cover, and simmer ½ hour. Add potatoes; cover; simmer 1 hour. Serves 4.

COLOMBIAN TONGUE

Smoked-tongue slices are served with a piquant mushroom wine sauce.

1 smoked beef tongue (3 pounds)	1 tablespoon flour
Water	1 cup tongue broth
1 bay leaf	1 can (3 ounces) chopped mushrooms, drained
1 clove garlic	
½ teaspoon peppercorns	
1 onion, minced	Few sprigs parsley, chopped
1 tablespoon butter	¾ cup red wine

Simmer tongue, covered, in water to cover with seasonings 3 hours, or until very tender. Remove tongue from liquid, and discard skin and bones; keep tongue hot in liquid, or cool and reheat. Cook onion in butter until golden; blend in flour. Add remaining ingredients; simmer 10 minutes. Serve as sauce for sliced tongue. Makes 8 to 10 servings.

"When mighty roast beef was the Englishman's food, It ennobled our hearts, and enriched our blood."
RICHARD LEVERIDGE

SHEPHERD'S BEEF PIE

A ring of mashed potatoes
circles the edge of the casserole.

Combine cut-up cooked beef with gravy. Add cooked peas, carrots, or green beans. Pour hot into a casserole. Make a ring of seasoned mashed potatoes around the edge of the casserole. Bake in hot oven, 400°F., about 20 minutes.

BEEF IN SAVORY SAUCE

Cooked roast beef is heated
in an herb-wine-and-tomato sauce.

1 medium onion, chopped	1 can (2 or 3 ounces) mushrooms, undrained
2 tablespoons beef fat	
2 tablespoons flour	¼ cup tomato sauce
Pinch thyme	
⅓ cup dry red wine	8 slices roast beef
1 cup beef bouillon	Salt and pepper

Cook onion in fat until lightly browned. Stir in flour and thyme. Add wine, bouillon, mushrooms, and tomato sauce. Bring to boil, and simmer 5 minutes. Add beef; heat. Season. Serves 4.

BEEF ALLA ITALIANA

The seasonings are garlic and orégano.

1 clove garlic, minced	¾ teaspoon salt
2 tablespoons olive oil	½ teaspoon orégano
1 can (1 pound) tomatoes	2 cups diced cooked beef
1 can (8 ounces) tomato sauce	Chopped parsley
¼ teaspoon pepper	Hot cooked spaghetti or noodles

Cook garlic in oil until lightly browned. Add tomatoes, tomato sauce, pepper, salt, and orégano. Cook 25 minutes. Add beef. Cook over low heat about 15 minutes. Sprinkle with chopped parsley. Serve with spaghetti. Serves 4.

BEEF CASSEROLE

Cooked beef, gravy, and vegetables
with a cheddar-cheese topping.

2 cups diced cooked beef	1 box frozen peas and carrots, cooked
1 can (10¾ ounces) beef gravy	½ cup grated cheddar cheese
1 can (1 pound) onions, drained	

Combine meat, gravy, onions, and peas and carrots. Put in casserole, and sprinkle with cheese. Bake in moderate oven, 350° F., 35 minutes. Makes 4 servings.

DEVILED ROAST-BEEF SLICES

They're dipped in crumbs, fried,
and served with a tangy gravy.

4 slices roast beef (¼″ to ½″ thick)	½ teaspoon dry mustard
Prepared mustard	Dash of Tabasco
Fine dry bread crumbs	1 tablespoon Worcestershire
Beef drippings	Garlic salt
1 cup beef gravy	Pepper

Spread slices of roast beef with prepared mustard. Dip in crumbs. Fry in drippings till browned. To make gravy, add drippings to remaining ingredients, and heat. Makes 4 servings.

BEEF AND KIDNEY PIE

Most of the cooking is done
before the crust goes on the pie.

1 beef kidney (about 1¼ pounds)	2 cups beef gravy
	1 can (1 pound) onions, drained
Salt and pepper	2 potatoes, diced
2 to 3 cups diced cooked beef	2 carrots, diced
	Pastry (1 cup flour)

Remove outer membrane from kidney. Split kidney, and cut in cubes. Cover with water; add salt and pepper, and simmer 1 hour, or until tender. Add next 5 ingredients, and simmer until potatoes and carrots are tender. Season to taste with salt and pepper. Add more liquid, if necessary. Pour into 2-quart casserole. Cover with pastry; make a few cuts for steam to escape. Bake in hot oven, 425°F., 20 minutes, or until crust is browned. Makes 4 to 6 servings.

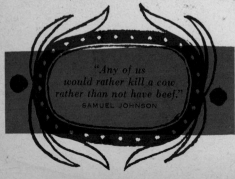

"Any of us
would rather kill a cow
rather than not have beef."
SAMUEL JOHNSON

CHICKEN

Chicken is the ever popular fowl. In the early days of the automobile, when
picnics were perhaps even more beloved than today, Mamma spent hours
preceding the event disjointing and frying several birds. (Of course
there had to be a drumstick for every child.) Then, when the golden-brown
pieces were cool, she carefully wrapped each in oilpaper,
ready for the picnic hamper. There are some nostalgic people who say that this
was chicken at its finest. But this deprecates the wonderful old-fashioned
Sunday dinner of roasted, stuffed chicken served with creamed pearl onions
and fresh hot rolls dripping with butter. In recent years, it's been the
fashion to cook chicken on the spit or to broil it. The results are delicious,
but there are many, many methods of preparing this delicate flesh
that shouldn't be neglected. The great cook book *Le Grand Livre de la
Cuisine,* by Prosper Montagne and Prosper Salles, lists some 400
ways to cook chicken, and these do not include another multitude of recipes
from Italian, German, Chinese, Japanese, and American cuisines. Chicken lends
itself to a wide choice of seasonings, flavorings, sauces, and accompaniments.
The next time you find yourself wondering what to serve, try chicken, and
try it a different way. The possibilities are almost endless.

43

BAKED CHICKEN WITH HERBS

The herbs are thyme, rosemary or sage, parsley, and chives.

1 frying chicken (about 2½ pounds), cut up	1 teaspoon thyme
5 tablespoons butter or margarine	1 teaspoon rosemary or sage
3 tablespoons flour	2½ cups milk
1 teaspoon salt	1 tablespoon chopped parsley
¼ teaspoon pepper	1 tablespoon chopped chives

Brown chicken in 2 tablespoons butter. Remove to 1½-quart casserole. Melt remaining butter in skillet; blend in flour. Add remaining ingredients, and cook until slightly thickened, stirring constantly. Pour over chicken. Bake, uncovered, in moderate oven, 325°F., about 50 minutes. Makes 4 servings.

CHICKEN, CREOLE STYLE

It simmers in onion, garlic, green pepper, and tomatoes.

1 frying chicken, cut up	½ cup chopped celery
¼ cup flour	1¼ teaspoons salt
¼ cup fat	Dash pepper
1 cup sliced onion	1 bay leaf, crumbled
1 clove garlic, minced	Dash Tabasco
1 green pepper, chopped	1 can (28 ounces) tomatoes

Dredge chicken pieces with flour, and brown lightly in hot fat. Remove chicken. Add onion, garlic, green pepper, and celery; cook slowly 5 minutes. Add remaining ingredients, breaking up tomatoes with a spoon. Bring to boil, and add chicken. Cover tightly, and simmer 40 minutes. Makes 4 servings.

CHICKEN ALLA MELANZANA

Browned chicken and eggplant baked with onion, olives, garlic, and wine.

3 tablespoons butter or margarine	1 clove garlic, minced
1 frying chicken (about 2½ pounds), cut up	1 cup water
	1 chicken bouillon cube
Salt and pepper	⅓ cup dry red wine
1 medium eggplant	¼ cup sliced stuffed green olives
Flour	
Vegetable oil	
1 onion, chopped	2 pimientos, cut in strips

Melt butter in large, heavy skillet. Add chicken, and fry until golden brown on all sides. Season with salt and pepper. Cover, and simmer 45 minutes, or until tender. Meanwhile, peel, and slice eggplant about ½" thick. Season with salt, dip in flour, and brown in oil until tender. Remove chicken, and put in shallow baking dish. To drippings in pan, add onion and garlic; brown about 5 minutes. Stir in 2 tablespoons flour; add water, bouillon cube, and wine. Bring to boil, and cook until thickened, stirring. Pour over chicken. Sprinkle with half of olives and pimiento. Cover with fried eggplant and remaining olives and pimiento. Bake in hot oven, 400°F., 25 minutes, or until thoroughly heated. Makes 4 servings.

CHICKEN À L'AFRIQUE

Chicken with a peanut-butter gravy and a garnish of hard-cooked eggs.

1 frying chicken (about 2½ pounds), cut up	3 cups water
	1 tablespoon ketchup
1 large onion, chopped	¾ cup chunk-style peanut butter
1 fresh or canned tomato, chopped	⅛ teaspoon cayenne
2 cloves garlic, minced	3 hard-cooked eggs, sliced
1 teaspoon salt	

Combine chicken, onion, tomato, garlic, salt, and 2 cups water. Bring to boil, cover, and simmer 30 minutes. Add ketchup. Blend peanut butter and remaining 1 cup water. Add to chicken mixture. Cover, and simmer 1 hour longer, stirring occasionally. Add cayenne and eggs. Makes 4 servings.

CHICKEN PARMESAN

Cheese, garlic, and sherry-mushroom sauce for chicken and spaghetti.

2 frying chickens (about 2½ pounds each), cut up	1½ cups chicken broth
Prepared garlic spread	¼ pound fresh mushrooms, sliced, or 1 can (4 ounces) sliced mushrooms
Grated Parmesan cheese	
3 tablespoons olive oil	⅓ cup sherry
2 tablespoons flour	Salt and pepper
	8 ounces spaghetti, cooked
	Chopped parsley

Coat chicken with garlic spread. Rub with about 3 tablespoons cheese. Cook lightly in oil about 5 minutes. Stir in flour; add broth, mushrooms, and sherry. Bring to boil. Cover, and simmer 45 minutes, or until tender. Season with salt and pepper. Mix spaghetti with sauce from chicken, and sprinkle with parsley. Put chicken on top. Serve with additional cheese. Serves 6 to 8.

MUSHROOM BARBECUED CHICKEN

Bottled barbecue sauce is used for this.

Cut 1 large frying chicken in quarters. Sprinkle with salt and pepper; roll in flour. Put in shallow baking pan. Put a thick slice of bacon on each. Cover pan with foil. Bake in hot oven, 400°F., about 40 minutes. Uncover; pour 1 can (3 ounces) sliced mushrooms over chicken. Dribble bottled barbecue sauce over top. Cover, and bake 10 minutes. Uncover, and broil 10 minutes, or until lightly browned. Makes 4 servings.

SKILLET CHICKEN IN SAGE-AND-MUSHROOM GRAVY

You use leaf sage and mushroom soup.

2 tablespoons butter	1 teaspoon leaf sage
1 frying chicken, cut up	½ teaspoon salt
1 can cream-of-mushroom soup	Dash pepper
	¼ cup water

Heat butter in large skillet, and lightly brown chicken. Then combine remaining ingredients; pour over chicken. Cover tightly; simmer 40 minutes, or until chicken is tender. Makes 4 servings.

SOUTHERN CHICKEN WITH PECANS

Chicken simmers in marjoram butter.

1 frying chicken (about 2½ pounds), cut up	¼ teaspoon marjoram
Flour	Cooked potato balls (12 to 16)
Salt and pepper	¾ cup shelled pecans
¼ cup butter or margarine	

Coat chicken with flour seasoned with salt and pepper. Brown in butter. Sprinkle with marjoram. Cover; cook over low heat 45 minutes. Add potato balls and pecans; heat. Serves 4.

ARROZ CON POLLO

Chicken, onion, pepper, tomatoes, and rice cooked together, then garnished with peas and pimiento.

1 frying chicken (about 2½ pounds), cut up	⅓ cup sherry
Salt	¼ teaspoon pepper
3 tablespoons olive oil	Pinch Spanish saffron
1 onion, chopped	½ teaspoon paprika
1 clove garlic, minced	2 whole cloves
1 green pepper, chopped	1 bay leaf
1 can (19 ounces) tomatoes	1 cup water
	1¼ cups uncooked long-grain rice
	1 cup cooked peas
	1 pimiento, cut up

Season chicken with salt. Brown in oil. Add onion, garlic, and green pepper, and brown 5 minutes longer. Add remaining ingredients, except rice, peas, and pimiento; cover; simmer 15 minutes. Add rice, bring to boil, stir. Cover; simmer 30 minutes. Garnish with peas and pimiento. Serves 4 to 6.

CHICKEN COCKTAIL

It's served with horse-radish, lemon, chili sauce.

Mix 1 cup chili sauce, 2 tablespoons each horse-radish and lemon juice, 1 teaspoon salt, and ¼ teaspoon pepper. Chill. Put in bowl in center of platter, and arrange diced cooked chicken around bowl. Serve with toothpicks for dipping chicken pieces in sauce.

MURGHA CURRY

Curry, apple, and ginger flavor creamed chicken and rice.

1 onion, minced	1 cup chicken
1 peeled apple,	broth
chopped	1 cup milk
¼ cup butter or	½ cup heavy
margarine	cream
⅓ cup flour	Juice ½ lemon
1 to 2 tablespoons	3 cups coarsely
curry powder	cut cooked
1½ teaspoons salt	chicken
Dash pepper	4 cups hot cooked
¼ teaspoon ginger	rice

Cook onion and apple in butter in top part of double boiler over direct heat until onion is yellowed. Blend in flour and seasonings. Slowly add broth, milk, and cream; cook over boiling water, stirring constantly, until mixture is thickened. Cover, and cook 10 minutes longer. Add lemon juice and chicken, and heat well. Serve with hot cooked rice. Makes 4 servings.

CHICKEN DIVAN

Broccoli, chicken, a rich sherry-cream sauce, and a sprinkling of cheese.

1 frying chicken	2 tablespoons
(about 2½	butter
pounds), split	3 tablespoons flour
2 cups water	Milk
Salt	Pepper
1 box frozen	2 tablespoons
broccoli spears	sherry
	Grated Parmesan
	cheese

Simmer chicken in water with 1 teaspoon salt 45 minutes, or until very tender. Save broth. Remove meat from bones in large pieces; then cut in long slices. Cook broccoli until just tender; drain, and put in shallow casserole. Melt butter in top part of double boiler; stir in flour. Measure chicken broth, and add enough milk to make 2 cups. Add to butter and flour. Cook, stirring constantly, until thickened. Add salt, pepper, and sherry. Cover broccoli with chicken, then with sauce. Sprinkle with cheese. Bake in hot oven, 400°F., about 12 minutes. Makes 2 servings.

CHICKEN ORÉGANO

A one-dish skillet or Dutch-oven meal.

Brown 1 frying chicken, cut up, in ½ cup olive or vegetable oil. Sprinkle with salt, pepper, 2 teaspoons orégano, and 1 teaspoon thyme. Add ½ cup water, 2 chicken-bouillon cubes, 4 sliced onions, and 4 quartered pared medium potatoes. Simmer, covered, 45 minutes, or until chicken and vegetables are done. Serves 4.

BOK YOU GUY

Chicken with soy-sauce gravy, raisin-rice, a topping of peanuts and coconut.

1 frying chicken	1 cup uncooked
(about 2½	rice
pounds), cut up	½ cup seedless
1½ cups water	raisins
3 tablespoons	½ cup salted
soy sauce	peanuts
3 tablespoons	Flaked coconut
cornstarch	

Simmer chicken in water with soy sauce 45 minutes, or until tender. Thicken with cornstarch mixed with a little cold water. Cook rice, and combine with raisins; sprinkle with peanuts and coconut. Serve with chicken and gravy. Makes 4 servings.

CHICKEN FILIPINO

You marinate chicken in lemon juice and soy sauce, then bake it.

⅓ cup soy sauce	1 frying chicken,
Juice 1 lemon	cut up
1 teaspoon poultry	Flour
seasoning	¼ cup fat for frying
½ teaspoon salt	2 onions, cut in
½ teaspoon pepper	half
1 teaspoon ginger	1 cup boiling
	water

Combine soy sauce, lemon juice, and seasonings. Pour over chicken, and allow to stand at least ½ hour. Lift chicken from sauce; roll in flour, and brown in hot fat. Place chicken, brown-sauce mixture, and remaining ingredients in covered roaster or casserole. Bake in moderate oven, 350°F., about 45 minutes, or until chicken is tender. Makes 4 servings.

DEEP-FAT FRIED CHICKEN

For a different flavor, add 1 teaspoon ground ginger to the flour.

Dredge 2 small frying chickens, split, with ½ cup seasoned flour. Heat deep fat to 370°F. on frying thermometer, or until a 1″ bread cube browns in 1 minute. Put chicken in fryer basket, 1 or 2 pieces at a time; lower carefully into hot fat. Fry chicken 12 to 15 minutes, or until golden brown and tender. Drain on absorbent paper. Keep hot until all pieces are fried. Serves 4.
Note: If preferred, use 1 quartered large fryer.

CHICKEN FLAMBÉ

Chicken is simmered in wine and served with flaming brandy sauce.

1 broiler (about	⅓ cup dry white
2 pounds),	wine
quartered	1 tablespoon flour
Salt and pepper	½ cup water
3 tablespoons butter	3 tablespoons
or margarine	brandy

Season chicken with salt and pepper. Brown in butter. Add wine. Cover, and simmer 45 minutes, or until tender. Remove chicken to hot platter. Stir flour into drippings in pan. Add water, and bring to boil. Add brandy, ignite, and serve blazing. Spoon sauce over chicken. Makes 4 servings.

BRAISED CHICKEN AND MUSHROOMS

Chicken and mushrooms are cooked in a white-wine-and-cream sauce.

1 frying chicken	¼ pound fresh
(about 2½	mushrooms,
pounds),	sliced, or 1 can
quartered	(4 ounces) sliced
3 tablespoons	mushrooms
butter or	¼ cup dry white
margarine	wine
Salt and pepper	1 tablespoon flour
1 onion, thinly	1 cup light cream
sliced	6 radishes, sliced

Brown chicken in butter. Season with salt and pepper. Remove from pan. Add onion and mushrooms. Cook about 5 minutes. Add chicken and wine; cover, and simmer 45 minutes, or until chicken is tender. Stir in flour; add cream, bring to boil, and simmer a few minutes. Garnish with radishes. Serves 4.

OVEN-FRIED CHICKEN

It's dipped in egg and crumbs.

1 frying chicken,	1 cup fine dry
quartered	bread crumbs
2 eggs, slightly	½ cup fat
beaten	¼ cup melted
1 teaspoon salt	butter or
¾ teaspoon pepper	margarine

Dip chicken in egg, then in seasoned crumbs. Brown quickly on all sides in hot fat in large skillet. Arrange chicken pieces, without overlapping, in shallow baking pan. Dribble with butter. Bake, uncovered, in moderate oven, 350°F., 30 minutes, or until tender. If desired, add 1 to 2 teaspoons ground marjoram, sage, or poultry seasoning to the bread crumbs. Makes 4 servings.

HAM-STUFFED CHICKEN

You use chicken thighs for this dish, two per serving.

Remove bone from chicken thighs, keeping skin intact. With skin side down, pound chicken to flatten slightly. In center of each, put a piece of cooked ham about 2"x1"x1". Fold chicken over, pull skin to cover, and fasten with skewer or strong wood toothpicks. Dip in slightly beaten egg, and roll in fine dry bread crumbs. Put in shallow baking dish, and pour over each a little melted butter. Cover, and bake in moderate oven, 325°F., about 1¼ hours. Remove skewers, and serve chicken plain or with gravy made with drippings.

BRUNSWICK CHICKEN STEW

It's made with onion, tomatoes, Lima beans, okra, and bread crumbs.

1½ teaspoons salt	⅓ cup sherry
¼ teaspoon pepper	1 tablespoon Worcestershire
1 fryer, cut up	1 box frozen Lima beans
2 tablespoons fat	
1 cup chopped onion	1 cup canned sliced okra
2½ cups water	1 box frozen cut corn
1 can (19 ounces) tomatoes	½ cup dry bread crumbs

Season chicken. Heat fat in Dutch oven; add onion and chicken. Cook until browned. Add water, tomatoes, sherry, Worcestershire. Cover; cook 40 minutes. Add beans and okra; simmer 10 minutes. Season; add corn and crumbs; simmer 10 minutes. Makes 6 servings.

FRIED CHICKEN WITH SQUAW RICE

The rice is cooked with green pepper, onion, salt, pepper, and turmeric.

1 frying chicken (about 2½ pounds), cut up	1 onion, chopped
	2 tablespoons chopped green pepper
¼ cup flour	
Salt and pepper	½ teaspoon turmeric
½ cup butter or margarine	
	2 cups water
1 cup uncooked rice	1 can (16 ounces) whole-kernel corn, drained

Roll chicken in flour seasoned with 1 teaspoon salt and ¼ teaspoon pepper. Brown in ¼ cup butter. Cover, and cook slowly 40 minutes, or until tender, turning pieces occasionally. Meanwhile, melt remaining ¼ cup butter in saucepan. Add rice and onion, and cook until rice is browned, stirring frequently. Add 1 teaspoon salt, ⅛ teaspoon pepper, the green pepper, turmeric, and water. Cover, bring to boil, and simmer 15 minutes, or until rice is tender. Add corn, and mix lightly. Pile rice and corn mixture on hot platter; arrange chicken around the edge. Makes 4 servings.

CHICKEN WITH DUMPLINGS

Onion, bay leaf, and lemon flavor the chicken while it's cooking.

1 frying chicken (about 2½ pounds), cut up	½ bay leaf
	2 slices lemon
3 cups water	Salt and pepper
1 onion, chopped	Dumpling batter

Simmer chicken with all ingredients, except dumplings, 35 minutes, or until tender. Remove bay leaf and lemon. Drop Dumpling batter on top of chicken with teaspoon. Cover tightly, and simmer 15 minutes without removing cover. Serve at once. Makes 4 servings.

Dumplings

1 cup sifted flour	1 teaspoon minced onion
1 teaspoon baking powder	
¾ teaspoon salt	2 egg yolks
Dash of mace or nutmeg	⅓ cup milk

Sift together dry ingredients. Add onion. Beat egg yolks with milk, and add to dry mixture. Mix lightly until blended.

CHICKEN RAGOUT

Chicken, gravy, sherry, seasonings,
and currant jelly blended together.

To 2 cups leftover chicken gravy or canned gravy add: ¼ cup sherry, 1 teaspoon Worcestershire, ½ teaspoon Accent, 1 tablespoon currant jelly, and salt and pepper. Heat, stirring to blend jelly. Add 2 cups cooked chicken, cut in strips. Heat. Makes 4 servings.

SHERRIED CHICKEN, POTATOES

Chicken, in a bed of mashed potatoes,
with sherry-mushroom sauce.

¼ cup butter or margarine	1 can (3 ounces) sliced mushrooms, undrained
¼ cup flour	
2 tablespoons chicken-stock base	2 envelopes instant mashed potatoes
1¼ cups water	Slices or pieces cooked chicken
½ cup heavy cream	3 tablespoons grated Parmesan cheese
¼ cup sherry	
Salt and pepper	Paprika

Make a sauce with first 6 ingredients. Add seasonings and mushrooms. Prepare potatoes as directed on the label, and put in shallow baking dish. Arrange chicken on potatoes. Cover with the sauce. Sprinkle with cheese and paprika. Bake in 425°F. oven 20 minutes; or broil until bubbly. Serves 6.

BARBECUED BROILED CHICKEN

The barbecue sauce contains mustard,
Worcestershire, vinegar, and butter.

1 broiling chicken (about 2 pounds), quartered	⅛ teaspoon pepper
	Dash cayenne
½ teaspoon dry mustard	1½ tablespoons vinegar
1 teaspoon Worcestershire	¼ cup melted butter or margarine
¾ teaspoon salt	

Put chicken, skin side down, on greased rack of broiler pan. Combine all other ingredients to make sauce; brush chicken with the sauce. Put about 4 inches from unit of preheated broiler. Broil 30 minutes, basting several times with more of the sauce. Turn chicken, and broil 15 minutes longer, basting with sauce. Makes 4 servings.

CHICKEN CHOW MEIN

It's seasoned with soy sauce.

1 onion, sliced	2 chicken bouillon cubes
2 cups sliced celery	1½ cups hot water
2 tablespoons fat	2 tablespoons soy sauce
1 can (19 ounces) bean sprouts, undrained	2 tablespoons cornstarch
1½ cups finely diced cooked chicken	¼ cup cold water
	Salt and pepper
	Chow-mein noodles

Cook onion and celery in fat 10 minutes. Add sprouts, chicken, bouillon dissolved in hot water. Bring to boil; simmer 5 minutes. Add soy sauce. Stir in cornstarch blended with cold water. Cook, stirring, until thickened. Season. Serve over noodles, with more soy sauce, if desired. Makes 4 servings.

CURRIED CHICKEN SALAD

Chicken is tossed with
celery and almonds.

3 cups diced cooked chicken	1 tablespoon minced onion
2 cups finely diced celery	¾ cup mayonnaise
⅓ cup slivered almonds, toasted	2 to 3 teaspoons curry powder
	1 teaspoon salt
Juice 1 lemon	Dash pepper
	Salad greens

Toss chicken with celery and almonds. Mix the remaining ingredients, except greens, and combine with chicken mixture. Chill. Serve on greens. Makes 4 to 6 servings.

CHICKEN KIEV

*Thin chicken cutlets are wrapped
around cubes of butter, then fried.*

1½ sticks butter	2 tablespoons
6 chicken breasts	cold water
Fine dry bread	Vegetable
crumbs	shortening
3 eggs	

Cut butter in half, lengthwise, then in
twelve 2″ pieces. Chill until very firm.
Cut chicken breasts in half; remove
bones. On wet board, pound chicken
into thin cutlets. Put a piece of butter
in center of each. Roll chicken around
butter; fold securely so butter cannot
escape during cooking. Secure with
toothpicks. Roll in bread crumbs; dip
in eggs beaten with cold water; roll
again in crumbs. Fry in hot deep shortening (375°F. on a frying thermometer)
3 to 5 minutes. Drain, and put on
cookie sheet in hot oven, 425°F., 5
minutes. Makes 6 servings.

BAKED CHICKEN-CHEDDAR
SANDWICHES

*Main dish sandwiches: chicken is in
mushroom sauce, has a cheddar topping.*

Dip 12 slices firm-type bread in mixture of 3 beaten eggs, ¾ cup milk, ½
teaspoon seasoned salt. Brown on both
sides in hot butter or margarine. Put 6
slices in shallow baking dish. Mix 1 can
cream-of-mushroom soup, ½ cup each
evaporated milk and chicken broth, ½
teaspoon bottled thick meat sauce, ¼
teaspoon pepper, 2 cups diced cooked
chicken. Spoon on toast slices; top
with remaining slices. Sprinkle with ½
cup grated cheddar. Bake in hot oven,
400°F., 15 to 20 minutes. Serves 6.

BACON-FRIED CHICKEN

*Bits of bacon adhere
to the chicken as it browns.*

Dredge 1 frying chicken, cut up, with
¼ cup seasoned flour. Spread ¼ pound
bacon, minced, over bottom of large,
cold skillet. Arrange chicken on top.
Do not cover. Cook very slowly 50 minutes, or until tender, turning chicken
as it browns. Makes 4 servings.

SMOTHERED FRIED CHICKEN

*In place of all water you can use
half white wine, half water.*

Dredge 1 frying chicken, cut up, with
½ cup seasoned flour. Brown quickly
on all sides in ½ cup hot fat in large,
covered skillet. Pour off fat. Add 2 cups
water. Cover, and simmer 30 minutes,
or until chicken is tender. Add more seasoning, if necessary. Makes 4 servings.

CHICKEN BAKED IN CREAM

*The seasonings are
celery salt and cayenne.*

1 frying chicken,	1 teaspoon celery
cut up	salt
¼ cup flour	¼ teaspoon
1 teaspoon salt	pepper
Dash cayenne	1 cup heavy cream

Dredge chicken pieces with mixture of
flour and seasonings. Put into 2-quart
casserole that has a tight-fitting cover.
Pour cream over chicken; cover, and
bake in moderate oven, 350°F., about
50 minutes, or until chicken is tender.
Uncover, and bake 15 minutes longer.
Makes 4 servings.

BAKED CHICKEN
AND VEGETABLES

They cook in garlic-mushroom sauce.

1 can (15½ ounces)	1 frying chicken,
meatless	cut up
spaghetti sauce	1 can (1 pound)
with mushrooms	onions
1 package dry	4 to 6 medium
garlic salad-	potatoes,
dressing mix	peeled

In 3-quart casserole, mix spaghetti
sauce and dry salad-dressing mix. Add
chicken and vegetables; stir to coat
each piece. Cover; bake in moderate
oven, 350°F., 2 hours. Makes 4 servings.

CHICKEN TETRAZZINI

Chicken, mushrooms, green pepper, and spaghetti in sherry-cream sauce.

¾ pound mushrooms, sliced	4 cups diced cooked chicken
1 small green pepper, slivered	2 pimientos, chopped
¼ cup butter or margarine	2 tablespoons sherry
3 tablespoons flour	6 ounces fine spaghetti, cooked
2 teaspoons salt	2 egg yolks, beaten
¼ teaspoon pepper	Grated Parmesan cheese
2½ cups light cream	

Cook mushrooms and green pepper in butter 5 minutes. Blend in flour and seasonings. Add cream; cook, stirring, until thickened. Add next 3 ingredients, and heat. Divide spaghetti into 6 broilerproof individual baking dishes. Add small amount of chicken mixture to egg yolks; stir into remaining mixture. Pour over spaghetti; sprinkle with cheese. Bake in slow oven, 300°F., about 45 minutes. Brown lightly under broiler. Makes 6 servings.

BATTER-FRIED CHICKEN

The batter contains soy sauce.

5-pound fowl, cut up	2 eggs, beaten
Salted water	⅔ cup milk
1 cup sifted flour	¾ teaspoon salt
2 tablespoons soy sauce	½ teaspoon pepper
	Fat for frying

Put fowl in kettle; cover with salted water, and bring to boil. Simmer, covered, 3½ hours, or until tender. Drain; reserve broth for other uses. (Fowl can be cooked a day ahead.) To make batter, combine remaining ingredients, except fat; beat with rotary beater until well blended. Melt fat to depth of 1½" in large, deep, heavy skillet. Heat fat to 370°F. on frying thermometer, or until a 1" bread cube browns in 1 minute. With tongs, dip each piece of chicken in batter. Fry in fat until golden brown on all sides. Drain on absorbent paper. Makes 4 servings.

Note: Bones can be removed from larger pieces before dipping in batter.

CHICKEN WITH YELLOW RICE

The rice is seasoned with garlic, salt, pepper, turmeric, and cayenne.

1 fryer, cut up	1 clove garlic, minced
½ cup fat	1½ teaspoons salt
1 cup uncooked rice	⅛ teaspoon pepper
2½ cups boiling water	1 teaspoon turmeric
	Dash cayenne

Brown chicken lightly on all sides in hot fat; put in 2-quart casserole. Sprinkle rice over and around chicken. Mix remaining ingredients; pour over chicken. Cover; bake in moderate oven, 350°F., about 45 minutes. Makes 4 servings.

PAPRIKA CHICKEN

Traditionally served over hot noodles.

3 medium onions, chopped	Salt and pepper
¼ cup butter or margarine	Flour
1 tablespoon paprika	1 cup chicken broth
½ teaspoon sugar	¾ cup heavy cream
1 frying chicken (about 2½ pounds), cut up	Hot cooked noodles

Cook onion slowly in butter until golden. Stir in paprika and sugar. Season chicken with salt and pepper; dip in flour. Cook slowly in onion mixture 15 minutes. Add broth; cover, and simmer 45 minutes, or until tender. Stir in cream; heat. Remove chicken, and strain sauce. Return chicken to sauce; heat, but do not boil. Serve with hot noodles. Makes 4 servings.

CHICKEN AND RICE SALAD

Chopped green onion and green pepper provide a touch of color.

¾ cup uncooked rice	1 tablespoon lemon juice
Salt	Small amount chopped green pepper
2 cups coarsely diced cooked chicken	¾ cup salad dressing or mayonnaise
1 cup diced celery	Pepper
2 green onions, chopped	Salad greens

Cook rice in boiling salted water until tender. Drain, and cool. Add chicken, celery, onion, lemon juice, and green pepper. Add salad dressing, and mix lightly. Season to taste with salt and pepper. Chill, and serve on greens. Makes 4 servings.

CHICKEN WITH OLIVE-AND-CAPER SAUCE

The sauce contains garlic and parsley as well as olives and capers.

1 frying chicken (about 2½ pounds), cut up	½ cup sliced stuffed green olives
¼ cup flour	2 tablespoons capers
1 teaspoon salt	1 tablespoon caper liquid
¼ teaspoon pepper	2 tablespoons water
3 tablespoons butter or margarine	¼ cup chopped parsley
1 clove garlic, minced	

Roll chicken in flour seasoned with salt and pepper. Brown in butter. Cover, and cook slowly 40 minutes. Add remaining ingredients; heat. Makes 4 servings.

BROILED CHICKEN IN CREAM

The chicken is brushed with parsley butter several times as it broils.

1 frying chicken (about 2½ pounds), quartered	2 sprigs parsley, chopped
	1 teaspoon salt
¼ cup melted butter or margarine	½ teaspoon pepper
	1 cup heavy cream

Arrange chicken, skin side down, on rack. Brush with mixture of butter and remaining ingredients, except cream. Put in preheated broiler about 4" from heat. Broil 50 to 60 minutes under medium heat, turning 3 or 4 times and brushing with butter mixture. Put chicken in skillet; add cream. Cover, simmer about 15 minutes. Put in serving dish, and cover with sauce from pan. Makes 4 servings.

BARBECUED CHICKEN, CHINESE STYLE

This comes out of the oven very brown, taking its color from the soy sauce.

⅓ cup soy sauce	¼ teaspoon pepper
3 tablespoons vegetable oil	1 clove garlic, minced
1 teaspoon dry mustard	1 frying chicken (about 2½ pounds), quartered
½ teaspoon ground ginger	

Mix soy sauce with all ingredients, except chicken. Brush all sides of chicken; let stand 30 minutes, brushing several times with sauce. Put chicken on rack in shallow pan, and bake in moderate oven, 350°F., 50 minutes, or until tender. Brush with sauce and pan drippings every 15 minutes, as long as any sauce remains. Makes 4 servings.

BUTTER-BROILED CHICKEN

You baste it every ten minutes.

Arrange 1 quartered frying chicken, skin side up, on rack. Sprinkle with salt and pepper; brush with melted butter. Preheat broiler; then place chicken in broiler so top surface is about 4 inches from unit. As chicken browns, brush with butter, turning about every 10 minutes. Cook until tender and well browned, 50 to 60 minutes. Season; serve with pan drippings. Serves 4.

CHICKEN WITH WELSH-RABBIT SAUCE

You use sharp cheddar for the sauce, and serve it on hot toast.

3 tablespoons butter or margarine	1 teaspoon Worcestershire
3 tablespoons flour	2 cups milk
1 teaspoon salt	½ pound sharp cheddar cheese, shredded
Dash cayenne	
⅛ teaspoon pepper	
1 teaspoon prepared mustard	Sliced cooked chicken
	Hot toast

To make sauce: melt butter, blend in flour and seasonings. Add milk; cook, stirring, until thickened. Add cheese; cook until cheese is melted. Arrange chicken on broilerproof platter; cover with the sauce. Broil until golden brown and bubbly. Serve on hot toast. Makes 4 to 6 servings.

OLD HOMESTEAD CHICKEN PIE

Chicken, onions, carrots, and peas are baked under a pastry crust.

1 stewing chicken (about 4 pounds), cut up	4 tablespoons butter
5 cups water	6 tablespoons flour
1 onion	3 cups chicken broth
2 stalks celery	Pepper
2 sprigs parsley	Pastry (recipe using 1 cup flour)
Salt	
1 can (1 pound) onions, drained	1 egg, slightly beaten
1 package frozen peas and carrots, cooked	

Simmer chicken, covered, in water with onion, celery, parsley, and 1 teaspoon salt, 3 hours, or until tender. Remove chicken; cool broth. Remove meat from bones, and cut into large pieces. Put in 2-quart baking dish with onions and peas and carrots. Skim fat from broth. Melt butter, and stir in flour. Add broth. Cook until thickened. Season to taste. Pour over chicken and vegetables. Keep hot. Cover with pastry. Make slits in crust to let steam escape. Brush crust with egg. Bake in hot oven, 425° F., about 30 minutes. Makes 6 servings.

CHILLED CHICKEN-CAPER CUPS

You serve them on salad greens with a mayonnaise-caper dressing.

1 stewing chicken (about 4 pounds), cut up	1 bay leaf
	Salt and pepper
5 cups water	Salad greens
1 onion	¾ cup mayonnaise
2 stalks celery	2 tablespoons capers

Simmer chicken, covered, in water with onion, celery, bay leaf, and 1 teaspoon salt 3 hours, or until tender. Drain, reserving liquid. Cool chicken; remove meat from bones, and cut into coarse dice. Arrange in 6 oiled custard cups or individual molds. Remove fat from top of liquid, and strain liquid; reduce to 2 cups by boiling uncovered. Season to taste with salt and pepper, and pour over chicken. Let stand until cool. Chill overnight, or until set. Unmold, and serve on salad greens with mayonnaise mixed with capers. Makes 6 servings.

CHICKEN PIQUANT

Chicken is baked with meatless spaghetti sauce and sherry.

1 frying chicken (about 2½ pounds), cut up	3 tablespoons butter
Salt and pepper	1 can (8 ounces) meatless spaghetti sauce
Fine dry bread crumbs	½ cup sherry

Sprinkle chicken with salt and pepper; roll in crumbs. Brown in butter. Put in 2-quart casserole. Mix spaghetti sauce and sherry; pour over chicken. Cover; bake in moderate oven, 350°F., 50 minutes, or until tender. Makes 4 servings.

CHICKEN WITH GINGER-CREAM SAUCE

The chicken simmers in the ginger sauce; the cream is added at the end.

1 frying chicken (about 2½ pounds), cut up	3 tablespoons butter or margarine
¼ cup flour	1 chicken bouillon cube
½ teaspoon salt	¾ cup water
Dash pepper	½ cup cream
1 teaspoon ginger	

Roll chicken in mixture of flour, salt, pepper, and ginger. Brown in butter. Stir in remaining flour mixture. Add bouillon cube dissolved in water, and bring to boil. Cover; simmer 45 minutes. Stir in cream. Heat. Serves 4.

COUNTRY CAPTAIN

Chicken, rice, tomatoes, onion, garlic, green pepper, curry, raisins, almonds.

1 frying chicken, cut up	1 teaspoon curry powder
2 tablespoons fat	½ teaspoon thyme
1 green pepper, chopped	Salt and pepper
1 clove garlic, chopped	2 cups cooked rice
1 onion, chopped	⅓ cup raisins
1 can (19 ounces) tomatoes	⅓ cup blanched almonds

Brown chicken well in fat in skillet. Remove chicken to casserole. Add to skillet green pepper, garlic, and onion. Add tomatoes, seasonings, rice, and half the raisins and almonds; simmer 10 to 15 minutes. Pour sauce over chicken, and cook, covered, in moderate oven, 325°F., 50 to 60 minutes. Do not thicken sauce. Serve with remaining raisins and almonds. Serves 4.

SOUTHERN-FRIED CHICKEN WITH CREAM GRAVY

You fry the chicken in a covered skillet so there's no spattering.

1 frying chicken (about 2½ pounds), cut up	¾ teaspoon pepper
Flour	Butter
1½ teaspoons salt	Vegetable shortening
	Cream Gravy

Shake moist pieces of chicken, a few at a time, in a plastic bag with ½ cup flour, the salt, and pepper until thoroughly coated. Melt equal amounts of butter and shortening to ½-inch depth in large, heavy, covered skillet. Put in chicken; cover, and brown quickly in hot fat on all sides. Reduce heat, and continue frying slowly 25 minutes, turning once or twice. Remove cover during last 10 minutes of cooking. Serve with **Cream Gravy:** Drain off all but 2 tablespoons fat from pan; stir in 2 tablespoons flour. Add 2 cups light cream gradually, stirring constantly. Season and cook until thickened. Makes 4 servings.

BROWNED CHICKEN WITH HOMINY DRESSING

The chicken is baked on top of the dressing.

1 broiling chicken (about 2 pounds), quartered	¼ teaspoon marjoram
Salt and pepper	1 can (1 pound, 13 ounces) whole hominy, drained
¼ cup butter or margarine	2 tablespoons fine dry bread crumbs
1 medium onion, chopped	
¼ teaspoon poultry seasoning	

Season chicken with salt and pepper. Brown in butter. Cover, and simmer 20 minutes. Remove from pan. To drippings in pan, add onion, and cook 5 minutes. Add 1 teaspoon salt, ⅛ teaspoon pepper, poultry seasoning, marjoram, and hominy. Cook about 5 minutes, stirring. Sprinkle with bread crumbs. Put in shallow baking dish; top with chicken. Bake in moderate oven, 375°F., 25 minutes, or until chicken is tender. Makes 4 servings.

FRANKFURTERS

The frankfurter, affectionately known as the "hot dog," ranks next to hamburger as the all-time favorite with American youth. The wiener roast at the beach campfire, at the outdoor grill or at the fireplace in the family living room is a sure-fire method for entertaining juveniles, and not a few of their elders enjoy sitting in on the party. What is better for a snack than a nicely roasted frankfurter, a bit crackly on the outside, nestled in a hot bun with plenty of good relish or mustard? In spite of our devotion, the frankfurter is not our invention. It came, as the name implies, from the city of Frankfurt, in Germany, a country that excels in creating all sorts of sausages. American butcher shops used to hang their wieners or frankfurters in great festoons from the ceiling. The sausages were sold by the yard, and lucky children who went shopping with Mother were offered free sausages as a treat. They ate them right on the spot. So great is our love for frankfurters that we have devised innumerable ways of using them. They go into soups and salads, into stews and casseroles; they are stuffed; they are skewered with vegetables; they are shredded, minced, and ground. Here are ways to dress up an old favorite and give it the appeal of the most elegant party dish.

FRANKFURTERS WITH RED CABBAGE

The cabbage comes in a jar.

Cook 1 pound frankfurters in 1 tablespoon margarine until lightly browned. Add 1 jar (16 ounces) red cabbage, undrained, and heat. Makes 4 servings.

INDIVIDUAL FRANKFURTER CASSEROLES

Frankfurters are baked in a relish-cheese sauce.

Make Cheese Sauce, page 240. When hot, add relish (about 1 tablespoon to 1 cup of sauce). Slice frankfurters to fit into individual casseroles. Cover with sauce, and sprinkle with crumbs. Put under broiler until nicely browned.

FRANKFURTER SMORGASBORD

Browned frankfurters with an assortment of relishes.

Slash top of each frankfurter, making shallow diagonal cuts about 1" apart. Brown lightly on all sides in a little fat. If preferred, brush frankfurters with fat, and cook on an outdoor grill. Serve hot on heated rolls with these relishes:

1. **Marinated Onion Rings:** Slice mild raw onions, separated into rings, and marinate in French dressing.

2. **Sautéed Peppers:** Cut strips of red and green sweet pepper, and sauté lightly in oil for a few minutes.

3. **Onion-Cucumber Relish:** Chop onions and cucumbers; dress with vinegar.

4. **Sweet-Sour Bacon Relish:** Heat equal parts of vinegar and brown sugar to the boiling point, then add chopped, dry, crisp bacon. Serve hot.

5. **Chili Pickle Relish:** Combine chili sauce and chopped pickle.

6. **Celery Horse-radish Mustard:** Add horse-radish to taste to prepared mustard, also a few celery seeds.

FRANKFURTERS, HOMINY, AND PEAS

This can be heated on top of the stove, or baked if you're using the oven.

Cook crisp, and drain 4 slices bacon. Pour off most of fat. In remainder, cook 1 pound frankfurters until lightly browned; remove from skillet. Put 1 can (29 ounces) whole hominy, drained, and 1 can (1 pound) peas, drained, in skillet. Pour ¼ cup melted butter over vegetables. Top with frankfurters, and sprinkle with crumbled bacon. Heat well. Or, bake in moderate oven, 375°F., about 30 minutes. Makes 4 servings.

PAPRIKA FRANKFURTERS

Browned, sliced frankfurters in paprika-seasoned sour cream.

1 pound frankfurters, sliced thin	2 tablespoons paprika
2 tablespoons fat	⅛ teaspoon pepper
1 onion, minced	1½ cups sour cream
½ teaspoon salt	

Brown frankfurters in fat; add onion, salt, paprika, and pepper; cook slowly until onion is tender. Add sour cream, stirring constantly. Cook until heated through. Serve on toast. Serves 6.

OPEN-FACE FRANKFURTER-CHEESE ROLLS

They're topped with a sprinkling of marjoram.

4 frankfurters (about ½ pound)	3 tablespoons melted butter or margarine
4 frankfurter rolls	1 teaspoon crumbled dried marjoram
¾ cup shredded sharp cheese	
¾ cup tomato sauce	Paprika

Cut frankfurters and rolls lengthwise. Put rolls on baking sheet, cut side up, and spread with mixture of cheese and tomato sauce. Put frankfurters, cut side up, on rolls. Brush with butter, and sprinkle with marjoram. Bake in hot oven, 425°F., 15 minutes, or until frankfurters are lightly browned. Sprinkle with paprika. Makes 4 servings.

BROILED FRANKFURTERS WITH HORSE-RADISH MAYONNAISE

The sauce contains mustard, too.

Make a sauce by thoroughly mixing ½ pint of mayonnaise, about 1½ teaspoons of prepared mustard, and 2 teaspoons of prepared horse-radish. Heat sauce, and put on broiled frankfurters. Makes enough sauce for 8 frankfurters.

GREEN PEPPERS STUFFED WITH FRANKFURTERS

The stuffing contains seasoned rice as well as diced frankfurters.

6 green peppers	Butter or margarine
1⅓ cups packaged precooked rice	Salt and pepper
	Garlic-seasoned
4 frankfurters, diced	bread crumbs

Parboil peppers. Prepare rice as directed on the package. Stuff peppers with frankfurters mixed with rice, a lot of butter, salt, and pepper. Top with crumbs. Set peppers in piepan with ¼" water, and bake in moderate oven, 350°F., about 40 minutes. Serves 6.

FRANKFURTERS AND BEANS, YANKEE STYLE

They're cooked with brown sugar and molasses.

3 cups dried marrow or pea beans	¼ cup brown sugar, packed
9 cups water	¼ cup butter or margarine, melted
1 tablespoon salt	1 can (1 pound) onions, drained
¼ teaspoon pepper	
1 teaspoon prepared mustard	1 pound frankfurters, cut in chunks
½ cup molasses	

Wash beans, and put in large kettle. Add water; bring to boil, and boil 2 minutes. Remove from heat, and let stand 1 hour. Cook beans until tender, adding water, if necessary. Add remaining ingredients, except onions and frankfurters; mix lightly. Put in large casserole or bean pot; cover, and bake in moderate oven, 350°F., 3 hours. Add onions and frankfurters during last 30 minutes of baking. Add water during baking, if necessary. Makes 8 servings.

BROILED FRANKFURTER SPECIAL

They're broiled with a delicious mixture of mayonnaise, mustard, bread crumbs, and chives.

Split 8 frankfurters, and broil for 5 minutes. Spread with a mixture of ½ cup mayonnaise, 1 tablespoon prepared mustard, ½ cup fine dry bread crumbs, and ½ teaspoon chopped chives. Broil 5 minutes longer. Makes 4 servings.

FRANKFURTERS BÉARNAISE

Have the frankfurters hot but not sizzling so they don't melt the sauce.

Gash 8 frankfurters, and make each into a circle, fastening with a toothpick. Spread with butter, and broil until nicely browned. Make Béarnaise Sauce, page 239. Place frankfurters on toast rounds, and top with sauce. Serves 4.

LIVERWURST FRANKFURTERS

Liverwurst is made into a paste with mustard and minced dill pickle.

Split frankfurters, and spread inside with a paste made with ¼ pound mashed liverwurst, 2 tablespoons each prepared mustard and minced dill pickle. Fry 8 slices bacon, and when frankfurters are nicely broiled, sprinkle with crushed bacon. Serve on toasted rolls. Makes 4 servings.

FRANKFURTER HASH

It has a topping of cheddar cheese.

4 cups finely diced cold boiled potato	½ pound frankfurters, thinly sliced
1 medium onion, chopped	3 tablespoons butter or margarine
3 tablespoons flour	½ cup shredded sharp cheddar cheese
Salt and pepper	
¼ cup milk	

Combine potato and onion. Sprinkle with flour, and season. Add milk and frankfurters. Put in shallow baking dish or piepan. Dot with butter. Bake in hot oven, 425°F., 30 minutes. Top with cheese. Bake 5 minutes longer, or until cheese is melted. Makes 4 servings.

FRANKFURTERS IN THE ROUND

They're broiled with cheese and topped with relish.

Butter sandwich rolls. Gash frankfurters, one to a roll; fasten ends of each together with toothpicks. Place frankfurters on buttered rolls with a good-sized piece of cheddar cheese in the middle, and broil until frankfurters are done to your liking. Top with your favorite relish and the roll top.

CHEESED FRANKFURTERS, POTATOES, AND PEAS

The cheese is made tangy with mustard and Worcestershire.

1 can (1 pound) whole potatoes	1 teaspoon prepared mustard
½ pound process American cheese, sliced	1 cup hot cooked peas
1¼ cups milk	½ pound frankfurters
1 teaspoon Worcestershire	1 teaspoon fat

Drain potatoes, and cut in large cubes. Put next 4 ingredients in skillet. Cover, and cook 5 minutes. Stir vigorously until ingredients are blended. Add potatoes and about ¾ cup of the peas; heat. Cut frankfurters in eighths, and brown lightly in the fat. Put potato mixture into serving dish, and sprinkle with remaining peas. Top with frankfurters. Makes 4 servings.

FRANKFURTERS AND EGGS, ITALIAN STYLE

Serve this with buttered, cooked escarole, or any salad greens.

2 slices bacon, cut up	6 stuffed olives, sliced
1 onion, minced	1 teaspoon capers
½ pound frankfurters, sliced	Salt and pepper
1 green pepper, cut in strips	Pinch orégano
	6 eggs, beaten
	2 tablespoons milk

Cook bacon slowly in heavy skillet. Add onion, and cook 3 minutes. Add frankfurters and green pepper, and cook until pepper is tender. Stir in remaining ingredients. Cook until eggs are set, stirring often. Makes 4 servings.

FRANKFURTERS IN WINE SAUCE

The wine is Burgundy.

Make 2 cups thick white sauce, and add ½ cup Burgundy. Cut 4 frankfurters into bite-size pieces. Add to sauce, and heat thoroughly. Makes 4 servings.

FRANKFURTERS À LA KING

Delicious with asparagus or peas.

1 can cream-of-celery soup	1 can (2 ounces) sliced mushrooms, drained
½ cup milk	1 pimiento, cut up
¾ pound frankfurters, sliced	2 hard-cooked eggs
	8 sandwich rolls

Heat soup with milk. Add frankfurters, mushrooms, and pimiento. Reserve one egg yolk; dice remaining egg white and egg, and add to the mixture. Heat. Scoop out centers from sandwich rolls; heat rolls in oven. Fill with mixture. Shred reserved egg yolk, and sprinkle over top. Makes 4 servings.

FRANKFURTER-MACARONI LOAF

A gelatin-based loaf served in slices.

1 envelope unflavored gelatin	2 teaspoons prepared mustard
1 cup milk	1 teaspoon salt
1 egg, slightly beaten	Dash Tabasco
4 cups cooked broken macaroni	1 cup grated process American cheese
½ cup mayonnaise	4½ frankfurters

Soften gelatin in milk in top part of double boiler. Add egg, and put over boiling water. Cook, stirring constantly, until slightly thickened and mixture coats spoon. Remove from heat, and add remaining ingredients, except frankfurters. Pack half of mixture into greased 9"x 5"x 3" loaf pan. Put 3 frankfurters lengthwise about ¾" apart at one end of mixture. Cut remaining whole frankfurter in half crosswise. Use these two pieces and remaining half frankfurter to fill other end of loaf. Cover with remaining macaroni mixture, and pack down. Chill several hours, or until firm. Unmold; slice. Serves 6.

FRANKFURTERS IN GARLIC BUTTER

You can use the leftover garlic butter to make garlic bread.

Slice 1 pound frankfurters, and sauté in ¼ pound of butter or margarine to which 1 glove of garlic has been added. Makes 4 to 6 servings.

FRANKFURTER RABBIT

Make this in individual ramekins so none of the sauce is lost.

Arrange sliced frankfurters on well-buttered toast. Top with Cheese Sauce, page 240, and good dash of Worcestershire. Slip under broiler until bubbly and nicely browned.

CRISPY FRANKFURTERS

They're rolled in a crust of crushed potato chips.

Split frankfurters, and brush generously with mayonnaise; then roll in crushed potato chips (½ cup mayonnaise and a 5-ounce package of potato chips will cover 6 to 8). Broil until golden.

FRANKFURTER, POTATO, AND CHEESE CASSEROLE

A ring of mashed potato with pimiento, cheese, and frankfurters baked in the center.

1 egg, beaten	¼ pound process
1 tablespoon	pimiento cheese,
chopped parsley	sliced
½ teaspoon salt	4 frankfurters
Dash each pepper	(about ½ pound)
and cayenne	1 small onion
2 cups hot mashed	2 tablespoons
potato	melted butter

Add egg, parsley, salt, pepper, and cayenne to potato. Beat well. Put in shallow 1-quart baking dish. Make a depression in the center, and build potato up around the sides of the dish with the back of a spoon. Put cheese in the depression. Lay scored frankfurters over cheese, and top with onion, sliced and separated in rings. Brush with butter. Bake in moderate oven, 375°F., 30 minutes. Makes 4 servings.

CREAMY FRANKFURTERS

You serve them on toast.

4 frankfurters	2 cups medium
Freshly ground	white sauce
black pepper	Buttered toast
Salt	

Dice frankfurters. Add to seasoned white sauce; stir constantly. When heated through, pour on toast. Serves 4.

FRANKFURTERS AND TOMATO-SCRAMBLED EGGS

You use tomato juice instead of milk when scrambling the eggs.

Dice frankfurters, 1 per person, and brown them lightly in butter. Add eggs, 2 per person, beaten with freshly ground pepper and tomato juice, as much liquid as you would use if scrambling eggs with milk. Cook slowly until eggs are of desired consistency.

FRANKFURTERS EN BROCHETTE

Frankfurters cooked on a skewer with onions, tomatoes, green pepper, bacon.

8 frankfurters	8 chunks green
8 canned white	pepper
onions	8 bacon slices
8 tomato quarters	French dressing

Cut frankfurters in chunks, and marinate with onions, tomatoes, peppers, and bacon in French dressing about half an hour. Arrange on skewers, alternating frankfurters with other ingredients. Broil over coals. Serves 4.

BARBECUED FRANKFURTERS

Be sure to serve some of the sauce over the cooked frankfurters.

1 onion, minced	½ teaspoon salt
2 tablespoons	¾ cup ketchup
vinegar	¼ cup fat
1 tablespoon	½ cup water
Worcestershire	8 frankfurters
½ teaspoon	(about 1
chili powder	pound)

Put all ingredients, except frankfurters, in skillet. Bring to boil. Add frankfurters, and simmer 10 minutes. Serves 4.

FRANKFURTER-STUFFED TOMATOES

You serve them cold.

Chop 4 frankfurters. Combine with celery that has been chopped and parboiled 3 minutes. Add mayonnaise, salt, and pepper, and use to stuff 4 good-sized tomatoes. Chill. Makes 4 servings.

SCALLOPED FRANKFURTERS AND TOMATOES

There's a topping of buttered crumbs.

1 can (19 ounces) tomatoes, drained	2 cups soft bread crumbs
4 frankfurters, cut bite-size	Salt and pepper
	Sugar
	Butter

In a well-buttered casserole, combine tomatoes, frankfurters, and 1 cup of the bread crumbs. Add salt, pepper, and a little sugar. Sprinkle 1 cup buttered bread crumbs on top, and bake in a hot oven, 400°F., about 30 minutes. Makes 4 servings.

FRANKFURTER ALL-IN-ONE

A hearty dish with potatoes, sauerkraut, onion, tomatoes, and bacon in addition to frankfurters.

4 slices bacon	2 pounds frankfurters
1 large onion, minced	8 potatoes, boiled in jackets
1 clove garlic, minced	¼ cup butter, melted
1 can (29 ounces), or 1¾ pounds fresh sauerkraut	2 tablespoons caraway seed
1 can (19 ounces) tomatoes, undrained	

Cut bacon in small pieces; brown with onion and garlic in Dutch oven. Add sauerkraut and tomatoes; cover, and cook slowly on top of stove or in slow oven, 300°F., 1¼ hours. Add frankfurters; cook 45 minutes. Arrange frankfurters in center of hot platter, and surround with peeled potatoes, rolled and heated in butter and sprinkled with caraway seed. Makes 8 servings.

CHEESE FRANKFURTERS

The frankfurters are stuffed with potatoes and onion, topped with cheese.

8 frankfurters	Salt and pepper
1½ cups mashed potato	Butter
	Cheddar cheese, coarsely grated
1 tablespoon minced onion	

Split frankfurters, stuff with mashed potato to which onion, salt, pepper, and plenty of butter have been added. Now sprinkle with cheese. Broil until a golden brown. Remove, and serve immediately. Makes 4 servings.

CREAMY FRANKFURTERS AND CORN

Mushroom soup makes a quick sauce for this creamed dish.

1 pound frankfurters	½ can cream-of-mushroom soup
3 tablespoons butter	¼ cup milk
1 can (17 ounces) whole-kernel corn	Pepper

Cut frankfurters in ½" slices. Melt butter; add frankfurters and drained corn. Cover, and cook about 10 minutes, stirring often. Add mushroom soup and milk, and stir constantly until soup is thoroughly heated. Then add a bit of pepper. Makes 6 servings.

FRANKFURTER DELIGHT

Frankfurters baked in a mushroom-sour-cream sauce.

8 frankfurters	Paprika
Butter	1 cup sour cream
2 tablespoons flour	½ cup chopped mushrooms
3 tablespoons water	1 tablespoon onion juice
½ teaspoon salt	

Cut frankfurters in bite-size pieces. Brown in butter. Place flour in a double boiler. Add water. Make a smooth sauce; add seasonings and sour cream slowly, stirring constantly. When the sauce has thickened, remove from heat, and add mushrooms and onion juice. Pour the sauce over the browned frankfurters in a casserole. Cover, and bake 30 minutes at 300°F. Makes 4 servings.

FRANKFURTERS AND ONIONS

Sliced, cooked, and seasoned onions
are served over the frankfurters.

4 cups sliced onion	2 tablespoons Worcestershire
1 clove garlic, minced	1 tablespoon prepared mustard
2 tablespoons fat	1 pound frankfurters, split
½ teaspoon salt	
Dash pepper	

Cook onion and garlic in fat until golden brown. Sprinkle with salt and pepper. Cover, and simmer 10 minutes. Add Worcestershire and mustard. Heat frankfurters in colander over boiling water. Put on hot platter, and top with onion mixture. Makes 4 servings.

STUFFED FRANKFURTERS

The stuffing is your
favorite kind, packaged or homemade.

Make stuffing with ½ package stuffing mix, following directions on the package. Or make 2 cups of your favorite stuffing for meat, see page 237, and bake the stuffing about an hour in a moderate oven, 325°F. Remove from oven, and set aside until it is cool enough to handle. Make a pocket in each of 8 frankfurters, and broil 5 minutes. Stuff the frankfurters, and return to broiler. Broil until nicely browned. Top with a generous dab of mayonnaise. Makes 8 servings.

FRANKFURTER AND CORN-MEAL PATTIES

You mix ground frankfurters with
cooked corn meal and fry the patties.

¾ cup yellow corn meal	½ pound frankfurters, cooked and ground, or minced very fine
2 teaspoons salt	
3 cups boiling water	¼ cup fat

Gradually add meal to salted boiling water, stirring constantly. Cook until thick. Remove from heat. Add frankfurters, mixing well. Drop by heaping tablespoonfuls onto platter; let stand until cold. Cook patties slowly in hot fat until they're browned on both sides. Makes 4 servings.

FRANKIE AND JOHNNY

Frankfurters plus johnnycake.

1 cup coarsely ground white or yellow corn meal	1 cup boiling water
	¼ cup milk
	2 tablespoons fat
1 teaspoon salt	1 pound frankfurters
Butter	

Mix corn meal, salt, and 1 tablespoon butter in a bowl. Add actively boiling water, and mix well. Stir in milk. Heat fat in 8"x 8"x 2" baking pan. Pour in batter and smooth to fill pan. Heat until edges are bubbly. Bake in very hot oven, 475°F., about 30 minutes. Cool in pan; cut in squares, split, and spread generously with softened butter. Brown under broiler. Slice frankfurters lengthwise, and brown in butter. To serve, place them between squares of johnnycake, sandwich-fashion. Serves 4.

FRANKFURTERS WITH CHEESE AND RICE

The cheese is cheddar,
the rice is precooked.

1 pound frankfurters	1 box (1⅓ cups) precooked rice
½ pound sharp cheddar cheese	½ cup milk

Cut the frankfurters bite-size. Melt cheese. Combine these with rice, and add milk. Simmer about 10 minutes. Makes 4 servings.

BARBECUED FRANKFURTERS AND LIMA BEANS

They're heated in a sweet-
and-sour tomato sauce.

1 onion, minced	1 tablespoon Worcestershire
1 clove garlic, minced	1 can (8 ounces) tomato sauce
2 tablespoons fat	1 can (21 ounces) dried Lima beans
¼ cup brown sugar, packed	1 pound frankfurters, cut in 2" pieces
2 tablespoons vinegar	
½ teaspoon dry mustard	

Cook onion and garlic in fat in skillet until lightly browned. Add sugar, seasonings, tomato sauce; bring to boil, and simmer 5 minutes. Add beans and frankfurters; heat. Makes 4 servings.

FRANKFURTER, ONION, AND POTATO SKILLET

They simmer in seasoned bouillon.

1 onion, chopped	½ teaspoon salt
2 tablespoons butter	Dash pepper
½ pound frank-	1 cup bouillon
furters, cut in	3½ cups cooked
½″ slices	diced potato

Cook onion in butter until lightly browned. Add next 4 ingredients. Bring to boil. Add potato; simmer until almost dry. Makes 4 servings.

FRANKFURTERS AND NOODLES

They're cooked with tomatoes, brown sugar, and American cheese.

1 onion, chopped	4 frankfurters,
¼ cup butter	cut in 1″ pieces
1 can (19 ounces)	½ cup grated
tomatoes	process American
4 ounces wide	cheese
noodles	Salt and pepper
2 teaspoons	¼ teaspoon
brown sugar	Accent

Cook onion in butter in skillet 5 minutes. Add next 3 ingredients; bring to boil, and simmer, uncovered, 20 minutes, stirring frequently. Add remaining ingredients, and heat. Makes 4 servings.

FRANKFURTER-CHEESE ROLL-UPS

Frankfurters, stuffed with cheese, are baked in dough until golden brown.

1 box hot-roll mix	8 long strips sharp
Melted butter	cheddar cheese
8 frankfurters	Evaporated milk
Prepared mustard	

Prepare roll mix as directed on the box. Let rise once; roll out to about ½″ thickness; cut in strips about 7″x 4″; brush with melted butter. Split frankfurters lengthwise, but do not cut through; spread with mustard, and insert a cheese strip in each. Overlap dough around frankfurters, and pinch the ends together. Put on greased baking sheet; cover with towel, and let rise until double. Brush with milk. Prick with fork. Bake in 450°F. oven 15 to 20 minutes. Makes 8 servings.

FRANKFURTERS AND FRENCH DRESSING

You must marinate the frankfurters for some time before cooking them.

Marinate frankfurters in French dressing about 2 hours. When ready to serve, sauté in butter to which 1 tablespoon French dressing has been added. This can also be an oven dish, but frankfurters must be turned often.

POLKA-DOT POTATO SALAD

A hot salad with sliced frankfurters and a vinegar-mustard dressing.

3 tablespoons	½ cup water
bacon fat	⅓ cup vinegar
1½ tablespoons	2 cups sliced
flour	cooked potato
1 tablespoon sugar	1 small onion,
1 teaspoon salt	minced
Dash pepper	Chopped parsley
1 tablespoon pre-	4 frankfurters
pared mustard	1 tablespoon butter

Heat fat; add flour, sugar, and seasonings; stir in water and vinegar. Cook until slightly thickened. Add potato, onion, and parsley. Heat thoroughly. Cut frankfurters in ¼″ slices, brown lightly in hot butter, and stir into potato mixture. Serve at once. Makes 4 servings.

FRANKFURTER AND LENTIL STEW

There are tomatoes, onion, and garlic in it, too.

¾ cup dried lentils	1 can (19 ounces)
2 cups water	tomatoes
1 onion, minced	1 teaspoon salt
1 small clove	½ teaspoon
garlic, minced	sugar
1 tablespoon butter	1 bay leaf
1 pound	1 whole black
frankfurters,	pepper
scored, then	¼ teaspoon
sliced	pepper

Wash lentils, and boil 2 minutes in water. Remove from heat, and soak 1 hour. Simmer until tender, adding more water if necessary. Brown onion and garlic in butter. Add remaining ingredients; simmer ½ hour. Add lentils with any liquid; heat. Serves 4.

HAM

In Paris during the Easter season an annual *Foire de Jambons,* or Ham
Fair, is held. Hams from all over the world are entered and, ah, there
is much joy in tasting snippets of ham from China, from Westphalia in Germany,
from Prague, from England, Ireland, France, Spain, Italy, and the peppery
ham from our own Kentucky. A ham fair might be an excellent idea for
America. Surely with the wide number of fine local smoked, cured, and aged
hams produced in many of our rural areas we could present an impressive array.
Consider the famous Virginia ham, cured and aged for months, and the
Smithfield from the same state; the tasty country hams from the Carolinas and
Kentucky; hams from the German region in Iowa, and from Pennsylvania and
West Virginia. Many of these must be soaked, then simmered in hot water before
they are baked, but what a wealth of flavor they offer. Here are ways to use
ham that will help you get the most from this excellent cured meat.

63

GLAZED BAKED HAM

*A carving tip: let it
stand 15 minutes before slicing.*

When buying a ham be sure to note
if it is fully cooked, the ready-to-eat
kind; or uncooked that must be cooked
before eating. Put ham on rack in shallow
pan, fat side up. The best way to
be sure the ham is done is to use a
meat thermometer. Bake in moderate
oven, 325°F., allowing 10 minutes to
the pound for the ready-to-eat kind and
baking to 130°F.; and allowing about
20 minutes to the pound for the uncooked
kind, baking to 160°F. When
ham is done, pour off drippings in pan,
and remove any skin that might be on
end of ham. Score fat with sharp knife.
Insert whole cloves, if desired, and
brush or spread with one of the glazes
listed below. Bake in hot oven, 400°F.,
15 minutes, or till well glazed.

GLAZES FOR HOT
BAKED HAM

Molasses: Mix ½ cup each vinegar and
molasses.

Marmalade: Use ½ cup orange, peach,
or apricot marmalade.

Honey: Use ¾ cup strained honey.

Mustard Molasses: Mix ½ cup sugar, ⅓
cup molasses, and ½ teaspoon dry
mustard.

Sweet-pickle: Use liquid drained from
gherkins or other sweet pickle.

Jelly: Mash 1 cup cranberry, currant,
or other tart jelly.

MANDARIN-ORANGE-
GLAZED HAM

Orange sections are studded with cloves.

Over top of scored hot baked ham, pour
a little of the syrup from a can of mandarin
oranges. Pat on some light-brown
sugar. Bake in hot oven, 400°F., about
15 minutes. Remove from oven, and in
the center of each diamond, put a mandarin
orange stuck with a whole clove.

TROPICAL GLAZED HAM

Butterscotch with pineapple.

Mix ½ cup undrained crushed pineapple,
¾ cup packed light-brown sugar,
and 2 teaspoons dry mustard. Spread
on hot baked ham, and bake in hot
oven, 400°F., 15 minutes, or until well
glazed.

VIRGINIA HAM SALAD

*The special Virginia
touch is chopped salted peanuts.*

2 cups diced cooked ham	1 cup diced celery
½ cup chopped salted peanuts	Mayonnaise Salad greens

Mix first 3 ingredients. Moisten with
mayonnaise; serve on greens. Serves 4.

HAM SALAD RING

*You can serve mayonnaise or salad
dressing in the center of the ring.*

2 envelopes unflavored gelatin	¼ cup salad dressing
½ cup cold water	Dash each cayenne and onion salt
1¾ cups boiling water	1 green pepper, chopped
¼ cup vinegar	¾ cup diced celery
¼ cup mustard pickle relish	1 cucumber, diced
2 cups diced cooked ham	Salt and pepper Salad greens

Soften gelatin in cold water; add boiling
water, and stir until dissolved; add
vinegar. To ¼ cup of this gelatin mixture,
add relish; cool. Pour into 5-cup
ring mold. Chill until set. Mix ham,
salad dressing, cayenne, onion salt,
and remaining gelatin mixture; chill until
slightly thickened. Add vegetables,
and season with salt and pepper. Pour
into mold. Chill until firm. Unmold on
greens. Serve with mayonnaise or salad
dressing, if desired. Makes 8 servings.

HAM AND POTATOES AU GRATIN

They have a cheese topping.

3 tablespoons butter or margarine	5 cups diced cooked potato
3 tablespoons flour	2 cups diced cooked ham
⅛ teaspoon pepper	½ cup shredded American cheese
2½ cups milk	

Melt butter; stir in flour and pepper. Add milk, and cook until thickened, stirring. Add potato, and put with ham in 2-quart casserole. Top with cheese, and bake in hot oven, 400°F., about 20 minutes. Makes 4 servings.

HAM-CORN POTATO SOUP

This is a hearty main-dish soup served with browned rye-bread cubes.

Baked-ham bone	2 cups milk
6 cups water	¼ cup minced parsley
4 cups diced potato	Salt and pepper
1 onion, chopped	4 slices rye bread, cubed
1 can (1 pound) cream-style corn	¼ cup ham fat

Break bone at joints; cover, and simmer in water 1½ hours. Remove bone, and take off meat. Add meat, potato, and onion to stock. Cook until potato is tender. Add corn, milk, and parsley. Season. Heat, and serve with bread cubes browned in the ham fat. Makes 4 large servings.

SWEET-AND-SOUR HAM WITH VEGETABLES

Vegetables are tossed in ham drippings and served around the meat.

1 onion	2 teaspoons dry mustard
3 or 4 potatoes	¼ cup brown sugar
Salted water	2 tablespoons vinegar
1 slice ready-to-eat ham (1½ pounds)	

Cut onion and potatoes in chunks. Cook in small amount of lightly salted water until tender; drain. Sprinkle ham with mustard, brown sugar, and vinegar. Broil one side, turn, and spoon the pan juice over top, and broil until lightly browned. Put ham on serving platter. Pour ham drippings over drained potatoes and onion, and toss a minute over low heat. Serve around ham. Serves 3 to 4.

BROILED HAM-BURGERS

Seasoned ham patties broiled with pineapple and served on rolls.

2 cups ground cooked ham	1 egg, slightly beaten
2 teaspoons instant minced onion	2 tablespoons pineapple juice
2 tablespoons chopped parsley	4 slices pineapple
1 tablespoon prepared mustard	4 sandwich rolls

Combine all ingredients, except pineapple and rolls. Shape into 4 patties. Broil about 5 minutes on each side. Put a slice of pineapple on top of each patty; broil until lightly browned. Serve on toasted rolls. Makes 4 servings.

HAM TETRAZZINI

Spaghetti, with ham, mushroom, and sherry sauce, is baked in the oven.

½ pound mushrooms, sliced	Salt and pepper
1 medium onion, minced	2 tablespoons sherry
⅓ cup butter or margarine	2 cups diced cooked ham
⅓ cup flour	1 package (8 ounces) thin spaghetti, cooked
2 cups milk	
1 cup light cream	¼ cup grated Parmesan cheese
6 stuffed olives, sliced	

Cook mushrooms and onion in the butter until lightly browned. Blend in the flour. Gradually add milk and cream; cook, stirring, until thickened. Add olives, and salt and pepper to taste. Add sherry, ham, and spaghetti; mix well. Pour into large shallow baking dish. Sprinkle with cheese. Bake in hot oven, 400°F., 20 minutes, or until bubbly. Makes 6 servings.

"Sit down and feed, and welcome to our table."
WILLIAM SHAKESPEARE

*"Tell me what you eat,
and I will tell you
what you are."*
ANSELME BRILLAT-SAVARIN

BAKED HAM SLICE WITH APPLES AND SWEET POTATOES

They're cooked in layers with brown sugar and cinnamon.

1 slice ready-to-eat ham (about 1½ pounds)	Juice 1 lemon
	4 sweet potatoes, cooked
½ cup brown sugar	4 apples, sliced
Few cloves	Dash cinnamon
½ cup water	2 tablespoons butter

Sprinkle ham with some of the brown sugar, and insert cloves in fat of ham. Pour water and lemon juice around ham. Bake in moderate oven, 350°F., about 15 minutes. Cover ham with alternate layers of sliced sweet potatoes and apples; sprinkle each layer with brown sugar and cinnamon; dot with butter. Bake 30 minutes, or until apples are tender. Makes 4 servings.

STUFFED HAM SLICES

Two good-sized slices of ham are stuffed, sandwich-fashion, then baked.

2 center-cut ready-to-eat ham slices, 1″ thick (about 3 pounds)	1 cup chopped celery leaves
	6 sprigs parsley, chopped
24 whole cloves	1 teaspoon salt
½ pound fresh spinach	¼ teaspoon pepper
	Dash cayenne
Chopped tops from 1 bunch green onions	Dash mace or nutmeg

Score edges of ham slices, and insert 12 cloves in the fat of each. Mix remaining ingredients, and put between ham slices. Insert several skewers to hold slices together. Put on rack in shallow baking pan, and bake in moderate oven, 325°., about 1½ hours. Makes 6 servings.

SAVORY BROILED HAM

Dry mustard, brown sugar, and vinegar are what make this savory.

1 center-cut ready-to-eat ham slice (about 2 pounds)	2 teaspoons dry mustard
	¼ cup brown sugar
	2 tablespoons vinegar

Put ham in shallow baking pan. Sprinkle with remaining ingredients. Broil under moderate heat until well browned. Turn, and baste with drippings in pan. Broil until lightly browned. Makes 4 servings.

BONELESS-BUTT BOILED DINNER

Ham plus onion, carrots, potatoes, and cabbage wedges.

1 smoked boneless butt (2 pounds)	4 to 6 medium potatoes
Water	1 medium head cabbage, cut in wedges
1 onion, sliced	
8 carrots	

Cover meat with water, add onion, and bring to boil. Simmer 2 hours, or until almost tender. Add carrots and potatoes, and simmer 15 minutes. Add cabbage, and cook 15 minutes longer, or until all is tender. Makes 4 servings.

HAM HAWAIIAN

Ham, green pepper, and pineapple mixture is served over hot rice.

¼ cup butter or margarine	1½ tablespoons cornstarch
½ medium green pepper, chopped	1½ tablespoons vinegar
2 cups slivered cooked ham	1½ teaspoons prepared mustard
1 can (9 ounces) sliced pineapple	⅛ teaspoon pepper
2 tablespoons brown sugar	¾ cup cold water
	1⅓ cups packaged precooked rice
	⅛ teaspoon ground cloves

Melt half of butter in skillet. Add green pepper and ham; cook 5 minutes. Drain pineapple, reserving liquid. Cut slices in bite-size pieces. Mix liquid and next 6 ingredients. Stir into ham mixture; cook, stirring, until thickened. Add pineapple; heat. Prepare rice as directed on the package, adding remaining butter and the cloves after rice has stood. Serve with ham mixture. Serves 4.

BAKED HAM SLICE WITH BANANAS

The ham is baked with mustard,
peanut butter, and brown sugar.

Put 1 slice ready-to-eat ham, ½" thick
and weighing about 1½ pounds, in baking dish. Spread with 1 teaspoon prepared mustard and ¼ cup peanut
butter. Sprinkle with 2 tablespoons
brown sugar. Bake in moderate oven,
350°F., 30 minutes. Arrange 4 peeled
bananas around ham, and sprinkle with
2 tablespoons brown sugar. Bake about
10 minutes longer. Makes 4 servings.

HAM AND BEAN BAKE

The ham is ground baked ham, the
beans are red kidney and Lima beans.

⅔ cup chopped baked-ham fat	Dash pepper
1 onion, chopped	1 teaspoon Worcestershire
2 tablespoons ketchup	¾ cup ground baked ham
1 tablespoon molasses	1 can (21 ounces) dried Lima beans
1 teaspoon dry mustard	1 can (21 ounces) red kidney beans
½ teaspoon salt	

Fry ham fat until crisp. Pour off drippings. Add onion, and cook slowly 5
minutes. Add remaining ingredients.
Pour into shallow baking dish. Bake in
350°F. oven 25 minutes. Serves 4.

HAM CROQUETTES

These are delicious with a creamy
horse-radish or mustard sauce.

¼ cup butter or margarine	1½ cups ground cooked ham
¼ cup flour	Salt and pepper
1 onion, minced	Fine dry bread crumbs
1 cup milk	Water
2 eggs	Fat for frying
Juice ½ lemon	

Melt butter; blend in flour and onion.
Add milk, and cook, stirring constantly,
until very thick. Stir into 1 egg beaten
with lemon juice. Add ham, and salt
and pepper to taste. Pour into a shallow
dish; cool. Shape into 4 croquettes.
Chill. Dip in crumbs, then in 1 egg
beaten with 2 tablespoons water. Dip
again in crumbs, and let stand ½ hour.
Fry in hot deep fat (390°F. on a frying
thermometer) 2 minutes. Makes 4.

HAM A LA CRÈME

The milk-and-cream sauce contains
green onions, tomato purée, and wine.

6 green onions, chopped fine	2 tablespoons tomato purée
¼ cup butter or margarine	¼ cup white wine
¼ cup flour	Salt and pepper
¾ cup each milk and light cream	8 thin slices baked or boiled ham

In top part of double boiler over direct
heat, cook onions in butter 5 minutes.
Blend in flour. Add milk and cream;
cook, stirring, until thickened. Put over
boiling water, and stir in purée and
wine. Add salt and pepper to taste.
Cut ham in strips, and put in shallow,
broilerproof dish. Pour sauce on ham,
and put under broiler until lightly
browned and bubbly. Makes 4 servings.

SPICED HAM AND BANANAS

Halved bananas, sprinkled with
brown sugar and lemon juice, are
baked over a center-cut ham slice.

Few whole cloves	Brown sugar
1 center-cut ready-to-eat ham slice (about 2 pounds)	½ cup water
	Juice 1 lemon
	2 or 3 firm ripe bananas
Prepared mustard	

Insert cloves in fat of ham. Put ham
in a shallow baking dish, and spread
with mustard. Sprinkle with brown sugar.
Add water and half of lemon juice.
Bake in slow oven, 300°F., about 50
minutes. Peel bananas, cut in halves
lengthwise, and arrange on ham.
Sprinkle with brown sugar and remaining lemon juice. Bake 10 to 15 minutes
longer, basting bananas several times
with the drippings in pan. Serves 4.

"Cheese and ham
are good companions."
OLD FRENCH PROVERB

CREAMY HAM AND EGGS

Cream and cream cheese make this smooth, rich, and delicious.

1 package (3 ounces) cream cheese	¼ teaspoon salt
	Dash of pepper
2 tablespoons butter	1 cup diced cooked ham
½ cup light cream	5 eggs, well beaten
	Toast points

Mix cheese, butter, cream, and seasonings in top part of double boiler. Put over boiling water, and heat until cheese is softened. Add ham and eggs; stir until eggs are set. Serve on toast points. Makes 4 servings.

HAM BLANKETS WITH CHICKEN

Chicken-stuffed ham slices are cooked on a bed of diced potato.

3 cups diced cooked potato	Salt and pepper
3 tablespoons butter	8 small slices cooked chicken
3 tablespoons flour	8 slices boiled or baked ham
2 cups milk	Paprika
1 cup diced sharp cheddar cheese	

Put ¾ cup potato in each of 4 flat individual baking dishes. Melt butter in saucepan; blend in flour. Gradually add milk, and cook, stirring, until thickened. Add cheese, and stir until cheese is melted. Season to taste with salt and pepper. Reserve about ½ cup sauce, and pour remainder over potato. Put a slice of chicken at one side of each ham slice, and fold ham over to form a triangle. Arrange two on each dish of potato. Top with remaining ½ cup sauce, and sprinkle with paprika. Put in hot oven, 400°F., 10 minutes, or until thoroughly heated. Or broil until lightly browned. Makes 4 servings.

HAM AND EGG BAKE

Diced cooked ham and beaten eggs spiked with Worcestershire.

6 eggs	Salt and pepper
2 cups diced cooked ham	Worcestershire
	Chopped parsley

Beat eggs slightly. Add ham, and seasonings. Pour into 8″ piepan. Bake in slow oven, 325°F., 20 minutes, or until set. Sprinkle with chopped parsley. Makes 4 servings.

HAM IN RAISIN SAUCE

It's served over hot noodles.

⅓ cup seedless raisins	2 tablespoons vinegar
2 cups water	2 cups chunky nuggets of cooked ham
1 cup brown sugar, packed	
2 tablespoons cornstarch	1 package (8 ounces) wide noodles, cooked
Pinch salt	
¼ teaspoon ginger	

Cook raisins in water 5 minutes. Mix sugar, cornstarch, salt, ginger, and vinegar. Stir into raisin mixture. Cook, stirring, until slightly thickened. Add ham; heat. Put hot cooked noodles in deep platter. Cover with ham and sauce. Makes 4 servings.

DEEP-DISH HAM PIE

It has a cheese-pastry lattice top.

¼ cup butter or margarine	1 can (3 ounces) sliced mushrooms, undrained
¼ cup flour	
¼ teaspoon dry mustard	2 to 3 cups diced cooked ham
1 teaspoon instant minced onion	1 cup cooked peas
	Salt and pepper
2 cups milk	Cheese Pastry

Melt butter; stir in flour, mustard, onion. Add milk; cook until thickened, stirring. Add remaining ingredients, except salt, pepper, and Pastry; heat, and season to taste. Put in casserole, cover with Pastry, cut in strips, and bake in hot oven, 425°F., 20 minutes, or until lightly browned. Makes 4 servings.

Cheese Pastry: Mix ¼ teaspoon salt with 1 cup flour. Cut in ⅓ cup shortening. Add ¼ cup grated sharp stale cheese. Add 2 tablespoons ice water, or just enough to moisten dough.

HAM-STUFFED EGGS

Serve these as appetizers, or as a garnish for main-dish salads.

6 hard-cooked eggs	Mustard pickle relish
½ cup minced cooked ham	Mayonnaise
	Paprika
	Chopped parsley

Halve eggs. Remove yolks, and mash. Mix yolks with ham. Season to taste with pickle relish and mayonnaise. Stuff egg-white halves with mixture. Sprinkle the stuffed eggs with paprika and chopped parsley.

HAM AND CORN FRITTERS

These are especially good served with applesauce.

1 can (8¾ ounces) cream-style corn	2 cups sifted flour
2 eggs	1 teaspoon salt
¾ cup milk	¼ pound boiled ham, diced
2 teaspoons baking powder	Fat for frying

Mix all ingredients, except fat. Drop by heaping tablespoonfuls into hot deep fat (365°F. on a frying thermometer), and fry until golden brown and done. Makes 4 servings.

HAM AND VEAL LOAF

You can serve it hot or cold with a whipped-cream, horse-radish sauce.

1½ pounds ground raw ham	1 teaspoon celery salt
½ pound ground raw veal	⅛ teaspoon pepper
2 eggs	¾ cup milk
Dried bread rolled to make 1½ cups fine crumbs	Whipped-cream Horse-radish Sauce, page 239

Mix all ingredients, except Sauce. Shape into two rolls to fit into two greased No. 2½ cans. (These cans hold 3½ cups.) Shake mixture; then press down lightly. Cover each can with foil or several layers of waxed paper, and tie securely. Put on rack in large kettle; surround with water half the depth of the cans. Cover kettle, and bring water to boil. Reduce heat, and simmer 3 hours. Turn hot or cooled loaves onto board; slice; cut slices in half, if preferred. Serve with Sauce. Serves 8.

INDIVIDUAL HAM LOAVES

You serve them with a mustard sauce.

Mix 1 pound ground raw smoked ham, 1½ pounds ground fresh pork, 2 beaten eggs, 1 cup cracker crumbs, 1 cup milk, 1 teaspoon dry mustard, ¼ cup horse-radish, 1 grated small onion, ¼ teaspoon each salt and pepper. Pack into 12 sections of 3″ muffin pan. Put on shallow baking pan, and bake in moderate oven, 350°F., about 1 hour. Serve hot with: **Mustard Sauce:** Mix 1 cup water, ½ cup brown sugar, ¼ cup vinegar, 2 teaspoons dry mustard, ¼ teaspoon salt, and a dash each pepper and cayenne. Bring to boil, and thicken with 3 tablespoons cornstarch blended with a little cold water. Makes 6 servings.

HAM-CHICKEN MOUSSE

This main dish, served on salad greens, is fine for a buffet supper.

1 envelope un-flavored gelatin	1 cup ground cooked ham
2 tablespoons cold water	1 cup ground cooked chicken
¾ teaspoon salt	1 green onion, minced
Dash cayenne	¼ cup salad dressing
3 egg yolks, slightly beaten	⅓ cup heavy cream, whipped
1 cup hot chicken broth	Salad greens

Soften gelatin in cold water. In top part of double boiler, mix seasonings and egg yolks. Stir in broth, and cook over boiling water until thickened. Add gelatin, and stir until dissolved. Cool. Fold in remaining ingredients, except greens. Pour into 1-quart mold, and chill until firm. Unmold on greens; garnish with tomato wedges, if desired. Makes 4 servings.

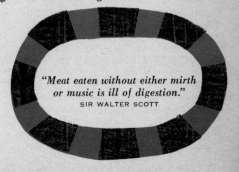

"Meat eaten without either mirth or music is ill of digestion."
SIR WALTER SCOTT

"The skin of the ham is the bottle that holds the perfume within."
OLD SPANISH PROVERB

HAM-ASPARAGUS ROLLS

The rolls are topped with a cheddar white sauce.

16 stalks cooked asparagus	½ cup grated sharp cheddar cheese
4 thin slices boiled ham	1 cup medium white sauce
	Toast points

Put 4 stalks asparagus on each ham slice; roll up. Broil 5 minutes on each side. Add cheese to sauce. Serve ham rolls on toast with the sauce. Serves 4.

HAM BAKED IN CLARET

The ham, a center-cut slice, is topped with chopped tart apples.

1 center-cut ready-to-eat ham slice, 1" thick (about 2 pounds)	2 cups chopped peeled tart apples
1 teaspoon dry mustard	½ cup brown sugar, packed
	1 cup claret

Put ham in large shallow baking dish. Sprinkle with mustard. Top with apples, and sprinkle with brown sugar. Pour claret over ham. Cover, and bake in moderate oven, 350°F., 1 hour. Uncover, and bake 30 minutes. Serves 4.

CREAMY HAM IN CROUSTADES

You need unsliced bread to make the croustades.

3 tablespoons butter or margarine	Dash pepper
3 tablespoons flour	Salt
3 cups milk	2½ cups cooked ham pieces
1 teaspoon prepared horse-radish	Croustades
	Cooked peas

Melt butter in saucepan, and blend in flour. Gradually add milk, and cook, stirring constantly, until thickened. Add seasonings and ham; heat. Serve in Croustades with a garnish of peas. Makes 4 servings.

Croustades

Cut unsliced white bread 2" thick; remove crusts. Cut into oblongs, and hollow out, leaving a shell ⅜" thick. Brush with melted butter, and bake in moderate oven, 375°F., 12 to 15 minutes, or until golden brown.

SCALLOPED HAM AND POTATOES

Traditional scalloped potatoes are a one-dish meal when you add ham.

1 center-cut ready-to-eat ham slice (about 2 pounds)	2 tablespoons flour
	1 teaspoon salt
	Dash pepper
4 cups thinly sliced potato	2 tablespoons melted butter
1 tablespoon instant minced onion	1½ cups hot milk
	Paprika

Cut ham in serving pieces, and put in 2-quart casserole. Mix remaining ingredients, except milk and paprika. Put on ham. Add milk, and sprinkle with paprika. Cover, and bake in moderate oven, 375°F., 45 minutes. Uncover, and bake 15 minutes longer. Serves 4.

CREOLE JAMBALAYA

Diced ham and rice in onion, green pepper, and tomato sauce, with a garnish of shrimp.

¼ cup butter or margarine	¼ teaspoon pepper
2 tablespoons flour	1 can (19 ounces) tomatoes
1 cup chopped onion	1 can (8 ounces) tomato sauce
1 clove garlic, minced	1½ cups water
½ green pepper, chopped	1 cup diced cooked ham
1 cup uncooked rice	1 can (5 ounces) medium shrimp, undrained
2 teaspoons salt	

Heat butter in large heavy skillet. Add flour, onion, garlic, and green pepper. Cook slowly 5 minutes. Add remaining ingredients, except the shrimp. Cover; cook until rice is tender, about 25 minutes. Add shrimp. Makes 4 servings.

HAMBURGER

J·L

If there were to be a national contest to select America's favorite food,
the hamburger would win. Everywhere, from Maine to California,
the familiar hamburger abounds. Truly, for a quick snack few foods are more
satisfying than a good ground-beef patty, cooked just to the rare
stage, oozing rich meat juice. But, surprisingly enough, in being so
devoted to the hamburger, the American public tends to forget the great
versatility of this dependable food. What a wealth of ways there are to prepare
ground chuck or round or sirloin. From elegant steak tartare laced with raw onion,
capers, anchovies, and raw egg to rich meat loaves and exotic curried meat balls,
these are dishes fit for any time or occasion. Ground beef blends
well with a wide choice of flavorings and seasonings. Add cheese, Roquefort,
Gruyère, or cheddar, for a zippy flavor. Try it with herbs or with a good
wine sauce. Buy ground beef fresh and don't overcook it.

71

HAMBURGER FLUFFS

The lightest meat balls ever.

1 pound ground beef	½ medium onion, minced
2 tablespoons flour	Pinch thyme
½ teaspoon Worcestershire	Pinch marjoram
½ teaspoon pepper	¾ cup undiluted evaporated milk
1 teaspoon salt	¾ cup water

Put beef in large bowl; add all ingredients, except milk and water. Whip mixture with large spoon or electric mixer. Add milk and water slowly, beating constantly. When all liquid has been absorbed, cover bowl, and let stand in refrigerator a few hours. (Mixture can be cooked at once, but texture improves on standing.) Drop in 16 mounds on hot well-greased griddle. Brown 1½ minutes on each side. Makes 4 servings.

HAMBURGER CASSOULET

A main-dish soup.

¾ pound ground beef	1½ teaspoons salt
1 small clove garlic, minced	Dash pepper
Few sprigs parsley, chopped	2 eggs
	Flour
¼ teaspoon marjoram	2 bouillon cubes
¼ teaspoon basil	4 cups water
¼ teaspoon onion salt	1 cup canned tomatoes
	1 small bay leaf, crumbled
	2 tablespoons rice

Mix first 6 ingredients, ½ teaspoon salt, pepper, and 1 egg. Shape into 32 tiny balls; dredge with flour. Bring bouillon cubes, water, tomatoes, 1 teaspoon salt, and bay leaf to boil in kettle. Add meat balls and rice. Cover, and simmer 45 minutes. Just before serving, stir in remaining egg, slightly beaten. Serves 4.

INDIVIDUAL BEEF LOAVES

They cook on a parsley-onion bed.

1½ pounds ground beef	¾ cup tomato juice
1 egg	2 tablespoons flour
1 cup soft bread crumbs	2 tablespoons fat
½ green pepper, chopped	2 onions, sliced
1 onion, chopped	2 sprigs parsley, chopped
1½ teaspoons salt	1 beef bouillon cube
¼ teaspoon pepper	½ cup boiling water

Mix first 8 ingredients. Shape in 6 loaves. Sprinkle with flour. Heat fat in kettle, and brown loaves on all sides. Remove loaves, and pour off fat. Put sliced onion and parsley in kettle, and arrange loaves on top. Dissolve bouillon cube in water. Pour over contents of kettle. Cover, and simmer 30 minutes. Put loaves on hot platter, and pour drippings over top. Makes 6 servings.

HAMBURGER STEAK

Ground beef shaped into a big steak.

Shape 3 pounds of ground beef into an oval steak about 2" thick. Put in a shallow pan. Broil top about 5 minutes. Finish cooking in hot oven, 425°F., 10 to 20 minutes, or until of desired doneness. (To test for doneness, carefully cut into steak.) Season with salt and pepper. Makes 8 to 10 servings. If desired, serve with the following sauces: Mushroom Sherry Sauce, page 239; Creole Sauce, page 239; or Spicy Barbecue Sauce, page 239.

POT-ROASTED BEEF LOAF

Really a one-dish meal.

¼ cup fine dry bread crumbs	2 tablespoons chopped parsley
½ cup water	2 tablespoons butter
2 pounds ground beef	12 small carrots
2 eggs	6 new potatoes
2 teaspoons salt	1 pound green beans
¼ teaspoon pepper	
1 onion, minced	

Soak bread crumbs in water. Mix with next 6 ingredients. Shape in a loaf. Brown in butter. Cover, and cook over low heat 1 hour, adding a little water if necessary. Add vegetables, cook 45 minutes longer. Serves 5 or 6.

BEEF-MUSHROOM CASSEROLE

Sliced onions and mushroom soup top herbed hamburger in a casserole.

Mix 1 pound ground beef, 1 teaspoon salt, ¼ teaspoon pepper, ¾ teaspoon marjoram. Press into 1½-quart casserole. Cover with 2 cups thinly sliced onions. Pour 1 can cream-of-mushroom soup over top. Cover; bake in 325°F. oven about 1¼ hours. Serves 4.

CREAMED HAMBURGER AND CABBAGE

The sauce is seasoned with celery seed, Worcestershire, and paprika.

¾ pound ground beef	½ teaspoon paprika
1 tablespoon instant minced onion	¼ teaspoon salt
	¼ teaspoon pepper
4 cups chopped cabbage	1 teaspoon Worcestershire
½ teaspoon celery seed	1 can cream-of-celery soup
	¼ cup milk

Cook beef in skillet until it loses its red color, breaking up meat with fork. Add onion and cabbage; cook until lightly browned. Add remaining ingredients, cover, and simmer about 10 minutes. Makes 4 servings.

HAMBURGER ROLL

Herb-biscuit dough and hamburger filling, wrapped jelly-roll style.

1 pound ground beef	Chopped parsley
1 teaspoon salt	¼ teaspoon dry mustard
¼ teaspoon pepper	2 tablespoons flour
1 can (2 ounces) mushroom pieces	⅓ cup water
1 onion, minced	Herb-biscuit Dough, page 20
¼ cup chopped sweet pickle	1 can (10¾ ounces) beef gravy

Cook beef, stirring with fork, until it loses its red color. Add all ingredients, except last 4. Simmer 10 minutes. Pour off most of fat, if any. Blend in flour; add water, and cook until thickened, stirring constantly. Cool. Roll Herb-biscuit Dough in 12"x 9" rectangle. Spread mixture on dough to within ½" of edges. Moisten edges with water; roll like jelly roll, and pinch edges together. Bake in greased shallow pan in hot oven, 425°F., 30 minutes. Slice, and serve with heated gravy. Serves 4.

SHERRIED HAMBURGER CASSEROLE

A smooth sherry-mushroom sauce and a topping of crisp-bacon crumbles.

4 slices bacon	¼ teaspoon each pepper and orégano
1 onion, minced	
1 clove garlic, minced	1 can (3 ounces) sliced mushrooms, drained
¼ cup fine dry bread crumbs	
1 pound ground beef	1 can mushroom soup
1 egg	½ cup dry sherry
1 teaspoon salt	

Cook bacon in skillet until crisp; drain. Pour off most of fat. Put onion and garlic in skillet, and cook over low heat 5 minutes; add crumbs, and cook a few minutes longer. Mix with beef, egg, and seasonings. Shape into 12 balls, and brown on all sides in a little hot bacon fat. Put in 1½-quart casserole. Mix last 3 ingredients, and pour over top. Sprinkle with crumbled bacon. Cover; bake in moderate oven, 375°F., about 45 minutes. Makes 4 servings.

BEEF MOUNDS WITH NOODLES

Beef is seasoned with tomato sauce and garlic.

Beat 1 can (8 ounces) tomato sauce into ¾ pound ground beef. Add 2 slices dry bread soaked in ½ cup hot water, dash cayenne, ½ teaspoon garlic salt. Shape in 4 mounds in shallow baking pan, and bake in hot oven, 400°F., about 20 minutes. Mix drippings in pan with 4 cups hot cooked noodles. Add some chopped parsley. Put noodles in serving dish, and top with hamburger mounds. Makes 4 servings.

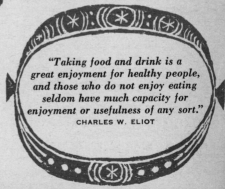

"Taking food and drink is a great enjoyment for healthy people, and those who do not enjoy eating seldom have much capacity for enjoyment or usefulness of any sort."
CHARLES W. ELIOT

SWEDISH MEAT BALLS

Beef balls, with a bit of veal
and pork added, and a cream gravy.

¼ pound veal	3 tablespoons butter
¼ pound fresh	or margarine
pork	1 pound ground
1 egg, slightly	beef
beaten	1½ teaspoons salt
1 cup milk	½ teaspoon pepper
½ cup fine dry	¼ teaspoon nutmeg
bread crumbs	2 tablespoons flour
2 tablespoons	1 cup hot water
minced onion	¾ cup light cream

Have butcher grind veal and pork, or force through food chopper 3 or 4 times, using medium blade. Combine egg, milk, and bread crumbs; let stand a few minutes. Brown onion in 1 tablespoon butter. Combine with soaked crumbs, meats, seasonings, nutmeg. Mix with spoon until smooth. Shape in 3 dozen balls about 1" in diameter. Brown in remaining butter. Pour off most of fat. Sprinkle meat balls with flour, and shake pan. Add hot water. Cover, and simmer 35 to 40 minutes. Add cream, and heat. Serve meat with the gravy. Makes 6 servings.

BLUE-CHEESE MEAT LOAF

Have this hot one day, cold the next.
It's wonderful either way.

3 cups crumbled	¼ teaspoon pepper
blue cheese	1 teaspoon
2 pounds ground	Worcestershire
beef	1 can (1 pound)
1 clove garlic,	tomatoes, par-
minced	tially drained

Let cheese stand about 15 minutes, to bring to room temperature. Mix well with remaining ingredients. Pack in 9"x 5"x 3" loaf pan. Bake in moderate oven, 350°F., about 1 hour. Serves 6.

"There is no love sincerer
than the love of food."
GEORGE BERNARD SHAW

FRENCH BREAD FARCI

Loaves of bread stuffed with meat, then
brushed with garlic butter and baked.

½ pound each	2 tablespoons
sausage meat	prepared mustard
and ground beef	Chopped parsley
1 onion, chopped	½ teaspoon salt
2 loaves brown-	Dash each pepper,
and-serve French	orégano
bread	1 small clove garlic
⅓ cup water	2 tablespoons
1 egg	melted butter

Cook sausage in skillet, breaking up meat with fork. Add beef and onion, and cook, stirring with fork, until lightly browned. Cut ends from each loaf of bread; reserve. Hollow out inside to make crumbs. Mix crumbs and rest of ingredients, except last 2. Add meat; pack bread shells with the mixture. Replace ends, and skewer in place. Crush garlic, and add to butter. Brush on bread. Bake in hot oven, 400°F., 15 to 20 minutes. To serve, cut in 2" slices. Makes 6 servings.

EAST INDIAN MEAT BALLS

For a one-dish meal, serve these on
rice with chutney and coconut.

1 large onion,	¼ cup slivered
chopped (reserve	blanched almonds
2 tablespoons for	1½ cups water
meat mixture)	Salt
2 tablespoons butter	½ cup soft bread
½ teaspoon each	crumbs
cinnamon and	¼ cup milk
mace	1 pound
¾ teaspoon curry	ground beef
powder	2 tablespoons
1 teaspoon whole	chopped parsley
black pepper (in	1 egg
cheesecloth bag)	1 teaspoon
⅓ cup seedless	Worcestershire
raisins	¼ teaspoon pepper

In large skillet, cook onion in butter until lightly browned. Add next 7 ingredients and ½ teaspoon salt. Cover, and simmer 15 minutes. Remove pepper bag. Mix 1 teaspoon salt and remaining ingredients. Shape in 1" balls. Brown on all sides in a second skillet, using a small amount of fat, if necessary. Pour off any fat, and add meat balls to first mixture. Cover, and simmer 20 minutes. Makes 4 servings.

SAUERBRATEN HAMBURGERS

They simmer in vinegar, cloves,
bay leaf, and gingersnaps.

1½ pounds ground beef	⅓ cup milk
1 medium onion, minced	1½ cups water
	½ cup vinegar
1 egg	10 whole cloves
1 teaspoon salt	1 bay leaf
¼ cup fine dry bread crumbs	8 gingersnaps, crumbled

Mix lightly first 6 ingredients. Shape into 4 large patties. Brown on both sides in hot greased skillet. Add remaining ingredients. Bring to boil; cover, and simmer 1 hour. Serves 4.

HAMBURGERS CHÂTEAUBRIAND

Good, hearty ground-beef steaks that
should appeal to the men of the house.

2 chicken bouillon cubes	¼ teaspoon pepper
¾ cup boiling water	2 teaspoons Worcestershire
1½ pounds ground beef	1 egg
¾ teaspoon salt	2 cans (3 ounces each) sliced mushrooms
¾ teaspoon poultry seasoning	2 tablespoons flour
	Hot toast triangles

Dissolve bouillon cubes in boiling water; cool. Add beef, seasonings, and egg; mix thoroughly. Shape into 4 thick steaks, and put in shallow baking pan. Broil under medium heat to desired doneness (about 5 minutes on each side for medium). Remove to hot platter. Drain mushrooms, reserving liquid. Cook in drippings in baking pan. Blend in flour. Add mushroom liquid, and cook till thickened. Serve hamburgers on toast, with gravy. Makes 4 servings.

BURGUNDY PECAN-BURGERS

Burgundy wine and pecans give
the perfect touch of sweetness.

1 pound ground beef	½ cup coarsely chopped pecans
1 teaspoon salt	⅓ cup red Burgundy wine
¼ cup pepper	

Mix all ingredients, except wine. Shape in 8 thin patties. Brown on both sides in skillet. Add Burgundy; cover, and simmer 5 minutes, or until of desired doneness. Makes 4 servings.

"That all-softening,
overpowering knell,
the tocsin of the soul —
the dinner bell."
LORD BYRON

HAMBURGER STEAKS FLAMBES

They give dinner a festive touch.

1½ pounds ground beef	¼ teaspoon pepper
¼ teaspoon marjoram	3 tablespoons olive oil
1½ teaspoons salt	½ cup brandy

Mix first 4 ingredients, and shape into 4 steaks. Pan-fry in hot olive oil until well browned on both sides and of desired doneness. Put on a hot platter. Pour brandy, slightly warmed, over top, and ignite. Spoon over steaks until flames are out. Makes 4 servings.

BEEF-VEGETABLE LOAF

You can serve it hot or cold.

½ green pepper	1 egg
1 onion	¾ cup tomato juice
1 carrot, peeled	1¼ teaspoons salt
1 potato, peeled	Dash pepper
1 pound ground beef	¼ cup fine dry bread crumbs

Force vegetables through food chopper, using fine blade. Do not drain. Add to remaining ingredients, and mix lightly but thoroughly. Pack into 9″x 5″x 3″ loaf pan. Bake in moderate oven, 325°F., about 1½ hours. Cool 10 minutes before removing from pan. Serves 6.

HAMBURGER BEARNAISE

A classic steak sauce enhances
large, large hamburger patties.

Season 1½ pounds ground beef with 1½ teaspoons salt and ¼ teaspoon pepper. Shape into 4 large patties, but handle as little as possible, and broil or pan-fry to desired doneness. Serve with Béarnaise Sauce, see page 239. Makes 4 servings.

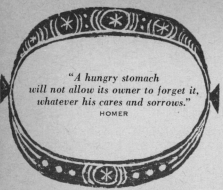

HAMBURGER CUPS WITH MUSHROOMS

They're served with savory butter.

1½ pounds ground beef	⅓ cup butter, melted
12 large mushrooms	2 tablespoons each chopped parsley,
Salt and pepper	green-onion tops

Shape beef in 6 thick patties, making large depression in center of each. Put in shallow baking dish. Wash mushrooms, and cut off part of stems. Put mushrooms around meat. Bake in hot oven, 400°F., 10 to 20 minutes, depending on degree of doneness desired. Turn mushrooms once during cooking; sprinkle beef and mushrooms with salt and pepper. Remove meat to hot platter, put 2 mushrooms in center of each hamburger, and top with savory butter made by mixing remaining ingredients. Makes 6 servings.

STEAK TARTARE

For those who like their beef raw.

For each serving allow 6 ounces freshly ground lean round or sirloin steak. Have butcher grind beef twice. Handle as little as possible, but arrange each serving in a mound. Make an indentation in each, and drop in a raw egg yolk. Garnish with capers or anchovy fillets. Have available: Worcestershire, mustard, salt, a pepper mill, bottled thick meat sauce, ketchup, and separate dishes of capers, caraway seeds, and finely chopped onion. Let each guest season his beef to taste. Serve plenty of buttered, thinly sliced rye bread or crisp toast.

HAMBURGER PIE

Cheesed potato forms the crust.

1 pound ground beef	½ cup milk
1 teaspoon salt	1 egg
¼ teaspoon pepper	1 envelope instant mashed potatoes
1 teaspoon instant minced onion	¾ cup shredded sharp cheddar cheese
¼ cup fine dry bread crumbs	Paprika

Mix meat, salt, pepper, onion, bread crumbs soaked in milk, and egg. Spread in 9″ piepan. Bake in moderate oven, 350°F., 35 minutes. Top with potatoes made according to package directions. Sprinkle with cheese. Bake 10 minutes, until cheese is melted and potatoes are hot. Sprinkle with paprika. Serves 4.

HAMBURGER PIZZA

*The crust is meat,
the filling Italian tomatoes.*

1 pound ground beef	1 clove garlic, minced
1 teaspoon salt	½ cup water
¼ teaspoon pepper	1 can (17 ounces) Italian tomatoes, drained
¼ cup fine dry bread crumbs	⅓ cup grated Parmesan cheese
1 small onion, chopped	Orégano

Mix beef, salt, pepper, bread crumbs, onion, garlic, and water. Pat into 9″ piepan; bake in moderate oven, 375°F., 15 minutes. Pour off fat. Cover with tomatoes; sprinkle with cheese and orégano; bake 15 minutes longer. Cut in wedges. Makes 4 servings.

BARBECUED HAMBURGER STEAKS

They have a vinegar-ketchup sauce.

2 pounds ground beef	¼ cup vinegar
2 tablespoons butter	1 onion, chopped
	1 tablespoon pre- pared mustard
Salt and pepper	1 tablespoon Worcestershire
½ cup ketchup	

Shape meat into 6 oval steaks. Brown in butter. Sprinkle with salt and pepper. Pour off fat. Mix remaining ingredients, and pour over meat. Cover; simmer 8 to 10 minutes, depending on desired doneness, basting meat several times with sauce. Makes 6 servings.

POT-ROASTED MEAT LOAF WITH VEGETABLES

The vegetables are onions, carrots, green beans, and new potatoes.

1½ pounds ground beef	1 egg
Salt and pepper	2 tablespoons fat
1 onion, grated	4 small white onions
½ teaspoon poultry seasoning	4 carrots, halved
¼ cup fine dry bread crumbs	½ pound green beans
½ cup water	4 small new potatoes

Lightly but thoroughly mix meat with 1½ teaspoons salt, ¼ teaspoon pepper, onion, poultry seasoning, crumbs soaked in water, and egg. Shape into loaf. Brown in fat in Dutch oven. Put rack or trivet under meat. Add a few tablespoons water; cover, and cook slowly about ¾ hour. Add vegetables, season; cook ½ hour longer, or until vegetables are tender. Remove meat and vegetables, and make a little gravy with pan drippings, if desired. Serves 4.

HAMBURGER PEPPER STEAKS

You simmer ground beef and green peppers in sherry-soy sauce.

2 pounds ground beef	1 tablespoon cornstarch
2 tablespoons butter	2 teaspoons sugar
¼ cup soy sauce	½ cup water
2 tablespoons sherry	4 green peppers, cut in eighths

Shape meat into 6 oval steaks. Brown lightly in butter. Mix remaining ingredients, except peppers, and pour over meat. Add green peppers. Cover; cook over medium heat 8 to 10 minutes, or until meat is of desired doneness and peppers are still crisp. Makes 6 servings.

DE LUXE HAMBURGER PATTIES

They're served on rolls with tomato and Bermuda-onion slices.

Shape 1½ pounds ground beef into 4 patties. Broil, fry, or grill to degree of desired doneness. Sprinkle with salt and pepper. Put meat patties on bottom halves of toasted sandwich rolls. On each of top halves, put a slice of Bermuda onion and a slice of tomato. Makes 4 servings.

HAMBURGER KEBABS

Delicious when broiled in the oven; superspecial done over charcoal.

1½ pounds ground beef	1 tablespoon sour cream
⅛ teaspoon cloves	1 onion, minced
⅛ teaspoon crushed cardamom seeds	⅛ teaspoon crushed cumin seed or ground cumin
Dash each pepper, cayenne, ginger	8 mushroom caps
1½ teaspoons salt	8 chunks green pepper

Lightly but thoroughly mix all ingredients, except mushroom caps and green pepper. Shape into 12 balls. Thread on skewers, 3 to a skewer, with a mushroom cap and green-pepper chunk between meat balls. Broil to desired doneness. Makes 4 servings.

BAKED HAMBURGER POTPOURRI

A careful, not random, selection of a little of this, a little of that.

½ pound each ground beef and ground lean pork	⅓ cup seedless raisins
¼ pound ground smoked ham	1 clove garlic, minced
1 teaspoon salt	1 egg
¼ teaspoon pepper	½ cup milk
¼ cup slivered blanched almonds	½ cup sherry
	Few sprigs parsley, chopped

Cook all ingredients, except last 4, in skillet about 10 minutes, breaking up meats with fork until they lose color. Cool slightly, and add remaining ingredients. Pour into 1-quart baking dish. Bake in moderate oven, 350°F., 20 minutes, or until firm. Serves 4.

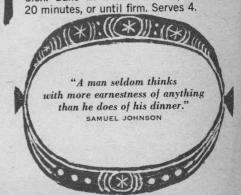

"A man seldom thinks with more earnestness of anything than he does of his dinner."
SAMUEL JOHNSON

SPANISH BEEF PIES

*Trust the Spanish to find a way to
combine olives with hamburger.*

1 onion, chopped	½ cup canned corn
½ green pepper, chopped	¼ cup each pitted ripe olives and seedless raisins
1 tablespoon butter or margarine	2 boxes piecrust mix
½ pound ground beef	2 hard-cooked eggs
½ teaspoon salt	White of egg
Dash pepper	

Cook onion and green pepper in butter
until lightly browned. Add beef, and
cook, breaking up with fork, until meat
loses its red color. Pour off fat, if any.
Add remaining ingredients, except last
3; mix well. Prepare mix, and roll, one
half at a time, to ⅛" thickness. Using
a 6" saucer, cut twelve rounds. Put
a spoonful of meat mixture on half
of each round, and top with slice of
egg. Brush edges with cold water.
Fold over, and crimp edges with fork.
Cut a few slits in top for steam to
escape. Brush with white of egg, slightly beaten. Bake in very hot oven,
450°F., about 15 minutes. Makes 12.

SMOTHERED HAMBURGER STEAKS

They simmer with onions in beef gravy.

1½ pounds ground beef	¼ cup fine dry bread crumbs
1½ teaspoons salt	4 medium onions, sliced
¼ teaspoon pepper	1 can beef gravy
½ cup water	

Mix all ingredients, except last 2.
Shape into 4 large patties. Brown on
one side in greased skillet. Turn, add
onion, and brown lightly. Add gravy,
cover, and simmer about 30 minutes.
Makes 4 servings.

BARBECUED MEAT BALLS

They're glazed in a spicy sauce.

½ cup soft stale-bread crumbs	Flour
¼ cup milk	2 tablespoons butter
1 pound ground beef	¼ cup each molasses, vinegar, ketchup
1 teaspoon salt	¼ teaspoon Tabasco
½ teaspoon Accent	¼ teaspoon orégano
1 small onion, minced	

Soak bread crumbs in milk; mix with
beef, salt, Accent, and onion. Form into
12 balls. Roll in flour, and brown in
butter. Combine remaining ingredients,
and pour over meat. Simmer 10 minutes, stirring several times until meat
balls are glazed. Makes 4 servings.

CREAMY HAMBURGER SAUCE

To serve on potatoes, rice, or noodles.

1 pound ground beef	1 can cream-of-mushroom soup
1 onion, chopped	¾ cup water
1 cup sliced celery	1 to 2 teaspoons chili powder
2 tablespoons fat	1½ teaspoons salt
1 can (3 ounces) sliced mushrooms, drained	¼ teaspoon pepper

Cook beef, onion, and celery in fat until
lightly browned, stirring often. Add rest
of ingredients; bring to boil. Cover, and
simmer about 35 minutes. Thicken, if
desired. Makes 4 servings.

BEEF PATTIES PARMIGIANO

They're cooked with tomato sauce.

1½ pounds ground beef	3 tablespoons butter or margarine
1 teaspoon salt	1 can (8 ounces) tomato sauce
½ teaspoon pepper	4 slices Mozzarella cheese
1 egg, beaten	
2 tablespoons milk	
Fine dry bread crumbs	Parmesan cheese

Mix meat, salt, and pepper. Form into
4 patties. Mix egg and milk. Dip patties
in mixture, then in crumbs. Fry in butter in broilerproof skillet over medium
heat until browned on both sides. Pour
tomato sauce over patties; top each
with Mozzarella and Parmesan. Broil
until Mozzarella melts. Serves 4.

LAMB

About 150 years ago the chophouse was a popular institution with American men in our Eastern cities. Here the merchant, lawyer, and doctor gathered regularly to eat hearty thick mutton chops rolled around kidneys, grilled to a crusty brown and still rare and juicy in the center. People in some areas still know the joys of excellent lamb and mutton, but by and large, Americans don't appreciate it. Possibly this is because they don't know how to prepare it properly. Good heavy lamb or mutton, well fatted and aged just as beef should be aged, is a special treat. But it should never be cooked to the well-done stage. Whether grilled or roasted, it's best when pink or red rare. Tiny young lamb chops should be well done, but never to the point of dryness. Lamb and mutton take well to a variety of seasonings: try a touch of tarragon or rosemary. As an excellent accompaniment for leg of lamb, try white beans dressed with the meat juices, a bit of garlic, and tomato.

MIXED GRILL SUPREME

Lamb chops, lamb kidney, sausage, bacon, mushrooms, and tomatoes.

4 large mushrooms	Onion salt
4 small link sausages	Salt and pepper
4 slices bacon	8 small rib lamb chops
4 lamb kidneys	4 tomato halves, scored
¼ cup melted butter or margarine	4 slices toast
	Watercress

Remove stems from mushrooms, and wipe caps with damp cloth. Put, rounded side up, on broiler pan with sausages and bacon. Wash, and split kidneys, and remove fat and membrane. Put, split side up, on broiler pan. Brush mushrooms and kidneys with melted butter. Sprinkle mushrooms with onion salt, and kidneys with salt and pepper. Broil under medium heat about 4 inches from unit, turning foods as they brown, and brushing mushrooms and kidneys again with butter. Remove and keep warm. Broil chops and tomatoes, brushing tomatoes with butter and sprinkling with salt and pepper. Serve chops on toast triangles. Garnish servings with other broiled foods and watercress. Makes 4 servings.

RED-WINE SHISH KEBAB

Marinated cubes of lamb are strung on skewers with vegetables.

2 pounds boneless lamb shoulder	1 clove garlic, crushed
1 cup dry red wine	Whole boiled small onions
3 tablespoons red-wine vinegar	Whole small or quartered tomatoes
½ cup olive oil	
1 onion, sliced	Green-pepper chunks
Bay leaf, thyme, cumin, orégano, or marjoram	Cubes of eggplant or zucchini

Cut lamb in 1½" cubes. Mix next 6 ingredients, and pour over lamb. Marinate in refrigerator at least 1 day before using, basting occasionally. String meat on skewers, alternating with pieces of vegetables. Broil to desired doneness over a charcoal fire outdoors or in an indoor broiler, basting occasionally with the marinade. Makes 4 servings.

CURRIED BREAST OF LAMB AND NOODLES

There are raisins in the well-seasoned sauce.

2 pounds breast of lamb	1 clove garlic, minced
¼ cup flour	¼ cup seedless raisins
2½ cups water	
2 teaspoons salt	1 tablespoon ketchup
1 to 2 tablespoons curry powder	1½ cups wide noodles
1 onion, chopped	

Have lamb cut as for stewing. Roll pieces in flour, and brown slowly without added fat. Pour off any fat which collects. Add 1½ cups water, seasonings, onion, garlic. Cover; cook 1½ hours. Add 1 cup water and remaining ingredients. Cover; cook 20 minutes, stirring occasionally, and adding more water if necessary. Makes 4 servings.

LEG OF LAMB, CREOLE

You marinate the lamb in creole sauce for some time before roasting it.

½ cup chili sauce	1 tablespoon sugar
2 tablespoons vinegar	1 teaspoon salt
½ cup dry red wine	½ teaspoon pepper
2 tablespoons olive oil	1 bay leaf
1 cup beef broth or bouillon	2 onions, minced
	2 cloves garlic, minced
	8-pound leg of lamb

Mix all ingredients, except lamb. Pour over meat. Let stand in refrigerator at least 6 hours, basting meat occasionally with the sauce. Put lamb on rack in roasting pan. Add sauce, and roast, uncovered, in moderate oven, 325°F., about 4 hours, basting occasionally with the sauce. Add boiling water if liquid evaporates. Remove lamb. Thicken gravy. Makes 8 to 10 servings.

HEARTY LAMB LOAF

*There's ground pork as well
as ground lamb in this meat loaf.*

1½ pounds ground raw lamb	1 onion, minced
½ pound ground pork	4 slices bread, soaked in water and drained
½ green pepper, minced	1 egg
3 sprigs parsley, minced	2 teaspoons salt
	¼ teaspoon pepper

Mix all ingredients lightly but thoroughly. Pack in a 9″x 5″x 3″ loaf pan. Bake in moderate oven, 350°F., about 1½ hours. Makes 8 servings.

LAMB HASH DE LUXE

*Serve this plain or on
warm slices or fingers of toast.*

1 onion, minced	1 cup lamb stock
3 tablespoons butter	1 cup undiluted evaporated milk
3 cups diced cooked lamb	2 egg yolks, slightly beaten
1 cup diced cooked potato	Salt and pepper
1 pimiento, chopped	Hot toast

Cook onion in the butter 2 or 3 minutes. Add lamb, potato, pimiento, and stock. Bring to boil. Mix milk and egg yolks; season with salt and pepper. Stir into hash mixture, and simmer a few minutes. Serve on hot toast. Makes 4 to 6 servings.

SOUDZOUKAKIA SMYRNAKA

*A Greek dish with ground lamb,
bread crumbs, wine, tomato sauce.*

1 pound ground lamb	½ teaspoon caraway seed
½ cup soft bread crumbs	Olive oil or butter
½ cup dry white wine	1 can (8 ounces) tomato sauce
2 cloves garlic, minced	½ teaspoon sugar
Salt and pepper	½ cup water
	Hot cooked rice

Mix all ingredients, except last 4. Shape into 6 rolls about 5″ long and 1″ in diameter. Brown rolls lightly in olive oil. Add tomato sauce, sugar, and water. Heat slowly to boiling. Simmer 5 minutes. Serve with rice. Serves 4.

LAMB BALLS, TOMATO CURRY

*Tiny ground-lamb balls are
served with curried canned tomatoes.*

1½ pounds ground raw lamb	1½ cups milk
1 onion, minced	2 teaspoons salt
¾ cup soft stale-bread crumbs	¼ teaspoon pepper
	Vegetable oil
	Tomato Curry

Mix all ingredients, except oil and Curry. Shape into balls, and brown on all sides in hot oil. Reduce heat, and cook, covered, until done. Serve with Curry. Serves 6.

Tomato Curry

1 can (28 ounces) tomatoes	¼ teaspoon pepper
1 teaspoon each salt, sugar, instant onion, curry powder	¼ cup soft stale-bread crumbs

Simmer all ingredients 15 minutes.

LAMB-STUFFED GREEN PEPPERS

*Ground cooked lamb is mixed with
rice before being put into the peppers.*

4 large green peppers	¼ teaspoon pepper
1½ cups ground cooked lamb	1 can (8 ounces) tomato sauce
¼ cup uncooked rice	1 cup water
1 small onion, minced	Dash cayenne
1½ teaspoons salt	2 basil leaves or pinch dried basil

Cut off tops, and remove seeds from peppers. Mix lamb, rice, onion, salt, and pepper. Stuff peppers about three-fourths full. Stand upright in small heavy saucepan with tight-fitting lid. Pour combined sauce, water, and remaining seasonings over peppers. Cover, and cook very slowly 40 minutes, or until rice is tender. Add more water, if necessary. Serves 4.

*"Better cross an angry man
than a hungry one."*
DANISH PROVERB

ARMENIAN LAMB PATTIES

The patties are cooked in garlic oil.

1 pound ground raw lamb	Few sprigs parsley, minced
1 small onion, minced	1 cup soft bread crumbs
1½ teaspoons salt	Vegetable oil
¼ teaspoon pepper	Clove of garlic, halved

Mix lamb, onion, seasonings, parsley, and crumbs. Add 2 tablespoons oil. Shape into 4 patties. Heat small amount of oil in skillet. Add garlic. Brown patties quickly on both sides in hot oil. Reduce heat, and cook slowly 10 minutes. Makes 4 servings.

BROILED BONED LEG OF LAMB

*The lamb is broiled
exactly as if it were a steak.*

Have butcher bone a leg of lamb. Open the meat out flat, rub with a cut clove of garlic, and brush with a little oil. Broil 45 minutes to 1¼ hours, depending on degree of doneness desired.

SPINACH-STUFFED LAMB

*You use boneless lamb shoulder
with a pocket in it.*

Have 4 to 5 pounds lamb shoulder boned, leaving a pocket. Wash, drain, and chop ½ pound spinach. Cook 3 minutes in 2 tablespoons butter with 2 tablespoons chopped celery, 1 tablespoon chopped green pepper, 1 teaspoon instant minced onion. Add 2 cups soft stale-bread crumbs, ¼ cup butter, ½ teaspoon salt, ¼ teaspoon pepper. Mix well. Fill pocket in meat, and sew or skewer opening. Rub with salt and pepper. Put on rack in baking pan, sear in very hot oven, 500°F., 15 minutes. Reduce heat to 325°F., and roast about 3 hours. Makes 6 servings.

SPICY ROAST LAMB SHOULDER

*The seasonings are ginger,
paprika, pepper, and marjoram.*

Boned and rolled shoulder of lamb (about 3¼ pounds)	1 teaspoon each pepper, paprika
2 teaspoons salt	2 teaspoons leaf marjoram
1 teaspoon celery salt	2 cloves garlic, minced
½ teaspoon ginger	2 tablespoons water

Put meat, fat side up, on rack in roasting pan. Mix seasonings and water, and spread on meat. Roast in 325°F. oven 2½ to 3 hours. Remove to a warm platter. Drain off all except 2 tablespoons of the brownest drippings; add 2 tablespoons flour, and brown lightly. Add 2 cups hot water, and cook until thickened. Season. Serve with the meat. Makes 8 servings.

Note: Seasonings can be omitted, if desired. Roast meat as above.

BAKED LAMB CHOPS AND GREEN ONIONS

*They bake in cream with a
sprinkling of Parmesan cheese.*

4 thick loin lamb chops	Salt and pepper
6 green onions, thinly sliced	2 tablespoons grated Parmesan cheese
¼ cup cream	

Put chops in shallow casserole; cover with onions, and add cream. Season, sprinkle with cheese, and bake in moderate oven, 350°F., 1 hour. Serves 4.

LAMB AND BEAN STEW

The beans are red kidney beans.

2 cups cubed roast lamb	1 can (19 ounces) tomatoes
2 tablespoons lamb fat	1 green pepper, chopped
1½ teaspoons salt	1 can (21 ounces) red kidney beans
Dash cayenne	

Brown lamb in fat in large saucepan. Add remaining ingredients, except beans. Bring to boil; cover, and simmer 1 hour. Add beans, and simmer 35 minutes longer, or until liquid is nearly absorbed. Makes 4 servings.

LAMB AND PARSLEY PINWHEELS

Rolled, stuffed lamb is simmered in seasoned lamb broth and served cold.

2 breasts of lamb	1 large bunch parsley
¼ teaspoon pepper	1 teaspoon celery salt
1 tablespoon salt	1 onion

Have lamb boned, but keep the bone. Spread out flat, cut out excess fat, and sprinkle with pepper and half the salt. Wash, and drain parsley; cut off stems. Cover meat with parsley; roll tight, and tie securely. Cover bones with boiling water; add remaining salt, celery salt, and onion. Bring to boil, skim, and add meat roll; reduce heat, and simmer 2 hours, or until meat is tender. Let cool in the broth. Then wrap in waxed paper, and chill. Serves 10.

LAMB BISCUIT ROLL, BROWN SAUCE

Seasoned ground lamb, with chopped mushrooms, olives, and pickles, is rolled in dough, jelly-roll fashion.

2 cups ground roast lamb	2 tablespoons chopped stuffed olives
¾ teaspoon salt	
¼ teaspoon pepper	2 tablespoons chopped sweet pickles
1 tablespoon lamb fat	¼ teaspoon dry mustard
1 can (2 ounces) chopped mushrooms, drained	Biscuit dough (recipe using 1½ cups flour)
1 small onion, minced	1 tablespoon milk
1 sprig parsley, chopped	Brown gravy

Put all ingredients, except biscuit dough, milk, and gravy in heavy skillet. Cook over low heat 10 minutes. Cool. Turn dough out on lightly floured board, and roll into rectangle ¼″ thick. Spread meat mixture over dough to within ½″ of edge. Roll up like jelly roll; moisten edges with water, and seal. Put roll in greased shallow pan, and brush with milk. Bake in hot oven, 425°F., about 30 minutes, or until crust is browned. Slice while hot, and serve with brown gravy. Makes 4 to 6 servings.

BARBECUED LAMB BREAST

The lamb is cut into serving pieces before being cooked.

3 pounds breast of lamb	1½ teaspoons each salt and chili powder
1 onion, sliced	Dash cayenne
2 cloves garlic, minced	¼ teaspoon pepper
¼ cup vinegar	½ cup ketchup
1 tablespoon Worcestershire	½ cup water

Cut lamb in serving pieces, trimming off any excess fat. Brown lamb slowly on all sides in Dutch oven. (Or brown in skillet, and transfer to a casserole.) Pour off fat. Mix remaining ingredients, and pour over meat. Cover, and bake in moderate oven, 350°F., 1¼ hours. Uncover, and bake about 15 minutes longer. Makes 4 servings.

LEBANESE KIBBE

A lamb-and-cereal mixture alternates with a lamb-onion-and-nut mixture.

½ cup cracked-wheat cereal	4 tablespoons butter or margarine
1¾ cups cold water	1½ pounds ground lamb
Salt	¼ cup pine nuts
2 onions, minced	¾ teaspoon pepper

Cook cereal in cold water with ½ teaspoon salt in top part of double boiler over boiling water 30 minutes, stirring occasionally. Cool. Cook onion in 2 tablespoons of the butter 5 minutes. Add ¾ teaspoon salt, half the lamb, the pine nuts, and ¼ teaspoon pepper. Mix cooled cereal, remaining lamb, ½ teaspoon salt, and ½ teaspoon pepper. Press half this mixture into 10″x6″x2″ baking dish. Spread with lamb and onion mixture. Top with remaining wheat mixture, and dot with remaining butter. Bake in moderate oven, 375°F., about 1 hour. Makes 6 servings.

"New meat begets new appetite."
JOHN RAY

"Who has but one lamb
makes it fat."
FRENCH PROVERB

FOIL-BAKED CHOPS
AND VEGETABLES

*The vegetables are potatoes,
carrots, onions, and green pepper.*

Cut 4 strips of heavy foil 18" long. Put
2 shoulder lamb chops in center of
each strip. Put 1 medium potato, peeled
and quartered, 1 small carrot, halved
crosswise, 1 medium onion, quartered,
and ¼ green pepper, cut in chunks, on
each pair of chops. Sprinkle with salt
and pepper. Wrap, securing with a double fold. Bake on cookie sheet in 275°F.
oven about 3 hours. Unwrap, put contents on a serving plate, and pour drippings over all. Makes 4 servings.

PRESSED LAMB LOAF

*A lamb-and-herb loaf
which you serve cold.*

4 pounds lamb shoulder	Marjoram Thyme
Water	Caraway seed
Salt and pepper	

Put lamb in a kettle, and cover with
water. Add seasonings, bring to boil,
and simmer 3 to 4 hours. Remove meat,
and chop fine. Moisten with broth, and
pack into 9"x 5"x 3" loaf pan. Cover with
waxed paper, and weight down. Chill.
Unmold, and slice. Serves 6 to 8.

LAMB TOURNEDOS

*Thick loin lamb chops are boned,
then wrapped in bacon, and broiled.*

Carefully bone thick loin lamb chops,
and wrap each piece of meat in a
strip of bacon; secure with a toothpick.
Broil under medium heat 6 to 8 minutes on each side. Season to taste.

LAMB AND VEGETABLE
SALAD

*Lamb and vegetables are
marinated in French dressing.*

1½ cups diced
  cooked lamb
	¼ cup French
	  dressing

½ cup each diced
  cooked potato,
  carrots, and peas
  or green beans
	2 sweet pickles,
	  chopped
	1 hard-cooked egg,
	  chopped
	½ cup mayonnaise
	Salad greens

Marinate meat and vegetables in
French dressing ½ hour. Add remaining
ingredients, except greens, and mix
lightly. Serve on greens. Serves 4.

LOCH LOMOND STEW

Lamb and vegetables, teamed with barley.

⅓ cup barley	2 sprigs parsley, minced
1 quart water	

2 cups cubed
  roast lamb
	½ cup chopped
	  celery tops

1 tablespoon lamb fat	2 teaspoons salt 4 potatoes, halved
2 onions, sliced	6 carrots, quartered

Soak barley in water 1 hour. Brown
lamb in fat in heavy kettle. Add undrained barley and remaining ingredients, except potatoes and carrots. Bring
to boil; cover, and simmer 1½ hours.
Add the potatoes and carrots. Continue
cooking 30 minutes longer, or until
vegetables are tender, adding a little
more water, if necessary. Serves 6.

ARABIAN LAMB AND CHICKEN

Cinnamon gives it a special flavor.

1 pound boneless
  lamb shoulder,
  cut in cubes
	¼ cup butter
	  or margarine

1 fryer, cut up	1 cup uncooked rice
3½ cups water	¼ teaspoon each
2 teaspoons salt	cinnamon and
2 onions, sliced	pepper Ripe olives

Put lamb and fryer in kettle. Add water
and salt; bring to boil, and simmer, covered, 1 hour, or until meats are tender.
Drain, reserving broth. In same kettle,
cook onion in butter 5 minutes. Add
meats, rice, 3 cups broth, and the
spices. Cover, and simmer 20 minutes,
or until rice is tender and liquid absorbed. Serve garnished with whole ripe
olives. Makes 4 to 6 servings.

POPPY-SEED LAMB PIE

There are vegetables in the pie, too.

⅓ cup lamb fat or margarine	1 can (1 pound) onions, drained
⅓ cup flour	2 cups cubed roast lamb
3 cups lamb broth or bouillon	Salt and pepper
1 teaspoon bottled sauce for gravy	1 tablespoon poppy seed
1 box frozen peas	1 stick pastry mix

Make gravy with fat, flour, broth, and sauce for gravy. Add vegetables and lamb; season to taste. Put in 2-quart casserole. Add poppy seed to pastry mix, stir in liquid as directed on pastry-mix label. Roll out on floured board to fit top of casserole. Cut vents to allow steam to escape, and put on lamb mixture. Bake in hot oven, 425°F., about 25 minutes. Makes 6 servings.

ALBANIAN LAMB WITH OKRA

Meat and vegetables are served over rice or cracked wheat.

2 pounds boneless lamb shoulder	¼ teaspoon pepper
3 tablespoons vegetable oil	1 cup water
3 medium onions, sliced	1 pound small okra pods, or 1 can (19 ounces) okra, drained
1 can (19 ounces) tomatoes	
1 teaspoon salt	Hot cooked rice, or cracked wheat

Cut meat in serving-size pieces. Brown on all sides in hot oil. Add onion, and cook 5 minutes longer. Add tomatoes, salt, pepper, and water. Cover, and simmer 45 minutes, or until meat is tender. Add okra. Cook about 30 minutes. Serve with rice or cracked wheat. Makes 6 servings.

ROAST CROWN OF LAMB

It's stuffed with ground roast trimmings, sausage meat, and crumbs.

Have butcher prepare crown of lamb, and grind trimmings. Mix ground meat with equal amount of sausage meat, bread crumbs, or packaged poultry stuffing. Season to taste with salt, pepper, and poultry seasoning. Moisten with hot water. Put roast on rack in shallow pan, and put cubes of salt pork on each bone end. Fill center with prepared meat. Roast, uncovered, in slow oven, 300°F., about 2 hours.

CREAMED LAMB IN PUFF SHELLS

The shells are sugarless dessert puffs.

2 tablespoons lamb fat	½ green pepper, chopped
4 tablespoons flour	1 pimiento, chopped
2 cups milk	2 cups cubed roast lamb
½ teaspoon salt	
Dash pepper	Cream Puff Shells, page 266
1 teaspoon Worcestershire	Parsley

Melt fat in top part of double boiler. Blend in flour. Add milk gradually, and cook over boiling water, stirring constantly, until thickened. Add remaining ingredients, except shells and parsley. Continue cooking over boiling water until thoroughly heated. Cut a small piece from top of each shell, and fill with creamed lamb. Garnish with parsley. Makes 4 to 6 servings.

RICE-STUFFED LAMB SHANKS

The rice stuffing is mixed with celery leaves.

4 short-cut lamb shanks (about 2½ pounds)	2 slices lemon
	3 whole cloves
	1 teaspoon salt
	¼ teaspoon pepper
1 tablespoon olive oil	1 cup uncooked rice
Boiling water	Celery leaves

Brown meat on all sides in hot oil in heavy kettle. Cover with boiling water; add lemon, cloves, salt, and pepper. Cover, and simmer 1½ hours. Lift out shanks; cool slightly, and remove bones. Skim fat from broth, bring broth to boil; add rice, and cook until tender, about 20 minutes, adding more water if necessary. Drain rice, reserving broth. Mix rice with a few chopped celery leaves; season. Stuff bone shanks with the mixture, put in shallow baking dish, and add 1 cup broth. Bake in moderate oven, 350°F., 15 minutes. Serves 4.

"Their hearts and sentiments were free,
Their appetites were hearty."
ROBERT WILLIAM BUCHANAN

ROAST LEG OF LAMB WITH POTATOES AND ONIONS

You parboil the potatoes before adding them to the meat.

8-pound leg of lamb	1 can (1 pound)
6 potatoes, pared	onions, drained
	Salt and pepper

Put lamb on rack in roasting pan. Roast in moderate oven, 325°F., 4 to 4½ hours. About 1 hour before meat is done, parboil potatoes 15 minutes. Drain, and put in pan with meat. Roast 45 minutes longer, basting potatoes occasionally with drippings in pan, and turning to brown evenly. Add onions during last ½ hour, and baste occasionally. Season vegetables. Makes 6 servings, with meat left over.

OVEN-BRAISED BREAST OF LAMB

It's cooked with potatoes and onions and seasoned with marjoram.

3 pounds breast of lamb	¼ teaspoon pepper
4 potatoes	½ teaspoon marjoram
8 onions	¼ cup boiling
2 teaspoons salt	water

Trim excess fat from lamb, and cut meat in serving-size pieces. Put in 3-quart casserole; sear in very hot oven, 475°F., about 30 minutes. Pour off accumulated fat; cover, and bake 30 minutes. Add potatoes, onions, salt, and pepper; cover, and bake 1 hour. Pour off fat; add marjoram, water. Cover; bake about 20 minutes. Serves 4.

LAMB CHUTNEY

The chutney is heated with lamb gravy.

¼ cup chopped chutney	1½ cups leftover lamb gravy
	8 slices leftover roast lamb

Mix chutney and gravy; heat to boiling. Add lamb; heat gently. Serves 4.

LAMB AND VEGETABLE POTAGE

The vegetables are split peas, celery, carrots, onions, and potatoes.

Bone from roast lamb	2 onions, chopped
2 quarts water	2 cups cubed
1 cup dried split peas	potatoes (3 medium)
2 stalks celery with leaves, chopped	3 teaspoons salt
	¼ teaspoon pepper
2 large carrots, sliced	Lamb scraps

Crack bone in several places. Put in kettle with water and peas. Bring to boil; cover, and simmer 2 hours. Add remaining ingredients, and simmer 30 minutes longer, or until vegetables are tender. Remove bone. Makes 2 quarts.

LAMB AND RED NOODLES

Tomato paste gives this its red color.

2 cups diced roast lamb	1½ teaspoons salt
2 tablespoons lamb fat	Dash pepper
	2 teaspoons paprika
2 cloves garlic, minced	1 package (8 ounces)
1 can (6 ounces) tomato paste	wide noodles
3½ cups water	Grated Parmesan cheese

Brown lamb lightly in fat. Add garlic, tomato paste, water, and seasonings. Bring to boil; cover, and simmer 1 hour. Add noodles, and continue cooking until noodles are tender, stirring occasionally to prevent sticking. Add more water, if necessary. Sprinkle with cheese just before serving. Makes 4 servings.

SADDLE OF LAMB, BÉARNAISE

Wine-and-butter basting gives flavor to the lamb.

6-pound loin of lamb	¼ cup melted butter or margarine
1 clove garlic	Béarnaise Sauce,
¼ cup dry white wine	page 239

Have lamb cut and tied by butcher. Rub with garlic, and put on rack in roasting pan. Roast in moderate oven, 325°F., about 2½ hours, basting occasionally with wine and butter, mixed. Serve with Sauce. Makes 8 servings.

BRAISED LAMB IN SOUR CREAM

*Dry white wine gives piquancy
to the sour-cream sauce.*

2 pounds lamb neck	2 bouillon cubes, dissolved in 1 cup boiling water
¼ cup flour	
2 teaspoons salt	
¼ teaspoon pepper	1 onion, minced
Pinch each thyme and tarragon	Juice ½ lemon
	1 cup sour cream
2 tablespoons butter	2 tablespoons dry white wine
¼ teaspoon caraway seed	

Trim some of fat from lamb, and cut meat in 1″ pieces. Dredge with flour seasoned with salt, pepper, and herbs. Brown in hot butter in heavy skillet. Add remaining ingredients; cover, and simmer 1½ hours. Makes 4 servings.

TURKISH LAMB PILAF

*You'll find currants and lots
of spices in this lamb-and-rice dish.*

2 onions, chopped	½ teaspoon pepper
¼ cup butter or margarine	
⅓ cup pine nuts	½ teaspoon mixed cloves, cinnamon, and allspice
1 cup uncooked rice	
½ cup dried currants	
	⅛ teaspoon sage leaves
4 cups chicken or lamb broth	2 cups slivered roast lamb
1 chopped fresh or canned tomato	Salt

Cook onion in the butter 5 minutes. Add nuts and rice; cook 5 minutes longer. Add remaining ingredients, except lamb and salt. Cover, and simmer 25 minutes, or until liquid is absorbed. Add lamb and salt. Heat. Serves 6.

GRILLED LAMB NECK WITH KIDNEYS AND BANANAS

*Allow one neck slice, one lamb
kidney, and half a banana per person.*

Split kidneys, and quarter bananas. Arrange lamb slices on greased broiler rack, season, and broil 5 to 8 minutes under moderate heat; turn. Put kidneys and bananas on broiler rack, brush with melted butter, and broil 5 minutes. Turn, and broil 5 minutes longer. Season kidneys and top side of neck slices.

SHERRIED LAMB AND MUSHROOMS

*You add a sprinkling of
grated Parmesan cheese with the sherry.*

½ pound mushrooms, sliced	8 slices roast lamb
2 tablespoons butter	1 tablespoon grated Parmesan cheese
1 teaspoon instant minced onion	
1 cup lamb gravy	1 tablespoon sherry

Cook mushrooms in the butter until lightly browned. Add remaining ingredients, except cheese and sherry. Heat well. Add cheese and sherry. Serves 4.

LAMB AND SUCCOTASH STEW

*Lamb, Lima beans, and corn are
combined in a quick-cooking stew.*

Brown 1½ pounds stewing lamb, cubed, 1 sliced onion, and 1 sliced green pepper in a little fat cut from the lamb. Add 1 cup water; simmer 20 minutes. Add 2 diced stalks celery with leaves, 1 box frozen Limas, 1 bay leaf, salt, pepper, ½ teaspoon celery salt. Cook 45 minutes. Add 1 box frozen cut corn; simmer 5 minutes. Serves 4.

LAMB IN CURRANT-ORANGE SAUCE

*Currant jelly and orange juice are
added to the lamb gravy.*

½ cup leftover lamb gravy	8 slices leftover roast lamb
¼ cup currant jelly	
½ cup orange juice	½ teaspoon prepared mustard
	Salt and pepper

Heat first 3 ingredients until jelly is melted. Add lamb, mustard, and salt and pepper. Heat well. Serves 4.

*"As much valour is to be found
in feasting as in fighting . . ."*
ROBERT BURTON

LAMB AND BEAN RAGOUT

An oven-baked stew with onions and tomatoes as well as lamb and beans.

1 cup dried white beans	1 bay leaf
Water	1½ teaspoons salt
2 pounds boneless lamb shoulder, cut in cubes	½ teaspoon each pepper and paprika
¼ cup bacon fat or butter	½ teaspoon herb seasoning
2 onions, sliced	1½ cups lamb or chicken broth
1 clove garlic, minced	
1 can (19 ounces) tomatoes	3 tablespoons flour

Wash beans; cover with water. Bring to boil, and boil 2 minutes. Let stand 1 hour; cook until tender. Brown lamb in hot fat. Add onions and garlic; cook a few minutes. Add drained beans, and all ingredients, except flour. Cover, and bake in moderate oven, 350°F., 2 hours. Thicken broth with flour blended with ¼ cup cold water. Stir into lamb mixture; bake 15 minutes. Serves 6.

LAMB AND EGGPLANT CASSEROLE

It has a beaten-egg topping.

1 small eggplant, peeled, and cut in ½" slices	2 cups chopped or ground roast lamb
1 onion, sliced	¼ cup olive oil
1 can (19 ounces) tomatoes, drained	4 eggs, slightly beaten
1 green pepper, cut in strips	Salt and pepper

Arrange all ingredients, except eggs, in alternate layers in 2-quart casserole. Cover, and bake in moderate oven, 350°F., 1 hour. Season eggs with salt and pepper, and pour quickly on ingredients in casserole. Cover, and bake 10 to 15 minutes. Serves 4 to 6.

RARE ROAST LEG OF LAMB

There are many who say you don't know how good lamb really is until you've eaten it rare.

5-pound leg of lamb	½ cup dry red wine
4 cloves garlic	
Salt and pepper	1 tablespoon butter
Flour	

Cut slits in lamb, and insert garlic cloves. Put on rack in roasting pan, and sprinkle with salt, pepper, and flour. Roast in moderate oven, 350°F., 20 minutes. Add wine, and roast 40 minutes longer, basting occasionally with drippings in pan. Remove to a hot platter, and top with butter. Slice very thin, and serve with the drippings. Makes 6 to 8 servings.

BARBECUED LAMB ON RICED POTATO

Vinegar, sugar, and cayenne flavor the tomato sauce.

1 onion, chopped	½ teaspoon salt
½ cup tomato sauce	⅛ teaspoon cayenne
¾ cup water	2 cups cubed roast lamb
1 teaspoon sugar	
1 tablespoon vinegar	Hot riced potato

Mix first 7 ingredients in skillet, and cook 5 minutes. Add meat; cover, and simmer 15 minutes. Serve over hot riced potato. Makes 4 servings.

LAMB STEAKS IN MARINADE

The marinade is oil, vinegar, minced onion, parsley, and rosemary.

2 pounds lamb sliced from leg, 1" thick	½ teaspoon salt
	1 onion, minced
3 tablespoons each olive oil and vinegar	Few sprigs parsley, chopped
	Few rosemary leaves, chopped
	Butter or margarine

Pound meat to about ¾" thickness. Put in bowl. Mix remaining ingredients, except butter, and pour over meat. Refrigerate several hours, or overnight. Sauté meat quickly on both sides in small amount of hot butter in skillet. Put on hot platter. Heat marinade in skillet, and pour over meat before serving. Makes 4 servings.

PORK

Anyone who comes from an old-fashioned farm background remembers the varied activity at pig-slaughtering time. There was so much to do that the whole family joined to help. The men, of course, took care of the actual slaughtering, and the women prepared the sausages, bacon, hams, and put the chops down in lard. Nothing was wasted. The pig's head was simmered gently in a great pot with herbs and seasonings; then the meat and juices were left to chill and turned into that delectable cold jellied dish, head cheese. Ears were boiled, then dipped in crumbs and broiled to be eaten with a spicy devil sauce; tails were cooked for hours with sauerkraut and beer or wine; pig's feet were pickled, or maybe fixed Italian style, boned and stuffed with chopped pork to make an unusual sausage. Even the fat was used. What wasn't rendered to make fine lard for pastries was used to preserve the chops and pork steaks. In the old-fashioned process, these were cooked down slowly and packed into great crocks; then melted lard was poured over the meat and into every crack and crevice. Stored in a cool spot, a deep cellar or springhouse, the cooked chops and steaks would keep all winter. They needed only reheating and crisping for dinner. Farm people who raise their own pigs know what wonderful eating they provide. As it has so often been said, the pig is good from snout to tail. Not only is the entire animal delicious, the meat of the pig also lends itself to many variations in cooking and saucing: Italians like to bone the leg and stuff it with Italian parsley, garlic, and orégano or basil; in Central America pork is often cooked with chilies, both hot and sweet, and a tomato sauce; Caribbean recipes for pork usually call for lime or orange juice; and the number of sauces for spareribs alone would almost fill a book. Here is a variety of ways to prepare the popular cuts from this accommodating animal.

PORK, APPLESAUCE, AND KRAUT CASSEROLE

Browned chops bake on tomato-seasoned applesauce and sauerkraut.

2 onions, sliced	2 cups (1-pound
¼ cup butter	can) applesauce
or margarine	¼ cup horse-radish
1 can (19 ounces)	1 can (1 pound)
tomatoes	sauerkraut
2 teaspoons sugar	6 large lean pork
Salt and pepper	chops
Dash orégano	1 tablespoon fat
1 cup soft bread	
crumbs	

Brown onions lightly in butter. Add tomatoes, sugar, 1 teaspoon salt, ¼ teaspoon pepper, and remaining ingredients, except last 2. Pour into large shallow baking dish. Brown chops on both sides in fat; sprinkle with salt and pepper. Put in baking dish. Cover with foil, and bake in moderate oven, 350°F., 1¾ hours. Serves 6.

ROAST PORK, ITALIAN STYLE

It has a mushroom and red-pepper sauce spiced with orégano, garlic.

Put 4-pound boned and rolled loin of pork on rack in roasting pan. Roast in moderate oven, 325°F., 2½ hours, or until meat thermometer registers 185°F. Remove meat from pan, and keep warm. Put 2 tablespoons pork fat from roasting pan in saucepan. Add 2 crushed cloves garlic, ¼ teaspoon crushed dried hot red pepper, 1 teaspoon orégano, and ¼ teaspoon fennel seed. Cook 5 minutes. Add 2-ounce can mushroom stems and pieces, drained; 7½-ounce jar roasted peppers, cut in ¼" strips; ¾ cup tomato purée; and 2 tablespoons chopped parsley. Skim remaining fat from meat drippings, and add drippings to mixture in saucepan. Simmer, season, and serve as sauce. Makes 6 to 8 servings.

ROAST PORK, SPANISH STYLE

It's basted with sherry.

Make a paste of ¼ teaspoon each powdered sage and ginger, 1 crushed garlic clove, 1 teaspoon each salt and flour, and enough sherry to moisten. Spread on fat side of 4-pound pork loin. Bake on rack in moderate oven, 325°F., 3 hours, or until meat thermometer registers 185°F., basting frequently with additional sherry during the roasting. Make gravy with drippings in pan. Serves 6 to 8.

PORK HOCKS WITH VEGETABLES

Hocks are cooked with bay leaf, garlic.

4 pork hocks	¼ teaspoon
Water	pepper
1 bay leaf	4 sweet potatoes
1 clove garlic	4 large white
2 teaspoons salt	turnips

Put hocks in kettle, and cover with water. Add seasonings, cover, and simmer 2 hours. Add potatoes, and turnips cut in quarters. Cook ½ hour. Skin hocks, and arrange on hot platter with vegetables. Serves 4.

SAVORY PORK TENDERLOIN

Browned pork slices simmer with highly seasoned tomatoes.

Roll 8 thin slices pork tenderloin in flour. Brown on both sides in a little fat. Drain off fat, and sprinkle meat with salt and pepper. Add 1 chopped medium onion, 1 teaspoon each Worcestershire and sugar, ½ teaspoon chili powder, and 1 cup canned tomatoes. Cover; simmer 1 hour, turning meat occasionally. Serves 4.

PORK, STROGANOFF STYLE

Pork strips with mushrooms and sour cream, served on rice.

Dredge 1 pound lean pork, cut in thin strips, with ¼ cup seasoned flour. Brown in 2 tablespoons hot fat. Add 1 cup water, 1 beef bouillon cube, 3 tablespoons ketchup or tomato purée, 1 teaspoon Worcestershire, and 1 can (3 ounces) sliced mushrooms with the liquid. Cover, and simmer about 30 minutes. Just before serving, stir in 1 cup sour cream. Serve at once with hot rice. Makes 4 servings.

90

SMOTHERED PORK CHOPS

The drippings, thickened or plain, are poured over the chops.

Dredge 6 pork chops (about 2¼ pounds) with seasoned flour. Brown on both sides in small amount of fat in skillet. Pour off fat. Add ½ cup water. Bring to boil; cover; lower heat, and simmer 1 hour. If necessary, thicken drippings. Season, and pour over chops. Serves 6.

ROAST PORK WITH SAGE ONIONS

Onions are fried in pork drippings.

3 pounds loin of pork	½ to 1 teaspoon powdered sage
Salt	3 tablespoons
8 medium onions	drippings from roast
	Pepper

Put pork on rack in shallow baking pan. Rub with salt. Roast in moderate oven, 325°F., 2 hours, or until meat thermometer registers 185°F. Peel onions, and cut in sixths. Sprinkle with sage, and fry in drippings in skillet until golden brown and tender. Season. Carve pork, and serve with onions. Makes 4 servings.

CHILI-PORK MEAT BALLS IN TOMATO SAUCE

The meat balls: pork, beef, crumbs, cheddar cheese, eggs, and seasonings.

To 1 can (29 ounces) tomatoes, add: ¼ cup instant minced onion, 2 teaspoons salt, 1 teaspoon sugar, ¼ teaspoon each garlic salt, pepper, and red hot sauce, and 1 teaspoon each chili seasoning and orégano. Bring to boil, cover, and simmer 30 minutes. Add browned meat balls (see below), and simmer, covered, 45 minutes. Serve on rice. Makes 6 to 8 servings.

Chili-Pork Meat Balls: Mix well 1 pound ground lean pork, ½ pound ground beef, 1 tablespoon instant minced onion, ¼ teaspoon each pepper and garlic salt, 2 tablespoons chili seasoning, 1 tablespoon shredded dried parsley, 1 teaspoon salt, ½ teaspoon orégano, 1½ cups fine dry bread crumbs, ¾ cup grated sharp cheddar, and 2 beaten eggs. Shape in 1½" balls. Brown in fat.

STUFFED PORK TENDERLOIN

The stuffing: Brussels sprouts and Italian chestnuts.

1 large pork tenderloin, split lengthwise	½ cup chopped, peeled, cooked Italian chestnuts
Salt and pepper	3 tablespoons melted butter or margarine
1 cup chopped cooked Brussels sprouts	

Lay tenderloin out flat, and sprinkle both sides with salt and pepper. Mix remaining ingredients, and spread on meat. Roll up crosswise, and tie. Put on rack in baking pan, and bake in very hot oven, 450°F., 15 minutes. Reduce heat to 325°F., and bake 1 hour, basting occasionally with pan liquid. Untie, and slice. Serves 4.

BAKED PORK AND RICE

Diced cooked pork is baked with rice in a cheese-wine sauce.

1 cup uncooked rice	Few sprigs parsley, chopped
¼ cup butter or margarine	1 teaspoon instant minced onion
¼ cup flour	⅛ teaspoon powdered sage
1¼ cups chicken broth	1 cup grated sharp cheddar cheese
½ cup dry white wine	2 cups diced cooked pork
1 can (3 ounces) sliced mushrooms	Salt and pepper Paprika

Cook, and drain rice. Make a sauce with next 4 ingredients. Add mushrooms, parsley, onion, sage, and half the cheese. Stir until cheese is melted; add rice and pork; season. Put in shallow baking dish, and sprinkle with remaining cheese and paprika. Bake in moderate oven, 375°F., about 30 minutes. Makes 6 servings.

HOW TO COOK PORK

Pork should always be well done, therefore low or moderate temperatures are recommended. Full flavor emerges at the well-done stage; also, prolonged heat kills trichinae organisms, if present.

CHINESE PORK-FRIED RICE

Pork and rice topped
with fried-egg strips.

1 pound boneless pork	Salt and pepper
1 clove garlic, minced	1 can (3 ounces) sliced mushrooms
1 onion, chopped	1¾ cups water
1 cup uncooked rice	1 egg
	Soy sauce

Cut pork in thin strips. Brown in skillet with garlic and onion. Add rice, and cook until lightly browned, stirring frequently. Add 1 teaspoon salt, ¼ teaspoon pepper, mushrooms, and water. Bring to boil; cover; simmer 25 minutes, or until rice is tender. Beat egg with salt and pepper. Put in hot greased 8″ skillet. Fry until firm, turning once; cut in strips. Put rice mixture in serving bowl; arrange egg on top. Serve at once with soy sauce. Serves 4.

HERB-STUFFED PORK BIRDS

They brown, then simmer in stock.

8 very thin end pork chops	Salt
1 onion, chopped	Dash pepper
2 tablespoons chopped parsley	½ teaspoon poultry seasoning
2 tablespoons chopped celery and leaves	2 cups soft bread crumbs
2 tablespoons butter	Water
	2 tablespoons flour
	2 tablespoons fat
	⅓ cup stock

Cut bones out of chops. Pound meat slightly. Make stuffing: cook onion, parsley, and celery in butter; add ½ teaspoon salt, pepper, and poultry seasoning; mix with bread crumbs; add a little water to moisten. Put some stuffing on each chop. Roll, and tie with string. Roll in flour; brown in fat in heavy skillet. Add stock; cover; simmer 1¼ hours. Makes 4 servings.

PORK SUPPLIES
Pork is relatively scarce only in summer, because most pigs are born in the spring and fall, and go to market in the fall, late winter and early spring.

PORK AND POTATO SCALLOP

Browned pork chops baked
on onion-scalloped potatoes.

Peel, and slice very thin, enough medium potatoes to make 4 cups. Slice thin 1 small onion. Measure 2 tablespoons flour. Put a layer of potato and onion in 2-quart casserole. Sprinkle with some of the flour, salt, and pepper. Repeat, ending with layer of potatoes. Add 1½ cups hot milk, or enough to almost cover potatoes. Brown 4 pork chops (about 1½ pounds) on both sides in hot skillet. Arrange chops on top of potatoes. Bake, covered, 45 minutes. Uncover, and bake 15 minutes longer, or until potatoes are tender. Makes 4 servings.

SWEET-AND-SOUR PORK WITH VEGETABLES

The vegetables: carrots, green beans.

Trim excess fat from 2 pounds pork shoulder, and cut meat in small cubes. Try out a piece of fat in skillet. Add meat; brown on all sides. Add 1 chopped onion; brown lightly. Add 1 teaspoon salt, ¼ teaspoon pepper, 1 cup water, ¼ cup vinegar, 2 tablespoons brown sugar, 1 chicken bouillon cube. Cover; simmer 20 minutes. Add 4 peeled carrots, cut in chunks and cooked, 1 box frozen whole green beans, partially .thawed. Cook 5 minutes. Thicken with 1 teaspoon cornstarch mixed with a little cold water. Serve plain or on rice. Serves 4 to 6.

TOMATO PORK TENDERLOIN

Pork simmers in tomato
juice, water, and a bouillon cube.

1 pork tenderloin	1 clove garlic, minced
Salt and pepper	
2 tablespoons flour	1 bouillon cube
3 tablespoons fat	1 cup water
1 small onion, chopped	½ cup tomato juice

Slice tenderloin in 2″ pieces, and flatten slightly. Season, and roll in flour. Brown on both sides in fat. Remove meat, and lightly brown onion and garlic. Add remaining ingredients, and bring to boil, stirring. Return pork to skillet, cover, and simmer 30 minutes. Makes 4 servings.

BREADED PORK CHOPS WITH APPLE RINGS

If you like gravy, use a can of mushroom soup thinned with milk.

Dredge 8 thin, center-cut pork chops (about 2 pounds) with seasoned flour. Dip in 1 egg beaten with 2 tablespoons water. Roll in fine, dry bread crumbs. Fry in hot, deep fat (375°F. on a frying thermometer) until golden brown and done. Meanwhile, core 2 large unpeeled red apples. Cut in ½" slices. Cook in 2 tablespoons butter in skillet until tender. Arrange chops and apples on hot platter. Serves 4.

PORK-VEGETABLE BAKE

The vegetables: onions, green pepper, potato, eggplant, okra, and tomatoes.

Cube 1 pound boneless pork, and brown in hot greased skillet. Add 2 onions, sliced thin, and 1 green pepper, cut in rings; cook 5 minutes. Season. Grease a 3-quart casserole, and line with 1 potato, sliced thin. Sprinkle with ½ cup uncooked rice and half of 1 can (29 ounces) tomatoes. Season. Add 1 small eggplant, peeled and diced, and pork mixture. Sprinkle with ½ cup uncooked rice and 1 cup drained canned okra. Add rest of can of tomatoes; season. Cover, and bake at 375°F. 1 hour. Uncover; bake 15 minutes. Serves 6.

BAKED PORK AND NOODLES

With the pork and noodles: celery, peas, mushrooms, and cheese.

Trim meat from bones, and remove excess fat from 3½ pounds pork shoulder. Try out some of the fat in skillet. Cut meat in small cubes; brown in the fat. Add 1 chopped onion, 1 cup sliced celery, 1 teaspoon salt, ½ teaspoon thyme, ¼ teaspoon pepper, 1 can mushroom soup, 1 cup water. Cover; simmer 1 hour. Cook, and drain 3 cups wide noodles. Add to first mixture with 1 can (8½ ounces) peas, undrained, 1 can (3 ounces) chopped mushrooms, undrained, 2 diced pimientos, ½ cup grated cheddar cheese. Pour into large shallow baking dish. Top with buttered bread crumbs; bake in 375°F. oven, 30 minutes. Makes 6 to 8 servings.

FOOD VALUE OF PORK
Like all meats, pork is a fine source for protein, iron, and niacin. In addition, it contains thiamin.

SPICY PORK KEBABS

Pork cubes coated with spiced peanut butter and broiled on skewers.

2 pounds lean boneless pork	½ teaspoon pepper
¼ cup smooth peanut butter	4 onions, grated
1 teaspoon ground coriander	1 clove garlic, minced
1½ teaspoons salt	1½ tablespoons lemon juice
½ teaspoon cayenne	1 tablespoon brown sugar
1 teaspoon ground cumin	3 tablespoons soy sauce

Cut pork in 1½" cubes. Mix remaining ingredients, and add pork; stir until well coated. Cover, and refrigerate several hours. Thread on skewers, and broil in broiler or over coals 20 to 25 minutes. Serves 6.

PORK-STUFFED PEPPERS, CHINESE STYLE

Peppers, stuffed with ground pork, are served with soy gravy on rice.

1 pound ground pork	2 tablespoons cornstarch
1 teaspoon salt	4 green peppers
¼ teaspoon pepper	1 chicken bouillon cube
1 tablespoon instant minced onion	Water
Soy sauce	2 cups hot cooked rice

Mix first 4 ingredients. Add 1 tablespoon each soy sauce and cornstarch. Cut off tops of peppers, scoop out seeds. Wash, and dry peppers, and fill with meat mixture. Put in greased skillet. Dissolve bouillon cube in ½ cup hot water. Pour into skillet; cover, and simmer 1 hour. Remove peppers. Blend remaining cornstarch, 1 teaspoon soy sauce, ¼ cup water. Add to liquid; cook until thickened. Put peppers on rice; pour liquid over. Makes 4 servings.

ROAST PORK WITH BROWNED VEGETABLES

*Potatoes, carrots, and onions
are cooked around the meat.*

Put 5-pound pork loin roast, fat side up, in open roasting pan. Rub with cut clove of garlic. Roast in moderate oven, 325°F., about 4¼ hours. About 1¼ hours before meat is done, put 12 each peeled small potatoes, carrots, and white onions around roast. Season with salt and pepper to taste. Turn vegetables occasionally. Serves 6 with some meat left over.

APPLE-STUFFED CROWN ROAST OF PORK

*To be fancy, fasten paper
frills to the roast's rib tips.*

1 onion, chopped	1 teaspoon grated
¼ cup diced celery	lemon rind
2 cups diced	Juice ½ lemon
tart apple	1 teaspoon salt
2 tablespoons	½ teaspoon crum-
butter or	bled leaf sage
margarine	4 cups bread cubes,
¼ cup molasses	toasted
¼ cup hot water	7-pound crown
	roast of pork

Cook onion, celery, and apple in butter 5 minutes. Remove from heat, and add remaining ingredients, except pork. Fill roast lightly with stuffing, heaping it up in the center. Roast, uncovered, in moderate oven, 325°F., about 4 hours. Serves 8.

Herb-stuffed Crown Roast of Pork: Follow above recipe, substituting the following stuffing: Cook 2 chopped onions, ¼ cup chopped parsley, 1 cup chopped celery in ½ cup margarine. Add 5 cups soft stale-bread crumbs, ½ teaspoon each sage and thyme, salt and pepper to taste. Moisten with a small amount of meat stock or water.

PORK IN MUSHROOM SAUCE

*Pork cubes simmer in mushroom
soup, Worcestershire, and marjoram.*

Cut 2 pounds lean boneless pork in 1½" cubes. Brown on all sides in 2 tablespoons vegetable oil. Pour off fat, and add 2 cans mushroom soup, 1 teaspoon Worcestershire, pinch marjoram, and ½ cup water. Cover, and simmer 1 hour. Serves 6.

BAKED FRESH HAM, SOUTHERN STYLE

*It stands overnight in spiced broth,
then bakes with cloves and sugar.*

5 pounds fresh	2 tablespoons salt
ham	1 tablespoon dry
Whole cloves	mustard
2 bay leaves	1 tablespoon
1 dried hot red	horse-radish
pepper	1 clove garlic
1 piece stick	½ cup brown
cinnamon	sugar, packed

Put meat in kettle, and cover with boiling water. Add 6 cloves and next 4 ingredients. Simmer 3 hours. Cool in broth overnight. Remove rind, and rub ham with mustard and horse-radish, mixed. Insert garlic next to bone. Bake on rack in slow oven, 300°F., 2 hours. Score fat with knife, and insert cloves at regular intervals. Sprinkle with sugar. Bake 1 hour longer. Makes 8 servings.

PORK CHOPS WITH ORANGE-RAISIN SAUCE

*The chops, topped with orange
sections, simmer in the sauce.*

4 pork chops	⅛ teaspoon
Flour	allspice
1 tablespoon fat	1¼ cups hot
Salt	water
1 or 2 oranges	Juice 1 lemon
2 tablespoons sugar	¼ cup orange juice
1 tablespoon	¼ cup seedless
cornstarch	raisins

Roll chops in flour; brown on both sides in hot fat. Sprinkle with salt. Section oranges, and put several sections on each chop. Mix sugar, cornstarch, and allspice; add water, and cook until thickened. Add juices and raisins. Pour over chops. Cover, and simmer about 1 hour. Makes 4 servings.

PORK STEAKS, BOUILLON

The bouillon is seasoned with thyme.

Dredge 4 pork-shoulder steaks with flour, and brown on both sides in 2 tablespoons hot fat. Season, and sprinkle with 1 chopped onion. Add 1 cup bouillon, ¼ teaspoon thyme. Cover, and simmer 35 to 40 minutes, turning several times. Serves 4.

CURRIED PORK

It's cooked with apple and onion.

Brown 1 pound diced lean pork in 1 tablespoon fat. Peel, and dice 2 apples. Add with 1 chopped onion to pork; brown lightly. Add 2 tablespoons flour, 1 to 2 teaspoons curry powder, ¼ teaspoon ginger, ⅛ teaspoon garlic salt, 2 cups bouillon, 1 tablespoon lemon juice. Cover; simmer 35 minutes. Serve on hot cooked rice. Serves 4 to 6.

PORK ALL-IN-ONE

Diced pork, onions, green pepper, pimientos, tomato sauce, and noodles.

Put 2 cups diced cooked pork, 2 chopped onions, 1 chopped green pepper, ¼ cup vegetable oil in Dutch oven. Cook 5 minutes. Add 1 jar (4 ounces) pimientos, cut up, 1 teaspoon salt, dash pepper, 1 can (8 ounces) tomato sauce, 3 cups water, 2 cups wide noodles. Cover; simmer 30 minutes. Serve with grated Parmesan cheese. Makes 6 servings.

BARBECUED PORK CHOPS

Chops marinate in barbecue sauce, then are basted with it as they bake.

In saucepan, mix ¾ cup each vinegar and ketchup, 1½ cups water, 1 chopped medium onion, 1 minced clove garlic, 2 teaspoons salt, ½ teaspoon pepper, 1 tablespoon Worcestershire, ¼ teaspoon Tabasco, and 3 tablespoons brown sugar. Simmer, uncovered, 20 minutes, stirring occasionally. Pour over 8 thick center-cut pork chops (about 3 pounds) in a deep bowl; cool. Refrigerate several hours. Arrange chops in shallow baking dish. Add sauce. Bake, uncovered, in 350°F. oven, 1½ hours, basting occasionally. Serves 4.

SPICY PORK

It simmers in orange juice with cloves, brown sugar, and cinnamon.

Insert 1 whole clove in the center of each of 6 pork chops. Rub chops well with 1 teaspoon each salt and paprika, and dash pepper, mixed. Brown on both sides in a little fat. Mix 1 can (6 ounces) frozen orange juice, 1 tablespoon brown sugar, and ¼ teaspoon cinnamon. Pour over chops. Cover; simmer 30 minutes. Serves 6.

PORK SHOULDER STUFFED WITH SAUERKRAUT

It's sprinkled with rosemary.

Buy a boned shoulder of pork allowing ½ pound for each serving. Sprinkle the inside with salt and pepper, and fill the pocket with sauerkraut. Sew or skewer the opening. Sprinkle with salt, pepper, and rosemary; dredge with flour. Roast in moderate oven, 325°F., until meat thermometer registers 185°F. (A 4-pound roast takes about 4 hours.)

PORK-VEGETABLE SKILLET

Diced pork, onion, green peppers, and carrots served on rice.

2 teaspoons sugar	1 teaspoon Worcestershire
1 pound boneless pork, diced	Dash Tabasco
¼ cup flour	1 onion, sliced
2½ cups water	4 green peppers
1 teaspoon salt	3 carrots, sliced
Dash pepper	Hot cooked rice

Melt sugar, and cook until dark brown in large skillet. Add pork, and cook until browned. Stir in flour, and brown lightly. Add water, seasonings. Cover; simmer ½ hour. Add onion; simmer ½ hour. Add peppers, cut in eighths, and carrot. Simmer ½ hour. Serve on rice. Makes 4 servings.

TO STORE COOKED PORK
Let it come to room temperature, then put it in a covered container (so it will retain its moisture) and place it in the coldest part of the refrigerator

CREOLE PORK CHOPS

They're cooked with tomatoes,
green pepper, and onion.

Dredge 4 pork chops with 2 table-spoons flour. Brown on both sides in 1 tablespoon fat. Add 1 can (19 ounces) tomatoes, ½ green pepper, chopped, 1 chopped medium onion, 1¼ teaspoons salt, and 1 tablespoon Worcestershire. Cover, and simmer about 1 hour. Serve on 8 ounces elbow macaroni, cooked. Makes 4 servings.

PORK WITH MUSHROOMS

Simmered in sherry and soy sauce.

Cut 1 pound lean boneless pork in thin strips. Brown in 3 tablespoons margarine. Season. Add 1 chopped onion, 2 or 3 sliced stalks celery, 1 pound sliced fresh mushrooms, pinch each ginger and nutmeg. Simmer, covered, 20 minutes. Add 2 tablespoons each sherry and soy sauce. Cover; simmer 10 minutes. Serve on hot cooked rice. Makes 4 servings.

PORK TETRAZZINI

Sherry-creamed pork and mushrooms
baked with spaghetti and Parmesan.

Cook ¾ pound sliced mushrooms and 1 slivered green pepper in ¼ cup butter 5 minutes. Blend in 3 tablespoons flour, 2 teaspoons salt, ¼ teaspoon pepper. Add 2½ cups light cream; cook until thickened. Add 4 cups diced cooked pork, 2 chopped pimientos, 2 tablespoons sherry. Divide 6 ounces fine spaghetti, cooked, into 6 broiler-proof individual baking dishes. Add pork mixture to 2 beaten egg yolks; mix well; pour over spaghetti. Sprinkle with grated Parmesan. Bake in 300°F. oven, 45 minutes. Broil until lightly browned. Makes 6 servings.

SERVINGS PER POUND
Roast Fresh Pork, with bone   2 or 3
Roast Fresh Pork, no bone   3 or 4
Spareribs   1 or 2

SPARERIBS SOYA

There's ginger, garlic, and lemon
juice blended with the soy sauce.

Cut 5 pounds spareribs in 2-rib portions. Roll in ¼ cup flour. Melt 1 tablespoon fat in Dutch oven, and brown spareribs, a few pieces at a time. When all are browned, pour off fat. Mix 1 tablespoon ginger, ½ cup soy sauce, juice 1 lemon, and 2 cloves garlic, crushed. Pour over ribs. Cover; bake in moderate oven, 325°F., 2½ hours, basting with the sauce several times. Serves 6.

STUFFED PORK CHOPS WITH VEGETABLES

The stuffing: onion, celery,
green pepper, and bread crumbs.

Slit 4 thick loin pork chops from fat side to bone to form a pocket in each. Brown on both sides in Dutch oven. Remove; cook 1 chopped small onion, 2 tablespoons each finely chopped celery and green pepper in ¼ cup margarine 5 minutes. Add 1½ cups soft bread crumbs, 1 teaspoon salt; fill pockets in chops; fasten with skewers. Put in Dutch oven with 6 potatoes, sliced thin; 4 carrots, cut in strips. Season. Cover; bake in 350°F. oven, 1 hour. Remove skewers. Makes 4 servings.

CURRIED PORK AND SMOKED-HAM LOAF

A meat loaf to be served cold.

Force 1 pound each fresh lean pork and boiled smoked ham ends through food chopper twice, using medium blade. Add 1 minced clove garlic, 1 chopped small onion, 3 teaspoons salt, 1 teaspoon pepper, 2 teaspoons curry powder, 1 to 2 teaspoons crumbled sage, 1 egg white, ½ cup evaporated milk. Mix lightly but thoroughly; shape in a rounded loaf about 9" long. Lay 4 slices bacon out on a square of cheesecloth; put meat loaf on bacon. Roll up in cloth; tie ends with cord; put on trivet in large kettle. Add 2 quarts boiling water, ¼ cup vinegar, 1 teaspoon salt. Cover; simmer 2½ hours. Remove from liquid; let stand until cold. Chill; unwrap; cut in thin slices. Makes 6 to 8 servings.

BAKED PORK TENDERLOINS

They bake in mushroom soup.

Season 2 small pork tenderloins, and roll in flour. Brown on all sides in 2 tablespoons hot oil. Remove to shallow baking dish. Lightly brown 1 stalk celery, diced, and 1 small onion, chopped, in drippings. Put with meat. Mix 1 envelope mushroom-soup mix and 1½ cups water. Pour over meat. Cover, and bake at 350°F. 2 hours. Serves 6 to 8.

FRESH-PORK TIMETABLE
Roast all cuts to 185°F.
Loin: 4-6 lbs., 3-4 hrs.
Boston Butt: 4 lbs., 3½ hrs.
Bone-in Picnic: 5 lbs., 3½ hrs.
Rolled Boned Picnic: 4 lbs., 4 hrs.
Ham: 5 lbs., 4½ hrs.

PORK HAWAIIAN

It's cooked with pineapple and soy sauce and served on rice.

Cut 1½ pounds lean pork shoulder in ½″ strips. Mix until smooth: 1 beaten egg, 1 tablespoon milk, 3 tablespoons flour, ½ teaspoon salt. Dip strips in the mixture; fry in 3 tablespoons margarine until browned and done. Cook 1 minced clove garlic in 1 tablespoon margarine 1 minute. Add 1 bouillon cube, 1 cup hot water, 1 cup pineapple tidbits, ½ cup juice, 1 sliced carrot, 2 tablespoons each vinegar and soy sauce, 1 tablespoon sugar, 1 green pepper, cut in eighths. Simmer 5 minutes. Add meat; thicken with 2 tablespoons cornstarch in cold water. Serve on rice. Makes 4 servings.

PORK ORIENTAL

You use mushrooms, green onions, and mixed Chinese vegetables.

1 pound lean pork, cut in thin strips	2 stalks celery, sliced
1 tablespoon vegetable oil	8 green onions with tops, sliced
Salt	1 can (1 pound) mixed Chinese vegetables, drained
1 cup water	
1 tablespoon chicken-stock base	2 teaspoons cornstarch
1 can (3 ounces) un-drained mushrooms	Hot cooked rice or chow-mein noodles

Brown pork in oil. Sprinkle lightly with salt, and add next 2 ingredients. Cover, and simmer 15 minutes. Add next 4 ingredients, and simmer 5 minutes. Thicken with cornstarch blended with a little cold water. Serve on rice or noodles. Makes 4 servings.

PORK CHOW MEIN

Pork, onion, celery, and bean sprouts cooked in soy sauce and molasses.

Cook 2 sliced onions and 2 cups sliced celery in 1 tablespoon vegetable oil 5 minutes. Add 2 cups each diced cooked pork and water, 3 tablespoons soy sauce, 1 tablespoon molasses. Simmer 15 minutes. Add 1 can (19 ounces) bean sprouts, drained; heat. Stir in 3 tablespoons cornstarch blended with a little cold water. Cook until thickened. Serve on chow-mein noodles. Serves 4.

SPARERIBS WITH LENTILS

Spareribs bake on bay-seasoned lentils.

Put 1½ cups lentils in kettle; add water to cover. Add 1 sliced onion, 1 bay leaf, 1 teaspoon salt, ⅛ teaspoon pepper. Cover; simmer 1 hour, or until lentils are tender. Pour, undrained, into baking pan. Cut 1½ pounds spareribs in portions. Brown on all sides; season, and put on lentils. Bake, uncovered, in moderate oven, 350°F., about 1½ hours. Makes 4 servings.

PORK WITH TOMATO RICE

Diced boneless pork and brown rice.

½ cup brown rice	½ teaspoon celery salt
1 tablespoon margarine	¼ teaspoon pepper
1 pound boneless pork, diced	1 teaspoon Worcestershire
1 small onion, chopped	2 cups tomato juice

Brown rice lightly in margarine. Remove rice from skillet, and brown pork. Add rice and remaining ingredients. Cover, and cook slowly 1 hour, stirring occasionally. Serves 4.

GEORGIA PORK CHOPS

Chops, topped with an onion slice,
in peanut butter-mushroom sauce.

Brown 4 large lean pork chops on both sides in small amount of fat. Pour off fat. Top each chop with a thick slice of onion. Mix ¼ cup peanut butter, ½ can mushroom soup, ¼ cup milk, 1 teaspoon each Worcestershire and salt, and ⅛ teaspoon pepper. Pour over chops. Cover, and cook slowly 45 minutes. Serves 4.

PIGS' KNUCKLES, SAUER-KRAUT, AND DUMPLINGS

They're seasoned with caraway seed.

Put 3 pounds pigs' knuckles, 2 pounds sauerkraut, and 6 cups water in kettle; cover, and simmer 3½ hours, or until meat is tender. Add 2 tablespoons caraway seed, and salt to taste. Drop Herb Dumpling batter, page 20, by tablespoonfuls into kettle. Cover, and steam 12 to 15 minutes without removing cover. Serves 4.

SWEET-SOUR SPARERIBS

They bake with celery, onion, green pepper, pineapple, and vinegar.

Put 3 pounds spareribs, meaty side up, in shallow pan. Season. Bake in hot oven, 400°F., 30 minutes. Cook 1 chopped onion, 2 chopped stalks celery, chopped ½ green pepper in 2 tablespoons fat, 5 minutes. Blend in 1 tablespoon cornstarch. Add 1 can (9 ounces) pineapple tidbits, undrained, 1 cup water, ¼ cup vinegar, 1 tablespoon soy sauce. Bring to boil; pour over ribs. Bake in moderate oven, 350°F., 1 hour, basting occasionally with liquid in pan. Makes 4 servings.

GOOD WITH PORK
Applesauce, Sautéed Apple Rings, Cranberry Sauce, Spiced Crab Apples, Sautéed Pineapple and Bananas, Spiced Peaches, Tart Jelly.

ROAST PORK AU VIN BLANC

It has white-wine sour-cream gravy.

Rub a 5-pound pork loin with half a lemon, a cut clove of garlic, crumbled marjoram, and salt and pepper. Roast in a moderate oven, 375°F., 2½ to 3 hours, or until a meat thermometer registers 185°F. Remove meat, and keep warm. Heat ⅓ cup dry white wine in pan. Stir in ¾ cup sour cream, and season. Serve with the pork. Serves 6 to 8.

ROTISSERIE-BARBECUED PORK CHOPS

They have a chili-soy-ketchup sauce.

½ cup brown sugar, packed	3 tablespoons Worcestershire
½ cup ketchup	1 teaspoon chili powder
¼ cup soy sauce	½ teaspoon pepper
¼ cup water	1 onion, minced
Juice 1 lemon	6 large pork chops
1 teaspoon salt	

In small saucepan, mix all ingredients, except pork chops; simmer about 15 minutes. Pour over pork chops, cool, and refrigerate several hours. Center chops on spit of rotisserie, being careful to balance chops well, and lock. Put in preheated rotisserie, and roast at moderate heat 1 hour, or until done, basting frequently with sauce. Makes 6 servings.

PORK CHOPS WITH PINEAPPLE RINGS

Cranberry juice gives the pineapple a pretty pink color.

6 large pork chops	6 slices canned pineapple
Salt and pepper	¼ cup bottled cranberry cocktail

Heat a large heavy skillet. Rub fat edge of one chop over bottom to grease. Put chops in skillet, and cook over medium heat until browned on both sides. Pour off fat. Season, and cover. Cook over low heat 45 minutes, turning when half done. Remove chops to hot platter. Put pineapple and cranberry cocktail in skillet; heat, turning slices once. Arrange on platter with chops; garnish with parsley, if desired. Makes 6 servings.

VEAL

A fine piece of veal, well cooked, is as good as a feast. Yet in this country
veal runs a poor fourth, after beef, pork and lamb, in
popularity. A main reason for its unpopularity is the sad treatment it receives
in most of our kitchens. Much veal is poorly seasoned and cooked until
it is tasteless and tough. Among classic European dishes are
Wiener Schnitzel, Scaloppine alla Marsala, and Blanquette de Veau, all delectable
indeed. Our own ancestors were more appreciative than we of the fine
qualities of veal. Cook books of 200 years ago suggest treating it with care
and seasoning it daintily with lemon or sweet herbs; saucing it with
cream and white wine; and serving it up garnished with truffles and
mushrooms, all excellent suggestions. Veal is young meat. Treat it tenderly; don't
rush the cooking; do not overcook it. Try thin scallops sautéed in butter
until crisp and brown around the edges, but tender and moist
inside, and flavored with a bit of lemon or cream or Marsala or sherry. Try a well-
seasoned pot roast of veal served cold with a tuna or salmon sauce
and a bowl of good mayonnaise. This is a wonderful summer dish.

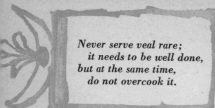

*Never serve veal rare;
it needs to be well done,
but at the same time,
do not overcook it.*

Veal Cutlets *are thin slices cut across the leg. They should be cut very thin, about ¼", and then pounded to ⅛" thickness.*

WIENER SCHNITZEL

Breaded veal cutlets with lemon, anchovy, capers, and chopped parsley.

Beat 2 eggs lightly; set out a bowl of flour seasoned with salt and freshly ground black pepper and another bowl of fine bread crumbs. Heat oil and butter mixed in a large skillet. You will need at least ½" fat in pan. Dip 4, or 1½ pounds, veal cutlets in flour, then in beaten egg, and finally in bread crumbs. Sauté cutlets in hot oil and butter until well browned on both sides and tender. Arrange cutlets on a hot platter, and on each place a slice of lemon topped with a rolled anchovy. Surround with mounds of chopped hard-cooked egg and tiny mounds of capers, and sprinkle with chopped parsley. Makes 4 servings.

Cutlets à la Holstein: Prepare cutlets as for Wiener Schnitzel (see above). Remove cooked cutlets to a hot platter, and top each with a fried egg. Crisscross each egg with 2 anchovy fillets, sprinkle with chopped parsley and capers; serve with lemon wedges.

SWISS VEAL

Veal strips, simmered in wine and sour cream, served on rice.

Cut 2 pounds thin veal cutlets in narrow strips. Dust with seasoned flour, and brown them quickly in 6 tablespoons hot, bubbly butter, turning to be sure they color evenly. Reduce heat, and add ½ cup white wine. Simmer gently a few minutes until the veal is tender. Taste for seasoning, and add more salt and freshly ground black

pepper. Add 1½ cups sour cream, and heat. Serve on saffron rice; garnish with parsley. Serves 6 to 8.

VEAL CUTLETS, SICILIAN STYLE

A large veal-cutlet roll stuffed with cold cuts and eggs, and baked.

3 very thin veal cutlets, cut across leg	Chopped parsley
	1 teaspoon basil
½ pound salami	5 or 6 hard-cooked eggs
½ pound mortadella or bologna	¼ cup olive oil
½ pound prosciutto or cooked ham	Salt and pepper
	5 or 6 bacon slices
¼ cup fine dry bread crumbs	2 cups tomato sauce
3 cloves garlic, minced	2 whole garlic cloves

Leave veal slices in one whole piece, but remove bone. Pound them very thin. Arrange slices on heavy waxed paper, side by side the long way, so they overlap slightly. Pound overlapping areas thoroughly to press them together. On veal, arrange rows of overlapping slices of salami. Top with rows of sliced mortadella or bologna, and finally with sliced prosciutto or cooked ham. Sprinkle surface with fine bread crumbs, minced garlic, chopped parsley, and basil. Down the center place a row of shelled, hard-cooked eggs. Sprinkle with oil, salt, and freshly ground black pepper. Roll up very carefully in the paper as for jelly roll, making certain that eggs stay in place in center. Remove paper, and tie the rolled meat firmly in several places. Place roll in baking dish, and strip top with bacon. Over all, pour tomato sauce with whole garlic cloves added. Bake in moderate oven, 350°F., 1 hour, basting from time to time with sauce. Remove to a hot platter, and slice, or serve from baking dish. Makes 8 servings.

Veal Scallops *(Scaloppine, Escalopes, Collops) are small slices of veal cut very thin and then flattened even more with a meat pounder. Be sure they are paper thin. If your butcher doesn't pound them enough, do it yourself. Place each scallop between two pieces of waxed paper, and pound with a meat pounder or any heavy flat object.*

Veal scallops are easy to prepare and lend themselves to a variety of seasonings. They take only a few minutes to cook, and an elegant meal built around scallops can be assembled in a mere half hour.

VEAL SCALLOPS, PLAIN

They're dredged with flour, then browned in hot butter and oil.

Dredge 8, or 1½ pounds, very thin veal scallops lightly with flour. Melt 3 tablespoons each butter and oil in large skillet. When bubbly and hot, brown scallops quickly on both sides. Reduce heat, and cook gently until meat is tender. (This will take a very few minutes.) Season. Makes 4 servings.

VEAL SCALLOPS WITH MARSALA

The traditional Veal Scaloppine of southern Italy.

Dust 8, or 1½ pounds, thin veal scallops with flour, and brown quickly on both sides in 3 tablespoons each butter and oil. Season with salt and freshly ground black pepper, and add a touch of ground ginger. Cover with Marsala wine, and continue cooking until Marsala is reduced one-half. Turn scallops once during this process. When wine is reduced and meat is tender, remove scallops to hot platter, and add another ¼ cup Marsala to pan. Bring juices to a boil, add ¼ cup chopped parsley, and pour over meat. Serve with rice. Makes 4 servings.

VEAL SCALLOPS MILANESE

Veal soaks in milk; then is covered with bread crumbs and sautéed.

Place 8, or 1½ pounds, very thin veal scallops in a dish, and cover them with ¾ cup milk. Soak for 1 hour. Drain milk from scallops, and add it to 2 beaten eggs. Heat 6 to 8 tablespoons butter in a large skillet until bubbly and hot. Dip scallops in flour, then in egg-milk mixture, and finally in fine bread crumbs. Sauté in hot butter until perfectly browned on both sides and tender. Season to taste with salt and freshly ground black pepper, and drain on absorbent paper. Makes 4 servings.

Veal Scallops Parmesan: Follow above recipe, but mix ½ cup grated Parmesan cheese, ⅓ cup chopped parsley, and 1 tablespoon chopped fresh basil or 1 teaspoon dry basil with ⅔ cup fine bread crumbs in which you dip scallops. After meat is cooked, remove to hot platter and rinse pan with ½ cup dry white wine. Pour juices over scallops.

VEAL SCALLOPS WITH LEMON

They are marinated in lemon juice.

Place 8, or 1½ pounds, very thin veal scallops on large, shallow plate, and cover with fresh lemon juice. Place another plate on top, and let meat stand for ½ hour. Remove from lemon juice, dust lightly with flour, and cook as in Veal Scallops, Plain. Season, and add ¼ cup finely chopped parsley. Toss scallops in parsley. Makes 4 servings.

VEAL SCALLOPS WITH WHITE WINE AND TARRAGON

Leftover scallops are delicious cold.

Dust 8, or 1½ pounds, very thin veal scallops with a little flour. Brown quickly on both sides in 3 tablespoons each hot melted butter and oil. Season to taste with salt; add 1 tablespoon fresh or 1½ teaspoons dried tarragon and just enough white wine to cover meat. Lower heat a bit, and continue cooking, turning scallops once or twice to be sure they are evenly bathed. When wine has cooked down and meat is tender, remove scallops to a hot platter, and add ¼ cup more white wine to pan. Turn up heat, and cook rapidly for a minute or two. Pour juices over the scallops. Makes 4 servings.

Veal Scallops with Vermouth and Tarragon: Substitute dry vermouth for white wine in recipe above.

Veal Scallops with Dill: Follow directions for Scallops with White Wine and Tarragon, but substitute dill weed for tarragon.

VEAL SCALLOPS, NIÇOISE

Garlic-oil sautéed veal with
white-wine and anchovy sauce.

Peel 3 cloves garlic, and chop very fine. Sauté in ⅓ cup olive oil until browned and crackly. Dust 8, or 1½ pounds, thin veal scallops with flour, and sauté in garlic-flavored oil until nicely browned on both sides. Season to taste with salt and freshly ground black pepper, and add ½ cup of dry white wine. Continue cooking until wine is reduced a little and the meat is tender. Turn scallops to bathe them thoroughly. Open a small can anchovy fillets, and chop coarsely. Add chopped anchovy and ¼ cup coarsely chopped parsley to pan. Heat through, and turn scallops to blend them well with seasonings. Makes 4 servings.

VEAL AND BACON TERRINE

A cold jellied loaf
made with veal scallops.

Buy 2 pounds very thin veal scallops and 1½ pounds of thinly sliced Canadian bacon. Chop ¾ cup each tiny green onions and parsley. Line bread pan or mold, both bottom and sides, with regular bacon slices. In bottom, put a layer of veal scallops, and sprinkle lightly with chopped green onion and parsley, freshly ground black pepper, a pinch of thyme, and piece of bay leaf, crumbled. Place layer of sliced Canadian bacon on this and another layer of veal scallops. Repeat the seasonings. Continue these layers until all the veal and Canadian bacon are

used. Strip top with regular bacon slices, and add ½ cup of dry white wine or dry vermouth. Place lid on mold, or cover with several layers heavy foil. Bake in a slow oven, 300°F., for 2 hours. Remove mold from oven, and take off lid. Add several layers of heavy foil, and place a plate on top. Put canned goods, a heavy electric iron, or any weighty object on plate. Let terrine stand until thoroughly cool and weighted down. Place in refrigerator to chill. When ready to serve, turn meat with jellied broth that has formed around it onto a decorative plate, and serve cut in very thin slices. Makes 6 to 8 servings.

Veal Birds are scallops of veal spread with stuffing, and then rolled and tied or fastened with toothpicks.

VEAL BIRDS, HUNGARIAN

Mushroom-stuffed veal, on noodles,
with cream and paprika.

Chop 1 pound mushrooms and stems very fine. Melt 6 tablespoons butter in skillet, and sauté mushrooms until a good deal of liquid forms in pan. Stir in 2 tablespoons flour, 1 teaspoon salt, ½ teaspoon freshly ground black pepper, and continue cooking until mushrooms are almost a paste. Spread 8 very thin veal scallops with mushroom paste. To each scallop, add 1 teaspoon finely chopped onion and 1 tablespoon chopped parsley. Roll firmly, and tie with string. Heat 4 tablespoons each butter and oil in skillet. Brown rolls in hot butter and oil, rolling them about to be sure they are evenly colored. Season with salt, and add 1 tablespoon or more, to taste, of Hungarian paprika. Pour 1 cup heavy cream into pan; cover, and simmer gently 8 to 10 minutes. Turn the rolls several times as they cook. Arrange rolls on buttered noodles. If you like a thickened sauce, add small balls of butter and flour kneaded together to the pan, and stir and cook until cream is thickened and smooth. Taste for seasoning, and pour over rolls and noodles. Garnish with buttered crumbs and chopped parsley. Makes 4 servings.

VEAL BIRDS WITH HAM

*Veal scallops, rolled around
ham and sage leaves.*

Buy 8 very thin scallops and 8 thin slices ham the same size. On each scallop, place a piece of ham, and pound thoroughly to press the two together. Top ham with a leaf of sage, and roll up scallop firmly. Tie with string. In large skillet, heat 4 tablespoons each butter and oil. Dust rolls with flour, and brown in hot butter and oil, making sure they are evenly colored. Season with a little salt (amount depends on saltiness of ham) and freshly ground black pepper, and add ⅓ cup white wine. Cover skillet, and cook gently 8 to 10 minutes, turning rolls once or twice during cooking. Makes 4 servings.

*Veal is a year-round
meat and it is delicate,
tender, and juicy
when properly cooked.*

ROAST LEG OF VEAL, LARDED

*It's larded with salt pork and ham
and roasted with wine.*

3-pound leg of veal, boned, rolled, and tied	1 teaspoon freshly ground black pepper
¼ pound lean salt pork	½ teaspoon ground ginger
3 or 4 slices prosciutto or cooked ham	½ teaspoon nutmeg Basil
3 cloves garlic, cut in small pieces	Olive or corn oil ½ cup tomato juice
1 teaspoon salt	½ cup sherry or Madeira wine

Have the butcher lard meat with strips of pork and small rolls of ham. Or do this yourself with a larding needle. Jab meat in several places with a sharp knife, and insert garlic pieces. Combine salt, black pepper, ginger, and nutmeg, and rub mixture on veal. Arrange in baking dish, and sprinkle with a little basil and a lot of oil. Mix ½ cup tomato juice with wine; add to pan. Insert meat thermometer in flesh, and roast in a moderate oven, 350°F., 30 minutes. Baste with pan juices, and continue roasting another 30 minutes. Baste again, adding more wine and tomato juice, if needed. Lower heat to 300°F., and continue cooking another 30 minutes, or until meat thermometer registers 165°F. Serve with the pan juices as sauce. Makes 6 servings.

Note: This roast is equally delicious sliced thin and served cold.

VEAU SAUMONÉ WITH DILL

*Cold roast leg of veal with
dill-salmon sauce.*

3- or 4-pound leg of veal, boned, rolled, and tied	2 cans (7 ounces each) salmon
1 cup white wine	1 teaspoon salt
Parsley	1 teaspoon freshly ground black pepper
Fresh dill or dried dill	2 egg yolks Vegetable oil

Place meat in deep casserole or baking dish with tight cover, and add wine, 3 sprigs parsley, 2 sprigs fresh dill or 1 teaspoon dried dill, salmon, salt, and pepper. Cover tightly, and bake in a moderate oven, 350°F., 2½ to 3 hours, or until meat is tender. Let cool in juices, then remove to refrigerator to chill. Put salmon and juices through food mill or fine sieve, or purée them in blender. Beat egg yolks until light and lemon-colored, and gradually add oil, about ½ cup. Slowly beat in puréed salmon mixture. Taste for seasoning, and add chopped parsley and fresh dill or dried dill. (You can do this whole process in blender.) When ready to serve, cut veal into thin slices, and arrange them on a platter. Pour sauce over meat. Makes 8 servings.

Veau Saumoné with Tarragon: Substitute fresh or dried tarragon for the dill in above recipe.

> *Veal becomes elegant
> in the company it keeps:
> blended with herbs, wine,
> cheese, smoked meats.*

VEAL CHOPS SOUBISE

*Browned chops topped with onions
and broiled with cheese sauce.*

6 good-sized veal chops	Flour
Milk	2 tablespoons oil
Butter	Salt and pepper
4 large onions, finely chopped	½ cup grated Parmesan cheese
	Grated Swiss cheese

Soak chops in enough milk to cover for 1 hour. Meanwhile, melt 4 tablespoons butter in heavy skillet, and steam onions in butter over a very low heat. They should be transparent and just tender, not browned. Remove onion, and reserve liquid. Remove chops from milk, and dry on absorbent paper. Dust lightly with flour, and brown on both sides in 4 tablespoons butter heated with oil. Lower heat, season chops with 1 teaspoon salt and ½ teaspoon freshly ground black pepper. Continue to cook, turning once, until chops are tender. Arrange chops in flat baking dish. Pour liquid from onions and blend it with milk in which chops were soaked. You will need about 1½ cups liquid. To pan in which chops were cooked, add enough butter to make 3 tablespoons fat. Blend in 4 tablespoons flour, and simmer gently 3 or 4 minutes. Slowly add milk-onion liquid, stirring constantly. Cook, and stir until sauce is smooth and thickened. Season to taste with salt and freshly ground black pepper, and add Parmesan cheese. Continue cooking until cheese is thoroughly blended into sauce. Spread each chop with drained steamed onion. Pour sauce over all, and sprinkle liberally with Swiss cheese. Run under broiler, or heat in a very hot oven, 475°F., until cheese melts and browns lightly. Makes 6 servings.

BROILED VEAL CHOPS

*You spread them with parsley
or chive butter before serving.*

Allow 1 thick rib or loin chop or 2 medium chops per serving. Since veal has little fat, chops must be well lubricated and cooked some distance from heat. Brush well with butter or oil, and arrange 6″ or 7″ from broiling unit. Cook slowly. A 1″ chop will take 15 to 18 minutes. Turn once during cooking time, brush again with oil or butter, and just before chop is done, season to taste with salt and freshly ground black pepper. Remove to hot platter, and spread with parsley or chive butter.

STUFFED VEAL CHOPS

The stuffing is ham and cheese.

Cut pockets in 4 fairly thick veal chops. Stuff each chop with 2 thin slices prosciutto or cooked ham and a slice Swiss cheese. Melt 4 to 8 tablespoons butter with 2 tablespoons oil. When hot, dust chops with flour, and brown quickly on both sides. Season to taste with salt and freshly ground black pepper, and add 1 finely chopped garlic clove and ½ cup dry vermouth. Cover pan, lower heat, and simmer 15 to 18 minutes, turning chops once during the cooking. When meat is tender, arrange chops on a hot platter. Add ¼ cup each chopped parsley and chopped chives and a little more vermouth to the pan. Stir, and heat through, and pour over chops. Makes 4 servings.

OSSO BUCCO

*Veal shanks simmer in
seasoned tomato-wine sauce.*

Dredge 4 veal shanks (about 2″ thick each) with seasoned flour, and brown on all sides in 4 tablespoons hot olive oil. Add 1 chopped clove garlic, 1 chopped medium onion, ½ cup white wine, ½ cup tomato purée, and 1 teaspoon basil. Cover, and simmer gently 1 hour. Remove cover, and add 2 chopped anchovy fillets, ¼ cup chopped parsley, and grated rind 1 lemon. Heat through, and blend thoroughly. Makes 4 generous servings.

POJARSKI CUTLETS

*Ground veal patties
with sour-cream gravy.*

1 cup soft stale- bread crumbs	⅓ cup heavy cream Salt
Milk	Dash nutmeg
1 pound ground veal	1 cup sour cream Pepper
Butter	

Soak bread crumbs in milk; squeeze dry.
Mix with veal, 3 tablespoons melted
butter, heavy cream, 1 teaspoon salt,
and nutmeg. Form mixture into 8 flat
patties. Melt 5 tablespoons butter in
large skillet, and cook patties very
slowly, turning to cook on both sides.
Do not let them get crusty. When the
meat is done, remove to hot platter.
Add sour cream to pan, and season to
taste with salt and pepper. Stir, and
heat through, but do not let it boil.
Pour over patties. Makes 4 servings.

OLD-FASHIONED VEAL LOAF

*Two parts veal to one part pork,
with bread crumbs and seasonings.*

2 pounds ground veal	½ cup chopped parsley
1 pound ground pork	2 eggs, beaten
1 cup fine soft stale- bread crumbs	1 teaspoon thyme 1 teaspoon salt
2 cloves garlic, finely chopped	1 teaspoon freshly ground black
¼ cup grated onion	pepper Bacon

Mix thoroughly all ingredients, except
bacon. Form into a firm loaf shape.
Place a layer of bacon slices on bottom
of shallow roasting pan or baking dish,
and arrange loaf on top. Strip the top
of meat with more bacon slices. Roast
in a moderate oven, 350°F., 1½ hours,
basting occasionally with pan juices.
Makes 8 servings.

Veal Loaf with Italian Sausages: Make
veal and pork mixture in recipe above.
Boil 6 to 8 Italian sausages 10 minutes. Cool, and remove skins. Arrange
half of the veal-pork mixture on bacon
slices in bottom of baking dish. Put
skinned sausages on meat, and add the
rest of mixture. Press down firmly. Top
with more bacon, and bake as above.

JELLIED VEAL LOAF

*An old American favorite
for picnics and buffet suppers.*

4 pounds neck of veal	1 teaspoon thyme 2 or 3 carrots
2 pounds shin of veal with bone	Celery stalks Cold water
1 veal knuckle	1½ tablespoons salt
1 onion, stuck with cloves	Pepper Hard-cooked eggs
1 bay leaf	Worcestershire

Place meat and bones in deep kettle,
and add onion, bay leaf, thyme, carrots,
and some celery stalks or leaves. Cover
with cold water, and bring to a boil.
Boil rapidly 5 minutes, then skim off
any scum that has formed. Add salt
and a few grinds of black pepper. Lower
heat, cover, and simmer for 2½ hours,
or until meat is very tender. Remove
the meat, and set broth aside to cool.
When meat is cool enough to handle,
separate all lean, and discard bone,
fat, and gristle. Chop lean meat rather
coarsely. Oil a mold, and place a layer
of chopped veal in bottom. Add a layer
of sliced hard-cooked eggs and more
chopped meat. Continue until the meat
is used. Skim fat from broth, strain it,
and return to heat to cook down. Season with Worcestershire. Cool reduced
broth, and pour over meat in mold.
(Broth should just barely reach top of
chopped veal.) Place in refrigerator to
chill and gel. Turn out on a platter,
and serve. Makes 12 servings.

Individual Jellied Veal Loaves: Arrange
layers of meat and egg in recipe above
in 12 individual molds. Top with broth,
chill, and gel, and turn out on lettuce
on salad plates. Add mayonnaise blended with chopped chives and parsley.

VEAL MEXICAN

Veal cubes simmer with spices,
tomato sauce, and green chilies.

2½ pounds shoulder of veal, cut in good-sized cubes	1 teaspoon orégano
	1 teaspoon salt
	Dash Tabasco
Butter or lard	2 cups tomato sauce
3 cloves garlic	1 can (6 ounces) green chilies, chopped fine
1 tablespoon chili powder	Hot cooked rice

Brown veal on all sides in butter. Add remaining ingredients, except chilies and rice. Cover, and simmer very gently about 2 hours, or until veal is thoroughly tender. Add chilies to veal, and heat through. If necessary, add more chili powder. Serve on rice. Serves 6.

Aillade: Prepare dish as above, but omit the chili powder and chilies, and add 4 more cloves garlic.

VEAL SHOULDER WITH CHEESE SAUCE

You use both Swiss and Parmesan cheese.

Place a 3- to 4-pound boned, rolled, and tied shoulder-of-veal roast in roasting pan, and insert meat thermometer in flesh. Roast in a moderate oven, 325°F., basting often with a mixture of melted butter and white wine. When veal has reached an internal temperature of 160°F. (in about 2 hours), remove, and cut into even slices. Arrange slices, alternating them with slices of baked ham, in baking dish. Pour pan juices over meat. In a skillet, melt 4 tablespoons butter, and blend in 4 tablespoons flour. Cook a few minutes, and slowly add 1½ cups scalded milk.

Cook, and stir until smooth and thickened. Continue cooking a few minutes, stirring constantly. Beat 2 egg yolks lightly, beat in ¼ cup of slightly warmed cream. Slowly add this mixture to sauce, blend it in thoroughly, and heat well, but do not let it boil or sauce will curdle. Stir in ½ cup grated Swiss cheese. Season to taste with salt. Sprinkle meat liberally with grated Swiss cheese, pour sauce over, and sprinkle top with grated Parmesan cheese. Run under broiler until lightly browned and bubbly. Remove from broiler, sprinkle with chopped parsley, and serve at once from the baking dish. Makes 8 servings.

STUFFED BREAST OF VEAL

It's stuffed with sausage meat
and baked with wine on a
bed of carrots and onions.

1½ pounds sausage meat	1 teaspoon salt
3 cups bread crumbs	1 teaspoon thyme
	Chopped parsley
½ cup sliced green onion	1 breast of veal with pocket
6 anchovy fillets, chopped	4 large onions, sliced
1 egg, slightly beaten	4 carrots, cut in strips
½ teaspoon freshly ground black pepper	Butter
	1 cup white wine or broth

Mix first 8 ingredients plus ¼ cup chopped parsley. Stuff pocket of veal breast with mixture, and sew it up or fasten with skewers. Mix onions, carrots, and 4 or 5 sprigs of parsley, chopped. Spread on bottom of baking pan. Dot bed of vegetables with butter, and place veal on top. Add wine, and sprinkle meat with salt and freshly ground black pepper if you use wine or if broth is not seasoned. Rub veal breast with butter; roast in very hot oven, 450°F., basting from time to time. After 30 minutes, or as soon as the veal begins to brown nicely, cover pan, and lower heat to 325°F. Continue roasting for 1¾ to 2 hours. About 15 minutes before meat is done, remove cover to finish browning on top. Makes 6 servings.

BOILED BREAST OF VEAL

It cooks with bacon, garlic sausage, and vegetables.

Place 1 small (about 3 pounds) breast of veal and ½ pound lean bacon in large kettle. Add 1 tablespoon salt and water to cover. Cover, and bring to a boil. Lower heat, and simmer gently 1¼ hours. Add 4 peeled onions, 6 peeled carrots, 1 stalk of celery, and 2 or 3 sprigs of parsley, and continue cooking 30 minutes. Add 1 pound of garlic sausage or Kolbasy, 3 white turnips, peeled and halved, and 6 medium potatoes, peeled. Cook 20 minutes, and add 1 small head of cabbage, quartered. Cook a final 15 minutes, adding 1 can (1 pound) tiny French-style peas during last few minutes. Remove veal breast to hot platter, and arrange sausage, bacon, and vegetables around it. Garnish with parsley, and serve with a hot mustard. Makes 6 servings.

LIVER STEAK BÉARNAISE

Thick slices of liver, crusty brown on the outside, pink in the center.

Broil 8 ounces of calves' liver per serving, cut 1″ to 1½″ thick, over charcoal or in a broiler until crusty brown outside and still pink and rare in center. Brush with mixture of melted butter and oil several times during broiling. Season to taste. If broiling over charcoal, move coals close to meat for last minute to char outside a bit. Serve sprinkled with chopped parsley and pass Béarnaise Sauce, page 239, or else:

Quick Béarnaise Sauce: In small pan cook 1 teaspoon tarragon, 2 teaspoons chopped green onion, 2 teaspoons chopped parsley, 3 tablespoons wine vinegar, and 1 tablespoon water. Cook gently until almost a glaze. Put 3 egg yolks in blender with 2 teaspoons lemon juice, ½ teaspoon salt, and a few grains cayenne. Flick the blender on and off rapidly, just long enough to blend eggs. Melt ¼ pound butter and bring just to boiling point. With blender turned on high, add melted butter steadily until sauce is thoroughly blended and thickened. Add tarragon mixture, and beat until well mixed. Makes enough sauce for 6 servings.

Remember that veal is just as delicious cold as it is hot. It is also good when reheated.

SWISS LIVER

Sautéed strips of liver with sour-cream sauce.

Cut 1½ to 2 pounds calves' liver in ½″ slices, then into strips, and dust with seasoned flour. Heat 3 tablespoons each butter and oil. When hot and bubbly, add 3 tablespoons finely chopped onion, 3 tablespoons of chopped parsley, and liver strips. Sauté liver quickly, turning strips to brown on all sides. Do not overcook. They should be pink in the center. Salt and pepper to taste, and add 1 cup sour cream. Heat cream through, but do not let it boil. Serve on fried toast. Makes 4 servings.

BROILED SWEETBREADS

They're breaded and broiled.

Soak 2 pairs sweetbreads in ice-cold water 2 or 3 hours. Drain, and blanch in boiling salted water 3 minutes. Remove sweetbreads, and when cool enough to handle take out tubes and membranes. Dip sweetbreads in melted butter, and place on broiling rack about 5″ from heat. Broil 4 minutes. Remove, and dip again in melted butter, and then in seasoned fine bread crumbs. Return to broiler with uncooked side toward heat. Continue broiling, brushing with melted butter, until crumbs are brown. Serve with Hollandaise Sauce, page 240, or Béarnaise Sauce, page 239. Makes 4 servings.

Broiled Sweetbreads, Southern Style: Top 4 slices hot toast with heated Virginia ham slices, and top with broiled sweetbreads (see above).

BROILED DEVILED CALVES' BRAINS

They're dipped in toasted bread crumbs so they have a crispy crust.

Soak 4 calves' brains in cold water 15 minutes; plunge in ice water 45 minutes. Remove the membranes. Drop brains in ¼ pound melted butter, then in 1 cup toasted crumbs, and broil until crispy and hot on all sides. Serve with melted butter and capers, or with Béarnaise Sauce, page 239. Serves 4.

VEAL, GUINEA FASHION

Banana skins stuffed with cooked veal and topped with banana slices.

3 onions, chopped	¼ pound mush-
3 green peppers, chopped	rooms, sliced
	1½ to 2 cups
3 tomatoes, peeled, seeded and chopped	diced cooked veal
	Salt and pepper
	6 bananas
4 tablespoons vegetable oil	Melted butter

Sauté onion, green pepper, and tomato in oil over very low heat about 20 minutes; add mushrooms. Continue cooking 5 minutes. Add veal, and salt and pepper to taste. Turn up heat, and cook, and blend until heated through. Remove peels from bananas by cutting one long slit from end to end in each skin. Gently force out fruit, leaving the skin intact. Wash skins, and arrange in a baking dish, slit side up, so each skin forms a boat. Stuff with veal mixture, and top each with overlapping slices of banana. Brush well with butter, and bake in a moderate oven, 350°F., 15 minutes. Makes 6 servings.

VEAL SALAD

It contains diced cooked veal, onion, celery, and toasted almonds.

Mix 2 cups diced cooked veal, ¼ cup each chopped onion and celery, and ½ cup toasted blanched almonds. Blend ⅔ cup mayonnaise with 1 teaspoon tarragon and 1 tablespoon lemon juice. Add enough mayonnaise to veal mixture to bind. Heap on a bed of greens, and garnish with the rest of the mayonnaise, peeled tomato wedges, ripe olives, and toasted almonds. Serves 4.

VEAL KIDNEYS EN BROCHETTE

Whole kidneys grilled on skewers and served with Béarnaise Sauce.

Use 1 whole kidney per person, and leave on most of outer layer of fat. Arrange whole on skewers; season; and grill over or under medium heat 12 to 14 minutes, turning several times. Pierce with cooking fork on all sides 2 or 3 times during broiling. Cut in half, and serve on very hot plates with Béarnaise Sauce, page 239.

KIDNEYS PIQUANT

Sliced roasted veal kidneys heated with wine and cognac.

4 veal kidneys	1 teaspoon salt
Butter	Juice 2 lemons
⅔ cup white wine	Fried toast
¼ cup cognac	Chopped parsley
2 teaspoons dry or very hot prepared mustard	

Remove fat from kidneys, and place kidneys in a well-buttered baking dish. Top each with 2 teaspoons butter, and roast in a very hot oven, 450°F., 10 to 12 minutes. Remove kidneys, and cut into thin slices. (You may finish this dish at the table with an electric skillet or chafing dish; otherwise finish on top of stove.) Cook wine and cognac until liquid is reduced one half. Add juices from baking dish, mustard, salt, 2 tablespoons butter, lemon juice, kidneys. Cook rapidly until just heated through and blended. Serve on fried toast, and sprinkle with chopped parsley. Makes 4 servings.

BARBECUES

G rilling, or barbecuing, is simply cooking over an open flame and it is the oldest method of cooking meats. For centuries it remained the standard way to prepare roasts, chops, and fowl. When the indoor stove was invented, with its built-in oven, grilling went out of style for a time. Apparently housewives decided it was too inconvenient to cope with the open flame. Professional cooks never abandoned grilling, and the hungry American male, when he hankered for a steak properly grilled to a crusty brown and tender, rare, and juicy inside had to hunt up a good restaurant. Now at last thanks to modern barbecuing equipment, grilling has returned to the American home. Across the land we are enjoying succulent roasts, steaks, fowl, and fish done to a turn. And grilling is not just a summertime activity. Many homes have built-in charcoal grills in the kitchen, and others boast electric rotisseries. It's no longer a fad to cook on the spit; it's part of our everyday life.

ROLLED ROAST OF BEEF

Serve with:
Roasted Sliced Potatoes and Onions
Grilled Green Peppers
Whole Tomatoes   Green Onions
Pumpernickel with Cheese Spread
Cupcakes and Whole Strawberries

Have roast at room temperature, and spit it right through middle. Start it over a hot fire, then maintain fire at medium for balance of cooking. Cook until meat thermometer reaches 5° to 10° below temperature desired. Douse, or lower fire, and allow meat to turn until ready to serve. This develops the juices and raises the temperature. If you like beef blood-rare, cook it to 120°F.; rare, 125°F., and so on. Allow about 15 minutes to the pound, depending on the thickness. **Potatoes and onions:** On squares of heavy foil, alternate thick slices of potato with onion. Sprinkle with salt, pepper, and orégano, and add a pat of butter. Wrap, and cook on grill about 1 hour. For **peppers,** cut in quarters, and discard seeds and veins. Marinate in French dressing overnight, then cook in hinged broiler until peppers are tender. Arrange on hot dish, pour over remaining marinade, sprinkle with chopped green onion, and serve. To make **spread,** mix sour cream with crumbled blue cheese.

CHARCOAL ROAST RIBS OF BEEF

Select a big roast, have it at room temperature, and spit it diagonally for better balance. (Start at point where rib end connects with backbone, and have spit emerge near tip of rib on other side.) Cook as directed for rolled roast. A 5-rib roast takes 2 hours to cook very rare, 3 to 4 to be very well done.

ROAST CORNED BEEF

Boil beef as usual, but don't overdo it. Then spread with mixture of 3 tablespoons prepared mustard, 1 pressed clove garlic, and ½ cup brown sugar. Spit as for roast beef, and cook over low fire until brown.

CHARCOAL-BROILED SALISBURY STEAK

Serve with:
Roast Corn
Toasted Cheese Bread
Sweet Onions with Orégano
Cherry Tomatoes
Brownies

Combine 3 pounds ground beef from round, rump, or shoulder with 1 tablespoon salt, ½ teaspoon freshly ground pepper, and 2 eggs. Form into a large patty, 1½" to 2" thick. Brush with soft butter or beef drippings, and broil in hinged broiler until done as desired. Serves 6. To roast **corn,** pull back husks, and remove silk, then replace husks, and tie with strip of outer husk. Soak in cold water for at least ½ hour, then roast around edge of fire, turning a few times. Outer husks will burn off and so will "tie" so that a little of the corn will be exposed. A few browned spots are delicious. To toast **cheese bread** split a long loaf French or Italian bread, and toast over coals on both cut and crust sides. Then spread with ¼ pound butter mixed with ½ pound grated cheddar cheese. Put near fire so cheese will melt. (If you want the topping bubbly brown, fill fine-meshed hinged broiler, preferably "basket" type, with hot coals, and hold it over top of bread.) For **onions,** peel, and thinly slice large sweet red ones. Sprinkle with salt and a little crumbled orégano; cover with mixture of 1 part vinegar to 2 parts water. Chill half a day before serving.

LAMB OR MUTTON STEAK

Have steaks cut 1½" thick. Grill, basting with garlic-butter and red-wine mixture, 8 minutes per side for rare.

BROILED LAMB OR MUTTON CHOPS

Have chops very thick, and cook exactly as you would steak. Do not overcook if you want them juicy and tender. A 1½" chop will cook medium rare in 10 to 15 minutes.

FOIL-BAKED VEAL CHOPS

Serve with:
Kidney-bean Salad
Cheese French Bread in Foil
Ice Cream, Chocolate Sauce

Brown 1½" thick chops quickly on both sides over charcoal. Put each chop on square of heavy foil, add 1 large pat of butter, and salt, pepper, tarragon. Wrap well, and finish cooking on grill, about 20 minutes, turning once or twice. **Salad:** Combine 2 cans (16 ounces each) drained kidney beans with 1 diced long cucumber, 3 peeled and diced tomatoes (discard pulp and seeds), 1 each chopped onion and green pepper. Serve in lettuce cups. Serves 6. Spread sliced **bread** with 1 cup grated Parmesan cheese mixed with ¼ pound butter and 1 tablespoon prepared mustard. Put the loaf back together again, wrap in foil, and heat at edge of grill for about ½ hour, turning at least once.

STEAK TERIYAKI

Serve with:
Broiled Pineapple
Toasted Corn Bread
Lima-bean Salad
Crackers and Cheese

Slice sirloin or tenderloin steak ½" or thinner, and cut in strips 1" wide. Soak bamboo skewers in water so they will not burn. Weave steak strips back and forth on skewers, leaving space for a handle. Marinate in mixture of ½ cup soy sauce, 1 mashed clove garlic, and ¼ cup sake or sweet sherry. Broil until done as desired, basting several times with marinade. Broil **pineapple** by brushing slices of canned or fresh with butter or oil, and cooking in a hinged broiler until brown on both sides. Split **corn bread** before toasting it over coals. For **salad**, combine 3 cups cooked Lima beans, 1 cup diced celery, ¼ cup each minced parsley and chives, and 2 teaspoons minced dill. Dress with ½ cup each mayonnaise and sour cream, 1 tablespoon of lemon juice, and salt and pepper to taste. Serves 6 to 8.

STATESIDE TERIYAKI

Slice steak ¾" thick, and cut in 1½" squares. Marinate as above, but add 1 teaspoon grated green or crystallized ginger to mixture. Thread on skewers, alternating with stuffed green olives and canned pineapple chunks. Broil, using marinade to baste.

CHICKEN OR PORK TERIYAKI

Marinate, and cook squares of raw chicken or pork as in recipe above.

CHARCOAL-ROASTED PORK LOIN

Serve with:
Foil-baked Apples
Foil-roasted Yams
Roast Corn   Coleslaw
Blueberry Cupcakes

Rub outside of whole or half loin with salt, pepper, and orégano, and spit parallel to backbone. Roast over slow fire until thermometer reaches 170° to 175°F., which is well done as pork should be, but juicy. A loin, any length, will take from 2 to 2¾ hours to cook. Core **apples**, 1 to a serving, and fill centers with mixture of sugar and butter, mixed if you like with a little cinnamon or nutmeg. Wrap in foil, and cook on outside of the fire about 30 minutes. Test by forking through foil.

BARBECUED SPARERIBS, CHINESE STYLE

Leave spareribs in one piece, and marinate 4 or 5 hours in mixture of: ½ cup water or chicken stock; ¼ cup soy sauce; ¼ cup each orange marmalade or honey, and tomato ketchup; and 2 crushed cloves garlic. Drain, weave on spit, or broil over a slow fire 1 to 1½ hours, basting with marinade occasionally. Cut apart to serve.

Note: The spit method of cooking spareribs requires practically no attention, but they have to be watched and turned constantly when they are broiled.

BARBECUED BREAST OF LAMB

Cooked as spareribs, above, but use Shish-kebab marinade, page 113.

HAMBURGERS WITH CHILI-CHEESE SAUCE

Serve with:
Shoestring Potatoes
Tomato and Green-pepper Salad
Ice-cream Cones

Make the hamburgers 4 to a pound, forming into fat patties. Tuck a chip of ice and about ½ teaspoon butter into center of each, brush outside with melted shortening, and broil over medium-hot fire until done to your liking. Serve on toasted buns with **cheese sauce** made by adding 1 cup grated cheddar cheese and 1 teaspoon chili powder to 2 cups medium cream sauce. This can be done at the grill, in a double boiler. The **potatoes** come from a can, and the **salad** is served on lettuce with mayonnaise rather than French dressing.

GREEN-CHILI AND CHEESE HAMBURGERS

Rinse 3 or 4 canned green chilies (a 4-ounce can) of seeds, and dice. Also dice ½ pound of cheddar cheese. Mix these with 2 pounds ground beef and 2 teaspoons salt. Form in 6 or 8 patties and broil.

EGG, GREEN-ONION, AND CAPER HAMBURGERS

Grill hamburgers, and top each with a fried egg. Pour on Green-onion and Caper Sauce: melt ¼ pound butter with 1 tablespoon tarragon vinegar and 1 tablespoon each minced green onions and capers.

GRILLED FRANKFURTERS OR SAUSAGES

Frankfurters, Polish sausage, or any favorite sausage can be broiled over charcoal. They can be split or not, as you wish, and brushed with oil or butter for extra-nice browning. Serve with 2 or 3 kinds of mustard, and sauerkraut cooked at the grill.

CHARCOAL-ROASTED TURKEY

Serve with:
Stuffed Celery
Avocado and Papaya Salad
Barley Casserole
Toasted Angel-food Cake
with Sour-cream Sauce

A 16-pound turkey (eviscerated weight) will take about 3 hours to roast and, with a minimum of attention, will be beautifully browned and juicy. It can be cooked stuffed or not, as you desire. If stuffed it will take a little longer. It is also harder to balance a stuffed turkey, at least until the flesh firms, because the dressing shifts as the spit turns. Truss turkey securely, having both wings and legs close to body and neck skin skewered on at back. Drive spit from a point just in front of tail, having it go through back and come out at about top of wishbone. This is a man's job, and will probably require the aid of a hammer. Connect spit to motor, and roast over medium fire until meat thermometer, in thickest part of thigh, registers 175°F., or until leg moves easily in joint. Internal temperature, as in all roast meats, will climb after cooking has ceased. If desired, fire can be lowered when thermometer reaches 170°F., and turkey allowed to turn over very little heat for ½ hour or longer, when it will be beautifully done. It is not necessary to baste turkey during cooking, though it may be done. A mixture of equal parts olive oil and vermouth, or melted butter and white wine with a little rosemary added, is good. For **barley casserole**, brown uncooked pearl barley in butter, then cook according to instructions on box, using chicken stock instead of water. Put in casserole, mix with melted butter, sliced sautéed mushrooms, chopped chives and parsley, and reheat before serving. Slice **angel-food cake**, and toast over charcoal at dessert time. For **sour-cream sauce**, brown ½ cup slivered almonds in butter, mix with 1 cup sour cream, and 2 tablespoons brown sugar. Makes 6 sauce servings.

ROAST CHICKEN

Serve with:
Risotto
Dill-Green Bean Salad, page 114
Peach Shortcake

Cook chicken like Charcoal-roasted Turkey, see page 112, allowing 45 minutes to 1 hour and 45 minutes. Baste with one of bastes suggested for turkey or with mixture of 1 part each of soy sauce, sherry, and oil. Chicken can be stuffed, or a bunch of sweet herbs can be put into its cavity before roasting. Try parsley, celery, green onion, and tarragon tied together with a thread. **Risotto:** Cook 1 cup uncooked rice and ¼ cup minced onion in ¼ cup butter until colored. Add 2 cups chicken stock (make it from the wing tips, neck, and gizzard); cover, and cook until rice is tender. Add ¼ cup grated Parmesan cheese and 2 tablespoons of butter. (Chopped cubed giblets can also be added.) Serves 6.

BROILED CHICKEN ORIENTALE

Serve with:
Fried Rice
Three-minute Asparagus
Mandarin Oranges
Sesame-seed Cookies

Make a marinade with ½ cup bland vegetable oil (not olive), ¼ cup soy sauce, ¼ cup sherry or whisky or gin, 1 large clove garlic, mashed, and 2 tablespoons grated green or crystallized ginger. Let split chickens or chicken breasts stand in this several hours, turning once or twice. Broil, using remaining marinade to baste. **Fried rice:** Cook 2 tablespoons chopped green onions in 3 tablespoons oil until wilted, then add 3 cups cooked white rice. Cook 5 minutes, stirring, then add 1 large egg that has been mixed with 2 teaspoons soy sauce. Cook, stirring, until egg is set, and serve sprinkled with chopped almonds. Makes 6 servings. For **asparagus,** slice in very thin diagonal slices, and cook 3 minutes only in boiling salted water; add butter.

SHISH KEBAB

Serve with:
Pilaf   Green Salad
Assorted Cheeses

Use lamb, mutton, beef, or even veal, cut in 1½″ cubes. For vegetables, have any or all of the following: quartered tomatoes or whole small ones, slices of onion or whole parboiled small ones, cubes of eggplant or zucchini, and pieces of green pepper. Pieces of bacon can be used; bay leaves can be threaded next to the meat. A simple marinade and a good one, is 1 part lemon juice to 3 parts olive oil. When stringing meat and vegetables on skewers, push close together if you want meat rare and juicy; leave space between if you want it crispy and well done. It will take from 10 to 30 minutes, depending on your taste. **Pilaf:** Make like Risotto, see top left, but omit cheese, and, instead, season with a little orégano or herb blend for rice.

6 MORE SKEWER COMBINATIONS

Cubes of cooked pork alternating with cubes of cooked sweet potato and canned pineapple.
Cubes of liver wrapped in bacon, and alternating with parboiled baby onions and canned or parboiled new potatoes.
Whole peeled jumbo shrimp, with green-pepper squares and pineapple chunks.
Cubes of fish with onion, tomato, green pepper, and bacon. These are called "fish kebabs."
Oysters or scallops wrapped in bacon, with mushroom caps.
Cubes of raw turkey breast, with bacon and pitted ripe olives.

MIXED GRILL

For each serving, have 1 thick loin lamb chop wrapped around a lamb kidney, then wrapped in a strip of bacon and skewered before broiling; 1 or 2 broiled pork sausages; ½ broiled tomato; 2 or 3 large mushroom caps dipped in butter, then broiled; and ½ broiled potato, brushed with butter and broiled until brown on both sides.

GRILLED MEATS, DIABLE

Serve with:
Mushrooms in Foil
Avocado Salad   Fruit

This classic way with grilled meats is especially good for beef ribs (cut from a cooked rib roast, with plenty of meat left on), or with cooked turkey or chicken breasts, or any sliced cooked meat, including such things as canned luncheon meats. The procedure is the same: Melt ¼ pound butter; add ½ teaspoon dry mustard. Dip meat in this, then roll in fine crumbs. Put in hinged broiler, and cook over medium-slow fire until brown. **Sauce Diable:** Cook 2 tablespoons minced green onions in 2 tablespoons butter until wilted; add 3 tablespoons vinegar, 1 teaspoon Worcestershire, dash Tabasco, 2 teaspoons prepared mustard, and 1 can bouillon. Simmer till reduced to ¾ cup. **Mushrooms:** put each serving on square of heavy foil, adding a pat of butter, salt, pepper, and lemon juice. Fold in a packet, sealing edges, and broil 10 minutes, turning once. Serve in foil.

MARINATED SHRIMP

Serve with:
Grilled Corn on the Cob
Green Salad, French Dressing
Onion-butter Bread
Fresh Pears   Gorgonzola Cheese

Select jumbo shrimp (8 to 12 to a pound), split shells down back with scissors, and wash out black veins. Marinate for 2 hours in marinade given for Broiled Chicken Orientale, see page 113. Broil over medium fire in hinged broiler about 5 minutes. **Onion-butter Bread:** slice French bread almost through. Spread onion-salted butter between slices; foil-wrap; heat.

SHRIMP, ITALIAN STYLE

Cook as above, but use a marinade of ½ cup olive oil, 2 crushed cloves garlic, 1 teaspoon salt, 1 tablespoon each lemon juice and minced parsley.

BROILED LOBSTER

Serve with:
Foil-baked Potatoes
Dill-Green Bean Salad
Assorted Cupcakes or Petits Fours

Have a live lobster, if possible. Split; remove intestinal vein and stomach. Brush meat well with softened butter, and cook 1 or 2 minutes, flesh side down; then turn and cook shell side about 15 minutes, basting top generously with butter. Lobster will be done when meat is opaque. Do not overcook. (Cooked lobsters should be broiled only until hot and browned.) For **salad,** sprinkle cooked green beans with dill, then cover with French dressing.

BROILED FISH FILLETS

Serve with:
Shoestring Potatoes
Stuffed-tomato Salad   Garlic Bread
Strawberries and Cream

Have hinged grill very well greased so fillets won't stick, and spread each with softened butter. Broil over medium fire until brown, basting with more butter mixed with white wine or lemon juice until flesh separates easily with fork and the transparent look is gone. Serve sprinkled with minced parsley and/or chives, and with a big wedge of lemon. The **tomatoes** are peeled, their pulp scooped out, and filled with a mixture of minced celery, green pepper, and green onion, topped with mayonnaise. Serve on lettuce.

BROILED WHOLE FISH

Any fish can be broiled whole, if it fits your grill. It can be split or not, but the former lets the flesh brown. A basket grill makes turning easier. Have grill well greased, and brush fish with butter or oil mixed with lemon juice. Broil, flesh side down, until flesh separates easily with a fork. A 5-pound fish will take 20 to 50 minutes, depending on its shape; a small one, even if not split, will cook in 12 to 15 minutes. Serve with lemon wedges.

CHAFING DISH SPCIALTIES

The chafing dish was a must for the elegant hostess of the late Victorian and
Edwardian eras. Intimate little supper parties were the fashion,
with the lady presiding at the chafing dish concocting something special,
a Welsh rabbit or oyster stew, for her admiring guests. Many sophisticated
young bachelors and men about town learned the art of chafing-dish cookery and
invited daring young women to share a supper *à deux* in their quarters.
There they displayed their culinary prowess while toasting the lady with champagne
or Rhine or Moselle. One such gentleman, a bit of a wag, published a book
of his recipes, each named for a conquest: "Lady Effingham's Eggs" and the
"Duchess of Cambridge's Frog Legs," to name two. Cooking in a
chafing dish still has a sophisticated air about it. There is something charming
about gathering around a table to watch the hostess put the finishing touches to her
creation: a dash of wine or cognac, or a lacing of fine liqueur. If you build up
a repertoire of special dishes suitable for Sunday lunches or buffet suppers,
you have then acquired a quick and graceful knack for entertaining. Somehow,
the chafing dish has an extra personal touch so flattering to guests.

115

SCRAMBLED EGGS WITH AVOCADO

*You add diced avocado
just before serving the eggs.*

¼ cup butter or margarine	¾ teaspoon salt
8 eggs	¼ teaspoon pepper
¼ cup light cream	1 small avocado, peeled and diced

Melt butter in top pan over boiling water. Beat eggs with cream and seasonings. Pour into pan, and cook, stirring occasionally, until of desired consistency. Add avocado. Serves 4.

Scrambled Eggs with Mushrooms: Use above recipe, omitting avocado. Cook ¼ pound mushrooms, sliced, in the butter over direct heat before adding the eggs. If desired, serve eggs in sautéed large mushroom caps.

Scrambled Eggs with Crab Meat: Use recipe for Scrambled Eggs with Avocado, omitting avocado. Add 1 can (6½ ounces) crab meat, flaked and heated slightly, to cooked eggs. Add 1 tablespoon sherry. Serve in toast cups, or Croustades, page 70.

Scrambled Eggs with Sweetbreads: Use recipe for Scrambled Eggs with Avocado, omitting avocado. Add ½ pound sweetbreads, cooked, diced, and reheated, to cooked eggs.

Scrambled Eggs with Cheese: Use recipe for Scrambled Eggs with Avocado, omitting avocado. Add ¼ cup each grated Gruyère and Parmesan cheese to eggs before cooking. Garnish scrambled eggs with chopped chives.

Scrambled Eggs, Hunter Style: Use recipe for Scrambled Eggs with Avocado, omitting avocado. Serve in Croustades, page 70; top with sautéed chicken livers and a little chopped fresh tarragon.

Scrambled Eggs with Anchovies: Use recipe for Scrambled Eggs with Avocado, omitting avocado. Add 6 or 8 anchovies, minced, to cooked eggs.

Scrambled Eggs with Ham: Use recipe for Scrambled Eggs with Avocado; omit avocado. Add 1 cup diced cooked ham.

WELSH RABBIT

You can make it with beer or milk.

2 tablespoons butter or margarine	1 teaspoon Worcestershire
1 pound sharp cheddar cheese, shredded	½ cup beer, ale, or milk
½ teaspoon dry mustard	2 eggs, slightly beaten
Dash cayenne	8 slices toast
½ teaspoon salt	Parsley

Melt butter in top pan over direct heat. Add cheese, and heat, stirring occasionally, until cheese is melted. Put over boiling water, add seasonings, and pour in the liquid mixed with eggs. Cook until thick, stirring frequently. Serve on toast with garnish of parsley. Makes 4 servings.

ONIONS IN CHEESE SAUCE

*Sliced onions are simmered
in tangy American cheese.*

4 onions, sliced	1 teaspoon prepared mustard
2 tablespoons butter or margarine	1 teaspoon Worcestershire
1 tablespoon flour	¾ pound process American cheese, cubed
½ teaspoon paprika	
¾ teaspoon salt	1 tall can evaporated milk
Dash pepper	Toast

Cook onion in the butter in top pan over direct heat until limp. Blend in flour and seasonings. Add cheese and milk. Heat, stirring occasionally, until cheese is melted and blended, and mixture bubbles. Put over boiling water; cover, and cook until onions are tender. Serve on toast. Makes 4 to 6 servings.

CREAMY EGGS AND CHEESE

*Use any process cheese,
the sharper the better.*

2 tablespoons butter	2 tablespoons water
½ cup shredded sharp process cheese	5 eggs, beaten
	Salt
	Pepper

Melt butter in top pan over direct heat. Add cheese and water; cook, stirring occasionally, until cheese is melted and smooth. Add eggs, and salt and pepper to taste. Cook over boiling water until eggs are just set, stirring frequently. Makes 4 servings.

MACARONI PARMESAN

*The Parmesan cheese is
mixed with sour cream.*

1 cup small soft-bread cubes	½ cup grated Parmesan cheese
2 tablespoons butter	2 egg yolks
⅛ teaspoon garlic salt	½ teaspoon paprika
8 ounces elbow macaroni	½ teaspoon salt
1 cup sour cream	¼ teaspoon pepper

Brown bread cubes in butter; add garlic salt, and set aside. Cook, and drain macaroni. Put in top pan over boiling water. Mix remaining ingredients, and stir into macaroni. Sprinkle with browned bread cubes. Makes 4 servings.

SAUTÉED CHICKEN LIVERS AND GREEN BEANS

*The sautéed chicken livers and
beans simmer in chicken broth.*

1 pound chicken livers	¼ cup butter
¼ cup flour	¾ cup chicken broth or bouillon
1 teaspoon salt	
¼ teaspoon pepper	1 box frozen cut green beans, cooked
½ teaspoon poultry seasoning	

Cut livers in half, and dredge with flour seasoned with salt, pepper, and poultry seasoning. Heat butter in top pan over direct heat until it begins to brown. Add livers, and sauté until lightly browned. Add broth, and simmer a few minutes. Put over boiling water; add beans, cover, and heat thoroughly. Makes 4 servings.

CLAM SPAGHETTI

*Cooked spaghetti is tossed with
onion-and-garlic-seasoned clams.*

2 tablespoons olive oil	1 tablespoon instant minced onion
Few sprigs parsley, chopped	1 can (10½ ounces) minced clams, undrained
1 clove garlic, minced	
½ teaspoon salt	8 ounces spaghetti, cooked
⅛ teaspoon pepper	

Heat oil in top pan over direct heat. Add parsley and garlic; cook about 5 minutes. Add seasonings, onion, and clams. Heat. Add spaghetti, and toss until well mixed. Heat over boiling water. Makes 4 servings.

RICE NEPTUNE

Rice with minced clams and shrimp.

1 can (10½ ounces) minced clams	½ teaspoon salt
1 small onion, minced	¼ teaspoon pepper
¼ cup butter	1⅓ cups packaged precooked rice
2 pimientos, cut in strips	1 box (10 ounces) frozen cleaned, shelled shrimp, cooked
¼ cup minced parsley	

Drain clams, reserving liquid. Cook onion in the butter in top pan over direct heat about 10 minutes. Add enough water to clam liquid to make 1½ cups. Add to onion mixture with pimientos and parsley. Heat to boiling. Add seasonings; put over boiling water, and stir in rice with fork. Cover, and let stand 5 minutes. Add clams and shrimp; heat. Makes 4 to 6 servings.

*"For whom he means
to make an often guest,
one dish shall serve;
and welcome make the rest."*
JOSEPH HALL

CHICKEN CHINOIS

You use soy sauce and ginger.

¼ cup butter or margarine	¼ teaspoon pepper
¼ cup flour	¼ teaspoon ginger
2 cups chicken broth or bouillon	½ teaspoon paprika
¼ teaspoon garlic salt	Salt to taste
1 tablespoon soy sauce	3 cups diced cooked chicken
	Hot cooked rice

Melt butter in top pan over direct heat. Blend in flour, broth, and seasonings. Cook, stirring occasionally, until thickened. Add chicken; put over boiling water; cover, and heat. Serve with rice, and additional soy sauce, if desired. Serves 4 to 6.

EGGS AND FRANKFURTERS

They're cooked with bacon, green pepper, olives, and capers.

2 slices bacon diced	6 stuffed olives, sliced
1 onion, minced	1 teaspoon capers
½ pound frankfurters, sliced	Salt and pepper
1 green pepper, cut in strips	Pinch orégano
	6 eggs
	2 tablespoons milk

In top pan, cook bacon until crisp. Add onion, and cook 2 or 3 minutes. Add frankfurters and green pepper; cook 5 minutes. Stir in olives, capers, and seasonings. Beat eggs with milk, and add to other ingredients. Put over boiling water, and cook, stirring occasionally until of desired consistency. Makes 4 servings.

"A little dish oft furnishes enough, And sure enough is equal to a feast."
HENRY FIELDING

MUSHROOM CREAMED BEEF

Delicious on baked potatoes, rice, noodles, or toast.

¼ pound dried beef	½ cup light cream or milk
2 tablespoons butter	Pepper
2 cans cream-of-mushroom soup	Worcestershire

Cover beef with boiling water, and let stand 5 minutes. Drain. Cut in pieces, and put in top pan with butter. Cook over direct heat until beef is frizzled. Add remaining ingredients, and put over boiling water. Heat, stirring occasionally. Makes 4 servings.

CHINESE FRIED RICE

It's cooked with meat or chicken and topped with thin strips of egg.

½ cup diced cooked chicken, ham, or pork	1 pimiento, chopped
3 tablespoons butter	1 teaspoon dried green pepper
1 can (3 ounces) sliced mushrooms, drained	3 tablespoons soy sauce
1 green onion, chopped	1 cup rice, cooked
	1 egg, beaten

Put all ingredients, except last 2, in top pan over direct heat. When butter is melted, stir rice in lightly with fork. Put over boiling water, and heat well. Meanwhile, cook egg in a greased skillet until firm, but not browned. Cut in thin strips, and put on rice. Makes 4 to 6 servings.

POACHED EGGS ALLA ROMANO

They're poached in spaghetti sauce and served topped with grated cheese.

1 can (8 ounces) meatless spaghetti sauce	Salt and pepper
4 eggs	4 slices toast
	Grated Romano cheese

Heat spaghetti sauce in top pan over direct heat. Carefully drop eggs, one at a time, into sauce. Sprinkle with salt and freshly ground pepper. Cover, and poach 5 minutes for medium-done eggs. Put one egg and some of the sauce on each slice of toast. Sprinkle with cheese. Makes 4 servings.

MEXICAN HOMINY

You add onion, green pepper,
and chili powder to hominy.

1 onion, minced	1 can (29 ounces)
1 green pepper,	whole hominy,
chopped	drained
¼ cup butter	1 teaspoon chili
or bacon fat	powder
½ teaspoon salt	Dash pepper

Cook onion and green pepper in the butter in top pan over direct heat about 10 minutes. Add remaining ingredients, and heat. Serves 4.

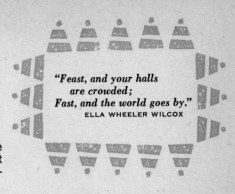

"Feast, and your halls
are crowded;
Fast, and the world goes by."
ELLA WHEELER WILCOX

CURRIED CHICKEN

It's served on rice
with a sprinkling of cashew nuts.

1 can each cream-	¾ cup light cream
of-chicken and	2 cups diced cooked
cream-of-	chicken
mushroom soup	½ cup broken
1 tablespoon	cashew nuts
curry powder	Hot cooked rice

Put all ingredients, except last 3, in top pan over boiling water. Cover, and heat, stirring occasionally. Add chicken, and heat. Sprinkle with nuts, and serve with rice. Makes 4 servings.

CHAFING DISH SCALLOP STEW

You use both milk and cream.

1 pound scallops	¼ teaspoon each
¼ cup butter	pepper and
1 tablespoon	paprika
Worcestershire	Salt, celery salt,
3 cups milk and 1	garlic salt, and
cup light cream,	seasoned salt to
scalded	taste

Cut scallops in small pieces, and put in top pan with butter over direct heat. Cook about 5 minutes. Add remaining ingredients, and keep hot over boiling water. Makes 4 servings.

Clam Stew: Use Scallop Stew recipe, substituting 2 dozen shucked raw soft-shell clams with liquid for the scallops.

Lobster Stew: Use Scallop Stew recipe, substituting 1½ cups diced cooked lobster meat for scallops.

Crab-meat Stew: Use Scallop Stew recipe, substituting 1½ cups diced cooked crab meat for scallops.

ONIONY SCRAMBLED EGGS

The onions are green onions, chopped.

2 tablespoons	¼ cup milk
butter	6 eggs, slightly
¼ cup chopped	beaten
green onion	Salt and pepper

Melt butter in top pan over direct heat. Add onion, and cook a few minutes. Put over boiling water; add milk and eggs. Cook, stirring occasionally, until thickened. Season to taste. Serves 4.

SHERRIED SPAGHETTI

It's served with grated
Parmesan or Romano cheese.

⅓ cup olive oil	8 ounces spaghetti,
1 clove garlic,	cooked
minced	Grated Parmesan or
⅓ cup cooking	Romano cheese
sherry	Salt and pepper

Heat oil and garlic in top pan over direct heat. Add the sherry, spaghetti, and ½ cup cheese. Season to taste. Toss well, and reheat over boiling water. Serve with cheese. Serves 4.

CURRIED RICE

Serve this with cold lamb or chicken.

2 tablespoons butter	1½ cups stock or
1 to 2 teaspoons	water
curry powder	1⅓ cups packaged
1 teaspoon instant	precooked rice
minced onion	Salt and pepper

Put all ingredients, except rice and salt and pepper, in top pan over direct heat, and bring to boil. Put over boiling water, and stir in rice with fork. Cover, and let stand 5 minutes. Season to taste. Makes 4 servings.

SHRIMP FONDUE

*Shrimp soup, Swiss cheese, and white
wine, as a dunk for cubes of bread.*

1 can frozen shrimp soup	2 tablespoons dry white wine
1 cup shredded Swiss cheese	Cubes of rye or French bread

Heat shrimp soup in top pan over boiling water. Add cheese, and stir occasionally until melted. Stir in wine. Serve as a dunk with the cubes of bread. Makes 4 servings.

SHRIMP NEWBURG

You flame the shrimp in cognac.

Sauté 2 pounds of cleaned raw shrimp in ½ cup of butter in a chafing dish for 10 minutes. Pour on 2 jiggers of cognac, and flame. Heat 1 pint of heavy cream in another pan, beat a quarter of it into 6 beaten egg yolks; combine with remaining cream, season with salt and paprika, and cook gently, stirring, until the sauce thickens. Pour over hot shrimp. Makes 6 servings.

LOBSTER NEWBURG

*Lobster in a sherry
egg-and-cream sauce.*

2 cups sliced cooked lobster meat	1 cup light cream
¼ cup melted butter	3 egg yolks, slightly beaten
2 tablespoons sherry	Salt, pepper, and nutmeg
	Toast points

Cook lobster in butter in top pan over direct heat, 5 minutes. Add sherry, and cook 1 minute. Put over boiling water; add cream and egg yolks. Cook, stirring, until slightly thickened. Season, and serve on toast. Makes 4 servings.

ZIPPY EGGS

*Mustard, Worcestershire, red hot
sauce, and pepper provide the zip.*

½ pound sharp cheddar cheese, cut in chunks	Dash red hot sauce
	¼ teaspoon pepper
1 can cream-of-celery soup	½ cup milk
1 teaspoon prepared mustard	6 hard-cooked eggs, cut in quarters
1 teaspoon Worcestershire	Toasted French bread

Melt cheese in top pan over boiling water. Add soup, seasonings, and milk; cover, and heat, stirring occasionally. Add eggs, and reheat. Serve on toast. Serves 4.

SCOTCH WOODCOCK

*You serve this tomato, cheese, and
egg dish on toasted crackers.*

1 can (28 ounces) tomatoes	2 eggs, beaten
	Salt and pepper
½ pound process American cheese, diced	Cayenne
	Crisp toasted crackers

Put tomatoes in top pan over direct heat. When heated, add cheese, and cook, stirring occasionally, until cheese is melted. Put over boiling water, and add eggs. Cook, stirring, until just thickened. Season to taste. Serve on crackers. Makes 6 to 8 servings.

CHILI TUNA PAPRIKA

*You can serve it on toast
or in puff shells.*

¼ cup butter or margarine	1 teaspoon Worcestershire
2 tablespoons flour	½ cup chili sauce
¾ teaspoon salt	1 can (7 ounces) tuna, drained and flaked
⅛ teaspoon pepper	
1 teaspoon paprika	
¼ cup cream or evaporated milk	Toast, or Cream-puff Shells, page 266
1 cup milk	

Melt butter in top pan over direct heat. Blend in flour and seasonings. Add cream, milk, and Worcestershire; cook until thickened, stirring occasionally. Add chili sauce and tuna; heat, and serve on toast, or in Cream-puff Shells. Makes 4 servings.

120

GOLDEN BUCK

*A cheese rabbit
topped with poached eggs.*

2 tablespoons butter	Salt, pepper,
½ pound process	dry mustard
American cheese,	Buttered toast
shredded	4 eggs, poached
⅓ cup milk	Chopped parsley

Melt butter in top pan over direct heat. Add cheese, and heat until melted. Add milk, and cook until thickened. Put over boiling water, and add seasonings to taste. Serve on toast, topping each portion with a poached egg. Garnish with chopped parsley. Serves 4.

FUSILLI WITH GREEN SAUCE

*Fusilli is the macaroni
shaped in spirals.*

⅓ cup butter or	Grated Parmesan
margarine	cheese
1 clove garlic,	8 ounces fusilli
minced	macaroni, cooked
¾ cup minced	
parsley	

Melt butter in top pan over direct heat. Add garlic, and cook about 5 minutes. Add parsley, ½ cup cheese, and fusilli. Toss well; heat over boiling water. Serve with additional grated Parmesan cheese. Makes 4 servings.

SOUTH-OF-THE-BORDER RABBIT

*A cheddar rabbit with green pepper,
onion, ketchup, and kidney beans.*

1 green pepper,	½ teaspoon
chopped	Worcestershire
½ onion, minced	2 tablespoons
¼ cup butter or	ketchup
margarine	1 can (1 pound)
¼ cup undiluted	red kidney
evaporated milk	beans, undrained
½ pound sharp	Toast points or
cheddar cheese,	crisp crackers
cut in pieces	

About 15 minutes before serving time, cook green pepper and onion in the butter in top pan over direct heat. When ready to serve, add milk and cheese; cook until cheese is melted, stirring occasionally. Put over boiling water; add Worcestershire, ketchup, and beans; cover, and heat. Serve on toast. Makes 6 servings.

PEARS BURGUNDY

*You serve cinnamon-sprinkled
sour cream on the side.*

⅓ cup sugar	1 can (29 ounces)
⅓ cup currant	pear halves,
jelly	drained
½ cup pear liquid	⅓ cup Burgundy
¼ teaspoon red	Sour cream
food coloring	Cinnamon

About ½ hour before serving time, put sugar, jelly, liquid, and coloring in top pan. Put over direct heat, and stir occasionally until jelly is melted. Add pears, and let bubble up. Cover, and simmer while serving main part of meal. When ready to serve, add Burgundy. Pass sour cream sprinkled with cinnamon. Makes 4 servings.

CURAÇAO PEACHES AND PINEAPPLE

They have a cream-cheese topping.

1 package (3	Dash salt
ounces)	1 can (9 ounces)
cream cheese	crushed pine-
½ cup heavy	apple, undrained
cream, whipped	¼ cup curaçao
Sugar	½ cup toasted
Dash almond	chopped
extract	blanched almonds
1 can (29 ounces)	
sliced peaches	

Mash cream cheese with fork, and beat until smooth. Fold in cream, 1 tablespoon sugar, and flavoring. Drain peaches, reserving ½ cup syrup. Put syrup, ½ cup sugar, salt, and pineapple in top pan over direct heat. Let bubble up. Put over boiling water, and add peaches; heat covered. Add curaçao. Sprinkle nuts on fruit, and serve with topping. Serves 6.

*"And nearer as they came,
a genial savour of certain stews,
and roast-meats, and pilaus,
Things which in hungry
mortals' eyes find favour."*
LORD BYRON

PEAR HONEY

Serve it as desert or as sauce.

⅓ cup each water and sugar	¼ teaspoon ginger
Grated rind ½ lemon	2 cups shredded winter pears

Put all ingredients, except pears, in top pan over direct heat. Stir occasionally until heated and sugar is dissolved. Add pears; cover, and simmer while serving main course. Serves 4.

CHERRIES JUBILEE

Flaming cherries spooned over ice cream.

1 can (17 ounces) dark sweet cherries	1 tablespoon cornstarch
2 tablespoons sugar	⅓ cup rum or brandy
Dash salt	1 quart ice cream

Drain cherries, and pit. Add enough water to syrup to make 1 cup. In top pan mix sugar, salt, and cornstarch. Add syrup. Cook over direct heat until slightly thickened. Add cherries, and heat. Add liquor, ignite, and spoon over ice cream. Makes 4 servings.

BANANAS AU RHUM

Bananas in flaming rum sauce.

¼ cup butter or margarine	¼ cup brown sugar
6 peeled ripe bananas, halved	Cinnamon
	½ cup rum

Melt butter in top pan over direct heat. Add bananas; sprinkle with half the sugar and a dash of cinnamon. Cook until bananas are lightly browned. Turn, and sprinkle again with sugar and cinnamon. When soft, add rum, and ignite. Serve with liquid. Serves 4.

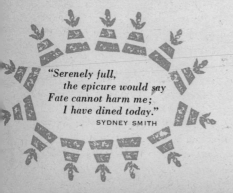

*"Serenely full,
    the epicure would say
Fate cannot harm me;
    I have dined today."*
SYDNEY SMITH

CREPES SUZETTE

*Thin dessert pancakes
served, flaming, in a liqueur sauce.*

4 eggs, well beaten	1 teaspoon salt
1 cup milk	2 teaspoons sugar
1 cup flour	Melted butter
1 tablespoon cognac	Sauce

Mix well all ingredients, except Sauce. Let stand in refrigerator 2 or 3 hours. When thicker than heavy cream, add a little more milk. Heat a 7″ or 8″ skillet, and brush with melted butter. Put in 1 generous tablespoon batter. Working quickly, tip, and tilt the pan so that the batter flows evenly over the bottom. Cook quickly. As soon as the pancake browns on one side, turn quickly, and brown the other. Proceed until all of batter is used. Reheat the Sauce. Makes about 32 crêpes.

Sauce: Cream ½ pound sweet butter until light and fluffy. Add grated rind of 1 small orange and 1 lemon, and ¼ cup sugar. Melt in top pan of chafing dish over direct heat. Add the juice of 1 orange, and heat to reduce mixture to one half. Add 2 ounces (¼ cup) each cognac and curaçao or Cointreau and 1 ounce (2 tablespoons) kirsch. Ignite with match flame. Then add the crêpes, one at a time. Bathe each in the sauce, fold in quarters, and put to one side of the pan. When all are ready to serve, sprinkle with a little sugar, pour on about 2 ounces of cognac, and ignite.

CREPES CARLOS

*Thin dessert pancakes, spread with
apricot preserves and served, flaming,
with pineapple chunks and rum sauce.*

Prepare crêpes as directed above. Peel and cut a pineapple in chunks (or use frozen or canned chunks). Cook slowly in ¼ cup butter until brown, adding more butter if necessary, and ¼ cup Jamaica rum. Spread crêpes with apricot preserves, and fold each in quarters. Put in a large chafing dish, arranging them on one side. At the other side, put the cooked pineapple. Pour all the pan juices over the crêpes, and heat gently over direct heat. When ready to serve, add 2 more jiggers of rum, and ignite.

MAIN DISH
CASSEROLES

T he term "casserole" has an odd history. It comes from the French, but in
France a casserole is a saucepan or pot for the top of the stove.
The covered container for oven cooking, if in metal or porcelain, is called a
cocotte; if it is made of earthenware, it is called a *terrine*. "Casserole" has
taken on even more complicated meanings in our cuisine. We often
assume that a casserole is a dish combining meat or fish and vegetables, or several
vegetables, and when we speak of having a "casserole dinner" we mean one
hot dish that is a meal in itself. Casserole can even mean a combination of already
partly prepared foods that takes only a few minutes to heat up: the career
girl's quick meal. Casserole cooking is ideally suited to foods that
need the application of low heat over a long period of time: meats that are best
braised, dried beans, fowl, or dishes that include flavors that require blending
and mellowing. Here is a wide range of casseroles for every taste and occasion.

CREAMY BAKED CHICKEN

*It's mixed with cream soup, peas,
and pimientos, and baked over rolls.*

1 frying chicken, cut up	¼ cup milk
1 cup water	3 sprigs parsley, chopped
1 stalk celery	2 pimientos, cut up
1 onion	1 can (8 ounces) peas
Salt	
1 can cream-of-chicken soup	6 frankfurter rolls, partially split

Steam chicken in water with celery, onion, and a little salt until tender, about 45 minutes. Remove chicken from bones, and cut in chunks; strain stock. Combine ½ cup of stock, chicken soup, and milk; heat. Add cut chicken, parsley, pimiento, and peas. Put rolls, cut side up, in baking dish; pour mixture between and over top. Bake in 400° F. oven 15 minutes. Serves 6.

BACON AND POTATO BAKE

*You season it with celery
and seasoning salts and paprika.*

4 large potatoes, pared	1 teaspoon celery salt
3 onions, sliced	½ teaspoon paprika
⅓ cup flour	Water
2 teaspoons seasoned salt	½ pound sliced bacon

Quarter potatoes; put in shallow 2-quart casserole with onion. Sprinkle with flour and seasonings, toss until vegetables are well coated, and press them down in dish. Add water to half the depth of vegetables. Arrange bacon on top. Cover; bake in hot oven, 400° F., 30 minutes. Uncover; bake 20 minutes. Makes 4 servings.

BEEF-VEGETABLE BAKE

The vegetables: mushrooms, beans, corn.

2 onions, chopped	1 can (2 or 3 ounces) chopped mushrooms
1 green pepper, chopped	
3 cloves garlic, minced	1 can (15½ ounces) cut green beans
2 tablespoons fat	1 can (12 ounces) whole-kernel corn
1 pound ground beef	
1 can (28 ounces) tomatoes	1½ teaspoons salt
2 tablespoons chili powder	12 ounces thin spaghetti, cooked
1 cup mushroom, bean, corn liquid	2 cups shredded sharp cheddar cheese

Cook onion, pepper, and garlic in fat. Add meat, and cook until it loses its red color, stirring. Add tomatoes, chili powder, and liquid. Simmer, covered, 30 minutes. Add remaining ingredients, except cheese. Put half of mixture in baking dish; sprinkle with half the cheese. Add remaining mixture, and sprinkle with remaining cheese. Bake in 375° F. oven about 45 minutes. Serves 8 to 10.

LASAGNA

*You use noodles, tomato-meat sauce,
and three different kinds of cheese.*

8 ounces lasagna noodles	1 pound Ricotta cheese
2 tablespoons salt	8 ounces Mozzarella cheese, sliced
Boiling water	
1 tablespoon olive oil	Tomato-Meat Sauce
	½ cup grated Parmesan cheese

Cook noodles in boiling salted water 25 minutes, or until tender, stirring frequently. Drain; add oil. Arrange in shallow 2½-quart baking dish, making 3 layers each of cooked noodles, Ricotta, Mozzarella, Sauce, and grated cheese. Bake in moderate oven, 325° F., about 45 minutes. Makes 6 servings.

Tomato-Meat Sauce: Brown 1 minced medium onion and 2 minced cloves garlic lightly in ¼ cup olive oil in large saucepan. Add 1 pound ground beef, and brown lightly. Add 1 can (28 ounces) tomatoes, 1 can (6 ounces) tomato paste, 2 teaspoons salt, ⅛ teaspoon cayenne, 1 teaspoon sugar, pinch basil, 1 bay leaf, and 2 cups water. Simmer, uncovered, about 1½ hours.

BAKED TOMATO FARFALLE AND CHEESE

Farfalle is the macaroni made in the shape of bowknots.

8 ounces farfalle	1 can (19 ounces)
Salt	tomatoes
1 onion, chopped	1 can (6 ounces)
2 tablespoons butter	tomato paste
½ cup water	¼ teaspoon pepper
1 green pepper,	¾ pound sharp
cut up	cheddar cheese

Cook farfalle in boiling salted water until tender; drain, and put in shallow 2-quart casserole. Cook onion in butter until brown; add water, 1 teaspoon salt, and next 4 ingredients. Bring to boil, and pour on farfalle. Cut 8 thin slices of cheese; set aside. Shred remaining cheese. Add to farfalle, and stir lightly. Bake in moderate oven, 325°F., about 1 hour. Stir once during baking. Top with sliced cheese. Bake until cheese melts. Serves 4 to 6.

PORK CHOPS À L'AUVERGNE

Layers of pork chops and cabbage with a wine, cream, and sage sauce.

1 large white	½ teaspoon
cabbage	crumbled dried
Salt	sage leaves
Freshly ground	½ cup dry white
pepper	wine
1 cup heavy cream	¼ cup freshly
4 pork chops	grated Parmesan
Butter or margarine	cheese

Wash, quarter, core, and cut up cabbage. Soak 1 hour in salted water. Drain, and rinse in cold water. Put in saucepan, and sprinkle with salt and pepper. Add cream; bring to boil, and simmer 30 minutes. Trim excess fat from chops, and fry until golden brown in 2 tablespoons butter. Cover, and cook slowly until very tender. Season. Remove chops. Add sage and wine to skillet. Scrape skillet to remove all browned bits. Add to cabbage with more seasoning, if necessary. Put a layer of cabbage in shallow casserole. Cover with chops. Add remaining cabbage, and pour liquid over top. Sprinkle with cheese, and dot with 2 tablespoons butter. Bake in moderate oven, 350°F., about 45 minutes. Makes 4 servings.

BEEF AND LIMA CASSEROLE

The beef is boneless chuck.

1 pound dried	½ teaspoon pepper
Lima beans	¼ cup flour
2 pounds boneless	⅓ cup butter
beef chuck	or margarine
1 tablespoon salt	3 onions, sliced

Wash beans; add 6 cups water; boil 2 minutes. Let stand 1 hour; then cook until just tender. Cut meat in 1″ cubes; roll in seasoned flour. Brown in butter in skillet; add onions; brown. Add 2 cups water; bring to boil. Arrange alternate layers of meat and beans in 3-quart casserole. Add skillet liquid and enough water to cover. Cover; bake in 300° F. oven 2 hours. Serves 6.

BARBECUED PORK BIRDS

The sauce is a sweet-and-sour one with vinegar and brown sugar.

8 center-cut pork	1 clove garlic
chops (about 2	¾ cup water
pounds)	½ cup ketchup
Italian herb	2 tablespoons
seasoning	vinegar
Salt and pepper	1 tablespoon
Flour	brown sugar
2 tablespoons butter	1 teaspoon
1 onion, chopped	Worcestershire

Trim off bones and any excess fat from chops. Split almost all the way through, and open out. Pound lightly to flatten. Sprinkle with seasoning, salt and pepper. Roll up, and tie with string. Dredge with flour, and brown in butter. Put in casserole, and add onion and garlic. Mix remaining ingredients; pour over birds. Boil; cover, and bake in moderate oven, 375° F., about 1 hour. Serves 4.

OYSTERS AUX CROUTONS

You can prepare this
several hours before you bake it.

1 quart bread cubes	Juice ½ lemon
½ cup butter	1 small onion, grated
Salt and cayenne	½ cup cream
1 pint raw oysters, drained	Paprika

Remove crusts from bread; cut in ¼" cubes. Melt half the butter in a large skillet; add half the bread. Sprinkle with salt and cayenne. Toss lightly over low heat until bread cubes are crisp and golden brown. Then brown remaining bread in butter. Cover bottom of baking dish with bread cubes. Add half the oysters. Sprinkle with salt and cayenne, few drops of lemon juice, and a bit of grated onion. Add another layer of bread cubes, remaining oysters, and seasonings. Top with remaining bread cubes. Pour cream over all, and sprinkle with paprika. Bake in moderate oven, 325°F., 35 minutes. Serves 6.

KIDNEY-BEAN AND SAUSAGE BAKE

It's cooked with onions, mustard-
pickle relish, and Worcestershire.

2 cans (1 pound, 5 ounces each) kidney beans	2 tablespoons mustard-pickle relish
1 can (1 pound) onions, drained	1 pound brown-and-serve sausage
1 teaspoon Worcestershire	

Drain liquid from 1 can beans; leave other undrained. Put in shallow 2-quart casserole. Add onions, Worcestershire, and relish. Top with sausage, and bake in hot oven, 425°F., 25 minutes, or until sausages are browned. Serves 4.

SALMON MOUNDS WITH CURRY MUSHROOM SAUCE

For the sauce, you mix mushroom
soup, milk, curry powder, and paprika.

1 onion, minced	¼ cup minced parsley
¼ cup melted butter or margarine	¼ teaspoon salt
1 can (1 pound) salmon	Dash nutmeg
Milk	1 can cream-of-mushroom soup
3 cups soft bread crumbs	¾ teaspoon curry powder
2 eggs	½ teaspoon paprika
¼ teaspoon poultry seasoning	2 stuffed olives

Cook onion in butter until golden. Drain salmon, reserving liquid. Add enough milk to liquid to make ½ cup. Mix onion, salmon, liquid, crumbs, eggs, poultry seasoning, parsley, salt, and nutmeg. Shape into 6 mounds in large shallow baking dish. Mix ½ cup milk, soup, curry powder, and paprika. Pour around salmon. Top each salmon mound with a slice of olive. Bake, uncovered, in moderate oven, 350°F., about 45 minutes. Makes 6 servings.

Tuna Mounds: Use above recipe; substitute 2 cans (7 ounces each) tuna for the salmon. Drain tuna. Use ½ cup milk for the liquid.

CHEESE-PORK SPAGHETTI

It's spiced with
soy sauce and Worcestershire.

1 pound end pork chops, boned	1 tablespoon Worcestershire
1 tablespoon fat	½ teaspoon sugar
1 large onion, chopped	½ teaspoon pepper
½ cup diced celery	1½ teaspoons salt
1 can (19 ounces) tomatoes	8 ounces spaghetti
2 tablespoons soy sauce	1 cup shredded sharp cheddar cheese

Cube pork, and brown in fat. Add onion and celery; cook 5 minutes. Add remaining ingredients, except spaghetti and cheese, and simmer 30 minutes. Cook, and drain spaghetti. Mix with sauce in 2-quart casserole. Sprinkle with cheese. Bake in moderate oven, 350° F., about 30 minutes. Serves 6.

PAELLA

A rice dish with chicken, sausage, and three different kinds of seafood.

2 frying chickens (about 2 pounds each)
Vegetable oil
Salt
1½ cups uncooked rice
2 cloves garlic, minced
1 bay leaf, crumbled
Large pinch saffron
¼ teaspoon pepper
1 cup canned tomatoes

3 cups water
1 green pepper, slivered
1 pimiento, sliced
Dash cayenne
1 pound hot Spanish or Italian sausage
1 dozen little-neck clams, shucked
1 pound shrimp, cooked, shelled, and cleaned
1 lobster tail, cooked, cut up
1 cup peas, cooked

Cut chickens in 20 pieces. Fry in shallow hot oil in skillet until browned. Put in large casserole, and sprinkle with 1 teaspoon salt. Put rice and garlic in skillet, and cook until rice is lightly browned. Add 2½ teaspoons salt and next 8 ingredients. Bring to boil, and pour on chicken. Cover, and bake in hot oven, 425°F., 25 minutes. Cut sausage in 1″ pieces, and fry until browned. Add sausage and remaining ingredients to casserole, stirring lightly with fork. Reduce heat to 375° F., and bake, covered, 15 minutes, or until thoroughly heated. Serves 8 to 10.

CHEESE SPOON SPREAD

The cheese is process American.

¾ cup corn meal
1 teaspoon salt
⅛ teaspoon pepper
1 tablespoon sugar
1 cup water

2 tablespoons butter
2 cups milk
½ pound process American cheese
3 eggs, beaten

In saucepan mix corn meal, salt, pepper, sugar, water, butter, and 1 cup of the milk. Bring to boil, and cook, stirring, until thickened. Cut two thirds of cheese in small pieces. Stir into corn-meal mixture. Add remaining 1 cup milk and the eggs. Mix well, and pour into 4 individual baking dishes, or 1½-quart casserole. Slice remaining cheese, and put on top of baking dishes. Bake in moderate oven, 325°F., about 35 minutes for individual dishes, 45 minutes for large one. Serves 4.

TUNA-CHEESE PUFF

This dish stands before baking so all the flavor soaks into the bread.

8 slices firm-type bread
1 can (7 ounces) tuna fish
4 slices process American cheese
2 tablespoons soft butter
⅔ cup nonfat-milk powder

½ teaspoon dry mustard
¼ teaspoon salt
⅛ teaspoon pepper
Dash paprika
Few sprigs parsley, chopped
1½ cups water
2 eggs, slightly beaten

Trim crusts from bread. Put half of bread in shallow baking dish. Drain, and flake tuna, and put on top of bread. Cover with cheese. Spread remaining bread with butter, and put on cheese. Mix remaining ingredients, and pour over top. Let stand 15 minutes. Bake in moderate oven, 350°F., 50 minutes. Serves 4.

SAVORY BEEF PIE

It has salami, onion, and carrots, too.

Pastry (recipe made with 2 cups flour)
3 cups diced cooked beef
½ cup diced salami
1 onion, chopped

¼ cup fat
¼ cup flour
1 teaspoon salt
¼ teaspoon pepper
2 cups stock or bouillon
1½ cups cooked diced carrots

Line a 10″x 6″x 2″ baking dish with pastry. Brown beef, salami, and onion in fat. Blend in flour and seasonings. Gradually add stock; cook, stirring, until thickened. Add carrots; pour into lined baking dish. Top with pastry, lattice fashion. Crimp edges. Bake in hot oven, 425° F., 30 minutes. Serves 6.

CREOLE STUFFED PEPPERS

The stuffing: seasoned beef and rice.

4 large green peppers	½ teaspoon Accent Seasoned salt, and pepper to taste
1 pound ground beef	Creole Sauce
2 cups cooked rice	

Split peppers; wash, and remove seeds and membrane. Parboil 5 minutes; drain. Cook beef until it loses its red color. Pour off fat. Mix beef, rice, and seasonings. Add ¼ cup Sauce. Pack peppers with the mixture. Put in large shallow baking dish. Pour about three-fourths of remaining Sauce around peppers. Cover; bake in moderate oven, 350°F., 45 minutes. Serve with remaining Sauce, heated. Serves 8.

Creole Sauce: Cook 1 chopped onion and ½ cup diced celery in 2 tablespoons butter 5 minutes. Add 1 can (15½ ounces) spaghetti sauce, 1 can (8 ounces) tomato sauce, 1 cup water, 1 bay leaf, 2 whole cloves, and salt and pepper. Simmer 15 minutes.

BLUE-CHEESE LIMA BAKE

As the cheese melts, its piquant flavor permeates the beans.

1 box frozen Lima beans, cooked	2 tablespoons fine dry bread crumbs
1 cup crumbled blue cheese	2 tablespoons melted butter
¼ cup consommé or bean liquid	⅛ teaspoon paprika

Put beans and cheese in 1-quart casserole. Add consommé. Mix remaining ingredients, and sprinkle on top. Bake in moderate oven, 375°F., about 25 minutes. Makes 4 servings.

BAKED PORK AND BEANS

Marrow or pea beans, bake with: pork, molasses, ketchup, brown sugar.

1 pound dried marrow or pea beans	¼ cup molasses
	¼ cup ketchup
6 cups water	2 teaspoons Worcestershire
1 clove garlic, minced	1 teaspoon salt
1 onion, sliced	Dash pepper
1 small dried hot red pepper or dash cayenne	1 teaspoon dry mustard
	¼ cup minced onion
1 bay leaf	2 tablespoons brown sugar
1 pound salt pork	

Wash beans; put in large kettle, and add water. Bring to boil, and boil 2 minutes. Let stand 1 hour. Add garlic, sliced onion, hot pepper, bay leaf, and pork (left in one piece). Bring again to boil; reduce heat, and simmer 1½ hours, or until tender but not mushy. Drain, reserving liquid. Skim off any fat. To 1 cup liquid, add molasses, ketchup, Worcestershire, salt, pepper, mustard, and minced onion; mix well. Put beans in 2-quart shallow baking dish. Pour liquid on beans. Remove rind from pork, and cut pork in slices. Put on beans. Sprinkle with brown sugar. Bake, uncovered, in hot oven, 400°F., about 1¼ hours, adding more liquid if necessary. Makes 6 to 8 servings.

SAVORY SAUSAGE AND SPLIT-PEA CASSEROLE

The topping is a generous sprinkling of grated cheddar cheese.

1 pound split peas	½ teaspoon seasoned salt
5 cups water	¼ teaspoon pepper
1 teaspoon salt	½ teaspoon Worcestershire
1 pound pork-sausage meat	1 cup grated cheddar cheese
2 tablespoons minced onion	

Cook peas with water and salt 35 minutes, or until peas are just tender. Drain, reserving ½ cup of the liquid. Brown sausage meat, breaking up with fork. Mix peas lightly with sausage and fat, ½ cup liquid, and remaining ingredients, except cheese. Put in shallow baking dish. Sprinkle with cheese. Bake in hot oven, 400°F., about 30 minutes. Makes 6 generous servings.

SAVORY TURKEY SQUARES WITH MUSHROOM SAUCE

The turkey squares have the texture of baked turkey stuffing.

3 cups coarsely chopped or ground cooked turkey	2 tablespoons minced parsley
2 cups soft bread crumbs	3 eggs, slightly beaten
1 cup turkey broth or 1 chicken bouillon cube and 1 cup water	1 tablespoon lemon juice
1 teaspoon Accent	2 tablespoons instant minced onion
⅔ cup minced celery	1 pimiento, chopped
	⅔ cup cream
	Salt and pepper
	Mushroom Sauce

Mix all ingredients, except seasonings and Mushroom Sauce. Season. Pour into 12"x 7"x 2" baking dish, and put in pan of hot water. Bake in moderate oven, 350°F., 50 to 60 minutes. Cut in squares, and serve with Sauce. Makes 6 to 8 servings.

Mushroom Sauce: In saucepan blend ¼ cup soft turkey fat or butter and ¼ cup flour; heat until bubbly, stirring. Gradually stir in 2 cups turkey broth, and cook, stirring, until thickened. Drain 1 can (3 ounces) chopped mushrooms. Add to sauce, and season with salt, pepper, poultry seasoning.

EGGPLANT PARMIGIANA

This contains two kinds of cheese: Parmesan and Mozzarella.

1 large eggplant	¼ cup grated Parmesan cheese
¾ cup olive oil	½ pound Mozzarella cheese, sliced thin
1½ cups canned tomato sauce, or Tomato-Meat Sauce, page 124	

Pare eggplant, and cut in ¼" slices. Fry on both sides in oil in skillet until brown, and drain well on absorbent paper. Put layer of eggplant slices in shallow baking dish; cover with some of the sauce, a little of the Parmesan cheese, and a few slices of Mozzarella. Repeat layers until all ingredients are used, ending with Mozzarella. Bake in hot oven, 400°F., 15 minutes, or until thoroughly heated. Serves 4 generously.

YANKEE LOBSTER PIES

Sherry-creamed lobster with cheese, potato-chip, and cracker-meal topping.

¾ cup butter or margarine	½ cup cracker meal
½ cup sherry	1 teaspoon paprika
2 cups cut-up cooked lobster	3 tablespoons crushed potato chips
2 tablespoons flour	2 tablespoons grated Parmesan cheese
½ teaspoon salt	
1½ cups light cream	
4 egg yolks	

Melt ¼ cup butter; add sherry; boil 2 minutes. Remove from heat, and add lobster. Melt ¼ cup butter in top of double boiler over simmering water. Stir in flour and salt. Add cream and sherry mixture, drained from lobster. Cook, stirring until thickened. Beat egg yolks; gradually stir in hot sauce. Return to double boiler, and cook over simmering water 3 minutes, stirring. Add lobster, and put into 4 individual baking dishes. Mix remaining ingredients with remaining ¼ cup melted butter. Sprinkle over top. Bake in slow oven, 300° F., about 15 minutes, or until thoroughly heated. Makes 4 servings.

BEEF-POTATO BAKE

Ground beef and cooked potatoes are baked with spaghetti sauce.

Cook 8 peeled potatoes 15 minutes. Put in casserole. Partially cook ½ pound ground beef. Add 1 can (15½ ounces) spaghetti sauce, 1 minced clove garlic, 1 minced onion, and 1 tablespoon chopped parsley; bring to boil. Pour over potatoes. Sprinkle with ¼ cup grated Parmesan or Romano cheese. Bake in moderate oven, 350°F., about 1 hour. Makes 4 servings.

HERB CHICKEN CASSEROLE

*Buttered, herbed chicken
is steamed in consommé.*

1 frying chicken, cut up	1 teaspoon salt
¼ cup soft butter or margarine	½ teaspoon pepper
	1 large carrot, sliced
1 tablespoon paprika	2 slices bacon, diced
1 teaspoon thyme	½ cup consommé

Wash, and dry frying chicken. Mix butter and seasonings, and spread on chicken pieces. Put in casserole. Add remaining ingredients. Cover; bake in 400° F. oven 1 hour, or until chicken and carrot are tender. Serves 4.

CORNED-BEEF AND VEGETABLE BAKE

*Corned beef, potatoes, and corn
with a sprinkling of cheddar cheese.*

1 tablespoon instant minced onion	1 teaspoon salt
	¼ teaspoon pepper
1 can (12 ounces) corned beef, broken in pieces	3 tablespoons melted butter
	3 tablespoons flour
2 cups diced cooked potato	1 can (16 ounces) whole-kernel corn, undrained
1¼ cups evaporated milk	⅓ cup shredded cheddar cheese

Mix onion, corned beef, potato, ½ cup milk, ½ teaspoon salt, ⅛ teaspoon pepper. Press against sides and bottom of shallow 2-quart casserole. Melt butter in skillet; blend in flour and remaining salt and pepper. Add liquid from corn and remaining milk; cook, stirring, until thickened. Add corn; pour into lined casserole. Sprinkle with cheese. Bake in moderate oven, 350°F., about 30 minutes. Makes 6 servings.

PIQUANT LIVER AND VEGETABLES

You can use beef, pork, or lamb liver.

2 ounces (¼ cup) diced salt pork	3 carrots, scraped
	1 can (4 ounces) sliced mushrooms
¾ pound beef, pork, or lamb liver	1 cup canned tomatoes
2 teaspoons salt	2 stalks celery, diced
¼ teaspoon pepper	
2 tablespoons flour	4 small white onions, peeled
3 medium potatoes	

Brown pork; remove from skillet. Remove membrane and large tubes from liver; cut liver in 1″ cubes. Dredge liver with 1 teaspoon salt, ⅛ teaspoon pepper, and the flour mixed together. Brown on all sides in hot fat. Peel, and quarter potatoes. Quarter carrots. Drain mushrooms, reserving liquid. Put tomatoes and 1 cup mushroom liquid and water in skillet; bring to boil. Add remaining salt and pepper. Put liver, pork, and vegetables in 1½-quart casserole; pour tomato mixture over top. Cover; bake in hot oven, 400°F., 1½ hours. Uncover last half hour. Serves 4.

CASSOULET

*A slow-cooking dish with beef, sausage,
and kidney beans baked in red wine.*

1 pound dried red kidney beans	2 cloves garlic, minced
6 cups water	½ teaspoon crushed dried rosemary
½ pound pork-sausage links	
1 pound boneless beef chuck, cubed	2 teaspoons salt
	¼ teaspoon pepper
	¾ cup dry red wine
2 medium onions, chopped	1½ cups bean liquid

Wash beans, and bring to boil with water; boil 2 minutes. Let stand 1 hour. Then simmer until almost tender. Cut sausages in half, and fry in skillet until browned. Remove sausage. Brown beef, onion, and garlic in fat remaining in pan; put in 3-quart casserole. Add seasonings and wine. Cover, and bake in moderate oven, 350°F., 1 hour. Add beans, sausage, and bean liquid. Recover, and bake 1½ hours longer, or until beans and meat are very tender. Makes 6 servings.

MANICOTTI

Fluffy pancakes with a cheese filling are baked in tomato sauce.

1 cup sifted flour	¼ teaspoon pepper
1 cup water	½ pound
Salt	Mozzarella, cut in
7 eggs	12 strips
2 pounds Ricotta	3 cans (8 ounces
Grated Parmesan or	each) tomato
Romano cheese	sauce

To make pancakes: Combine flour, water, and ¼ teaspoon salt; beat until smooth. Beat in 4 eggs, one at a time. Heat a 5″ to 6″ skillet, and grease with a few drops oil. Put about 3 tablespoons batter in hot skillet, and roll pan around to distribute evenly. Cook over low heat until firm (do not brown). Turn, and cook lightly on other side. Continue making pancakes until all batter is used. This amount will make 12 to 14 pancakes. (Do not grease skillet a second time.)

To make filling: Mix ½ teaspoon salt, 3 eggs, Ricotta, ¼ cup grated cheese, and the pepper. Put about 2 tablespoons filling and a strip of Mozzarella on each pancake, and roll up. Pour 1 can tomato sauce into large shallow baking dish. Put pancakes, seam side down, in sauce. Cover with remaining 2 cans sauce, and sprinkle with ½ cup grated cheese. Bake in 350° F. oven, 45 minutes. Makes 6 generous servings.

DRIED-BEEF CASSEROLE

The beef is baked between two layers of chow-mein noodles.

¼ pound dried beef	1 can cream-of-
Boiling water	mushroom soup
½ cup diced celery	¼ teaspoon
1 can (8½ ounces)	garlic salt
peas, undrained	¼ teaspoon pepper
1 can cream-of-	1 can (3½ ounces)
chicken soup	chow-mein
	noodles

Tear beef in pieces. Cover with boiling water; drain, and mix with remaining ingredients, except noodles. Arrange half of noodles in shallow casserole. Add beef mixture, and top with noodles. Bake in moderate oven, 375°F., about 30 minutes. Makes 6 servings.

SEAFOOD SUPREME

This baked dish contains crab meat, lobster tails, cod, and shrimp soup.

2 cans (6½ ounces	1 can cream-of-
each) king crab	mushroom soup
meat or 2 boxes	½ cup heavy
(6 ounces each)	cream
frozen crab meat,	2 tablespoons
thawed	sherry
2 lobster tails,	Dash pepper
cooked and	2 tablespoons fine
cut up	dry bread crumbs
1 pound cod fillets,	¼ cup grated
poached	Parmesan cheese
1 can frozen shrimp	Paprika
soup, thawed	2 tablespoons butter

Flake crab meat, removing membrane. Add all but last 4 ingredients; mix well. Pour into shallow baking dish. Sprinkle with crumbs, cheese, and paprika. Dot with butter. Bake in moderate oven, 350°F., about 30 minutes. Makes 6 servings.

DEVILED-HAM AND CORN PUDDING

A little sugar makes it sweet; evaporated milk makes it creamy.

Drain, and reserve liquid from 1 can (16 ounces) whole-kernel corn. Add liquid to 1 cup evaporated milk with enough water to make 2 cups. Beat 4 eggs; add corn, milk mixture, 2 tablespoons melted butter, 1 large or 2 small cans deviled ham, 1 tablespoon sugar, ½ teaspoon salt, ⅛ teaspoon pepper. Mix well; turn into 1½-quart casserole. Set in pan of hot water, and bake in moderate oven, 350°F., 1 hour, or until knife inserted in center comes out clean. Makes 4 servings.

BAKED VEAL PAPRIKA

You garnish it with sour cream.

¼ pound lean salt pork	3 beef bouillon cubes
3 pounds boneless stewing veal	1½ cups hot water
Flour	1½ teaspoons salt
1 pound fresh mushrooms, sliced	½ teaspoon pepper
	2 tablespoons paprika
1 onion, sliced	1 cup sour cream
	Chopped parsley

Cut pork in small pieces, and fry in large heavy kettle until crisp; remove. Cut veal in 1½" pieces, and roll in flour. Brown lightly in pork fat. Then add mushrooms and onion. Cook 15 minutes, stirring often. Dissolve bouillon cubes in water, and add with pork and seasonings to first mixture. Put in 2½-quart casserole; cover, and bake in moderate oven, 350°F., 1½ to 2 hours, or until veal is very tender. Just before serving, top with sour cream; sprinkle with parsley. Makes 6 servings.

CARAWAY ONION-CHEESE PIE

The cheese is cheddar.

2 cups thinly sliced onion	3 eggs, slightly beaten
2 tablespoons butter	1½ cups shredded cheddar cheese
9" unbaked pastry shell	¾ teaspoon salt
¾ teaspoon dry mustard	¼ teaspoon pepper
1 tablespoon cold water	1 teaspoon caraway seed

Cook onion in butter until tender, but not brown. Put in pastry shell. Mix mustard with cold water until blended; add remaining ingredients, except caraway seed. Pour over onions. Sprinkle with seed. Bake in hot oven, 400° F., about 40 minutes. Makes 6 servings.

CHICKEN AND OYSTER CASSEROLE

The casserole has a heavy-cream sauce and a topping of toasted almonds.

1 large frying chicken, cut up	½ cup boiling water
¼ cup flour	½ cup heavy cream
Salt and pepper	18 oysters
2 tablespoons shortening	2 tablespoons toasted slivered almonds

Reserve back, wings, and neck of chicken for later use. Wash remaining pieces, and dry. Dredge with flour mixed with ½ teaspoon salt and ⅛ teaspoon pepper. Brown on all sides in hot fat. Remove to 1½-quart casserole. Add boiling water; cover, and bake in moderate oven, 350°F., 1 hour, or until tender. Add cream, ¾ teaspoon salt, ⅛ teaspoon pepper, and the oysters. Cover, and bake 10 minutes longer. Sprinkle with almonds, and serve at once, with hot baking powder biscuits, if desired. Makes 4 servings.

BEEF PINWHEEL CASSEROLE

It's beef, onion, peas, tomatoes, and biscuit dough.

1½ cups ground cooked beef	1 can (1 pound) peas
1 onion, chopped	1 can (1 pound) tomatoes
¼ teaspoon each thyme and pepper	1½ tablespoons flour
1½ teaspoons salt	Biscuit dough, made with 2 cups biscuit mix or 2 cups flour
2 tablespoons fat or drippings	

Cook beef, onion, and seasonings in fat a few minutes. Reserve 1 cup. To remainder, add peas and tomatoes. Blend flour with a little cold water; stir into mixture; cook until slightly thickened. Pour into 2-quart casserole. Roll biscuit dough into a 24"x 6" rectangle. Spread with reserved meat mixture. Roll up jelly-roll fashion. Form in ring around edge of casserole; press ends together. With scissors, cut slices through ring almost to center, about 1" apart. Turn each slice slightly on its side. Bake in very hot oven, 450°F., 20 to 25 minutes. Makes 4 servings.

The memory of the big iron Dutch oven quietly simmering on the back of the stove lingers on for those who were born before the era of "quick cooking." What wonderful aromas came from that homely black utensil. You could sniff for hours before dinnertime, slowly building up a glowing appetite. Rich smells of onion, garlic, herbs, turnip, and other vegetables mingled with savory aromas of meat: the glorious pot roast. Strangely enough, to many people, "pot roast" automatically means beef. Yet the term refers only to a *method* of cooking. Veal, pork, chicken, or any type of meat can be prepared as a pot roast. Roasting in the pot is especially suited to meat or fowl that needs tenderizing by long, slow cooking with a little moisture in a covered pot. Pot roasts can be prepared on top of the stove, over a slow burner, or in a slow oven. Here are a number of fine pot roasts prepared with a variety of meats. They range from the old-fashioned Yankee pot roast to duck cooked Spanish style. Or for a change, try liver, kidney, or heart cooked in the pot. A flavorful summer pot roast, served cold, is the Italian *vitello tonato,* veal with tuna sauce. These are rules to remember when pot-roasting: season well for a savory dish; don't cook the roast too fast; don't let it get dry; don't overcook.

POT

ROASTS

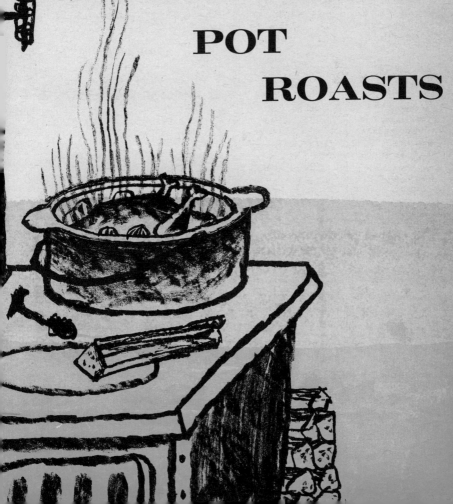

PEPPERY BEEF

You can serve this stuffed, rolled brisket of beef either hot or cold.

4 pounds boneless fresh beef brisket	2 tablespoons fine dry bread crumbs
1 tablespoon whole black peppers	1 teaspoon garlic salt
1½ teaspoons salt	1 cup hot water
¼ teaspoon ground allspice	1 onion, sliced

Have butcher pound brisket flat. Put on board, and with a heavy knife, score the meat lengthwise and crosswise on both sides. Put the peppers in a small cloth bag, and crush with hammer or mallet. Sprinkle meat with crushed peppers, salt, allspice, crumbs, and garlic salt. Roll very tightly lengthwise. Cut in two crosswise pieces. Tie firmly with string. Put on a rack in heavy kettle. Add hot water and the onion; cover, and simmer for about 4 hours, adding more water, if necessary. Serve hot, or cool in broth; chill. Serves 8.

BEEF WITH RED WINE

This dish has the French touch, with wine and a little salt pork.

3 pounds beef for pot roast	1 onion, sliced
¼ pound salt pork, diced	1 bay leaf, crumbled
Salt and pepper	½ clove garlic, minced
½ cup water	Flour
1 cup dry red wine	

Brown meat on all sides with the salt pork in a heavy kettle. Sprinkle with salt and pepper. Place a rack in bottom of kettle under meat; add remaining ingredients. Cover, and simmer 3 to 3½ hours. Remove meat, and thicken liquid with a flour-and-water paste. Add salt and pepper to taste. Makes 4 servings.

BEEF BRISKET WITH MUSHROOM GRAVY

You use sliced fresh mushrooms for the gravy.

4 pounds boneless fresh beef brisket	¼ pound mushrooms, sliced
1 onion, sliced	2 tablespoons butter
Salt and pepper	
Flour	

In large heavy kettle, brown beef in its own fat. Pour off fat. Add onion; cover, and cook over low heat 1 hour. Put meat in shallow pan to cool. Cut into attractive serving-size slices. Return to kettle, and sprinkle with salt and pepper. Cover, and simmer 2 hours, or until tender. Turn slices once. Remove meat to hot platter. To make gravy: skim off fat; add a little flour-and-water paste, and cook until slightly thickened. Add mushrooms browned lightly in the butter. Makes 6 servings.

SAUERBRATEN

You marinate the beef for two or three days before cooking it.

4 to 5 pounds round of beef	½ teaspoon dried thyme
2 onions sliced	1 sprig parsley
1 carrot, sliced	4 tablespoons margarine
1 stalk celery, sliced	3 tablespoons flour
2 cups red wine vinegar	2 tablespoons red currant jelly
1 tablespoon salt	Gingersnaps
1 tablespoon mixed pickling spice	

Put meat in a deep bowl or crock. Mix vegetables, vinegar, seasonings, herbs; pour over meat. Store, covered, in the refrigerator for 2 or 3 days, turning meat once or twice. Remove meat from marinade, and wipe dry. Brown on all sides in 1 tablespoon margarine in heavy kettle. Remove meat, and melt remaining 3 tablespoons margarine in kettle. Blend in flour. Add the strained marinade and the meat. Cover, and simmer 2½ hours, or until meat is tender. Remove meat, and blend jelly and 4 or 5 gingersnaps into liquid in pan. If necessary, add more gingersnaps to thicken mixture, or add more jelly. Serve meat sliced with the gravy. Makes 4 servings, with meat left over.

GINGER BEEF

Tomatoes and beef broth provide the liquid necessary for pot-roasting.

4 pounds beef for pot roast	2 cloves garlic, minced
1 teaspoon turmeric	1 cup canned tomatoes
2 teaspoons ginger	1 cup broth or bouillon
2 teaspoons salt	2 dried red peppers, crushed
2 tablespoons fat	
2 onions, chopped	

Rub meat with next 3 ingredients. Brown on all sides in fat in heavy kettle. Put meat on rack in kettle. Add remaining ingredients, cover, and simmer 3½ hours. Serves 6.

POT ROAST, CHINESE STYLE

Ginger and soy sauce provide the Oriental touch in this beef roast.

3 pounds beef for pot roast	½ teaspoon ginger
2 tablespoons flour	¼ cup soy sauce
1 tablespoon fat	2 large onions, sliced
½ cup water	Hot cooked rice

Dredge meat with flour, and brown on all sides in fat in heavy kettle. Put a rack in kettle under meat; add water, ginger, and soy sauce. Cover, and simmer 2½ to 3 hours. Add onion; simmer half-hour longer, or until onion is tender. Remove the meat, and slice it. Pour the drippings and onion over the sliced meat. Serve with fluffy dry rice. Makes 4 servings.

YANKEE POT ROAST

It's beef cooked with onion, turnip, carrot, celery, and parsley.

4 pounds beef for pot roast	½ cup diced turnip
1 teaspoon salt	½ cup diced carrot
¼ cup water	¼ cup cut celery, with leaves
1 medium onion, sliced	2 tablespoons chopped parsley

Brown meat on all sides in heavy kettle, adding a small amount of fat if necessary. Sprinkle with salt. Put a rack in kettle under meat; add water and onion. Cover, and simmer 3½ to 4 hours. Add remaining ingredients. Simmer ½ hour, or until vegetables are done. Then remove meat, and thicken liquid with a flour-and-water paste, if desired. Season to taste. Makes 6 servings.

BARBECUED SHORT RIBS

The barbecue sauce calls for mustard, Worcestershire, celery, salt, pepper.

3 pounds beef short ribs	½ cup sliced celery
1 onion, chopped	1½ teaspoons salt
½ cup water	⅛ teaspoon pepper
2 tablespoons Worcestershire	
1 teaspoon prepared mustard	

Brown short ribs on all sides in heavy kettle; pour off fat. Add remaining ingredients; cover, and simmer 2 hours, or until tender, turning meat several times and adding more water if necessary. Makes 4 servings.

BEEF LOAF WITH CARROTS

Ground beef is shaped into a loaf, then pot-roasted with whole carrots.

½ cup tomato juice	¼ teaspoon dried sage
½ cup fine dry bread crumbs	2 tablespoons instant minced onion
1 pound ground beef	
Salt	Flour
Dash of cayenne	1 tablespoon fat
⅛ teaspoon seasoned salt	¾ cup water
	8 carrots, peeled

Mix tomato juice and crumbs; let stand 5 minutes. Add beef, 1 teaspoon salt, cayenne, seasoned salt, sage, and onion. Mix well, and shape into loaf; dredge with flour, and brown slowly on all sides in fat in heavy kettle. Slip low rack under loaf, and add water. Put carrots around meat, and sprinkle with ½ teaspoon salt. Cover, and cook over very low heat about 1 hour, adding water if needed. Makes 4 servings.

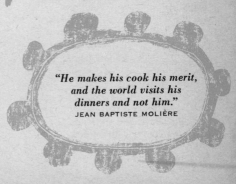

"He makes his cook his merit, and the world visits his dinners and not him."
JEAN BAPTISTE MOLIÈRE

FRUITED SPICED BEEF

*You use dried mixed fruit and
a generous amount of pickling spice.*

5 pounds beef for pot roast	2 tablespoons mixed pickling spice
2 tablespoons fat	2 teaspoons salt
2 cups water	1 pound dried mixed fruit

Brown the meat on all sides in hot fat in large heavy kettle. Remove meat, and pour off fat. Add water, and bring to boil. Put meat on rack in kettle; add pickling spice. Cover, and simmer 2½ hours. Add salt and fruit, and simmer 1 hour longer, or until meat is tender. Slice meat, and serve with the liquid poured over top. Garnish with cooked dried fruit. Makes 6 servings, with meat left over.

COFFEE POT ROAST WITH VEGETABLES

*Coffee gives this an elusive
and tantalizing flavor.*

2 pounds beef for pot roast	6 carrots, peeled and diced
1 cup each tomatoes, water, black coffee	2 cups diced potato
Salt and pepper	1 box frozen peas
1 onion, chopped	

Brown meat on all sides in heavy kettle, adding a small amount of fat if necessary. Add tomatoes, liquids, salt, pepper. Bring to boil; cover, and simmer 1 hour. Add onion and carrot; simmer 15 minutes. Add potato, and cook until vegetables are tender. Add peas; cook a few minutes. If desired, thicken gravy with flour blended with a little cold water. Makes 6 servings.

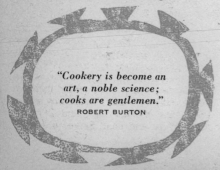

"Cookery is become an art, a noble science; cooks are gentlemen."
ROBERT BURTON

BEEF IN SPAGHETTI SAUCE

*An Italian-style dish with garlic,
herb seasoning, and Parmesan cheese.*

4 pounds beef for pot roast	1 teaspoon salt
2 tablespoons olive oil	¼ teaspoon pepper
1 onion, chopped	2 cans (8 ounces each) tomato sauce
1 clove garlic, minced	Water
1 teaspoon Italian mixed dried-herb seasoning	1 pound spaghetti
	Grated Parmesan or Romano cheese

Brown meat on all sides in oil in heavy kettle. Put meat on rack in kettle. Add next 5 ingredients. Mix tomato sauce with 1 cup water, and pour over meat. Cover, and simmer 3½ hours, or until meat is tender, adding 2 more cups of water at intervals during the cooking. Cook, and drain spaghetti. Remove meat to a hot platter, slice, and top with some of the sauce. Toss remaining sauce with the spaghetti, and serve with grated Parmesan or Romano cheese. Makes 6 servings.

SAVORY STUFFED HEART

Beef heart simmers on a bed of rice.

1¼ cups rice, uncooked	Salt and pepper
Few celery leaves, chopped	1 beef heart
3 onions, chopped	2 tablespoons fat
1 teaspoon poultry seasoning or ½ teaspoon each thyme and sage	2 cups beef bouillon, broth, or water

Cook, and drain rice. Mix with next 3 ingredients; season to taste with salt and pepper. Remove large tubes and as much fat as possible from heart. Season well inside and out with salt and pepper. Fill with some of rice mixture, and sew edges together. Brown well in hot fat in heavy kettle. Cover, and cook slowly without added water 2 hours. Remove meat, and pour off all fat. Put remaining rice mixture in kettle; add bouillon, and season to taste. Put heart on top, cover, and simmer 1 hour, or until meat is tender. Makes 8 servings.

WEST INDIAN POT ROAST

*Pot roast of beef is
cooked with coconut liquid.*

1 can flaked coconut	Flour
1¼ cups boiling water	2 tablespoons fat
	Salt and pepper
	1 onion, sliced
3 pounds beef for pot roast	1 clove garlic, minced

Put coconut in bowl, and cover with boiling water; let stand until cold. Strain, reserving liquid. Dredge meat with flour, and brown on all sides in fat in heavy kettle. Pour off fat, and put meat on rack in kettle. Season with salt and pepper, and add coconut liquid, onion, and garlic. Simmer, covered, 3 to 3½ hours, or until tender. Remove meat, and thicken liquid, if desired. Makes 4 servings.

VITELLO TONATO

*It has a sauce of puréed
anchovies and tuna fish.*

3½ pounds veal cut from the leg	2 egg yolks
Celery	1½ cups uncooked rice
Olive oil	6 green onions, sliced
3 carrots	
10 fillets of anchovy	1 red onion, chopped
½ a sour pickle	½ green pepper, chopped
2 cans (7 ounces each) tuna fish	12 each ripe and green olives, chopped
1 cup dry white wine	
2 cloves garlic	¼ cup minced parsley
Salt, pepper, thyme	Tarragon vinegar

Simmer veal, 4 celery stalks, ½ cup olive oil, 1 carrot, next 5 ingredients, and seasonings about 3 hours. When tender, cool in pot. Purée ingredients, except meat, in an electric blender, or force through a food mill. Beat egg yolks, and stir in ½ cup oil, a few drops at a time. When thickened, beat in puréed mixture. Cook, and cool rice. Add 2 chopped carrots; 1 cup diced celery; green and red onion; green pepper; olives; parsley; oil, vinegar, and salt and pepper to taste. Add a little purée. Serve veal sliced very thin with the purée as a sauce, and with the rice salad. Garnish with artichokes and pimientos, if desired. Serves 8.

"Good cooks always have
good tempers."
OLD SAYING

SWEET-SOUR POT ROAST

*Sugar provides the sweet,
and vinegar provides the sour.*

4 pounds beef for pot roast	¾ cup vinegar
	Cold water
2 tablespoons fat	½ cup brown sugar
1 medium onion, sliced	
	Dash allspice
Salt and pepper	Flour

Brown meat slowly in fat. Add onion, and cook 5 minutes longer. Sprinkle lightly with salt and pepper. Add vinegar, ½ cup water, sugar, and allspice. Cover, and simmer 4 hours, or until tender. Remove meat, and thicken gravy with flour mixed with a little cold water. Makes 6 servings.

VEAL BREAST FILIPINO

*You marinate the veal in soy sauce,
vinegar, and herbs, then pot-roast it.*

2 pounds veal breast	¼ cup flour
¼ cup soy sauce	3 tablespoons fat
1 tablespoon vinegar	¾ cup boiling water
½ teaspoon each salt and pepper	1 can (8 ounces) white onions, drained
1 teaspoon ginger	

Put veal in deep bowl. Mix soy sauce, vinegar, and seasonings. Pour over veal, and let stand at least 30 minutes, turning meat several times. Lift meat from marinade; roll in flour, and brown in hot fat. Put a rack under meat in kettle. Add marinade and boiling water. Cover, and simmer for about 2 hours. Add onions, and heat. Serves 4.

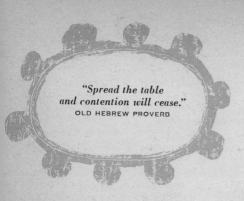

SPICY RUMP OF VEAL

*There's brown sugar in this
in addition to the spices.*

5 pounds rump of veal	2 tablespoons vegetable oil
1 tablespoon each brown sugar, dry mustard, and salt	2 tablespoons vinegar
	1 teaspoon basil
½ teaspoon pepper	1 clove garlic, minced
	½ cup water

Rub veal with mixture of sugar and seasonings. Brown on all sides in oil in heavy kettle. Put meat on rack. Add remaining ingredients, cover, and simmer 2½ hours, or until meat is tender, basting occasionally with liquid in kettle, and adding more water if necessary. Makes 8 servings.

VEAL NECK WITH TOMATO GRAVY

*If you like, you can add vegetables
to this dish.*

3 pounds veal neck	¼ teaspoon each dried thyme and marjoram
Seasoned flour	1 bay leaf
2 tablespoons fat	Salt and pepper
1 clove garlic, minced	1 can (8 ounces) tomato sauce
	½ cup water

Roll meat in seasoned flour, and brown on all sides in hot fat in heavy kettle. Pour off fat. Add remaining ingredients, cover, and simmer 1½ to 2 hours. Serve meat with liquid in kettle; thicken with a flour-and-water paste, if desired. Makes 4 servings.

VEAL SHOULDER, ITALIAN STYLE

You use a lot of garlic for this dish.

4½ to 5 pounds boned and rolled veal shoulder	2 tablespoons olive oil
1 tablespoon flour	1 tablespoon minced parsley
1 teaspoon salt	1 teaspoon dried rosemary
½ teaspoon freshly ground pepper	3 cloves garlic, minced
	1 cup water

Rub veal with next 3 ingredients. Brown on all sides in oil in heavy kettle. Put meat on rack in kettle. Add remaining ingredients. Cover, and simmer 3 hours, or until tender. Makes 8 servings.

VEAL BREAST PIQUANT

*It has a hot sauce with garlic,
chili powder, Worcestershire, vinegar.*

3 pounds veal breast	Dash pepper
2 tablespoons fat	2 teaspoons salt
2 onions, chopped	3 tablespoons vinegar
1 clove garlic, minced	1 tablespoon Worcestershire
1½ teaspoons chili powder	¼ cup ketchup
	1 cup water

Brown veal on all sides in fat in heavy kettle. Mix remaining ingredients, and pour over meat. Cover, and simmer 1½ hours, basting occasionally with the liquid. Serves 4.

VEAL WITH OLIVE SAUCE

*You add wine, olives, and grated lemon
rind to the sauce at the last minute.*

3 pounds veal breast	⅓ cup dry red wine
2 tablespoons fat	10 stuffed olives, chopped
Salt and pepper	Grated rind of ½ small lemon
1 cup broth	
1 tablespoon cornstarch	

Brown veal on all sides in fat in heavy kettle. Season. Add broth; cover and simmer 1½ hours, or until tender, basting occasionally with liquid in kettle. Remove veal, and thicken liquid with cornstarch blended with a little cold water. Add remaining ingredients, and more salt and pepper, if necessary. Pour on veal. Serves 4.

138

VEAL WITH RAISIN SAUCE

The sauce contains mushrooms, currant jelly, and sour cream as well as raisins.

3 pounds veal breast	2 tablespoons sherry or white wine
2 tablespoons flour	1 bay leaf
4 tablespoons butter or margarine	¾ cup raisins
1 can (13¾ ounces) condensed chicken broth	1 can (4 ounces) sliced mushrooms, drained
	1 tablespoon currant jelly
	1 cup sour cream
	Salt and pepper

Rub veal on both sides with the flour, and brown in 2 tablespoons hot butter in heavy kettle. Add broth, sherry, and bay leaf. Cover, and simmer 2 hours, or until meat is tender. Cook raisins and mushrooms lightly in remaining 2 tablespoons butter; stir in jelly. Remove meat, and slice. Add raisin mixture and sour cream to liquid in kettle. Heat gently, and season to taste with salt and pepper. Serve as sauce for the veal. Makes 6 servings.

LAMB PAPRIKA

You add the sour cream at the last minute to the wine-and-water cooking liquid.

3 pounds lamb neck	¼ cup each dry white wine and water
Seasoned flour	½ teaspoon caraway seed
2 tablespoons vegetable oil	½ teaspoon oregano
2 medium onions, chopped	1 cup sour cream
1 clove garlic, minced	Hot cooked noodles
	Paprika

Dredge lamb with seasoned flour, and brown on all sides in oil in heavy kettle. Pour off fat, and add remaining ingredients, except last 3. Cover, and simmer 2 hours, or until meat is tender, basting occasionally with the liquid in kettle, and adding more water if necessary. Remove lamb, and add sour cream to liquid. Heat gently, adding seasoning to taste. Pour over lamb, and serve with noodles sprinkled with paprika. Makes 4 servings.

BREAST OF LAMB ROSÉ

It takes its name from rosé wine, used in the sauce.

3 pounds breast of lamb	¼ cup currant jelly
Salt and pepper	¼ cup boiling water
1 cup chicken stock or other stock	½ cup rosé wine
	Few sprigs parsley, chopped

Brown meat on all sides in heavy kettle. Pour off fat, and sprinkle meat with salt and pepper. Add stock, cover, and simmer 2 hours, or until meat is tender. Dissolve jelly in boiling water; add wine and parsley; pour over meat. Simmer about 15 minutes longer, basting several times with the liquid in kettle. Serve meat with the liquid; thicken, if desired, with a small amount of flour blended with cold water. Serves 4.

HERBED LAMB SHOULDER

The herbs are garlic, rosemary, thyme, marjoram, sage, and bay leaf.

4 pounds boned and rolled lamb shoulder	1 teaspoon each dried rosemary, thyme, and marjoram
1 clove garlic	1 bay leaf
2 tablespoons fat	Salt and pepper
½ teaspoon dried sage	½ cup water

Rub lamb with cut clove garlic; brown on all sides in hot fat in heavy kettle; remove meat, and pour off fat. Put rack under meat in kettle. Add herbs, and sprinkle meat with salt and pepper. Add water; cover, and simmer 3 hours, or until meat is tender. Remove meat, and thicken liquid with a flour-and-water paste. Season with salt and pepper to taste. Makes 6 servings.

"Cease your chatter and mind your platter."
OLD SAYING

SPARERIBS HAWAIIAN

*Pineapple, both the juice and the
fruit, is Hawaii's contribution.*

4 pounds spareribs	1 teaspoon each
2 onions, chopped	paprika, chili
2 cloves garlic,	powder, sugar,
minced	dry mustard
1½ cups	2 tablespoons
pineapple juice	cornstarch
½ cup vinegar	1 can (9 ounces)
1 teaspoon salt	crushed pine-
Dash pepper	apple, undrained

Brown spareribs on all sides in heavy
kettle. Remove meat, and pour off fat.
Return ribs to kettle; add onion and
garlic. Mix pineapple juice, vinegar,
and seasonings; pour over meat. Cover,
and simmer 2 hours, or until meat is
tender, basting occasionally with liquid.
Remove ribs. For sauce, thicken liquid
with blended cornstarch and pineapple.
Serves 4 to 6.

PORK LOIN WITH SAUERKRAUT

*The sauerkraut is seasoned
with caraway seed and apple.*

4 pounds pork	1 can (29 ounces)
loin	sauerkraut
Salt and pepper	1 raw potato,
¼ cup water	peeled and
1 onion, sliced	grated
1 tablespoon	1 apple, peeled
caraway seed	and sliced

Brown meat on all sides in heavy kettle.
Sprinkle with salt and pepper. Put a
rack in kettle under meat; add water
and onion. Cover, and simmer 2½
hours. About ½ hour before meat is
tender, add remaining ingredients. Continue simmering until tender. Season
to taste. Serves 6.

MEXICAN PORK LOIN IN
PEPPER SAUCE

*The sauce contains hot sausage
in addition to green peppers.*

5 tablespoons	2 tomatoes,
olive oil	peeled and
3 cloves garlic,	chopped
minced	1 cup chicken
¼ pound hot	bouillon
sausage	6 green peppers,
4 pounds pork	sliced thin
loin	Flour
3 onions, chopped	Salt and pepper

BREAST OF LAMB
WITH DILL SAUCE

*This popular pickling spice
is a natural with lamb.*

3 pounds breast	1 teaspoon salt
of lamb	4 whole black
1 cup water	peppers
1 teaspoon dill seed	Dill Sauce

Put lamb in kettle, and add water and
seasonings. Cover, and simmer 1½
hours, or until meat is tender, adding
more water if necessary. Remove meat,
and strain liquid. Prepare Sauce, using
liquid; pour over meat. Serves 4 to 6.

Dill Sauce: Melt 2 tablespoons butter,
and blend in 2 tablespoons flour. Add
1¼ cups strained liquid, 1 teaspoon
sugar, and 1 teaspoon vinegar. Cook
until thickened. Beat 1 egg yolk, stir
in small amount of sauce; add to remainder of sauce, and mix well. Season
with salt and pepper to taste.

Heat 3 tablespoons of oil in heavy
kettle. Add garlic, and sausage, cut in
small pieces. Cook until well browned;
remove sausage. Brown pork loin on
all sides. Remove pork, and pour off
fat. Return pork to kettle with half the
onion, the tomatoes, bouillon, and sausage. Cover, and simmer about 2½
hours. In skillet, heat remaining 2
tablespoons oil. Add remaining onion
and the peppers. Cook, stirring occasionally, until tender; season. Remove
pork, and slice. Arrange on hot platter;
thicken the liquid in kettle with a
flour-and-water paste; add salt and pepper, and pour some of the gravy over
pork. Top with peppers and onion.
Serve remaining gravy in bowl. Makes
6 servings.

SPICED FRESH HAM

Ham is cooked with lemon, spices, herbs.

1 fresh ham (about 5 pounds)	1 bay leaf, crumbled
1½ cups water	1 tablespoon slivered lemon rind
1 teaspoon each salt, dried thyme, sage, whole cloves	2 tablespoons lemon juice
1½ teaspoons whole allspice	1 onion, chopped
	1 large carrot, diced

Brown meat on all sides in heavy kettle. Pour off fat, and put a rack under meat in kettle. Add remaining ingredients; cover, and simmer 4 hours, or until meat is tender, basting occasionally with liquid in kettle and adding more water if necessary. Thicken liquid, if desired. Makes 8 servings.

VEAL KIDNEYS AU CITRON

These pot-roasted kidneys are served with lemon wedges.

4 veal kidneys with the fat	Salt and pepper
¼ cup water	Lemon wedges

Put kidneys in large heavy kettle. Add water; cover, and cook over very low heat 3 hours, or until no blood comes out when kidneys are pierced with a fork. Remove fat; slice kidneys; season, and serve with lemon. Serves 4.

DANISH CALF HEARTS

They're served in a rich cream sauce.

2 calf hearts (about 1½ pounds)	4 whole black peppers
6 sprigs parsley, chopped	Dash pepper
2 onions, sliced thin	2 small carrots, diced
1 tablespoon fat	1 stalk celery, diced
½ bay leaf	1 cup water
1 teaspoon salt	¼ cup heavy cream

Wash hearts, and remove large tubes. Stuff hearts with parsley and half the onion; close with skewers, or sew with string. Brown on all sides in fat in heavy kettle. Add remaining onion, seasonings, carrot, celery, and water. Cover, and simmer 2 hours, or until hearts are very tender. Strain broth, add cream; pour over hearts. Serves 4.

LAMB LIVER WITH RICE

Tender slices of liver in brown gravy, served over fluffy, hot rice.

2 lamb livers (about 2 pounds)	1 bay leaf
1½ cups boiling water	⅛ teaspoon dried thyme
Flour	¼ teaspoon pepper
¼ cup bacon fat or other fat	2 teaspoons salt
3 sprigs parsley	1 onion, sliced
	Hot cooked rice

Cover livers with the water. Let stand 5 minutes. Drain, reserving water. Dry livers, and dredge with 2 tablespoons flour. Brown in hot fat in heavy kettle. Add herbs, seasonings, onion, and reserved water. Cover, and simmer 1½ hours, or until done. Remove livers, and slice. Thicken liquid with a flour-and-water paste. Season to taste, and serve with the liver on hot rice. Serves 6.

PORK LIVER, VEGETABLES

The vegetables are onion, carrots, parsnips, and potatoes.

1½ cups boiling water	2 teaspoons salt
1 pork liver (about 2 pounds)	¼ teaspoon pepper
2 tablespoons flour	1 onion, sliced
¼ cup bacon fat	2 cups sliced carrots
3 sprigs parsley	1½ cups sliced parsnips
1 bay leaf	4 potatoes, cubed
⅛ teaspoon thyme	

Pour water over liver; drain, reserving water. Remove tough outer membrane from liver; dry meat, and dredge with flour. Brown on all sides in fat. Add reserved water, and seasonings. Cover, and simmer 1 hour. Add vegetables, and simmer about 30 minutes longer. Makes 6 servings.

"The pleasure of the table is of all ages, conditions, countries and times."
BRILLAT-SAVARIN

STUFFED CHICKEN

*Vegetables are pot-roasted
with the chicken.*

1 roasting chicken (about 4 pounds)	4 carrots, cut in pieces
Stuffing, pages 236-237	4 small white onions
Vegetable oil	¼ pound whole green beans
Salt and pepper	1 cup Fordhook Lima beans
¾ cup water	
4 medium potatoes, peeled	

Fill chicken with stuffing, and sew up openings. Tie legs together. Brown on all sides in small amount of oil in heavy kettle. Pour off fat, and put chicken on rack in kettle. Season with salt and pepper. Add water; cover, and simmer 1 hour. Add vegetables, and season. Simmer, covered, 1 hour longer, or until chicken and vegetables are tender. Makes 4 servings.

COLD HERBED CHICKEN

*Good in summer with a salad of
cooked vegetables.*

1 roasting chicken (about 4 pounds)	¼ teaspoon pepper
Salt	¼ teaspoon thyme
Few sprigs parsley	Hot water
1 onion	Watercress
	Tomato wedges

Wash chicken, and sprinkle cavity with 1 teaspoon salt. Put parsley, onion, pepper, and thyme in cavity. Tie chicken in compact shape to fit kettle being used. Put chicken on rack in kettle. Add 1 teaspoon salt, and hot water to level of rack. Add neck and giblets. Cover, and simmer 2 hours, or until very tender, adding water to keep level with rack. Cool chicken, and slice from bones. Garnish with cress and tomato wedges. Makes 4 servings.

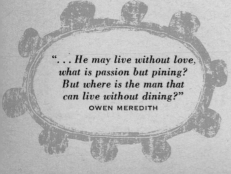

"... He may live without love,
what is passion but pining?
But where is the man that
can live without dining?"
OWEN MEREDITH

DUCK, SPANISH STYLE

*The sauce is highly seasoned
and, being Spanish, contains sherry,
as well as tomato sauce.*

1 duck (4 to 5 pounds)	¼ teaspoon garlic salt
1 onion, chopped	1 can (8 ounces) tomato sauce
1 cup chicken broth or stock	1 tablespoon paprika
1 teaspoon salt	1 can (4 ounces) mushroom stems and pieces, drained
¼ teaspoon pepper	
½ teaspoon celery salt	¼ cup dry sherry

Brown duck slowly on all sides in heavy kettle; pour off fat. Put duck on rack in kettle, and add remaining ingredients, except last 2. Simmer, covered, 1½ hours, or until duck is tender, basting frequently with the liquid in kettle. Remove duck to a hot platter. Add mushrooms and sherry to contents of kettle; heat, and pour over duck. Makes 4 servings.

CHICKEN, JAMAICA STYLE

*It features a whole chicken,
browned and then pot-roasted with
dried red peppers and allspice.*

1 roasting chicken (about 4 pounds)	2 dried red peppers, crushed
2 tablespoons butter or margarine	1 tablespoon vinegar
1½ cups chicken broth	¼ teaspoon allspice
¾ cup sliced celery	½ cup sliced green olives
1 medium onion, chopped	1 medium green pepper, sliced
½ teaspoon garlic salt	2 tablespoons cornstarch
	Salt and pepper

Brown chicken on all sides in butter in heavy kettle. Put chicken on rack in kettle. Add next 7 ingredients; cover, and simmer 1½ hours, or until chicken is tender. Add olives and green pepper, and cook 10 minutes longer. Remove chicken to a hot platter, and thicken liquid in kettle with cornstarch blended with a little cold water. Season to taste with salt and pepper, and pour over chicken. Makes 4 servings.

FISH

Our seas, lakes, and rivers offer a magnificent choice of fish, a delectable form of food of which we are not sufficiently appreciative. The New England colonists were much more fish conscious than present-day Americans, and it's to the colonists that we owe such classics as chowders, fish cakes, and salt cod. Perhaps many American cooks neglect fish because they don't quite understand what to do with it. Too often they dip fish in crumbs and fry it until it is hard, dry, and tasteless; or they boil it until it is a flavorless mush. Different kinds of fish have distinctive flavors and textures and these characteristics easily disintegrate with overcooking. Fish is delicate. It must be treated with care. Cook it just until the flesh flakes easily with a toothpick or fork. Never overcook it and never let it get dry. You can make your selection from the amazing variety of salt-water fish: fresh tuna, haddock, cod, mackerel, red snapper, porgy, sea trout, sea bass, blue fish, butterfish, and many more. From lakes and rivers come whitefish, pike, pickerel, perch, trout, salmon, smelt. You will find that all sorts of fish combine wonderfully with many seasonings and sauces. Potatoes drenched with butter and chopped parsley are a standard accompaniment. Remember, too, that serving a dry white wine greatly enhances all fish dishes.

143

FISH AND CHIPS

The fish is flounder;
the chips are potato strips.

1½ pounds flounder fillets, cut in serving-size pieces	1 tablespoon melted butter
Salt and pepper	1½ pounds (5 medium) potatoes
¾ cup sifted flour	Fat for frying
1 egg, slightly beaten	Tarragon or dill vinegar
½ cup milk	

Sprinkle fish with salt, pepper. Sift flour with ¾ teaspoon salt. Combine egg, milk, and butter. Add flour mixture, and beat until smooth. Peel potatoes, and cut each into 6 to 8 lengthwise pieces. Wash, and dry. Fry in hot deep fat until golden brown. Drain on absorbent paper, sprinkle lightly with salt, and keep hot in oven. Dip fish in batter, and fry in same fat until brown. Serve potatoes and fish very hot with vinegar. Serves 4.

BARBECUED HALIBUT STEAKS

You can use this barbecue
sauce with any kind of white fish.

1 small onion, minced	2 tablespoons brown sugar
½ green pepper, chopped	½ cup water
3 tablespoons butter or margarine	1 teaspoon dry mustard
½ cup chili sauce	1 tablespoon Worcestershire
½ cup ketchup	½ teaspoon each salt and pepper
Juice 2 lemons	4 halibut steaks (2 pounds)

Cook onion and green pepper in butter 5 minutes. Add remaining ingredients, except fish, and simmer 10 minutes. Broil halibut until done, brushing from time to time with the barbecue sauce. Makes 4 servings.

SOUTHERN FISH CHOWDER

The fish is pollack fillets; seasonings
include bay leaf and Tabasco.

2 pounds pollack fillets	2 cups tomato purée
⅓ cup bacon drippings or margarine	1½ quarts water
	1 tablespoon Worcestershire
⅓ cup flour	12 whole cloves
1½ cups chopped onion	Dash Tabasco
1 clove garlic, minced	1 tablespoon paprika
⅔ cup chopped green pepper	1 bay leaf
	1 tablespoon salt
1½ cups diced potato	¼ teaspoon pepper
	1 lemon, sliced

Cut fish in 1" pieces. Cook drippings and flour slowly in large heavy kettle until flour is golden brown. Add onion, garlic, and green pepper. Cook 5 minutes; add potato, tomato purée, water, and seasonings. Cover, and simmer ½ hour. Add fish; cover, and poach 8 minutes; add lemon slices. Serves 4 to 6.

SOUR-CREAM BUTTERFISH

It's fried, then served with a parsley,
onion, and sour-cream sauce.

2 pounds butterfish	1 cup sour cream
Salt and pepper	1 tablespoon minced parsley
¾ cup sifted flour	
1 egg, beaten	1 tablespoon minced green onion
½ cup milk	
1 tablespoon melted butter	Juice ½ lemon
Fat for frying	Dash cayenne

Sprinkle fish with salt and pepper. Combine flour, egg, milk, and butter; add ½ teaspoon salt, and beat until smooth. Dip fish in batter, and fry in hot deep fat until golden brown. For sauce, combine sour cream, ½ teaspoon salt, and remaining ingredients. Heat slightly. Serves 4.

POMPANO, TARTAR SAUCE

The pompano is fried in butter.

Fry fish as in Fish and Chips, above left. Serve with **Tartar Sauce:** Combine ⅔ cup mayonnaise, ½ teaspoon minced onion, 1 teaspoon minced parsley, 1 tablespoon each chopped capers, pickle relish, chopped stuffed olives, and dash cayenne. Chill. Serves 4.

STUFFED SOLE FILLETS

The stuffing is carrots, parsley,
pimientos, green onions, and crumbs.

2 pounds sole	2 pimientos, minced
Melted butter or	2 green onions,
margarine	chopped, or 1
2 carrots, peeled	small onion,
and shredded	minced
6 slices bread,	Salt and pepper
cubed	to taste
2 tablespoons	
chopped parsley	

Cut fillets in serving pieces, if necessary. Mix ¼ cup melted butter and remaining ingredients. Divide onto fillets, and roll up from small end, securing with toothpicks. Put in baking dish, and brush with melted butter. Bake in moderate oven, 375°F., 30 minutes. Serves 6.

Quick Stuffed Fillets: Use above recipe. Prepare ½ package stuffing mix, and use to stuff fillets. Proceed as directed.

CURRIED COD

A quick-and-easy dish that
cooks in just 15 minutes. The secret:
the cod is cut in cubes.

3 onions, chopped	4 whole cloves
1 clove garlic,	1 stick cinnamon
minced	½ cup undiluted
1 small green	evaporated milk
pepper, chopped	1 pound cod fillets,
1 tablespoon	cubed
curry powder	Salt
¼ cup butter or	Hot cooked rice
margarine	

Cook first 4 ingredients in the butter 5 minutes. Add next 4 ingredients; cover, and simmer 10 minutes. Season. Serve with rice. Serves 4.

MARINATED WHITING

You broil the fish after it has
been marinated in French dressing.

Cut 1½ pounds whiting fillets in serving-size pieces. Refrigerate fish in ½ cup highly seasoned French dressing for several hours. Arrange fish on broiler rack; broil under medium heat 5 minutes on each side, brushing with dressing used for marinating. To serve, pour drippings over fish; sprinkle with paprika. Serves 4.

OVEN FISH CHOWDER

The fish is cod or haddock which is
baked in a creamy white-wine broth.

2 pounds cod or	¼ teaspoon dried
haddock fillets	dill seed
4 potatoes, sliced	¼ teaspoon white
Few chopped	pepper
celery leaves	½ cup dry white
1 bay leaf	wine
2½ teaspoons salt	2 cups boiling
4 whole cloves	water
1 clove garlic	2 cups light cream
3 onions, sliced	Chopped parsley
¼ pound butter	
or margarine	

Put all ingredients, except the cream and parsley, in 3-quart casserole. Cover, and bake in moderate oven, 375°F., 1 hour. Heat light cream to scalding; add to chowder. Serve with garnish of chopped parsley. Makes 6 servings.

DUTCH FISH AND SHRIMP

The shrimp, in a creamy sauce, is
poured over the fish which is flounder.

2 cups water	1 egg yolk
Salt	½ cup heavy
1 pound flounder	cream
3 tablespoons butter	1 cup cooked
or margarine	shrimp
2 tablespoons flour	Pepper
Juice 1 lemon	Chopped parsley

Bring water to boil in skillet. Add 1 teaspoon salt. Simmer fish in the water 10 minutes, or until done. Remove fish, and put on a hot platter; keep warm. Reserve 1¼ cups liquid. Make a sauce with butter, flour, and liquid. When thickened, stir in lemon juice and egg yolk mixed with cream. Cook 5 minutes longer. Add shrimp, and season to taste. Heat, and pour over fish. Sprinkle with parsley. Serves 4.

FISH CASSEROLE

A one-dish meal with cod or haddock, potatoes, and vegetables.

2 pounds cod or haddock fillets	¼ teaspoon white pepper
4 potatoes, sliced	2½ teaspoons salt
3 onions, sliced	¼ pound butter or margarine
Few celery tops	½ cup dry white wine
1 bay leaf	
4 whole cloves	2 cups boiling water
1 clove garlic	
¼ teaspoon dried dill seed	2 cups light cream
	Chopped parsley

Put all ingredients, except last 2, in 3-quart casserole. Cover; bake in 375°F. oven 1 hour. Add scalded cream. Top with parsley. Serves 6.

TROUT, ANCHOVY SAUCE

In addition to anchovies, the sauce contains white wine, mint, and parsley.

4 trout	½ cup white wine
Seasoned flour	1 teaspoon chopped fresh or dried mint
Olive oil	
3 tablespoons butter or margarine	
4 anchovy fillets, cut fine	1 tablespoon chopped parsley
	Juice 1 lemon

Roll fish in seasoned flour. Heat enough olive oil to cover bottom of skillet. Pan-fry fish about 5 minutes on each side. Meanwhile, melt butter, add anchovy fillets, and heat 5 minutes. Add wine, mint, and parsley, simmer 3 minutes; add lemon juice. Put fish on hot platter, and pour sauce over all. Serves 4.

DEVILED HALIBUT STEAKS

They are spread with a mustard mixture, then broiled.

Mix 2 tablespoons prepared mustard, 1 tablespoon oil, 2 tablespoons chili sauce, 2 tablespoons horse-radish, and 1 teaspoon salt. Spread half of mixture on 4 halibut steaks (about 2 pounds). Put on greased broiler rack, and broil about 6 minutes under medium heat. Turn fish, spread with remaining sauce, and broil 5 or 6 minutes. Serves 4.

SWORDFISH AMANDINE

Almonds browned in butter are a perfect garnish for fish.

½ cup chopped almonds	Sherry
	Pepper
8 tablespoons butter or margarine	2 green onions, chopped
Parsley	8 slices crumbled crisp bacon
1 lemon	
4 swordfish steaks	Paprika

Brown almonds lightly in 2 tablespoons butter. Set aside. Melt remaining 6 tablespoons butter; add few sprigs parsley, chopped, and grated rind and juice of ½ lemon. Put fish on foil-covered broiler pan. Put 1 tablespoon sherry on each steak, and sprinkle with pepper. Spoon some of butter mixture over each. Broil under medium heat 10 minutes, basting with sherry-butter mixture. Turn fish; baste. Broil 10 minutes longer. Sprinkle with almonds, green onion, bacon. Garnish with lemon slices, paprika. Serves 4.

Salmon Amandine: Follow above recipe, substituting 4 salmon steaks.

FISH WITH EGG SAUCE

You can serve any kind of fish fillets with this sauce which contains dry white wine as well as eggs.

1½ pounds fish fillets	½ teaspoon Worcestershire
1 clove garlic, minced	1 teaspoon prepared mustard
Salt and pepper	
½ cup boiling water	1½ cups milk
¼ cup butter or margarine	3 hard-cooked eggs, diced
3 tablespoons flour	3 tablespoons dry white wine
	Paprika

Cut fish in serving pieces, and arrange on greased rack in large skillet. Sprinkle fish with garlic, salt, and pepper. Put boiling water in bottom of skillet. Cover, and simmer 15 minutes. Meanwhile, melt butter in saucepan. Blend in flour and seasonings. Add milk, and cook until thickened, stirring constantly. Add eggs and wine; season with salt and pepper. Cover fish with sauce, and sprinkle with paprika. Serves 4.

PORGIES EN PAPILLOTES

En papillotes means in paper. Fish is baked in brown paper or foil.

4 porgies, about 1 pound each	¼ cup softened butter or
Salt and pepper	margarine
Brown paper or foil	2 tablespoons minced parsley

Sprinkle cleaned fish inside and out with salt and pepper. Cut paper or foil large enough to wrap individual fish, and spread center of each piece with 1 tablespoon butter. Lay fish on spread section, and sprinkle with parsley. Wrap up, and tie with string, if necessary. Bake on cookie sheet in moderate oven, 375° F., 1 hour, or until done. Serve on paper. Makes 4 servings.

Fillets en Papillotes: Cut fillets in serving pieces. Season, and spread with parsley-green onion butter. Wrap up, and bake as above.

SMELTS WITH CAPER SAUCE

Smelts have a crisp corn-meal crust.

2 pounds smelts	Fat for frying
⅓ cup evaporated milk	¼ cup butter or margarine
⅓ cup flour	Juice ½ lemon
⅓ cup yellow corn meal	1 tablespoon capers
2 teaspoons salt	1 tablespoon minced parsley
⅛ teaspoon pepper	

Dip fish in evaporated milk, then roll in combined flour, corn meal, and seasonings. Heat enough fat to cover the bottom of frying pan. Fry fish 5 minutes on each side, or until well-browned and done. Meanwhile, melt butter; add lemon juice, capers, and parsley. Pour over hot fish. Serves 4.

GOLDEN FILLETS

Sole or flounder fillets are served with parsleyed lemon butter.

Season sole or flounder fillets. Fry in hot butter 3 to 5 minutes on each side. Serve with **Maître d'Hôtel Butter:** Melt ½ cup butter; add 1 tablespoon lemon juice, ⅛ teaspoon each salt and pepper, and 1 teaspoon minced parsley.

BAKED WHOLE FISH

Use snapper, bluefish, or haddock.

Stuff whole fish lightly with well-seasoned bread stuffing. Cut 3 or 4 gashes in skin, and insert thin slices of salt pork or bacon. Put a pinch of thyme or marjoram, 1 minced onion, 3 tablespoons minced parsley, and 2 tablespoons fat in baking pan. Put fish in pan; bake in 350°F. oven until fish flakes easily with a fork.

MACKEREL, MUSTARD SAUCE

You broil the fish, brushing it often with the sauce.

2 large or 4 small mackerel (about 3 pounds)	2 teaspoons prepared mustard
¼ cup melted butter or margarine	Juice ½ lemon
½ teaspoon paprika	½ teaspoon salt
	⅛ teaspoon pepper

Put fish on greased broiler rack. Combine remaining ingredients, and brush on fish. Broil under medium heat, 8 to 12 minutes, brushing with sauce several times. Serves 4.

SPINACH-STUFFED FISH FILLETS

Fillets are baked in spaghetti sauce.

2 medium onions, chopped	1 pound spinach, cooked and drained
1 tablespoon butter	1 can (15½ ounces) meatless spaghetti sauce
2 pounds sole or flounder fillets	

Cook onion in butter until tender, but not brown. Spread each fillet with cooked spinach, and sprinkle with onion. Roll up, and put in shallow baking dish. Pour on spaghetti sauce; bake in moderate oven, 350°F., about 20 minutes. Makes 6 servings.

PERCH, ITALIAN STYLE

*Garlic and orégano
provide the Italian touch.*

2 tablespoons minced parsley	1½ pounds ocean-perch fillets
1 clove garlic, minced	1 teaspoon salt
3 tablespoons olive oil	⅛ teaspoon pepper
1 cup hot water	Pinch of orégano

Cook parsley and garlic in olive oil in skillet 3 minutes. Add hot water, and bring to boil. Add fish and seasonings. Cover, bring again to boil, and cook 5 to 10 minutes. Serve with the liquid. Makes 4 servings.

SESAME BAKED FISH

*Sesame seeds are toasted, then
mixed with butter and added to the fish.*

2 pounds fish fillets or steaks	¼ teaspoon pepper
Salt	¼ cup sesame seed, toasted in 350°F. oven 10 minutes
Melted butter or margarine	
3 cups soft bread cubes	½ teaspoon thyme

Put fish in a shallow baking dish. Sprinkle with salt, and pour on ¼ cup melted butter. Mix 1 teaspoon salt, ⅓ cup melted butter, and remaining ingredients. Spread on fish. Bake in moderate oven, 375°F., about 30 minutes. Makes 6 servings.

STUFFED MACKEREL

*Onion, parsley, mushrooms, and mint
go into the bread-crumb stuffing.*

Split mackerel (about 4 pounds)	¼ pound fresh mushrooms, sliced
Salt and pepper	
1 small onion, chopped	6 tablespoons fat
1 tablespoon chopped parsley	1 cup soft bread crumbs
	1 teaspoon chopped fresh or dried mint

Sprinkle fish inside and out with salt and pepper. Cook onion, parsley, and mushrooms in 3 tablespoons hot fat 5 minutes. Add to crumbs and mint; season to taste with salt and pepper. Stuff fish with the mixture, and sew openings closed, or use toothpicks. Cut several gashes in skin. Put remaining 3 tablespoons fat in baking pan, and add fish. Bake in 350° F. oven 45 to 50 minutes. Serves 4.

HALIBUT WITH WINE SAUCE

*The wine is any dry white wine, such
as sauterne, Chablis, or Rhine wine.*

1½ pounds halibut steaks	1 teaspoon salt
¼ cup butter or margarine	Dash pepper
	2 cups milk
¼ cup flour	2 hard-cooked eggs, chopped
¼ teaspoon dry mustard	¼ cup dry white wine
½ teaspoon Worcestershire	1 tablespoon minced parsley
	Paprika

Poach fish as in Poached Cod Steaks, page 152. Melt butter; blend in flour and seasonings. Add milk, and cook until thickened, stirring. Add eggs and wine. Pour sauce over fish. Sprinkle with parsley and paprika. Serves 4.

FISH GUMBO

*This is a hearty fish
soup, with haddock or cod and
vegetables, served over rice.*

1 onion, chopped	1 bay leaf
1 green pepper, chopped	½ teaspoon thyme
¼ cup butter or margarine	1 dried red pepper, crushed
1 can (19 ounces) tomatoes	1 can (19 ounces) okra, undrained
1 teaspoon salt	1 pound haddock or cod, cubed
½ teaspoon celery salt	Hot cooked rice

Cook onion and green pepper in the butter 5 minutes. Add remaining ingredients, except last 3. Simmer, uncovered, about 30 minutes. Add okra and fish; simmer 10 minutes. Serve with rice. Serves 4.

FILLETS OF SOLE EN CASSEROLE

The sole is poached, then
served with a creamy wine sauce.

Few sprigs parsley, chopped	2 pounds sole fillets
2 green onions, chopped	3 tablespoons butter or margarine
1 teaspoon salt	2 tablespoons flour
⅛ teaspoon white pepper	1 cup heavy cream
1 cup white wine	1 egg yolk
½ cup water	

Put first 6 ingredients in skillet, and bring to boil. Add fish, and poach about 10 minutes. Remove fish to a shallow, broilerproof casserole; reduce liquid to 1 cup. In top part of double boiler melt 2 tablespoons butter, and blend in flour. Add fish liquid and half the cream. Cook, stirring, until thickened. Mix remaining cream and egg yolk. Pour small amount of sauce over mixture, stirring. Pour back into double boiler, and cook a few minutes longer, stirring. Add remaining 1 tablespoon butter, and pour over fish. Brown under broiler. Serves 6.

HORSE-RADISH SOLE

The horse-radish sauce
has a sour-cream base.

Poach fish as in above recipe. Serve hot with following sauce: Mix 1 cup sour cream, 2 tablespoons grated lemon rind, 3 tablespoons prepared horse-radish, and ¾ teaspoon salt.

PIQUANT WHITEFISH

Capers give it a pleasant tartness.

1 pound whitefish fillets	2 teaspoons Worcestershire
1 tablespoon oil	½ cup ketchup
1 tablespoon vinegar	¼ cup water
2 tablespoons minced onion	1 tablespoon capers
1 teaspoon salt	1 cup cooked green peas

Cut fish in serving-size pieces. Bring oil, vinegar, onion, salt, Worcestershire, ketchup, and water to boil in top part of double boiler. Add capers and fish. Cover, and cook over boiling water 25 minutes, stirring several times. Add peas; heat. Serves 4.

MARINATED FISH

The marinade is oil, wine vinegar,
garlic, and rosemary.

1½ pounds small fish	1 tablespoon chopped fresh rosemary or 1 teaspoon dried
Corn meal or fine dry bread crumbs	1 cup wine vinegar
2 cloves garlic	Salt and pepper
¼ cup olive oil	Watercress

Dip fish in corn meal. Brown 1 clove garlic in oil; remove garlic; add fish, and cook until done. Sprinkle flat dish with rosemary; put fish on top, and sprinkle with more rosemary. To oil remaining in skillet, add second clove of garlic, and brown lightly. Remove garlic, and add vinegar; heat gently. Pour over fish. Season. When cold, cover, and chill overnight. Garnish with cress. Makes 4 to 6 servings.

SOLE IN VERMOUTH

The sole is poached in the vermouth,
then browned under the broiler.

1 cup dry vermouth	⅔ cup butter or margarine
1½ pounds sole fillets	1 tablespoon heavy cream
4 egg yolks	Salt and pepper

Heat vermouth in a skillet. Wrap fish loosely in cheesecloth, and poach in the vermouth about 10 minutes. Put fish on a broilerproof platter. Reduce vermouth to about ⅔ cup. In top of double boiler, combine egg yolks, butter, cream, and vermouth. Cook over hot, not boiling, water, stirring until thickened. Season. Pour over fish, and brown quickly under broiler. (Don't worry if sauce curdles slightly.) Serves 4.

MUSTARD FISH AND CHIPS

*Fish fillets are spread with mustard
sauce, then baked with French fries.*

Put 1 pound fish fillets in baking dish.
Mix ¼ cup salad dressing, 2 teaspoons
prepared mustard, and 2 tablespoons
minced onion. Spread on fish. Sprinkle
with paprika. Bake in 500°F. oven, 15
minutes, along with 1 box frozen French
fries. Serves 2.

BAKED STUFFED FISH STEAKS

*The stuffing is potato seasoned with
onion and herbs.*

Wipe 4 halibut steaks (about 3 pounds)
with damp cloth. To make stuffing: Fry
1 minced large onion in ⅓ cup butter
until tender, but not browned. Add 3
cups chopped cooked potato, ¼ teaspoon thyme, ½ teaspoon marjoram,
and salt and pepper to taste. Mix lightly, and spread on 2 steaks. Top with
remaining steaks, and put in shallow
baking dish. Brush with melted butter.
Bake in moderate oven, 350°F., about
45 minutes. Makes 4 servings.

DEEP-FRIED SWORDFISH

*You cut the fish into bite-sized
pieces before frying it.*

1½ pounds	Fine dry bread
swordfish steaks	crumbs
2 eggs	Vegetable oil
3 tablespoons	or shortening
water	Salt

Cut steaks in bite-size chunks. Dip in
egg and water, beaten together, then
in crumbs. Fry until golden brown in
hot deep oil. Drain on absorbent paper,
and sprinkle with salt. Serve very hot
with Tartar Sauce, page 240, if desired
Makes 4 servings.

HADDOCK-POTATO PATTIES

*Flaked fish and seasonings
are mixed with mashed potatoes.*

4 medium potatoes	1 teaspoon
1 pound haddock	poultry
fillets, cooked	seasoning
and flaked	Salt and pepper
1 egg, beaten	Flour
2 tablespoons	Fat for frying
minced onion	

Cook potatoes, and mash. Add fish, egg,
onion, poultry seasoning, and salt and
pepper to taste. Shape into 8 flat patties, and roll in flour; pan-fry in hot fat
until browned. Serves 4.

FLOUNDER, MONTEREY

*White wine and ginger give the sauce
and the fish a distinctive flavor.*

1½ pounds flounder	⅛ teaspoon ginger
fillets	¼ cup butter or
Salt and pepper	margarine
⅓ cup dry	1 tablespoon
white wine	instant minced
Juice 1 lemon	onion
1 bay leaf,	2 sprigs parsley,
crushed	chopped

Season fish with salt and pepper. Cut
into serving-size pieces. Roll up; secure with toothpicks. Put remaining ingredients in skillet; bring to boil. Add
fish, and simmer, covered, 10 minutes.
Spoon some of sauce over fish once
or twice. Serves 4.

SALMON STEAKS WITH
EGG-AND-CAPER SAUCE

The salmon is poached.

Water	1 slice lemon
1 slice onion	4 salmon steaks
1 teaspoon salt	(1½ pounds)
6 whole black	Egg-and-Caper
peppers	Sauce
Few celery leaves	Minced parsley

Half-fill deep skillet with water. Add
onion, salt, peppers, the leaves, and
lemon. Boil 5 minutes; reduce heat.
Slip fish into water, and simmer gently
about 10 minutes, or until fish flakes
easily when tested with a fork. Remove
fish, and serve with Sauce made as in
Fish with Egg Sauce, page 146; omit
wine; add 1 tablespoon capers with
eggs. Top with parsley. Serves 4.

HOT PERCH SANDWICHES

Perch, tomato halves, and
a mustard-tartar sauce are baked
in foil-wrapped rolls.

1 egg, beaten	2 tablespoons
Salt and pepper	pickle relish
1 pound ocean-	1 onion, minced
perch fillets	3 tablespoons
½ cup fine dry	mayonnaise
bread crumbs	1 tablespoon
Vegetable oil	prepared mustard
6 sandwich rolls	6 slices tomato,
	cut in half

Mix egg, ½ teaspoon salt, and ⅛ teaspoon pepper. Dip fish in egg mixture, and roll in crumbs. Fry in hot oil until well browned. Split rolls, and remove some of the centers. Mix relish, onion, mayonnaise, and mustard; spread on rolls. Put fish on rolls, top with tomatoes, and season. Replace roll tops, and wrap each in foil. Put in moderate oven, 350°F., 10 minutes. Makes 6.

Fish-Stick Sandwiches: Use above recipe; substitute 1 box fish sticks, thawed, for the fried perch. Heat fish as directed on package; allow 2 sticks per sandwich.

CREAMED FINNAN HADDIE

Flaked fish is served in
a hard-cooked egg and cream sauce.

1½ pounds	¼ cup butter or
boneless finnan	margarine
haddie	¼ cup flour
2 cups milk	¼ cup cream
1 bay leaf	Dash cayenne
1 pinch thyme	1 pimiento,
10 whole black	chopped
peppers	2 hard-cooked
1 slice onion	eggs, chopped

Soak fish in milk 1 hour, with bay leaf, thyme, peppers, and onion. Then put over very low heat, and simmer gently 10 minutes. Flake fish. Strain milk, and reserve. Melt butter, and blend in flour. Add milk and cream slowly; cook until thickened, stirring. Add fish and remaining ingredients. Serves 4.

Creamed Smoked Whiting: In above recipe, substitute 1½ pounds smoked whiting for finnan haddie.

CHILI BAKED PERCH

In addition to chili sauce,
this contains Burgundy and onion.

Put 1 pound ocean-perch fillets in shallow baking dish. Mix ¾ cup chili sauce, ¼ cup red Burgundy, and 2 tablespoons instant minced onion. Spread on fish, and sprinkle with ¾ cup grated process American cheese. Bake in very hot oven, 450°F., 15 to 20 minutes. Makes 3 or 4 servings.

HURRY-UP FISH CHOWDER

It takes less than 30 minutes to cook.

2 ounces salt	1 quart water
pork, diced	1 pound fish
2 cups diced	fillets
potato	1 tall can un-
1 carrot, sliced	diluted evap-
1 stalk celery,	orated milk
chopped	Salt and pepper
2 onions, sliced	4 soda crackers,
⅛ teaspoon	crumbled
leaf thyme	Paprika

Brown pork; remove from fat. To fat add potato, carrot, celery, onion, thyme, water. Cover; cook 10 minutes, or until vegetables are tender. Add fish; simmer 8 minutes, and break fish apart with fork. Add milk, and season to taste. Heat well, but do not boil. Add pork and crackers. Sprinkle with paprika. Serves 4.

SWORDFISH, TOMATO SAUCE

You add the juice of a lemon, always
right with fish, to the tomato sauce.

1½ pounds sword-	2 cloves garlic,
fish, 1½" thick	minced
7 tablespoons	Juice 1 lemon
olive oil	1 can (8 ounces)
1 cup finely	tomato sauce
chopped parsley	Salt and pepper

Cut fish in servings; put in baking dish. Simmer next 3 ingredients 10 minutes. Add lemon juice and sauce; heat. Season, and pour over fish. Bake in 425° F. oven 25 minutes. Serves 3 or 4.

CODFISH KEDGEREE

Fish, rice, hard-cooked eggs,
and cream are all cooked together.

1 pound cod fillets, cooked and flaked	3 tablespoons minced parsley
2 cups hot cooked rice	½ cup light cream
	1 tablespoon butter
4 hard-cooked eggs, chopped	1 teaspoon salt
	Dash pepper

Put fish in top part of double boiler with remaining ingredients. Heat thoroughly. A pinch of curry powder can be added, if desired. Serves 4.

FLAKED HADDOCK, NEWBURG

The haddock, in a sherry-and-
cream sauce, is served on toast.

3 tablespoons butter or margarine	¾ cup light cream
	⅓ cup milk
1½ tablespoons flour	1½ pounds haddock fillets, cooked and flaked
1 teaspoon salt	
½ teaspoon paprika	3 tablespoons sherry
¼ teaspoon nutmeg	2 egg yolks
Dash cayenne	4 slices hot toast

Melt butter, and blend in the flour and seasonings. Add cream and milk slowly; cook until thickened, stirring constantly. Add fish, and heat. Add sherry mixed with egg yolks, and cook 2 or 3 minutes longer. Serve on toast. Serves 4.

MAYONNAISE SWORDFISH

Crumbs, any kind you like, give
the swordfish a nice crisp crust.

Season 2 pounds swordfish with salt and pepper. Spread generously with mayonnaise, and sprinkle lightly with instant minced onion, then with packaged corn-flake crumbs, fine dry bread crumbs, or cracker crumbs. Bake in hot oven, 400° F., 30 minutes. Serves 4.

HERB-BROILED SALMON

The herbs are marjoram,
parsley, and watercress or chives.

2 pounds salmon steaks, about ¾" thick	¼ teaspoon pepper
	½ teaspoon marjoram
1 tablespoon grated onion	2 tablespoons minced parsley
Juice 1 lemon	1 tablespoon minced watercress or chives
6 tablespoons melted butter or margarine	
1 teaspoon salt	

Arrange fish on greased broiler rack. Mix remaining ingredients, and pour half over steaks. Broil about 6 minutes under medium heat; turn, and pour remaining sauce over fish. Broil 5 or 6 minutes longer. Serves 4.

POACHED COD STEAKS, CONTINENTAL

Blue cheese, vinegar, mustard, and
paprika go into the butter sauce.

2 cups boiling water	⅓ cup butter or margarine, melted
1 slice lemon	
1 teaspoon salt	½ cup crumbled blue cheese
1 slice onion	
Few celery leaves or parsley sprigs	2 teaspoons vinegar
	2 teaspoons prepared mustard
4 cod steaks (about 2 pounds)	½ teaspoon paprika

Simmer first 5 ingredients 10 minutes. Add fish, and simmer 10 minutes longer. Lift fish to a hot platter. Mix remaining ingredients. Pour over fish. Serves 4.

FISH FILLETS IN MUSHROOM-CHEESE SAUCE

To make the sauce, you add grated
cheddar and sherry to mushroom soup.

1½ pounds fish fillets	1 cup grated sharp cheddar cheese
Salt	
1 can cream-of-mushroom soup	¼ cup sherry
	Dash pepper
	Paprika

Cut fish in serving pieces, and arrange in baking dish. Season. Mix remaining ingredients, except paprika. Spread on fish. Top with paprika; bake in 375° F. oven 25 minutes. Serves 4.

Of all shellfish, shrimp is our most popular. The large sort, caught in the Atlantic and Gulf waters, is shipped all over the country. Even the most remote midland restaurant now lists fresh Gulf shrimp on the menu. If, on the other hand, you are a fan of the tiny tender Pacific shrimp, you must indulge your appetite when near the Western coast. These are not shipped in quantity. Though widespread shipment and consumption of shrimp has brought a new interest in ways to prepare it, we still rely too much on frying this tender morsel. Good crisp fried shrimp are excellent, but all too often they are dipped in a heavy, soggy batter and cooked too long. The average shrimp takes only a few minutes, about three to five, to cook. Overcooking kills the taste. Whether you are deep-frying, sautéeing, grilling or poaching in court bouillon, cook the shrimp only until opaque all through.

SHRIMP

HOW TO COOK SHRIMP

To shell or not to shell and when to clean.

Most cooks feel that shrimp have more flavor if cooked in the shells. However, they can be shelled before cooking, the shells boiled for 5 minutes then discarded, and the shrimp cooked in the same water.

As far as cleaning is concerned, it's easier to pull out the vein before cooking, but on the other hand the shrimp will lose their beautiful smooth pink backs, as the flesh curls away from the slit. So, if looks are important, as when they are served whole for an appetizer, it's best to clean after cooking.

To boil, add just enough boiling water to cover: about a quart for each pound. To each quart of water add 1 teaspoon salt and, if desired, 1 teaspoon pickling spice, a few onion slices, half a lemon, and an herb bouquet. Bring liquid again to a boil, and boil shrimp from 2 to 5 minutes, depending on size. Do not cook longer. Drain, and prepare according to recipe.

SHRIMP COCKTAIL SUPREME

You can substitute cut-up anchovies for the caviar, if you like.

Arrange chilled cooked shrimp, preferably small ones, on lettuce leaves in cocktail glasses. For 6 cocktails make a sauce with 1 cup sour cream, ¼ cup mayonnaise, 1 tablespoon lemon juice, and 2 or 3 ounces black or red caviar. Or snip 6 anchovy fillets in little pieces, and use them instead. Pour over the shrimp, and serve garnished with a twisted slice of lemon.

BOILED SHRIMP IN SHELLS

Serve them hot dripping with butter, or cold in French dressing.

Cook them as above, in the shells, and serve hot with melted butter and bibs. Or serve cold, with French dressing, and omit butter.

SHRIMP PASTE

An appetizer to spread on crackers.

Grind 2 pounds cooked shrimp 3 times, or pound in a mortar. Cream with ½ cup butter, ¼ teaspoon dry mustard, a pinch ground mace, 1 tablespoon sherry, and salt and black pepper to taste. Pack in a bowl or pot with a cover; chill. Makes about 3 cups.

SHRIMP CAKES

They have an olive and dill sauce.

¼ cup chopped onion	Salt and pepper
Butter or margarine	1 pound shrimp, cooked and chopped
3 tablespoons flour	
1 teaspoon prepared mustard	Cracker crumbs
1 cup cream	Olive-Dill Sauce

Cook onion in 4 tablespoons butter until wilted. Stir in flour, mustard, cream, and seasonings. When thick and smooth, add shrimp. Chill; form in cakes, roll in cracker crumbs, and sauté in a lot of butter. Serve with Sauce: Combine 1 cup mayonnaise, ½ cup chopped ripe olives, 1 tablespoon dill weed, and 1 tablespoon lemon juice. Makes 4 servings.

SHRIMP COCKTAIL

The delicate sauce lets the true flavor of the shrimp come through.

For 6 cocktails, allow 1 pound cooked shrimp, cut in pieces if large. For the sauce, combine 1 cup mayonnaise, ½ cup sour cream, ¼ cup ketchup, 1 tablespoon lemon juice, and salt to taste. Season with chives, curry powder, dill or garlic, if desired, according to taste. Or add diced ripe avocado or minced celery or green pepper to the shrimp. Serve in lettuce-lined dishes or cocktail glasses, or heap on halved, unpeeled ripe avocados.

GARLIC-GINGER SHRIMP

Garlic and ginger are
added to a sherry-soy marinade.

Split, and clean jumbo shrimp. Marinate 3 or 4 hours, turning occasionally, in equal parts sherry or sake, soy sauce, and peanut or sesame oil, to which 1 pressed clove garlic and 1 tablespoon grated fresh or crystalized ginger have been added. Broil in range or over charcoal 4 minutes on each side.

QUICK SHRIMP SAUTÉ

A dish to cook at the table in a
chafing dish or an electric skillet.

Shell, and devein desired number of shrimp. For each pound, melt ½ cup butter or margarine, add either 1 crushed clove garlic or ¼ cup finely minced onion, and shrimp. Cook quickly until pink; add ¼ cup cognac, flame, season, and serve at once on toast (½ cup heavy cream can be added if you wish more sauce). One pound shrimp makes 4 servings.

SHRIMP FRIED RICE

Shrimp and rice cooked
with water chestnuts and eggs.

Melt ¼ cup (½ bar) butter or margarine in large skillet. Add 2 cups cold cooked rice, 1 pound cooked chopped shrimp, and ½ cup minced water chestnuts. Cook until well heated, then stir in 2 eggs that have been beaten with 2 tablespoons soy sauce. Reheat, stirring until eggs are set; garnish with chopped green onions. Serves 6.

SHRIMP-PEPPER PAN ROAST

Jumbo shrimp, white wine, green
pepper, cognac, ketchup, and cream.

In the top pan of chafing dish or in electric skillet, put ¼ pound butter or margarine. When melted, add 3 pounds cleaned raw jumbo shrimp, 1 cup white wine, 1 chopped green pepper, 1 teaspoon salt, 2 tablespoons cognac, and ¼ cup water. Bring to boil; add ¼ cup ketchup and 2 cups cream. Allow to heat for 2 or 3 minutes, and serve immediately over hot buttered toast in individual shallow baking dishes. Makes 6 to 10 servings.

SHRIMP REMOULADE

A puréed egg, anchovy, wine, and
herb sauce with chilled shrimp.

3 hard-cooked egg yolks	1 tablespoon each minced parsley, green onion
1 raw egg yolk	¾ cup olive oil
1 tablespoon prepared mustard	3 tablespoons tarragon vinegar
2 teaspoons horse-radish	3 tablespoons white wine
1 teaspoon anchovy paste	1 pound shrimp, cooked and cleaned
¼ teaspoon ground mace	

Rub hard-cooked egg yolks smooth with wooden spoon. Add next 7 ingredients. Gradually work in olive oil, vinegar, and wine. Mix well, or purée in blender. Serve with chilled shrimp. Serves 4.

SHRIMP JAMBALAYA

Shrimp with chopped ham,
tomatoes, rice, and seasonings.

2 pounds shrimp	2 cups tomatoes
2 tablespoons flour	Pinch cayenne
2 tablespoons lard	1½ cups uncooked rice
1 cup chopped cooked ham	½ teaspoon thyme
½ cup chopped onion	2 teaspoons chili powder
1 clove garlic, finely minced	1 teaspoon salt
	Boiling water

Shell, and devein shrimp and, if large, cut in pieces. Brown flour in hot lard. Add ham, onion, garlic, and shrimp. When onion begins to color, add next 6 ingredients. Add boiling water to moisten well, and cook, covered, until rice is tender. More water will have to be added as moisture is absorbed, and any stirring should be done gently with a fork. Jambalaya should be moist, but not mushy. Serves 8.

SHRIMP IN OTHER LANGUAGES
Chinese : har
German : garneelen
Norwegian : standreker
Danish : rajer
Greek : natantia
Spanish : camarones
French : crevettes
Italian : gamberi or scampi

TWICE-FRIED SHRIMP

*You serve them on toothpicks
as an appetizer.*

Shell 2 pounds jumbo shrimp; split up backs, removing veins. Flatten each shrimp; roll well in seasoned flour. Dip in slightly beaten egg, then fry in hot deep fat (375°F. on a frying thermometer) 1 minute only. Drain. In a chafing dish or electric skillet, melt ¼ cup butter. Add ¼ cup olive oil, 2 large cloves garlic (put through a garlic press or thoroughly mashed with ½ teaspoon of salt), 1 tablespoon minced parsley, and ½ teaspoon minced sweet basil. Heat, add fried shrimp, and reheat. Serve on toothpicks as an appetizer. Makes 8 servings.

SHRIMP AND SPAGHETTI

*Cooked shrimp heated in garlic and
tomatoes, then tossed with spaghetti.*

Crush 1 large clove garlic, and cook in ½ cup each butter or margarine and olive oil until soft. Mash smooth; add 1 pound chopped cooked shrimp and 2 fresh tomatoes that have been peeled, seeded, and cut in pieces. Heat; add 3 tablespoons minced parsley, salt, and pepper, and mix with 1 pound of spaghetti, cooked **al dente**. Makes 6 servings.

CRÊPES WITH SHRIMP

*Shrimp-stuffed crêpes are broiled
with Hollandaise and whipped cream.*

1 pound shrimp	3 tablespoons
¼ cup butter	sherry
or margarine	½ cup thick white
1 cup minced	sauce
mushrooms	12 Crêpes, page 124
2 tablespoons	½ cup Hollandaise
minced onion	Sauce, page 240
½ cup cream	½ cup heavy
	cream, whipped

Shell and clean shrimp, and sauté in butter, with mushrooms and onion. After 5 minutes, add cream, sherry, and white sauce. Put a spoonful on each crêpe, roll, and arrange, seam down, in shallow, well-greased baking dish. Combine Hollandaise (leftover can be used) with whipped cream. Spread over crêpes, and brown under broiler. Makes 4 servings.

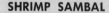

What is the difference between prawns and shrimp? In San Francisco and points north, prawns are large or jumbo shrimp; in England they are Dublin Bay prawns, which M. André Simon, founder of The Wine & Food Society, claims are biologically the same as scampi and langoustine, though he admits that

SHRIMP SAMBAL

A condiment to serve with curry.

Shred 1 pound cooked shrimp, and cook in 3 tablespoons butter or margarine a few minutes. Add ½ cup grated coconut, 3 chopped green chilies, 2 cloves pressed garlic, 1 tablespoon grated green ginger. Add salt to taste, and chill before serving. Serves 4.

MARINATED SHRIMP WITH CHILIES

The garnish is onion and orange slices.

Cook 2 pounds split jumbo shrimp and a crushed garlic clove in ¼ cup olive oil 5 minutes. Discard garlic. Combine with 2 chopped green chili peppers, and French dressing: ¾ cup olive oil, ¼ cup lemon juice, dash cayenne, and 1 teaspoon salt. Chill; garnish with onion and orange slices. Serves 8.

SHRIMP WITH
WILD RICE, ROMAGNA

*This dish uses two popular
Italian herbs: orégano and basil.*

2 packages (10 ounces each) frozen, shelled and cleaned shrimp	2 cans (8 ounces each) tomato sauce
1 cup uncooked wild rice	1 sauce-can water
	½ teaspoon orégano
1 clove garlic, minced	½ teaspoon sweet basil
¼ cup olive oil	1 green pepper, cut in chunks
	Salt and pepper

Thaw shrimp. Cook rice in boiling salted water; drain, and put in 2-quart casserole. Cook garlic in olive oil 5 minutes. Add all ingredients, except shrimp and salt and pepper. Bring to boil, and simmer 10 minutes. Add shrimp, and salt and pepper to taste. Pour on rice. Cover, and bake in moderate oven, 350°F., about 30 minutes. Makes 6 servings.

those of the Adriatic are larger and of a finer flavor. Famed Chef Conil says Dublin Bay prawns are langoustines, but not to be confused with scampi. Not being marine biologists, we allow that jumbo shrimp or prawns or scampi may be cooked the same way, even if not related.

SHRIMP SPREAD

Ground shrimp, cream cheese,
minced onion, and sour cream.

1 package (8 ounces) softened cream cheese	½ cup finely minced green onion
1 pound shrimp, cooked, cleaned, and ground	½ cup sour cream or mayonnaise
	Salt and pepper

Combine all ingredients. Add garlic, dill, curry powder or chili powder, if desired. Spread on crisp crackers, toast triangles, or dark bread for an appetizer. Makes about 3 cups.

CHINESE FRIED SHRIMP

They're fried in batter and served
with hot mustard and ketchup.

2 pounds large or jumbo shrimp	3 tablespoons corn meal
3 eggs	1 teaspoon salt
1 cup milk	Fat for frying
1 cup flour	Ketchup
2 tablespoons cornstarch	Dry mustard
	Beer

Remove shells from shrimp, but not tails. Split down back, and pull out veins. Flatten with bottom of a glass. Make a batter by beating eggs, and adding next 5 ingredients. Holding by the tail, dip each shrimp in batter, then drop into hot deep fat (375°F. on frying thermometer), and cook until brown. Drain on absorbent paper. Serve with ketchup, and dry mustard mixed with stale beer until of proper consistency. Makes 6 to 8 servings.

CHEESE-FRIED SHRIMP

They're fried in
crumbs and Parmesan cheese.

Prepare shrimp for frying as above; dip first in mayonnaise (**not** salad dressing), then in 2 parts crumbs to 1 part grated Parmesan cheese. Fry as above.

BROILED SHRIMP AND PROSCIUTTO

The shrimp are marinated in cognac,
wrapped in prosciutto, and broiled.

Marinate peeled and cleaned shrimp in cognac. Wrap each in thin slice prosciutto, string on skewers, alternating with small pieces bay leaf, and cook over charcoal or in broiler 3 minutes. Remove; roll in melted butter, then in crumbs, and return to broiler 4 minutes. Serve with lemon wedges.

SWEET-AND-SOUR SHRIMP

They're cooked with
ginger and pineapple chunks.

Split 2 pounds cleaned cooked shrimp, and combine with 2 cups pineapple chunks, 2 tablespoons grated green or crystallized ginger, 1 green pepper, cut in long slivers; heat all together 2 minutes in ¼ cup butter, margarine, or oil. Add 1 cup pineapple juice, ¼ cup sugar, ½ cup vinegar, 1 tablespoon soy sauce, and 2½ tablespoons cornstarch mixed with ½ cup water. Cook until thick and clear. Serve with hot cooked rice. Makes 6 servings.

SHRIMP BISQUE

Serve it hot with croutons, or
cold sprinkled with parsley or chives.

1 pound shrimp	½ cup each minced onion, carrot
4 cups water	
Salt	2 tablespoons minced parsley
Herb bouquet (parsley, thyme, bay leaf)	3 tablespoons butter or margarine
2 tablespoons uncooked rice	1 cup heavy cream
	Milk

Cook shrimp in water, 1 teaspoon salt, and herb bouquet 5 minutes. Strain stock, and to it add rice. Simmer until rice is soft. Sauté onion, carrot, and minced parsley in butter until soft. Add to stock, along with shrimp. Whirl in blender until smooth, doing half at a time, or grind shrimp before adding, and force mixture through a sieve. Add cream, more salt if necessary, and 1 teaspoon curry powder, if desired. Add milk to desired consistency. Reheat, or chill. If served hot, garnish with croutons; if cold sprinkle with finely minced parsley or chives. Serves 6.

SIZE OF SHRIMP

There are jumbo (15 or less to the pound), large, medium, and small (about 40 to the pound). Largest are the most expensive. Except in markets near fishing grounds, shrimp you buy are just the tails.

7 SHRIMP SALADS

For each salad, you start with ½ cup of minced celery, 1 pound of boiled, cleaned shrimp, and ½ to ¾ cup of mayonnaise.

Add the following ingredients for each pound shrimp:

Shrimp and Rice Salad: 1 cup chilled cooked rice.

Shrimp and Olive Salad: ½ cup sliced ripe or stuffed green olives.

Herbed Shrimp Salad: 1 tablespoon each minced chives and parsley.

Shrimp and Pepper Salad: ¼ cup minced green pepper.

Shrimp and Cucumber Salad: 1 chopped seeded cucumber.

Shrimp, Egg, and Onion Salad: 3 chopped hard-cooked eggs and ½ cup chopped green onions.

Shrimp-Macaroni Salad: 3 cups cooked elbow macaroni, ½ cup mayonnaise, 1 tablespoon crushed dill seed, 2 tablespoons chopped onion.

SHRIMP VICTORIA

Shrimp and mushrooms, in sour-cream sauce, served on rice.

Shell 2 pounds shrimp, and remove veins. Clean, and quarter 1 pound mushrooms. Sauté ½ cup minced onion in ¼ pound butter or margarine until wilted. Add mushrooms, cook 2 minutes, then add shrimp. Cook another 4 minutes, stirring. Add 2 tablespoons flour, 1 teaspoon salt, a dash freshly ground pepper, and 3 cups sour cream. Cook gently, stirring, until heated. Serve with rice. Serves 6.

SHRIMP DIP, HAWAIIAN

Water chestnuts, pineapple, and soy sauce strike the Hawaiian note.

Mix well: ½ pound chopped cooked shrimp, 1 can (5 ounces) chopped water chestnuts, 1 cup sour cream, 1 package (3 ounces) cream cheese, 1 cup drained crushed pineapple, and 3 tablespoons soy sauce. Makes 3 cups.

SHRIMP AND ARTICHOKE SALAD

A luncheon main dish, or a first course for dinner.

On individual plates, arrange beds of very finely minced lettuce. On these lay large artichoke bottoms (canned or cooked), and heap with shrimp salad. (To each cup diced shrimp, add ¼ cup finely diced celery and ½ cup mayonnaise. Season with a few drops lemon juice, salt, and pepper. Sieve hard-cooked egg yolk over shrimp.

SHRIMP LOUIS

The famous crab-meat salad adapted for shrimp.

Arrange a bed of lettuce on each plate. On this, place large cooked shrimp, preferably split. Pour over dressing, and garnish with quartered, shelled hard-cooked eggs, also artichoke hearts or asparagus spears, if you wish. For dressing: combine 1 cup of mayonnaise, ½ cup chili sauce, and ¼ cup each minced green onion and minced green pepper. Makes 6 servings.

EXOTIC SHRIMP SALAD

It contains water chestnuts and curry-soy mayonnaise.

2 pounds cooked cleaned shrimp	2 teaspoons curry powder
1 cup sliced water chestnuts	2 tablespoons soy sauce
¼ cup each minced green onion and celery heart	Lettuce
	Litchi nuts
1 cup mayonnaise	Toasted slivered almonds

If shrimp are large, cut in pieces, and combine with water chestnuts, green onion, and celery heart. Make dressing with next 3 ingredients. Mix with shrimp, pile in nests of lettuce, and garnish with nuts. Serves 6.

SHRIMP KEBABS

Skewered shrimp with olives and bacon.

Peel jumbo shrimp, and remove veins. String on skewers, alternating with squares of bacon and pitted large ripe olives or cubes of pineapple. Dip in melted butter or oil, and broil over charcoal, or under broiling unit in range 4 minutes on each side.

SHRIMP CHOWDER

Shrimp, potato, onion, stock, milk, and salt pork.

Cook 2 pounds shrimp as on page 154. Drain, reserve liquid; shell, and clean shrimp. Dice ¼ pound salt pork, and cook until brown and crisp. Reserve, and in the fat cook ½ cup minced onion until wilted. Combine onion, 2 cups shrimp stock, 2 cups diced potato. Cover, and simmer until potato is tender; then add shrimp, 3 cups rich milk, and diced pork. Heat. Makes 6 to 8 servings.

SHRIMP STEW

You use half heavy cream, half milk.

Cook 2 pounds shrimp as on page 154. Clean, and cut in pieces if large. Add to 2 cups strained shrimp stock and 2 cups each heavy cream and milk. Season. Heat; put in a tureen, add a little butter, sprinkle with minced parsley. Serves 6 to 8.

SHRIMP CURRY

Suggested condiments: French-fried onions, coconut, chutney, bananas.

2 pounds shrimp	3 tablespoons flour
1 cup chopped onion	Curry powder
	1 cup tomatoes
3 tablespoons butter	Juice ½ lemon
1 clove garlic	Hot cooked rice
1 teaspoon salt	Condiments

Cook shrimp, as on page 154, and save liquid. Cook onion in butter until wilted. Grind garlic in mortar with salt, and add to onion, with flour and 2 tablespoons curry powder. Cook 2 minutes; then add tomatoes, lemon juice, 3 cups water in which shrimp were cooked, and simmer 10 minutes. Add shrimp, and heat well. Correct seasoning, adding more curry, if desired. Serve with rice and condiments. Makes 8 servings.

PORTUGUESE SHRIMP SALAD

Shrimp plus olives, eggs, green onions, and green chilies.

Combine 1 pound cooked shrimp, cut in pieces, with ½ cup chopped green olives, 2 tablespoons chopped green onions, 2 tablespoons chopped green chilies, 2 chopped hard-cooked eggs, and ½ cup mayonnaise. Serve on lettuce or mixed salad greens. Serves 4.

SHRIMP TERIYAKI

They marinate in pineapple juice, soy sauce, and oil.

Split shrimp up back with scissors, and pull out veins. Marinate in equal parts pineapple juice, soy sauce, and bland vegetable oil. Thread shrimp on split bamboo or wooden sticks that have been soaked in water. Broil, or grill 3 or 4 minutes on each side, and serve on the sticks.

ICED CURRIED SHRIMP

The garnish: cucumber slices and pineapple chunks.

1 clove garlic, finely minced	Dash Tabasco
1 small onion, chopped	Salt
	Mayonnaise
3 tablespoons butter	Lemon juice
3 tablespoons flour	2 pounds shrimp, cooked, peeled
1 to 2 teaspoons curry powder	Toasted almond slivers
1 cup canned tomatoes	Sliced cucumber
	Pineapple chunks

Make a sauce by cooking garlic and onion in butter. Add next 4 ingredients and 1 teaspoon salt. Cook until thick; then force through sieve. Cool, and add to an equal amount mayonnaise. Add lemon juice and more salt and curry to taste. Mix with shrimp. Pack in round-bottomed bowl, and chill. Turn out on plate; sprinkle with slivers of toasted almonds, and surround with cucumber and pineapple. Serves 8.

FOOD VALUE OF SHRIMP

They are high in protein, minerals, vitamin B complex; neither freezing nor canning destroys their food value. One-quarter pound of shrimp, an average main-dish serving, comes to only 120 calories.

SHRIMP FLAMBÉES

They're grilled on bamboo sticks, then flamed in cognac.

Select jumbo shrimp, and remove shells and veins. String on bamboo sticks. Dip in melted butter, and grill or broil 3 or 4 minutes on each side. Put on a platter, pour on 1 jigger hot cognac for each pound of shrimp, and flame. Serve on the bamboo sticks.

SESAME SHRIMP

They marinate in soy sauce and bourbon and are toasted in sesame seed.

Marinate peeled jumbo shrimp in equal parts of sesame oil, bourbon whisky, and soy sauce for 2 hours. Grill, or broil 3 or 4 minutes on each side. Dip again in marinade, roll in sesame seed to cover, and return to grill or broiler until seeds on both sides of shrimp are lightly colored.

SHRIMP HAWAIIAN

Sautéed shrimp on pineapple with a sprinkling of toasted almonds.

Marinate 2 pounds peeled, cleaned shrimp in ¼ cup each soy sauce and pineapple juice. Sauté in ½ cup butter or margarine. Serve on 6 slices sautéed pineapple; sprinkle with toasted slivered almonds. Serves 6.

CREAMED SHRIMP WITH AVOCADO

You serve it on hot buttered toast.

To make creamed shrimp, mix 2 cups cream sauce or Béchamel Sauce, page 240, with each pound cleaned, shelled cooked shrimp, cut in pieces if large. Cover buttered toast with sliced avocado, and ladle on creamed shrimp. One pound shrimp serves 4.

SHRIMP IN THE OVEN

They have a garlic and white-wine sauce.

Allow 6 jumbo shrimp for each serving. Split ¾ of the way down back, but do not remove shells. Arrange in individual dishes with cut side spread open, and so that wide part is in center, tails sticking up. For each serving, mix 3 tablespoons melted butter or margarine, 2 tablespoons olive oil, ¼ teaspoon salt, 1 small clove garlic put through a press or mashed to a paste in the salt, 1 tablespoon white wine, and 1½ teaspoons minced parsley. Pour over shrimp; bake in a 400°F. oven 8 minutes. Serve at once.

SHRIMP CREOLE

Shrimp, onion, green pepper, tomatoes, and herbs simmered in consommé.

1 cup minced onion	Salt
½ cup minced green pepper	Dash cayenne
	Herb bouquet
¼ cup shortening	(parsley, thyme,
4 tomatoes,	bay leaf)
peeled, chopped	2 pounds shrimp
2 cups consommé	Hot cooked rice
or fish stock	

Sauté onion and green pepper in shortening. Add tomatoes, consommé, ½ teaspoon salt, cayenne, and herb bouquet. Simmer 40 minutes; discard bouquet; add cleaned raw shrimp, and simmer 6 minutes. Correct seasoning, and serve with rice. Serves 6.

SHRIMP À LA BÉARNAISE

The Béarnaise sauce is blended with tomato purée.

½ pound fresh mushrooms	Dash nutmeg
	Salt and pepper
¼ cup butter or margarine	Béarnaise Sauce, page 239
2 pounds shrimp	¼ cup tomato
1 tablespoon each lemon juice, minced parsley	purée

Chop mushrooms, and cook in butter, with shelled, cleaned shrimp, 5 minutes. Add remaining ingredients, except Sauce and purée. Arrange shrimp in baking pans. Mix together a batch of Béarnaise Sauce. Add tomato purée. Pour over shrimp, and brown slightly under broiler. Serves 6.

TUNA FISH

If you were able to peek into the cupboards of all the kitchens across the country, you would undoubtedly find a can or two of tuna on the shelves of more than half. This is by far our most popular fish, and interestingly enough, it is the *canned* tuna people prefer, not the fresh, which has an entirely different flavor. This tasty canned fish is used in a variety of dishes: in appetizers, in sandwiches, plain with mayonnaise, or mixed in salad with celery and onions, in cream sauces, in casseroles, in many combinations with other foods. The most expensive is imported from France and put up in olive oil. Spain and Italy also ship tuna in olive oil. The Japanese put up white meat in brine; this is a good choice for dieters. American canneries prepare several types: all white meat, mixed white and dark meat, all dark (the least expensive), chunked or flaked (the economy choice for sandwiches), and kippered and smoked. Here are more ways to fix this versatile, popular fish.

161

"That fish will soon be caught that nibbles at every bait."
THOMAS FULLER

ORIENTAL TUNA

A spread or a stuffing for tomatoes.

Combine 1 can tuna, flaked, 2 tablespoons very finely minced onion, ½ cup minced water chestnuts, 3 tablespoons mayonnaise, 1 teaspoon soy sauce, ½ teaspoon lemon juice, ½ teaspoon curry powder. Mix well. Makes about 1½ cups.

TUNA COCKTAIL

It's dressed with horse-radish mayonnaise and garnished with almonds.

Combine 1 can tuna (white preferred), and ½ cup minced celery. Mix ½ cup mayonnaise, 2 teaspoons grated horse-radish, 2 teaspoons grated onion, and 2 tablespoons lemon juice; combine with tuna. Garnish with slivered almonds. Makes 4 servings.

TUNA ANTIPASTO

A fine first course for dinner, or a main course for lunch.

Arrange the following in individual dishes, or cover a large tray or platter with shredded lettuce, then arrange the ingredients in rows:

1 can tuna, broken into large flakes (white preferred)	3 hard-cooked eggs, quartered
1 can drained anchovies, rolled or flat	6 slices salami
	2 peeled tomatoes, sliced
If you like, add:	Ripe olives
6 pickled artichoke hearts	Sliced onions
Green beans	Gorgonzola or Provolone cheese

Serve with crusty bread and cruets of oil and vinegar. Serves 6.

RICH TUNA SALAD

Tuna, celery, shallots or green onions with cream and mayonnaise.

Combine 1 can tuna (white preferred), flaked, with ½ cup finely minced celery, 1 tablespoon finely minced shallots or green onions, salt and pepper to taste, and ¼ cup mayonnaise to which have been added 1 teaspoon fresh lemon juice and ¼ cup heavy cream, whipped.

TUNA APPETIZERS

Large flakes of tuna with a dill-cream dressing.

Arrange large flakes of tuna (white preferred) on lettuce leaves on 4 individual plates. Whip ¼ cup heavy cream, fold in ½ cup mayonnaise, 2 teaspoons lemon juice, and 1 teaspoon crushed dill seed or dill weed. Place a mound on each plate, and decorate top with a bit of pimiento or sliced stuffed olive. Serves 4.

Cold Tuna Tarts: Make 6 shallow tart shells, and cool. Fill with Rich Tuna Salad. Dust with paprika, and top with a curled anchovy. Serves 6.

Tuna San Francisco: For each serving, cover a salad plate with finely sliced lettuce. On this put a large thick slice peeled tomato, topped with an artichoke shell. Fill artichoke with Rich Tuna Salad, and pour ¼ cup Thousand Island dressing over all.

TUNA-CAPER APPETIZERS

They're decorated with hard-cooked egg slices.

Mash 1 can of tuna with 2 tablespoons butter (¼ bar) and 2 teaspoons capers. Spread on 1½" rounds of bread, and decorate each with a thin slice of hard-cooked egg and a whole caper. Makes about 24.

Tuna Dinner Canapés: Toast large rounds of bread, allowing 1 for each guest. Just before serving, put toast circles on individual plates, and spread each generously with Rich Tuna Salad. Top with a slice of peeled tomato, and on that place a deviled-egg half (cut crosswise), the cut side down. Drizzle a little thin mayonnaise over all, and garnish plates with salad greens.

APPLE-TUNA SALAD

*Leave the apples unpeeled
for a bright touch of color.*

Drain 1 can tuna (white meat preferred), and separate into large flakes. Combine ½ cup minced celery, 1 cup diced unpeeled apples, 2 tablespoons chopped salted peanuts, and enough mayonnaise or salad dressing to moisten (about ⅓ cup). Carefully fold in the tuna, and put in lettuce-lined salad bowl. Serves 3 or 4.

SALAD NIÇOISE

*Tuna with beans, potatoes, eggs,
tomatoes, onion, anchovies, olives.*

1 head lettuce, sliced	3 large tomatoes, quartered
2 cans tuna (white preferred)	1 large sweet red onion, sliced
1 cup sliced cooked potatoes	1 can flat anchovy fillets, drained
1 cup cooked green beans	12 black olives (preferably European type)
3 hard-cooked eggs, quartered	French dressing

Arrange lettuce in large shallow bowl. Break tuna into good-sized chunks, and arrange in middle. Surround with ring of potatoes, then with beans; surround with eggs and tomatoes, alternating. Break onion into rings, and cover ingredients; then lay anchovies on top. Garnish with olives. At the table, pour on a generous amount of French dressing, made with some olive oil for flavor, and mix gently. Serves 6.

HOT TUNA-SHRIMP SALAD

It bakes with a butter-crumb topping.

2 cans tuna	½ cup sour cream
½ pound cut cooked shrimp	1 cup mayonnaise
¼ cup minced green pepper	Dash Tabasco
¼ cup minced green onion	⅓ cup fine dry bread crumbs
1 cup minced celery	2 tablespoons melted butter

Drain, and separate tuna chunks. Mix carefully with all ingredients, except last 2. Turn into buttered 1½-quart casserole. Combine crumbs and butter, and sprinkle over top. Bake in hot oven, 400°F., 15 minutes, or until well heated. Serves 6.

TUNA COLESLAW WITH GRAPES

It has mayonnaise sour-cream dressing.

2 cups finely sliced cabbage	2 tablespoons minced onion
1 cup seedless grapes (or Tokays, Black Ribiers, or Muscats, cut in half and seeded)	¼ cup mayonnaise
	⅓ cup sour cream
	1 teaspoon lemon juice
	Salt and pepper
	1 can tuna

Mix all ingredients, except tuna. Separate tuna chunks, and fold in lightly but well. Serves 6.

TUNA-STUFFED TOMATO SALAD

*Tuna is mixed with celery
and sliced ripe olives.*

6 large tomatoes	⅓ cup mayonnaise
Salt	1 can tuna, flaked
1 tablespoon minced onion	Pepper
½ cup minced celery	Celery leaves
½ cup sliced ripe olives	Lettuce or curly endive

Peel tomatoes, cut thin slice from top, and scoop out pulp. Sprinkle with salt, and turn upside down to drain. Combine other ingredients, except celery leaves and lettuce, adding curry, chili, or mixed herbs, if you wish, and fill tomatoes. Top with celery leaf, and garnish plate with lettuce. Serves 6.

TUNA-STUFFED CUCUMBERS

*Serve the cucumber boats as a
salad and the cups as an appetizer.*

Peel cucumbers, split lengthwise, and scoop out seedy portion. Or cut crosswise in 1" sections, and scoop out part of insides, making small cups. Fill with Rich Tuna Salad, page 162.

*"It always is the biggest fish
you catch that gets away!"*
EUGENE FIELD

163

TUNA RADICCIO

An Italian-inspired tuna salad.

1 quart curly endive, escarole, or dandelion greens	¼ cup minced green onion
	½ cup olive oil
1 can tuna	1 clove garlic, pressed
8 anchovy fillets, chopped	2 to 3 tablespoons vinegar
¼ cup minced green olives	Salt and pepper
¼ cup minced parsley	¼ cup shredded salami
1 hard-cooked egg, chopped	½ cup sliced radishes
	¼ cup sliced green pepper

Wash greens, and shred. Mix well with other ingredients. Serves 6.

TUNA-WALNUT SPREAD

You use mayonnaise and lemon juice for moistening.

Flake 1 can tuna well. Combine with 1 cup finely chopped or ground walnuts, 1 teaspoon lemon juice, and enough mayonnaise to moisten (about ¼ cup if the tuna is drained, less if it isn't). Makes about 2 cups.

TUNA DIP, FINES HERBES

The herbs: parsley, thyme, tarragon.

1 can tuna	2 tablespoons minced chives (or 1 teaspoon dried)
1 package (3 ounces) cream cheese	1 teaspoon minced tarragon (or ¼ teaspoon dried)
¼ cup sherry	Salt
2 tablespoons minced parsley	Sour cream

Combine all ingredients, using enough sour cream to make of dunking consistency. If you wish, add 1 or 2 tablespoons of chopped capers or nuts. Makes about 1 cup.

*"Ye monsters of the bubbling deep,
Your Maker's praises spout;
Up from the sands ye codlings peep,
and wag your tails about."*
COTTON MATHER

TUNA MAYONNAISE

Serve it on sliced eggs, tomatoes, cucumbers, cold green beans, or lettuce.

Put 1¼ cups mayonnaise into the blender. Add a small (3¼-ounce) can of tuna and an anchovy, and whirl until smooth. Makes about 1½ cups.

TUNA AND AVOCADO SANDWICHES

There's crisp bacon in them, too.

Divide 1 large ripe peeled and sliced avocado among 4 slices buttered toast. Spread with mayonnaise, cover with lettuce leaves; then divide 1 can tuna, broken into large flakes, among sandwiches. Put 2 half-slices crisp bacon on each, cover with top slice of toast, and cut in diagonal halves. Makes 4.

BREAKFAST TUNA, WITH VARIATIONS

The variations come in the seasonings.

1 can tuna	Seasonings
2 cups medium white sauce	3 English muffins
	6 poached eggs

Flake tuna, and add to white sauce. Season with salt and pepper to taste, and any seasoning that you wish: a little curry, or anchovy paste, a few fines herbes, minced parsley, some dill or saffron. Split, and toast muffins; poach eggs, preferably in rings to keep them in shape, and assemble: a toasted muffin half, creamed tuna, and finally poached eggs. Serves 6.

CURRIED TUNA

You serve it on rice with chutney.

2 cups chopped onion	2 cups canned tomatoes
1 cup chopped apple	Salt
½ cup butter or margarine	2 cans tuna
	Hot cooked rice
2 tablespoons curry powder	Chutney

Sauté onion and apple in butter until wilted. Add curry powder and tomatoes; cover, and simmer half hour. Salt to taste. Separate tuna into flakes, add, and cook just enough to heat tuna. Serve with rice, chutney, and any other desired condiments. Serves 4.

TUNA PIZZA

The pastry is hot-roll mix.

1 package hot-roll mix	2 cans tomato sauce
4 tablespoons olive oil	1 teaspoon orégano
1 clove garlic, crushed	Salt and pepper
2 cans tuna chunks	½ pound Mozzarella cheese, sliced
Pitted ripe olives	

Prepare hot-roll mix according to directions on package. Divide in half. Roll each into large round, about ¼" thick. Put on greased cookie sheet or two 12" pizza pans. Combine 3 tablespoons olive oil and garlic, and paint surface of dough liberally. Drain tuna, reserving liquid. Separate tuna chunks, and arrange on pizzas so that surfaces are fairly well covered. Arrange olives in spaces left. Combine oil drained from tuna, any garlic oil remaining, tomato sauce, orégano, salt and pepper to taste, and spread over tuna. Top with cheese, paint tops with 1 tablespoon olive oil, and bake in hot oven, 425°F., 20 minutes, or until nicely browned around edges. Serves 6 to 12.

TUNA CASSEROLE

A basic tuna and noodle recipe with suggestions for variations.

½ pound noodles	2 cans tuna
Salt	2 tablespoons sherry
1 clove garlic, minced	Pepper
½ cup minced green onion	3 tablespoons bread crumbs
3 tablespoons butter	2 tablespoons minced parsley
¼ cup flour	2 tablespoons melted butter
2 cups milk	

Cook noodles in salted water, and drain. Sauté garlic and onion in butter until wilted; add flour, blend over heat, and add milk. Cook, stirring, until thickened and smooth; add tuna, sherry, salt and pepper to taste. Other ingredients of your choice may be added with the tuna (nuts, sliced olives, cooked peas or beans, quartered artichoke hearts). Put in 1½-quart casserole. Mix crumbs, parsley, and butter; sprinkle on top. Reheat in 350°F. oven 15 minutes. Serves 6 to 8.

"The man what weds for greedy wealth, He goes a fishing fair, But often times he get a frog, Or very little share."
UNKNOWN

RISI E BISI CON TONNO

Rice and peas with tuna served with grated Parmesan cheese.

Combine 3 cups hot cooked rice, 3 cups hot cooked peas, 1 or 2 cans tuna, ¼ cup minced onion sautéed in ¼ cup butter, salt and pepper to taste. Serve with grated Parmesan cheese. Serves 6 to 8.

BRANDADE DE THON

Tuna, white beans, and cheese baked with a crumb topping.

Cook 1 cup dried white beans and 4 cloves garlic in water until tender (about 2 hours). Drain, and purée, or whirl in blender until smooth, with 2 tablespoons cream or olive oil, 1 can tuna, and a little bean liquid. When smooth, season to taste with salt, and add ¼ cup each grated Swiss and Parmesan cheese. Put in a shallow baking dish, dot with 2 tablespoons of butter, and sprinkle with ½ cup of soft, stale bread crumbs. Bake in moderate oven, 375°F., 20 minutes, or until hot and brown. Serves 6.

TUNA MARKA

Tuna, green onions, water chestnuts, and ginger sour cream on rice.

2 cans tuna (white preferred)	2 teaspoons slivered fresh or candied ginger
½ cup chopped green onion	2 cups sour cream
1 tablespoon butter	Salt and pepper
½ cup sliced water chestnuts	Hot cooked rice

Drain tuna oil into pan, add onion and butter, and cook until wilted. Add tuna, broken in large flakes, water chestnuts, ginger, sour cream, and salt and pepper to taste. Heat (do not boil) over low heat. Serve with rice. Serves 6.

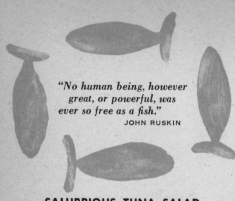

"*No human being, however great, or powerful, was ever so free as a fish.*"

JOHN RUSKIN

SALUBRIOUS TUNA SALAD

Tuna, cottage cheese, celery, green pepper, onion, and olives.

Combine 1 can tuna, drained and flaked, with ½ pint cottage cheese, 2 tablespoons each of chopped celery, green pepper, onion, and ripe olives. Add salt and pepper to taste, and a little dill weed, chili powder, or curry powder, if you like. Serve on lettuce with crisp crackers. Serves 4 to 6.
Note: If dietetic tuna is used, this is a good low-calorie, high-protein dish.

PICKLED TUNA WITH SOUR CREAM

You add onions, lemon, and bay leaf to wine vinegar for the pickling mixture.

2 cans tuna	2 bay leaves
2 large onions, sliced thin	2 teaspoons mixed pickling spice, crushed
1 lemon, sliced thin	1 cup sour cream
¼ cup water	
⅓ cup wine vinegar	

Break undrained tuna into large pieces. Toss lightly with onion and lemon. Mix water, vinegar, bay leaves, and spice; simmer 5 minutes. Pour over tuna mixture, toss lightly, and stir in sour cream. Chill. Use as appetizer or salad. Makes 4 to 6 servings.

TUNA PAPRIKA

Tuna in sour cream and paprika.

Cook 1 cup minced onion in 2 tablespoons butter until wilted. Add 2 tablespoons flour, ½ cup chicken stock, ½ teaspoon salt, 3 tablespoons paprika, and cook slowly 10 minutes. Add 1½ cups sour cream and 2 cans tuna (white preferred). Heat, and serve with noodles or rice. Serves 4 to 6.

TUNA AND POTATO TART

Eggs are baked in the tuna-potato filling.

1 tablespoon chopped onion	2 tablespoons minced parsley
Butter	1 baked 10″ pastry shell
1 can tuna	6 eggs
2 cups seasoned mashed potato	

Cook onion in 1 tablespoon butter until wilted. Add tuna, potato, parsley, and salt and pepper if needed. Put in baked shell, make 6 depressions in potato mixture, drop a raw egg in each, and drizzle melted butter over each. Bake in moderate oven, 375°F., until eggs are set. Serves 6.

CREAMED TUNA

Season with sherry, herbs, or spices.

Combine 1 can tuna, flaked, with 1½ to 2 cups medium white sauce, seasoned with sherry, herbs, or spices. Makes 2 to 2½ cups.

Creamed Tuna and Eggplant: Peel a medium-sized eggplant, and cut in ½″ slices. Dip in slightly beaten egg, and then in cracker crumbs. Sauté in hot bacon fat until brown on both sides, about 8 minutes. Serve as a bed for Creamed Tuna. Sprinkle with minced dill, chives, or chopped ripe olives, if desired. Serves 4 to 6.

Hot Tuna Tarts: Make tart shells, and, while still warm, fill with Creamed Tuna, seasoned as you wish. Garnish to suit your imagination and taste.

Tuna Shortcake: Cover split, buttered biscuits with Creamed Tuna (above).

TUNA TURNOVERS

Each of these makes a hearty serving.

Make pastry with 1 cup sifted flour, ½ teaspoon salt, and ⅓ cup shortening. Roll in a 12″ square, and cut in 4 squares. Mix 1 can tuna, 1 teaspoon instant minced onion, 1½ teaspoons Worcestershire, ¼ cup mayonnaise, ¼ teaspoon salt, dash pepper. Spread on lower half of each square; fold top half over mixture, and seal edges with tines of fork. Bake on cookie sheet in 400°F. oven 20 minutes. Makes 4.

TUNA AND CABBAGE PIROG

Dilled tuna, cabbage, and
onion baked in pastry.

1 package	1 or 2 cans tuna
hot-roll mix	2 tablespoons
4 cups finely	dill weed
chopped cabbage	Salt and pepper
1 onion, chopped	1 egg
¼ cup butter	1 tablespoon water

Prepare hot-roll mix according to directions on box. Cook cabbage and onion in butter until wilted. Add tuna, flaked, and dill weed. Season to taste. After dough has risen, divide in half, and roll each half into a rectangle about 9"x 11". Put one in shallow baking pan, and spread with tuna-cabbage mixture. Moisten edges, and top with second rectangle; seal. Brush top with egg beaten with water, and bake in hot oven, 400°F., 15 to 20 minutes. Cut in squares. Serves 12.

TUNA WILD RICE, AMANDINE

You can use brown or white
rice instead of wild if you like.

Blanch, and sliver ½ cup almonds, and brown lightly in 3 tablespoons butter or margarine. Cook ¾ cup wild rice, drain well, and mix with almonds and butter. Add salt if necessary. Separate 1 can tuna (white preferred) into large flakes, and combine with 2 cups medium white sauce and 2 tablespoons sherry. Pack rice mixture into 3-cup bowl, unmold on round platter, and surround with tuna mixture. Serves 4. **Note:** A good way to cook wild rice is to cover it with boiling water, cover pan, and let stand 20 minutes, then drain. Repeat 3 times, or until rice is done to your liking.

TUNA KEDGEREE

Tuna, rice, chopped eggs, and cream.

2 cans tuna	2 tablespoons
2 cups cooked rice	minced parsley
2 hard-cooked	(optional)
eggs, chopped	½ teaspoon
¼ cup cream	curry powder
Salt and pepper	(optional)

Flake tuna, combine it and its juices with the other ingredients, and heat well. Serves 6 for breakfast, 4 for lunch.

JAPANESE TUNA AND EGGS

A tuna, bean-sprout, and green-
onion omelet with soy sauce.

Pour boiling water over ¼ pound bean sprouts, let stand 1 minute, and drain (or use a 1-pound can, drained). Mix with ½ cup thinly sliced green onions, 5 slightly beaten eggs, 1 tablespoon soy sauce, and 1 can tuna, broken into pieces. Put 2 tablespoons oil in 10" skillet, add mixture, and cook until set and brown on the bottom. Fold. Serves 4.

TUNA EGGS FOO YOUNG

They're served with thickened
soy sauce and chicken broth.

Make like Japanese Tuna and Eggs above, but add ½ cup minced water chestnuts, and cook by spoonfuls on griddle or in skillet. Turn, and brown other side, and serve with a sauce made by seasoning 1 cup of chicken stock with 2 tablespoons soy sauce, and thickening with 4 teaspoons of cornstarch moistened in 2 tablespoons of cold water. Cook until thickened and clear. Serves 4.

CHICKEN IN TUNA SAUCE

Sauce is moistened with white wine
and water in which the chicken cooked.

Cook a large plump roasting chicken or capon in ½ white wine and ½ water, using just enough to cover in pot the size of the chicken. When tender, chill, and slice. Make the sauce by blending together 1 can tuna, 1 tablespoon olive oil, juice of 1 lemon, 6 anchovies, ½ cup mayonnaise, and enough chicken liquid to make a sauce the consistency of thin mayonnaise. Chill, and serve with chicken; garnish platter with lemon slices. Serves 6.

"There are as good fish
in the sea as ever
came out of it."
SIR WALTER SCOTT

SWEET-AND-SOUR TUNA

*It's cooked with pineapple, green
pepper, green onions, and tomatoes.*

1 can (9 ounces) pineapple tidbits	1 green pepper, sliced thin
½ cup vinegar	2 tomatoes, peeled, seeded, and cut in eighths
¼ cup sugar	
1 tablespoon soy sauce	2 cans tuna
2 tablespoons cornstarch	Hot cooked rice or fried Chinese noodles
4 green onions, sliced diagonally	

Drain syrup from pineapple, and combine it with vinegar and sugar. Mix soy sauce with cornstarch, and add. Cook, stirring, until clear and thickened. Add onion, green pepper, tomatoes, and pineapple, and simmer 4 minutes. Add tuna, broken into large flakes, and heat. Serve with rice. Serves 4 to 6.

TUNA AND CHILI FONDUE

*Tuna and green chilies
baked in cheese custard.*

1 can tuna	1 teaspoon chili powder
½ cup minced celery	12 slices bread
2 tablespoons minced onion	2 cups grated cheddar cheese
¼ cup minced canned green chilies	3 eggs, beaten
	1 cup milk
¼ cup mayonnaise	¼ cup cream
¼ teaspoon salt	¼ teaspoon salt
	Dash Tabasco

Combine first 7 ingredients. Spread on half the bread, and make sandwiches. Cut each in quarters, and arrange in layers in square baking dish, putting cheese between layers and on top. Combine remaining ingredients, and pour over all. Bake in slow oven, 300°F., 50 minutes, or until set. Serves 6.

*"They say fish should swim thrice . . .
first it should swim in the sea,
then it should swim in butter,
and . . . it should swim in good claret."*
JONATHAN SWIFT

TUNA FLORENTINE

*Tuna, Swiss, and Parmesan cheeses
on a bed of chopped spinach.*

1 pound spinach, cooked, chopped, and seasoned	¼ cup grated Swiss cheese
	⅓ cup grated Parmesan cheese or ½ cup grated cheddar
2 tablespoons butter	
3 tablespoons flour	
2 cups rich milk	
	2 cans tuna

Put spinach in large shallow baking dish, and keep hot. Make a roux with butter and flour; add milk, Swiss cheese, 2 tablespoons Parmesan, and oil and juice from the tuna. Cook over hot water 20 minutes. Add tuna, flaked, and pour over spinach. Sprinkle top with remaining Parmesan cheese and put under broiler until brown and bubbly. Makes 6 servings.

FRESH TUNA TARRAGON

It has a white-wine sauce.

Marinate 2 pounds tuna steaks in white wine to cover (about 1½ cups) 2 hours. Drain. To marinade, add 1 tablespoon dried tarragon, and let soak. Dry steaks, dust lightly with flour, sprinkle with salt, and brown on both sides in ¼ cup butter or oil. Add wine and tarragon mixture, and cook at high heat until wine is reduced one half. Remove fish to a hot platter, pour over wine and tarragon sauce, and serve. Makes 4 to 6 servings.

BROILED FRESH ALBACORE

*It marinates in oil with a bay
leaf, rosemary, and lemon juice.*

Skin fish, removing any dark meat lying under it. Cut into steaks 1½" thick. Remove dark meat near bone. Marinate in mixture of ¼ cup each olive oil and salad oil, bay leaf, some freshly ground pepper, ½ teaspoon salt, a sprig (or ½ teaspoon) rosemary, and juice of 1 lemon. Turn after 1 hour, and marinate another hour. Grill over medium charcoal fire or in oven broiler 4 to 5 minutes on each side. Serve with lemon butter. Garnish with cress. Allow ½ pound trimmed steak for each person.

CHEESE

Cheese is one of the oldest forms of preserved food. Centuries ago, possibly on the steppes of central Asia, some tribe of herdsmen devised a way to ferment and age milk in cakes that could be eaten weeks and even months later. Without realizing it they had created one of mankind's richest and most highly concentrated foods. Since that day, people have gone on inventing cheeses. Some are dry and crumbly; others creamy or buttery; some are mild; others sharp. Most are made from cow's milk, but some are made from goat's or mare's milk. Every kind has its use. Here are the world's famous cheeses: Roquefort from France, aged in limestone caves; Gruyére and Emmenthal, the cheese with the large holes, from Switzerland; Camembert and Brie, both rich and creamy, from France. America's greatest cheese is the familiar cheddar, an outstanding treat both plain and in cooking. At its best it is well-aged, sharp and dry.

BRANDIED CHEDDAR CHEESE

You serve it at room temperature as a spread for crackers.

4 cups (1 pound) shredded cheddar cheese	1 teaspoon sugar
	Dash cayenne
2 tablespoons butter	½ cup brandy

Have cheese and butter at room temperature. Add sugar, cayenne, and ¼ cup brandy; mix, or beat with electric mixer until quite smooth. Gradually add remaining ¼ cup brandy, mixing until creamy. Store in covered crock in refrigerator. Makes about 2 cups.

LIPTAUER CHEESE

A cocktail spread featuring cottage cheese, anchovies, capers, and chives.

1 can (¾ ounce) anchovy fillets	1 carton (8 ounces) cottage cheese, sieved
1 tablespoon each dry mustard, caraway seed, capers, and chopped chives	1 cup soft butter or margarine
	Paprika
	Chopped parsley

Drain anchovies, and mince. Mix with remaining ingredients, except last 2. Mound in serving dish. Garnish with paprika, parsley. Chill. Makes 2 cups.

POT-CHEESE DUMPLINGS

You serve them with melted butter and sour cream.

1 pound dry pot cheese	3 quarts boiling water
2 eggs	Butter or margarine
1 cup sifted flour	½ pint sour cream
1 teaspoon salt	

Mash cheese; add eggs, and mix well. Stir in flour and salt. Drop by table-spoonfuls into rapidly boiling water; cover, and boil 15 minutes. Drain, and serve with melted butter and sour cream. Makes 4 servings.

CHEDDAR-CHEESE STICKS

Crisp cheese hot breads, to serve as appetizers or snacks.

2 cups sifted flour	1½ cups (6 ounces) shredded sharp cheddar cheese
¾ teaspoon salt	
Dash paprika	
Butter or margarine	Water

Sift dry ingredients. Cut in ½ cup butter. Add cheese, and mix well; then add enough water to hold ingredients together. Roll out on floured board to rectangle 14"x 8". Dot with 2 tablespoons butter; fold corners into center. Roll out again; dot with 2 tablespoons more butter; fold again. Wrap in waxed paper; chill about half hour. Roll out ¼" thick. With pastry wheel, cut in scalloped strips, 4"x ½". Put on ungreased cookie sheet. Bake in hot oven, 400°F., 8 to 10 minutes. Makes about 4½ dozen.

CHEESE FRITTERS

They're delicious with tart jelly.

1 egg, beaten	Dash red hot sauce
½ cup milk	2 cups biscuit mix
1 teaspoon Worcestershire	1½ cups diced process American cheese
1 tablespoon instant minced onion	Fat for frying
	Tart jelly

Mix first 5 ingredients, and add to biscuit mix. Mix well, and stir in cheese. Drop by tablespoonfuls into hot deep fat (365°F. on a frying thermometer), and fry until golden brown. Drain on absorbent paper. Serve with tart jelly. Makes about 20.

CHEESE WAFFLES

Shredded American cheese is added to plain waffle batter.

3 eggs, separated	2 tablespoons sugar
2 cups milk	1 teaspoon salt
2 cups shredded process American cheese	2 teaspoons baking powder
	½ cup butter or margarine, melted
2 cups sifted flour	

Beat egg yolks with rotary beater. Combine with milk and cheese. Add to sifted dry ingredients, mixing just until blended. Add butter. Fold in stiffly beaten egg whites. Bake in hot waffle iron. Makes 8 to 10.

CHEESE SHRIMP CHOWDER

Cheddar cheese and shrimp, plus onion,
potato, celery, milk, and sherry.

3 medium potatoes, diced	8 ounces cheddar cheese, diced
1 cup sliced celery with tops	¼ teaspoon pepper
1 large onion, chopped	1 can (4½ ounces) medium shrimp, undrained
2 cups boiling water	2 to 4 tablespoons dry sherry
1 tall can evaporated milk	Chopped parsley

Put first 4 ingredients in saucepan; bring to boil, and simmer, covered, 15 minutes, or until potatoes are tender. (Do not drain.) Add milk, cheese, and pepper; heat gently, stirring, until cheese is melted. Add shrimp and sherry. Serve in bowls with sprinkling of parsley. Makes about 2½ quarts.

CHILLED ROQUEFORT BOUILLON

It's served with sour cream
and a sprinkling of chopped chives.

1 envelope unflavored gelatin	Juice ½ lemon
	¼ cup crumbled Roquefort cheese
½ cup cold water	Sour cream
2 cans beef bouillon	Chopped chives

Soften gelatin in water; dissolve over low heat. Stir into bouillon; add lemon juice. Chill until slightly thickened. Lightly fold in cheese. Serve in bouillon cups with sour cream and a sprinkling of chives. Serves 4 to 6.

BLUE CHEESE-ONION SOUP

You use beef stock or
bouillon for the base.

4 cups thinly sliced onion	5½ cups beef stock, or 4 beef bouillon cubes and 5½ cups water
⅓ cup butter or margarine	
¼ teaspoon pepper	¾ cup crumbled blue cheese

Cook onion in butter in kettle until golden brown. Add pepper and stock, and bring to boil. Simmer, covered, 1 hour. Ladle into deep soup bowls, and sprinkle cheese on top. Serve with toasted small slices of French bread or croutons, if desired. Serves 6.

CHEESE SOUP AUX CROUTONS

The cheese is sharp cheddar.

1 onion, sliced	1 teaspoon Worcestershire
1 cup chopped celery	2 bouillon cubes
¼ cup butter or margarine	2 cups water
	1 carrot, diced
¼ cup flour	1 quart milk
½ teaspoon dry mustard	1½ cups (6 ounces) shredded sharp cheddar cheese
½ teaspoon each garlic salt and Accent	Salt and pepper
	Croutons

In large saucepan, cook onion and celery in butter about 5 minutes. Blend in flour and seasonings. Add next 3 ingredients. Bring to boil, and simmer, covered, 15 minutes. Add milk, and heat almost to boiling. Add cheese; stir until melted. Season. Serve with croutons. Makes 1½ quarts.

CHEESE-CHICKEN SANDWICH, LA SALLE

Blue cheese, chicken, and creamy sauce.

6 slices white bread	¼ teaspoon pepper
6 tablespoons butter	¼ cup heavy cream
Cooked chicken	1¾ cups milk
½ cup crumbled blue cheese	1 teaspoon instant minced onion
3 tablespoons flour	2 egg yolks, beaten
¾ teaspoon salt	¼ cup grated Parmesan cheese

Cut crusts from bread, and spread slices with 2 tablespoons butter. Arrange flat in shallow baking dish. Top with chicken slices; sprinkle with blue cheese. Melt remaining butter; blend in flour and seasonings. Add liquids and onion; cook, stirring, until thickened. Stir small amount into egg yolks. Return mixture to saucepan; cook 2 or 3 minutes, stirring. Pour over ingredients in baking dish. Sprinkle with grated cheese. Bake in hot oven, 425°F., about 15 minutes. Serves 6.

SWISS-CHEESE SOUFFLÉ

*You put a dash of Tabasco
or red hot sauce in it.*

½ cup milk	1 teaspoon salt
1 cup stale-bread crumbs	4 eggs, separated
1 tablespoon butter	Dash paprika
½ pound process Swiss cheese, shredded	Dash Tabasco or red hot sauce

Heat first 3 ingredients in top part of double boiler over boiling water. Stir in cheese. Add salt to egg whites; beat until stiff. Beat yolks well; add remaining seasonings; fold into sauce. Pour sauce over whites, folding in carefully. Bake in buttered 1½-quart casserole in 350°F. oven 25 to 30 minutes. Serves 4.

CHEESE-HOMINY PUFF

Cheddar is the cheese.

¾ cup hominy grits	¼ cup butter or margarine
1 cup boiling water	
1½ teaspoons salt	1 cup grated sharp cheddar cheese
2 cups milk	
	4 eggs, separated

Cook hominy with water and salt in top part of double boiler 2 minutes, stirring. Add milk; cook 30 minutes, stirring occasionally. Add butter and cheese; stir until melted. Add beaten egg yolks, and fold in stiffly beaten whites. Bake in buttered 1½-quart casserole in moderate oven, 350°F., about 45 minutes. Makes 4 servings.

SPAGHETTI PARMESAN

*Garlic spaghetti is tossed in olive
oil and grated Parmesan cheese.*

Cook 8 ounces spaghetti, following directions on package, and adding 1 clove garlic, minced, to water. Drain. Add ¼ cup olive oil and 1½ cups grated Parmesan; toss. Serves 4.

CHEDDAR-CHEESE SOUFFLÉ

*A slow-cooking soufflé
that bakes for 1½ hours.*

½ pound sharp cheddar cheese, cut up	1½ teaspoons salt
	⅛ teaspoon cayenne
1 tall can evaporated milk	½ teaspoon dry mustard
1 milk-can water	6 egg yolks
1 tablespoon instant minced onion	6 egg whites

Combine all ingredients, except egg whites, in bowl. Blend one half at a time in electric blender. Beat egg whites until stiff, and fold into blended mixture. Bake in ungreased 2½-quart casserole in slow oven, 300°F., about 1½ hours. Serves 4.

TWO-CHEESE MEAT TARTS

*There's American cheese in the
shells and cream cheese in the filling.*

⅓ cup shortening	1 cup diced luncheon meat
¾ cup shredded process American cheese	½ cup crumbled cooked bacon
1¾ cups sifted flour	1 package (3 ounces) cream cheese
¼ teaspoon salt	
3 tablespoons cold water	2 tablespoons evaporated milk

Cut shortening and American cheese into flour and salt. With fork, lightly mix in water. Divide in 16 pieces, and roll out each to form a round about 3½" in diameter. Fit into medium muffin pans. Mix luncheon meat and bacon; put a spoonful into each shell. Mix cream cheese and milk; spread on meat in shells. Bake in 450°F. oven about 15 minutes. Makes 16.

CHEDDAR-CHEESE CORN

This is served on toast.

Melt 2 tablespoons butter; blend in 1 tablespoon flour, ½ teaspoon salt, and ⅛ teaspoon pepper. Add 1 teaspoon caraway seed and 1 cup light cream. Cook, stirring, until slightly thickened. Add 1 can (12 ounces) whole-kernel corn, undrained; heat. Top with ½ pound sharp cheddar cheese, sliced. Cover; heat slowly until cheese melts. Makes 4 servings.

WESTERN BURGERS

Seasoned crab meat and
cheddar cheese are broiled on rolls.

Mix 1 can (6½ ounces) crab meat, flaked; 1 teaspoon prepared mustard; and 2 tablespoons chili sauce. Split, and butter 4 sandwich rolls; spread with mixture. Top with cheddar-cheese slices; broil. Serves 4.

CREAM-CHEESE EGG ROLLS

Delicious with watercress or salad.

Mix well: 1 package (8 ounces) soft cream cheese, 3 chopped hard-cooked eggs, 1 grated small onion, ½ teaspoon salt, ¼ teaspoon pepper, ½ cup sliced stuffed olives. Scoop out some crumbs from 8 split sandwich rolls. Fill rolls with cheese mixture, and put halves together. Makes 8.

CHILI-CHEESE SANDWICHES

Cheddar plus onion rings,
green pepper, and chili sauce.

Trim crusts from 6 slices of bread; toast on one side. Spread untoasted side with mayonnaise. Top with onion rings. Cook ¼ cup chopped green pepper 5 minutes in 2 tablespoons butter. Stir in ½ cup chili sauce. Spread on sandwiches, and top each with two thin slices of cheddar cheese. Broil until cheese is melted. Serves 6.

CHEESE-PEACH SALAD

It's served with Mustard Mayonnaise.

Mix 1 cup cream-style cottage cheese and 2 tablespoons horse-radish. Put between 8 peach halves. Serve on lettuce with **Mustard Mayonnaise:** add 1 tablespoon prepared mustard to ½ cup mayonnaise; fold in ¼ cup heavy cream, whipped. Serves 4.

BLUE-CHEESE SPRING SALAD

Beans, cucumber, tomato, pepper,
and onion are tossed with the cheese.

Toss lightly: 1 cup cooked green Lima beans; 1 cucumber, peeled and diced; 1 ripe tomato, diced; ½ green pepper, cut in strips; 2 green onions, sliced; few sprigs of parsley; ¼ cup crumbled blue cheese; ⅓ cup French dressing. Serve on greens. Serves 6.

FROZEN ROQUEFORT SALAD

It contains cream cheese, too.

¼ pound Roquefort cheese, finely crumbled	¼ teaspoon each paprika, salt, and Worcestershire
1 package (3 ounces) cream cheese, softened	Dash cayenne
	¾ cup heavy cream, whipped
1 teaspoon vinegar	½ pimiento, chopped
1 tablespoon chopped chives	Salad greens

Turn refrigerator control to coldest setting. Mix all ingredients well, except last 3. Then fold in cream and pimiento. Pour into a refrigerator tray, and freeze until firm. Cut in squares, and arrange on greens. Serves 6.

BLUE-CHEESE SALAD BOWL

Cauliflower, Bermuda onion, olives,
and lettuce besides the blue cheese.

1 small head cauliflower	⅔ cup French dressing
½ Bermuda onion, thinly sliced	½ cup crumbled blue cheese
½ cup sliced stuffed olives	1 small head lettuce

Slice flowerets of cauliflower thin, and separate onion in rings. Add olives and dressing to cauliflower and onion; marinate in refrigerator for 30 minutes. Just before serving, add blue cheese and lettuce, broken in bite-size pieces. Toss lightly. Serves 6.

OREGON CHEESE SALAD

Pears are spread with a cheddar
cheese, sour-cream, and nut mixture.

Mix 1 cup each grated cheddar cheese, and chopped filberts or walnuts, ½ cup sour cream, and dash salt. Arrange 8 fresh or canned pear halves on salad greens. Sprinkle with orange juice, and spread with cheese mixture. Serve as is, or stud with grapes. Serves 4.

TWO BASIC GROUPS
NATURAL CHEESE: milk curds that have been heated, pressed, and, in most instances, cured. PROCESS CHEESE: natural cheese that has been shredded, blended, pasteurized.

CANELLONI, PARMESAN SAUCE

Tiny pancakes stuffed with a cheese, chicken, spinach, and sausage mixture.

½ pound sausage meat, cooked and drained	⅛ teaspoon thyme
	⅛ teaspoon pepper
1 box frozen spinach, cooked, chopped fine	Butter
	1 cup milk
	2 eggs, beaten
1 cup finely chopped cooked chicken	½ cup sifted flour
	1 teaspoon baking powder
¼ cup grated Romano cheese	½ teaspoon salt
	Parmesan Sauce

To make Stuffing, mix first 6 ingredients. **To make Pancakes:** Heat 2 tablespoons butter and the milk until butter is melted. Cool slightly. Add next 4 ingredients, and mix until smooth. Drop by spoonfuls onto hot buttered skillet to form 18 3" pancakes. Fry until browned on both sides. Cool, and spread each with Stuffing. Roll up, and put in broilerproof shallow baking dish. Cover with Sauce. Broil 5 minutes. Makes 6 servings.

Parmesan Sauce: Melt 3 tablespoons butter; blend in 3 tablespoons flour. Add 1½ cups light cream; cook, stirring, until thickened. Stir in ½ cup grated Parmesan cheese. Season.

CHEESE-POTATO CUSTARD

The cheese, cottage cheese, is blended with sour cream.

1 cup each cottage cheese and sour cream	1 onion, chopped
	2 pimientos, chopped
2 cups hot mashed potato	2 eggs, well beaten
	2 tablespoons butter
1 teaspoon salt	

Mix cheese and cream. Add next 4 ingredients; mix well. Fold in eggs. Pour into buttered 1½-quart casserole, and dot with butter. Bake in 350°F. oven 1 hour, or until set. Serves 4 to 6.

QUICHE LORRAINE

A main-dish cheese and bacon pie.

1½ cups (6 ounces) grated imported Swiss cheese	1 cup heavy cream
	½ cup milk
	½ teaspoon salt
8 slices crisp bacon, crumbled	¼ teaspoon pepper
	Dash cayenne
1 unbaked 9" pie shell	½ teaspoon dry mustard
3 eggs	

Sprinkle cheese and bacon in pie shell. Beat remaining ingredients together, and pour into pie shell. Bake in moderate oven, 375°F., 45 minutes, or until firm and browned. Makes 6 servings.

FONDUE NEUCHÂTELOISE

You make it with Swiss cheese, kirsch, and dry white wine.

1 cup Neuchâtel (or Rhine, Riesling, or any light dry white wine)	Salt, pepper, and nutmeg to taste
	2 to 3 tablespoons kirsch
1 clove garlic	1 loaf French bread or 4 hard rolls, cut in bite-sized pieces
4 cups (1 pound) shredded Swiss cheese	
1½ tablespoons flour	

Heat wine with garlic in top part of double boiler over boiling water. Remove garlic. Dredge cheese with flour. Add, a handful at a time, to wine, stirring after each addition until cheese is melted. Season to taste; add kirsch. **To serve:** Put on table over hot water. Holding a piece of bread on fork, each person, in rotation, dunks it in the cheese mixture with a stirring motion. **Note:** If the cheese mixture becomes too thick, thin with a little heated wine. Makes 4 servings.

CHEESE-BAKED FISH FILLETS

Fish bakes in a sauce of cheddar cheese, mushroom soup, and sherry.

Cut 1 pound fresh or frozen fish fillets in serving pieces, and arrange in shallow baking dish. Sprinkle lightly with salt. Mix 1 can (10½ ounces) mushroom soup, 1 cup grated sharp cheddar cheese, ¼ cup sherry, and ⅛ teaspoon pepper. Spread on fish. Sprinkle with paprika. Bake in moderate oven, 375°F., about 25 minutes. Serves 3.

CHEESE-TURKEY SHORTCAKES

*Turkey in cheese gravy on
hot biscuits with pimiento garnish.*

In top part of double boiler over boiling water, melt ½ pound process American cheese. Stir in ⅔ cup chicken broth. Add 2 cups diced cooked turkey, 1 teaspoon instant minced onion, and pepper to taste. Heat; serve on hot biscuits with a garnish of pimiento strips. Serves 4.

TWO-CHEESE FONDUE

You use Parmesan and Swiss cheeses.

3 tablespoons butter or margarine	¼ pound Parmesan cheese, grated
3 tablespoons flour	¼ pound Swiss cheese, grated
Dash cayenne	1" cubes rye or whole-wheat bread, toasted
¾ cup each light cream and chicken stock	
1 teaspoon instant minced onion	

Melt butter in top pan of chafing dish. Blend in flour and cayenne. Gradually add liquids. Add onion, and cook, stirring, until thickened. Put over hot water; add cheeses; cook until cheeses are melted. Hold bread on forks, and dip in sauce. Makes 4 to 6 servings.

DOUBLE-BOILER MACARONI AND CHEESE

*You stir in browned
bread cubes just before serving.*

2 cups elbow macaroni	½ teaspoon dry mustard
5 cups boiling water	½ pound sharp cheddar cheese, cubed
2 teaspoons salt	
1 tablespoon instant minced onion	1 teaspoon Worcestershire
½ cup powdered cream	1 cup soft bread cubes
3 tablespoons flour	2 tablespoons butter
¼ teaspoon pepper	Seasoned salt

In top part of 2½-quart double boiler, cook first 4 ingredients until macaroni is tender. (Do not drain.) Mix next 4 ingredients; stir into first mixture. Add cheese and Worcestershire. Put over boiling water; simmer, covered, 15 minutes, stirring occasionally. Brown bread cubes in butter; sprinkle with seasoned salt. Stir into mixture. Makes 4 to 6 servings.

MILE-HIGH CHEESE SOUFFLÉ

You start it in a 475°F. oven.

½ cup butter or margarine	2 cups milk
½ cup sifted flour	2 cups (½ pound) sharp cheddar cheese, cut fine
2 teaspoons salt	
½ teaspoon paprika	8 eggs, separated
Dash cayenne	

Melt butter in top part of double boiler over hot water. Add flour and seasonings; mix well. Stir in milk, and cook, stirring constantly, until sauce is thick and smooth. Add cheese, and stir until melted. Remove from heat. Beat yolks until light, and gradually stir into cheese sauce. Rinse beater; beat whites until stiff but not dry, and carefully fold sauce into whites. Pour mixture into 3-quart casserole that has been generously brushed with melted butter. Bake in very hot oven, 475°F., 10 minutes. Reduce heat to 400°F.; bake 25 minutes. Makes 6 servings.

HAM AND POTATOES, CHANTILLY

They bake in a cheddar-cream sauce.

3 large potatoes, cooked and riced	½ cup heavy cream
¼ cup hot milk	1 cup (¼ pound) shredded sharp cheddar cheese
2 tablespoons butter	
Salt and pepper	Paprika
½ cup finely chopped baked or boiled ham	

Mix potato, milk, butter, and seasonings to taste; beat until fluffy. Put in shallow 1-quart baking dish. Sprinkle with ham. Whip cream until stiff; fold in cheese, and season to taste. Spread on potatoes. Sprinkle with paprika. Bake in very hot oven, 450°F., 15 minutes. Makes 4 servings.

CREAMY ITALIAN DRESSING

*It's made with Parmesan or Romano, to
serve on lettuce or cooked vegetables.*

Prepare 1 envelope Italian salad-dressing mix with vinegar, water, and salad
oil as directed on the envelope. Measure ½ cup, and reserve remainder for
later use. To ½ cup, add ¼ cup each
sour cream and grated Parmesan or
Romano cheese; mix well. Serve on
salad greens or cooked vegetables.
Makes about 1 cup.

JELLIED TWO-CHEESE SALAD RING

*You can also serve the cheese ring
for dessert, surrounded with fruit.*

1 envelope un- flavored gelatin	½ cup crumbled Roquefort or blue cheese
⅓ cup cold water	½ teaspoon salt
1 cup cottage cheese, mashed	⅔ cup heavy cream
	Salad greens

Sprinkle gelatin over water; let stand
5 minutes. Dissolve over hot water.
Combine remaining ingredients, except
greens, and blend with gelatin. Pour
into oiled 1-quart ring mold, and chill
until firm. Unmold on greens, and fill
center with chicken, meat, or fish
salad. Makes 4 servings.

COTTAGE-CHEESE MOLD WITH FRUIT

*Serve this for dessert,
or on greens as a salad.*

1 envelope un- flavored gelatin	⅛ teaspoon paprika
¼ cup cold water	Dash of cayenne
2 cups cottage cheese	½ cup milk or cream
¾ teaspoon salt	Fruit

Soften gelatin in cold water, and dissolve over hot water. Mash cheese fine;
add seasonings, milk, and gelatin. Turn
into ring mold. Chill several hours.
Unmold, and fill center with fruit.
Makes 4 servings.

CHEESE-TOMATO SALAD

*Curried cottage cheese and
cucumber spread between tomato slices.*

Cut each of 4 large, unpeeled tomatoes
into 4 slices. Add ½ cup minced cucumber or celery to ½ pound cottage
cheese. Season with curry powder,
grated onion, salt, and pepper. Spread
each tomato slice, except tops, with
cheese filling. Stack slices on lettuce,
and replace tops. Insert sprigs of parsley in each top. Serve with mayonnaise or other dressing. Serves 4.

CHEESE-APPLESAUCE PIE

It has a cinnamon corn-flake shell.

1 cup packaged corn-flake crumbs	½ cup heavy cream
Sugar	2 tablespoons flour
1 teaspoon cinnamon	3 teaspoons grated lemon rind
2 tablespoons butter, melted	3 tablespoons lemon juice
2 cups cottage cheese	1 jar (15 ounces) applesauce
2 eggs	¾ cup chopped almonds
⅛ teaspoon salt	

Mix crumbs, 2 tablespoons sugar, cinnamon, and butter. Press firmly on bottom and sides of 9″ piepan. Press
cheese through fine sieve. Add eggs,
½ cup sugar, salt, cream, flour, 1 teaspoon lemon rind, and 1 tablespoon
juice. Beat until smooth; pour into pan.
Bake in slow oven, 325°F., about 1
hour. Cool. Mix remaining rind, juice,
applesauce, almonds. Spread over pie.

ROQUEFORT-SOUR CREAM DRESSING

*You can use the same recipe
with Gorgonzola or blue cheese.*

1 pint sour cream	2 tablespoons vinegar
½ teaspoon each garlic salt, celery salt, pepper, and paprika	1 teaspoon salt
	½ pound Roquefort cheese, crumbled
¼ cup mayonnaise	Romaine

Mix all ingredients, except last 2.
Carefully fold in Roquefort. Serve on
romaine or other lettuce. Serves 8.

CREAM CHEESECAKE

It has a cookie-dough crust and a whipped cream and almond topping.

Cookie-dough Crust	Grated rind ½
40 ounces cream	orange
cheese	5 eggs
1¾ cups sugar	2 egg yolks
3 tablespoons flour	1 cup heavy cream
¼ teaspoon salt	Toasted chopped
Grated rind 1 lemon	blanched almonds

Make Crust. Have ingredients, except ¾ cup of the cream, at room temperature. Beat cheese until fluffy. Mix sugar, flour, and salt; gradually blend into cheese, keeping mixture smooth. Add grated rinds. Add eggs and egg yolks one at a time, beating well after each. Stir in ¼ cup room-temperature cream. Turn into Crust. Bake in very hot oven, 475°F., 15 minutes. Reduce heat to 200°F.; bake 1 hour longer. Turn off heat; let stand 15 minutes. Remove from oven; cool. (This cake will shrink some.) Remove sides of pan. Top with ¾ cup cream, whipped, and almonds. Makes 12 servings.

Cookie-dough Crust: Mix 1 cup sifted flour and ¼ cup sugar. Add grated rind 1 lemon, 1 egg yolk, and ½ cup soft butter; mix well. Chill. Roll ⅓ of dough to cover bottom of 9″ spring-form cake pan. Bake in hot oven, 400°F., 8 minutes, or until lightly browned. Butter sides of pan; put bottom, with crust, inside it. Cool. Roll remaining dough into 2 strips, 3½″ wide 14″ long; press onto pan sides.

SAVORY CHEESE-NUT SLICES

Three different kinds of cheese, plus brandy and chopped nuts.

⅓ cup crumbled	1 teaspoon brandy
blue cheese	½ cup chopped
1½ cups (6 ounces)	nuts
shredded sharp	Toasted crackers
cheddar cheese	Dates, figs, or
1 package (3	raisins
ounces) cream	
cheese	

Have cheeses at room temperature; add brandy; mix with electric mixer or rotary beater till creamy. Put on waxed paper; form in 7″ roll; coat with nuts. Wrap in paper; chill firm. Slice; serve with crackers and fruit. Serves 6.

COTTAGE-CHEESE PUDDING

It's flavored with lemon juice and topped with slivered almonds.

½ cup each fine	½ teaspoon grated
dry bread crumbs	lemon rind
and brown sugar	1 tablespoon lemon
¼ cup butter or	juice
margarine, melted	¼ teaspoon salt
2 cups cottage	½ cup heavy
cheese	cream, whipped
3 tablespoons flour	¼ cup slivered
2 eggs, separated	almonds
½ cup granulated	
sugar	

Mix crumbs, brown sugar, and butter; press firmly on bottom and halfway up sides of buttered 10″ x 6″ x 2″ baking dish. Beat cottage cheese until smooth. Add flour, and mix well. Beat egg yolks until thick and lemon-colored. Gradually beat in granulated sugar, lemon rind, juice, and salt. Add to cheese mixture. Beat egg whites until stiff but not dry. Fold with cream into cheese mixture. Pour into lined dish. Sprinkle with almonds. Put baking dish in pan half-filled with hot water. Bake in 350°F. oven about 55 minutes. Serve warm or cool. Serves 6 to 8.

CHEESE À LA CRÈME

Cottage and cream cheeses and chilled beaten cream.

1 package	1 pound creamed
(3 ounces)	cottage cheese
cream cheese	1 cup heavy cream

Beat cheeses until smooth and creamy. Gradually beat in cream, beating until thick. Line strainer or colander with several thicknesses of cheesecloth. Stand in bowl deeper than strainer. Pour in mixture; tie cloth. Let drain overnight in refrigerator. Untie; turn out on plate; remove cheesecloth. Surround with sugared whole berries or other fruit. Makes 6 to 8 servings.

JELLIED CHEESECAKE

*It contains pineapple and is
garnished with candied ginger.*

10 finely crushed graham crackers	1 box vanilla-pudding mix
2 tablespoons melted butter	2 cups cottage cheese, sieved
Sugar	2 egg whites
1 can (19 ounces) crushed pineapple	1 cup heavy cream, whipped
Milk	Sweetened whipped cream
2 envelopes un-flavored gelatin	Chopped candied ginger

Mix cracker crumbs, butter, and 2 ta-blespoons sugar. Press on bottom of 9" springform pan. Chill while preparing filling: Drain pineapple, and add enough milk to pineapple juice to make 2 cups. Put in saucepan, and sprinkle with gelatin. Stir in pudding mix, and cook, stirring, until thickened. Stir in cheese and pineapple. Cool, if necessary. Beat egg whites until almost stiff; gradually beat in ¼ cup sugar. Fold into first mixture with whipped cream. Pour into prepared pan; chill several hours, or until firm. Remove to plate; garnish with whipped cream and ginger. Serves 8.

CHEESE-JAM TURNOVERS

*You use cream cheese and
raspberry or strawberry jam.*

Cream cheese	½ teaspoon salt
½ cup butter or margarine	Raspberry or straw-berry jam
1½ cups sifted flour	1 egg, beaten

Mix well 8 ounces cream cheese and the butter. Blend in flour and salt. Chill several hours, or overnight. Roll dough into 15" square. Cut in 25 squares. Put a small amount of jam and a piece of cream cheese at one side of each square. Moisten edges, and fold over to form oblongs or triangles. Press edges together with fork, and brush with egg. Bake in 450°F. oven about 15 minutes. Makes 25.

STORAGE OF OPENED NATURAL CHEESE
Wrap it tightly in a double thickness of waxed paper, foil, or transparent saran; place in refrigerator. Small ends of natural cheese should be grated, then refrigerated, covered.

PASCHA

*Creamed, almondy cottage cheese,
delicious with toasted poundcake.*

2 egg yolks	⅓ cup heavy cream
½ cup sugar	Grated rind 1 lemon
1 pound dry cottage cheese (farmer cheese)	¼ teaspoon vanilla extract
⅓ cup butter or margarine	½ teaspoon almond extract

Beat egg yolks and sugar. Add cheese, butter, cream, and rind; mix well. Put in kettle, and bring to boil, and simmer 5 minutes; stir constantly. Cool slightly. Add flavorings. Line strainer or colander with several thicknesses of cheesecloth; stand in bowl deeper than strainer. Pour in mixture; tie cloth. Cover, and refrigerate. Let drain until moisture drips out. Untie; turn out on plate; remove cloth. Serves 6 to 8.

CREAM-CHEESE MOUSSE

*Mixed with the cheese are gelatin,
fruit juices, cream, and almonds.*

1 envelope un-flavored gelatin	½ teaspoon almond extract
1 cup pineapple juice	¼ teaspoon salt
1½ cups sugar	½ cup toasted slivered blanched almonds
1 cup orange juice	
Juice 1 lemon	1 cup heavy cream, whipped
12 ounces soft cream cheese	

Turn refrigerator control to coldest setting. Sprinkle gelatin on pineapple juice in saucepan. Add sugar; heat, stirring, until gelatin and sugar are dissolved. Cool. Add orange and lemon juice. Blend cheese with next 3 ingredients. Stir in first mixture; fold in cream; pour into freezing trays, and freeze until firm. Serves 8.

FRENCH-FRIED CAMEMBERT

*Serve this hot, for dessert, with
chilled grapes or apple slices.*

Chill 6 wedges (1¾ ounces each) Camembert cheese. Cut each in half lengthwise. Dip in 2 slightly beaten eggs and fine dry bread crumbs. Fry in hot deep shortening (400°F. on a frying thermometer) for just ½ minute. Makes 6 servings.

EGGS

Of all sorts of food, eggs contain the most highly concentrated nourishment and have the most varied uses. Besides being a treat just in themselves, they form the basis of soufflés, custards, and custard sauces; they go into cakes, cake icings, and meringues. As a food to be eaten unadorned, an egg is almost perfection. A true gourmet breakfast might be a fresh egg or two coddled in the shell and served piping hot in an egg cup with a salt mill, pepper mill, a bowl of fresh sweet butter, and a loaf of crusty home-baked bread. Put alongside a pot of steaming coffee or tea and a jar of fine bitter-orange marmalade and you have a meal of excellent simplicity. This is an old-fashioned breakfast, and it has never been improved upon. The egg goes equally well as a tasty main course at luncheon or supper. As an omelet it takes to all kinds of seasonings and fillings; in a quiche it is rich and creamy. One word of warning: do not cook eggs over high direct heat. In sauces it will curdle; as a dish in itself it will turn hard, rubbery, and tasteless. You have only to look at an egg to see what a delicate thing it is.

EGGS IN RED WINE BOURGUIGNON

The eggs are poached in wine which is then thickened for a sauce.

2 cups dry red wine	Salt and pepper
1 bay leaf	8 eggs
Pinch each dried	Buttered croutons
thyme and	1 tablespoon butter
tarragon	1 tablespoon flour

Simmer wine and seasonings 15 minutes in skillet. Poach eggs in the mixture. Remove eggs, and put on croutons. Melt butter in small saucepan; blend in flour. Add wine mixture, and cook, stirring, until thickened. Pour over eggs. Makes 4 servings.

EGG-HAM-VEGETABLE BAKE

The vegetables are peas, cauliflower, and mushrooms.

½ cup butter or margarine	¼ pound cooked ham, minced
6 eggs, separated	1 can (8½ ounces) peas, drained
½ cup sour cream	1 small cauli-
1¼ teaspoons salt	flower, cooked
¼ teaspoon pepper	and sliced
4 tablespoons flour	1 can (3 ounces)
¾ cup grated Parmesan cheese	sliced mushrooms, drained

Cream butter. Add egg yolks, cream, salt, pepper, flour, and 2 tablespoons cheese; mix well. Fold in stiffly beaten egg whites. Spread half of mixture in shallow baking dish. Sprinkle with ham and 2 tablespoons cheese. Cover with peas and 2 tablespoons more cheese; repeat with cauliflower, more cheese; then mushrooms and remaining cheese. Spread remaining egg mixture over top. Bake in moderate oven, 350°F., about 45 minutes. Makes 6 servings.

CHINESE EGG ROLLS

They're filled with seafood, celery, ham, onion, and Chinese vegetables.

3 eggs	¼ cup each
1 cup flour	minced cooked
2 tablespoons cornstarch	ham, water chestnuts, and
2 cups water	bamboo shoots
½ teaspoon salt	1 tablespoon
1 cup chopped	soy sauce
cooked shrimp,	2 tablespoons
crab meat, or	minced
lobster	green onion
½ cup finely diced celery	Fat for frying

Beat 2 eggs slightly. Beat in flour, cornstarch, water, and salt. Heat a greased 7" or 8" skillet. Add 1 tablespoon batter, and tip and tilt pan so that batter runs evenly over bottom of pan. Fry on one side only. Mix 1 egg and remaining ingredients, except fat. Shape into finger-size rolls. Lay on cooked sides of pancakes, and roll up, tucking in edges to seal in filling. (A little uncooked batter can be used for sealing.) Chill. Just before serving, brown in 2" hot fat. Makes about 30.

POACHED EGGS, PORTUGAISE

The eggs, topped with cheese sauce, are broiled on mounds of rice.

½ green pepper, chopped	2 cans (8 ounces each) tomato
1 small onion, chopped	sauce
Butter	2 tablespoons flour
1⅓ cups pack-	1 cup milk
aged precooked	½ cup grated
rice	sharp cheddar
Salt and pepper	cheese
1¾ cups water	6 eggs, poached
	Chopped parsley

Cook green pepper and onion in ¼ cup butter 5 minutes. Add rice, 1 teaspoon salt, ⅛ teaspoon pepper, water, and tomato sauce. Bring to boil; cover, and simmer 10 minutes, stirring occasionally. In a separate pan, melt 2 tablespoons butter, and blend in flour; add milk gradually, and cook, stirring until thickened. Stir in cheese, and add seasonings to taste. Make 6 rice mounds on a broilerproof baking dish. Put an egg on each, and cover with cheese sauce. Broil quickly until bubbly. Garnish with parsley. Serves 6.

BACON-EGG STRATA

Bread strips, diced bacon, and custardy eggs, all baked together.

8 slices bread, crust-trimmed	3 cups milk, scalded
¼ pound bacon, diced	1 teaspoon instant minced onion
4 eggs, slightly beaten	¾ teaspoon seasoned salt
	¼ teaspoon pepper

Cut each slice of bread in 3 strips, and arrange half in shallow baking dish. Cook bacon crisp, and spoon bacon and fat over bread. Cover with remaining bread. Mix remaining ingredients, and pour over mixture in baking dish. Put in pan of hot water, and bake in moderate oven, 350°F., 45 minutes, or until firm. Serves 6.

EGGS MOLLETS CHASSEUR

Poached eggs are broiled on a bed of green onion and mushrooms.

Cook 1 minced green onion with top and 3 chopped mushrooms in 1 tablespoon butter 5 minutes. Add ¼ cup chicken stock or bouillon, and simmer 10 minutes. Add 1 tablespoon sherry, and salt and pepper to taste. Pour into 9" piepan. Poach 4 eggs; put into pan, and season. Pour 2 tablespoons heavy cream over eggs, and sprinkle with 2 tablespoons grated Parmesan cheese. Broil until golden. Serves 4.

EGG AND POTATO PIE, INDIENNE

It's seasoned with curry.

½ teaspoon onion salt	1 tablespoon flour
6 potatoes, cooked, mashed, and seasoned	½ teaspoon salt
	½ teaspoon curry powder
6 hard-cooked eggs, cut in chunks	⅛ teaspoon pepper
	¾ cup milk
2 tablespoons butter	Few sprigs parsley, chopped

Add onion salt to potatoes, and line a shallow 1½-quart baking dish with the mixture. Fill center with the eggs. Melt butter, and blend in flour and seasonings. Gradually add milk, and cook, stirring constantly, until thickened. Add parsley, and pour over eggs. Bake in moderate oven, 375°F., about 30 minutes. Serves 6.

WAFFLE EGG OMELET

You serve it with jelly.

Make a smooth paste with ¼ cup each flour and hot water. Add 4 well-beaten egg yolks, ½ teaspoon salt, ⅛ teaspoon pepper, and 2 tablespoons melted butter or margarine. Mix well, and fold in 4 stiffly beaten egg whites. Put in moderately hot large waffle iron, and bake about 3 minutes. Cut in 4.

HUEVOS RANCHEROS

Eggs and onion-tomato-pimiento sauce.

1 clove garlic, minced	1 pimiento, chopped
2 onions, chopped	1 can (28 ounces) tomatoes
3 tablespoons butter	Salt
1 or 2 dried hot red peppers	8 eggs

Cook garlic and onion in 2 tablespoons butter until lightly browned. Add crumbled hot pepper, pimiento, and tomatoes. Simmer 45 minutes, or until thickened. Add salt to taste. Fry eggs in remaining butter. Serve with the sauce. Makes 4 servings.

SHIRRED EGGS CARUSO

They're garnished with chicken livers.

4 teaspoons melted butter	Salt and pepper
8 eggs	Sautéed chicken livers
8 tablespoons heavy cream	

Put 1 teaspoon butter in each of 4 individual baking dishes or ramekins. Break 2 eggs into each. Add 2 tablespoons cream, and sprinkle with salt and pepper. Bake in moderate oven, 350°F., 10 to 15 minutes. Garnish with chicken livers. Makes 4 servings.

SHERRIED SWISS EGGS

Eggs cooked first in sherried butter,
then grilled with Swiss cheese.

3 tablespoons butter or margarine	4 eggs
3 tablespoons sherry	Salt and pepper
	¼ cup grated Swiss cheese

Melt butter in broilerproof skillet; add sherry and eggs. Cook until whites are almost congealed; season, and sprinkle with cheese. Broil till cheese is melted. Makes 4 servings.

CRAB-STUFFED EGGS

They bake in sour-cream sauce.

Cut 8 hard-cooked eggs lengthwise; remove yolks, and reserve for sandwiches, salads, or other use. Mix 1 can (6½ ounces) crab meat, 1 tablespoon minced parsley, 1 egg yolk, ¾ teaspoon salt, dash pepper, dash dry mustard, and ¼ cup sour cream. Stuff eggs with mixture, and put in shallow baking dish. Mix 3 egg yolks, 1½ cups sour cream, ¾ teaspoon salt, dash pepper. Pour around eggs. Sprinkle with paprika. Bake in 350°F. oven about 30 minutes. Serves 4 to 6.

BARCELONA EGGS AND TUNA

They're cooked with green pepper and onion and served on toast.

In 2 tablespoons olive oil, cook 1 chopped medium green pepper and 1 chopped onion 5 minutes. Beat 8 eggs; add 1 can (9¼ ounces) tuna, flaked, ½ teaspoon salt, and ⅛ teaspoon pepper. Mix well, and pour into skillet with vegetables. Cook, lifting edges with spatula and tilting skillet to allow uncooked egg to run under. Divide in 4 portions, and turn each to brown. Serve on toast, spread with mayonnaise. Makes 4 servings.

"There is always a best way of doing everything, if it be to boil an egg."
RALPH WALDO EMERSON

EGGS HONGROISE

You serve them on toast in paprika-cream sauce.

1 small onion, minced	1½ cups milk
6 tablespoons butter or margarine	1 cup heavy cream
	½ cup chicken broth
4 tablespoons flour	Salt and pepper
2 tablespoons paprika	6 hard-cooked eggs, sliced
	Buttered toast

Cook onion in butter 5 minutes. Blend in flour and paprika. Gradually add liquids, and cook, stirring, until thickened. Season to taste. Add eggs, and heat. Serve on toast. Makes 4 servings.

HERB CUSTARD EGGS

The herbs are marjoram, thyme, sage.

4 eggs	¼ teaspoon each marjoram, thyme, and sage
¾ teaspoon salt	
Dash pepper	1⅓ cups milk

Slightly beat eggs, seasonings, herbs, and milk in top of well-greased double boiler. Cover; cook over boiling water, without stirring, 20 minutes, or until just set. After 15 minutes, remove cover, and if eggs have set, discontinue cooking. Serve at once. Spoon carefully onto hot plates. Makes 4 servings.

OMELET CHARENTIÈRE

It's made with bacon, green onions, and cream.

8 slices bacon, diced	3 tablespoons heavy cream
2 tablespoons butter	½ teaspoon salt
8 green onions (white part), sliced	¼ teaspoon pepper
	2 teaspoons prepared mustard
8 eggs, slightly beaten	Parsley

Cook bacon in large skillet until browned. Remove bacon, and drain on absorbent paper. Pour off fat. Melt butter in skillet; add green onion, and cook 2 or 3 minutes. Add bacon to eggs with remaining ingredients, except parsley. Pour into skillet, and cook, lifting edges of mixture with spatula to let egg run under. When firm and browned on bottom, fold over, and turn out on a hot platter. Garnish with parsley. Makes 4 servings.

HAM SOUFFLÉ

Especially good with cheese sauce.

¼ cup butter or margarine	1 cup ground cooked ham
¼ cup flour	6 egg whites
1 cup milk	Salt and pepper
4 egg yolks	

Melt butter; blend in flour. Gradually add milk, and cook, stirring, until very thick. Beat egg yolks until thick and lemon-colored. Stir into hot mixture; then add ham. Beat egg whites until stiff but not dry, and fold into hot mixture carefully but thoroughly. Season. Put in buttered 2-quart baking dish, and bake in moderate oven, 350°F., about 50 minutes. Serves 4 to 6.

Chicken Soufflé: Use above recipe, substituting 1 cup finely chopped or ground cooked chicken for the ham. Season with Worcestershire, poultry seasoning, salt, and pepper. If desired, serve with a sauce made by heating 1 can mushroom soup, ½ teaspoon Worcestershire, and ¼ cup cream.

Shrimp Soufflé: Use Ham Soufflé recipe, substituting 1 cup finely chopped cooked shrimp for the ham. Add a little lemon juice.

Lobster Soufflé: Use Ham Soufflé recipe, substituting 1 cup finely chopped cooked lobster for the ham. Add a little lemon juice.

Clam Soufflé: Use Ham Soufflé recipe, substituting 1 cup drained canned minced clams for ham.

Corn Soufflé: Use Ham Soufflé recipe, substituting 1 cup cream-style corn for the ham. Cook 1 minced small onion with the butter 5 minutes before adding flour.

EGGS ASTORIA

Poached eggs on toast with smoked salmon, anchovy paste, and white sauce.

Spread buttered toast very lightly with anchovy paste. Top with a slice or more of smoked salmon and a poached egg. Serve with hot white sauce made with part cream.

SPARAGI AL'UOVO

Asparagus and eggs, Italian style.

1 bunch asparagus (2½ pounds)	Salt and pepper
	⅓ cup grated Parmesan cheese
Salted water	
6 tablespoons olive oil	1 clove garlic
	8 eggs

Cook asparagus in boiling salted water until tender; drain well. Put whole asparagus spears in shallow baking pan. Pour 3 tablespoons of oil over asparagus, and sprinkle with salt, pepper, and cheese. Cut garlic in half, and cook slowly in remaining 3 tablespoons oil about 5 minutes; do not brown. Remove garlic. Put asparagus under broiler, and brown lightly under medium heat. While asparagus is browning, drop eggs into oil; cover, and cook slowly 3 minutes. Serve 2 eggs on each portion of asparagus. Makes 4 servings.

POACHED EGGS À LA RHINE

Poached eggs on toast with mushrooms, cheese sauce, and pimiento.

½ pound mushrooms, sliced	1 cup milk
	Grated Parmesan cheese
Butter	
4 slices hot buttered toast	Salt and pepper
	4 eggs, poached
2 tablespoons flour	Pimiento strips

Cook mushrooms in 2 tablespoons butter 5 minutes. Put toast on a broiler-proof platter or baking dish; cover with mushrooms. Melt 2 tablespoons butter, and blend in flour; add milk gradually, and cook, stirring, until thickened. Stir in ½ cup cheese, and seasonings to taste. Put an egg on each slice of toast, and cover with sauce. Sprinkle with cheese. Broil until golden, and garnish with pimiento. Serves 4.

VELVET EGGS

They heat in creamy cheese sauce and are served on chow-mein noodles.

3 onions, sliced	1½ cups milk
3 tablespoons butter or margarine	½ cup light cream
2½ tablespoons flour	½ cup grated Parmesan cheese
1 teaspoon seasoned salt	6 hard-cooked eggs, sliced
¼ teaspoon pepper	Chow-mein noodles

Cook onion in butter until tender, but not browned. Blend in flour and seasonings. Add liquids, and cook, stirring, until thickened. Add cheese and eggs; heat, and serve on noodles. Serves 4.

EGG-STUFFED FRENCH LOAF

Hard-cooked eggs, celery, and olives are baked in sliced French bread.

1 oval loaf of French bread	1½ cups diced celery
½ cup milk	⅓ cup diced stuffed olives
1 egg	6 hard-cooked eggs, chopped
1 clove garlic, minced	½ cup mayonnaise
Salt and pepper	2 tablespoons melted butter
½ teaspoon ground coriander seed	

Cut a slice from top of loaf of bread, and reserve. Scoop out enough crumbs from loaf to make 2 cups. Mix crumbs with all ingredients, except melted butter. Cut almost all the way through loaf to make 6 thick slices. Cut top to match. Fill loaf tightly with salad mixture. Add top pieces. Brush with butter; wrap in foil; bake in 425°F. oven 30 minutes. Serve hot. Serves 6.

GNOCCHI PARMESAN

Egg balls baked in cheese sauce.

½ cup milk	5 eggs
½ cup water	Boiling water
½ cup butter or margarine	Cheese Sauce, page 240
¼ teaspoon salt	½ cup grated Parmesan cheese
1⅓ cups unsifted flour	Paprika

Heat liquids and butter to boiling. Add salt and flour all at once, and stir vigorously until mixture leaves sides of saucepan and forms a ball. Remove from heat, and add eggs, one at a time, beating well after each. Drop mixture by half-measuring-teaspoonfuls into boiling salted water. When balls come to the surface, remove to a bowl of cold water. Drain well, and mix with Cheese Sauce. Put in a shallow baking dish, and sprinkle with cheese and paprika. Bake in moderate oven, 375°F., about 30 minutes. Serves 4.

CHICKEN-EGG OMELET

There are ripe olives in the filling.

Mix 8 beaten eggs, ½ cup milk, ½ teaspoon salt, ¼ teaspoon pepper. Heat 2 tablespoons butter or margarine in large skillet. Add egg mixture, and cook, lifting edges with spatula, and tilting skillet to allow uncooked egg to run under. Heat ¼ cup milk, ¼ teaspoon pepper, 1 can cream-of-chicken soup, 1 cup diced cooked chicken, 1 teaspoon Worcestershire, ½ cup chopped ripe olives. When omelet is done, cover half with some of the chicken mixture, fold over, and turn out on hot platter. Top with remaining sauce; sprinkle with parsley. Serves 4-6.

VENETIAN EGGS

The sauce contains sweet red peppers, tomatoes, anchovies, orégano.

3 sweet red peppers, chopped	¼ teaspoon orégano
4 peeled tomatoes, cut in chunks	1 tablespoon olive oil
6 anchovies, diced	12 eggs
Salt and pepper	Butter

Cook all ingredients, except eggs and butter, about 10 minutes. Fry eggs in butter. Serve with sauce. Serves 6.

EGGS FLORENTINE

They bake on spinach with Puffy Cream Sauce and cheese.

1 box frozen chopped spinach, cooked and drained	Puffy Cream Sauce
	¼ cup grated Parmesan cheese
4 eggs, poached	

Put spinach in hot, shallow, broiler-proof baking dish, and make 4 depressions in it. Put 1 egg in each depression. Cover with Sauce, and sprinkle with cheese. Put under broiler until delicately browned. Makes 4 servings.

Puffy Cream Sauce: Melt 3 tablespoons butter; blend in 3 tablespoons flour, ½ teaspoon salt, and dash cayenne. Gradually add 1¼ cups milk, and cook, stirring, until thickened. Remove from heat, and fold in ¼ cup heavy cream, which has been whipped.

CHEESE AND CHIVE OMELET

The cheese is cottage cheese.

6 eggs	⅛ teaspoon pepper
1 carton (8 ounces) creamed cottage cheese	1 or 2 tablespoons chopped chives
½ teaspoon salt	1½ tablespoons butter

Beat all ingredients, except butter, until fluffy. Heat butter in broilerproof skillet, and pour in egg mixture. Cook over low heat until firm and browned on bottom. Put under medium heat in broiler until lightly browned on top. Cut in wedges. Makes 4 servings.

SAILOR'S OMELET

It contains anchovy paste and smoked salmon.

Garlic	2 tablespoons chopped parsley
3 tablespoons anchovy paste	Dash cayenne
2 tablespoons heavy cream	4 slices smoked salmon
8 eggs	

Rub a bowl with garlic; put anchovy paste and cream into bowl; mix until smooth. Add eggs, parsley, cayenne. Beat well, and pour into greased skillet. Cook, lifting edges with spatula to allow uncooked egg to run under. When firm, fold, and serve garnished with salmon. Serves 4.

GOLDEN FLEECE

Baked cream cheese, milk, eggs, and seasonings.

2 packages (3 ounces each) cream cheese	4 eggs
	½ teaspoon salt
¾ cup milk	½ teaspoon dry mustard

Heat cheese in top of double boiler over hot water until softened. Remove from heat. Add remaining ingredients, and beat until blended. Pour into individual baking dishes or custard cups, and bake in pan of hot water in moderate oven, 375°F., 20 to 25 minutes. Makes 4 servings.

CHEDDAR EGGS

They have a touch of onion.

1 small onion, minced	½ cup shredded cheddar cheese
2 tablespoons butter	6 eggs, slightly beaten
¼ cup water	Salt and pepper

Cook onion in butter until lightly browned. Add water, cheese, and eggs. Cook over low heat to desired consistency, stirring constantly. Season. Serve at once. Makes 4 servings.

EGGS IN SOUR-CREAM SAUCE

You add pickle and paprika to the sour cream.

¾ cup chopped green onions and tops	Salt and pepper
	¼ cup minced sweet pickle
2 tablespoons butter	1 cup sour cream
8 eggs	Paprika

Cook onion in butter in skillet 5 minutes. Break eggs onto onion; sprinkle with salt and pepper. Mix pickle and sour cream; pour over eggs. Sprinkle with paprika; cover, and simmer about 15 minutes. Makes 4 servings.

"Omelettes are not made without breaking eggs."
ROBESPIERRE

EGGS BENEDICT

Poached eggs and ham on muffins topped with Hollandaise Sauce.

Pan-fry 8 small, thin ham slices until browned and done; keep warm. Split, butter, and toast 4 English muffins under broiler. In large skillet, poach 8 eggs in boiling salted water. Top each of 8 muffin halves with a ham slice, then a poached egg. Serve at once with Hollandaise Sauce, page 240, and a garnish of parsley. Makes 4 servings.

EGGS AU BEURRE NOIR

They have a browned-butter sauce.

4 eggs
3 tablespoons butter

1 tablespoon lemon juice or vinegar
Hot toast
Salt and pepper

Fry eggs gently in 2 tablespoons butter. Remove eggs, and keep hot. Add remaining 1 tablespoon butter to skillet, and brown. Add lemon juice slowly so it doesn't spatter, and heat. Put eggs on toast, and season. Pour sauce over eggs. Makes 4 servings.

SAVORY STUFFED EGGS

They bake with peas in mushroom sauce.

Cut 6 hard-cooked eggs in half lengthwise. Remove yolks, and cream with ¼ cup butter. Add ¼ teaspoon salt, 1 teaspoon each Worcestershire and prepared mustard, and 1 tablespoon minced parsley. Mix well. Fill egg whites with mixture; put in baking dish. Surround with 1 box frozen peas, partly cooked. Top with 1 can mushroom soup, mixed with ½ cup milk, dash pepper. Sprinkle with 1 cup grated cheddar cheese and a little paprika. Bake in 350°F. oven 30 minutes. Makes 4 servings.

EGGS MORNAY

Eggs in sherry-cheese sauce.

6 tablespoons butter or margarine
6 tablespoons flour
1¾ cups milk
1 cup chicken broth
4 ounces sharp cheddar cheese, diced

½ cup grated Parmesan cheese
¼ cup sherry
½ teaspoon Worcestershire
Salt and white pepper
12 eggs
Croutons
Chopped parsley

Make a sauce with first 8 ingredients. Add salt and pepper to taste. Hard-cook eggs, or cook less time, if preferred. Shell while warm, and put in shallow baking dish. Surround with the sauce, and sprinkle with croutons. Reheat, if necessary, in slow oven, 300°F. Sprinkle with parsley. Serves 6.

CUBAN EGGS

Stuffed eggs are baked in cheese-tomato sauce and served on rice.

8 hard-cooked eggs
½ teaspoon salt
Dash pepper
1 teaspoon dry mustard
1 tablespoon cream
1 cup grated sharp cheddar cheese

1 onion, minced
½ medium green pepper, minced
2 tablespoons butter
2 cans (8 ounces each) tomato sauce
Hot fluffy rice

Cut eggs in half lengthwise, and remove yolks. Mash yolks; add seasonings, cream, and half the cheese. Mix well, and stuff whites. Put in shallow baking dish. Cook onion and green pepper in butter 5 minutes. Add sauce, and heat. Pour over eggs. Sprinkle with remaining cheese. Bake in hot oven, 400°F., about 15 minutes. Serve with rice. Serves 4.

CREAMED EGGS SUPREME

The sauce is tangy with Worcestershire and Tabasco.

Melt ¼ cup butter; blend in ¼ cup flour. Add 1 teaspoon Worcestershire, 1½ cups milk, and ½ cup cream. Cook, stirring, until thickened. Add a dash Tabasco, 2 tablespoons chopped parsley, 1 chopped pimiento, and 8 hard-cooked eggs, cut in chunks. Heat. Season to taste. Makes 4 to 6 servings.

EGGS À LA SUISSE

They have a sherry-cream sauce.

Melt 1 tablespoon butter in skillet. Add ½ cup cream. Break in 4 eggs, one at a time. Sprinkle with salt, pepper, and a dash of cayenne. Cook until whites are nearly firm. Sprinkle with grated cheese. Cook until whites are firm. Serve on buttered toast. Pour cream from pan, mixed with a little sherry, over toast. Serves 4.

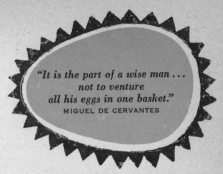

"It is the part of a wise man ... not to venture all his eggs in one basket."
MIGUEL DE CERVANTES

EGG-TUNA AMANDINE

A casserole with a crumb topping.

6 tablespoons butter or margarine	1 can (7 ounces) tuna, drained
¼ cup flour	¼ cup chopped almonds
½ teaspoon salt	1 pimiento, cut in strips
⅛ teaspoon pepper	4 hard-cooked eggs, diced
2 cups milk	½ cup soft bread crumbs
1 tablespoon lemon juice	

Make a sauce with 4 tablespoons butter, flour, seasonings, and milk. Add next 5 ingredients. Mix well. Put in 9″ piepan or shallow baking dish. Top with crumbs mixed with remaining butter, melted. Bake in 375°F. oven 30 minutes. Makes 4 servings.

EGG AND TOMATO SQUARES, MOUSSELINE

They contain Parmesan cheese, too.

1 can tomato soup	¼ teaspoon pepper
2 tablespoons butter	½ teaspoon Accent
1 teaspoon instant minced onion	½ teaspoon Worcestershire
¾ cup fine dry bread crumbs	¼ cup grated Parmesan cheese
¾ teaspoon seasoned salt	4 eggs, separated
	Mousseline Sauce, page 239

Mix first 8 ingredients in saucepan, and heat, stirring, until butter melts. Remove from heat, and add 2 tablespoons cheese and well-beaten egg yolks. Cool, and fold in stiffly beaten whites. Put in shallow baking dish, and sprinkle with remaining cheese. Bake in moderate oven, 350°F., 30 minutes, or until firm. Cut in squares, and serve with Mousseline Sauce. Serves 6.

EGG-SALMON QUICHE

A main-dish pie.

Unbaked deep 9″ pie shell	2 tablespoons chopped parsley
1 can (1 pound) salmon	6 eggs, beaten
Juice ½ lemon	1½ cups light cream or milk
1 onion, minced	1 teaspoon seasoned salt
2 tablespoons butter	¼ teaspoon pepper

Bake shell in very hot oven, 450°F., 5 minutes. Drain salmon liquid into bowl. Remove bones and skin, and flake salmon. Put in pie shell, and sprinkle with lemon juice. Cook onion lightly in the butter. Sprinkle onion and parsley on salmon. Mix salmon liquid, eggs, cream, and seasonings. Pour over salmon. Bake in moderate oven, 350°F., 50 minutes, or until firm. Let stand a few minutes; cut in wedges, and serve. Makes 6 servings.

BAKED EGG-SPINACH RING

You fill it with creamed eggs.

2 boxes frozen chopped spinach	¼ teaspoon pepper
3 eggs, beaten	1 teaspoon instant minced onion
¼ cup heavy cream	½ teaspoon Accent
¼ cup melted butter or margarine	1½ cups soft bread crumbs or cubes
1½ teaspoons seasoned salt	

Cook, and drain spinach. Blend in electric blender, or chop very fine. Mix all ingredients, and pour into well-greased 6-cup ring mold. Put in pan of hot water, and bake in moderate oven, 350°F., 1 hour, or until firm. Unmold on hot platter, and fill center with Creamed Eggs Supreme, page 186. Makes 6 servings.

JAPANESE EGG SALAD

It's made with rice and shrimp.

½ cup uncooked rice	4 hard-cooked eggs
1 tablespoon instant minced onion	Salad greens
1 cup well-seasoned French dressing	3 sweet gherkins, chopped
1 box (10 ounces) frozen peeled shrimp, cooked	2 tablespoons ketchup
	1 tablespoon capers

Cook, and drain rice. Add onion, ½ cup dressing, shrimp, and 2 eggs, diced. Mix lightly with fork, and chill. Put on greens in bowl. Sprinkle pickles around edge. Grate separately whites and yolks of 2 eggs. Sprinkle whites next to pickles; put yolks in center. Serve with remaining ½ cup dressing mixed with ketchup and capers. Serves 4 to 6.

MOLDED EGG-LOBSTER SALAD

You spice it with curry powder.

1 envelope un-flavored gelatin	1 tablespoon instant minced onion
2 cups milk	1 can (5½ ounces) lobster, diced
¾ cup mayonnaise or salad dressing	1 cup diced celery
1½ teaspoons seasoned salt	Juice 1 lemon
¼ teaspoon pepper	6 hard-cooked eggs
1 teaspoon curry powder	Salad greens

Sprinkle gelatin on 1 cup of the milk; heat, stirring to dissolve gelatin. To remaining milk, add mayonnaise and seasonings; beat until blended. Add next 3 ingredients and 4 eggs, diced. Pour into 6-cup mold; chill until firm. Unmold on greens, and garnish with remaining eggs, sliced. Serves 4.

EGG AND OLIVE MOLD

Eggs and olives are chilled in gelatin.

1 envelope unflavored gelatin	Small amount grated onion
½ cup cold water	¾ cup diced celery
½ teaspoon salt	¼ cup chopped stuffed olives
Juice 1 lemon	4 hard-cooked eggs, chopped
Dash Tabasco	Salad greens
1 cup mayonnaise	

Soften gelatin in cold water. Dissolve over hot water. Add salt, lemon juice, and Tabasco; cool. Stir mixture slowly into mayonnaise. Add remaining ingredients, except salad greens, and pour into 3-cup mold. Chill until firm. Unmold onto greens. Makes 4 servings.

SAVORY EGG SALAD

A hot salad featuring potatoes, too.

2 tablespoons butter	1 pimiento, chopped
2 tablespoons flour	1 cup diced celery
1½ teaspoons salt	⅓ cup minced ripe olives
Pepper	6 hard-cooked eggs, chopped
1 cup milk	
4 cups diced cooked potato	⅔ cup salad dressing
1 onion, minced	

Melt butter; blend in flour and seasonings. Gradually add milk, and cook, stirring, until thickened. Add potato, and heat gently. Just before serving, add remaining ingredients, reserving some of the chopped egg to garnish top. Mix lightly. Add more salt and pepper, if necessary. Serves 4.

EGGS IN ASPIC

The aspic is made with chicken broth and white wine.

4 hard-cooked eggs, halved lengthwise	¼ cup cold water
Anchovy fillets	1½ cups hot well-seasoned chicken broth
Chopped parsley and chives	¼ cup dry white wine
1 envelope un-flavored gelatin	

Put eggs, flat side down, in serving dish. Make a cross of anchovy fillets on each. Sprinkle with herbs. Soften gelatin in cold water. Dissolve in hot broth. Add wine; cool. Chill until slightly thickened. Spoon over eggs. Chill until firm. Makes 4 servings.

MAIN DISH SALADS and Dressings

The "salat," as it was once called, originated as long ago as Biblical times. For centuries the only version was the green salad still so popular: greens, herbs, maybe a little garlic or onion, and a dressing of oil and vinegar. By the late seventeenth century, daring cooks were adding other vegetables. Since then, ideas on what can go into a salad have embraced almost every sort of food: raw and cooked vegetables, meats, fowl, fish, cheese, fruit, rice, *pastas*. Probably the forerunner of our hearty salads, those including meats or fish, is the salmagundi. This old-time concoction was a cold pyramid of anchovies, hard-cooked eggs, ham, chicken, celery, parsley, and capers served with a cold egg dressing. Today, such rib-sticking mixtures augmented by greens and some vegetables often form the main course of a summer dinner or a luncheon. Here is a versatile selection of main dish salads. Try them, and then try creating your own.

189

CHEF'S SALAD

*Strips of ham, cheese,
and turkey with
tomatoes, eggs, radishes, cucumbers.*

Assorted greens	Tomato wedges
Strips of ham or	Sliced hard-
tongue, Swiss	cooked eggs
cheese, turkey,	French dressing
or chicken	Salt and freshly
Sliced radishes	ground pepper
and cucumbers	

Have ingredients in separate dishes,
and allow the family members or guests
to help themselves, or break greens
into pieces, toss with other ingredients,
and serve in large salad bowl.

HAM MOUSSE

*The gelatin base is
flavored with consommé.*

1 envelope un-	1 can consommé
flavored gelatin	1 cup ground
1/3 cup cold water	cooked ham
2 egg yolks	1 slice onion,
3/4 teaspoon salt	minced
Dash cayenne	1/4 cup mayonnaise
1 teaspoon dry	1/4 cup heavy
mustard	cream, whipped
	Lettuce

Soften gelatin in cold water. Mix egg
yolks, salt, cayenne, and mustard in
top part of double boiler. Beat until
thick and lemon-colored. Add consommé, and cook, stirring, over boiling
water until mixture thickens enough to
coat a metal spoon. Add gelatin, and
stir until dissolved. Cool. Add ham,
onion, mayonnaise, and cream. Pour
into 1-quart mold. Chill until firm. Unmold on bed of lettuce on serving
plate. Makes 4 servings.

LAMB, CUCUMBER, AND TOMATO SALAD

It has a sour-cream dressing.

2 cups diced	1 apple, diced
cooked lamb	4 cups broken
1 cucumber,	lettuce, romaine,
thinly sliced	and chicory
2 tomatoes, diced	Salt and pepper
	Sour cream

Mix all ingredients, except sour cream.
Moisten with cream; toss. Serves 4.

MACARONI, BEAN, AND EGG SALAD

*The dressing: two parts mayonnaise
to one French, and a dash of Tabasco.*

Mix 2 cups elbow macaroni, cooked,
1/2 cup mayonnaise, 1/4 cup French dressing, dash Tabasco, 1/3 cup diced sweet
pickles, 2 tablespoons vinegar, 6 hard-
cooked eggs, cubed, 1 can (1 pound)
red kidney beans, drained, and salt and
pepper to taste. Chill, and serve on
watercress. Serves 6.

FRANKFURTERS AND HOT POTATO SALAD

*The potato salad has
a sweet-and-sour dressing.*

3 tablespoons	1/2 cup water
bacon fat	1/3 cup vinegar
1 1/2 tablespoons	5 cups sliced
flour	cooked potato
1 tablespoon sugar	1 onion, minced
1 teaspoon salt	Chopped parsley
Dash pepper	8 frankfurters

Heat fat; add flour, sugar, and seasonings; stir in water and vinegar. Cook
until slightly thickened. Add potato,
onion, and parsley. Heat well. Cut several diagonal gashes, 1/4" deep, in
frankfurters. Brown lightly in a little
fat. Arrange on salad. Makes 4 servings.

COTTAGE CHEESE AND BLUEBERRY SALAD

It has a garnish of sliced peaches.

Mix 3/4 pound cottage cheese, 1 pint
fresh blueberries, salt to taste, and dash
cayenne. Spoon lightly in 6 mounds
onto watercress. Garnish with sliced
peaches and serve with mayonnaise.
Serves 6.

TUNA FISH SALAD

Add ¼ cup sliced stuffed olives for extra color if you like.

2 cans (7 ounces each) tuna, drained and flaked	Juice 1 lemon Salad dressing or mayonnaise Salad greens
1 cup diced celery or cucumber	

Mix first 3 ingredients. Add dressing to moisten. Chill, and serve on greens. Makes 4 servings.

Salmon Salad: Use recipe for Tuna Fish Salad, substituting 1 can (1 pound) salmon, drained and flaked.

HOT SEAFOOD SALAD

You can make this salad ahead.

3 slices white bread, toasted	1 can (5 ounces) shrimp
½ cup mayonnaise	2 tablespoons chopped parsley
¼ cup diced sweet pickles	2 hard-cooked eggs, sliced
1 small onion, chopped	¼ cup finely diced celery
1 can (6½ ounces) king crab meat	

Cut toast in ½" cubes. Mix with mayonnaise, pickles, and onion. Remove membrane from crab meat, and flake. Drain shrimp, and clean. Add seafood and parsley to toast mixture. Heat over hot water 20 to 30 minutes, or until hot. Serve garnished with egg slices and sprinkled with celery. Serves 4.

STUFFED-TOMATO SALAD

The tomatoes are stuffed with eggs, deviled ham, and the tomato pulp.

4 large tomatoes	Salt and pepper
6 hard-cooked eggs	Lettuce
Salad dressing	Capers
1 can (2½ ounces) deviled ham	

Cut slice from stem end of each unpeeled tomato. Scoop out pulp; turn tomatoes upside down to drain. Chop eggs; add tomato pulp, and moisten with salad dressing. Add deviled ham, and salt and pepper to taste. Fill tomato shells with mixture. Serve on lettuce, with a garnish of capers. Serves 4.

BROILED TURKEY SALAD

Turkey salad topped with potato chips and cheese, then broiled.

2 cups diced cooked turkey	⅓ cup sour cream
1½ cups diced celery	¼ cup toasted slivered almonds
¼ cup French dressing	2 cups finely crushed potato chips
Salt and pepper	1 cup grated cheddar cheese
½ cup salad dressing or mayonnaise	Salad greens

Marinate turkey and celery in French dressing 1 hour. Season. Mix salad dressing with sour cream. Top salad with mixture, and garnish with almonds. Chill. About 15 minutes before serving, put salad in 4 individual ramekins or a 9" piepan. Mix potato chips and cheese. Completely cover salad. Put under broiler until cheese is melted. Tuck greens under salad, and serve. Serves 4.

WHOLE-MEAL SALAD

Potatoes, eggs, celery, salami, liverwurst, cheese, and cabbage.

2 cups diced cooked potato	½ cup cubed sharp cheddar cheese
3 hard-cooked eggs, diced	1 cup shredded cabbage
1 cup diced celery	¼ cup olive oil
1 tablespoon minced onion	Salt and pepper
½ cup cubed hard salami	½ cup mayonnaise
½ cup cubed liverwurst	Salad greens Chopped parsley

Mix first 8 ingredients. Add olive oil, and salt and pepper to taste. Mix lightly but well. Add mayonnaise. Serve salad on greens with a sprinkling of parsley. Serves 4.

". . . four persons are wanted to make a good salad: a spendthrift for oil, a miser for vinegar, a counsellor for salt, and a madman to stir all up."
ABRAHAM HAYWARD

JELLIED SALMON SALAD

*It's made in a ring with tomato
wedges and avocado in the center.*

1 teaspoon instant minced onion	2 tablespoons capers
¼ cup cold water	⅓ cup chopped stuffed olives
1 envelope un-flavored gelatin	Salad greens
Juice 1 lemon	French dressing
2 cups mayonnaise	2 tomatoes, cut in wedges
1 can (1 pound) salmon, drained	1 small avocado, sliced
2 hard-cooked eggs, chopped	

Mix onion and cold water. Soften gela-tin in the mixture; dissolve over hot water or low heat. Add lemon juice, and stir into mayonnaise. Add next 4 ingredients. Pour into 5-cup ring mold, and chill until firm. Unmold on greens. Fill center with French-dressed toma-toes and avocado. Serves 4 to 6.

Jellied Tuna Salad: Use above recipe, substituting 2 cans grated-style tuna, drained, for the salmon.

BEEF AND POTATO SALAD, LORENZO

*It's served on watercress
with French Dressing de Luxe.*

2½ cups slivered cooked beef	3 diced sweet pickles
3 tomatoes, quartered	Chives and tarragon, to taste
4 cooked potatoes, diced	French Dressing de Luxe, page 194
Chopped parsley	Watercress

Mix all ingredients, except last 2. Add Dressing to moisten. Serve on bed of watercress. Serves 4.

*"Lettuce is like conversation:
it must be fresh and crisp,
so sparkling
that you scarcely notice
the bitter in it."*
CHARLES DUDLEY WARNER

CHOP SUEY SALAD

*Veal or chicken, bean sprouts,
pickles, and green onion, with
soy-French dressing and mayonnaise.*

2 cups diced cooked veal or chicken	½ cup chopped sweet pickles
¼ cup French dressing	1 green onion, chopped
1 teaspoon soy sauce	1 teaspoon salt
1 can (19 ounces) bean sprouts	Dash pepper
	⅓ cup mayonnaise
	Salad greens

Marinate veal or chicken in French dressing and soy sauce about 30 min-utes. Chill. Drain bean sprouts; add meat and remaining ingredients, ex-cept greens. Mix lightly. Serve on greens. Makes 4 servings.

FRUIT SALAD WITH COTTAGE CHEESE

It's garnished with avocado.

1 avocado	Salad greens
2 tablespoons lemon juice	1 pound cottage cheese
3 cups cantaloupe or honeydew balls	½ cup mayonnaise
1 cup fresh or frozen pineapple cubes	1 tablespoon honey
1 cup strawberries or blueberries	2 tablespoons chopped salted almonds

Peel avocado, and cut in strips. Sprinkle with lemon juice. Arrange fruits on greens. Garnish with avocado and cheese. Serve with dressing made by mixing remaining ingredients. Serves 4.

FISH AND POTATO SALAD

*You can use any baked or poached
fish fillets and diced cooked potato.*

2 cups flaked baked or poached fish fillets	1 tablespoon instant minced onion
2 cups diced cooked potato	1 teaspoon seasoned salt
½ cup diced celery	¼ teaspoon pepper
	Paprika
	French dressing
	Chopped parsley

Mix first 6 ingredients. Add a little paprika, and moisten with dressing. Chill. Sprinkle with parsley. Serves 4.

MEDLEY SUPPER SALAD

Chicken livers, red onion,
eggs, blue cheese, and greens.

½ pound chicken livers, diced	1 red onion, thinly sliced
2 tablespoons butter	3 hard-cooked eggs, cubed
Salt	½ cup crumbled blue cheese
1 clove garlic	½ cup French Dressing de Luxe, page 194
4 cups broken salad greens	

Cook chicken livers in the butter until lightly browned. Sprinkle lightly with salt; cool. Rub salad bowl with cut clove garlic. Mix all ingredients, except garlic; toss. Serves 4 to 6.

TURKEY OR CHICKEN SALAD

It's garnished with almonds.

2 cups diced cooked turkey or chicken	Salt and pepper
1 cup sliced celery	Salad greens
¼ cup French dressing	½ cup salad dressing or mayonnaise
2 cups seeded halved Malaga or Tokay grapes	⅓ cup sour cream
	¼ cup toasted slivered almonds

Marinate turkey and celery in French dressing 1 hour. Add grapes, and season to taste with salt and pepper. Arrange on greens. Mix dressing and sour cream. Top salad with the mixture, and garnish with almonds. Serves 4.

Curried Turkey Salad: Use recipe for Turkey Salad, substituting Curry Mayonnaise, page 194, for the salad dressing and sour cream. Substitute chopped salted cashew nuts for the almonds.

HOT SKILLET SALAD

Green pepper, onion, lettuce, and
tomatoes are cooked with eggs.

½ green pepper, chopped	6 eggs
1 onion, minced	2 tablespoons milk
2 cups shredded lettuce	1 teaspoon salt
2 ripe tomatoes, cut fine	Dash pepper
	2 tablespoons olive oil

Mix all ingredients, except oil. Heat oil in large skillet; add mixture; cook, stirring, until eggs are set. Serves 4.

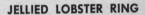

"A touch of raw celery saves many a salad from banality."
P. MORTON SHAND

JELLIED LOBSTER RING

The center is filled with French-
dressed onions and peas.

1 envelope un-flavored gelatin	2 tablespoons minced sweet pickles
¼ cup cold water	2 tablespoons chopped, pitted green olives
½ cup boiling water	¼ teaspoon salt
½ cup mayonnaise	Salad greens
¼ cup ketchup	1 box frozen peas, cooked
Juice 1 lemon	2 green onions, chopped
2 cups diced cooked lobster meat	French dressing
½ cup diced celery	

Soften gelatin in cold water; dissolve in boiling water. Add next 8 ingredients. Pour into 5-cup ring mold, and chill until firm. Unmold on greens. Fill center with peas and onions moistened with dressing. Makes 4 to 6 servings.

SHRIMP AND EGG BALLS

They're served with Roquefort-
Sour Cream Dressing.

1 can (5 ounces) shrimp, chopped	¼ teaspoon salt
2 slices cooked bacon, crumbled	⅛ teaspoon pepper
1 small onion, grated	¼ cup mayonnaise
3 hard-cooked eggs, diced	½ cup finely chopped parsley
½ teaspoon prepared mustard	Roquefort-Sour Cream Dressing, page 176

Mix all ingredients, except parsley and Dressing. Shape into 8 balls. Roll in parsley; chill. Serve with Dressing. Makes 4 servings.

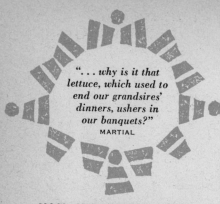

". . . why is it that lettuce, which used to end our grandsires' dinners, ushers in our banquets?"
MARTIAL

HAM AND CHEESE SALAD, JULIENNE

The ham and cheese, Swiss, are cut in very thin strips.

Cut ¼ pound boiled ham, ¼ pound Swiss cheese, and 4 stalks celery in thin strips. Add 2 peeled tomatoes, cut in eighths. Toss with French dressing and serve on lettuce. Makes 4 servings.

FRENCH DRESSING DE LUXE

French dressing, plus garlic, chili sauce, horse-radish, and paprika.

½ cup lemon juice or vinegar	1 teaspoon dry mustard
1½ cups olive or other salad oil	Dash cayenne
Several cloves garlic, gashed	⅓ cup chili sauce
2 teaspoons salt	1 tablespoon horse-radish
¼ teaspoon pepper	1 teaspoon paprika

Mix all ingredients in a 1-quart glass jar; cover tightly, and shake until well blended. Refrigerate. Makes 2 cups.

COTTAGE-CHEESE DRESSING

For fruit, vegetable, or green salads.

To ¾ cup French dressing, add 2 tablespoons each cottage cheese and chopped parsley, 1 tablespoon pickle relish.

FRUIT-SALAD DRESSING

You make it with mayonnaise, whipped cream, almonds, and jelly.

To ¾ cup mayonnaise, add ⅓ cup heavy sweet or sour cream, whipped, ¼ cup chopped salted almonds, and ¼ cup mashed currant jelly.

VINAIGRETTE DRESSING

Good on vegetables or greens.

To ¾ cup French dressing, add 1 chopped hard-cooked egg and 1 teaspoon chopped chives.

THOUSAND ISLAND DRESSING

Good with seafood, egg, vegetable, or mixed-green salads.

Mix 1 cup mayonnaise, ½ cup chili sauce, 2 tablespoons minced green peppers, 3 tablespoons chopped stuffed olives, 1 minced pimiento, 1 teaspoon grated onion or 2 teaspoons chopped chives. Makes about 2 cups.

OLIVE DRESSING

For fish, fruit, or vegetable salads.

To ¾ cup French dressing, add ¼ cup chopped stuffed green or ripe olives.

CHIFFONADE DRESSING

Try this on vegetable salads.

To ¾ cup French dressing, add 1 chopped hard-cooked egg, 1 teaspoon minced parsley, 1 tablespoon minced pimiento, 1 teaspoon minced green onion, and ⅛ teaspoon paprika.

HERB DRESSING

Meat or seafood salads take wonderfully to this dressing.

To ¾ cup French dressing, add 2 teaspoons chopped fresh dill, marjoram, rosemary, or summer savory.

SHARP-CHEDDAR DRESSING

For fruit, vegetable, or macaroni salads.

Finely shred ½ pound sharp cheddar cheese; soften at room temperature. Add 1 cup mayonnaise, 2 tablespoons vinegar, 1 minced clove garlic, ½ teaspoon salt, dash cayenne, and 2 teaspoons Worcestershire. Beat until blended. Makes about 2 cups.

CURRY MAYONNAISE

For fruit, vegetable, or macaroni salads.

Add 1 to 3 teaspoons curry powder to 1 cup mayonnaise.

CORN

Of all the strange, unknown plants that explorers found in the New World, corn is the most important. The Indians called it "maize," and the harvest of maize meant the difference between abundance and starvation. When the first young ears had formed, many tribes held a harvest festival, and everyone gorged on tender green corn. Some American families have perpetuated this rite. Each year when the first young corn appears, they hold a corn feast. They select the corn with care; it should be tender and milky with tiny even kernels and must be rushed to the kitchen as soon after picking as possible. Off come the husks and silk, and the ears are plunged into boiling water for a mere few minutes. What exquisite pleasure when eaten with plenty of butter, coarse salt, and freshly ground pepper. Although corn tastes superb "as is," its delicate, bland flavor is a good foil for chili and other hot and spicy dishes. Try these recipes for new ways to enjoy America's famous vegetable. You'll be amazed at its versatility.

CORN BISQUE

You use cream-style corn.

Melt 3 tablespoons butter or margarine.
Add 1 grated small onion. Blend in
3 tablespoons flour. Add 3 cups milk,
and cook until slightly thickened, stirring. Put 2 cups cooked cream-style
corn through coarse sieve. Add to milk
mixture with 1 teaspoon Worcestershire, seasoned salt and pepper to
taste. Heat, and serve with chopped
parsley or croutons. Makes 1 quart.

CHILLED CURRIED CORN SOUP

The garnish: fresh basil.

2 cups cooked cream-style corn	¼ teaspoon white pepper
1 teaspoon instant minced onion	1 teaspoon curry powder
1 teaspoon Worcestershire	½ cup milk
½ teaspoon salt	1 cup heavy cream
	Fresh basil

Blend all ingredients, except basil, in
electric blender until smooth. Chill.
Serve in cups with a basil leaf on each.
Makes about 3½ cups.

CORN AND TOMATO BISQUE

It's seasoned with curry.

1 onion, chopped	1 bay leaf
¼ cup butter or margarine	2 cups water
2 tablespoons flour	2 cups cream-style corn
1 tablespoon sugar	1 can (19 ounces) tomatoes
1¼ teaspoons seasoned salt	1 cup evaporated milk
¼ teaspoon pepper	2 egg yolks
Dash curry powder	Juice 1 lemon
6 whole black peppers	Chopped parsley

Cook onion in butter 5 minutes. Blend
in flour, sugar, and seasonings. Add
remaining ingredients, except last 4.
Simmer, uncovered, about 30 minutes.
Strain, and add milk and egg yolks,
beaten together. Simmer a few minutes
longer. Add lemon juice, and serve
with parsley. Makes 1½ quarts.

CORN-LOBSTER CRUMB PIE

The crumbs are corn flakes.

2 cups cooked whole-kernel corn	4 tablespoons butter or margarine
1 can (5½ ounces) lobster, drained	2 tablespoons flour
Few sprigs parsley, chopped	½ teaspoon each Worcestershire, dry mustard, salt
Juice ½ lemon	¼ teaspoon pepper
1 teaspoon instant minced onion	1 cup milk
	¼ cup corn-flake crumbs

Mix first 5 ingredients. Melt 2 tablespoons butter in saucepan; blend in
flour and seasonings. Add milk, and
cook, stirring, until thickened. Add to
first mixture. Mix well, and put in 9″
piepan. Sprinkle crumbs on top, and
dot with remaining butter. Bake in
moderate oven, 375°F., about 30 minutes. Makes 4 servings.

ROAST CORN-ON-THE-COB

It's roasted with the husks on.

Pull back husks from corn; remove silk.
Replace husks, and tie in place. Soak
corn in salted water 5 minutes; drain.
Roast on grill over hot fire 10 to 12
minutes, turning frequently. Remove
husks, and serve corn with butter, or
margarine, and salt.

BOILED CORN-ON-THE-COB

*One of the simplest and best ways to
serve fresh corn.*

Husk corn, and remove silk. (A dry
vegetable brush is handy to remove
stubborn silk.) Plunge corn into large
kettle of rapidly boiling water; cover,
and cook over high heat 8 to 10 minutes. Remove from water; drain, and
serve with butter.

GOOD-NEIGHBOR SKILLET

Mexican corn and Canadian bacon.

Fry 1 pound thinly sliced Canadian
bacon quickly on both sides. Remove,
and keep hot. In fat, cook ½ green
pepper, chopped, 5 minutes. Add ½
cup water, and 3 cups whole-kernel
corn, and simmer 10 minutes. Add 2
slivered pimientos. Put in serving dish;
top with bacon. Serves 4 to 6.

CORN AND SAUSAGE, CREOLE

Tomatoes, green pepper, and seasonings make up the creole sauce.

½ pound link sausages	2 cups cooked whole-kernel corn
1 onion, chopped	1 bay leaf
½ green pepper, chopped	½ teaspoon thyme
1 tablespoon flour	1 teaspoon salt
1 can (19 ounces) tomatoes	⅛ teaspoon pepper

Cut sausages in small pieces. Cook slowly in heavy skillet until browned. Add onion and green pepper, and continue cooking until sausage is well done. Blend in flour. Then stir in tomatoes gradually. Add corn, and cook until slightly thickened. Add seasonings; simmer 20 minutes. Serves 4 to 6.

HERBED CORN BAKED IN TOMATO CUPS

You can use either fresh or dried herbs; ½ teaspoon if you use dried.

1 onion, chopped	Dash pepper
3 tablespoons butter or margarine	¼ cup minced fresh herbs (parsley, thyme, basil, or summer savory)
2 cups whole-kernel corn	
½ teaspoon salt	4 large tomatoes

Cook onion in butter until lightly browned; add corn, salt, pepper, and herbs. Slice top off each tomato, and scoop out centers (save pulp for stewing or using in soups or casseroles). Fill tomatoes with corn mixture. Put in shallow baking dish, and bake in 375°F. oven 30 minutes. Serves 4.

CORN SQUARES WITH CREAMED HAM

You add whole-kernel corn to biscuit-mix batter to make the squares.

Mix until smooth: 2 cups biscuit mix, ¾ cup milk, 2 tablespoons each sugar and vegetable oil, 1 egg, and 1 teaspoon ground sage. Add 2 tablespoons instant minced onion; few sprigs parsley, minced; and 1 cup cooked whole-kernel corn. Spread in greased 13" x 9" x 2" baking pan, and bake in very hot oven, 450°F., about 20 minutes. Cut in 6 pieces. Serve with creamed ham made with 4 cups medium white sauce and 2 cups diced cooked ham. Serves 6.

CALIFORNIA SUCCOTASH

The California touch: slivered almonds and chopped ripe olives.

Cook 2 cups Lima beans in small amount of boiling water 10 minutes. Add corn cut from 4 ears; cook 10 minutes longer. Melt 3 tablespoons butter or margarine; add ¼ cup slivered blanched almonds, and brown lightly. Add with ¼ cup chopped ripe olives to drained succotash. Season. Serves 4.

SWEET-AND-SOUR CORN AND BEANS

Corn and green beans cooked with onion, bacon, sugar, and vinegar.

3 slices bacon	2 cups cooked whole-kernel corn
1 onion, minced	¼ cup vinegar
1 can (15½ ounces) cut green beans	Salt and pepper
1 tablespoon sugar	

Dice, and brown bacon; remove from fat. Add onion to fat; brown lightly. Add liquid from beans, and cook down to ⅓ cup. Add beans, bacon, and remaining ingredients. Heat. Serves 6.

CREAMY SKILLET CORN

Grated fresh corn in paprika cream.

Grate 6 to 8 ears of corn; add 2 tablespoons butter and ¼ cup heavy cream. Cook in skillet, stirring, about 8 minutes. Season; add paprika. Serves 4.

STEWED CORN AND TOMATOES

A recipe for fresh corn and fresh tomatoes.

Cook 1 minced green pepper in 2 tablespoons butter 2 or 3 minutes. Add 1 tablespoon instant minced onion, 1 teaspoon each salt and sugar, ⅛ teaspoon pepper, and 4 peeled and sliced ripe tomatoes. Cook 5 minutes. Add corn cut from 4 ears; cook gently 8 to 10 minutes. Makes 4 servings.

TO CHOOSE AND STORE FRESH CORN

To choose: Look for bright-green, snug husks, dark-brown silk (sign of well-filled kernels). Milk flows from kernels when pressed. *To store:* Cook fresh corn soon as possible; but refrigerate till then.

SAVORY BROILED CORN

*You spread it with herbed
tartar sauce before broiling.*

½ cup tartar sauce	½ teaspoon salt
½ onion, grated	Dash cayenne
¼ cup minced parsley	8 ears corn, cooked until almost tender

Combine tartar sauce, onion, parsley,
and seasonings. Arrange corn on baking sheet. Spread with tartar-sauce
mixture. Broil until lightly browned.
Makes 4 servings.

CREOLE CORN

*Corn cooked with onion, tomatoes,
sugar, salt, pepper, and green pepper.*

1 onion, chopped	¼ teaspoon pepper
2 tablespoons butter	2 cups whole-kernel corn
2½ cups chopped peeled tomatoes	½ green pepper, chopped
1 teaspoon sugar	
1 teaspoon salt	

Cook onion in butter until lightly
browned. Add tomatoes, sugar, seasonings, and corn; simmer 10 minutes.
Add green pepper; simmer 5 minutes
longer. Makes 6 servings.

FRESH-CORN SOUFFLÉ

*You grate the corn
before putting it in the soufflé.*

Melt 2 tablespoons butter or margarine
in heavy saucepan. Blend in 2 tablespoons flour, 1½ teaspoons salt, and
⅛ teaspoon pepper. Add 1 cup milk,
and cook, stirring, until thickened. Add
2 cups grated fresh corn, and mix well.
Stir in 2 egg yolks, beaten until thick
and lemon-colored. Fold in 2 stiffly
beaten egg whites. Pour into buttered
2-quart casserole. Bake in moderate
oven, 350°F., about 30 minutes. Makes
4 to 6 servings.

To make grated or cream-style corn:
See box immediately below.

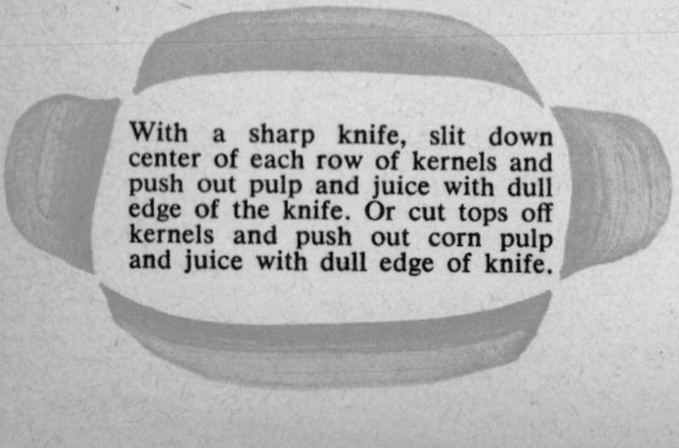

With a sharp knife, slit down
center of each row of kernels and
push out pulp and juice with dull
edge of the knife. Or cut tops off
kernels and push out corn pulp
and juice with dull edge of knife.

HERBED CORN AND PEAS

The herb is marjoram or orégano.

Combine 2 pounds peas, cooked, and
2 cups cooked whole-kernel corn. Add
⅓ cup water in which peas were
cooked, few sprigs chopped parsley,
and ½ teaspoon dried marjoram or
orégano. Heat, and season with butter,
salt, and pepper. Serves 6.

CORN AND CRAB-MEAT SCRAMBLED EGGS

*You sprinkle each serving with
curry powder and chopped parsley.*

Melt 2 tablespoons butter. Add 1½
cups cooked whole-kernel corn and 1
can (6½ ounces) crab meat, flaked.
Heat, stirring constantly. Mix 6 beaten
eggs, ¼ cup milk; add to corn and
crab meat. Cook until eggs are set,
stirring occasionally. Season. Serve at
once with a little curry powder and
chopped parsley. Serves 4.

CORN-STUFFED PEPPERS

Corn custard in green-pepper shells.

4 large green peppers	2 eggs, beaten
1¼ cups whole-kernel corn	¾ teaspoon salt
	⅛ teaspoon pepper
2 cups scalded milk	1 tablespoon instant minced onion

Slice tip end off peppers, and remove
seeds. Cut off part of stem, if necessary, to allow peppers to stand upright when inverted. Cook in boiling
salted water 5 minutes, and drain.
Combine remaining ingredients. Fill
pepper shells with corn mixture. Put
in baking dish; bake in 350°F. oven
about 30 minutes. Serves 4.

CORN AND SHRIMP PUDDING

It contains grated cheddar cheese.

2 cups cooked whole-kernel corn	1 teaspoon instant minced onion
1 can (5 ounces) shrimp, drained	¾ teaspoon seasoned salt
1 cup milk	¼ teaspoon pepper
2 eggs, beaten	Dash nutmeg
½ green pepper, minced	½ cup grated cheddar cheese

Mix all ingredients, and put in shallow
baking dish. Bake in moderate oven,
325°F., 1 hour, or until firm. Serves 4.

CORN AND CARROT PUDDING

*Whole-kernel corn and ground carrots,
baked with milk, eggs, and seasonings.*

2 tablespoons butter	1½ cups cooked
2 tablespoons flour	whole-kernel corn
1 teaspoon each	1½ cups finely
salt and sugar	ground raw
¼ teaspoon each	carrot
pepper, paprika	½ green pepper,
1 tablespoon instant	ground
minced onion	2 eggs, beaten
1 cup milk	

Make a sauce with butter, flour, seasonings, and milk. Add remaining ingredients, and mix well. Put in buttered 1½-quart casserole, and bake in 350°F. oven about 45 minutes. Serves 6.

BROILED CHILI CORN WITH BACON

*Corn, bacon, chili sauce, and onion
broiled in individual servings.*

Cut 8 bacon slices in half, and partially fry. Remove from skillet, and drain off all but 2 tablespoons fat. Add 1 medium onion, minced, and cook 5 minutes. Add 3 cups cooked whole-kernel corn, and season. Divide into 4 individual broilerproof baking dishes. Top with ½ cup chili sauce and bacon. Broil 10 minutes. Makes 4 servings.

CORN AND MEAT BALLS, MEXICALI

*The tomato sauce contains
green pepper, onion, chili powder.*

1 pound	1 onion, chopped
ground beef	1 can (8 ounces)
1 teaspoon	tomato sauce
seasoned salt	½ cup water
¼ teaspoon pepper	½ teaspoon
2 tablespoons flour	chili powder
2 tablespoons fat	1½ cups cooked
1 green pepper,	whole-kernel
chopped	corn

Mix first 3 ingredients, and shape in 12 balls; roll in seasoned flour, and brown on all sides in hot fat. Remove meat, and lightly brown green pepper and onion in the fat. Put meat back in skillet, and add remaining ingredients, except corn. Cover, and simmer 10 minutes. Add corn; heat. Serves 4.

TO STEAM CORN IN MILK
Remove just outer husks; remove silk; replace inner husks. Put in kettle; cover with milk; let stand 20 minutes. Drain most of milk; heat till cover is very hot. Lower heat, and steam 15-20 minutes.

VENEZUELAN BAKED CORN

*The seasonings are brown sugar,
salt, pepper, and nutmeg.*

1 small onion,	½ teaspoon each
minced	pepper and
2 tablespoons butter	nutmeg
2 tablespoons flour	1 cup milk
2 tablespoons	2 eggs, beaten
brown sugar	2 cups cooked
1 teaspoon salt	whole-kernel corn

Cook onion in butter 5 minutes. Blend in flour, sugar, and seasonings. Add milk, and cook, stirring, until thickened. Gradually stir mixture into eggs. Add corn, and mix well. Pour into 9″ piepan or other shallow dish, and bake in moderate oven, 325°F., 45 minutes, or until firm. Makes 4 to 6 servings.

INDIVIDUAL CORN CASSEROLES

*You use both whole-kernel
and cream-style corn.*

Reserve 4 slices from ½ pound bacon. Dice remainder, and fry until crisp. Drain off fat. To cooked bacon, add 2 cups each cooked whole-kernel corn and cream-style corn, 1 beaten egg, 2 tablespoons chopped parsley, ½ teaspoon salt, and ⅛ teaspoon pepper. Put in 4 individual casseroles; top with bacon. Bake in hot oven, 400°F., 30 minutes. Serves 4.

CORN IN CREAM

Seasoned with parsley and garlic salt.

In top part of double boiler, put ⅔ cup light cream, 2 tablespoons chopped parsley, 1 teaspoon salt, ¼ teaspoon pepper, dash garlic salt, and 4 cups whole-kernel corn. Cover; cook over boiling water 15 minutes, stirring occasionally. Serves 6.

Soak husked corn in cold water 10 minutes; put in skillet. Add ½ cup cold water; cover; cook 5 minutes. Uncover; let water evaporate. Add 1 teaspoon vegetable oil per ear, salt; cook 5 minutes.

CORN AND OKRA

First they fry, then they simmer.

Heat 4 tablespoons bacon fat or margarine in skillet. Add 1 pint fresh okra cut in ¼" slices, 1 minced small onion, and corn cut from 4 ears. Cook, stirring, 10 minutes. Season. Add 1 cup water; cover, and simmer about 25 minutes. Makes 4 servings.

CORN AND MUSHROOM BAKE

It contains onion, celery, parsley, pimiento, and cheddar cheese, too.

2 tablespoons butter	1 pimiento, chopped
1 can (3 ounces) sliced mushrooms, drained	½ teaspoon salt
	Dash pepper
1 onion, minced	1 egg, beaten
¼ cup finely minced celery	¼ cup milk
	½ cup soft bread crumbs, buttered
2 cups cream-style corn	½ cup shredded cheddar cheese
1 tablespoon minced parsley	

Melt butter in skillet. Add mushrooms, onion, and celery; cook until onion is golden. Add corn, parsley, pimiento, salt, and pepper. Combine egg and milk; add to corn mixture. Pour into 1-quart casserole; top with crumbs and cheese. Set casserole in baking pan. Add hot water to pan to depth of 1". Bake in moderate oven, 375°F., 40 minutes, or until firm. Makes 4 servings.

TWO-BEAN SUCCOTASH WITH PORK CUBES

You add cream to cooked Lima and green beans, then top with salt pork.

Cut ¼ pound salt pork in large cubes, and fry slowly until well browned and done. Cook ½ pound green beans, cut, and 2 cups Lima beans in small amount of boiling salted water about 15 minutes. Add corn cut from 4 to 5 ears to beans, and simmer 5 minutes. Add ½ cup cream; salt and pepper. Heat, and serve topped with pork. Serves 6.

FRESH-CORN PANCAKES

Serve them with butter and syrup.

Mix 2 cups fresh cream-style corn, 1 teaspoon each baking powder and sugar, ¾ teaspoon salt, dash pepper, 1 tablespoon each melted butter and cream. Beat 2 egg yolks until thick and lemon-colored and 2 whites until stiff. Stir yolks into first mixture, and fold in whites. Drop by spoonfuls onto hot, lightly greased griddle; brown on both sides. Makes 4 dozen 3" cakes. **Note:** If cakes seem too tender to handle, stir a little flour into batter.

CORN OYSTERS

A variation of corn pancakes.

Combine 2½ cups fresh cream-style corn, 1 egg, beaten, ½ cup milk, 1 teaspoon salt, 1 tablespoon sugar, and ¾ cup sifted flour. Mix well. Melt 2 tablespoons butter in skillet, and drop batter into skillet by tablespoonfuls. Brown on each side. Makes 12 large "oysters."

CORN WAFFLES

Use a waffle mix or your own recipe.

Add 1 cup cooked whole-kernel corn to 1 recipe waffle mix, or to your own favorite recipe. Bake as usual.

FRESH-CORN MUFFINS

You grate the fresh corn. For directions, see page 198.

Sift together: 2 cups sifted flour, 2 teaspoons baking powder, ½ teaspoon salt, and 2 tablespoons sugar. Cut in ¼ cup soft butter or margarine. Beat 2 eggs; add ¾ cup milk, and 1 cup grated fresh corn. Mix only enough to dampen dry ingredients. Fill hot greased 2¾" muffin pans two-thirds full; bake in 425°F. oven, 25 minutes. Makes 12.

CORN FRITTERS

Try using bacon fat for the fat.

Beat 1 egg. Add ½ cup milk and 2 cups corn cut from 6 to 8 ears corn. Add 1½ cups sifted flour, 2 teaspoons baking powder, 1 teaspoon salt, and dash pepper. Mix well. Stir in 1 tablespoon fat. Drop by tablespoonfuls into hot deep fat (375°F. on a frying thermometer), and fry until golden brown. Drain on absorbent paper. Serves 4.

ONIONS

The onion, praise heaven, has been around for untold centuries. Subtract the onion family from our food list and our meals would soon degenerate into dull, monotonous routines. What a magnificent family it is. First of all, there is the delicate, refined little chive or *ciboulette,* colorful and pungent as a garnish and a subtle addition to many soups, sauces, and salads. Then there is the young green onion (or spring onion or scallion, as it is sometimes called), the joy of the summer vegetable garden. It is exquisite plain with salt, in the summer salad bowl, in sauces, soups, and vegetable dishes. And don't forget the small white pearl onion; it is traditional with roast fowl at holiday time and brings back memories of family gatherings and the loaded table. Then there are the stand-bys: the yellow onion for general use; the Spanish or Bermuda for French-frying and with steaks and hamburgers; the red Italian, so good in salads and plain in a vinegary marinade.

GOURMET RELISH

Serve cold with rye-bread rounds and cheese.

4 cups thinly sliced, peeled Bermuda onions
1 teaspoon salt
⅛ teaspoon pepper
2 cups dry white wine
½ cup chopped parsley

Put onion and seasonings in wine, and chill well. Add parsley. Serves 8.

ONION-CUCUMBER SALAD

The dressing is tarragon vinegar.

2 mild onions
2 large cucumbers
½ cup tarragon vinegar
¼ cup cold water
1 teaspoon sugar
Salt and pepper

Peel, and cut onions and cucumbers into wafer-thin slices. Cover with salted ice water, and let stand in refrigerator several hours. Drain, and add remaining ingredients.

Onion-Cucumber Salad with Sour-cream Dressing: After draining vegetables in recipe above, add ½ cup sour cream, ½ cup tarragon vinegar, garnish of chopped chives.

BERMUDA CASSEROLE

Alternating layers of onion, bread, and cheese baked as a custard.

2 large Bermuda onions, sliced
4 slices stale white bread (without crusts), cubed
¾ cup grated sharp cheddar cheese
¾ cup rich milk
2 eggs, beaten
¾ teaspoon salt
⅛ teaspoon pepper
Butter or margarine
Cayenne

Parboil onion 10 minutes, and put in shallow baking dish, in layers with bread and cheese. Combine milk, eggs, salt, and pepper; pour over top layer, and dot with butter. Sprinkle with dash cayenne. Bake as custard in hot water in 375°F. oven 40 minutes. Serves 4.

BERMUDAS GLACÉS

Onions bake slowly in honey sauce.

6 Bermuda onions
2 tablespoons butter
¼ cup honey
½ teaspoon paprika
½ teaspoon salt
⅛ teaspoon pepper
3 tablespoons water

Halve onions, and put cut side up in large covered casserole. Top with remaining ingredients, and cover. Bake in moderate oven, 350°F., 1½ hours, basting with sauce. Serves 6.

CHICKEN-STUFFED ONIONS

They're served with sour-cream sauce.

6 large mild onions, peeled
½ cup chopped mushrooms
½ cup chopped cooked chicken
2 tablespoons soft butter
½ cup soft bread crumbs
Salt and pepper
½ cup chicken stock
Paprika
½ cup sour cream

Parboil onions 30 minutes. Scoop out centers, and make stuffing of chopped centers and remaining ingredients, except stock, paprika, and sour cream. Stuff onions. Put in buttered baking pan. Add stock; sprinkle with paprika; cover, and bake in hot oven, 400°F., about 30 minutes. Remove cover for last 10 minutes. Remove onions; add sour cream to pan; serve over onions. Makes 6 servings.

RUSSIAN ONIONS AND MUSHROOMS

Serve this dish with steak or roast beef.

1½ cups chopped onion
2 tablespoons butter or bacon fat
1 pound mushrooms, sliced
1½ teaspoons salt
¼ teaspoon pepper
½ teaspoon paprika
1 tablespoon flour
1 pint sour cream

Simmer onion in butter until golden. Add mushrooms and seasonings, and cook slowly 10 minutes. Add flour, stir; add sour cream slowly, and simmer 10 minutes. Makes 6 servings.

ONION SOUFFLÉ

Serve this handsome, fluffy dish the minute you take it from the oven.

2 cups sliced onion	½ cup cream
Salt	3 tablespoons flour
1 tablespoon brown sugar	Dash cayenne
4 tablespoons butter or margarine	¼ teaspoon pepper
	3 eggs, separated and beaten
	Paprika

Boil onion 15 minutes in salted water to cover. Reserve ½ cup liquid. Drain, and grind or chop onion. Add sugar and 1 tablespoon butter. Make 1 cup sauce using onion liquid, remaining butter, cream, flour, cayenne, pepper, and salt to taste. Add onion mixture to sauce, then add a little sauce to egg yolks; add yolks to sauce. Let cool slightly, and fold in stiffly beaten whites. Place in buttered soufflé dish. Sprinkle with paprika, and bake in 350°F. oven 45 minutes. Serves 6.

TURK'S ONION DELIGHT

A chopped onion and egg dish served with seasoned yogurt.

¼ cup chopped onion	Grated sharp cheddar cheese
2 tablespoons olive oil	Yogurt seasoned with dash each garlic salt, paprika
4 eggs	
Salt and pepper	

Simmer onion in olive oil until golden; put in buttered shallow baking dish. Break eggs gently on top; sprinkle with salt, pepper, and cheese, and bake in moderate oven, 375°F., 15 minutes. Serve with heated yogurt. Serves 4.

FRITTATA DI ITALIA

An Italian version of the onion omelet.

Sauté 2 large sweet onions, sliced, in 2 tablespoons olive oil. Season 6 eggs, and beat lightly. Stir in onion. Add 2 tablespoons oil to pan; add eggs, and cook over low heat until set. Turn carefully to other side; brown lightly. Serves 4.

PEANUT-CREAMED ONIONS

Some of the nuts go into the sauce, some are used for a topping.

18 peeled small white onions	1 cup of rich white sauce
½ cup salted peanuts, chopped fine	Salt and pepper
	Dash mace

Cook onions in salted water until tender. Drain, and add with half of peanuts to white sauce. Season, and top with remaining nuts. Bake in moderate oven, 375°F., 20 minutes. Serves 4.

ONIONS AND TOMATO, AMERICAN

Small white onions are cooked in a casserole with stock and tomato soup.

18 small white onions, peeled and cooked	1 tablespoon oil
¼ teaspoon pepper	1 can tomato soup
1 tablespoon butter	1 cup meat stock (or bouillon made with cube and onion water)

Put all ingredients in 1½-quart casserole. Mix well; cover, and bake in 375°F. oven about half hour. Serves 6.

CURRIED ONIONS

Thick Bermuda or Spanish onion slices are heated in curry white sauce.

Cut 3 large Bermuda or Spanish onions in thick slices. Cook in salted water until tender; drain, and add to 2 cups hot cooked rice. Stir in 1 cup light cream or evaporated milk, 2 tablespoons butter, ¼ teaspoon mace, ¾ teaspoon salt, and 1 tablespoon curry powder. Heat. Serves 4 to 6.

FRENCH-FRIED ONIONS

Delicious with steak or hamburger.

Peel Spanish or Bermuda onions, and cut in ¼" slices. Separate into rings; dip in evaporated milk, then in flour, and fry in hot deep fat (380°F. on a frying thermometer) until golden brown and done. Drain on absorbent paper, and sprinkle with salt.

DUTCH ONION PIE

The base of the pie's
filling is cottage cheese.

3 cups thinly sliced onion	¼ cup heavy cream
2 tablespoons butter	9″ baked pie shell
1 pound cottage cheese	Salt and pepper Cayenne

Fry onion in butter until soft. Moisten cheese with cream, and pour into shell; season lightly with salt and pepper. Cover with onion. Add more salt and pepper, and dash of cayenne. Bake in 400°F. oven 15 minutes. Serves 6.

HONEY-GLAZED ONIONS

You use small white onions.

24 small white onions, peeled	3 tablespoons butter or margarine
2 tablespoons honey	¼ cup hot water
2 tablespoons ketchup	Dash each salt and cayenne

Cook onions in salted water 20 minutes. Drain, and put in baking dish. Pour over sauce made of remaining ingredients, and cover. Bake in moderate oven, 350°F., about 1 hour, basting occasionally. Serves 4.

FRENCH ONION QUICHE

An onion and Swiss-cheese pie.

1 cup sliced mild onion	1 cup each milk and light cream
2 tablespoons butter	1 teaspoon salt
½ pound Swiss cheese, grated	¼ teaspoon pepper Dash nutmeg
9″ unbaked pie shell	3 strips crisp bacon, crumbled
3 eggs, beaten	

Sauté onion in butter until golden and soft. Put with cheese in pie shell. Combine remaining ingredients, and pour over cheese and onions. Bake in moderate oven, 375°F., 45 minutes, or until knife blade comes out clean. Cool slightly. Serves 6.

ONIONS, SWISS STYLE

A casserole dish with lots of Swiss cheese
and a crumb topping.

2 sweet onions, sliced thin	1 can cream-of-chicken soup
2 tablespoons butter	1 cup rich milk
Salt and pepper	1 cup buttered bread crumbs
2 cups grated Swiss cheese	

Separate onion slices into rings, and sauté in butter until golden; then cover pan, and simmer 10 minutes. Put in buttered baking dish; season, and cover with cheese. Dilute soup with milk, and pour over cheese. Top with crumbs, and bake in 375°F. oven half hour. Serves 4.

ONIONS AND EGGS, FAUST

The onions and eggs are
baked in seasoned white wine.

6 hard-cooked eggs	¼ teaspoon pepper
2 cups chopped onion	Paprika
2 tablespoons butter	Dry mustard
½ cup dry white wine	¼ cup chili sauce
¾ teaspoon salt	¼ cup buttered fine dry bread crumbs

Slice eggs, and put in buttered baking dish. Brown onion lightly in butter, and add remaining ingredients, except crumbs. Pour over eggs. Sprinkle with crumbs, and bake in hot oven, 425°F., about 15 minutes. Serves 4 to 6.

SHALLOTS AND TOMATOES

Use big, beefsteak
tomatoes for this cold dish.

3 tomatoes, large beefsteak type, peeled and sliced	¼ cup olive oil
2 shallots, diced fine	1 tablespoon basil vinegar (or pinch of crushed basil and 1 tablespoon cider vinegar
2 tablespoons chopped parsley	Salt and pepper

Put tomatoes in bowl, and sprinkle with shallots. Add remaining ingredients, mixed well. Chill before serving. Makes 4 servings.

SPANISH ONION BAKE

*You peel the onions
after they have been baked.*

6 Spanish or	Paprika
Bermuda onions	¼ cup melted
¼ cup water	butter or
Salt and pepper	margarine

Clean, and wipe, but do not peel onions. Cut off root end to just beyond skin joint. Put in buttered baking dish with water, and bake in moderate oven, 375°F., 1¼ hours. Remove skin by grasping top and slipping it off. Return to dish; season; pour butter over, and return to oven for 5 minutes. Serve in same dish. Makes 6 servings.

SOUTHERN ONION BREAD

You serve this as you do spoon bread.

2 tablespoons butter	1½ cups
or bacon fat	buttermilk or
¾ cup uncooked	sour milk
white corn meal	½ teaspoon soda
1 egg, beaten	1 teaspoon salt
¼ cup chopped	⅛ teaspoon
onion	pepper

Put butter in 1-quart casserole, and heat in oven. Mix rest of ingredients until smooth, and put in hot casserole. Bake in hot oven, 425°F., half hour, or until barely set. Makes 4 to 6 servings.

ONIONS AND NOODLES, MEXICANOS

*To make this in the true Mexican
manner, use lard in place of butter.*

3 cups finely	1 package (8
chopped mild	ounces) fine
onion	noodles
¼ cup butter	2 cups rich beef
	stock or
	consommé
	Chopped parsley

Sauté onion in butter a few minutes; add uncooked noodles. Stir, and cook 5 minutes. Add stock; cover, and simmer about ½ hour. Check for seasoning. Garnish with parsley. Serves 6.

ONIONS AND APPLES

A hot relish to serve with meat.

Put 2 cups sliced onion and 3 cups peeled sliced apple in skillet with 2 tablespoons butter or bacon fat; cover; simmer over low heat until apples are soft and onions tender (about 10 minutes). Season; add 2 tablespoons brown sugar, and serve with meat. Serves 4.

GERMAN ONION TART

*This has a sour-cream filling with
onions, nutmeg, ginger, caraway seed.*

3 cups thinly	1½ teaspoons salt
sliced white	¼ teaspoon
onion	pepper
3 tablespoons	⅛ teaspoon each
butter or	nutmeg, ginger
bacon fat	9″ pie shell, baked
1 pint sour	at 450°F.
cream	10 minutes
2 eggs, slightly	Caraway seed
beaten	Paprika

Sauté onion in butter slowly until soft and golden. Add all except last 3 ingredients to onion, and turn into pie shell. Sprinkle with caraway seed and paprika. Bake in hot oven, 450°F., 10 minutes; reduce heat to 350°F., and bake half hour longer, or until a knife blade comes out clean. Serves 6.

LEEK AND GREEN-PEA PURÉE

*The garnish is sour cream
topped with toasted poppyseed.*

6 leeks (white	2 cups rich milk
only), thinly	Salt and pepper
sliced	Dash curry powder
4 tablespoons butter	Sour cream
or margarine	Toasted poppy seed
4 cans green-pea	
soup	

Sauté leek gently in butter until soft but not brown. Combine soup, milk, and seasonings in top of double boiler. Add leek, and heat. Serve with garnish of sour cream and poppy seed. Makes about 2 quarts.

DANISH ONIONS

The Danish touch is blue cheese.

Boil 8 peeled medium onions in salted water until tender. Drain; mix with ¼ cup crumbled blue cheese and 2 cups rich white sauce. Season with salt, pepper, and cayenne. Simmer 5 minutes. Serve on potatoes. Makes 4 servings.

GARLIC SEASONING

Good on meats and vegetables.

Mix 2 cloves garlic, peeled and pressed, ½ cup salt, 1½ teaspoons each black pepper and ground ginger. Let stand for several days in covered jar before using on meats or vegetables.

ONION AND CHEESE SOUP

The cheese is a sharp cheddar.

1 cup chopped onion	Salt and pepper
2 tablespoons butter	2 cups grated sharp cheddar cheese
2 tablespoons flour	
1½ quarts rich milk, scalded	Paprika
	Minced chives

Sauté onion in butter until soft. Add flour, and mix; add milk gradually, stirring, and heat to just below boiling. Season, and stir in cheese. Serve with paprika and chives. Makes 2 quarts.

ITALIAN GARLIC SOUP

The liquid is rich chicken broth.

5 cloves garlic, peeled and pressed	Pinch each thyme and rosemary
1 tablespoon olive oil	½ cup light cream
2 quarts rich chicken broth	3 egg yolks, beaten
Salt and pepper	Toast
	¼ cup grated Parmesan cheese

Sauté garlic in oil until light brown. Add to hot broth with seasonings. Simmer 1 hour; strain, and return to heat. Add cream to egg yolks, then add a little broth; then add eggs to broth. Remove soup after 5 minutes, and pour over toast in tureen. Sprinkle with grated cheese. Makes about 2 quarts.

LEEK SOUP

This is a hearty main-dish soup.

6 leeks (white only), cut in thin rounds	6 cups chicken broth
1 white onion, sliced	½ cup chopped parsley
¼ cup butter or margarine	1 egg yolk, beaten
6 potatoes, peeled and sliced	Salt and pepper
	Dash nutmeg
	2 cups light cream
	Crumbled crisp bacon

Sauté leek and onion in butter until soft but not brown. Add potatoes, broth, and parsley, and simmer until vegetables are soft. Strain, and sieve vegetables, and return purée to stock. Add some broth to egg, stirring, then add egg to broth with seasonings. Add cream, and reheat, but do not boil. Garnish in tureen with bacon. Makes 2 quarts.

SOUTH AMERICAN ONION SOUP

Onions and almonds in rich stock.

6 onions, thinly sliced	2 quarts rich stock
3 tablespoons butter	Salt and pepper
1½ cups almonds, blanched and chopped fine	Rounds of crusty bread, toasted
	1 cup grated Gruyère cheese

Sauté onion in butter slowly until soft. Add nuts and stock; simmer half hour. Season, and serve with toast sprinkled with cheese. Makes about 2½ quarts.

CHIVE AND CRESS SOUP

A quick-cooking cream soup.

3 tablespoons butter or margarine	1 cup chopped watercress
½ cup minced chives	3 tablespoons flour
	4 cups milk
	Salt and pepper
	Dash cayenne

Melt butter over low heat in heavy pan. Add chives and cress, and cook 5 minutes. Add flour, and stir; add milk slowly, and cook, stirring, until thickened. Season. Makes 1 quart.

It's hard to imagine a time when potatoes were not a daily dish. Yet a little over 450 years ago they were known only to the Incas of Peru, who had an elaborate agricultural system and developed this tuberous vegetable until they had many, many varieties, all sizes, shapes, and even colors. Like tomatoes and corn, potatoes were native only to the New World and explorers took them to Europe. The Irish took to the simple, bland tuber and brought it back to America as the Irish potato, the variety most widely grown and eaten in this country. We regularly depend on three types: the common mature (or stored) potato for boiling, mashing, hash-browned, and cooking with roasts; the elongated baking potato with its fine mealy texture; and the new potato, waxy and smooth, which is delicious sautéed and the best choice for salads. There are probably more recipes for preparing potatoes than for any other vegetable in the world. No wonder they are almost as basic as bread in our diet.

POTATOES

CARAWAY POTATOES

Use small new potatoes in the jackets.

Scrub 8 small new potatoes, and cook in boiling salted water until tender. Drain, and peel. Melt 2 tablespoons butter, and add 1 tablespoon caraway seed. Add potatoes, and toss until well-coated with butter and seed. Sprinkle with paprika and parsley. Serves 4.

FRENCH-FRIED POTATOES

You fry them in shallow fat.

Peel potatoes. Heat ¾" fat in large skillet to 285°F. on a frying thermometer. Cut potatoes in ½" slices, then in ½" strips. Rinse in cold water, and dry. Put potatoes in hot fat; fry 20 to 30 minutes, or until tender and brown. Drain on absorbent paper. Sprinkle with salt.

Lattice-fried Potatoes: Cut peeled potatoes with lattice cutter, and fry a few minutes in fat heated to 385°F. on a frying thermometer.

POTATOES AND ONIONS, CHARLENE

The potatoes and onions are cooked in a rich cream sauce.

Peel, and quarter enough potatoes and onions to make 3 cups each. Simmer in just enough salted water to cover until cooked. Drain off liquid, and replace with 1½ cups rich milk and ½ cup cream. Add 3 tablespoons butter, and season to taste with salt, pepper, dash cayenne. Simmer until thoroughly heated. Makes 6 servings.

BAKED HERBED POTATOES

Diced potatoes are baked with onion, celery, butter, parsley, seasonings.

8 cups diced potato	¼ cup minced parsley
1 onion, minced	
1 cup minced celery and leaves	2 teaspoons salt
	¼ teaspoon pepper
⅓ cup melted butter or margarine	1 teaspoon poultry seasoning

Cook potato in small amount of boiling water 5 minutes; drain. Add remaining ingredients, and mix well. Put in shallow baking dish, and bake in moderate oven, 375°F., about 30 minutes. Makes 6 servings.

POTATOES BOULANGÈRE

You cook the potatoes in herb consommé.

2 onions, sliced thin	½ teaspoon salt
	¼ teaspoon pepper
2 tablespoons butter	
4 potatoes, sliced thin	1 bay leaf
	¼ teaspoon thyme
1 can consommé	Chopped parsley

Cook onion in butter 5 minutes. Add remaining ingredients, except parsley. Cover, and simmer 25 to 30 minutes. Garnish with parsley. Serves 4.

BAKED POTATOES

To keep the skins soft during the baking, rub them with a little fat.

Scrub medium or large potatoes, and dry. Arrange on small baking sheet, piepan, or rack in oven. Bake in very hot oven, 450°F., 45 to 50 minutes, or until done. Cut a 1½" cross in center top of each potato. Hold with clean towel, and press at bottom until potato bursts through top. Fluff up potato with fork, and add a square of butter.

POTATO SOUFFLÉ

Cream and beaten egg whites make it smooth and fluffy.

3 tablespoons butter or margarine	1 teaspoon instant minced onion
3 tablespoons flour	1 cup mashed potato
	3 eggs, separated
1 cup light cream	Salt and pepper

Melt butter, and blend in flour. Add cream, and cook, stirring, until thickened. Add onion and potato; heat, stirring. Quickly stir in beaten egg yolks. Season, and fold in stiffly beaten egg whites. Pour into 1½-quart soufflé dish or casserole, and bake in moderate oven, 350°F., 30 minutes, or until puffed and firm. Makes 4 servings.

CHANTILLY POTATOES

A large mound of mashed potatoes
baked with a cheddar-cream coating.

Cook, drain, and mash enough potatoes to make 3 cups. Season with butter, salt, and pepper; shape in a mound on a piepan. Whip ½ cup heavy cream until stiff. Season with salt, paprika, and a dash cayenne. Fold in ½ cup grated cheddar cheese. Spread on potato mound. Bake in a moderate oven, 375°F., about 15 minutes. Serves 4.

POTATO MOUNDS, AMANDINE

Riced potatoes sprinkled
with buttered almonds and baked.

1½ pounds potatoes	1 egg Salt and pepper
4 tablespoons butter or margarine	¼ cup slivered blanched almonds
¼ cup hot milk	

Peel potatoes; cut in pieces, and cook in boiling salted water until tender. Drain, and force through ricer. Add 2 tablespoons butter, milk, and egg; beat until light and fluffy. Season. Drop from spoon in 12 mounds on greased baking sheet. Mix remaining 2 tablespoons butter and almonds; sprinkle on mounds. Bake in hot oven, 400°F., 15 minutes, or until lightly browned. Makes 4 servings.

HASH-BROWNED POTATOES

Make them plain, or add some
minced onion or parsley if you like.

3 cups chopped cold boiled or baked potato	Salt and pepper Instant minced onion or chopped parsley (optional)
3 tablespoons flour	
¼ cup milk	Bacon fat

Mix first 3 ingredients. Season to taste with salt, pepper, and onion. Heat 2 tablespoons fat in heavy 9″ skillet. Add potato mixture, and pack with spatula in a large cake. Cook over medium heat until brown and crusty, shaking the pan to keep potato from sticking. Turn out on flat plate. Wipe pan free of crumbs, and add 1 tablespoon fat. Slide potato back into hot pan, brown side up. Cook until bottom is brown, packing edges with spatula and shaking pan. Makes 4 servings.

POTATO PANCAKES

They contain a little onion.

4 large potatoes	1 egg, beaten
1 small onion	2 tablespoons flour
½ cup milk	
1 teaspoon salt	Fat for frying

Peel, and grate potatoes and onion into milk. Mix with remaining ingredients, except fat. Drop by tablespoonfuls into hot fat in skillet. Brown on both sides, and serve at once. Makes 6 servings.

HERBED PAN-ROASTED POTATOES

You sprinkle them with
paprika, parsley, thyme or marjoram.

Boil peeled medium potatoes 10 minutes. Drain, and arrange around roast of meat about 1 hour before meat is done. Turn occasionally, and baste with drippings in pan. When done, remove roast to hot platter. If potatoes are not browned enough, put under broiler in same pan, turning to brown. Sprinkle with paprika, minced parsley, crumbled thyme or marjoram, and arrange around roast.

POTATO RAGOUT

Sliced potatoes, onion,
bacon, tomatoes, thyme, and parsley.

4 medium potatoes	Salt and pepper
1 onion, sliced	1 teaspoon chopped fresh thyme or pinch dried thyme
1 or 2 cloves garlic, minced	
½ cup butter or margarine	
4 slices bacon	Few sprigs parsley, chopped
3 tomatoes, diced	

Peel potatoes, and slice thin. Brown onion and garlic lightly in butter. Add potato and diced bacon. Cook until the potatoes are lightly browned. Add remaining ingredients, and cover. Cook slowly 20 minutes, stirring occasionally. Makes 4 servings.

A giant Idaho or Maine potato,
a pink-skinned Bermuda, a mealy Green
Mountain, or a firm White Pearl, the
potato is truly what the French have
called it, pomme de terre, *the apple*
of the earth.

POTATOES BAKED IN SPAGHETTI SAUCE

*You sprinkle them with onion,
garlic, and parsley before baking.*

8 medium potatoes	1 clove garlic,
2 tablespoons	minced
olive oil	1 small onion,
1 can (10½ ounces)	minced
meatless	1 tablespoon
spaghetti sauce	chopped parsley

Peel potatoes, and cook in boiling salted water until partially tender. Drain, and coat with oil. Put in shallow baking dish. Pour spaghetti sauce over potatoes, and sprinkle with remaining ingredients. Bake in moderate oven, 350°F., 1 hour, or until potatoes are tender. Serves 4.

BAKED POTATOES RECTOR

*Baked potato mashed with cream and
onions, then returned to the shells.*

Bake large potatoes as on page 208. Cut a large oval piece of skin from the top of each potato, and scrape all the potato from the shell into a warm bowl. Season potato with salt, pepper, and paprika. Mash well, and beat in a little heavy cream. Add some chopped green onion, and fill potato shells lightly with the mixture. Put in hot oven until lightly browned.

PARSLEYED POTATO BALLS

You cut them with a melon-ball cutter.

4 large potatoes	¼ cup melted
2 sprigs parsley,	butter or
chopped	margarine

Peel potatoes, and put in cold water. With melon-ball cutter, cut potatoes in balls. Cook in boiling salted water until just tender. Drain, and shake over low heat to dry out slightly. Add parsley and butter. Makes 4 servings.

As chips or chippers, potatoes are indispensable as a snack. Hash-browned or scalloped for dinner and served from a hot earthenware dish, they lend an air of richness to the meal, and of the delights of French fries, it is unnecessary to speak.

CURRIED POTATOES

They simmer in chicken broth.

Cook 1 minced small onion in ¼ cup butter or margarine 5 minutes. Add 3 cups diced cooked potato, and cook until butter is absorbed. Add 1½ teaspoons each curry powder and lemon juice, ½ cup chicken broth; season. Cook a few minutes. Serves 4.

CRISP NEW POTATOES

*They're rolled in fat and flour,
then baked with stuffed olives.*

12 small new	1 teaspoon salt
potatoes	Dash pepper
2 tablespoons	½ teaspoon
melted fat	paprika
2 tablespoons	¼ cup chopped
flour	stuffed olives

Boil potatoes; peel; roll in fat, then in mixed flour and seasonings. Put in shallow baking dish, sprinkle with olives, and bake in hot oven, 425°F., about 20 minutes. Makes 4 servings.

RISSOLÉ POTATOES

*Fried-potato cubes served
with green pepper and pimiento.*

3 cups cold	½ medium green
cooked-potato	pepper, chopped
cubes	2 pimientos,
Fat for frying	chopped
	2 tablespoons butter

Fry potato in hot deep fat (375°F. on a frying thermometer) until crisp and golden brown. Drain on absorbent paper, and put in hot serving dish. Cook pepper and pimiento in butter 2 or 3 minutes. Sprinkle on potato. Serves 4.

DOUBLE-BOILER CREAMED POTATOES

A recipe featuring dry nonfat milk.

½ cup dry	Small amount
nonfat-milk	grated onion
powder	3 cups finely diced
3 tablespoons flour	raw potato
1 teaspoon salt	1 tablespoon butter
¼ teaspoon pepper	1¼ cups water

In top part of double boiler, mix nonfat milk, flour, and seasonings. Add onion and potato; stir until coated. Add butter and water, and cook over boiling water 1 hour, or until potato is tender; stir occasionally. Serves 4.

GOLDEN POTATOES

They're fried with corn meal.

6 boiled potatoes	¼ cup yellow
1 onion, grated	corn meal
Salt and pepper	2 tablespoons fat

Dice potatoes into bowl containing onion, seasonings, and corn meal; mix well. Heat fat in skillet. Add potato mixture, and cook until brown and crusty, stirring often. Serves 4.

SOUR-CREAM POTATO PATTIES

You start with grated cooked potato.

2 cups grated	About 1 cup
cooked potato	sour cream
½ teaspoon salt	Fat for frying
1 cup sifted flour	

Mix first 3 ingredients. Add enough sour cream to make a soft dough, as for biscuits. Roll to ⅛" thickness on floured board. Cut with floured 2" cutter. Fry in small amount of hot fat in skillet until golden brown on both sides and done. Serves 6.

BORDEAUX POTATOES

Sliced potatoes and seasoned tomatoes.

4 potatoes, peeled	2 fresh or canned
and cooked	tomatoes, diced
1 clove garlic	Salt, pepper,
1 tablespoon	and thyme to
vegetable oil	taste

Slice potatoes thin. Brown garlic lightly in oil, and remove. Add tomatoes and seasonings; cook 5 minutes. Add potatoes, and cook 5 to 10 minutes longer. Makes 4 servings.

TWO-CHEESE POTATOES

The cheeses: cottage and American.

6 cooked medium	1 teaspoon
potatoes, diced	Worcestershire
½ pound (1 cup)	¾ cup milk
cottage cheese	2 tablespoons
1 medium onion,	chopped parsley
grated	¼ cup shredded
2 teaspoons salt	process Ameri-
Dash cayenne	can cheese

Put potato in shallow, 2-quart baking dish. Mix remaining ingredients, except American cheese; pour over potato. Top with American cheese. Bake in hot oven, 400°F., about 15 minutes. Makes 4 servings.

Envisage, if you can, a world without potatoes. No potatoes, for instance, in an Irish stew, or in a well-browned corned-beef hash. It is unthinkable.

POTATO WAFFLES

Riced potato is added to waffle batter.

3 eggs	1 tablespoon
1 cup sifted flour	melted fat
2 teaspoons	2 cups cold, riced
baking powder	cooked potato
½ teaspoon salt	Butter
1 cup milk	Maple syrup

Beat eggs until light. Add sifted dry ingredients, milk, and fat; mix until smooth. Add potato, and mix well. Bake in hot waffle iron. Serve hot with butter and syrup. Serves 4.

NEW POTATOES AND PEAS IN CREAM

Small cooked peeled potatoes and frozen peas are heated in peppered cream.

1 pound small	1 box frozen peas
new potatoes	⅔ cup heavy
1 teaspoon salt	cream
2 cups boiling	⅛ teaspoon
water	pepper

Peel potatoes, and cook with salt in water until almost tender. Add peas; continue cooking until vegetables are tender. Drain; add cream and pepper; heat well. Makes 4 servings.

MEXICAN PANNED POTATOES

They're cooked with onion, garlic, chili powder, orégano.

1 onion, minced	¼ teaspoon
1 small clove	orégano
garlic, minced	1 teaspoon salt
2 tablespoons	1 cup water
bacon fat	4 medium pota-
1 teaspoon chili	toes, peeled
powder	and quartered

Brown onion and garlic lightly in fat. Add seasonings and water; bring to boil. Add potatoes, and simmer, stirring occasionally, 30 minutes, or until potatoes are tender. Serves 4.

POTATOES BAKED IN CREAM

Chopped cooked potato, cream, and nutmeg bake in individual servings.

3 cups finely chopped cold cooked potato	⅛ teaspoon nutmeg
Salt and pepper	½ cup heavy cream

Mix all ingredients. Pile lightly in 4 buttered individual baking dishes. Bake in very hot oven, 450°F., 15 minutes, or until lightly browned. Serves 4.

POTATO DUMPLINGS

Riced potatoes must stand overnight before being made into dumplings.

8 medium potatoes	2 eggs, beaten
½ cup sifted flour	1½ teaspoons salt

Cook unpeeled potatoes in boiling salted water until tender; drain. Peel, and force through ricer onto platter. Let stand at room temperature, uncovered, overnight. Add flour, eggs, salt; mix well. Form in 8 balls; drop into large kettle of boiling salted water. Boil, uncovered, 20 minutes, or until done. Drain. Serves 4.

POTATOES HUNGARIAN

They're baked in layers with sliced eggs, sour cream, crumbs, paprika.

6 medium potatoes	Dash pepper
4 hard-cooked eggs	6 slices toast, crushed fine, or 1 cup fine dry bread crumbs
¼ pound butter or margarine	
1 pint sour cream	
1½ teaspoons salt	Paprika

Peel, cook, and slice potatoes. Slice eggs. Melt butter; add cream and seasonings; mix well. Put potatoes, eggs, cream mixture, and crumbs in layers in shallow baking dish. Repeat, ending with crumbs. Sprinkle with paprika. Bake in moderate oven, 350°F., about 30 minutes. Serves 6.

Consider the economy of potatoes. Even the jacket is edible, and good for you, too. No wonder it is a favorite with the thrifty Scots.

POTATOES WITH CAPER BUTTER

You make caper butter by blending butter, capers, and a little vinegar.

4 medium potatoes	1 tablespoon vinegar
¼ cup butter or margarine	1 tablespoon capers

Peel potatoes, and cook in boiling salted water until tender. Drain. Heat butter in saucepan until golden brown. Remove from heat; gradually add vinegar, then capers. Pour over potatoes. Makes 4 servings.

CUSTARD POTATOES

Sliced potatoes are baked in a custard sauce.

1 cut clove garlic	2 eggs, beaten
Butter	1 cup milk
4 medium potatoes	2 tablespoons heavy cream
Salt and pepper	

Rub a shallow baking dish with garlic, and butter dish well. Peel potatoes, and slice very thin. Put in dish, and season. Mix eggs, milk, and cream; pour over potatoes. Dot with butter. Bake in moderate oven, 350°F., 45 minutes, or until potatoes are tender. Before serving, dot again with butter. Makes 4 servings.

HOT MASHED-POTATO SALAD

Seasoned mashed potatoes, onions, and celery garnished with pepper rings.

To 6 cups hot mashed potatoes, add ½ cup diced celery, ¾ cup salad dressing, 1 minced onion, ¼ cup each milk and vinegar, 1 tablespoon dry mustard, and salt and pepper to taste. Mix well, and garnish with paprika and green-pepper rings. Makes 6 servings.

GERMAN POTATO SALAD

Diced bacon, onion, and vinegar heated and tossed with sliced potatoes.

Peel, cook, and drain 6 medium potatoes. Cut in very thin slices. Put in shallow baking dish, and season with salt and pepper. Dice 4 slices bacon, and cook with 1 sliced onion. Add 2 tablespoons vinegar, and heat to boiling. Pour over potatoes. Cover, and let stand in slow oven, 300°F., until warm. Toss lightly. Serves 6.

Rice was being grown and harvested in the Orient at least 5,000 years ago. From Asia, its cultivation has spread to all regions where soil and climate are suitable and its use has spread even farther. Today there is no part of the civilized world where rice is not a staple. The reason for its popularity is no mystery: rice is one of the few foods that can be used in any course of the meal. It goes into soups, stuffings, and breads; it can be a vegetable or be combined with meat or fish; and it is the base of one of the finest desserts, rice pudding. This creamy confection, studded with plump raisins and gently flavored with spices, is a favorite with all age groups. Here is a variety of recipes drawing on the cuisines of many areas: curry from the Orient; jambalaya from Creole cookery; pilaf from the Middle East; paella from Spain. Try them all to find how many things rice can do.

RICE

SAVORY RICE

*You serve this
with grated Italian cheese.*

Prepare 1½ cups packaged precooked rice as directed on the label. Add 1 can (8 ounces) spaghetti sauce, and mix well. Reheat. Serve with a generous sprinkling of grated Parmesan or Romano cheese. Makes 4 servings.

GREEK RICE AND PORK PILAF

*It contains bacon, onion, sweet red
peppers, and green peas, too.*

¼ pound lean pork, diced	Salt and pepper
3 slices bacon, diced	2 cups hot water
1 onion, chopped	2 small sweet red peppers, cut in 1" pieces
1 cup uncooked rice	½ cup green peas, cooked

In a skillet, cook first 3 ingredients until pork is browned. Add rice, salt, and pepper; cook a few minutes. Pour off excess fat. Add hot water and the peppers. Bring to boil; cover; simmer till rice is done. Add peas. Serves 4.

RICE, KIDNEY BEANS, AND PORK CUBES

*Diced salt pork is a
topping for the rice and beans.*

Dice ½ pound lean salt pork, and fry until crisp. Remove pork, and keep hot. Cook 1 minced clove garlic in the fat 5 minutes. Add a drained can (1 pound, 4 ounces) red kidney beans, 3 cups cooked rice, a little minced parsley, and salt and pepper to taste. Heat well. Serve topped with the pork cubes. Makes 4 servings.

HOPPIN' JOHN

*A Southern dish
featuring black-eyed peas and rice.*

Cover 1 pound dried black-eyed peas with 6 cups cold water. Bring to boil; boil 2 minutes; let stand 1 hour. Add ½ pound sliced bacon or salt pork and 2 dried hot red peppers. Simmer about 30 minutes, or until peas are tender, adding more water, if necessary. Cook 2 chopped medium onions in 2 tablespoons fat 5 minutes. Add to peas with 1 cup uncooked rice. Cook, stirring occasionally, until rice is tender. Water should be absorbed. Top with pimiento strips. Serves 8.

HAM-CHEESE RICE

The cheese is a sharp cheddar.

1 small onion, minced	2 cups milk
Butter or margarine	½ pound sharp cheddar cheese
3 tablespoons flour	½ cup diced cooked ham
1 teaspoon salt	1 can (8 ounces) peas, drained
⅛ teaspoon pepper	4 cups hot cooked rice
½ teaspoon dry mustard	3 tablespoons fine dry bread crumbs
1 teaspoon Worcestershire	

Cook onion in 4 tablespoons butter 5 minutes. Blend in flour and seasonings. Add milk; cook, stirring, until thickened. Dice half of cheese, and add to mixture; stir until blended. Add ham and peas. Slice remaining cheese. Put half of rice in shallow baking dish. Cover with layer of sliced cheese; pour half of hot mixture over top. Repeat. Sprinkle with crumbs; dot with 2 tablespoons butter. Bake in hot oven, 400°F., about 20 minutes, or until mixture is lightly browned and bubbly. Makes 4 to 6 servings.

Tuna-Cheese Rice: In above recipe, in place of ham add 1 can (7 ounces) tuna, drained and flaked, to hot mixture with the peas. Pour over rice, and proceed with rest of recipe as directed.

RICE AND HAMBURGER BALLS

They're simmered in spaghetti sauce.

Mix 1 pound ground beef, 1 minced onion, 1 teaspoon salt, ¼ teaspoon each pepper and poultry seasoning, 1 egg, ⅓ cup each water and packaged precooked rice. Bring 1 can (15½ ounces) spaghetti sauce and ⅓ cup water to boil in large saucepan. Drop meat mixture in sauce by large spoonfuls. Cover; simmer about 30 minutes. Makes 4 servings.

Instant or Precooked: needs only to steam in boiling water before serving. Brown Rice: the whole, unpolished grain of rice with only the hull removed. Its texture is chewy; its flavor is nutlike.

GREEN RICE

Hot cooked rice is mixed with sour cream and parsley.

1⅓ cups packaged precooked rice	½ cup sour cream
¾ teaspoon salt	⅔ cup chopped parsley
1⅓ cups boiling water	Dash cayenne

Prepare rice with salt and water as directed on the label. Add remaining ingredients, and reheat. Serves 4.

RICE-LAMB BAKE

A good recipe for leftover lamb.

2 medium onions, chopped	1 can (28 ounces) tomatoes, drained
2 tablespoons lamb fat	1½ teaspoons salt
2 cups ground roast lamb	1 teaspoon paprika
2 cups cooked rice	1 teaspoon Worcestershire
	1 slice bacon, diced

Cook onion in fat 5 minutes. Add remaining ingredients, except bacon. Put in baking dish. Sprinkle with bacon. Bake in moderate oven, 375°F., about 45 minutes. Serves 4.

RICE AND HAM STUFFED PEPPERS

There's half a pound of American cheese blended into the stuffing.

Cut 4 large green peppers in halves crosswise. Remove seeds. Cook peppers in 2 cups boiling water 5 minutes. Drain, reserving liquid. Cook 1 cup rice until tender; drain. Sauté 1 minced onion in 2 tablespoons butter 5 minutes. Add ¾ cup water and ½ pound diced process American cheese. Stir until blended. Add 1 cup diced cooked ham, rice, 2 tablespoons minced parsley, and salt and pepper to taste. Fill pepper halves. Put on rack in skillet with 1½ cups pepper liquid. Simmer, covered, about 15 minutes. Serves 4.

RICE AND BEEF, ORIENTAL

You use ginger and soy sauce for the seasonings.

In 2-quart casserole, mix 1¼ cups packaged precooked rice, 1 pound ground beef, 2 sliced medium onions, 1-pound can bean sprouts (drained), 1 box frozen cut green beans, 1 can beef bouillon, ⅓ cup soy sauce, ½ cup water, and ½ teaspoon ginger. Cover, and bake in hot oven, 425°F., about 40 minutes. Serves 4 to 6.

RICE AND PORK CASSEROLE

Browned pork chops and rice are baked in seasoned chicken broth.

4 pork chops	2 green onions, sliced
Salt and pepper	1 tomato, peeled and diced
2 chicken bouillon cubes	½ green pepper, chopped
2 cups hot water	Paprika
1 cup uncooked rice	

Brown chops, and put in shallow baking dish. Season. Dissolve bouillon cubes in water; pour over chops. Add next 3 ingredients; sprinkle with green pepper and paprika. Cover tightly (with foil if cover is not available), and bake in moderate oven, 350°F., about 1 hour. Serves 4.

BAKED RICE, PORK, AND CABBAGE

Cabbage leaves are stuffed with a mixture of rice and pork.

¾ pound boneless lean pork	8 cabbage leaves
½ cup uncooked rice	1 small onion, minced
1½ teaspoons salt	1 tablespoon vegetable oil
¼ teaspoon pepper	1 can tomato soup
	¾ cup water

Cut pork in ½" cubes, and mix with rice, salt, and pepper. Cook cabbage leaves in boiling salted water until limp. Fill each leaf with about ⅓ cup of the meat mixture, and roll up loosely. Put, seam side down, in baking dish. Cook onion in oil 5 minutes. Add soup and water; mix well, and pour over cabbage rolls. Cover, and bake in moderate oven, 375°F., about 1½ hours. Makes 4 servings.

YELLOW RICE

The herb turmeric is the ingredient that gives the rice its yellow color.

Put 1 cup uncooked rice in 1½-quart casserole with 2 cups boiling water, 1 teaspoon each salt and turmeric, and 2 tablespoons butter or margarine. Cover, and bake in moderate oven, 350°F., about 1¾ hours. Serves 4.

ITALIAN RICE SOUP WITH CHICKEN LIVERS

The chicken livers are chopped and mixed with egg yolk.

½ cup uncooked rice	4 chicken livers, cooked
1 tablespoon butter or margarine	1 egg yolk
4 cups chicken broth	Chopped parsley
Salt and pepper	Grated Parmesan cheese

Lightly brown rice in the butter. Add broth; bring to boil, and season with salt and pepper. Cover, and simmer until rice is done. Meanwhile, chop chicken livers, and mix with beaten egg yolk. Remove rice from heat; add liver mixture. Serve in bowls with a sprinkling of parsley and grated cheese. Makes 4 to 6 servings.

GEORGIAN RICE AND CHICKEN

Raisins and almonds are in the sauce.

2 frying chickens, cut up	½ cup seedless raisins
½ cup butter or margarine	½ cup blanched almonds
2 medium green peppers, chopped	1 teaspoon curry powder
1 clove garlic, minced	1 teaspoon dried thyme leaves
2 onions, chopped	Salt and pepper
1 can (19 ounces) tomatoes	2 cups rice, partially cooked

Fry chicken in butter until golden brown. Remove chicken to a large casserole. Pour off butter. To skillet, add green pepper, garlic, onion, tomatoes, ¼ cup each raisins and almonds, and seasonings. Simmer 10 to 15 minutes. Put rice in casserole with chicken. Pour sauce over top. Cover, and bake in hot oven, 400°F., 30 minutes, or until chicken is tender. Garnish with remaining raisins and nuts. Serves 6.

BAKED RICE AND TURKEY

There are layers of curried rice, diced turkey, cream-of-mushroom soup, and crumbs.

1½ cups packaged precooked rice	2 cups diced cooked turkey
1½ cups boiling water	6 olives, sliced
¾ teaspoon salt	1 can cream-of-mushroom soup
2 tablespoons instant minced onion	½ cup milk
	½ cup grated cheddar cheese
1 teaspoon curry powder	¼ cup corn-flake crumbs

Prepare rice with water and salt as directed on the label. Add onion and curry powder; put in shallow baking dish. Cover with turkey, and sprinkle with olives. Mix soup and milk; pour over top. Sprinkle with cheese and crumbs. Bake in moderate oven, 350°F., about 30 minutes. Serves 6.

RICE FLUFF, CHEESE SAUCE

Egg whites make a fluffy rice dish which is served with a mustard-cheese sauce.

1 cup uncooked rice	½ teaspoon Worcestershire
1 tablespoon butter	1 tablespoon instant minced onion
1 tablespoon flour	
¾ teaspoon salt	2 eggs, separated
¼ teaspoon paprika	¾ cup grated sharp cheddar cheese
1 teaspoon dry mustard	
2 cups milk	

Cook, and drain rice. Keep warm in moderate oven, 350°F. Melt butter; blend in flour, salt, paprika, mustard. Add milk, Worcestershire, and onion; cook, stirring, until slightly thickened. Add a little of mixture to beaten egg yolks; return to sauce; cook 2 minutes. Stir in cheese. Beat egg whites until stiff. Fold into rice, and bake 3 minutes. Cover with cheese sauce, and serve at once. Makes 4 servings.

RICE AND CHICKEN PILAF

There's a topping of chopped walnuts.

3 cups diced cooked chicken	1 cup uncooked rice
1 onion, chopped	2½ cups chicken broth or bouillon
½ cup butter or margarine	½ cup drained canned tomatoes
¼ teaspoon each pepper and garlic salt	Salt
½ teaspoon thyme	½ cup chopped walnuts

Cook chicken and onion in butter until lightly browned. Add remaining ingredients, except last 2. Cover, and simmer 30 minutes, stirring occasionally. Add salt to taste, and the nuts. Serves 4.

DRIED-BEEF AND CHEESE RICE

A tangy cheese sauce with dried beef is served over the rice.

½ green pepper, chopped	2 cups milk
1 onion, chopped	1 cup shredded sharp cheddar cheese
¼ cup butter or margarine	
¼ pound dried beef	Salt and pepper
3 tablespoons flour	1 cup uncooked rice
	Chopped parsley

Cook green pepper and onion in butter a few minutes. Add beef, torn in pieces, and heat. Stir in flour; add milk, and cook until thickened, stirring constantly. Add cheese, and heat gently until cheese melts. Season. Cook, and drain rice; serve with the sauce and a sprinkling of parsley. Makes 4 servings.

PARMESAN RICE WITH CHICKEN

Rice is cooked in chicken broth with Parmesan cheese added.

1 onion, chopped	½ teaspoon turmeric
3 tablespoons butter or margarine	½ cup diced cooked chicken and giblets
1¼ cups uncooked rice	⅔ cup grated Parmesan cheese
1 quart chicken broth	Salt and pepper

Cook onion in butter until lightly browned. Add rice, and brown. Add broth and turmeric; cover; simmer 20 minutes. Stir in chicken and ⅓ cup cheese. Cook 15 minutes. Season. Put in serving dish, and sprinkle with remaining ⅓ cup cheese. Serves 4.

ONION RICE

Especially good with pot roast or meat loaf.

Heat 1 can condensed onion soup and ⅓ cup water to boiling. Stir in 1½ cups packaged precooked rice. Cover; turn off heat, and let stand 5 minutes. Fluff with fork; add pepper to taste, and serve with grated Parmesan cheese, if desired. Serves 4.

CURRIED RICE AND PEAS

Serve this with roast lamb, poultry, or pork.

2½ cups boiling water	1½ teaspoons curry powder
1 teaspoon salt	1 box frozen peas
1¼ cups uncooked rice	1 pimiento, cut in strips
¼ cup butter or margarine	

Mix first 5 ingredients in Dutch oven or covered casserole. Cover, and bake in hot oven, 400°F., about 45 minutes. Cook, and drain peas; mix lightly into rice. Top with pimiento. Serves 6.

SPANISH RICE

You can use either white or brown rice for this recipe.

Brown 1 cup white or brown rice, 1 chopped onion, and 1 chopped green pepper lightly in ¼ cup butter or margarine. Add 1 crumbled bay leaf, 2 whole cloves, 1 teaspoon each salt and sugar, ¼ teaspoon pepper, 1 can (19 ounces) tomatoes, and 2 cups boiling water. Bring to boil, and simmer, covered, 30 minutes, or till water is absorbed, stirring occasionally. Serves 4.

Frankfurter Spanish Rice: In above recipe, add 4 frankfurters, cut in chunks, to rice mixture before simmering. Serve with grated cheese and minced parsley.

PERFECTLY COOKED RICE

To prevent gumminess, don't remove lid and don't stir rice while it's boiling. To prevent sogginess, always add boiling water to rice while it is cooking.

RICE PANCAKES

You start with pancake mix.

Mix well: 1 cup pancake mix, 1 egg, and 1½ cups milk. Stir in 1 cup cooked rice. Fry on hot, well-greased griddle until browned on both sides. Serve at once with butter and syrup. Makes about 3 dozen 3″ pancakes.

PEANUT RICE

Good with poultry.

Cook ¾ cup minced celery in 3 tablespoons butter 5 minutes. Add 1 teaspoon instant minced onion, 2 cups hot cooked rice, and ½ cup finely chopped salted peanuts. Toss lightly, and serve with a sprinkling of chopped parsley. Makes 4 servings.

RICE MUFFINS

Delicious for any meal of the day.

1½ cups sifted flour	3 tablespoons soft shortening
2 teaspoons baking powder	1 cup cold cooked rice
½ teaspoon salt	1 egg, beaten
2 tablespoons sugar	1 cup milk

Sift dry ingredients. Cut in shortening. Add rice, egg, and milk; mix only enough to moisten dry ingredients. Half-fill 2¾″ muffin pans. Bake in 425°F. oven 25 minutes. Makes 12.

RICE, VIENNESE STYLE

This contains lots of paprika, a favorite Viennese seasoning.

1 small onion, minced	2 cups hot consommé
Butter or margarine	1 cup canned peas, heated
1 cup uncooked rice	1 teaspoon paprika
Salt and pepper	

Brown onion lightly in 1 tablespoon butter; then add rice, and cook until glazed. Season with salt and pepper. Add consommé; bring to boil, and simmer until rice is done. (Consommé should be entirely absorbed.) With a fork, carefully stir in peas. Add 2 tablespoons butter, and sprinkle with paprika. Serves 4 or 5.

RICE-TUNA FRITTERS

A fine luncheon or supper dish.

1½ cups water	¼ cup milk
⅔ cup uncooked rice	2 eggs, separated
1 teaspoon salt	2 tablespoons flour
1 can (7 ounces) tuna fish	Dash pepper
	Fat for frying

In saucepan, bring to a boil water, rice, and salt. Cover, and cook over low heat 15 minutes. Remove from heat. Mix tuna, milk, egg yolks, flour, and pepper; add to rice; mix well. Beat egg whites until stiff; fold into rice mixture; drop from tablespoon into hot deep fat (365°F. on a frying thermometer), and fry until brown. Serves 4.

SAUTÉED BROWN RICE AND MUSHROOMS

Chili powder provides a special zest.

1 medium onion, minced	3 cups cooked brown rice
¼ green pepper, minced	¾ teaspoon salt
¼ cup butter or margarine	⅛ teaspoon pepper
1 can (3 ounces) mushroom stems and pieces, drained	½ teaspoon chili powder

Cook onion and green pepper in the butter 5 minutes. Add remaining ingredients, and cook until lightly browned, stirring gently. Serves 4.

RICE-WALNUT FRITTERS

You add rice and nuts to batter.

1 cup sifted flour	2 tablespoons oil
1 teaspoon baking powder	2 cups cooked brown rice
1 teaspoon salt	½ cup chopped walnuts
3 eggs, slightly beaten	Fat for frying
½ cup milk	Maple syrup

Sift dry ingredients into a bowl. Add eggs, milk, and oil; beat until smooth. Stir in rice and nuts. Drop by spoonfuls into hot deep fat (365°F. on a frying thermometer), and fry until golden. Serve with syrup. Makes 22.

RICE WAFFLES

Serve them hot with butter and syrup.

Beat until smooth: 4 cups biscuit mix, 3⅓ cups milk, 2 eggs, and 4 tablespoons vegetable oil. Add 2 cups cooked rice, and cook on hot waffle iron. Serve hot with butter and syrup. Makes 10 waffles, 11"x 6".

FRENCH RICE SALAD

*Warm rice is chilled
in a dressing of vinegar and oil.*

1 cup uncooked rice	12 radishes, sliced
Oil and vinegar	2 tablespoons chopped walnuts
Salt and pepper	
½ pound Bel Paese cheese, cubed	Handful of watercress, chopped

Cook rice; while still warm, dress with oil and vinegar, salt and pepper. Chill. Add rest of ingredients. Serves 4.

CURRIED RICE SALAD

*Crushed pineapple
is tossed with the rice.*

Toss lightly: 3 cups cold cooked rice, 1 cup chopped celery, ¼ cup chopped green pepper, 1 teaspoon instant minced onion, 1 teaspoon curry powder, ½ teaspoon dry mustard, ¾ teaspoon salt, ⅛ teaspoon pepper, ¾ cup mayonnaise, juice ½ lemon, and 1 can (9 ounces) crushed pineapple (drained). Serve on salad greens with a garnish of chopped salted cashew nuts. Serves 6.

CHEESE AND BACON RICE SALAD

You can serve this hot or cold.

1 cup uncooked rice	½ cup chopped sweet pickles
2 cups boiling water	¼ pound sharp cheddar cheese, cut in ½" cubes
1½ teaspoons salt	
⅛ teaspoon pepper	1 cup thinly sliced radishes
6 strips bacon, cooked crisp	3 green onions, sliced
2 tablespoons bacon fat	½ green pepper, chopped
¼ cup mayonnaise	

Cook rice in the water with salt and pepper until tender. Crumble bacon; add with remaining ingredients to warm rice. Serve at once, or chill and serve on salad greens. Serves 4 to 6.

KITCHENETTE RICE PUDDING

*Traditional rice pudding, but made
in a double boiler.*

Scald 1 quart milk in top of double boiler. Add ¼ cup rice (not processed) slowly, stirring constantly. Add ¼ cup sugar, ¼ teaspoon each salt and nutmeg, and ⅓ cup seeded raisins. Cook, covered, over simmering water 1½ hours, stirring frequently. Pour mixture slowly over 1 slightly beaten egg. Return to boiler; cook 2-3 minutes. Serves 6.

PINEAPPLE RICE PUDDING

You use canned crushed pineapple.

Mix 2 cups cooked rice, 2 tablespoons sugar, 1 can (1 pound 14½ ounces) crushed pineapple. Chill; fold in 1 cup heavy cream, whipped. Chill. Serves 6.

Glorified Rice Dessert: Use above recipe. Add 16 halved marshmallows to first mixture. Proceed as directed. Garnish with maraschino cherries.

SWEET SCRAMBLED RICE

You cook this in a skillet.

¼ cup raisins	2 tablespoons chopped nuts
¼ cup rum	
1 cup uncooked rice	Grated rind 1 lemon
¼ teaspoon salt	1 egg, beaten
Sugar	½ cup butter or margarine
3 cups milk	Cinnamon

Soak raisins in rum several hours. Cook rice, salt, and 1 cup sugar in milk in top part of double boiler over boiling water 30 minutes, or until rice is tender and milk is absorbed, stirring occasionally. Add raisins, nuts, lemon rind, and egg. Melt butter in skillet; add rice mixture, and cook, letting brown crust form. Turn, and brown remainder. Sprinkle with sugar and cinnamon. Serves 4 to 6.

YIELD OF RICE

Regular Milled: 1 cup = 3 cups cooked
Parboiled: 1 cup = 4 cups cooked
Brown: 1 cup = 4 cups cooked
Instant or Precooked:
*   1 cup = 2 cups cooked*

BAKED RICE CUSTARD

You can use brown or white sugar; brown gives it a butterscotchy flavor.

Bring to boil: ¾ cup packaged precooked rice, 3 cups milk, and ¼ cup raisins. Mix: 2 beaten eggs, ⅔ cup granulated or brown sugar, ½ teaspoon salt, ¼ teaspoon nutmeg. Add hot mixture, stirring. Pour into baking dish, and bake in pan of hot water in 375°F. oven 35 minutes; stir several times during first part of baking. Serves 6.

OLD-TIME RICE PUDDING

You can make this recipe with either white or brown rice.

½ cup uncooked rice (not processed)	½ teaspoon salt
	½ teaspoon nutmeg
	2 quarts milk
½ cup sugar	¾ cup raisins

Mix rice, sugar, salt, and nutmeg in a shallow 2½-quart baking dish. Add 1 quart milk. Then, to prevent spilling, add second quart of milk after placing dish in the oven. Bake in moderate oven, 325°F., 2½ hours, stirring twice during first hour. Stir the brown crust into pudding several times during the remainder of baking. Add raisins half hour before pudding is done. Then allow crust to form again. Serve with cream, if desired. Makes 6 to 8 servings.

Butterscotch Rice Pudding: In Old-time Rice Pudding recipe, substitute 1 cup brown sugar for the white. Omit raisins. Serve cold.

Date Rice Pudding: In Old-time Rice Pudding recipe, substitute ¾ cup chopped pitted dates for the raisins.

Chocolate Rice Pudding: Mix ¼ cup cocoa with the rice and sugar mixture. Increase sugar to ⅔ cup, and omit raisins. Serve cold with whipped cream.

Apricot or Prune Rice Pudding: Substitute well-drained soaked dried apricots or prunes for the raisins in Old-time Rice Pudding. Cut fruit in strips.

CUSTARD RICE PUDDING

It has raisins in it, and a sprinkling of nutmeg.

½ cup uncooked rice	1½ teaspoons grated lemon rind
3 eggs, beaten	
½ cup sugar	½ cup raisins
¼ teaspoon salt	3½ cups milk
1 teaspoon vanilla extract	Nutmeg

Cook, and drain rice. Mix with remaining ingredients, except nutmeg. Pour into shallow baking dish, and sprinkle with nutmeg. Set in pan of hot water, and bake in slow oven, 300°F., about 1½ hours. Serve warm or cool. Serves 6.

Queen of Rice Puddings: Use above recipe, separating eggs. Use only yolks in pudding. When pudding is done, spread top with soft currant jelly. Top with a meringue made with the 3 egg whites and 6 tablespoons sugar. Brown in 400°F. oven about 5 minutes.

RICE IMPERIAL

Candied fruit, soaked in brandy, and whipped cream are stirred into gelatin rice pudding.

1 cup chopped candied fruit	1 envelope unflavored gelatin
¼ cup brandy	4 egg yolks
1 cup uncooked rice	1 cup sugar
Boiling water	1 teaspoon vanilla extract
Milk	1 cup heavy cream, whipped
¼ teaspoon salt	

Soak fruit overnight in brandy. Cook rice in boiling water about 10 minutes. Pour off water, and finish cooking rice in 1⅓ cups milk to which salt has been added. Put aside to cool. Meanwhile, sprinkle gelatin on ⅔ cup cold milk in top part of double boiler. Cook over boiling water, adding egg yolks, sugar, and vanilla. Stir constantly, and cook until thickened. Mix with rice. Cool, and stir in undrained fruit and then the whipped cream. Chill. Makes 6 to 8 servings.

TOMATOES

Your great-grandfather, along with many Americans, believed that the tomato, or "love apple" as it was commonly called, was deadly poison. Many people grew tomatoes in their flower gardens, but only as decorative plants, not as food. The American Indian, of course, knew its value and used it fearlessly and plentifully. The tomato was one of the Western Hemisphere's contributions to the world. Spanish explorers took it to Spain and from there it was transplanted to Italy. Perhaps Italians were more venturous in their eating habits. It was not long before they were using it in sauces and salads. Today it's impossible to imagine Italian cuisine without the tomato. The English adopted the fruit for a popular English breakfast dish: grilled tomatoes with rashers of bacon or grilled kidneys. This is still an outstanding breakfast combination. Modern Americans have made up for lost time by using tomatoes in an amazing variety of ways: they go into juice and into soups and sauces; they are baked, grilled, fried and stewed, and eaten raw in salads; they make ketchup, chili sauce, and pickles; and they even go into a pie.

CUCUMBER TOMATO-JUICE COCKTAIL

A tangy drink with Tabasco, Worcestershire, and horse-radish.

1 medium cucumber	Juice 1 lemon
2¼ cups tomato juice	2 teaspoons prepared horse-radish
2 tablespoons chopped green onions and tops	½ teaspoon salt
	⅛ teaspoon pepper
1 teaspoon Worcestershire	Dash Tabasco
	Lemon wedges

Peel cucumber, and grate. Add remaining ingredients, except lemon wedges. Cover, and refrigerate 2 hours. Strain through a coarse sieve, and serve with lemon. Makes 4 servings.

SHERRIED TOMATO-SHRIMP BISQUE

The garnish is lemon slices and chopped parsley.

2 cans (19 ounces each) tomatoes	Pinch thyme
2 cups beef broth or bouillon	2 teaspoons salt
1 cup cut celery and leaves	3 tablespoons uncooked rice
2 onions, sliced	1½ pounds shrimp, cooked and cut in pieces
2 carrots, sliced	2 cups light cream
2 sprigs parsley	Sherry
4 whole cloves	Croutons
6 whole black peppers	Thin slices lemon
Small piece bay leaf	Chopped parsley

Put tomatoes, broth, vegetables, seasonings, and rice in kettle; bring to boil. Cover, and simmer 1 hour. Force through fine sieve, or put in blender, and run until smooth. Just before serving, add shrimp; heat. Heat cream, and add to tomato mixture. Season to taste. Serve at once with dash of sherry and a sprinkling of croutons. Garnish with lemon slices and finely chopped parsley. Makes about 2½ quarts.

JELLIED TOMATO MADRILÈNE

Serve with salad or cottage cheese.

Combine 2 cans (12½ ounces each) consommé Madrilène and 2 cups of tomato juice. Soak 2 envelopes of unflavored gelatin in ¾ cup of the mixture. Heat remaining mixture; then add gelatin, and stir to dissolve. Add juice of 1 lemon. Pour into a 2-quart mold; chill until firm. Unmold. Serves 8.

COLD TOMATO HERB SOUP

You use juice and fresh tomatoes.

2 beef or chicken bouillon cubes	1 clove garlic
1 cup boiling water	3 tablespoons lemon juice
3 cups tomato juice	Dash Tabasco
1 onion, grated	2 tablespoons minced fresh herbs (parsley, basil, savory, etc.)
1 cup chopped celery	½ cucumber, sliced
1 green pepper, minced	2 peeled ripe tomatoes, sliced
1 teaspoon salt	

Dissolve bouillon cubes in water; cool slightly. Add tomato juice, onion, celery, green pepper, and salt. Cut garlic in half, and put toothpick through both halves; then add to mixture. Mix lightly. Cover, and refrigerate several hours, or overnight. Just before serving, remove garlic; add remaining ingredients. Serve over ice. Makes 1½ quarts.

GAZPACHO

A cold soup of Spanish derivation.

1 medium loaf French bread (about 1 pound)	½ cup wine vinegar
2 cloves garlic	Salt and pepper
3 tomatoes, peeled	Croutons
1 large onion	Finely diced cucumber, tomato, onion, parsley, hard-cooked egg
1 cucumber, peeled	
½ cup olive oil	

Cut up bread; soak in water, and squeeze almost dry. Put in blender with garlic and coarsely cut tomatoes, onion, and cucumber. Run blender until contents are thoroughly mixed. With blender still turned on, remove cover, and add oil gradually. Pour into bowl; stir in vinegar, and salt and pepper to taste. Chill. Serve in large flat bowls. Put croutons and finely diced remaining ingredients in individual bowls to be passed at the table. Serves 4 to 6.

CREAM OF FRESH-TOMATO SOUP

You season it with basil or mint.

2 cups chopped ripe tomatoes	2 tablespoons butter
1 onion, sliced	2 tablespoons flour
½ bay leaf	2 cups milk
½ teaspoon salt	Chopped fresh basil or mint
⅛ teaspoon pepper	

Simmer tomatoes with onion, bay leaf, salt, and pepper about 10 minutes. Strain. Melt butter, and stir in flour; add milk, and cook until thickened, stirring constantly. Slowly stir in hot tomatoes. Sprinkle with herb. Serves 4.

TOMATO BOUILLON

Use either fresh or canned tomatoes.

1 can (19 ounces) tomatoes, or 2 cups chopped ripe tomatoes	¼ teaspoon celery seed
	¼ teaspoon whole black peppers
1 can beef broth	3 whole cloves
1 small onion, sliced	Salt
	Chopped parsley

Heat all ingredients, except salt and parsley. Simmer about 10 minutes. Strain. Season to taste with salt. Serve topped with parsley. Makes 4 servings.

FRIED GREEN-TOMATO AND CUCUMBER SLICES

You dip them in rolled oats.

Slice 2 large green tomatoes about ½" thick. Peel 1 large yellow ripe cucumber; slice, and remove seeds. Season. Dip slices in evaporated milk, then in quick-cooking rolled oats (rub oats between hands to make them fine). Fry slowly in hot oil until brown and tender. Makes 4 servings.

STEWED GREEN TOMATOES AND PEPPERS

They're cooked with sliced onion.

1 onion, sliced	2 green peppers
3 tablespoons butter or margarine	6 large green tomatoes
	Salt and pepper

Cook onion in butter in skillet 3 minutes; do not brown. Wash, and core peppers and tomatoes; cut into eighths lengthwise. Add to onion. Cover, and cook slowly, stirring often, about 20 minutes, or until peppers are just tender. Season. Makes 4 servings.

TOMATOES, CORN, AND OKRA

The seasoning is paprika.

1 onion, chopped	Salt, pepper, and paprika
2 tablespoons butter	
1 pound okra, sliced	1 cup whole-kernel corn
4 medium tomatoes, peeled and quartered	

Cook onion in butter until golden. Add okra, and cook about 5 minutes, stirring. Add tomatoes, and cook until okra is tender. Season. Add corn; cook 5 minutes longer. Makes 4 servings.

FRIED TOMATOES WITH CREAMY GRAVY

The tomatoes are dredged with flour and fried in bacon fat.

Remove ends from 4 large tomatoes, and cut tomatoes in half. Season tomatoes, and dredge with flour. Brown on both sides in 3 tablespoons bacon fat. Remove to hot platter. Blend 1 tablespoon flour into drippings in pan. Add 1½ cups milk. Cook until thickened, stirring constantly. Add more seasoning if necessary. Pour over tomatoes. Makes 4 servings.

GREEN BEANS AND GLAZED-TOMATO SAUCE

The tomatoes are glazed in sugared, salted butter.

1 pound whole green beans	½ cup sugar
	Dash salt
2 tablespoons butter	1 quart chopped peeled tomatoes

Cook whole beans, covered, in small amount of boiling, salted water until tender. Meanwhile, melt butter in skillet; stir in sugar and salt, and add tomatoes. Cook over low heat until liquid has boiled down, turning tomatoes frequently to glaze on all sides. Drain beans, and top with tomatoes. Serves 4.

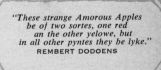

"These strange Amorous Apples be of two sortes, one red an the other yelowe, but in all other pyntes they be lyke."
REMBERT DODOENS

CHILI-STEWED FRESH TOMATOES

Tomatoes seasoned with chili.

Peel, and cut up 6 tomatoes. Simmer with ¾ teaspoon salt, ¼ teaspoon pepper, 1 teaspoon chili powder, and 2 teaspoons sugar in covered pan 30 minutes. Makes 4 servings.

TOMATOES AND EGGPLANT

They're cooked Creole style.

¼ pound salt pork, diced	2 cups canned or diced fresh tomatoes
2 tablespoons olive oil	Dash cayenne
1 onion, chopped	1 eggplant (about 1½ pounds), pared, diced
1 medium green pepper, chopped	

Fry salt pork until browned. Add oil, onion, and green pepper, and fry until tender. Add tomatoes and cayenne, and simmer 30 minutes. Add eggplant; cover; cook 30 minutes. Serves 4 to 6.

GREEN-TOMATO MINCEMEAT

*It's made with apples,
raisins, and beef suet, plus tomatoes.*

4 quarts (after grinding) green tomatoes	1 cup vinegar
4 quarts chopped peeled tart apples	2 tablespoons cinnamon
2 pounds raisins, chopped or coarsely ground	2 tablespoons salt
	1 teaspoon ground cloves
	1 teaspoon allspice
1 cup ground beef suet	2 pounds brown sugar
	½ cup molasses

Force tomatoes through food chopper. Drain. Put in large kettle, and cover with boiling water. Boil 5 minutes. Drain, and repeat. Drain, and add remaining ingredients. Bring to boil; simmer until thick. Put in sterilized jars, seal. Makes about 8 pints.

For pie: Sprinkle mincemeat with seedless raisins, and dot with 2 tablespoons butter. Adjust top crust, and bake in hot oven, 425°F., about 30 minutes.

*"Oh, herbaceous treat! 'Twould
tempt the dying anchorite to eat;
Back to the world he'd turn his
fleeting soul, And
plunge his fingers in the salad bowl."*
SYDNEY SMITH

PIQUANT RELISH

Good with frankfurters, hamburgers.

¼ cup hot vinegar	¼ cup chopped celery
1 cup seeded tomatoes	½ teaspoon each celery and mustard seed
⅔ cup diced cucumber	Salt and pepper
½ cup chopped onion	

Mix all ingredients. Makes 2 cups.

SUMMER RELISH

Keeps well in the refrigerator.

1 quart peeled and chopped ripe tomatoes, drained	2 tablespoons salt
	2 tablespoons mustard seed
1½ cups finely chopped celery	⅓ cup brown sugar
1 cup finely chopped onion	¼ teaspoon cloves
	¼ teaspoon mace
1 apple, chopped	½ teaspoon cinnamon
2 tablespoons horse-radish	Dash cayenne
	1½ cups vinegar

Mix all ingredients thoroughly. Cover, and refrigerate. If too juicy, drain off some liquid. Makes about 1½ quarts.

CURRIED TOMATO RELISH

There's a touch of garlic in it.

3 medium tomatoes, peeled	2 teaspoons curry powder
1 teaspoon sugar	2 teaspoons vinegar
¼ teaspoon garlic salt	½ teaspoon salt

Cut tomatoes in small pieces, and simmer 10 minutes. Add remaining ingredients, and cook 5 minutes. Cool. Makes about 1 cup.

SWEET SPICY TOMATO RELISH

The spice is clove.

7 pounds ripe tomatoes	4 pounds sugar
	1 tablespoon salt
3 cups cider vinegar	¼ cup whole cloves

Peel, and chop tomatoes. Cover with vinegar, and allow to soak overnight. Drain. Put tomatoes, sugar, and salt in kettle; add cloves, tied in a piece of cheesecloth. Cook to consistency of preserves. Let stand overnight. Heat to boiling; remove cloves. Pour into hot sterilized jars; seal. Makes 5 pints.

GREEN-TOMATO PICKLE

It's packed in spiced vinegar.

4 quarts thinly sliced green tomatoes	1 teaspoon celery seed
1 quart thinly sliced onions	1 tablespoon each whole black peppers, mustard seed, dry mustard
⅓ cup cooking salt	1 lemon, sliced
3 cups vinegar	3 cups brown sugar, packed
1 teaspoon whole allspice	

Put tomatoes and onions in large bowl, and sprinkle with salt; cover, and let stand overnight. Drain. Heat remaining ingredients to boiling. Add tomatoes and onions. Bring to boil, and simmer about 10 minutes, stirring gently several times. Pour into hot sterilized jars, and seal. Makes about 5 pints.

ALGERIAN-STYLE EGGS

They're baked on top of garlic tomatoes and green pepper.

1½ cups drained canned tomatoes	2 tablespoons butter
1 clove garlic, crushed	6 eggs
1 green pepper, sliced	1 teaspoon salt
	Dash pepper

Heat tomatoes with garlic. Put in buttered 8″ piepan. Cook green pepper in butter until tender. Put on top of tomatoes. Beat eggs with salt and pepper until well mixed. Pour over tomatoes. Bake in moderate oven, 350°F., 25 minutes, or until set. Makes 4 servings.

SAVORY TOMATOES, BEANS, AND SQUASH

You use either green or wax beans and yellow squash.

1 onion, sliced	2 teaspoons salt
1 clove garlic, minced	2 tablespoons vegetable oil
¼ cup minced parsley	1 pound green or wax beans, cut
¼ teaspoon pepper	3 tomatoes, diced
¼ teaspoon thyme	2 cups diced yellow squash
¼ teaspoon sage	

Cook onion, garlic, parsley, and seasonings in oil in large skillet about 3 minutes. Add vegetables, and water to half the depth of mixture. Cover, and simmer 20 minutes. Serves 4 to 6.

"Tomatoes can be prepared in so many delicious ways that one can eat them every day . . . and not get tired of them."
GEORGE WASHINGTON CARVER

RED AND GREEN TOMATO PIE

It has a cheese topping.

Pastry	⅛ teaspoon pepper
Evaporated milk	⅓ cup mayonnaise
4 cups sliced red and green tomatoes	⅓ cup grated Parmesan cheese
1½ teaspoons salt	1 clove garlic, minced

Line deep 9″ piepan with pastry; crimp edges, and brush with evaporated milk. Bake in very hot oven, 450°F., 5 minutes. Fill shell with tomatoes, and sprinkle with salt and pepper. Mix remaining ingredients, and spread on tomatoes. Bake in moderate oven, 350°F., 40 minutes, or until tomatoes are done. Makes 6 servings.

BROILED OR GRILLED TOMATOES

Cook them with salt, pepper, and onion salt, or with a variety of toppings.

Cut out core from stem end of firm tomatoes. Cut in halves. Put on baking sheet. Make crisscross cuts on top surface of each. Dot with butter and sprinkle with salt, pepper, and onion salt. Or use any of the toppings listed below. Broil under moderate heat 10 minutes, or until tomatoes are tender and topping is lightly browned. If preferred, tomatoes can be baked instead, in a hot oven, 425°F.

Toppings

Garlic spread.
Anchovies and oil from can.
Peanut butter and crumbled bacon.
French dressing or mayonnaise.
Cheese spread.
Mustard and a dash Worcestershire.
Or spread with soft butter, and add one of the following: Bread crumbs, onion salt, sage, and thyme; thinly sliced onion and paprika; grated cheese and soft bread crumbs; grated Parmesan cheese; chopped green onion or chives; chopped fresh herbs such as thyme, rosemary, marjoram, dill, basil, or sage.

TOMATO-CHEESE SALAD

The cheese is cottage cheese.

2 cups cottage cheese	6 stuffed olives, chopped
1/3 cup mayonnaise	Salt and pepper
1 green onion, chopped	6 large tomatoes
	Salad greens

Mix cottage cheese, mayonnaise, green onion, and olives. Season with salt and pepper. Cut a thin slice from stem ends of tomatoes; remove cores; cut each tomato into three slices. Put slices together with cheese mixture to make 6 servings. Serve on greens, and top with remaining cheese. Serves 6.

BAKED STUFFED TOMATOES

Save the tomato centers to put in the stuffing.

Cut a thin slice from stem ends of 4 large unpeeled tomatoes. Scoop out centers, leaving outer wall. Pour 1 can mushroom soup into shallow baking dish, and put tomato shells in dish. Sprinkle inside of tomatoes with salt and pepper. Fill with stuffing. Sprinkle with buttered crumbs. Bake in moderate oven, 375°F., 30 minutes. Serves 4.

Corned-beef Hash Stuffing: Cook 1 chopped onion in 2 tablespoons shortening 5 minutes. Add tomato centers, and cook until thick. Add 1 can (1 pound) corned-beef hash and 2 tablespoons chopped parsley. Mix well.

Savory Crumb Stuffing: Cook 1 chopped onion and 1/4 cup chopped celery in 1/4 cup butter about 5 minutes. Add tomato centers, and simmer about 10 minutes. Add 4 cups soft bread crumbs, 1 teaspoon poultry seasoning, salt, and a dash of cayenne. Mix well.

Macaroni or Rice Stuffing: Cook 1 chopped onion, 1/2 chopped green pepper, and 1/4 cup chopped celery in 2 tablespoons shortening about 5 minutes. Add tomato centers, and cook 10 minutes. Combine with 2 cups cooked macaroni or rice. Season to taste.

Vegetable Stuffing: Simmer tomato centers, and combine with a cooked vegetable: Lima beans, chopped broccoli or spinach, peas, or green beans. Season with salt, pepper, onion salt.

TOMATOES WITH SOUR CREAM

You add chives to the sour cream.

Sprinkle sliced tomatoes with salt and freshly ground pepper. Serve with sour cream and chopped chives.

COUNTRY SALAD BOWL

It contains tomato, cucumber, green pepper, and sweet onion.

Arrange slices of tomato, cucumber, green pepper, and sweet onion in salad bowl. Sprinkle with salt, pepper, and a little sugar. Add malt, wine, cider, tarragon, garlic, or any other herb vinegar to taste. Chill about half an hour.

TOMATOES WITH HERBS

There's a choice of herbs.

Use one of the small varieties: Red Cherry, Yellow Pear, or Yellow Plum. Chill well, and serve whole, in salad or as appetizers, sprinkled generously with salt and minced fresh sweet basil, marjoram, thyme, rosemary, or dill. Add French dressing or mayonnaise.

COLD STUFFED TOMATOES

The stuffing can be coleslaw, cottage cheese, or your favorite salad.

Cut out stem-end core of unpeeled tomatoes. Starting at center of other end, cut in quarters or eighths 3/4 of way down. Pull gently apart. Fill center with creamy potato salad, tuna or shrimp salad, coleslaw, chicken salad, cottage cheese, or vegetable salad. Serve in lettuce cups, and garnish with mayonnaise or sour cream.

DESSERT TOMATOES

They're served with cream and sugar.

Select firm red ripe tomatoes. Cover with boiling water; drain, and peel. Chill several hours. Cut in thick slices. Serve in chilled dishes with heavy cream and a sprinkling of sugar.

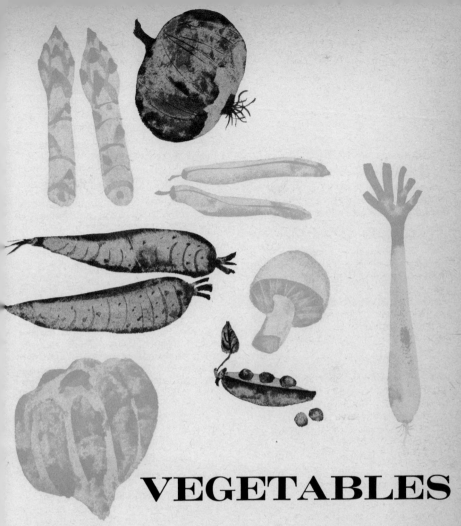

VEGETABLES

Of the many fine foods we have in America, vegetables are probably the least
appreciated and the most neglected. Europeans know the importance of
these plant foods and sometimes even serve them as a separate course in the meal.
For example, fresh, juicy asparagus is served alone, after the meat course.
The Chinese and Japanese cook vegetables quickly, just to the bitey stage, with
the true garden flavor and bright color still intact. We need to learn
more about the interesting combinations of vegetables: beans and peas mixed
with a bit of onion and grated cheese; spinach with mushrooms; eggplant, tomato,
zucchini, onion, and garlic blended together, a favorite in southern France
where it is called *ratatouille*. Seasonings need not be limited to salt
and pepper. Parsley, chives, tarragon, and basil are good additions, and try
garnishing with buttered crumbs, tiny croutons, bits of crisp bacon, or toasted
nuts. Try to prepare vegetables to bring out their flavors. Here in this chapter
are fine suggestions; follow these and then create your own versions.

227

HOT GERMAN BEANS

Cook 1 pound green or wax beans, and drain, reserving liquid. Dice 4 slices bacon, and cook with 1 chopped onion until onion is golden. Add liquid from beans, and reduce to about ¼ cup. Add 1 tablespoon sugar, ¼ cup vinegar, ⅛ teaspoon thyme, ½ teaspoon Accent, and beans. Heat; season to taste. Makes 4 servings.

PAPRIKA LIMAS AND LEEKS

Cook 2 boxes frozen Fordhook Limas as directed on the package. Drain, reserving ½ cup liquid. Simmer 2 small thinly sliced leeks in 2 tablespoons butter 5 minutes. Blend in 1 tablespoon flour. Add bean liquid, and cook until thickened. Add ½ teaspoon paprika, beans, and salt and pepper; heat. Makes 6 servings.

ASPARAGUS AND CARROTS

Cook 2 cups sliced carrots until almost tender. Add 1 box frozen cut asparagus; sprinkle with salt and pepper, and cook until tender. Drain. Pour over a little melted butter, and sprinkle with chopped parsley. Makes 4 to 6 servings.

ASPARAGUS, HERB BUTTER

Cook 1 box frozen or ½ pound fresh asparagus until tender. Cream ¼ cup soft butter, dash each cayenne and paprika, and a pinch each rosemary and thyme. Blend in juice ½ lemon. Serve on drained hot asparagus. Makes 2 or 3 servings.

ASPARAGUS AND MUSHROOMS

Wash 1 pound fresh asparagus, and cut in 1½" pieces. In skillet bring ¼ cup water and 3 tablespoons vegetable oil to boil. Add asparagus, 1 small minced onion, 1 can (4 ounces) drained sliced mushrooms, salt, pepper. Cook, covered, 8 to 10 minutes, shaking skillet occasionally. Add ¼ cup light cream. Makes 3 to 4 servings.

GREEN BEANS, CAPE COD STYLE

Wash 1 pound green beans, and remove stem ends; cut beans in half lengthwise. Put in saucepan; barely cover with boiling water. Cook, covered, 20 minutes, or until just tender. Drain. Add 2 tablespoons cream, 2 teaspoons sugar, 2 tablespoons butter; season; toss lightly. Makes 4 servings.

GREEN BEANS, LYONNAISE

3 slices bacon, diced	1 pound green beans, Frenched, or 2 boxes frozen French-cut green beans, cooked
1 medium onion, sliced	

Cook bacon until crisp; remove and reserve. Add onion, and cook until lightly browned. Add beans; heat, and season with salt and pepper. Garnish with bacon. Makes 6 servings.

GREEN BEANS WITH EASY HOLLANDAISE

2 quarts whole green beans	Dash cayenne
½ cup butter or margarine	2 tablespoons lemon juice
	2 egg yolks

Cook beans, covered, in small amount of boiling salted water until tender.
To make sauce: Melt butter in double boiler over 1" boiling water. Add cayenne, lemon juice, and egg yolks. Reduce heat; beat well with rotary beater until thick. Serve immediately over hot, drained beans. Makes 6 servings.

SAVORY LIMAS AND TOMATOES

Cook 1 minced small onion and ½ minced clove garlic in 2 tablespoons butter. Add ¼ cup minced green pepper, 1 can (19 ounces) tomatoes, 2 cups cooked Limas, ¾ teaspoon seasoned salt, ⅛ teaspoon each pepper and marjoram, ½ teaspoon Accent. Simmer, uncovered, 15 minutes. Makes 4 servings.

BEANS AU GRATIN

1 box each frozen cut green beans, wax beans, Lima beans	Dash pepper Dash Worcestershire
4 tablespoons butter or margarine	1 cup medium cream
2 tablespoons flour	½ cup grated Parmesan cheese
1 teaspoon salt	

Cook beans separately according to package directions; drain. Mix lightly, and put in shallow baking dish. Melt 2 tablespoons butter; stir in flour, salt, pepper, and Worcestershire. Add cream, and cook until thickened, stirring. Pour over beans. Dot with remaining butter, and sprinkle with cheese. Bake in moderate oven, 375°F., until hot and browned. Makes 6 servings.

GREEN BEANS AND MUSHROOMS

Cook ¼ pound sliced mushrooms and ½ small minced onion in 2 tablespoons butter. Add 1 box of frozen or ¾ pound fresh green beans, ½ cup water, and salt and pepper. Bring to boil; cover, and cook until tender. Add ¼ cup heavy cream, and heat. Makes 4 servings.

HARVARD BEETS

½ cup sugar	½ cup vinegar
2 tablespoons cornstarch	2 tablespoons butter
1 teaspoon salt	2 cans (1 pound each) sliced
Dash pepper	beets

Mix first 6 ingredients in saucepan. Add 1 cup liquid drained from beets. Cook until thickened, stirring constantly. Add beets, and simmer 10 minutes. Makes 8 servings.

BEETS IN WINE

Heat 2 tablespoons butter, ¼ cup dry red wine, 3 tablespoons honey, ¼ teaspoon ground cloves, ½ teaspoon grated orange rind. Add 1 can (1 pound) tiny beets, drained; heat, then let stand in a warm place 15 minutes to blend flavors. Makes 4 servings.

BEETS AND APPLESAUCE

Cook, drain, and peel 6 medium beets. Mash with potato masher, or put through ricer. Add 1 cup fresh or canned applesauce, and heat. Season to taste with salt, pepper, and butter. Makes 4 servings.

SOUR-BEET SHREDS

4 cups shredded raw beets	2 tablespoons water
2 tablespoons butter	1 tablespoon vinegar
1 teaspoon sugar	Salt and pepper

Put all ingredients, except salt and pepper, in heavy saucepan. Cover, and cook over medium heat 10 minutes, or until beets are tender but still crisp. Stir twice with fork during cooking. Season. Makes 4 servings.

BROCCOLI WITH SOUR CREAM

2 pounds fresh broccoli or 2 boxes frozen broccoli spears	2 tablespoons tomato paste
	¼ teaspoon dried basil
Salt	2 teaspoons minced drained capers
1 cup sour cream	
¼ cup mayonnaise	

Discard some of the larger leaves and a little of the stalk from fresh broccoli. Cook broccoli, covered, in 1" boiling salted water, 10 to 15 minutes. (Cook frozen broccoli as directed on the box.) Drain, and cool. Mix ¾ teaspoon salt and remaining ingredients; chill. Serve on cold cooked broccoli. Makes 4 servings.

BROCCOLI, ITALIAN STYLE

2 tablespoons vegetable oil	Dash cayenne
1 clove garlic, cut in half	1 bunch broccoli, cooked

Heat oil, garlic, and cayenne 5 minutes; remove garlic, and pour over hot broccoli. Makes 3 or 4 servings.

BROCCOLI PIQUANT

Cook 1 box frozen cut or chopped broccoli according to package directions. Meanwhile, cook 2 diced slices of bacon and ½ minced clove garlic until bacon is crisp. Add 2 tablespoons vinegar; heat. Brown ¼ cup soft bread crumbs in 1 tablespoon butter. Pour sauce over broccoli, and sprinkle with crumbs. Makes 3 servings.

BROCCOLI, SPANISH STYLE

Cook 2 boxes frozen broccoli spears until barely tender. While still warm, dress with the following: Mix ¼ cup each olive oil and lemon juice, 1 crushed clove garlic, ½ teaspoon salt, and ⅛ teaspoon pepper. Sieve 1 hard-cooked egg yolk over top, and garnish with strips of pimiento. Serves 4.

BRUSSELS SPROUTS AND CHESTNUTS

Cook 1 box frozen or 1 pint fresh Brussels sprouts until tender. Shell ½ pound chestnuts. (To shell, gash the end of each nut, and heat in oil in oven about 10 minutes. Remove shells and skins with a sharp knife.) Cook in boiling salted water about 10 minutes. Combine Brussels sprouts and chestnuts, and pour over ¼ cup melted butter. Season. Makes 4 servings.

BRUSSELS SPROUTS IN BROWNED BUTTER

Cook and drain 2 boxes frozen Brussels sprouts. Brown ¼ cup butter in skillet. Add juice 1 lemon, sprouts, and salt and pepper; heat. Serves 4.

NORWEGIAN CREAMED CABBAGE

Cook 1 quart finely shredded cabbage in boiling, salted water, barely to cover, 5 minutes. Drain. Add ½ cup sour cream, ½ teaspoon caraway seed, and salt and pepper. Cook in top of double boiler over boiling water 10 minutes. Makes 4 servings.

CABBAGE, CHEESE SAUCE

¼ pound bacon	¼ pound sharp
2 cups medium	cheddar or
white sauce	process cheese,
1 medium head	shredded
cabbage	Salt and pepper

Fry bacon until crisp; remove from pan. Use fat for making white sauce. Cut cabbage in wedges; cook in small amount of salted water until tender, about 10 minutes. Add cheese to white sauce, and heat until melted; season. Put drained cabbage on platter; cover with cheese sauce, and sprinkle with crumbled bacon. Makes 4 servings.

SWEET-AND-SOUR RED CABBAGE

1 onion, chopped	1 cup water
3 tablespoons butter	3 tablespoons
or margarine	brown sugar
9 cups shredded red	1 tablespoon
cabbage	caraway seed
1 large tart apple,	1¼ teaspoons salt
diced	¼ teaspoon pepper
3 tablespoons	⅓ cup seedless
vinegar	raisins

Cook onion in butter 5 minutes. Add cabbage; cover, and cook 5 minutes longer. Add remaining ingredients; cover; simmer 10 minutes. Serves 6.

CABBAGE, TOMATOES, AND GREEN PEPPER

Cook 3 sliced onions in 2 tablespoons butter 3 minutes. Put 1 green pepper, cut in chunks, on top; cover, and cook 5 minutes. Add 2 large tomatoes, cut in half, skin side down. Quarter ½ medium head cabbage, and put with tomatoes. Season. Cover; simmer about 15 minutes. Serves 4.

BRAISED CARROTS AND CELERY

Cook 4 carrots, peeled and cut in chunks, 15 minutes. Drain. Cut celery stalks in 2″ pieces. Measure 2 cups. Lightly brown carrots, celery, and 1 chopped small onion in 2 tablespoons butter. Add ¾ cup water, and season with salt and pepper. Cover, and cook until vegetables are tender. Uncover, to evaporate liquid. Sprinkle with chopped parsley. Makes 4 servings.

CARROTS PARMESAN

Drain hot cooked carrot strips, and put in serving dish. Pour over melted butter or margarine, and sprinkle generously with grated Parmesan cheese.

MASHED CARROTS AND POTATOES

Cook, drain, and mash 6 medium carrots. Prepare 1 envelope instant mashed potatoes. Mix both vegetables, and season to taste with salt, pepper, and butter. Makes 4 to 6 servings.

CAULIFLOWER WITH CHEESE

1 large head cauliflower	½ cup shredded process cheese
2 tablespoons melted butter	Paprika

Cook cauliflower in salted water until tender, about 20 minutes. Drain, and put in serving dish. Pour over melted butter; sprinkle with cheese and paprika. Makes 4 to 6 servings.

CAULIFLOWER WITH ALMOND BUTTER

Trim off outer leaves of 1 small cauliflower. Wash, and cook in boiling, salted water 10 minutes, or until tender. Drain. Cook ¼ cup slivered almonds in 3 tablespoons butter until lightly browned. Put cauliflower in dish; top with butter and nuts. Serves 4.

CAULIFLOWER POLONAISE

Cook 1 box frozen cauliflower according to package directions. Meanwhile, combine 3 tablespoons melted butter, 1 teaspoon chopped parsley, and 1 chopped hard-cooked egg. Pour over drained cauliflower. Sprinkle with 2 tablespoons finely crushed potato chips. Makes 3 servings.

CUCUMBERS IN CHEESE SAUCE

2 large cucumbers	½ cup shredded sharp cheddar cheese
2 tablespoons butter	
1 cup medium white sauce	

Peel cucumbers, and cut in ¼" slices. Cook in butter until lightly browned and tender. Add white sauce, and sprinkle with cheese. Heat. Serves 4.

BRAISED CUCUMBERS

3 medium cucumbers	1 beef bouillon cube
2 tablespoons butter or margarine	1 tablespoon boiling water
	Salt and pepper

Peel cucumbers; cut once lengthwise and crosswise. Brown lightly in butter. Add bouillon cube dissolved in water. Cook, covered, over low heat about 5 minutes. Season. Makes 4 servings.

EGGPLANT, CREOLE STYLE

1 medium eggplant, peeled and cubed	1 can (8 ounces) tomato sauce, or 2 tomatoes, peeled
1 green pepper, cut in strips	
1 onion, chopped	Salt and pepper

Cook vegetables and tomato sauce, covered, over low heat about 10 minutes. Season. Makes 4 servings.

FRENCH-FRIED EGGPLANT STICKS

1 medium eggplant (about 1½ pounds)	6 tablespoons cold water
½ cup prepared pancake mix	Fat for frying

Pare eggplant; cut in ½" slices, then in ½" strips. Combine pancake mix and water, and stir until well mixed. Dip eggplant strips in batter; then fry in hot deep fat (375°F. on a frying thermometer) until golden brown. Drain on absorbent paper. Makes 4 servings.

FRIED GREEN PEPPERS

Remove seeds from 6 large green peppers, and cut peppers in eighths. Cover with boiling water, and cook, covered, 3 minutes. Drain, and fry slowly in hot margarine or fat until lightly browned. Season. Makes 4 servings.

BAKED STUFFED MUSHROOMS

Remove stems from 1 pound large mushrooms. Wash, and dry caps. Wash stems, and chop. Dice 3 slices bacon, and cook with mushroom stems and 2 tablespoons chopped green pepper. Add 1 tablespoon instant minced onion, 1 crumbled slice bread, ½ teaspoon seasoned salt, ¼ teaspoon Accent. Stuff mushroom caps. Put in shallow baking dish, brush with vegetable oil, and add small amount of water. Bake in moderate oven, 375°F., about 25 minutes. Makes 6 servings.

DEVILED MUSHROOMS, CASINO

20 large whole mushrooms	¼ cup cream
Salt and pepper	1 teaspoon dry mustard
¼ cup melted butter or margarine	Few grains cayenne
Toast	½ teaspoon paprika
1 cup chopped mushrooms	1 teaspoon Worcestershire

Wipe mushrooms with a damp cloth; season, and broil carefully, basting with melted butter until tender. Put on 4 toast rounds. Cook chopped mushrooms in butter until they are delicately browned. Season. Add cream and remaining ingredients. Reheat; pour over mushrooms on toast. Serve at once. Makes 4 servings.

CURRIED PEAS AND ONIONS

Cook 1 box frozen peas as directed on the package. Drain off all but about 1 tablespoon liquid. Add 1 can (1 pound) onions, drained, 3 tablespoons butter, and 1 teaspoon curry powder. Heat, stirring lightly once or twice. Season. Makes 4 to 6 servings.

MUSHROOM-PIMIENTO PEAS

Cook 1 box frozen peas as directed on the label. Add 3 tablespoons butter, 1 can drained sliced mushrooms, and 2 chopped canned pimientos; heat. Makes 3 servings.

MASHED RUTABAGA WITH ONION

1 medium rutabaga	2 tablespoons butter
2 onions	½ teaspoon salt
	¼ teaspoon pepper

Cook rutabaga and onion in small amount of boiling salted water until tender. Drain. Mash; add butter and seasonings, and beat well. Makes 4 to 6 servings.

RUTABAGA WITH SALT PORK

4 cups cubed rutabaga	1 onion, minced
¼ pound salt pork, finely chopped	Salt and pepper to taste

Cook rutabaga in boiling water until tender. Cook pork until brown and crisp; add onion, and cook a few minutes longer. Add drained rutabaga. Cook 5 minutes, stirring often to brown cubes slightly. Season with salt and pepper. Makes 4 to 6 servings.
Note: White turnips can be used.

CREAMED SPINACH AND MUSHROOMS

2 pounds spinach	1 tablespoon flour
2 tablespoons butter	Dash nutmeg
¼ pound mushrooms, sliced	Salt and pepper
	¼ cup milk or light cream

Wash spinach, and cook without adding water until tender; drain. Chop. Melt butter; add mushrooms, and cook until tender, about 4 minutes. Blend in flour, nutmeg, salt, and pepper. Add milk, and cook until thickened, stirring. Add spinach, and heat well. Makes 4 to 6 servings.

WILTED SPINACH AND CARROT

4 slices bacon	¼ cup water
½ cup vinegar	2 boxes frozen spinach
2 tablespoons sugar	1 carrot, shredded
1 teaspoon salt	
Dash pepper	

Fry bacon until crisp. Remove. Add vinegar, sugar, salt, pepper, and water to fat; bring to boil. Add spinach, and cook, breaking up with fork. Stir in carrot, and serve with crumbled bacon sprinkled on top. Makes 4 to 6 servings.

WILTED RAW SPINACH

Prepare a hot sauce with 2 tablespoons bacon fat or butter, 2 tablespoons flour, 1 small minced onion, 1 cup water, ½ teaspoon dry mustard, and 2 tablespoons vinegar. Pour over ¾ pound cleaned, drained, and chopped fresh spinach. Mix well, and season to taste with salt and pepper. Serve at once. Makes 4 servings.

PANNED GARDEN GREENS

Cook 2 quarts finely chopped beet or turnip tops, cabbage, escarole, romaine, lettuce, spinach, chard, or mustard greens quickly in 2 tablespoons bacon fat or butter in large heavy saucepan 3 to 5 minutes, stirring constantly. Season. Makes 4 servings.

HERB-FRIED SUMMER SQUASH

Cut 2 pounds summer squash in ½" slices. Roll in flour seasoned with salt, pepper, and 1 teaspoon herbs such as thyme, marjoram, or sage. Dip slices in slightly beaten egg; roll in fine dry bread crumbs, and fry in hot deep fat (350°F. on a frying thermometer) 8 minutes, or until squash is brown and tender. Makes 4 servings.

FRIED SUMMER SQUASH AND ONIONS

Wash, and dice 2 pounds summer squash. Put in skillet with 3 thinly sliced onions, 3 tablespoons butter or margarine, ½ teaspoon salt, ¼ teaspoon pepper. Cover, and cook 20 to 30 minutes. Makes 4 servings.

SCALLOPED HUBBARD SQUASH

1 onion, chopped	3½ cups mashed
1 green pepper,	cooked Hubbard
chopped	squash, or 2
3 tablespoons butter	boxes thawed
or margarine	frozen squash
	Salt and pepper
	½ cup fine dry
	bread crumbs

Cook onion and green pepper in butter until tender. Add squash, and salt and pepper to taste. Put in shallow baking dish, and sprinkle with crumbs. Bake in hot oven, 400°F., about 30 minutes. Makes 4 servings.

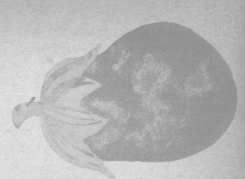

BAKED WINTER SQUASH

Split acorn squash, or cut Hubbard squash in serving pieces. Remove seeds; sprinkle with salt and pepper; put a small piece of butter in each, and a little honey, if desired. Bake in moderate oven, 375°F., 45 minutes, or until tender.

SQUASH, GREEN-BEAN SAUTÉ

1 onion, chopped	1 tablespoon
⅓ cup olive oil	chopped parsley
3 small or 2 medium	1 cup boiling water
summer squash	Salt and pepper
½ pound green	
beans	

Cook onion in oil until lightly browned. Cut squash in ¼" slices. Add squash, green beans, cut in 1" pieces, parsley, and water to onion. Cover, and cook over low heat 10 minutes, or until vegetables are tender. Season with salt and pepper. Makes 4 servings.

BAKED ZUCCHINI

2 medium zucchini	2 cups bread cubes
(about 1 pound)	½ teaspoon poultry
1 clove garlic,	seasoning or
minced	orégano
2 tablespoons butter	Salt and pepper
or margarine	

Wash, and cook unpeeled zucchini 10 minutes in small amount of boiling salted water. Drain, and cut in half lengthwise. Scoop out pulp; chop. Cook garlic in butter a few seconds. Stir in chopped pulp, bread cubes, poultry seasoning, and salt and pepper. Stuff zucchini with mixture; put in greased baking dish, and bake in moderate oven, 350°F., 20 minutes, or until zucchini is tender. Makes 4 servings.

CANDIED SWEET POTATOES

6 sweet potatoes	¼ cup water
1 cup brown sugar, packed	½ teaspoon salt
¼ cup butter or margarine	2 whole cloves

Cook, and drain potatoes. Peel; cut in halves lengthwise, and put in shallow baking dish. Mix remaining ingredients, and boil 5 minutes. Pour over potatoes. Bake in moderate oven, 375°F., about 30 minutes, basting occasionally. Makes 6 servings.

SCALLOPED SWEETS AND CRANBERRIES

6 sweet potatoes	¾ teaspoon grated orange rind
1½ cups whole cranberry sauce	¾ teaspoon cinnamon
¾ cup water	1½ tablespoons butter
½ cup brown sugar, packed	

Cook, and drain potatoes. Peel; cut in half lengthwise, and arrange in baking dish. In saucepan mix remaining ingredients, except butter. Simmer, uncovered, 5 minutes. Add butter; stir until butter is melted. Pour over potatoes, and bake, uncovered, in moderate oven, 350°F., 20 minutes, or until glazed and hot. Makes 6 servings.

VEGETABLE MEDLEY

Cut 2 peeled carrots in small chunks. Put in saucepan with ¼ pound green beans, cut, and 1 box frozen baby Lima beans. Add small amount boiling water, and ½ teaspoon salt. Cover, and cook until vegetables are tender. Ten minutes before vegetables are done, add 1 sliced small summer squash, and 4 sliced green onions. Cover, and cook 10 minutes. Drain, and season with butter, salt, and pepper. Makes 4 to 6 servings.

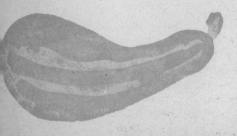

SWEET-POTATO PUFF

2 pounds sweet potatoes	⅛ teaspoon each pepper, nutmeg, ginger, allspice, and cinnamon
⅓ cup hot light cream	2 tablespoons molasses
Butter or margarine	
½ teaspoon salt	

Cook potatoes until tender; drain, peel, and mash. Beat until light and fluffy. Beat in cream, ¼ cup butter, and seasonings. Put in 1½-quart baking dish. In small saucepan, bring 1 tablespoon butter and the molasses to boil. Dribble over top of potatoes. Bake, uncovered, in hot oven, 400°F., 15 to 20 minutes. Makes 6 servings.

VEGETABLE HOT POT

3 tablespoons butter or margarine	1½ cups shelled green peas
8 medium potatoes, peeled	¾ pound whole green beans
8 small carrots, peeled	1 cup water
Salt and pepper	2 tomatoes, cut in half
1 bunch green onions	

Heat butter. Cut potatoes in half, and put cut side down in butter; brown lightly. Add carrots; sprinkle with salt and pepper; cover; cook 5 minutes. Add onions, peas, beans, and water; cover; cook slowly 25 minutes. Put tomatoes, cut side up, on top of other vegetables; cover; cook 5 minutes longer. Add more water if necessary. Makes 4 servings.

VEGETABLE GOULASH

In saucepan mix: 1 cup each cooked Lima beans, diced raw potato, fresh or canned corn; 1 can (19 ounces) tomatoes, 1 sliced medium onion, 1 diced green pepper, 1 teaspoon sugar, small piece bay leaf, salt and pepper. Cover; bring to boil, and simmer 20 minutes, or until potato is tender. Melt 2 tablespoons butter in saucepan; blend in 2 tablespoons flour. Pour off liquid from vegetables. Cook until thickened; season to taste, and pour over vegetables. Makes 4 servings.

STUFFINGS and Sauces

In leading Paris restaurants the *saucier* is second in rank only to the head chef. The *saucier* prepares sauces and often all stuffings, and on his skill depends the success of many of the most elaborate dishes in French cuisine. Sauces and stuffings have much in common: they give additional flavor and body to dishes; they enhance or glamorize what might otherwise be rather plain fare; and, in terms of preparation, both must be well seasoned and perfectly blended so that the flavors melt together. A good *saucier* has an excellent "nose" and a keen sense of taste. The day's first task for the sauce chef is to make the basic, or "mother," sauces. From these he can create many others by simply adding a seasoning, a wine, some cream and eggs, or meat or fish stock. With Bordeaux wine added, *Espagnole*, or basic brown sauce, becomes *Bordelaise;* with onions added, basic white sauce becomes *Sauce Soubise;* these and many other variations can be made in just a few moments. The art of the *saucier* is applied in the same way to stuffings, which can be varied by adding different seasonings, herbs, bits of chopped meat, or nuts. Bread stuffings need not always be made of plain white bread; brown bread is good, and sometimes rye. Learn to make these stuffings and sauces; they offer you a wide choice on which to build. Then, remember the French *saucier's* trick of variations and try experimenting. Use your "nose" and taste buds. Always be sure you season well and season with flavorings that blend together.

"Poultry is the lightest and best of all aliments."
CLAUDIUS GALEN

Poultry Stuffings

ORANGE-RICE STUFFING

1 cup finely diced celery with leaves	2 tablespoons grated orange rind
1 small onion, minced	⅛ teaspoon each thyme and marjoram
⅓ cup butter or margarine	½ teaspoon Accent
1 cup water	Dash pepper
1¼ cups orange juice	2 cups packaged precooked rice

Cook celery and onion in butter 5 minutes. Add remaining ingredients, except rice, and bring to boil. Add rice; mix just to moisten. Cover; remove from heat. Let stand 5 minutes. Makes about 5 cups.

CHESTNUT STUFFING

1 cup butter or margarine	¾ cup chopped celery and leaves
1 cup minced onion	2 quarts soft stale-bread crumbs or cubes
1 teaspoon each thyme and sage	
1½ teaspoons salt	1 pound Italian chestnuts, cooked, shelled, and chopped
¾ teaspoon pepper	
⅓ cup chopped parsley	

Melt butter in skillet, and add all ingredients, except last 2. Cook 5 minutes. Add crumbs and chestnuts. Makes about 10 cups.

Bacon-Chestnut Stuffing: In recipe above, omit butter, and cook all ingredients, except crumbs and chestnuts, with ¼ pound each diced bacon and ham. Add crumbs and chestnuts.

OLIVE STUFFING

12 slices day-old firm-type bread	⅓ cup butter or margarine
3 onions, minced	¾ cup chopped green olives
½ cup chopped parsley	2 teaspoons poultry seasoning
1 cup chopped celery	1 egg, beaten
	Salt and pepper

Trim crusts from bread. Cut bread in small cubes. Cook onions, parsley, and celery in the butter 8 minutes. Add bread and remaining ingredients; mix lightly. Makes about 8 cups.

Cranberry Stuffing: Use above recipe, omitting onions, olives, and poultry seasoning. Add 1 cup ground raw cranberries mixed with ⅓ cup sugar and ⅓ cup chopped almonds. Use as stuffing for duck.

Corn Stuffing: Use recipe for Olive Stuffing, omitting olives. Add 2 cups drained whole-kernel corn.

Oyster Stuffing: Use recipe for Olive Stuffing, omitting olives. Add 1 pint small oysters, drained; cook with onion, parsley, and celery.

CELERY-ONION STUFFING

2 cups chopped celery and leaves	1 teaspoon salt
2 cups chopped onion	¼ teaspoon pepper
	¼ cup butter or margarine
1 teaspoon each thyme and sage	½ cup chicken broth or water
½ teaspoon celery salt	3 cups soft stale-bread cubes

Cook celery, onion, and seasonings in butter 5 minutes. Add remaining ingredients, and mix thoroughly. Makes about 5 cups.

Peanut Stuffing: In recipe above, omit thyme and sage, and reduce onion to ½ cup. Add 1 cup chopped peanuts after cooking celery and onion.

Celery-Almond Stuffing: Follow recipe for Celery-Onion Stuffing, but reduce onion to ½ cup. Add ½ cup toasted slivered almonds after cooking celery and onion.

CREAMY BRAZIL-NUT STUFFING

¾ pound shelled Brazil nuts	1 or 2 leaves fresh sage
1¼ cups butter or margarine	Heavy cream
2 quarts tiny bread cubes	Salt and pepper

Cut nuts in small chunks. Brown lightly in ¼ cup of the butter. Dry out bread cubes in oven. Brown in remaining butter. Mix nuts, bread, and sage. Add cream to moisten, and salt and pepper to taste. Makes about 8 cups.

Meat Stuffings

RAISIN-RICE STUFFING

1¼ cups rice	½ teaspoon bouquet garni (a blend of dried herbs)
⅓ cup melted butter or margarine	
1 onion, grated	Grated rind ½ orange
1 teaspoon salt	¼ cup raisins
1 tablespoon minced parsley	

Cook rice; drain. Add to remaining ingredients; mix lightly. Makes 5 cups.

SPANISH-RICE STUFFING

1 cup uncooked rice	1 can (3 ounces) chopped mushrooms, drained
3 tablespoons olive oil	1 can (1 pound) tomatoes
2 large onions, chopped	1 egg, beaten
1 green pepper, chopped	1 teaspoon salt
1 clove garlic, minced	2 teaspoons seasoning salt
1 pimiento, diced	½ teaspoon Accent
	⅛ teaspoon pepper

Cook rice; drain, and mix with remaining ingredients. Makes about 6 cups.

MINT STUFFING

Cook 1 small onion, chopped, and ¼ cup chopped celery and leaves in ¼ cup butter or margarine 5 minutes. Mix with ½ cup chopped fresh mint leaves or 1 tablespoon dried mint, and 3 cups soft stale-bread cubes. Makes 3 cups.

APPLE AND ONION STUFFING

2 large onions, chopped	½ teaspoon Accent
¼ cup butter or margarine	2 teaspoons celery seed
2 cups diced tart apple	½ teaspoon marjoram
4 cups soft stale-bread crumbs	¼ teaspoon pepper
1½ teaspoons salt	½ cup apple cider or apple juice

Cook onion in butter 5 minutes. Add remaining ingredients, and mix well. Makes about 4 cups.

SAUERKRAUT STUFFING

1 can (1 pound, 11 ounces) sauerkraut, drained	1 tart apple, peeled, cored, and chopped
2 tablespoons brown sugar	¼ cup dried currants
1 clove garlic, minced	1 cup chopped water chestnuts
1 onion, chopped	⅛ teaspoon thyme
Salt and pepper	

Chop sauerkraut. Add remaining ingredients, and mix thoroughly. Makes about 5 cups.

Fish Stuffings

VEGETABLE STUFFING

2 carrots, shredded	⅓ cup melted butter or margarine
2 tablespoons minced parsley	6 slices crust-free bread, cubed
2 pimientos, minced	Salt and pepper
2 chopped green onions with tops	

Mix all ingredients. Makes 3 cups.

*"That is your poem —
too tenuous for a book;
You are a very gentle perfect
cook."*

WALTER LOWENFELS

SHRIMP STUFFING

9 slices firm-type bread	1 onion, chopped
6 tablespoons butter or margarine	Juice ½ lemon
	1 egg, beaten
½ pound shrimp	2 tablespoons milk
2 tablespoons chopped parsley	½ teaspoon thyme
	1 teaspoon salt
	⅛ teaspoon pepper

Trim crusts from bread, and spread slices with half the butter. Toast buttered side under broiler; then cut in cubes. Peel shrimp; remove vein; cut in small pieces. Cook shrimp, parsley, and onion in remaining butter about 5 minutes. Mix bread, shrimp mixture, remaining ingredients. Makes 5 cups.

Clam Stuffing: Use recipe above, but substitute 1 can (10½ ounces) minced clams, drained, for shrimp.

CHEESE STUFFING

1 medium onion, thinly sliced	½ cup grated process American cheese
¼ cup butter or margarine	
1½ cups soft stale-bread cubes	Salt and pepper
	⅛ teaspoon each rosemary, thyme

Cook onion in butter 5 minutes. Mix with other ingredients. Makes 2 cups.

PIQUANT STUFFING

1 tablespoon grated onion	Juice ½ lemon
2 cups soft stale-bread crumbs	Few sprigs parsley, chopped
⅓ cup melted butter or margarine	½ teaspoon celery salt
	2 teaspoons capers
	Salt and pepper

Cook onion and crumbs in butter until crumbs are lightly browned. Mix with other ingredients. Makes 2 cups.

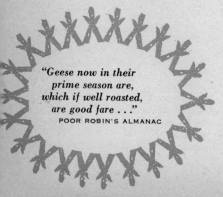

"Geese now in their prime season are, which if well roasted, are good fare . . ."
POOR ROBIN'S ALMANAC

FINES HERBES-MUSHROOM OMELET STUFFING

¼ pound mushrooms, chopped	Salt and pepper
2 tablespoons butter	Chopped fresh parsley, chives, tarragon, and chervil
3 eggs	

Cook mushrooms in 1 tablespoon of the butter until browned. Beat eggs, and season with salt and pepper and herbs to taste. Add mushrooms. Melt remaining 1 tablespoon butter in skillet. Add egg mixture, and cook until firm. Cool; then cut in strips. Makes about 2 cups.

Meat Sauces

SAVORY BUTTER

Cream ⅓ cup butter until fluffy. Add 1 tablespoon each minced green-onion tops or chives, celery leaves, and parsley; dash garlic salt, ½ teaspoon each salt and crumbled leaf sage. Also good on fish. Makes about ⅓ cup.

HOT MUSTARD SAUCE

Mix ¼ cup English-type or Dijon prepared mustard, 1 teaspoon dry mustard, ¼ cup salad dressing or mayonnaise, 2 tablespoons sour cream. Makes about ⅓ cup.

HORSE-RADISH SAUCE

Brown 1 chopped onion in ¼ cup butter. Stir in 2 tablespoons flour; add 2 cups strained meat stock, ½ cup horse-radish, 1 cup vinegar, 2 cloves, ¼ cup sugar. Season. Simmer about 10 minutes. Serve with boiled beef. Makes about 3 cups.

MUSHROOM SAUCE

Lightly brown ½ pound sliced mushrooms in 3 tablespoons butter. Blend in 2 tablespoons flour; brown slightly. Add 1¼ cups cold water, 2 bouillon cubes, ⅛ teaspoon pepper. Cook, stirring, until thickened. Makes 2 cups.

SPICY BARBECUE SAUCE

saucepan heat ½ cup butter, 1 tea-
...oon each salt, sugar, and instant
...nced onion, 2 tablespoons vinegar
...lemon juice, 1 tablespoon Worces-
...rshire, ½ cup water and ¼ teaspoon
...pper. Also good for barbecuing poul-
...y. Makes about 1 cup.

MUSHROOM SHERRY SAUCE

...ok ½ cup minced fresh mushrooms
...d 1 tablespoon minced onion in ¼
...p butter until tender. Add ½ tea-
...oon salt and 2 tablespoons sherry.
...rve on hamburgers or steak. Also
...od with fish. Makes about ⅓ cup.

CREOLE SAUCE

...ok ½ cup chopped onion and 1
...inced clove garlic in 3 tablespoons
...getable oil until golden. Add ½ cup
...opped green pepper, 1 bay leaf, 1
...an (19 ounces) tomatoes, 1 teaspoon
...lt, ⅛ teaspoon pepper, 1 can (3
...unces) chopped mushrooms, dash cay-
...nne. Simmer, uncovered, 20 minutes.
...rve with meat loaf, hamburgers, om-
...ets, or fish. Makes about 2 cups.

WHIPPED-CREAM HORSE-RADISH SAUCE

...hip ½ cup heavy cream. Fold in 1
...easpoon grated onion, 1 tablespoon
...orse-radish, 1 teaspoon salt. Serve on
...old ham or other meat. Also good on
...sh. Makes about 1 cup.

RAISIN SAUCE

...n saucepan mix ½ cup brown sugar,
...2 teaspoon dry mustard, 1 tablespoon
...our. Add ¼ cup each seedless raisins
...nd vinegar, 1½ cups water. Cook,
...tirring, until syrupy and slightly thick-
...ned. Makes about 1½ cups.

TOMATO BARBECUE SAUCE

...n saucepan mix ¼ cup butter, 1 tea-
...poon onion salt, ¾ cup ketchup, ½
...easpoon salt, and 1 tablespoon each
...repared mustard and Worcestershire.
...eat until butter is melted. Also good
...or barbecuing chicken. Makes 1 cup.

*"After dinner sit
a-while
After supper walk
a mile."*
OLD ENGLISH PROVERB

Fish Sauces

MOUSSELINE SAUCE

Melt 2 tablespoons butter; blend in 2
tablespoons flour. Add 1 cup chicken
stock; cook, stirring, until thickened.
Pour hot over 2 beaten egg yolks, stirring. Season. Add 2 tablespoons lemon
juice, ¼ teaspoon grated lemon rind,
1 tablespoon chopped parsley. Makes
about 1 cup.

BÉARNAISE SAUCE

Add 1 teaspoon each minced parsley
and fresh tarragon to 1 recipe Hollandaise, page 240. Or, make Hollandaise with 2 tablespoons tarragon vinegar instead of lemon juice, and add
1 teaspoon minced parsley.

MAÎTRE D'HÔTEL BUTTER

Melt ¼ cup butter. Add dash Tabasco,
1 tablespoon lemon juice, ½ teaspoon
salt, 1 tablespoon chopped parsley.
Also good on meats. Makes ¼ cup.

RAVIGOTE SAUCE

To 1 cup hot thin white sauce (made
with 1 tablespoon each butter and
flour, 1 cup milk), add 1 tablespoon
tarragon vinegar, juice 2 lemons, 1 tablespoon each minced green onion,
tarragon, and chervil. Keep hot 5 minutes; strain. Add 1 tablespoon capers
and chopped white of 1 hard-cooked
egg. Makes about 1 cup.

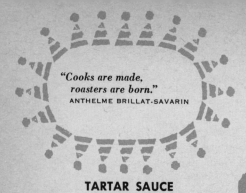

*"Cooks are made,
roasters are born."*
ANTHELME BRILLAT-SAVARIN

DRAWN BUTTER SAUCE

Melt ¼ cup butter over hot wat
Blend in 2 tablespoons flour, ½ t
spoon salt, dash each pepper and
prika. Add 1 cup water; cook, stirri
until thickened. Add 1 to 2 teaspoo
lemon juice. Makes about 1 cup.

Vegetable Sauces

TARTAR SAUCE

Mix ⅔ cup mayonnaise, ½ teaspoon
minced onion, 1 teaspoon minced parsley, 1 tablespoon chopped capers,
pickle relish, and stuffed olives, dash
cayenne. Makes ⅔ cup.

HERBED MAYONNAISE

Mix 1 cup mayonnaise or salad dressing, juice 1 lemon, 2 tablespoons
chopped chives, 4 chopped sprigs parsley, 2 teaspoons prepared mustard.
Chill. Serve on chilled shrimp or lobster. Makes about 1 cup.

CHEESE SAUCE

Add ⅓ cup shredded cheese (sharp
cheddar, Romano, Parmesan, processed
American), ½ teaspoon dry mustard,
and a dash garlic salt to 1 cup hot
seasoned medium white sauce. Also
good on croquettes or rice. Makes about
1 cup.

SEAFOOD COCKTAIL SAUCE

Mix ½ cup chili sauce, 1 tablespoon
each lemon juice and horse-radish, ½
teaspoon salt, ⅛ teaspoon pepper.
Chill. Makes about ½ cup.

BÉCHAMEL SAUCE

Simmer, uncovered, for 20 minutes: 1½
cups chicken stock, 1 slice onion, 1
slice carrot, a small piece of bay leaf,
1 parsley sprig, and 6 whole black
peppers. Strain (there should be 1 cup).
Melt ¼ cup butter; blend in ¼ cup
flour. Stir in strained stock and 1 cup
milk or milk and cream. Cook, stirring, until thick. Season. Also good on
chicken or croquettes. Makes 2 cups.

HOLLANDAISE SAUCE

In top part of double boiler, beat
egg yolks with wooden spoon. Add
teaspoon salt, dash cayenne, and
tablespoon lemon juice. Stir in ½ c
melted butter. Add 3 tablespoons h
water. Put over hot (not boiling) wat
and cook, stirring, 4 or 5 minutes,
until thickened. Also good on fis
Makes about ⅔ cup.

CURRY SAUCE

Add 1 to 3 teaspoons curry powd
and 1 tablespoon lemon juice to 1 c
hot seasoned medium white sauce. Als
good on omelets. Makes 1 cup.

MUSHROOM-CHEESE SAUCE

Wash, and slice ¼ pound mushroom
Cook until lightly browned in 1 te:
spoon butter. In top part of doub.
boiler mix 1 beaten egg, 1 cup mil
¾ teaspoon dry mustard, and ¼ te:
spoon paprika. Heat over boiling wa
ter; add ½ pound process America
cheese, cut in pieces. Stir until chees
is melted and sauce is thickened. Ad
mushrooms, and heat. Makes 2 cup:

VINAIGRETTE SAUCE

Mix, and chill 1 teaspoon salt, ⅛ tea
spoon pepper, dash cayenne, ¼ tea
spoon paprika, 3 tablespoons tarrago
vinegar, ½ cup olive or vegetable oi
1 tablespoon minced green pepper,
tablespoon chopped sweet pickle,
tablespoon minced parsley, 2 teaspoon
chopped chives, and a few drops o
onion juice. Serve on asparagus o
broccoli. Makes about ⅔ cup.

CAKES and FROSTINGS

W hat's for dessert?" is among the commonest questions asked in the American home, and if the answer is "cake," smiles of satisfaction go round the table. Few sweets are more satisfying than a good home-baked cake of fine texture and brimming with the goodness of creamy butter, fresh eggs and topped off with a luscious frosting. How does one make sure of such success in baking? You, the baker, must be as accurate as a scientist working in a laboratory. Be sure your oven is set at the right temperature. Follow directions to the letter and measure ingredients carefully. And here is a final suggestion: use good ingredients and use genuine, not imitation, flavorings. They make a world of difference in the taste.

NUT CAKE

*Serve it plain or
sprinkled with confectioners' sugar.*

1 cup soft butter or margarine	2 teaspoons bakin powder
1¾ cups sugar	¾ teaspoon salt
1 teaspoon vanilla extract	¾ cup milk
3 eggs and 1 yolk	1 cup finely chopped nuts
3 cups sifted cake flour	

Cream butter; gradually add sugar, ar
beat until light and fluffy. Add vanill.
Add eggs and yolk, one at a time, bea
ing thoroughly after each additio▪
Add sifted dry ingredients alternate▪
with milk, beating until smooth. Fol
in nuts. Pour into 9″ tube pan, line
on the bottom with paper. Bake i
moderate oven, 375°F., 1 hour, or u▪
til done. Cool in pan 10 minutes; r◾
move to rack.

LIME OR LEMON PARTY CAKE

*A sprinkling of silver shot
gives it a festive look.*

⅔ cup shortening Sugar	3 teaspoons baking powder
1 teaspoon vanilla extract or grated rind 1 lime or lemon	1 teaspoon salt 1 cup milk 5 egg whites Cream Filling, page 252
2⅔ cups sifted cake flour	Lime or Lemon Frosting, page 252

Cream shortening; add 1¼ cups sugar
gradually, beating until light and fluffy.
Add flavoring. Then sift in dry ingredients alternately with milk, beating until smooth. Beat egg whites until
foamy, and add ½ cup sugar gradually.
Continue beating until mixture stands
up in peaks; fold into batter. Pour
into two 9″ layer pans, lined on the
bottom with paper. Bake in moderate
oven, 375°F., about 30 minutes. Cool.
Spread Filling between layers and
Frosting on top and sides of cake.

RAISIN-FILLED SPICE LAYERS

The filling has sour cream in it.

¾ cup shortening	1⅔ cups light- brown sugar, packed
2½ cups sifted cake flour	1 cup milk
3½ teaspoons baking powder	3 eggs
1 teaspoon salt	Raisin Filling, page 252
½ teaspoon cinnamon	Confectioners'-suga frosting, or
¼ teaspoon nutmeg	7-Minute Frost-
⅛ teaspoon each cloves and allspice	ing, page 251

TWO-EGG BUTTER LAYERS

You use all butter for the shortening.

Stir ½ cup butter just to soften. Sift
in 2½ cups sifted cake flour, 3 teaspoons baking powder, 1 teaspoon salt,
1½ cups sugar. Add ¾ cup milk, 1
teaspoon vanilla. Mix until dry ingredients are dampened; then beat 2 minutes at low speed of electric mixer or
300 vigorous strokes by hand. Add 2
eggs and 2 tablespoons milk. Beat 1
minute longer in mixer or 150 strokes
by hand. Pour into two 9″ layer pans,
lined on the bottom with paper. Bake
in moderate oven, 375°F., 20 to 25
minutes. Cool on racks. Frost with Semisweet Frosting, page 251, or as desired.

Put shortening in mixing bowl, and
mix just to soften. Sift dry ingredients
except sugar, on top of shortening▪
Add sugar, forcing through sieve to
remove lumps, if necessary, and ¾ cup
milk. Beat 2 minutes at low speed o▪
electric mixer or 300 vigorous strokes
by hand. Add eggs and remaining milk
and beat 1 minute longer in mixer o▪
150 strokes by hand. Pour into two 9″
layer pans, lined on the bottom with
paper. Bake in moderate oven, 375°F.,
about 25 minutes. Turn out on cake
racks; remove paper, and cool. Spread
Raisin Filling between layers and frosting on top and sides of cake.

ANGEL FOOD CAKE

It takes a cup of egg whites.

cup sifted cake flour	¼ teaspoon salt
cup egg whites (7 or 8 whites)	1¼ cups sifted sugar
teaspoon cream of tartar	1 teaspoon vanilla extract

Sift the flour several times. Beat egg whites until frothy. Add cream of tartar and salt; beat until stiff, but not dry. Gradually beat in sugar. Add vanilla. Then fold in flour in fourths. Pour into an ungreased 9″ tube pan; bake in moderate oven, 325°F., about 1 hour. Invert pan on rack. Let stand until cold. Serve plain or spread top with Chocolate Glaze, page 251.

Chocolate Angel Food: Use above recipe, substituting ¼ cup cocoa for ¼ cup of the flour. Sift cocoa with the flour. Proceed as above; cool. Spread top of cake with Chocolate Glaze, page 251.

SUNSHINE CAKE

You make a design on top by dusting sugar through holes in a paper doily.

1½ cups egg whites (9 or 10 whites)	Grated rind 1 orange or 1 teaspoon orange extract
½ teaspoon salt	1⅓ cups sifted cake flour
1 teaspoon cream of tartar	⅔ cup egg yolks (8 or 9 yolks)
1⅓ cups sifted sugar	Confectioners' sugar

Beat whites until frothy; add salt and cream of tartar gradually, beating constantly until stiff but not dry. Add sugar gradually, beating constantly, until all sugar is used and mixture holds its shape when bowl is tilted. Blend in orange rind. Sift flour onto mixture gradually; carefully and gently fold in until well blended after each addition. Beat egg yolks until thick and lemon-colored, and gradually fold into first mixture. Pour into ungreased 10″ tube pan, and bake in moderate oven, 325°F., 1 hour and 15 minutes. Invert on rack, and cool before removing from pan. Dust sifted confectioners' sugar through the holes in a fancy paper doily placed on the top of the cake; then carefully remove doily.

RAISIN-SPICE LOAF CAKE

The spices are cinnamon, nutmeg, and allspice.

1 cup brown sugar, packed	½ teaspoon nutmeg
1 cup seeded raisins	½ teaspoon allspice
1¼ cups water	2 cups sifted flour
½ cup shortening	1 teaspoon soda
1 teaspoon cinnamon	1 teaspoon baking powder
	½ teaspoon salt

Boil first 7 ingredients 5 minutes. Chill. Sift dry ingredients; stir into first mixture. Pour into greased, waxed-paper-lined loaf pan, 9″x 5″x 3″. Bake in moderate oven, 350°F., 55 to 60 minutes. Turn out on rack; remove paper; cool. Serve plain, or frost as desired.

DAFFODIL CAKE

Two batters, one yellow, one white, baked together in a tube pan.

1 cup egg whites, (8 or 9)	1 teaspoon vanilla extract
½ teaspoon salt	4 egg yolks
1 teaspoon cream of tartar	Grated rind ½ orange
1 cup sugar	Yellow Jacket Frosting, page 252
1 cup sifted cake flour	

Beat egg whites with salt until frothy. Add cream of tartar, and beat until stiff, but not dry. Gradually add sugar, and beat until very stiff and glossy. Fold in flour in thirds. Add vanilla. Beat egg yolks until thick and lemon-colored. Divide batter, and fold egg yolks and rind into half. Put by tablespoonfuls into an ungreased 9″ or 10″ tube pan, alternating the yellow and white mixtures. Bake in slow oven, 300°F., about 1 hour. Invert on rack to cool. Remove from pan, and frost top and sides of cake.

"Bless the food that comes to me
With those who share and serve it;
And if there be a good dessert
Oh grace me to deserve it!"
A. F. BROWN

CINNAMON-MOLASSES LAYERS

They have a cream-cheese frosting.

¾ cup shortening	1 teaspoon
⅔ cup sugar	cinnamon
3 eggs	¾ teaspoon salt
¾ cup molasses	1 cup milk
2¾ cups sifted	Cream-cheese
flour	Frosting,
1 teaspoon soda	page 251

Cream shortening; add sugar gradually, beating until light. Then add eggs, 1 at a time, beating thoroughly after each. Add molasses, and mix well. Sift in dry ingredients alternately with milk, beating until smooth. Pour into 2 round 9″ layer pans, lined on the bottom with paper. Bake in moderate oven, 350°F., 35 to 40 minutes. Cool; frost.

BUTTERSCOTCH BANANA CAKE

The filling is butterscotch; the bananas go into the cake itself.

¾ cup shortening	1 teaspoon soda
2¼ cups sugar	1 teaspoon baking
1½ teaspoons	powder
vanilla extract	¾ teaspoon salt
Grated rind 1 lemon	⅓ cup buttermilk
3 eggs	Butterscotch Filling,
1½ cups mashed	page 252
bananas (3 or 4)	7-Minute
3 cups sifted cake	Frosting,
flour	page 251

Cream shortening; add sugar gradually, beating until light. Add vanilla and lemon rind, then eggs, one at a time, beating thoroughly after each. Add bananas. Sift in dry ingredients alternately with buttermilk, beating until smooth. Pour into three 9″ pans, lined on the bottom with paper. Bake in moderate oven, 350°F., about 30 minutes. Cool. Spread Filling between layers and Frosting on top and sides of cake.

Good cooks are educated people
Schooled at their aunts' and
mothers' knees. Instinctively
they behave in kitchens
As in a busy hive behave the bees.
ANONYMOUS

COCONUT LAYER CAKE

It has orange filling and fluffy frosting sprinkled with coconut.

1 cup shortening	¾ teaspoon salt
2 cups sugar	1 cup milk
½ teaspoon	Orange Filling,
almond extract	page 252
4 eggs	Fluffy Frosting,
3 cups sifted	page 252
cake flour	2 cups grated
2¼ teaspoons	fresh coconut
double-acting	or 1 can
baking powder	flaked coconut

Cream shortening; add sugar gradually, beating until light. Add flavoring then eggs, 1 at a time, beating well after each. Add sifted dry ingredients alternately with milk, beating until smooth. Pour into 3 round 9″ layer pans, lined on the bottom with paper. Bake in moderate oven, 375°F., about 25 minutes. Cool. Spread Filling between layers, and Frosting on top and sides of cake. Sprinkle with coconut.

BURNT-SUGAR CAKE

A three-layer cake with caramel frosting and pecan garnish.

Sugar	3 cups sifted cake
½ cup boiling	flour
water	3 teaspoons baking
⅔ cup butter or	powder
margarine	1 teaspoon salt
1 teaspoon vanilla	1 cup milk
extract	Caramel Frosting,
2 eggs, separated	page 251
	Pecan halves

Heat ½ cup sugar slowly in small saucepan, stirring. When sugar is melted and begins to smoke, add water slowly and carefully, stirring. Cook until syrup measures ½ cup, stirring until sugar is dissolved. Cool. Cream butter; add 1 cup sugar gradually, beating until light and fluffy. Add vanilla, then yolks, one at a time, beating thoroughly after each. Stir in cold syrup. Add sifted dry ingredients alternately with milk, beating until smooth. Beat egg whites until stiff but not dry. Fold into flour mixture. Pour into 3 round 9″ layer pans, lined on the bottom with paper. Bake in moderate oven, 375°F., about 20 minutes. Cool; frost. Top with nuts.

GOLDEN HONEY-NUT CAKE

Vegetable oil is in the shortening.

4 eggs	3¾ cups sifted
1 cup sugar	flour
½ cup vegetable	2 teaspoons baking
oil	powder
Grated rind	¾ teaspoon salt
1 lemon	1 cup coarsely
2 cups honey	chopped
½ teaspoon soda	walnuts

Beat eggs, sugar, oil, and lemon rind. Heat honey almost to boiling, and beat in soda. Add to first mixture. Add sifted dry ingredients, and beat until blended. Add nuts. Pour into 13″ x 9″ x 2″ pan lined with waxed paper. Bake in moderate oven, 350°F., about 1 hour. Turn out on rack, peel off paper, and let stand until cold. Store airtight for several days before serving. Serve plain, sprinkle with confectioners' sugar, or spread top and sides of cake with thin confectioners'-sugar frosting flavored with grated lemon rind.

ORANGE RUM CAKE

You should let this cake stand a day or two before serving it.

1 cup butter or	1 teaspoon soda
margarine	½ teaspoon salt
2 cups sugar	1 cup buttermilk
Grated rind 2 large	1 cup finely
oranges and	chopped walnuts
1 lemon	Juice 2 large
2 eggs	oranges
2½ cups sifted	Juice 1 lemon
flour	2 tablespoons
2 teaspoons baking	rum
powder	

Cream butter; gradually add 1 cup sugar, and beat until light. Add fruit rinds, and eggs, one at a time, beating thoroughly after each. Add sifted dry ingredients alternately with buttermilk, beating after each addition until smooth. Fold in nuts. Pour into greased 9″ or 10″ 2-quart tube pan. Bake in moderate oven, 350°F., about 1 hour. Strain fruit juices into saucepan. Add remaining 1 cup sugar and rum; bring to boil. Remove cake from oven, and pour syrup slowly over cake in pan. If all the liquid is not absorbed, pour remainder on later. (This is a moist cake, so it must be eaten with a fork.)

"The most indispensable quality of a cook is exactitude: It should also be that of the guest."

ANSELME BRILLAT-SAVARIN

APPLESAUCE-NUT LOAF CAKE

It's spiced with nutmeg, cloves, and cinnamon.

½ cup shortening	1 teaspoon baking
1 cup brown sugar,	powder
packed	½ teaspoon each
1 cup canned	ground cloves
applesauce	and cinnamon
2¼ cups sifted	¼ teaspoon nutmeg
flour	1 cup chopped nuts
½ teaspoon each	Caramel Frosting,
soda and salt	page 251

Cream shortening and sugar; add applesauce. Sift dry ingredients, and gradually beat into first mixture. Add nuts. Pour into greased 9″x 5″x 3″ loaf pan. Bake in moderate oven, 325°F., 1 hour. Turn out on rack to cool; frost.

ALMOND CHIFFON CAKE

Egg whites make it light and fluffy.

2¼ cups sifted	¾ teaspoon almond
cake flour	extract
1½ cups sugar	1 cup egg whites
3 teaspoons	(7 or 8 whites)
baking powder	½ teaspoon cream
1 teaspoon salt	of tartar
½ cup vegetable	Butter-Cream
oil	Frosting, page 250
5 egg yolks	½ cup toasted
¼ cup cold water	sliced blanched
½ cup milk	almonds

Sift dry ingredients into mixing bowl. Make a well in the center, and add oil, yolks, water, milk, and flavoring. Beat until smooth. Beat whites with cream of tartar until they form very stiff peaks. Gradually add first mixture; carefully fold in with rubber spatula until well blended after each addition. Pour into ungreased 10″ tube pan. Bake in moderate oven, 325°F., 55 minutes; then increase heat to 350°F., and bake 10 to 15 minutes longer. Invert cake in pan on cake rack to cool. Frost; sprinkle with nuts.

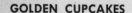

GOLDEN CUPCAKES

Eggs and butter make them golden.

Cream ½ cup soft butter or margarine; gradually add 1 cup sugar; beat until light and fluffy. Add ½ teaspoon vanilla extract, then 2 eggs, one at a time, beating well after each addition. Sift 1½ cups sifted cake flour, 1¼ teaspoons baking powder, ¼ teaspoon salt. Add to first mixture alternately with ⅓ cup milk, beating until smooth. Half-fill 12 greased 2¾" cupcake pans with batter. Bake in moderate oven, 375°F., about 20 minutes. Cool slightly; remove to racks. Frost as desired.

MARASCHINO-CHERRY CAKE

It has marshmallow frosting.

½ cup shortening	3 teaspoons baking powder
1¼ cups sugar	¾ teaspoon salt
½ teaspoon almond extract	¼ cup cherry juice
16 maraschino cherries, cut fine	½ cup milk
	4 egg whites
2 cups plus 6 tablespoons sifted cake flour	7-Minute Frosting, page 251
	16 (¼ pound) marshmallows, cut in quarters

Cream shortening; add sugar gradually, beating until light. Add flavoring. Mix cherries with 2 tablespoons flour. Sift remainder with baking powder and salt. Add cherries, and dry ingredients to creamed mixture alternately with combined cherry juice and milk, beating until smooth. Fold in egg whites, beaten until stiff but not dry. Pour into two 8" layer pans, lined on the bottom with paper. Bake in moderate oven, 350°F., about 35 minutes. Cool. Make Frosting, and beat in marshmallows while hot. Spread between layers and on top and sides of cake.

LORD BALTIMORE CAKE

The filling contains nuts, candied cherries, and macaroon crumbs.

½ cup shortening	½ cup each chopped nuts, dry macaroon crumbs
2 cups sifted cake flour	
2 teaspoons baking powder	¼ teaspoon orange extract
¾ teaspoon salt	12 cut candied cherries
1 cup sugar	
5 egg yolks	2 teaspoons lemon juice
¾ cup milk	
1 teaspoon vanilla extract	7-Minute Frosting, page 251

Put shortening in mixing bowl, and mix just to soften. Sift dry ingredients on top of shortening; add egg yolks, half the milk, and vanilla. Beat 2 minutes at low speed of electric mixer or 300 vigorous strokes by hand. Add other half of milk, and beat 1 minute longer in mixer or 150 strokes by hand. Pour into two 9" layer pans, lined on the bottom with paper. Bake in moderate oven, 375°F., about 20 minutes. Cool. Make Frosting. To one half, add remaining ingredients. Spread between cake layers. Use remaining frosting for top and sides of cake.

BUSY-DAY POUNDCAKE

Have the butter and eggs at room temperature.

3 sticks (¾ pound) butter	6 eggs
1 pound confectioners' sugar	1 sugar-box sifted all-purpose flour (Use empty sugar box. Do not shake down. Level off with spoon.)
1 teaspoon vanilla extract	
½ teaspoon mace	

In electric mixer, cream butter and sugar until light and fluffy. Add vanilla and mace. Add eggs, one at a time, beating thoroughly after each. Add flour, and mix only until blended. Put in buttered and floured 10-inch tube pan. Bake in moderate oven, 325°F., about 1½ hours. Let stand in pan 5 minutes. Then turn out on cake rack to cool.

POUNDCAKE

*Serve it plain, or dusted
with confectioners' sugar.*

1 cup soft butter	1½ teaspoons
Flour	vanilla extract
¼ teaspoon soda	5 large eggs,
1½ cups sugar	separated
1½ tablespoons	⅛ teaspoon salt
lemon juice	1 teaspoon cream
	of tartar

Grease a 9″ tube pan or 9″x 5″x 3″ loaf pan with 1 tablespoon of the butter. Dust with flour, and tap to remove excess. Sift 1½ cups sifted flour, soda, and ¾ cup of the sugar into bowl. Add remaining butter, and mix in well with fingers. Add lemon juice and vanilla, then egg yolks, one at a time, mixing with the fingers until well blended. Beat egg whites with salt until stiff, but not dry. Gradually beat in remaining ¾ cup sugar; fold in cream of tartar. Add to first mixture, and fold in with hands until whites are thoroughly mixed in. Spoon into pan, and even with back of spoon. Jolt pan on table to remove air bubbles. Bake in moderate oven, 325°F., 1 hour, or until done. Then turn off heat, and let stand in oven 10 to 15 minutes. Remove to cake rack, and let stand 10 minutes longer. Loosen with spatula, and turn out on waxed-paper-covered rack; cool. Dust with confectioners' sugar, if desired. Store airtight.

KENTUCKY CHRISTMAS CAKE

*Try heating pieces in a double
boiler and serving with hard sauce.*

Follow recipe for Poundcake, omitting lemon juice and vanilla. Add 2 teaspoons nutmeg soaked 10 minutes in ¼ cup bourbon whisky. Warm 1 pound pecans, coarsely chopped, and ½ pound seeded raisins, cut in half, in oven. Dredge with ¼ cup sifted flour, and coat well. Fold into cake batter. Spoon into buttered and floured 10″ tube pan. Bake in moderate oven, 325°F., 1 hour and 15 minutes, or until done. Let stand in pan 30 minutes on rack. Remove to waxed-paper-covered rack to cool. Turn right side up. Store airtight. If desired, cake can be decorated before baking with candied cherries and pecan halves.

STRAWBERRY-BLONDE CAKES

*They're baked in piepans and
contain brandied fruit and nuts.*

Follow recipe for Poundcake, omitting lemon juice and vanilla. The day before making cake, mix 1½ cups coarsely chopped pecans; 1 cup dried currants; 1 tablespoon nutmeg; and ½ cup brandy, whisky, or sherry. Let stand overnight; liquid should be absorbed. Next day, make cake, and fold in soaked mixture, ¼ cup diced citron, 1 cup cut pitted dates, and ½ cup drained whole-strawberry preserves. Bake in 4 buttered and floured 8″ piepans in moderate oven, 325°F., 50 to 60 minutes. Cool in pans; remove, and brush with brandy. Store airtight.

CHOCOLATE MARBLE CAKE

It has chocolate frosting and nuts.

½ cup	½ cup egg
shortening	whites
1½ cups sugar	2 squares
1¼ teaspoons	unsweetened
vanilla extract	chocolate, melted
2 cups sifted	3 tablespoons
cake flour	water
¾ teaspoon	Rich Chocolate
salt	Frosting,
2 teaspoons	page 251
baking powder	¼ cup chopped
½ cup milk	pecans

Cream shortening; add 1¼ cups sugar gradually, beating until light; add vanilla. Add sifted dry ingredients alternately with milk, beating until smooth. Fold in stiffly beaten whites. Divide batter. Add remaining sugar to chocolate and water; stir until thick; cool; blend into half batter. Alternate light and dark batters in greased, paper-lined 9″ x 5″ x 3″ loaf pan. Cut through batter with knife to improve marbling. Bake in moderate oven, 350°F., about 1 hour. Turn out on rack; remove paper; cool, and frost. Sprinkle with nuts.

*"He who receives his friends
and gives no personal attention
to the meal prepared for them
is unworthy of having friends."*
ANSELME BRILLAT-SAVARIN

CANDIED FRUITCAKE

The fruit: pineapple, cherries, dates.

Sift 2 cups sifted flour, 2 teaspoons baking powder, and ½ teaspoon salt into large bowl. Add 1 pound (2½ cups) candied pineapple, coarsely cut, 1 pound (2 cups) whole candied cherries, and 1¼ pounds (3½ cups) pitted dates, coarsely cut. Mix well with hands to coat each piece of fruit with flour. Beat 4 eggs until frothy; gradually beat in 1 cup sugar. Add to fruit, and mix well. With hands, mix in 2 pounds (8 cups) pecan halves. Grease, and line with brown paper, two 9″ clamp or clampless springform pans; grease paper. Divide dough into pans, and press down firmly with fingers. If necessary rearrange fruit and nuts to fill any empty spaces. Bake in slow oven, 275°F., about 1¼ hours. Let cakes stand in pans about 5 minutes. Turn out on racks, and pull off brown paper. Cool cake before slicing.

SOUTHERN LANE CAKE

A special-occasion white cake with a rich fruit-and-nut frosting.

CAKE: Cream 1 cup butter well; add 2 cups sugar gradually, beating until fluffy. Add 1 teaspoon vanilla. Sift together 3¼ cups sifted flour, 3½ teaspoons baking powder, and ¾ teaspoon salt. Add to butter mixture alternately with 1 cup milk, beating till smooth. Beat 8 egg whites till stiff, but not dry. Fold in. Pour batter into 4 round 9″ layer pans, lined on the bottom with paper. Bake in 375°F. oven 15 minutes. Turn cakes out on racks; cool; spread Frosting (next column) between layers and on top and sides of cake.

"*All human history attests That happiness for man, — the hungry sinner! — Since Eve ate apples, much depends on dinner.*"
LORD BYRON

LANE FROSTING: Beat 8 egg yolks; add 1¼ cups sugar, ½ cup butter; cook, stirring, 5 minutes. (Do not let yolks become scrambled in appearance. Mixture should be almost translucent.) Remove from heat, and add 1 cup each chopped pecans, chopped seeded raisins, shredded coconut, and finely cut candied cherries, ¼ teaspoon salt, and ⅓ cup bourbon or rye.

ORIENTAL FRUITCAKE

Two fruitcake layers and a white one with orange filling, fluffy frosting.

FOR FRUITCAKE LAYERS

½ cup shortening	1 cup chopped walnuts
1 cup sugar	1 cup golden raisins, halved
3 eggs	½ cup each currants, minced candied orange peel, citron, and cherries
½ cup molasses	
2 cups sifted flour	
½ teaspoon each soda, salt, allspice	
¼ teaspoon each cloves and mace	½ cup milk
1 teaspoon cinnamon	

Cream shortening; gradually add sugar, and beat until light. Add eggs, one at a time, beating thoroughly after each. Beat in molasses. Sift dry ingredients. Stir in nuts and fruits. Add to creamed mixture with milk; mix well. Divide into 2 square or round 9″ layer pans, lined on the bottom with paper. Bake in slow oven, 275°F., about 1½ hours.

FOR WHITE-CAKE LAYER

⅓ cup shortening	1⅓ cups sifted cake flour
¾ cup sugar	1½ teaspoons baking powder
¼ teaspoon almond flavoring	
½ teaspoon vanilla	½ cup milk
½ teaspoon salt	2 egg whites

Cream shortening; gradually add ½ cup sugar, and beat until light. Add flavorings, and sifted dry ingredients alternately with milk, beating after each addition until smooth. Beat egg whites until foamy; gradually add ¼ cup sugar, and beat until stiff. Fold into batter. Pour into 9″ square or round layer pan, lined on the bottom with paper. Bake in 375°F. oven 25 minutes. To fill and frost, see next page.

To fill and frost: Spread Orange Filling, page 252, between layers, having white layer in center. Spread Fluffy Frosting, page 252, on top and sides of cake, and decorate with walnut halves.

MILLINOCKET FUDGE CAKE

A tender, moist, dark-red cake.

½ cup soft butter or margarine	1¾ cups sifted flour
1½ cups sugar	1½ teaspoons cream of tartar
2 eggs	1 teaspoon soda
1 teaspoon vanilla extract	¾ teaspoon salt
2 squares unsweetened chocolate, melted and cooled	½ cup milk
	¾ cup boiling water
	Fudge Frosting, page 251

Cream butter and sugar. Add eggs and vanilla; beat until light. Blend in chocolate. Add sifted dry ingredients alternately with milk; beat until smooth. Stir in water. (Batter will be thin.) Pour into 9"x 9"x 2" pan, lined on bottom with paper; bake in 350°F. oven 1 hour. Cool; frost.

CHOCOLATE SHADOW CAKE

Really dark and velvety.

6 squares unsweetened chocolate	3 eggs
½ cup hot water	2 cups sifted cake flour
1¾ cups sugar	1 teaspoon soda
Soft butter or margarine	½ teaspoon salt
1 teaspoon vanilla extract	⅔ cup milk
	Fluffy Frosting, page 252

Melt 4 squares chocolate in the hot water in top part of double boiler over boiling water. Cook until thickened, stirring. Add ½ cup sugar, and cook 2 or 3 minutes, stirring. Cool. Cream ½ cup butter and 1¼ cups sugar. Add vanilla. Add eggs, one at a time, beating thoroughly after each addition. Add sifted dry ingredients alternately with milk, beating until smooth. Add chocolate mixture, and blend. Pour into two 9" layer pans, lined on bottom with paper. Bake in 350°F. oven about 45 minutes. Cool, and frost. When frosting is set, melt 2 squares chocolate and 2 teaspoons butter. Dribble over top of cake. Let chocolate set before cutting.

CHOCOLATE-NUT CAKE

A moist, open-textured red cake.

⅓ cup soft butter or other shortening	¾ cup buttermilk
¾ cup sugar	1 teaspoon vanilla extract
1 egg	1 cup coarsely chopped pecans or walnuts
2 squares unsweetened chocolate, melted	Semisweet Frosting, page 251
1⅓ cups sifted cake flour	8-10 pecan or walnut halves
¾ teaspoon soda	
½ teaspoon salt	

Cream butter and sugar. Add egg, and beat until light. Blend in cooled chocolate. Sift dry ingredients; add alternately with milk. Add vanilla, chopped nuts. Pour into 9"x 5"x 3" loaf pan, lined on the bottom with paper. Bake in moderate oven, 350°F., about 1 hour. Cool; frost; arrange nuts around edge.

SEMISWEET DEVIL'S FOOD

You use brown sugar and buttermilk.

1½ cups (9 ounces) semisweet chocolate pieces	1¾ cups sifted flour
⅓ cup soft butter or margarine	1¼ teaspoons soda
1½ cups brown sugar, packed	1 teaspoon salt
1½ teaspoons vanilla extract	½ cup buttermilk
2 eggs	¾ cup boiling water
	Semisweet Frosting, page 251

Melt chocolate over hot water; cool. Cream butter, sugar, and vanilla. Add eggs, one at a time, beating thoroughly after each. Stir in chocolate. Add sifted dry ingredients alternately with buttermilk; beat until smooth. Stir in water. Pour into two 9" layer pans, lined on bottom with paper. Bake in moderate oven, 375°F., 25 minutes. Cool; frost.

*"And spiced dainties, everyone,
From silken Samarcand
to cedar'd Lebanon."*
JOHN KEATS

RED DEVIL'S FOOD

A three-layered devil's food.

¾ cup soft butter or margarine	1⅓ cups milk
2 cups sugar	3 eggs
2⅔ cups sifted cake flour	3 squares unsweetened chocolate, melted and cooled
1½ teaspoons baking powder	1½ teaspoons red food coloring
¾ teaspoon each soda and salt	1 teaspoon vanilla extract

Cream butter. Sift dry ingredients into butter. Add 1 cup milk, and mix until flour is dampened. Beat 2 minutes. Add ⅓ cup milk and remaining ingredients. Beat 2 minutes. Pour into three 8" layer pans, paper-lined on bottom. Bake in 350°F. oven 30-35 minutes. Cool; frost as desired. Or spread tops and sides of cake with Fluffy Frosting, page 252.

SPICY FUDGE CUPCAKES

You need cinnamon and molasses.

⅓ cup shortening	2 cups sifted cake flour
1 cup sugar	
1 teaspoon vanilla extract	1 teaspoon each baking powder and cinnamon
2 eggs	½ teaspoon salt
2 squares unsweetened chocolate, melted	½ cup each hot water, buttermilk, molasses
½ teaspoon soda	

Cream shortening, sugar, and vanilla. Add eggs, one at a time, beating thoroughly after each addition. Add cooled chocolate, and blend. Add sifted dry ingredients alternately with liquids, beating until smooth. Half-fill greased 2½" cupcake pans with batter. Bake in 350°F. oven 25 minutes. Serve plain, or frost. Makes 28.

CHOCOLATE 7-LAYER CAKE

Must be kept in the refrigerator.

6 eggs, separated	¼ cup cornstarch
1¼ cups sugar	½ teaspoon salt
2 tablespoons lemon juice	Creamy Chocolate Frosting, page 251
¾ cup sifted flour	

Beat egg yolks until thick. Gradually add sugar, beating constantly with rotary beater; add half of lemon juice. Add sifted dry ingredients alternately with remaining lemon juice, beating until smooth. Fold in stiffly beaten egg whites. Spread a few tablespoons batter in each of two or three 8" layer pans, lined on bottom with paper. Bake in 450°F. oven 5 minutes. Turn out on racks. Repeat baking process until all the batter is used and 7 layers are baked. Cool, and frost. Chill.

CHOCOLATE CHIFFON CAKE

Light and mildly chocolate.

1¾ cups sifted cake flour	1 cup buttermilk
¾ teaspoon soda	2 eggs, separated
¾ teaspoon salt	2 squares unsweetened chocolate, melted, cooled
1½ cups sugar	
⅓ cup vegetable oil	Fudge Frosting, page 251

Sift flour, soda, salt, 1 cup sugar. Add oil and ½ cup buttermilk. Beat one minute. Add ½ cup buttermilk, yolks, and chocolate. Beat 1 minute. Beat whites until stiff, but not dry. Slowly beat in ½ cup sugar. Fold into batter. Pour into two 8" layer pans, lined on bottom with paper. Bake in 350°F. oven 30 minutes. Cool; frost.

BUTTER-CREAM FROSTING

1 cup sugar	2 egg whites
⅛ teaspoon cream of tartar	½ teaspoon vanilla extract
¼ cup water	⅔ cup butter

Combine first 3 ingredients in saucepan. Cook until a little of the mixture dropped in cold water forms a soft ball (240°F. on a candy thermometer). Beat egg whites until stiff, but not dry. Add syrup very slowly to egg whites, beating constantly. Add vanilla. Cool. Cream butter; add egg-white mixture, 2 or 3 tablespoons at a time, beating after each addition. Makes enough for tops and sides of two 9" layers.

7-MINUTE FROSTING

½ cups sugar	1½ teaspoons
⅓ cup water	light corn syrup
¼ teaspoon salt	1 teaspoon vanilla
egg whites	extract

Combine all ingredients, except vanilla, in top of double boiler. Beat with rotary beater until mixed. Put over rapidly boiling water; beat constantly for minutes, or until frosting forms peaks. Add vanilla; beat until cool and of spreading consistency. Makes enough frosting for tops and sides of two 9" layers or for large tube cake.

CARAMEL FROSTING

tablespoons butter or margarine	⅛ teaspoon salt
⅓ cup heavy cream	Few drops vanilla extract
⅓ cup brown sugar, packed	Sifted confectioners' sugar (about 3 cups)

Mix first 4 ingredients in saucepan. Bring to boil, stirring constantly. Remove from heat; add vanilla. Then add gradually enough sifted confectioners' sugar to make frosting of spreading consistency. Makes enough frosting for tops and sides of three 9" layers.

CREAM-CHEESE FROSTING

Mash 1 package (3 ounces) cream cheese. Add 1 tablespoon warm water and 1 teaspoon vanilla. Then add gradually about 3 cups sifted confectioners' sugar, beating until smooth and of spreading consistency. Makes enough frosting for tops and sides of two 9" layers or for large tube cake.

RICH CHOCOLATE FROSTING

1½ cups sifted confectioners' sugar	2½ tablespoons hot water
3 squares unsweetened chocolate, melted	3 egg yolks
	½ teaspoon vanilla extract
Dash of salt	¼ cup soft butter or margarine

Add half the sugar to the chocolate. Mix well, and add salt, water, and remaining sugar. Beat in egg yolks gradually. Add vanilla and butter, and beat until blended. Makes enough frosting for top and sides of 9"x 5"x 3" loaf cake or for tops of two 9" layers.

CREAMY CHOCOLATE FROSTING

Melt 4 squares unsweetened chocolate in top of double boiler over hot water. Beat 4 egg yolks with ⅔ cup sugar; add ½ cup heavy cream and ⅛ teaspoon salt. Pour slowly over chocolate, stirring constantly. Cook over hot water 5 minutes, or until thickened, stirring. Cream 1¼ cups unsalted butter; add chocolate mixture, 1 tablespoonful at a time, beating until blended. Chill until of spreading consistency.

FUDGE FROSTING

In saucepan combine 2 squares unsweetened chocolate, 1½ cups sugar, ½ cup milk, ¼ cup butter or margarine, 1 tablespoon corn syrup, and ¼ teaspoon salt. Bring to boil; cook until a small amount of mixture forms a soft ball when dropped in a little cold water (232°F. on a candy thermometer). Cool to lukewarm. Add 1 teaspoon vanilla; beat to spreading consistency. Makes enough frosting for top and sides of 9" square cake.

CHOCOLATE GLAZE

Melt together 2 tablespoons butter and 2 squares unsweetened chocolate. Beat in 2 tablespoons boiling water, 1 cup sifted confectioners' sugar, dash salt, and ¼ teaspoon vanilla extract. Makes enough for top of 9" angel cake.

SEMISWEET FROSTING

Melt 1 package (12 ounces) semisweet chocolate pieces and 3 tablespoons butter over hot water. Remove from heat; stir in ½ cup confectioners' sugar, ½ cup evaporated milk, 1 teaspoon vanilla, ¼ teaspoon salt. Beat until smooth. Makes enough frosting for tops and sides of two 9" layers.

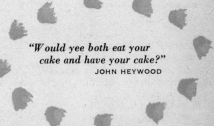

"Would yee both eat your cake and have your cake?"
JOHN HEYWOOD

ORANGE FILLING

Mix ½ cup sifted cake flour, 1 cup sugar, and ¼ teaspoon salt in heavy saucepan. Add ¼ cup water, and mix until there are no lumps. Add 1¼ cups orange juice, ¼ cup lemon juice, 2 tablespoons grated orange rind, and grated rind 1 lemon. Cook over low heat until mixture thickens and becomes almost transparent. Beat 4 egg yolks slightly; add hot mixture slowly, stirring constantly. Return to saucepan, and, stirring constantly, cook slowly about 5 minutes, or until sauce thickens again. Cool. Makes enough filling for two or three 9″ layers.

BUTTERSCOTCH FILLING

3 tablespoons butter or margarine	¼ cup flour
½ cup brown sugar, packed	½ teaspoon salt
1½ cups milk	1 egg, beaten
	½ teaspoon vanilla extract

Melt butter; add sugar, and cook 2 minutes in top of double boiler, over direct heat. Add 1 cup milk, and heat over boiling water. Mix remaining milk, flour, and salt until smooth. Stir into hot mixture. Cook 5 minutes, stirring constantly. Cover; cook 10 minutes longer, stirring occasionally. Add mixture to egg; return to double boiler, and cook 2 minutes. Cool; add vanilla. Makes enough filling for 9″ layer cake.

RAISIN FILLING

Mix 1 cup each sour cream and sugar, ½ teaspoon salt, 1 cup chopped seeded raisins in saucepan. Bring to boil, and cook about 10 minutes over medium heat, stirring constantly. Cool. Makes enough filling for 9″ layer cake.

"An' I had one penny in the world thou shouldst have it to buy gingerbread."
WILLIAM SHAKESPEARE

CREAM FILLING

Mix ⅓ cup sugar, 2½ tablespoons flour and ⅛ teaspoon salt in saucepan. Ad ¼ cup milk, and stir until smooth Add ¾ cup milk, and cook over lo heat until thickened. Add mixture 1 beaten egg; return to saucepan, an cook 2 minutes longer. Cool, and ad ½ teaspoon grated lemon or lime rin Makes 1 cup.

YELLOW JACKET FROSTING

In saucepan, mix 1⅔ cups sugar, tablespoons light corn syrup, and cup water. Cook, without stirring, unt a little of the mixture forms a har ball when dropped in cold wat (250°F. on a candy thermometer Beat 3 egg yolks and ¼ teaspoon sa until thick and lemon-colored. Gradu ally add syrup, and beat until thic and of spreading consistency. Ad grated rind ½ orange and ½ lemo and 1 teaspoon lemon juice. Make enough frosting for large tube cake o two 9″ layers.

FLUFFY FROSTING

1½ cups sugar	½ cup egg whites (about 4)
½ teaspoon cream of tartar	½ teaspoon vanill extract
⅛ teaspoon salt	
½ cup hot water	

Combine first 4 ingredients in sauce pan. Cook, without stirring, until little of the mixture dropped in col water will form a soft ball (240°F. in a candy thermometer). Meanwhile, bea egg whites until stiff but not dry. Add syrup very slowly to egg whites, beat ing constantly with rotary beater, or electric mixer at high speed. Add va nilla. Makes enough frosting for top and sides of two 9″ layers.

Lime or Lemon Frosting: Make half the above recipe, omitting cream of tarta and vanilla and substituting 2 table spoons lime or lemon juice for 2 ta blespoons of the water. Add ¼ tea spoon grated lime or lemon rind, and tint frosting pale green or yellow, with vegetable coloring.

COOKIES

Do you remember the joys of the cookie can or cookie jar? It usually stood in a far corner of the kitchen drainboard or in the pantry. It might be a big earthenware crock with a cover, or a ten-pound lard tin, painted bright red or blue. It was always full of tasty homemade cookies that you could munch on when you came home from school: sometimes ginger snaps, or maybe sugar cookies, or fat oatmeal cookies studded with raisins, or thin lemon-flavored wafers, delicate and melting in the mouth. Like candy making, cookie baking, and the full cookie jar, is an old custom that needs to be revived. It can be a family affair. Rolling the dough and wielding the cookie cutter are great fun for children. Then there's the chance to be creative if the cookie calls for decoration. Here are cookie recipes to call up memories for all of us. They are from all over the world: Germany, China, Russia, Poland, Mexico, and many other lands, together with our own national specialties. Try the familiar and then move on to the strange.

"I am glad that
my Adonis hath
a sweet tooth in his head."
JOHN LYLY

BARS AND SQUARES

ORANGE BARS

- 1 navel orange
- 1 cup seeded raisins
- ½ cup soft butter or margarine
- 1 cup granulated sugar
- 1 egg
- 2 cups sifted flour
- ½ teaspoon baking powder
- ¼ teaspoon salt
- 1½ cups confectioners' sugar

Cut orange in half, and squeeze out about 2 tablespoons juice; reserve. Force remainder, including rind, with raisins through food chopper. Cream butter; add granulated sugar and egg; beat until light. Add flour, baking powder, and salt; mix well. Stir in orange mixture. Spread in greased 13″x 9″x 2″ pan. Bake in hot oven, 425°F., about 25 minutes. Mix reserved juice with confectioners' sugar until smooth. Spread on baked mixture while still warm. Cool; cut into 39 3″ x 1″ bars.

MARBLE BROWNIES

- 1 cup soft butter or margarine
- 1½ teaspoons vanilla extract
- 2 cups sugar
- 4 eggs
- 2 cups sifted flour
- ½ teaspoon salt
- 2 cups chopped nuts
- 2 squares unsweetened chocolate, melted
- Rich Chocolate Frosting, page 251

Cream butter, vanilla, and sugar; add eggs, one at a time, beating well after each. Add flour and salt; mix well. Stir in nuts. Divide batter; add cooled chocolate to one part. Drop batter alternately by teaspoonfuls into greased waxed-paper-lined 13″x 9″x 2″ pan. Run knife through batter several times. Bake in moderate oven, 350°F., about 45 minutes. Turn out on rack. Remove paper. Frost. At serving time, cut in 3″x 1½″ bars. Makes 2 dozen.

SAUCEPAN BROWNIES

In saucepan over low heat, melt ⅓ cu butter or margarine and 2 squares u sweetened chocolate, stirring constan ly; cool. Beat in ½ teaspoon vanil extract and 1 cup sugar. Add 2 egg one at a time, beating well after eac Add ¾ cup sifted flour, ¼ teaspoo salt. Stir in ¾ cup chopped nut Pour into greased, waxed-paper-line 8″x 8″x 2″ pan. Bake in moderate ove 350°F., about 25 minutes. Turn out o rack; remove paper. Cool; cut i squares. Store airtight.

NEWTON SUGAR SQUARES

- 1 cup soft butter or margarine
- 1¼ cups sugar
- 2 eggs
- 2 cups sifted flour
- ¼ teaspoon soda
- ¼ teaspoon salt
- 1 teaspoon ginger
- 2 tablespoons buttermilk

Cream butter with 1 cup sugar; ad eggs, and beat until light. Add sifte dry ingredients and buttermilk; mi well. Spread in greased 15″x 10″x 1 pan, and sprinkle with remaining ¼ cup sugar. Bake in hot oven, 400°F about 20 minutes. Cool, and cut in 4 cookies about 2″ square.

FROSTED MOLASSES BARS

- 2¾ cups sifted flour
- ½ teaspoon soda
- ½ teaspoon salt
- ½ teaspoon cloves
- 1 teaspoon cinnamon
- 1 teaspoon allspice
- 1 cup molasses
- ¾ cup granulated sugar
- 1 egg, beaten
- 1 teaspoon grated lemon rind
- ½ cup chopped nuts
- ⅓ cup diced citron
- 1 cup confectioners' sugar
- 4 teaspoons water

Sift flour, soda, salt, and spices. Pu molasses in large saucepan, and hea to boiling. Remove from heat; adc granulated sugar; stir until dissolved Cool; then beat in egg and lemon rind Add dry ingredients, nuts, and citron mix well. Chill overnight. Divide dough in half, and put each half on a greasec cookie sheet. Cover with waxed paper and roll to a 10″x 9″ rectangle. Bake in hot oven, 400°F., about 12 minutes Mix sugar and water until smooth. Brush on cookies while warm. Cool then cut in 2½″x 1″ bars. Makes about 6 dozen. Store airtight.

HONEY-DATE BARS

cup honey	¼ teaspoon salt
eggs, well beaten	Two packages
teaspoon vanilla	(6½ ounces each)
extract	pitted dates,
⅓ cups sifted	cut up
flour	1 cup chopped nuts
teaspoon baking	Fine granulated
powder	sugar

Mix honey, eggs, and vanilla; beat well. Add sifted dry ingredients, dates, and nuts. Spread in greased 13"x 9"x 2" pan. Bake in moderate oven, 350°F., about 45 minutes. Cool in pan. Cut in "x 1" bars; roll in sugar. Makes 39.

SPICY PECAN SQUARES

cup soft butter	2 cups sifted flour
cup brown sugar,	½ teaspoon salt
packed	1 teaspoon
teaspoon vanilla	cinnamon
extract	1 cup ground
egg, separated	pecans

Cream butter; add sugar, vanilla, and egg yolk; beat until light. Add sifted dry ingredients and half the nuts; mix well. Press into greased 15"x 10"x 1" pan, and brush top with slightly beaten egg white; sprinkle with ½ cup nuts. Bake in 350°F. oven 25 minutes. Cut in 2" squares. Makes 36.

LAYERED BRAZIL-NUT BARS

¼ cup soft butter	½ cup flaked
cup plus 2	coconut
tablespoons sifted	1 teaspoon vanilla
flour	1 cup (6-ounce
½ teaspoon salt	package)
¾ cup brown	semisweet
sugar, packed	chocolate pieces
2 eggs, beaten	¼ cup light corn
1½ cups minced	syrup
Brazil nuts	1 tablespoon water

Mix butter, 1 cup flour, and ¼ teaspoon salt until blended. Press firmly into 9" square pan. Bake in moderate oven, 375°F., 15 minutes. Beat sugar into eggs. Add remaining ¼ teaspoon salt, 1 cup nuts, the coconut, and vanilla. Spread evenly over baked layer in pan. Return to oven, and bake 15 minutes longer. Cool in pan. Melt chocolate over hot water, and stir in corn syrup and water. Spread on baked mixture, and sprinkle with remaining ½ cup nuts. Let stand until topping is firm; cut in 3"x 1" bars. Makes 27.

COCONUT BARS

½ cup soft butter	1 teaspoon vanilla
1½ cups light-	extract
brown sugar,	2 eggs
packed	1 cup chopped nuts
1¼ cups sifted flour	1 can flaked
½ teaspoon salt	coconut

Cream butter and ½ cup of the sugar. Add 1 cup of the flour, and mix well. Pat into greased 13"x 9"x 2" pan. Bake in moderate oven, 375°F., 12 minutes. Mix remaining sugar, flour, and other ingredients. Spread evenly on mixture in pan. Bake 20 minutes. Cut in 54 bars. Cool. Store airtight.

MINCEMEAT DIAMONDS

1 tablespoon soft	¼ teaspoon
butter	nutmeg
1½ cups brown	3 tablespoons hot
sugar, packed	water
2 eggs	Chopped nuts
2 tablespoons	¼ cup seeded
molasses	raisins, chopped
2 cups sifted flour	1 box (9 ounces)
½ teaspoon each	mincemeat,
salt and soda	broken up with
1 teaspoon each	fork
cinnamon, cloves	Frosting

Mix first 4 ingredients well. Add sifted dry ingredients and water; mix until smooth. Add ⅓ cup chopped nuts, raisins, and mincemeat. Spread thin in 2 greased 13"x 9"x 2" pans. Bake in hot oven, 400°F., 12 to 15 minutes. Spread with Frosting while warm, and sprinkle with chopped nuts. Cool; cut in 2" diamonds. Makes 4 to 5 dozen. **Frosting:** Mix well: 3 cups confectioners' sugar, about ⅓ cup hot milk, 1 teaspoon vanilla extract, and dash salt.

CHOCOLATE DIAMONDS

2 squares
  unsweetened
  chocolate
	½ cup sifted flour
	¼ teaspoon salt
	½ teaspoon vanilla

½ cup butter or margarine	extract ⅔ cup chopped
1 cup sugar 2 eggs	nuts

Melt chocolate and butter over hot water. Add remaining ingredients, except nuts, and mix well. Spread in greased 15"x 10"x 1" pan. Sprinkle with nuts. Bake in hot oven, 400°F., about 12 minutes. Cool slightly, and cut in 1½" diamonds in pans. Makes about 4 dozen. Store airtight.

ROLLED

ROLLED SEED COOKIES

½ cup soft butter	½ teaspoon salt
6 tablespoons sugar	¼ cup water
1¾ cups sifted flour	1 teaspoon each

1½ teaspoons
  baking powder
	anise, poppy,
	  caraway seed

Cream butter; add sugar and sifted dry ingredients; blend with fingers or pastry blender. Add liquid to make a stiff dough. Divide dough in thirds; roll 1 portion to ⅛" thickness; sprinkle with anise seed; roll lightly; cut in small shapes. Put on greased cookie sheets; bake in hot oven, 400°F., 10 to 12 minutes. Roll second portion; sprinkle with poppy seed. Roll third portion; sprinkle with caraway seed, and proceed as above. Makes 4 to 5 dozen.

ORANGE-MOLASSES JUMBOS

1 cup soft butter or margarine	1 cup molasses 4 cups sifted flour
Sugar	1 teaspoon each

Grated rind 1
  orange
	salt, soda,
	  ginger

2 eggs	

Cream butter; add 1 cup sugar, rind and eggs. Beat until light. Add molasses and sifted dry ingredients; mix well. Chill 2 to 3 hours. Roll on floured board to ⅛" thickness; sprinkle with sugar, rolling lightly to make sugar stick; cut with floured 3½" cutter. Bake in moderate oven, 375°F., about 10 minutes. Makes about 3 dozen.

CRISP GINGER COOKIES

1 cup soft butter or margarine	4½ cups sifted flour 1 teaspoon soda
½ cup granulated sugar	1 teaspoon salt 1 teaspoon each

½ cup light-brown
  sugar, packed
	ginger and
	  cinnamon

⅓ cup molasses	½ teaspoon cloves
⅔ cup light corn syrup	

Cream butter; add sugars; beat until light. Add molasses and corn syrup; mix well. Add sifted dry ingredients and knead until smooth. Chill until firm. Roll out on lightly floured board to less than ⅛" thickness. Cut with floured fancy cutter. Bake in moderate oven, 350°F., about 8 minutes. Makes about 12 dozen. Store airtight.

JUMBLES

1 cup soft butter or margarine	1 egg 3 cups sifted cake
1 cup granulated sugar	flour ¼ teaspoon salt

Grated rind 1
  orange
	Confectioners'
	  sugar

Cream butter; add granulated sugar, rind, and egg; beat until light. Add flour and salt; mix well. Chill. Dredge board with confectioners' sugar. Roll half of dough to 8" square. Cut square in half, and cut each half in 14 strips, 4" long. Put on ungreased cookie sheets, joining ends to form rings. Repeat with rest of dough. Bake in hot oven, 400°F., 8 to 12 minutes. Makes 56. Store airtight.

COCONUT JUMBLES

½ cup soft butter	1 teaspoon baking
½ cup sugar	powder
1 tablespoon milk	¼ teaspoon salt
1 egg	1 cup flaked
1¼ cups sifted	coconut
flour	

Cream butter; add sugar, milk, and egg; beat until light. Add sifted dry ingredients; mix well. Chill overnight. Roll on floured board to ⅛″ thickness; cut with floured 2½″ doughnut cutter; sprinkle with coconut. Bake in moderate oven, 375°F., 10 to 12 minutes. Makes 3 dozen. Store airtight.

CHOCOLATE TOPPERS

⅔ cup soft butter	1½ cups sifted
1 cup sugar	flour
1 cup finely ground	½ teaspoon salt
walnuts	1½ cups semisweet
1 teaspoon vanilla	chocolate pieces

Cream butter; add sugar; beat until light. Add nuts, vanilla, flour, and salt. (Mixture will be dry.) Roll to ⅛″ thickness between 2 sheets of waxed paper. Cut with floured, small, fancy cookie cutter. Bake in hot oven, 400°F., 8 to 10 minutes. Cool. Melt chocolate, and spread on cookies. Makes about 60.

JELLY TEACAKES

4 cups sifted flour	4 egg yolks
1 cup soft sweet	2 teaspoons vanilla
butter	extract
Sugar	1 egg white
¼ teaspoon salt	½ cup finely
2 tablespoons	chopped nuts
heavy cream	Currant jelly

Mix flour, butter, 1¼ cups sugar, and remaining ingredients, except last 3. Chill several hours. Roll out on floured board to ⅛″ thickness. Cut with floured 2″ scalloped cutter. Cut holes in centers of half of cookies with tip of a pastry tube or with a thimble. Brush these with slightly beaten egg white; sprinkle with sugar and nuts. Bake all cookies in moderate oven, 350°F., about 10 minutes. Cool; spread jelly on plain cookies, putting a little more in the centers. Top with remaining cookies. Makes about 4 dozen. Store unfilled cookies airtight.

"Sugar and spice and all things nice."
ROBERT SOUTHEY

SHORTBREAD

6 cups sifted flour	1 pound soft butter
1 cup sugar	or margarine
	2 egg yolks

Mix first 3 ingredients very thoroughly with hands. Add egg yolks, one at a time, kneading dough well after each addition. Divide in 8 parts, and roll each into a square or circle about ½″ thick. Prick with fork. Bake in moderate oven, 350°F., 15 minutes. Reduce heat to 300°F., and bake about 30 minutes longer. Cut in eighths, and return to oven until edges are browned. Makes 64. Store airtight.

NUT SHORTBREAD

1 cup soft butter	2½ cups sifted
or margarine	flour
½ cup sugar	½ cup chopped
⅛ teaspoon salt	nuts

Mix all ingredients thoroughly with hands; chill. Roll to ½″ thickness. Cut with 1½″ cookie cutters, and bake in slow oven, 300°F., 20 to 25 minutes. Makes about 2 dozen. Store airtight.

SAND TARTS

½ cup soft butter	1 teaspoon baking
Sugar	powder
2 eggs, separated	1½ cups sifted flour
1 tablespoon milk	15 unblanched
½ teaspoon	almonds, split
vanilla extract	¼ teaspoon
½ teaspoon salt	cinnamon

Cream butter; add 1 cup sugar, egg yolks, milk, and vanilla; beat until light. Add sifted dry ingredients; mix well. Chill at least 3 hours. Roll dough very thin; cut with 3″ star cookie cutter. Put on greased cookie sheets; put a split almond on each cookie. Brush with unbeaten whites; sprinkle with 1 tablespoon sugar and the cinnamon. Bake in moderate oven, 375°F., about 8 minutes. Makes 2½ dozen.

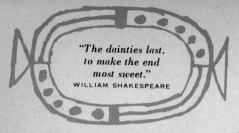

*"The dainties last.
to make the end
most sweet."*
WILLIAM SHAKESPEARE

FILLED OATMEAL COOKIES

1 cup soft butter or margarine	2 cups sifted flour
1 cup sugar	¼ teaspoon soda
1 teaspoon vanilla extract	¾ teaspoon salt
2 cups rolled oats, ground very fine	½ cup buttermilk Date-Nut Filling

Cream butter with sugar and vanilla. Add oats and sifted flour, soda, and salt alternately with buttermilk; mix well. Chill several hours. Roll very thin; cut with small cookie cutters. Bake in hot oven, 400°F., 8 to 10 minutes. Put together in pairs with Filling the day cookies are served. (Or fill, wrap, and freeze.) Makes about 7 dozen small finished cookies. Store airtight.

Date-Nut Filling: Cut 1 pound pitted dates in small pieces. Put in saucepan with 1½ cups sugar, ½ teaspoon salt, 2 teaspoons grated lemon rind, and 2 cups water. Bring to boil, and cook 10 minutes, or until thickened, stirring occasionally. Add 2 cups finely chopped nuts, and cool.

DROPPED

HERMITS

½ cup soft butter	1 teaspoon cinnamon
1 cup brown sugar, packed	¼ teaspoon each cloves and nutmeg
2 eggs	2 cups seeded raisins, chopped
2 cups sifted cake flour	½ cup chopped nuts
1 teaspoon baking powder	
½ teaspoon salt	

Cream butter; add sugar and eggs; beat until light. Add sifted dry ingredients, raisins, and nuts; mix well. Drop by teaspoonfuls onto greased cookie sheets; bake in moderate oven, 350°F., about 10 minutes. Makes about 4 dozen. Store airtight.

BROWN-EDGED COOKIES

1 cup soft butter or margarine	2 eggs
⅔ cup sugar	1½ cups sifted flour
1 teaspoon vanilla	¼ teaspoon salt

Cream butter; add sugar, vanilla, and eggs, one at a time, beating well after each addition. Add flour and salt; mix well. Drop by half-teaspoonfuls onto greased cookie sheets. Bake in moderate oven, 350°F., about 10 minutes. Makes about 3 dozen. Store airtight.

BUTTER-NUT WAFERS

½ cup soft butter	¾ cup sifted flour
1 cup light-brown sugar, packed	1 teaspoon baking powder
1 teaspoon vanilla extract	½ teaspoon salt
1 egg	½ cup finely chopped nuts

Cream butter; add sugar, vanilla, and egg; beat until light. Add sifted dry ingredients and nuts. Drop by scant teaspoonfuls onto cookie sheets. Bake in hot oven, 400°F., 5 minutes. Cool ½ minute. Remove to racks. Makes 96.

MELT-IN-THE-MOUTH COOKIES

½ cup butter	¾ cup sifted flour
1 cup light-brown sugar, packed	1 teaspoon baking powder
1 teaspoon vanilla extract	½ teaspoon salt
1 egg	½ cup finely chopped nuts

Cream butter; add sugar, vanilla, and egg; beat until light. Add sifted dry ingredients and nuts. Drop by scant teaspoonfuls onto cookie sheets. Bake in hot oven, 400°F., about 5 minutes. Cool ½ minute. Remove to racks. Makes about 8 dozen. Store airtight.

CHERRY-COCONUT MACAROONS

1 egg white	1 can flaked coconut
⅛ teaspoon salt	½ teaspoon vanilla
½ cup sugar	Candied cherries

Beat egg white with salt until foamy. Add sugar, 2 tablespoons at a time, and beat until mixture will stand in stiff peaks. Fold in coconut and vanilla. Drop by teaspoonfuls onto greased cookie sheets. Put a cherry half in center of each cookie. Bake in 350°F. oven 12 to 15 minutes. Makes 16.

COCONUT KISSES

½ teaspoon salt
4 egg whites
1¼ cups very fine
granulated sugar
1 teaspoon vanilla
extract
2 cups flaked
coconut

Add salt to egg whites, and beat until stiff, but not dry. Add sugar, 1 tablespoon at a time, beating until granules are dissolved. Add vanilla and coconut, mixing lightly. Drop by teaspoonfuls onto ungreased brown paper on cookie sheets. Bake in moderate oven, 350°F., about 20 minutes. Slip paper onto wet table or board. Let stand 1 minute. Loosen kisses with spatula; remove to wire racks. Makes about 4 dozen.

OATMEAL DROP COOKIES

½ cup soft butter
or margarine
1 cup sugar
1 egg
1½ cups sifted flour
½ teaspoon salt
½ teaspoon soda
¾ teaspoon
cinnamon
½ teaspoon each
cloves, allspice
1¾ cups quick-
cooking rolled
oats
⅔ cup raisins, cut
½ cup chopped
nuts
⅓ cup milk

Cream butter; add sugar and egg. Beat until light. Sift flour with salt, soda, and spices; add oats, raisins, and nuts. Add to first mixture alternately with milk, and mix well. Drop by teaspoonfuls onto greased cookie sheets. Bake in moderate oven, 350°F., about 15 minutes. Makes 3 dozen. Store airtight.

PINE-NUT COOKIES

4 eggs
1½ cups
granulated sugar
½ teaspoon grated
lemon rind
Few drops oil
of anise
2¼ cups sifted
flour
¼ teaspoon salt
Confectioners'
sugar
Pine nuts

Put eggs and granulated sugar in top of double boiler over hot water. Beat with rotary beater until mixture is lukewarm. Remove from water; beat until foaming and cool. Add flavorings, and fold in flour and salt. Drop by teaspoonfuls onto greased and floured cookie sheets. Sprinkle with confectioners' sugar and nuts. Let stand 10 minutes; bake in 375°F. oven about 10 minutes. Makes about 60.

MINCEMEAT HERMITS

1 cup sifted flour
¼ teaspoon each
soda, salt, and
nutmeg
½ teaspoon
cinnamon
⅓ cup soft butter
or margarine
⅓ cup dark-brown
sugar, packed
1 egg
½ cup mincemeat
1 tablespoon sour
cream
Vanilla Glaze

Sift flour, soda, salt, and spices. Cream butter and sugar. Add egg; beat until light. Add dry ingredients, mincemeat, and cream; mix well. Drop by teaspoonfuls onto cookie sheets. Bake in hot oven, 400°F., 10 to 12 minutes. Remove to racks, and spread with **Vanilla Glaze:** Mix well 1½ cups sifted confectioners' sugar, dash salt, 1 teaspoon vanilla, 2 tablespoons melted butter, and enough cream, about 2 tablespoons, to make a smooth paste. Makes about 3 dozen. Store airtight.

FRUIT DROPS

1 cup soft butter
or margarine
1 cup light-brown
sugar, packed
2 eggs, slightly
beaten
1 teaspoon vanilla
extract
3 cups sifted flour
½ teaspoon soda
¼ teaspoon salt
⅓ cup hot water
1 cup each chopped
dates, seeded
raisins, and nuts

Cream butter; add sugar, eggs, and vanilla; beat until light. Add sifted dry ingredients alternately with water; mix well. Stir in fruits and nuts. Drop by teaspoonfuls onto greased cookie sheets, and bake in hot oven, 400°F., 10 to 12 minutes. Makes about 4 dozen. Store airtight.

FUDGE WAFERS

1 cup soft butter	1 teaspoon vanilla
1 cup sugar	extract
1 egg	1½ cups sifted
2 squares unsweet-	flour
ened chocolate,	¼ teaspoon salt
melted	Brazil-nut slices

Cream butter; add sugar and egg; beat until light. Add chocolate and vanilla; blend. Add dry ingredients; mix well. Drop by scant teaspoonfuls onto cookie sheets. Press a nut slice in center of each. Bake in hot oven, 400°F., about 10 minutes. Makes about 7 dozen.

PEANUT-OATMEAL COOKIES

1 cup soft butter	1½ cups sifted flour
1 cup granulated	½ teaspoon soda
sugar	3 cups quick-
1 cup brown sugar,	cooking rolled
packed	oats
2 eggs	½ pound salted
1 teaspoon vanilla	Spanish peanuts

Cream butter; add sugars, eggs, and vanilla; beat until light. Add remaining ingredients; mix well. Drop by tea-spoonfuls onto greased cookie sheets. Bake in moderate oven, 375°F., about 10 minutes. Makes 12 dozen.

SPICE DROP COOKIES

½ cup shortening	1½ teaspoons
½ cup brown	baking powder
sugar, packed	2 teaspoons
2 eggs	cinnamon
1 cup chopped	¼ teaspoon each
seeded raisins	cloves, allspice
or pitted dates	1 tablespoon
1½ cups sifted flour	molasses
½ teaspoon salt	2 tablespoons milk

Cream shortening; add sugar, and eggs, one at a time, beating well after each addition. Add raisins, and sifted dry ingredients alternately with molasses and milk; mix well. Drop by teaspoon-fuls onto greased cookie sheets; bake in moderate oven, 375°F., 10 to 12 minutes. Makes about 3 dozen.

" 'Tis the Dessert that graces all the Feast, For an ill end disparages the rest."
WILLIAM KING

SESAME-SEED WAFERS

¾ cup soft butter	1¼ cups sifted
or margarine	flour
1½ cups light-	¼ teaspoon bakin
brown sugar,	powder
packed	½ cup sesame
2 eggs	seed, toasted in
1 teaspoon vanilla	325°F. oven

Cream butter; add sugar, eggs, an vanilla; beat until light. Add remain ing ingredients; mix well. Drop by tea spoonfuls onto greased cookie sheets Bake in moderate oven, 325°F., 1 minutes. Makes about 5 dozen.

SHAPED

PECAN DAINTIES

1 cup soft butter	1 tablespoon
½ cup sugar	water
2 cups sifted flour	2 cups pecans,
1 teaspoon vanilla	ground
extract	Pecan halves

Cream butter and sugar until light; add remaining ingredients, except pecan halves, and mix well. Chill until firm Shape in ¾" balls. Top each with a pecan half. Bake in moderate oven 325°F., 20 minutes. Makes 72 to 96.

Snow Mounds: Omit pecan halves, and roll warm baked cookies in very fine granulated sugar.

OATMEAL COOKIES

1½ cups brown	¾ teaspoon vanilla
sugar, firmly	extract
packed	1½ cups sifted
¾ cup melted lard	flour
6 tablespoons	¾ teaspoon soda
buttermilk	3 cups quick-
½ teaspoon salt	cooking rolled
	oats

Combine ingredients in order given, mixing thoroughly. Shape in small balls about 1" in diameter, and put on greased cookie sheets. Flatten each cookie to ⅛" thickness by pressing with a wet spatula. Bake in moderate oven, 375°F., 10 to 12 minutes. Makes 5 to 6 dozen. Store airtight.

RUM BALLS

cup finely crushed vanilla wafers	2 tablespoons cocoa
cup confectioners' sugar	2 tablespoons light corn syrup
½ cups chopped pecans	¼ cup rum
	½ cup fine granulated sugar

Mix crumbs, confectioners' sugar, 1 cup nuts, and cocoa. Add corn syrup and rum, and mix well. Shape in 1" balls. Roll half in granulated sugar, and remainder in the ½ cup nuts. Makes about 36. Store airtight.

GOLDEN NUGGETS

½ cup soft butter or margarine	½ teaspoon vanilla extract
⅓ cup sugar	2 teaspoons grated orange rind
1 egg	2 tablespoons orange juice
1¼ cups sifted flour	1½ cups coarsely chopped walnuts or pecans
¼ teaspoon salt	
¼ teaspoon cinnamon	

Cream butter; add sugar and egg; beat until light. Add sifted flour, salt, and cinnamon, and remaining ingredients, except nuts; mix well. Chill, and shape into 1" balls. Roll in nuts. Bake in moderate oven, 325°F., about 20 minutes. Makes about 2 dozen nuggets.

GLAZED ALMOND COOKIES

1 cup soft butter or margarine	¾ cup chopped blanched almonds
1 cup sugar	2⅔ cups sifted cake flour
½ teaspoon each almond and vanilla extracts	½ teaspoon salt
2 eggs, separated	48 whole almonds, unblanched

Cream butter; add sugar, flavorings, and egg yolks, one at a time, beating after each addition. Add chopped nuts, flour, and salt; mix well. Roll into balls about 1" in diameter; dip in unbeaten egg whites, and put, 2" apart, on greased cookie sheets. Flatten each ball by pressing thumb into center, making a depression. Put an almond in each depression. Bake in moderate oven, 350°F., about 10 minutes. Makes 4 dozen. Store airtight.

PEANUT-BUTTER FINGERS

½ cup soft butter	1 egg
½ cup peanut butter	½ cup finely cut raisins
2 teaspoons grated orange rind	1 cup sifted flour
½ cup brown sugar, packed	¼ teaspoon soda
½ cup granulated sugar	½ teaspoon baking powder
	½ teaspoon salt

Cream butter, peanut butter, and rind. Add sugars and egg; beat until light. Add remaining ingredients; mix well. Chill. Shape in rolls 2" long and ⅜" in diameter. Score lengthwise with tines of fork. Bake in moderate oven, 350°F., about 12 minutes. Makes 72.

PRESSED

BRAZIL-NUT COOKIES

⅔ cup soft butter or margarine	2 tablespoons orange juice
1 cup sugar	⅔ cup Brazil nuts, ground
1 egg	2 cups sifted flour
½ teaspoon rum flavoring	½ teaspoon baking powder
1 teaspoon grated orange rind	¾ teaspoon salt

Cream butter and sugar; add egg, rum flavoring, orange rind and juice; beat until light. Add nuts and sifted dry ingredients; mix well. Force through spritz gun or cookie press onto cookie sheets. Bake in hot oven, 400°F., 8 to 10 minutes. Makes about 5 dozen.

LEMON-CHEESE COOKIES

1 cup soft butter
    or margarine
1 package (3
    ounces) cream
    cheese, softened
1 cup sugar
1 egg yolk
½ teaspoon lemon
    flavoring

1 teaspoon grated
    lemon rind
2½ cups sifted flour
½ teaspoon salt
Colored sugar,
    cinnamon sugar,
    or finely chopped
    nuts

Cream butter, cheese, and sugar; add egg yolk and flavorings; beat until light. Add sifted flour and salt; mix well. Force through spritz gun or cookie press onto cookie sheets. Decorate as desired. Bake in moderate oven, 350°F., about 15 minutes. Makes about 6 dozen. Store airtight.

BLACK-EYED SUSANS

½ cup soft butter
    or margarine
½ cup granulated
    sugar
½ cup brown
    sugar, packed
1 egg
1 teaspoon vanilla
    extract

1 cup moist smooth
    peanut butter
1½ cups sifted
    flour
½ teaspoon soda
½ teaspoon salt
Semisweet
    chocolate pieces

Cream butter and sugars; add egg, vanilla, and peanut butter; beat until light. Add sifted dry ingredients, and mix well. Force through spritz gun or cookie press onto cookie sheets, using a disk that will make flower designs. Put a chocolate piece in center of each. Bake in moderate oven, 350°F., about 15 minutes. Makes about 60.

(Store cookies airtight in separate container.)

SLICED

BLACK AND WHITE PINWHEELS

½ cup soft butter
½ cup sugar
1 egg yolk
1 teaspoon vanilla
1½ cups sifted flour
¼ teaspoon salt

½ teaspoon
    baking powder
3 tablespoons milk
1 square unsweet-
    ened chocolate,
    melted

Cream butter; add sugar, egg yolk, and vanilla; cream until light. Add sifted dry ingredients and milk; mix well. Divide dough, and add chocolate to half. Roll each half between sheets of floured waxed paper to form a 10"x 9" rectangle. Remove top papers, and roll dough up tightly to form a roll about 2" in diameter. Wrap in paper, and chill several hours. Cut in ⅛" slices and bake in 375°F. oven 8 to 10 minutes. Makes about 4 dozen.

BUTTERSCOTCH COOKIES

Cream 1 cup butter; add ½ cup each granulated and light-brown sugar. Add 1 teaspoon vanilla, and 2 eggs, one at a time, beating well after each. Add 2¾ cups sifted flour, ½ teaspoon each salt and soda; ½ cup finely chopped nuts. Chill 2 hours. Shape in 2 loaves 2" square. Wrap in waxed paper; chill overnight. Slice ⅛" thick. Bake on sheets in hot oven, 400°F., 6 to 8 minutes. Remove to racks while hot. Makes about 6 dozen. Store airtight.

PRUNE COOKIES

Cream 1 cup soft butter, 1 cup packed brown sugar, ½ cup granulated sugar. Add 2 eggs, one at a time; beat after each. Add 1 tablespoon vinegar, 1 teaspoon vanilla, 1 cup chopped cooked prunes, 4 cups sifted flour, 1 teaspoon each soda and salt, 1 cup chopped nuts. Shape in 3 rolls 2" in diameter. Wrap in waxed paper; chill overnight. Cut in ⅛" slices; bake in hot oven, 400°F., 12 minutes. Makes about 12 dozen. Store airtight.

The art of pastry making goes back some centuries. It flourished first in Italy, and Catherine de Medici is supposed to have introduced it to France when she brought Italian chefs to that country. The French took to fancy pastries with delight, and by the late eighteenth century they were creating such masterpieces of decorated confection that pastry chefs of the day took special training in architecture. Today, individual pastries and creamy little pastries for dessert have become as important to the hostess as hors d'oeuvres. The modern housewife and hostess need not be a student of architecture to create delectable tidbits for her guests. Here are pastries as simple as you choose, and also elaborate confections on which you may lavish your creative artistry. Just remember that one of the major charms of this type of food is in its size. Keep your party pastries small and dainty.

PARTY PASTRIES

FLAKY FRENCH PASTRY

Refrigerate it, in
moistureproof paper, until you need it.

2 cups plus 2 tablespoons sifted flour	2 egg yolks
¾ teaspoon salt	¼ cup light cream
1 cup soft butter or margarine	2 tablespoons dry white wine

Sift flour and salt into bowl. Cut in butter. Add combined egg yolks, cream, and wine; mix with fork until blended and smooth. Knead lightly in bowl until bubbles begin to appear on the surface of dough. Cover, and chill 1 hour. Roll to ⅛" thickness on floured board. Fold twice lengthwise, and then twice crosswise. Chill 15 minutes. Roll, and fold twice more.

MAIDS OF HONOR

Tarts with cherry-jam filling and, on
top, a piece of decorated cake.

⅓ cup butter or margarine	Frosting
1 box pastry mix	Food coloring
Cherry jam	Candied violets, colored candies
1 small box white cake mix	

Cut butter into pastry mix. Add just enough of the liquid indicated on pastry-mix label to hold dough together. (Chill if necessary.) Roll out to ⅛" thickness, and cut in 24 rounds with 3½" cutter. Fit into 2½" muffin-pan sections. Put about 1 teaspoon jam into each. Prepare cake mix, and put a spoonful of batter on jam. Bake in moderate oven, 350°F., 20 to 25 minutes. Cool in pans, and remove to racks. Spread tops with tinted and flavored frosting. Decorate. Makes 2 dozen.

DEVONSHIRE BERRY TARTS

The filling is cream cheese.

Use half the recipe for Tart Pastry, page 267, substituting 1 egg yolk for the whole egg. Add just enough milk to hold mixture together. Prepare 6 tart shells. Wash, and hull 1 quart strawberries; put half through sieve. Add enough water to sieved berries to make 1½ cups. Mix ¼ cup cornstarch, dash salt, and ¾ cup sugar. Stir in sieved berries. Cook, stirring, until thickened. Cool. Mix 1 package (3 ounces) cream cheese with 2 tablespoons milk; spread in tart shells. Cover with whole berries, tips up. Top with sieved-berry glaze. Chill.

LINCOLN LOGS

Filling is brown sugar and cream.

2 eggs	¾ teaspoon baking powder
⅔ cup granulated sugar	¼ teaspoon salt
1½ teaspoons lemon juice	¼ cup hot milk
Grated rind ½ lemon	Confectioners' sugar
⅔ cup sifted cake flour	Filling
	Chocolate frosting

Beat eggs until very thick and cream-colored. Gradually add granulated sugar, and beat until blended. Stir in lemon juice and rind. Fold in next 3 ingredients. Then stir in milk. Pour into waxed-paper-lined 15"x 10" pan. Bake in hot oven, 400°F., about 15 minutes. Turn out on cloth sprinkled with confectioners' sugar, and peel off paper. Cut in half crosswise, and roll up each half in cloth from end. Remove cloths, and cool rolls. **Filling:** Mix 1 cup heavy cream, ⅔ cup brown sugar, and ½ teaspoon vanilla; chill 1 hour. Whip until stiff. Unroll cakes, and spread half of filling inside each. Reroll, and spread top with frosting. Run tines of fork lengthwise. Chill, and slice. Serves 10.

FROSTED FINGERS

You top them with petit-four frosting.

Bake a cake in 13"x9"x2" pan. Cool; cut in thirds; frost each with different tinted Petit-Four Frosting, page 265; mark off in 3"x 1" fingers, scoring through frosting. Decorate. Before serving, cut through scorings.

PETITS FOURS

Dainty, pretty pastries made from firm-textured white or yellow cake.

Make cake with mix or use bought poundcake or other firm-textured white or yellow cake. Cut slices about ¾" thick. Then cut cake in shapes with small cutters. Put together sandwich-fashion with jam or jelly between. To frost and decorate, put petits fours on rack with tray underneath. Spoon Frosting (see below) over cakes until coated, scraping frosting up from tray to re-use. When firm, decorate, using a pastry tube, with Decorating Frosting (below).

PETIT-FOUR FROSTING

1 cup granulated sugar	½ cup water
1/16 teaspoon cream of tartar	Sifted confectioners' sugar
⅛ teaspoon salt	Flavoring
	Food coloring

Bring to boil all ingredients, except last 3; cook to 226°F. on a candy thermometer. Cool to lukewarm (110°F.). Gradually add sugar, and beat until smooth and thick enough to almost hold its shape. Add flavoring. Divide into 4 parts. Leave one part white, and tint others pink, yellow, green.

DECORATING FROSTING

Mix until smooth two parts confectioners' sugar to one part of butter or margarine. Flavor, and color as desired. Or buy tubes of colored frostings.

DATE-CHEESE ROLL-UPS

1 cup butter or margarine	2 cups sifted flour
½ pound cream cheese	¼ teaspoon salt
	Confectioners' sugar
	Pitted dates

Cream butter and cheese together. Blend in flour and salt. Chill several hours, or until firm enough to roll. Roll to ⅛" thickness on board sprinkled with confectioners' sugar. Cut in 3"x 1" strips with pastry wheel. Put a date in center of each strip, and roll up. Put, folded side down, on cookie sheets. Bake in moderate oven, 375°F., about 15 minutes. If desired, sprinkle with confectioners' sugar. Makes about 8 dozen. Store airtight.

ORANGE TARTLETS

The filling: marmalade topped with nuts.

⅔ cup vegetable shortening	5 to 6 tablespoons orange juice
2 cups sifted flour	Orange marmalade
1 teaspoon salt	Chopped nuts
2 teaspoons grated orange rind	

Cut shortening into flour and salt. Add rind, and enough orange juice to hold mixture together. Roll out tiny pieces of dough to ⅛" thickness on floured board. Fit pieces over backs of tiny scalloped tart pans. Put on cookie sheet, and prick bottoms with fork. Bake in hot oven, 425°F., about 10 minutes. Cool slightly, and remove gently from pans. Cool; put marmalade in each. Sprinkle with nuts. Makes 48.

TEA TARTLETS

A custardy lemon-and-orange filling.

2 eggs, beaten	Juice 1 large lemon
¾ cup sugar	2 tablespoons butter
⅛ teaspoon salt	Rich pastry
Grated rind ½ orange	

Mix all ingredients, except pastry, in small double boiler. Cook over boiling water, stirring, until thickened. Cool. Line tiny scalloped tart pans with pastry. Bake in 450°F. oven about 12 minutes. Cool; remove from pans. Fill just before serving. Makes 24.

BANANA-AMBROSIA TARTS

Vanilla pudding topped with fruit.

Prepare 1 box vanilla-pudding mix with 2 cups milk as directed on the label. Cool, and pour into eight 4" baked tart shells. Peel 4 oranges, and remove sections. Just before serving, slice 2 or 3 ripe bananas. Arrange oranges and bananas on pudding in shells. Garnish with flaked coconut and maraschino cherries. Makes 8.

CREAM PUFFS

Fill them with vanilla, chocolate, or fluffy cream filling.

1 cup water	4 large eggs, beaten
½ cup butter or margarine	Cream Filling
¼ teaspoon salt	Confectioners'
1 cup sifted flour	sugar

In saucepan heat water, butter, and salt to full rolling boil. Reduce heat, and quickly stir in flour, mixing vigorously with wooden spoon until mixture leaves the sides of the pan in a ball. Remove from heat, and add eggs in 6 additions, beating after each addition until mixture is very smooth. (An electric mixer at a low speed makes this procedure easier.) Drop dough from metal mixing spoon onto greased baking sheets, forming mounds 3" apart. Bake in hot oven, 400°F., 40 to 45 minutes. Remove at once to racks, and cool away from drafts. Split, and fill with desired Cream Filling (see right). Sprinkle with confectioners' sugar, or frost as desired. Store in refrigerator. Makes 12 large or 16 medium cream puffs.

PETITS PUFFS

Omit frosting, use nonsweet filling, and you can serve as appetizers.

Use Cream Puff recipe. Level off 1¼ measuring-teaspoons dough onto greased baking sheet. Then, using this amount as a guide for size, drop remaining dough from ordinary teaspoon. Bake in hot oven, 400°F., about 20 minutes. Fill, and frost. Makes 8 dozen.

VANILLA CREAM FILLING

3 cups milk	½ teaspoon salt
¾ cup sugar	3 eggs, beaten
6 tablespoons cornstarch	1 tablespoon butter
	2 teaspoons vanilla

Scald milk in top of double boiler over boiling water. Mix sugar, cornstarch, and salt. Stir into milk. Cook, stirring until thick. Cover; cook 10 minutes longer. Add small amount of mixture to eggs; return to double boiler; cook 5 minutes. Add butter. Put in bowl, and sprinkle small amount of sugar over top to prevent skin from forming. Chill; add vanilla.

Chocolate Cream Filling: Use above recipe. Melt 3 squares unsweetened chocolate in milk, and beat until smooth. Proceed as directed above.

Fluffy Cream Filling: Use either recipe above, reducing milk to 2½ cups. Just before using, fold ½ cup heavy cream, whipped, into chilled mixture.

ÉCLAIRS

After giving them a cream filling, you frost the tops with chocolate.

Use Cream Puff recipe (left), forcing mixture through pastry tube; or shape with spatula into 16 fingers, 4" x 1". Bake as for Cream Puffs. Fill with Vanilla Cream Filling (above), and top with thin chocolate frosting. Makes 16.

WALNUT CRESCENTS

Pastries filled with coarse walnut paste.

Use pastry dough from the recipe for Hungarian Cheese Pastries, page 267, adding 1 teaspoon grated lemon rind. Cut chilled dough in 24 small pieces. Roll each piece out on board sprinkled with confectioners' sugar, to form thin rounds. Spread Walnut Filling almost to edge. Roll up, and twist ends slightly to form crescents. Put on cookie sheet, and brush with beaten egg. Bake in moderate oven, 375°F., 15 to 20 minutes. Cool, and sift confectioners' sugar over top.

Filling: Grind coarsely 1½ cups walnuts. Stir in 2 egg whites, ⅓ cup sugar, dash salt, 1 tablespoon milk.

PASTRY FOR TARTS

*If you make this ahead, keep it
chilled until you're ready to use it.*

⅔ cup soft shortening	¼ cup sugar
2 cups sifted flour	½ teaspoon salt
½ teaspoon baking powder	1 egg, beaten with 2 tablespoons milk

Cut shortening into sifted dry ingredients. With fork, lightly mix in egg and milk. Chill until ready to use.

PEACH CREAM TARTS

*You top the cream filling with a
peach half and peach preserves.*

Use above recipe. Divide dough in 12 parts. Roll each piece to form a round 4½" in diameter. Fit over back of 3½" tart pans, or trim edges with pastry wheel, and fit inside 3½" foil pans. Bake in hot oven, 425°F., 10 minutes. Cool, and remove from pans. Prepare, and chill Vanilla Cream Filling, page 266. Before serving, fill shells, and top each with a small, well-drained peach half. Spread with peach preserves; put chopped nuts around edge.

GLAZED CHERRY TARTS

*Red sour cherries and cherry syrup
go on top of the cream filling.*

Prepare tart shells as above and Vanilla Cream Filling, page 266, with 1 teaspoon vanilla and ½ teaspoon almond extract in place of 2 teaspoons vanilla. Drain 1 can (1 pound) pitted red sour cherries, reserving ¾ cup juice. In saucepan mix ¼ cup sugar, 2 tablespoons cornstarch, ⅛ teaspoon salt. Add cherry juice; cook, stirring, until thickened. Add cherries and 1 tablespoon lemon juice. Add red food coloring to tint desired shade. Cool. Before serving, fill tart shells, and top with cherry mixture. Makes 12.

STRAWBERRY ICE CREAM TARTS

Each is topped with a fresh berry.

Prepare tart shells as in Peach Cream Tarts. Just before serving, fill shells with strawberry ice cream, using 1 quart for 12 tarts. Top with a fresh strawberry with cap and stem.

DOUBLE-CHOCOLATE TARTS

*Chocolate filling plus chocolate
sauce and whipped cream.*

Prepare tart shells as in Peach Cream Tarts. Make Chocolate Filling, page 266. Chill. Before serving, fill sheets; dribble with chocolate sauce; top with sweetened whipped cream.

HUNGARIAN CHEESE PASTRIES

The filling: lemony cottage cheese.

½ cup plus 1 tablespoon soft butter or margarine	Heavy cream (about 1½ tablespoons)
1⅔ cups sifted flour	Filling Confectioners' sugar
⅛ teaspoon salt	Black-currant or other jelly
1 egg yolk, beaten	

Pastry: Cut butter into flour and salt. Add egg yolk, mixing with fork. Add just enough cream to hold mixture together. Chill overnight. Roll about one-third to form an 8" square a little more than ⅛" thick. Put in 8"x 8"x 2" pan. Roll more dough to form strips about 1" wide. Fit around sides of pan. Pour in Filling, and even top. Roll out remaining dough; cut in ¾" strips. Put on Filling, lattice-fashion. Bake in 350°F. oven about 40 minutes. Cool on rack. Just before serving, sift confectioners' sugar over top of each pastry. Cut in 2" squares, and garnish with jelly. Makes 16.

Filling: Press 1 pound dry cottage cheese through fine sieve. Add ¼ cup sugar, grated rind ½ lemon, 2 egg yolks, 2 tablespoons melted butter. Beat 4 egg whites stiff with ¼ teaspoon salt. Fold into mixture.

APRICOT CRESCENTS

They have a cream-cheese pastry.

½ cup soft butter or margarine	1 tablespoon cold water
6 ounces cream cheese, softened	Apricot preserves Minced nuts
¾ cup sifted flour	Confectioners' sugar
⅛ teaspoon salt	

Cut butter and cheese into flour and salt. Add water, and mix lightly with fork until blended. Chill until firm. Cut in 24 pieces, and roll each piece very thin on floured board, to form 2½" to 3" squares. Spread each with apricot preserves, and sprinkle with nuts. Roll up from one corner, and bend ends in slightly to form crescents. Put folded side down on cookie sheets, and bake in very hot oven, 450°F., about 10 minutes. Sift confectioners' sugar over cooled crescents. Makes 24.

ORANGE-PLUM TWISTS

You can serve them warm or cold.

¼ cup soft butter or margarine	1 egg
2 cups biscuit mix	⅓ cup heavy cream
2 tablespoons granulated sugar	½ cup damson plum preserves
1 teaspoon grated orange rind	Confectioners' sugar

Cut butter into biscuit mix. Stir in granulated sugar and rind. Beat egg and cream until blended; with fork, stir into first mixture. Put on floured board, and knead a few times. Roll out to form a rectangle 15"x 3". Spread with preserves, and fold twice lengthwise to form a 15"x 1" rectangle. Cut crosswise in 1" strips. Twist each strip twice to form a spiral. Put on foil-covered cookie sheet, and bake in very hot oven, 450°F., 10 to 12 minutes. Sift confectioners' sugar over warm twists. Makes 15.

BANBURY TARTS DE LUXE

Raisins, currants, candied pineapple, dates, and nuts in pastry envelopes.

¼ cup each currants, seedless raisins, chopped candied pineapple	2 eggs, slightly beaten
	2 tablespoons flour
	¼ teaspoon salt
½ cup chopped dates	Grated rind and juice 1 lemon
½ cup chopped nuts	Flaky French Pastry, page 264
1 cup light-brown sugar, packed	1 egg yolk
	1 tablespoon milk

Mix well all ingredients, except last 3. Roll pastry to ⅛" thickness, and cut in 4" squares. Put about 1 tablespoon of the mixture in the center of each square, and fold the corners to meet in center. Brush with egg yolk, beaten with milk; bake in 450°F. oven 12 to 15 minutes. Fills about 24.

COCONUT-DATE TARTS

The filling is dates and coconut, plus cherries, nuts, and preserves.

Make and bake as for Banbury Tarts, substituting the following filling: Mix well ¾ cup flaked coconut, ¼ cup each chopped candied cherries and brown sugar, ¼ cup pineapple or apricot preserves, ⅓ cup chopped nuts, ¾ cup chopped dates, 1 tablespoon flour, 1 egg, ¼ teaspoon salt, grated rind and juice 1 lemon. Fills about 18.

CHERRY-COCONUT PASTRIES

Cherry filling is baked on a sweet pastry base.

1 box pastry mix	1½ teaspoons vanilla extract
2 tablespoons sugar	
3 eggs, beaten	½ cup flaked coconut
1 cup brown sugar, packed	½ cup chopped nuts
½ teaspoon baking powder	½ cup chopped maraschino cherries
2 tablespoons flour	

Prepare pastry as directed on the label, adding sugar. Press into bottom and on sides of 9"x 9"x 2" pan. Bake in hot oven, 425°F., 10 minutes. Mix remaining ingredients; pour into crust. Bake in 325°F. oven 35 minutes. Cool; cut in 3"x 1½" bars. Makes 18.

PUFF PASTE

This takes time and trouble,
but it makes delectable pastries.

1 pound sweet butter	1 tablespoon lemon juice
4 cups flour	1¼ cups cold water (about)
1 teaspoon salt	

1. Shape the butter into a brick about 3″x 5″x ¾″.

2. Roll butter in 3 tablespoons of the flour, coating all sides. Wrap in waxed paper, and chill.

3. Put remaining flour in a large bowl. Make a well in the center. Add salt and lemon juice. Gradually begin to add water, only enough to make a rather firm, slightly sticky dough.

4. Knead dough thoroughly on floured board, 20 minutes. Pound it on the table at intervals to achieve the right consistency. It should be very elastic and smooth. Form it into a ball; place on well-floured cloth.

5. With a rolling pin, make the ball of dough into the shape of a four-leaf clover. Roll ends out, leaving the center thick. Well rolled, the dough will have a thick cushion in the center and 4 thinner "petals."

6. Put brick of butter in the center of the four-leaf clover. Fold "petals" over dough by stretching them over butter and sealing all the edges so that the butter is completely enclosed. Wrap in waxed paper, and chill for 20 minutes.

7. On a well-floured cloth, gently roll out the block of dough as evenly as possible into a rectangle slightly less than ⅓″ thick, and about 3 times as long as it is wide. Do not roll over ends in the length, but when dough is long enough, roll it lightly in the width, flattening ends to same thickness as the rest of the dough.

8. Fold dough into thirds, making 3 layers, and chill for 20 minutes. Turn folded sides toward you, and roll out dough, and fold again into thirds. (Rolling, folding, and turning is called a "turn.") It is necessary to make a total of 6 turns, after which the dough is ready for use. The dough should be chilled between each turn, and again after cutting.

FLORENTINE MERINGUE

Tart jam, meringue, and toasted
almonds on puff-paste pastry.

Roll ¼ recipe Puff Paste, at left, in an 18″x 6″ rectangle. Cut off ½″ strips from ends and sides. Put oblong on a cookie sheet. Moisten the edges with cold water. Press the strips around edge to form rim. Prick in several places. Bake in very hot oven, 450°F., 10 minutes, or until well puffed and slightly browned. Cool, and spread with tart jam. Beat 3 egg whites with ⅛ teaspoon salt until almost stiff. Gradually beat in 6 tablespoons sugar; continue beating until stiff, but not dry. Cover jam with the meringue, and sprinkle with shredded toasted almonds. Dust with confectioners' sugar. Bake in 425°F. oven 5 minutes. To serve, cut in squares or strips. Makes 17 strips, 5″x 1″.

CREAM HORNS

Puff-paste pastry with
whipped cream or Cream Filling.

Roll ¼ recipe Puff Paste, at left, in a 10″x 8″ rectangle. Cut in twelve 10″ strips. Roll over cone-shaped forms, having the edges overlap. Chill 20 minutes. Bake in very hot oven, 450°F., 10 minutes, or until well puffed and slightly browned. Brush with slightly beaten egg white diluted with 1 teaspoon water. Reduce the heat to 350°F., and bake until glazed and browned. Slip from the forms, and cool. Fill with whipped cream or with Cream Filling, page 266. Makes 12.

NAPOLEONS

*Vanilla cream filling between
thin layers of puff-paste pastry.*

Roll Puff Paste, page 269, ⅛″ thick.
Cut in 6 strips 3″ wide and 14″ long.
Put on cookie sheets, covered with 2
layers of brown paper, and prick with
fork. Cover with another cookie sheet
to keep flat. Bake in very hot oven,
450°F., 5 minutes. Reduce heat to
moderate, 350°F., and bake 15 minutes longer. Remove cookie sheet, and
bake 15 minutes longer, or until pastry
is dry and brown. When cold, trim off
edges. Make 2 piles of 3 strips each,
putting well-chilled Vanilla Cream Filling, page 266, between layers. Chill,
and cut each crosswise in 3 pieces
about 4″x 2″. Spread a thin confectioners' sugar frosting on top; draw
lines of chocolate frosting across top,
using writing tip with pastry bag. Chill.
Makes 6 napoleons.

TINY CHEESECAKES

*There's cream cheese both in the pastry
and the filling.*

Make ½ pastry recipe as in Date-
Cheese Roll-ups, page 265. Omit chill-
ing; shape in 24 balls. Put one in each
of 24 tiny muffin cups. Press against
sides of cups with fingers to line evenly. Cream 6 ounces cream cheese, 2
tablespoons sugar, 1 teaspoon vanilla,
and 1 egg. Spoon into lined cups.
Bake in moderate oven, 350°F., about
20 minutes. Cool. Spread top of each
with sour cream, and dot with a bit
of red jam. Makes 24.

BILLETS-DOUX

Almond-filled pastry envelopes.

¾ cup soft butter or margarine	Almond Filling
1½ cups sifted flour	¼ cup confec-tioners' sugar
¼ teaspoon salt	¼ teaspoon cinnamon
6 egg yolks	

Cut butter into flour and salt. Add egg
yolks, and mix well. Chill overnight.
Cut dough into 21 pieces, and roll
each piece thin on floured board, to
form a 5″ to 6″ square. Put a heaping
measuring tablespoonful of Filling in
center; fold in thirds, and fold ends
over to form a square envelope. Bake
in 350°F. oven about 20 minutes. Cool,
and sift sugar and cinnamon over top.
Makes 21 billets-doux.

Almond Filling: Beat 5 egg whites with
⅛ teaspoon salt until almost stiff.
Gradually beat in ⅔ cup granulated
sugar, and continue beating until stiff.
Beat in ½ teaspoon cinnamon. Fold in
¾ cup almonds, blanched and ground
coarsely.

SOUR-CREAM TWISTS

*You must refrigerate the dough for
an hour before shaping it into twists.*

3½ cups sifted flour	2 tablespoons lukewarm water
1 teaspoon salt	1 cup sour cream
1 cup soft butter or margarine	1 whole egg
1 envelope active dry yeast	2 egg yolks
	1 teaspoon vanilla extract
	1 cup sugar

Sift flour and salt into large bowl. Cut
in butter. Soften yeast in water in
small bowl. Add sour cream, egg, yolks,
and vanilla; mix well. Add to flour mixture; stir until blended. Cover, and put
in refrigerator 1 hour. Divide dough in
thirds; return two-thirds to refrigerator.
Roll other third on board, sprinkled
with ⅓ cup sugar, to form a rectangle
18″x 6″. Fold over in thirds from end.
Repeat rolling and folding twice more.
Then roll into a 16″x 4″ rectangle. Cut
in 4″x 1″ strips, and twist on sugar to
form spirals. Put on greased cookie
sheets, and bake in hot oven, 400°F.,
15 to 20 minutes. Repeat with remaining dough. Makes 48.

PIES

A s American as apple pie" may be a timeworn expression, but it reflects an
important truth about American cuisine. Here in this country the pie
as dessert achieves perfection. France has elegantly glazed fruit tarts, and flans
with cookie crusts filled with pastry cream and glazed fruits; England has
deep fruit tarts with crust toppings; Italy and Germany have tarts with pastry
bases. But none matches the tender lusciousness of a well-made American pie.
Imagine a fruit pie, such as an apple made with fine ripe Gravensteins
heaped with creamy butter and sugar and nestled in pastry dough of feathery
crispiness, served hot, perhaps with a big wedge of sharp cheddar cheese. What
could be more delectable? Well, a possible rival might be a delicate ripe
juicy peach pie served hot with thick cream. Or one of those fluffy lemon-meringue
pies, with crust so tender it melts in your mouth. It's a mouth-watering
experience just to repeat a list of pies that have been specially created in this
country: pumpkin pie, Southern pecan pie, lime chiffon pie, black-bottom pie,
shoofly pie; the list is almost endless. Try pie for a typical American treat.

BANANA-DATE-NUT PIE

*Quick to make, rich and delicious,
this pie is made ahead and chilled.*

1 package (1 pound) pitted dates	Baked 9" pie shell
2 cups water	2 ripe bananas
2 cups chopped nuts	½ cup heavy cream, whipped

Combine all but 6 dates, and the water in saucepan; cook until dates absorb water. Remove from heat; cool. Add nuts. Line pastry shell with sliced bananas, reserving few slices for top. Spread date mixture over them; chill. To serve, garnish with cream; remaining dates, slivered; and bananas.

MINCEMEAT PIE WITH CHEESE CRUST

It has a lattice top.

1½ cups sifted flour	4 cups prepared mincemeat or Green-Tomato Mincemeat, page 224
½ teaspoon salt	
⅓ cup shortening	
½ cup shredded process American cheese	

Sift flour and salt; cut in shortening. Add cheese, and toss with fork to blend. Sprinkle with cold water (about 2 tablespoons), and mix with fork until dry ingredients are moistened. Press into a ball. On floured board, roll ⅔ of dough to ⅛" thickness; press into 9" piepan. Fill with mincemeat. Roll remaining dough, and cut in strips ½" wide. Arrange on pie, lattice fashion. Trim lattice edges; crimp edges of crust with fingers. Bake in 400°F. oven 20 minutes, or until lightly browned.

Brandied Mince Pie: Follow recipe for Mincemeat Pie with Cheese Crust, adding ¼ cup brandy to mincemeat.

PUMPKIN PIE

*Serve this plain, or spread it
with sweetened whipped cream and
a sprinkling of chopped Brazil nuts.*

1½ cups canned pumpkin	Dash cloves
1 can (14½ ounces) evaporated milk	2 tablespoons butter
	2 eggs (1 white stiffly beaten)
¾ cup light-brown sugar, packed	½ teaspoon lemon extract
½ teaspoon salt	Deep unbaked 9" pie shell
½ teaspoon ground ginger	Grating of nutmeg
1 teaspoon cinnamon	

In saucepan combine pumpkin, milk, sugar, salt, spices, and butter. Mix well, and heat until butter is melted. Pour over slightly beaten egg and egg yolk; add flavoring. Fold in stiffly beaten egg white. Cool. Pour into unbaked shell; top with grated nutmeg, and bake in very hot oven, 500°F., 8 minutes. Reduce heat to moderate, 325°F.; bake 25 to 30 minutes longer, or until set. Cool.

BANANA MERINGUE PIE

*Sliced bananas line the bottom
of the pastry shell, and are topped
with custard and meringue.*

Sugar	½ teaspoon vanilla extract
6 tablespoons flour	
Salt	2 or 3 ripe bananas
2½ cups milk	Baked 9" pastry shell
3 eggs, separated	¼ teaspoon cream of tartar
1 tablespoon butter	

Mix ½ cup sugar, flour, and ¼ teaspoon salt in top part of double boiler. Add milk, and cook over boiling water until thickened, stirring constantly. Cover, and cook 10 minutes longer, stirring occasionally. Beat egg yolks. Add a small amount of milk mixture slowly to yolks; return to double boiler, and cook 2 minutes, stirring. Remove from heat; add butter and vanilla. Cool. Slice bananas into shell; pour cooked mixture over them at once. Add dash salt and cream of tartar to egg whites; beat until stiff. Gradually add 6 tablespoons sugar, continuing to beat until very stiff. Pile lightly on pie, and spread to edge. Bake in 325°F. oven about 18 minutes.

LEMON MERINGUE PIE

*You use egg whites left over
from the filling for the meringue.*

Sugar	¼ cup butter
Salt	or margarine
6 tablespoons	3 eggs, separated
cornstarch	Lemon juice
2 cups boiling water	Baked 9" pastry
Grated rind 1 lemon	shell

Mix 1¼ cups sugar, ⅛ teaspoon salt, and cornstarch. Add water and lemon rind. Cook until thickened, stirring; simmer 10 minutes. Add butter, but do not stir. Gradually stir into egg yolks mixed with ½ cup lemon juice. Strain into pastry shell, and bake in hot oven, 400°F., 10 minutes. Add ⅛ teaspoon salt and 1 teaspoon lemon juice to egg whites; beat until stiff. Gradually add 6 tablespoons sugar, continuing to beat until very stiff. Pile lightly on pie, and spread to edge. Reduce heat to 350°F.; bake 18 minutes.

LATTICE APPLE PIE

*You partially cook the apples
before putting them in the pie shell.*

1¼ cups sugar	Pastry for 9" pie
¼ cup water	with strips
Pinch of salt	½ teaspoon
3 pounds tart	cinnamon
apples	1 tablespoon butter
1 tablespoon butter	

Put sugar, water, and salt in large skillet; cover, and heat until sugar begins to dissolve. Peel, and core apples; cut in eighths. Drop enough pieces of apple in sugar syrup to cover bottom of skillet; cook gently until just tender, leaving cover on until apples begin to get tender. Remove apple pieces carefully to flat pan or tray; continue until all are done. Thicken syrup with flour mixed with a little water; there should be about ⅓ cup of thickened syrup; cool. Line deep 9" piepan with pastry. Fill with apples; cover with thickened syrup, and top with cinnamon and butter. Moisten edge of crust; cover with pastry strips, lattice fashion. Crimp edges firmly. Brush top with undiluted evaporated milk for glaze, if desired. Bake in very hot oven, 450°F., 15 minutes. Reduce heat to hot, 400°F., and continue baking 25 minutes longer, or until well browned.

BUTTERSCOTCH CREAM PIE

*This has a topping of
whipped cream and slivered almonds.*

½ cup granulated	½ teaspoon salt
sugar	2 eggs
⅓ cup hot water	Baked 9" pie
2 cups milk	shell
¼ cup butter or	1 cup heavy cream,
margarine	whipped
6 tablespoons flour	Toasted slivered
¾ cup brown	almonds
sugar, packed	

Put granulated sugar in small heavy saucepan or skillet, and cook without stirring until sugar melts and becomes golden brown. Remove from heat, and add water slowly; cook, without stirring, until sugar dissolves. Add milk, and heat almost to boiling. Melt butter in top part of double boiler. Remove from heat, and add mixture of flour, brown sugar, and salt; beat in eggs. Slowly add caramel-milk mixture. Cook over boiling water until thickened, stirring constantly; cover, and cook 10 minutes, stirring occasionally. Cool to room temperature. Pour into baked shell; chill several hours. Spread with whipped cream; sprinkle with nuts.

LEMON SPONGE PIE

You use both lemon juice and rind.

¾ cup sugar	1 cup milk
¼ cup melted butter	2 eggs, separated
or margarine	⅛ teaspoon salt
¼ cup flour	Pastry for 9" open
Grated rind and	pie
juice 2 lemons	

Mix sugar, butter, flour, lemon rind and juice, milk, and egg yolks. Beat egg whites with salt until stiff, but not dry. Fold into first mixture. Pour into pastry-lined piepan, and bake in 350°F. oven 40 minutes. Cool.

*"...The best
of all physicians
Is Apple-pie and cheese!"*
EUGENE FIELD

SOUTHERN PECAN PIE

For a brown crust, brush the edges with evaporated milk before baking.

½ cup sugar	1 tablespoon
1 cup dark	melted butter
corn syrup	1¼ cups pecan
¼ teaspoon salt	halves
1 tablespoon flour	Unbaked 9″ pie
2 eggs	shell
1 teaspoon vanilla	
extract	

Beat together sugar, syrup, salt, flour, and eggs. Add vanilla, butter, and pecans. Pour into shell. Turn up rounded side of some pecans. Bake in 300°F. oven 1 hour, or until set. Cool.

Chocolate Pecan Pie: Use above recipe, melting 2 squares unsweetened chocolate with the butter.

TURNOVER APPLE PIE

Although you bake the apples under the single crust, they end up on top.

5 cups thinly sliced	Sugar
tart apples	Cinnamon
Pastry for 8″ open	2 tablespoons butter
pie	

Fill piepan with apples. Roll out pastry; fit over top of apples, and trim edge. Bake in hot oven, 425°F., 25 minutes, or until apples are soft and pastry is baked. Remove from oven, and turn upside down on a warm serving plate. Lift up piepan, carefully scrape apples from crust, and mix with apples left in pan, mashing with spoon. Stir in ½ cup sugar, ⅛ teaspoon cinnamon, and 1 tablespoon butter. Spread apple mixture on crust, and sprinkle with sugar and cinnamon; dot with remaining butter. Put in warm place until butter is melted. Serve warm, with ice cream, if desired.

"And lords made love
— and ladies, pies."
FLORENCE LA GANKE HARRIS

SESAME CHOCOLATE PIE

Sesame seeds go into the crust and are also sprinkled over the top.

Sesame-seed pastry	2 eggs, separated
for 9″ open pie	2 tablespoons
(see below)	water
Sesame seeds	1 cup sour cream
1 package (6	¼ teaspoon salt
ounces)	⅓ cup honey
semisweet	
chocolate pieces	

Add 2 tablespoons sesame seed to pastry. Make, and bake a 9-inch pie shell; cool. Toast 2 tablespoons sesame seed in oven after turning off heat; set aside. Melt chocolate over hot water. Remove from hot water, and beat in egg yolks, one at a time. Gradually stir in water, and beat until smooth. Fold in cream. Beat egg whites with salt until stiff, but not dry. Gradually beat in honey, and continue beating until very stiff and glossy. Fold in chocolate mixture. Pour into pastry shell, and sprinkle with toasted sesame seed. Chill until firm.

BLACK-BOTTOM PIE

The crumb crust is made with gingersnaps; the filling contains a little rum.

1½ cups milk	2 tablespoons
1 envelope un-	dark rum
flavored gelatin	1½ squares
¾ cup sugar	unsweetened
¼ teaspoon salt	chocolate, melted
4 eggs, separated	Crumb crust, made
1 tablespoon	with gingersnaps
cornstarch	Whipped cream
	Shaved chocolate

Put milk in top part of small double boiler. Soften gelatin in milk. Add ¼ cup sugar, salt, egg yolks, and cornstarch. Beat to blend. Put over simmering water, and cook, stirring constantly, until thickened and mixture coats a metal spoon. Remove from heat, and add rum. Measure out ½ cup mixture, and blend in chocolate. Spread in bottom of crust. Chill remaining mixture until thickened, but not firm. Beat egg whites until foamy; gradually add remaining ½ cup sugar, beating until stiff, but not dry. Fold this meringue into gelatin mixture. Pile lightly on chocolate mixture. Chill firm. Top with whipped cream, shaved chocolate.

LEMON-BLUEBERRY PIE

You need lemon-pie mix for this one.

1 package	1 egg, slightly
lemon-pie mix	beaten
½ cup boiling	1 pint blueberries
water	Pastry for 9″ pie
¾ cup sugar	with strips

Dissolve capsule and tablet from lemon mix in water. Combine dry lemon mix, sugar, egg, and water mixture; stir in berries. Pour into pastry-lined piepan; top with pastry strips. Bake in hot oven, 425°F., 45 minutes; reduce heat to 350°F.; bake 15 minutes.

CONCORD GRAPE PIE

You use both the pulp and the skins of these beautiful dark-purple grapes.

7 cups stemmed	¼ teaspoon salt
Concord grapes	Grated rind of 1
3 tablespoons	orange
cornstarch	Pastry for 9″ pie
1½ cups sugar	with strips

Wash grapes; slip skins from pulp, reserving skins. Heat pulp to boiling, and rub through coarse sieve to remove seeds. Combine cornstarch, sugar, salt, and rind; add grape pulp. Cook until thickened, stirring constantly. Add skins; cool. Pour filling into pastry-lined piepan; cover with strips of pastry, lattice fashion. Bake in very hot oven, 450°F., 10 minutes; reduce heat to 350°F.; bake 25 minutes.

SHOOFLY PIE

You use dark molasses and brown sugar in this Pennsylvania Dutch pie.

¾ cup dark	¼ cup butter
molasses	or margarine
¾ cup boiling	½ cup brown
water	sugar, packed
½ teaspoon soda	Pastry for 9″ open
¼ teaspoon salt	pie
1½ cups sifted	
flour	

Mix first 4 ingredients. Then with hands, mix next 3 ingredients. Pour about one-third of molasses mixture into pastry-lined piepan. Sprinkle with one-third of flour mixture. Continue alternating layers, ending with flour. Bake in moderate oven, 375°F., 35 minutes. Serve warm or cold.

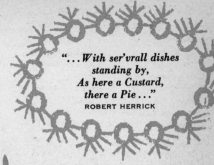

"...With ser'vrall dishes standing by, As here a Custard, there a Pie..."
ROBERT HERRICK

STRAWBERRY SNOWBANK PIE

Almond icing covers most of the top.

Baked 9″ pie	½ teaspoon
shell	cream of tartar
1 quart	Pinch of salt
strawberries	2 egg whites
1¼ cups sugar	¼ teaspoon
½ cup water	almond extract

Fill shell with whole unsweetened berries that have been washed, hulled, and drained; put prettiest berries in center. Mix sugar, water, and cream of tartar in saucepan; cover, and bring to boil; uncover, and cook until syrup spins long threads (240°F. on candy thermometer). Pour gradually into stiffly beaten salted whites, beating constantly until icing piles in peaks. Add extract; pile on pie, leaving center uncovered. Cool, but do not refrigerate.

Peach Snowbank Pie: Follow recipe for Strawberry Snowbank Pie, substituting 3 cups drained sliced peaches.

COFFEE NUT CREAM PIE

You use a pudding mix and instant coffee to make the filling.

1 package vanilla	½ cup heavy
pudding mix	cream, whipped
1½ cups milk	Baked 8″ pie
2 tablespoons	shell
instant coffee	¼ cup nuts

Combine pudding mix, milk, and instant coffee; cook as directed on package; cool. Fold in cream. Pour into shell; sprinkle with chopped nuts; chill.

Mocha Nut Cream Pie: In above recipe, use chocolate instead of vanilla pudding mix.

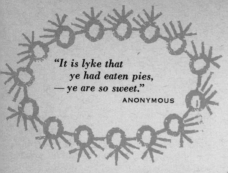

**"It is lyke that
ye are so sweet."**

ANONYMOUS

CRANBERRY-RAISIN PIE

*You cook the cranberries
and raisins in orange juice.*

1½ cups sugar	1 teaspoon each
¼ cup orange juice	grated orange
¼ teaspoon salt	and lemon rind
Water	2 tablespoons butter
3 cups cranberries	Pastry for 9″
1 cup seeded	covered pie
raisins	
1 tablespoon	
cornstarch	

Bring first 3 ingredients and 2 table-spoons water to boil in saucepan, stirring until sugar is dissolved. Add cranberries, and cook, stirring occasionally, until berries pop open. Add raisins. Blend cornstarch and 2 tablespoons water. Add to berry mixture, and cook until thickened, stirring. Remove from heat, and stir in fruit rinds and butter. Pour into bottom crust. Moisten edges with water, and cover with top crust which has been slit to allow steam to escape. Press edges together with tines of fork. Bake in hot oven, 425°F., about 25 minutes.

Cranberry Pie: Use above recipe, omitting raisins and increasing cranberries to 3½ cups.

CHOCOLATE ANGEL PIE

*It has a meringue crust, and
you must make it a day ahead.*

4 eggs, separated	3 squares unsweet-ened chocolate
¼ teaspoon salt	
½ teaspoon	2 tablespoons water
cream of tartar	1 cup heavy cream,
1½ cups sugar	whipped

Beat egg whites and ⅛ teaspoon salt until foamy; add cream of tartar. Continue beating, adding 1 cup sugar gradually, until very stiff. Spread 1″ layer on bottom of greased 9″ piepan. Pile remaining egg white evenly around sides of pan. Bake in very slow oven, 250°F., 1 hour; cool. Melt chocolate in top part of double boiler over boiling water. Beat egg yolks, remaining ½ cup sugar, ⅛ teaspoon salt, and water thoroughly; stir into chocolate. Cook over boiling water, stirring constantly, until very thick. Remove from heat, and cool. Fold in cream; pour into meringue. Chill overnight.

SOUR-CREAM RAISIN PIE

You can serve this warm or cold.

2 eggs	⅛ teaspoon salt
1 cup sugar	1 tablespoon lemon
1 cup sour cream	juice
1 cup cut seeded	Pastry for 9″
raisins	covered pie
¼ teaspoon nutmeg	

Beat eggs slightly; add sugar, and beat until light. Add remaining ingredients, except pastry. Pour into bottom crust. Moisten edges of pastry, and cover with top crust which has been slit to allow steam to escape. Press edges together with tines of fork. Bake in very hot oven, 450°F., 15 minutes. Reduce heat to moderate, 350°F., and bake about 30 minutes.

APRICOT-PRUNE PIE

*Cinnamon and nutmeg give
spice to the fruit filling.*

2½ cups cooked	½ cup sugar
dried apricots	⅛ teaspoon salt
and pitted prunes	¼ teaspoon each
Pastry for 9″	cinnamon and
covered pie	nutmeg
½ cup cooking	Juice 1 lemon
liquid from fruit	1 tablespoon butter
1 tablespoon	
cornstarch	

Put fruit in bottom crust. Mix liquid, cornstarch, sugar, salt, and spices. Cook until slightly thickened. Stir in lemon juice and butter; pour over fruit. Moisten edges of pastry, and cover with top crust which has been slit to allow steam to escape. Press edges together with tines of fork. Bake in hot oven, 425°F., about 45 minutes. Serve either warm or cold.

COTTAGE CHEESE PIE

This has dried currants in it, too.

1½ cups creamed cottage cheese	Juice of 1 lemon
1 tablespoon flour	3 eggs, separated
⅛ teaspoon salt	⅓ cup dried currants
1 cup heavy cream	Unbaked 9" pie shell
⅔ cup granulated sugar	Confectioners' sugar
Grated rind 1 lemon	

Force cheese through a fine sieve or food mill. Blend in flour and salt. Then stir in cream, granulated sugar, lemon rind and juice. Beat egg whites until stiff, but not dry; then beat yolks until thick and lemon-colored. Stir yolks and currants into cheese mixture. Fold in whites, and pour into pastry shell. Bake in very hot oven, 450°F., 10 minutes. Reduce heat to 350°F., and bake 45 minutes, or until firm. Cool, and sprinkle with confectioners' sugar.

DEVONSHIRE STRAWBERRY PIE

Cream cheese, fresh strawberries, strawberry syrup, and whipped cream.

1 quart strawberries	1 package (3 ounces) cream cheese
Water	
¼ cup cornstarch	Baked 9" pie shell
⅛ teaspoon salt	½ cup heavy cream, whipped
¾ cup sugar	
2 tablespoons milk	

Wash hulled berries, and put aside 6 for garnish. Put half of berries through sieve, and slice remainder. Add water to sieved berries to make 1½ cups mixture. In saucepan mix cornstarch, salt, and sugar. Add sieved berry mixture, and cook until thickened, stirring. Cool. Mix milk and cheese; spread on pastry shell; cover with sliced berries. Spread thickened mixture on top. Chill. Top with whipped cream and berries.

GLAZED STRAWBERRY PIE

You use strawberry jam for the glaze.

Spread 6 ounces cream cheese, softened, in bottom of baked 9" pie shell. Top with 1 pint washed, hulled strawberries, pointed ends up. Top with 1½ cups strawberry jam. Chill. Top with whipped cream.

NEVER-FAIL CUSTARD PIE

Never-fail because filling and crust bake separately.

2¼ cups milk	½ teaspoon vanilla extract
½ cup sugar	3 eggs
½ teaspoon salt	Unbaked 9" pie shell
Grating of nutmeg	

Scald milk; add sugar, salt, nutmeg, and vanilla. Mix well. Gradually pour over slightly beaten eggs, stirring constantly. Grease a deep 9" piepan with vegetable oil; pour in custard mixture. Put pan in larger shallow pan, and pour in hot water to depth of about 1". Bake in slow oven, 300°F., 55 minutes, or until set. Remove pan of custard from water; let stand until cold, then chill. Bake pie shell in a 9" piepan exactly like the one containing custard; cool. Just before serving, carefully loosen custard from sides of pan, using a small spatula. Shake gently to loosen custard from bottom; carefully but quickly slide from pan into shell. Let filling settle into crust a few minutes.

Coconut Custard Pie: Use the above recipe, sprinkling custard just before baking with ½ cup flaked coconut.

RHUBARB PIE

This one has a lattice-strip top.

3 tablespoons flour	Grated rind 1 orange
1 to 1¼ cups sugar	¼ cup orange juice
¼ teaspoon salt	Pastry for 9" pie with strips
4 cups diced rhubarb	2 tablespoons butter

Mix flour, sugar, salt, and rhubarb. Add orange rind, and juice. Turn into bottom crust. Dot with butter. Cover with strips of pastry, lattice fashion. Bake in 450°F. oven 20 minutes. Reduce heat to 350°F.; bake 20 minutes.

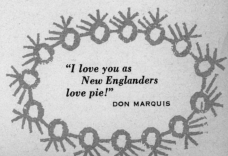

"I love you as New Englanders love pie!"
DON MARQUIS

VELVETY CHIFFON PIE

You can use a pastry shell or a
crumb crust for this popular favorite.

1 cup milk	4 eggs, separated
1 envelope un-	1 teaspoon vanilla
flavored gelatin	extract
¾ cup sugar	Baked 9" pie shell
¼ teaspoon salt	or crumb crust

Put milk in top part of small double boiler. Soften gelatin in milk. Add ¼ cup sugar, the salt, and egg yolks. Beat slightly to blend. Put over simmering water, and cook, stirring constantly, until thickened and mixture coats a metal spoon. Remove from heat, and add vanilla. Chill until thickened, but not firm. Beat egg whites until foamy; gradually add remaining ½ cup sugar, beating until stiff, but not dry. Fold this meringue into gelatin mixture. Pile lightly in pastry shell; chill until firm. Serve plain, or spread with sweetened whipped cream.

Coffee Chiffon Pie: Follow recipe for Velvety Chiffon Pie, adding 2 tablespoons coffee powder to hot mixture.

Nesselrode Chiffon Pie: Follow recipe for Velvety Chiffon Pie, substituting 2 tablespoons brandy for the vanilla. Fold ¼ cup diced candied fruits into filling with the meringue. Chill in crumb crust made with coconut macaroons. Garnish pie with whipped cream, candied cherries, and angelica.

Peanut Crunch Chiffon Pie: Follow recipe for Velvety Chiffon Pie. Beat ⅓ cup peanut butter into hot mixture with rotary beater. Spread firm pie with whipped cream, and top with ¼ cup crushed peanut brittle.

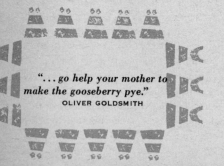

"...go help your mother to make the gooseberry pye."
OLIVER GOLDSMITH

STRAWBERRY CHIFFON PIE

A chiffon pie made
with water instead of milk.

1 box strawberry-	1 box (10 ounces)
flavored gelatin	frozen sliced
⅔ cup boiling	strawberries,
water	thawed
⅛ teaspoon salt	3 egg whites
2 tablespoons lemon	⅓ cup sugar
juice	Vanilla-wafer crust

Dissolve gelatin in boiling water. Add salt, lemon juice, and strawberries. Chill until thickened, but not firm. Beat egg whites until foamy; gradually add sugar, and beat until stiff, but not dry. Fold into gelatin. Pile in crust; chill until firm.

Raspberry Chiffon Pie: Use above recipe, substituting raspberry gelatin for the strawberry and 1 box raspberries for the strawberries.

Orange-Peach Chiffon Pie: Use above recipe with orange gelatin and 1 box frozen peaches, cut up.

LIME CHIFFON PIE

It's topped with whipped cream.

¼ cup lime juice	4 eggs, separated
½ cup water	Grated lime rind
1 envelope un-	Baked 9" pie
flavored gelatin	shell
1 cup sugar	Sweetened
¼ teaspoon salt	whipped cream

In top part of small double boiler, put lime juice and water. Soften gelatin in liquids. Add ½ cup sugar, salt, and egg yolks. Beat slightly to blend. Put over simmering water, and cook, stirring constantly, until thickened and mixture coats a metal spoon. Remove from heat, and add 2 teaspoons rind. Chill until thickened, but not firm. Beat egg whites until foamy; gradually add remaining ½ cup sugar, beating until stiff. Fold into gelatin mixture. Pile lightly in pastry shell; chill until firm. Spread with sweetened whipped cream; sprinkle with lime rind.

Lemon Chiffon Pie: Follow recipe for Lime Chiffon Pie, substituting lemon juice and rind for lime.

FROZEN
DESSERTS

Americans have, for generations, been avid eaters of frozen desserts of all kinds. Perhaps our hot summers are responsible, but whatever the reason, it is here that the ice-cream parlor reached its peak, that most of the amazing sundae concoctions were created, and that the mechanical refrigerator with its wide variety of frozen confections came into its own. Frozen desserts are popular not only with the family and guests, but even more popular with the housewife. They can be prepared well in advance; they are ready for the party or family dinner with no last-minute fussing. Given a minimum of care, they are almost foolproof, yet they can be elegant enough for the most important occasion. Here is a fine selection of recipes, including low-calorie ices for the weight conscious and smooth, rich concoctions such as frozen butterscotch-pecan roll. Try them for new ways to please your family and guests.

FROZEN PINEAPPLE CREAM CAKE

Coconut cream pudding with pineapple fills and frosts orange chiffon layers.

1 can (1 pound, 4½ ounces) crushed pineapple	⅓ cup chopped maraschino cherries
1 box coconut-cream pudding mix	1 pint heavy cream, whipped
	1 orange chiffon cake

Put pineapple in heavy saucepan, and stir in pudding mix. Cook until very thick and clear, stirring constantly. Cool; then chill. Fold in cherries and cream. Cut cake in 3 crosswise layers. Spread filling generously between layers and on top of cake. Freeze until filling is firm. Let stand a few minutes at room temperature before cutting. Makes 12 servings.

CITRUS MILK SHERBET

You use three citrus-fruit juices: orange, lemon, and grapefruit.

¾ cup light corn syrup	¼ cup each orange, lemon, and grapefruit juice
2 cups milk	
Grated rind 2 oranges	⅛ teaspoon salt
Grated rind ½ lemon	2 egg whites

Turn refrigerator control to coldest setting. Mix corn syrup, milk, rinds, and juices. Pour into refrigerator tray, and partially freeze. Remove to cold bowl, and beat until light and fluffy. Fold in stiffly beaten salted egg whites. Return to refrigerator tray, and freeze until firm. Makes 4 servings.

STRAWBERRY SHERBET

It's made with mashed fresh strawberries and pineapple juice.

1 teaspoon unflavored gelatin	1 can (18 ounces) pineapple juice
¼ cup cold water	1 pint fresh strawberries
¾ cup sugar	⅛ teaspoon salt
	1 egg white

Turn refrigerator control to coldest setting. Sprinkle gelatin on cold water, and let stand 5 minutes. Heat sugar and pineapple juice to boiling; stir into gelatin; chill. Wash, drain, and mash berries; force through sieve. Add to pineapple mixture, and pour into refrigerator tray. Partially freeze. Pour into chilled bowl, and beat until fluffy. Fold in stiffly beaten salted egg white. Return to refrigerator tray, and freeze until firm. Makes 6 servings.

LEMON-LIME SHERBET

Gelatin, milk, cream, sugar, salt, and frozen lemon-and-lime ade.

1 envelope unflavored gelatin	¼ teaspoon salt
2 cups milk	¼ cup sugar
2 cups light cream	1 can (6 ounces) frozen lemon-and-lime ade

Turn refrigerator control to coldest setting. In small saucepan, sprinkle gelatin on ½ cup milk, and let stand 5 minutes. Dissolve over hot water or very low heat. Mix with remaining ingredients. Freeze in refrigerator trays until frozen 1 inch in from edge of tray. Turn into chilled bowl, and beat with rotary beater until smooth, but not melted. Freeze in trays. Serves 6.

PEACH SHERBET

You make it in a crank-type freezer.

1 cup sugar	½ cup each orange and lemon juice
1 cup water	
2 cups fresh-peach pulp	1 egg white
	⅛ teaspoon salt

Boil sugar and water 5 minutes. Cool. **To make peach pulp:** Pit soft ripe peaches, and press through sieve or food mill. Mix all ingredients. Put in crank-type freezer, and freeze until firm. Makes about 1¼ quarts.

FROZEN APRICOT SANDWICHES

A whipped-cream and apricot mixture frozen between graham crackers.

1 cup heavy cream	1 jar (7¾ ounces)
2 tablespoons sugar	apricot-and-
2 tablespoons	apple (baby food)
lemon juice	18 graham crackers

Whip cream, and fold in remaining ingredients, except crackers. Arrange 9 crackers in 8″ square pan. Pour cream mixture over crackers, and cover with 9 remaining crackers to make sandwiches. Freeze until firm. Cut in 9 squares. Serve with warm chocolate sauce, if desired. Makes 9 servings.

FROZEN VANILLA CUSTARD

Vanilla, whipped cream, eggs, sugar, salt, and milk.

2 cups milk	1 cup heavy cream,
3 eggs, beaten	whipped
¾ cup sugar	1 tablespoon
⅛ teaspoon salt	vanilla extract

Turn refrigerator control to coldest setting. Heat milk in top part of double boiler over boiling water. Mix eggs, sugar, and salt. Gradually stir in hot milk. Return to double boiler, and cook over simmering water, stirring constantly, until mixture thickens and coats a metal spoon. Remove from heat, and cool. Fold in cream and vanilla. Pour into refrigerator tray, and freeze until firm. Makes 6 servings.

Frozen Banana-Raisin-Rum Custard: Use recipe for Frozen Vanilla Custard, omitting vanilla. Partially freeze. Soak 1 cup finely chopped raisins in ⅓ cup light rum 10 minutes. Fold raisins, 1 cup mashed ripe banana, and ½ cup chopped maraschino cherries into partially frozen ice cream. Freeze until firm. Makes 10 servings.

Frozen Caramel Custard: Use recipe for Frozen Vanilla Custard, decreasing milk to 1¾ cups and vanilla to 2 teaspoons. Increase sugar to 1 cup. Cook ½ cup of the sugar in small heavy skillet until golden brown and syrupy. Cool slightly; **gradually** add ¼ cup water, and cook, stirring, until syrup is melted. Add to custard mixture, and proceed as directed.

Frozen Nut-brittle Custard: Use recipe for Frozen Vanilla Custard. Fold ½ cup finely crushed nut brittle into mixture before freezing.

Frozen Nesselrode Pudding: Use above recipe, omitting vanilla. Partially freeze. Then fold in 1 cup minced candied fruit (cherries, ginger, orange peel, lemon peel, pineapple), ¼ cup chopped seeded raisins, and 2 tablespoons rum or 1 teaspoon rum extract. Freeze as directed. Makes 8 servings.

WATERMELON ICE

You need the juice from about one-fourth of a good-sized watermelon.

3 cups watermelon	1 envelope
juice	unflavored
½ cup sugar	gelatin
⅛ teaspoon salt	Juice 1 lemon

Mix first 3 ingredients. Remove about ¼ cup to small saucepan. Sprinkle gelatin on juice in saucepan, and let stand 5 minutes. Dissolve over hot water or very low heat. Add with lemon juice to first mixture. Freeze in crank-type freezer. Makes about 1 quart.
Note: To make juice, force melon pulp through a food mill or sieve.

GRAPE-LIME ICE

Just sugar, water, and fruit juices, perfect for those on low-fat diets.

2 cups water	1 cup grape juice
1 cup sugar	Juice 2 small limes

Turn refrigerator control to coldest setting. Boil water and sugar 5 minutes; cool. Add fruit juices. Pour into refrigerator tray, and partially freeze. Remove from tray to chilled bowl. Beat until fluffy and light in color. Return to tray; freeze until firm. Serves 6.

FRENCH VANILLA ICE CREAM

The French note: six egg yolks.

6 egg yolks	2 cups heavy
2 cups milk	cream
1 cup sugar	3 teaspoons
¼ teaspoon salt	vanilla extract

In top part of double boiler beat egg yolks and milk with rotary beater. Add sugar and salt; cook over simmering water, stirring constantly, until thickened and mixture coats a metal spoon. Let cool, then add cream and vanilla. Freeze in a crank-type freezer. Makes about 1½ quarts.

Banana Ice Cream: Use above recipe, omitting all but 1 teaspoon vanilla. Force 3 large ripe bananas through sieve, and add pulp to ice-cream mixture. Freeze.

Peach Ice Cream: Use recipe for French Vanilla Ice Cream, substituting 1 teaspoon almond extract for vanilla. Partially freeze. Add 2 cups sweetened crushed fresh peaches, or use thawed frozen. Finish freezing.

Strawberry Ice Cream: Use recipe for French Vanilla Ice Cream, omitting vanilla. Partially freeze. Add 2 cups sweetened crushed fresh strawberries, or use thawed frozen. Finish freezing.

Raspberry Ice Cream: Use recipe for French Vanilla Ice Cream, omitting vanilla. Partially freeze. Add 2 cups sweetened strained fresh raspberries, or use thawed frozen. Finish freezing.

COCONUT SNOWBALLS

Serve them with your favorite sauce.

Shape any flavor ice cream into balls; roll quickly in flaked coconut. Put in freezer until firm.

ORANGE VELVET ICE CREAM

It contains candied orange peel.

2 egg yolks	2 cups orange juice
1 cup light	1 cup heavy
cream	cream, whipped
¼ teaspoon salt	¼ cup finely diced
2 cups sugar	or shredded
1 cup water	candied orange
	peel

In top part of small double boiler beat egg yolks, light cream, and salt with rotary beater. Put over simmering water and cook, stirring constantly, until slightly thickened and mixture coats a metal spoon. Cool. Boil sugar, water, and juice 5 minutes; cool. Combine mixtures, and fold in cream. Partially freeze in crank-type freezer. Then add orange peel, and finish freezing. Makes about 2 quarts.

PHILADELPHIA ICE CREAM

It's made with all cream; there are no eggs or milk.

1 quart	⅛ teaspoon salt
light cream	1½ tablespoons
¾ cup sugar	vanilla extract

Scald cream. Add sugar and salt; cool, and add vanilla. Pour into container of crank-type freezer, and freeze until firm. Makes about 1½ quarts.

SWEET-CHOCOLATE ICE CREAM

You use half cream, half milk.

Two bars (4 ounces each) German's sweet chocolate	3 eggs
	1 cup sugar
	2 cups light cream
2 cups milk	1 tablespoon
⅛ teaspoon salt	vanilla extract

Put chocolate and milk in top part of double boiler over boiling water, and heat, stirring constantly, until chocolate is dissolved. Beat salted eggs and sugar; add cream and vanilla. Add chocolate mixture, and strain into container of crank-type freezer. Freeze until firm. Makes about 1½ quarts.

MOCHA MOUSSE

*It's made with unsweetened
chocolate and instant coffee.*

3 squares unsweetened chocolate	1 tablespoon instant coffee
⅓ cup water	1 teaspoon vanilla extract
¾ cup sugar	2 cups heavy cream, whipped
⅛ teaspoon salt	
3 egg yolks	

Turn refrigerator control to coldest setting. Put chocolate and water in saucepan. Bring to boil over low heat, stirring vigorously until blended. Add sugar and salt; simmer 3 minutes, stirring. Gradually stir into well-beaten egg yolks; add coffee, and cool. Fold in vanilla and cream. Freeze until firm in refrigerator trays. Serves 8.

CRANBERRY MOUSSE

*You use whole-cranberry sauce
and cream cheese.*

1 package (3 ounces) soft cream cheese	1 cup heavy cream, whipped
¼ cup sugar	1 can (1 pound) whole cranberry sauce
⅛ teaspoon salt	

Turn refrigerator control to coldest setting. Beat cream cheese until fluffy. Stir in sugar and salt, and fold into cream. Add cranberry sauce, and mix lightly. Pour into refrigerator tray, and freeze until firm. Makes 6 servings.

LEMON MOUSSE

Both lemon juice and rind are needed.

2 tablespoons cornstarch	⅓ cup lemon juice
¼ teaspoon salt	Grated rind 1 lemon
1 cup sugar	1 pint heavy cream, whipped
1 cup milk	
3 egg yolks, slightly beaten	

Turn refrigerator control to coldest setting. In top part of small double boiler mix cornstarch, salt, and sugar. Add milk. Cook over boiling water about 15 minutes, stirring frequently. Pour slowly over egg yolks, stirring constantly. Mix well, and return to double boiler; cook 1 minute, stirring. Add lemon juice and rind; chill. Fold in cream. Pour into refrigerator trays, and freeze until firm. Makes 8 servings.

FROZEN BUTTERSCOTCH-PECAN ROLL

*Whipped cream, brown sugar, and
nuts frozen in rolled cake.*

1 cup heavy cream	¼ teaspoon salt
¼ cup brown sugar, packed	3 eggs
½ cup chopped pecans	1 cup granulated sugar
1 tablespoon butter	⅓ cup water
1 cup sifted cake flour	1 teaspoon vanilla extract
1 teaspoon baking powder	Confectioners' sugar
	Butterscotch sauce

Mix cream and brown sugar; chill 1 hour. Brown nuts lightly in butter, and drain on absorbent paper. **To make cake:** Sift flour, baking powder, and salt. Beat eggs until very thick and lemon-colored. Gradually beat in granulated sugar. Blend in water and vanilla. Add dry ingredients, and beat only until smooth. Grease a 15½"x 10½" jelly-roll pan, and line bottom with brown paper; grease. Pour in batter. Bake in moderate oven, 375°F., 12 to 15 minutes. Turn out on a towel sprinkled with confectioners' sugar. Roll cake lengthwise in towel. Cool on rack. Whip cream mixture until stiff; fold in nuts. Unroll cake. Spread with cream mixture. Re-roll, and freeze. Cut in thick slices, and serve with butterscotch sauce. Makes 8 servings.

Macaroon Ice Cream Roll: Use cake recipe from Frozen Butterscotch-Pecan Roll. Fill with mixture of: 1 cup heavy cream, whipped, ½ cup finely crushed macaroons, and 2 tablespoons sugar. Freeze, and serve with partially thawed frozen raspberries.

SPUMONI

It contains maraschino cherries,
candied orange peel, almonds, brandy.

2 cups milk	8 maraschino
5 egg yolks,	cherries,
slightly beaten	finely chopped
⅛ teaspoon salt	2 tablespoons
1 cup sugar	minced candied
1 teaspoon	orange peel
vanilla extract	8 slivered blanched
1 cup heavy	almonds
cream	2 tablespoons
	brandy

Turn refrigerator control to coldest setting. In top part of double boiler mix milk, egg yolks, salt, and ¾ cup of the sugar. Cook over simmering water, stirring constantly, until thickened and mixture coats a metal spoon. Cool; add vanilla. Pour into refrigerator tray, and freeze until almost firm. Line a 2-quart melon mold with the mixture. Whip cream until stiff; fold in remaining ¼ cup sugar, cherries, peel, almonds, and brandy. Fill center of mold; cover, and freeze in freezer or freezing compartment of refrigerator until firm. Unmold on serving plate, and cut in wedges. (To loosen spumoni from the mold, put a cloth wrung out of hot water on the bottom of mold.) Serves 6 to 8.

MAPLE PARFAIT

Maple syrup, egg yolks, and cream.

Turn refrigerator control to coldest setting. In top part of small double boiler, beat 6 egg yolks and ⅔ cup maple syrup. Add dash salt, and cook over simmering water until slightly thickened, stirring. Cool. Fold in 1 pint heavy cream, whipped. Freeze in refrigerator tray until firm. Serves 6.

STRAWBERRY-ALMOND ROLL

Strawberries form the shell,
almond-whipped cream the filling.

1 box frozen	3 tablespoons
strawberries,	chopped blanched
thawed	almonds
8 tablespoons sugar	¼ teaspoon
Water	almond extract
1 teaspoon	½ cup heavy
unflavored gelatin	cream, whipped
Red food coloring	

Turn refrigerator control to coldest setting. Force berries through sieve. Add 5 tablespoons sugar, and water to make 2 cups. Sprinkle gelatin on 1 tablespoon cold water, and let stand 5 minutes. Dissolve over hot water. Stir into berry mixture. Pour into refrigerator tray, and freeze until mushy. Add small amount of red food coloring. Beat well, and turn into a 28-ounce can. (It will not fill can.) Put in freezer or freezing compartment of refrigerator until almost firm. Pack mixture onto sides of can, leaving center hollow. Add remaining sugar, nuts, and flavoring to whipped cream; pour into center. Cover with waxed paper; freeze. To serve, run a spatula around inside of can; wrap in hot cloth until dessert slides out. Cut in slices. Serves 4.

Raspberry-Almond Roll: Omit strawberries in the above recipe, and use 1 box of thawed frozen raspberries.

COFFEE TORTONI

It's frozen in individual servings.

1 egg white	1 teaspoon
1 tablespoon	vanilla extract
instant	⅛ teaspoon
coffee	almond extract
⅛ teaspoon salt	¼ cup toasted
6 tablespoons	blanched
sugar	almonds, finely
1 cup heavy cream	chopped

Turn refrigerator control to coldest setting. In small bowl mix egg white, coffee, and salt. Beat with rotary beater until almost stiff; gradually beat in 2 tablespoons of the sugar, and beat until stiff. Whip cream, and fold in remaining 4 tablespoons sugar and flavorings. Fold in meringue and nuts. Spoon into ¼-cup paper or foil cups, and freeze until firm. Makes 8 servings.

PUDDINGS
AND
SAUCES

The English bride of times past always included in her trousseau a large collection of pudding forms, and she was expected to know how to prepare the puddings to fill them and to make sauces that were appropriate. The forms were variously shaped. Some represented the British lion, some the unicorn, others were like sheaves of wheat or bunches of asparagus, and there were gay flower designs: roses, carnations, and lilies. The puddings that came from them were as delightful to look at as to eat. Puddings should be beautiful to behold. Heap a smooth creamy pudding into fine-stemmed sherbet glasses, or pile it in a sheer crystal serving bowl and serve it at the table. Turn molded pudding onto your prettiest platter and decorate it. Depending on the time of the year and the formality of the occasion, you might prepare a satisfying old-fashioned plum pudding; a light meringue fantasy; a rich, creamy Bavarian dish; or a delicate orange fluff.

285

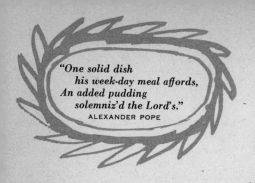

"One solid dish
his week-day meal affords,
An added pudding
solemniz'd the Lord's."
ALEXANDER POPE

MOLASSES DUFF

A steamed pudding with sherry sauce.

1 egg	¼ teaspoon salt
2 tablespoons sugar	1 teaspoon soda
½ cup molasses	½ cup boiling
2 tablespoons	water
melted butter	Sherry Sauce,
1½ cups sifted flour	page 292

Beat egg until thick and lemon-colored; gradually beat in sugar and molasses. Stir in butter. Add sifted dry ingredients alternately with boiling water to egg mixture. Pour into a greased 1½-quart mold; cover tightly with lid or double thickness of waxed paper or foil, secured with rubber bands. Place on rack in bottom of large kettle, and add boiling water to half-cover mold. Cover and steam 1½ hours. Turn out immediately, and serve with Sauce. Serves 6 to 8.

ORANGE FLUFF PUDDING

A jellied, spongelike pudding with
a garnish of orange slices and grapes.

5 eggs, separated	½ cup boiling
½ cup sugar	water
1 envelope un-	Grated rind
flavored	of 1 orange
gelatin	⅛ teaspoon salt
Juice 1 lemon	Orange slices
Juice 1 orange	Green grapes

Beat egg yolks until thick and lemon-colored; gradually beat in sugar. Soften gelatin in fruit juices, and dissolve in boiling water; add to egg-yolk mixture with grated orange rind. Refrigerate until mixture just starts to congeal. Fold in the egg whites, beaten with salt until stiff. Pour into 2-quart ring mold. Refrigerate for at least 4 hours. Unmold, and decorate with orange slices and grapes. Serves 6 to 8.

LEMON-SOUFFLÉ BREAD PUDDING

The cooking secret: measure the
bread cubes carefully.

2 cups crust-trimmed bread cubes	Juice and grated rind 1 lemon
¾ cup sugar	½ cup butter
	4 eggs, separated
	⅔ cup milk

Mix together bread cubes, sugar, juice, and rind. Stir in melted butter. Beat yolks until thick and lemon-colored; add milk, and pour over the bread. Fold in stiffly beaten egg whites. Pour into buttered 1½-quart casserole. Bake in a moderate oven, 350°F., 30 minutes. Serve hot, with cream flavored with nutmeg, if desired. Serves 6.

ORANGE MERINGUE

It's covered with orange
sauce and garnished with almonds.

6 egg whites	¼ teaspoon
¼ teaspoon cream of tartar	orange extract
½ teaspoon salt	Orange Sauce, page 292
1 cup sugar	Toasted almond slivers

Beat egg whites until frothy; sprinkle over cream of tartar and salt; beat until stiff, but not dry. Gradually beat in sugar, and add extract. Pour into a buttered 9"x 5"x 3" loaf pan, and put in pan of hot water. Bake in moderate oven, 350°F., 1 hour. Place pan on cake rack to cool. At serving time, remove from pan to an oblong platter. Spoon Sauce over, and sprinkle with almonds. Serves 8.

SABAYON

A hot, fluffy pudding made
with Marsala, port, or sherry wine.

5 egg yolks	⅛ teaspoon salt
1 tablespoon cold water	½ cup Marsala, port, or sherry
¾ cup sugar	wine

In the top of a double boiler, beat egg yolks with water until they are foamy and light. Whisk in sugar, salt, and wine. Beat over hot water, not boiling, until thickened and fluffy. This will take only a few minutes. Pile into sherbet glasses; serve hot. Serves 6.

abayon with Fresh Strawberries or eaches: Follow recipe for Sabayon, age 286. Cool and fold in 5 stiffly eaten egg whites. Pile in a pretty erving bowl, and garnish with fruit.

Chocolate Sabayon: Follow recipe for Sabayon, page 286; stir 2 ounces grated weet chocolate into the dessert when t is taken from the heat.

Frozen Sabayon: Follow recipe for Sabayon, page 286. Cool, and add 1 pint heavy cream, whipped, ¼ cup diced candied cherries, ½ cup diced candied pineapple, and ½ cup chopped pecans. Freeze in parfait glasses, and garnish with candied cherries and bits of angelica. Or pour into ice-cube trays, and freeze in refrigerator, or in mold in freezer. Makes 10 to 12 servings.

BLACK AND WHITE DELIGHT

Prunes, bananas, marshmallows, and sweetened whipped cream.

1 cup diced cooked prunes	1 tablespoon lemon juice
2 bananas, sliced	1 cup heavy cream, whipped
12 large marshmallows, cut in quarters	2 tablespoons sugar

Mix prunes, bananas, and marshmallows; sprinkle with lemon juice. Lightly fold in cream and sugar. Pile in sherbet glasses. Serves 6.

RUSSIAN CREAM

A sour-cream gelatin dessert.

1 cup light cream	2 tablespoons cold water
¾ cup sugar	1 cup sour cream
1½ teaspoons unflavored gelatin	Frozen fruit

Heat light cream and sugar in double boiler until lukewarm. Add gelatin softened in cold water; stir until dissolved. Remove from heat, and cool. Fold in sour cream beaten to a smooth, fluffy consistency. Pour into individual molds. Refrigerate 3 or 4 hours. Unmold, and serve with frozen fruit. Serves 4.

BAVARIAN CREAM

A gelatin dessert to serve plain or with fruit or crème de menthe.

1 envelope unflavored gelatin	¼ teaspoon salt
1 cup milk	1 teaspoon vanilla extract
4 eggs, separated	1 cup heavy cream, whipped
½ cup sugar	

Soften gelatin in milk. Add beaten egg yolks, ¼ cup sugar, and salt. Cook over simmering water, stirring constantly, until thickened and smooth. Add vanilla. Cool. Stir occasionally to prevent a crust from forming. Fold in meringue made from egg whites and ¼ cup sugar, and the cream. Pour into 2-quart mold; refrigerate at least 4 hours. Unmold. Serves 8.

Charlotte Russe: Line charlotte mold or springform with ladyfingers. Fill with Bavarian Cream (above); refrigerate at least 4 hours.

Chocolate Bavarian Cream: Melt 2 ounces unsweetened chocolate; add to Bavarian Cream custard. Proceed as in Bavarian Cream recipe (above).

Praline Bavarian Cream: In Bavarian Cream recipe (above), add ⅔ cup praline along with the meringue and whipped cream. Also sprinkle soft unmolded pudding with praline.

To make praline: In a heavy skillet, place 1 cup unblanched almonds, 1 cup filberts, and 2 cups sugar; cook gently over moderate heat until sugar melts and caramelizes, and skins of nuts burst. Pour on lightly buttered cookie sheet. When cold and brittle, break into small pieces; place in towel and pound to a powder with a mallet, or grind. Will keep indefinitely in a tightly covered glass jar.

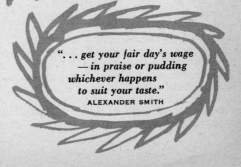

"... get your fair day's wage
— in praise or pudding
whichever happens
to suit your taste."
ALEXANDER SMITH

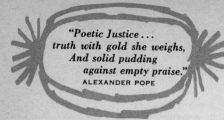

BRIDE'S PUDDING

A fluffy white pudding served with
an apricot-brandy sauce or berries.

2 envelopes un-flavored gelatin	1 pint heavy cream, whipped
½ cup cold water	1 teaspoon vanilla extract
⅓ cup boiling water	1 can flaked coconut
6 egg whites	
¼ teaspoon salt	Apricot-Brandy
¾ cup sugar	Sauce, page 292

Soften gelatin in cold water; pour over boiling water, and stir until dissolved. Cool. Beat egg whites with salt until frothy; gradually beat in sugar. Continue beating until mixture holds a peak when beater is lifted. Slowly beat in gelatin. Fold in whipped cream and vanilla. Butter well a 9″ springform pan; sprinkle thickly with coconut, reserving some for the top. Pour in egg-white mixture; sprinkle with coconut. Chill for at least 4 hours. Cut in wedges, and serve with Sauce or fresh or frozen raspberries. Serves 10 to 12.

TOPSY-TURVY CHERRY PUDDING

Red sour cherries and cherry
syrup are baked over batter.

1¼ cups sugar	1 can (1 pound) red sour cherries, drained
2 tablespoons butter	
1 cup sifted flour	½ cup cherry juice
⅛ teaspoon salt	
1 teaspoon baking powder	Whipped cream or ice cream
¾ cup milk	

Cream 1 cup of the sugar with butter. Sift flour; measure, and sift with salt and baking powder; add alternately with milk to butter mixture. Pour into a buttered shallow baking dish. Combine cherries with remaining ¼ cup sugar and cherry juice. Heat to boiling point. Pour over batter. Bake in 350°F. oven 30 minutes. Serve with cream or ice cream. Serves 6.

A SIMPLE LEMON SOUFFLÉ

A fairly firm soufflé served with
a dusting of confectioners' sugar.

4 eggs, separated	Juice and grated rind of 1 lemon
1 cup granulated sugar	⅛ teaspoon salt
	Confectioners' sug

Beat egg yolks until thick and lemo colored; gradually beat in ½ cup gran lated sugar; add lemon juice and rin Beat egg whites with salt until froth gradually beat in remaining ½ cu sugar. Continue beating until mixtu will hold a peak when beater is lifte fold into egg-yolk mixture. Pour into straight-sided 1½-quart baking dis preferably pottery, lightly buttered an sprinkled with sugar. Place dish in pa of hot water, and bake in moderat oven, 325°F., 40 minutes. Remove fro oven; dust with confectioners' suga and serve at once. Makes 6 serving **Note:** The French enjoy a soufflé tha has a crusty top and sides and a cen ter soft enough to serve as a sauce To obtain this result, bake it at 375°F for only 20 minutes.

FRENCH VANILLA SOUFFLÉ

For a truly impressive-looking
soufflé, bake it with a collar.

2 tablespoons cornstarch	¼ teaspoon salt
1 cup cold milk	5 egg whites
4 egg yolks	1 teaspoon vanilla extract
½ cup sugar	Confectioners' suga

Blend cornstarch with milk; heat to boiling, and boil 1 minute; pour over the egg yolks which have been beaten with ¼ cup sugar and the salt. Cool Beat egg whites stiff; gradually beat in remaining ¼ cup sugar. Fold into the egg-yolk mixture. Add vanilla. Pour into a straight-sided 2-quart baking dish, preferably pottery, buttered and sprinkled with sugar. Mixture should fill it two-thirds full. Or use a smaller dish, and firmly tie a collar of buttered heavy waxed paper around it. Collar should be 3″ or 4″ above the rim of the dish. Set dish in a pan of hot, not boiling, water, and bake in a 325°F. oven 30 to 40 minutes. Dust with sifted confectioners' sugar. Serves 6 to 8.

hocolate Soufflé: Add 2 ounces un-weetened chocolate to the cornstarch nd milk in preceding recipe; stir until hocolate is melted.

lack-bottom Soufflé: Cover bottom of ouffle dish with melted sweet choco-ate. Cover with Vanilla Soufflé mixture, age 288; bake as directed.

pricot or Peach Soufflé: Pour ½ Vanilla souffle, page 288, into dish; arrange rained canned apricots or peaches, cut n quarters, on mixture. Top with re-naining mixture, and bake as directed.

BANANA FLUFF PUDDING

A chilled banana, gelatin, and whipped-cream pudding.

1 envelope un-flavored gelatin	1 tablespoon grated orange rind
¼ cup cold water	Dash of salt
4 medium bananas	¾ cup confection-ers' sugar
1 cup orange juice	1 cup heavy cream, whipped
2 tablespoons lemon juice	

Soften the gelatin in cold water; dis-solve over hot water. Mash bananas, and add fruit juices, rind, salt, and sugar. Add the gelatin, and chill until slightly thickened. Fold in whipped cream. Chill well. Serves 6 to 8.

CRANBERRY PUDDING

Steamed pudding made with molasses and whole raw cranberries.

1⅓ cups sifted flour	⅓ cup boiling water
1 teaspoon soda	2 cups whole raw cranberries
½ teaspoon salt	Butter Sauce, page 291
½ cup molasses	

Sift dry ingredients. Add molasses and water; stir in cranberries. Pour into buttered 1½-quart mold; cover tightly with a lid or double thickness of waxed paper or foil; secure with rubber bands or string. Place on rack in large kettle, and add boiling water to half-cover mold. Cover, and steam 2 hours. Un-mold; serve hot with Sauce. Serves 6.

COCONUT-CREAM MOLD

It's decorated with fruit and served with a warm sauce.

2 envelopes un-flavored gelatin	¼ teaspoon salt
⅓ cup cold water	1 pint heavy cream, whipped
1 cup scalded milk	1 can flaked coconut
1 cup sugar	Fruit
1 teaspoon vanilla extract	Hot Butter-Cream Sauce, page 292

Soften gelatin in cold water; dissolve in scalded milk; add sugar, and stir until mixture just begins to congeal. Chill until mixture just begins to congeal. Fold in vanilla, salt, whipped cream, and coconut. Pour into a 2-quart ring mold. Refrigerate at least 4 hours. Unmold on large serving plate, and decorate with small bunches of grapes, maraschino cherries with stems, or with other fruit in season. Serve with Sauce. Makes 8 servings.

INDIAN PUDDING

A hot pudding to be served with sauce, ice cream, or frozen whipped cream.

¼ cup corn meal	3 cups scalded milk
2 tablespoons sugar (optional)	2 tablespoons butter
½ teaspoon salt	⅓ cup molasses
½ teaspoon ground ginger	½ cup cold milk
¼ teaspoon cinnamon	Brandy Hard Sauce, page 292

In the top of a double boiler mix corn meal, sugar, salt, and spices. Add scalded milk, butter, and molasses. Heat, and cook over boiling water 20 minutes, stirring frequently. Pour into a buttered 1½-quart baking dish; add cold milk. Bake in slow oven, 300°F., about 3 hours. Serve the pudding hot with Brandy Hard Sauce, ice cream, or frozen whipped cream. Makes 4 gen-erous servings.

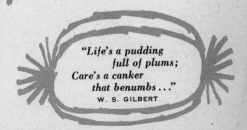

"Life's a pudding full of plums; Care's a canker that benumbs..."
W. S. GILBERT

DANISH RUM PUDDING

*Raspberry sauce goes with
this chilled gelatin pudding.*

1 envelope un- flavored gelatin	¼ cup medium dark rum
1¼ cups milk	1 cup heavy
¼ teaspoon salt	cream, whipped
1 cup sugar	Raspberry Sauce,
4 eggs, separated	page 292

Soften gelatin in milk in top part of
double boiler. Heat with salt and ½
cup sugar to the boiling point; pour
over slightly beaten egg yolks; return
to heat, and cook, stirring constantly,
until mixture coats a spoon. Add rum.
Refrigerate. When mixture just begins
to congeal, fold in egg whites beaten
until stiff with remaining sugar, and
whipped cream. Pour into 2-quart mold.
Chill 4 hours, or overnight. Serve with
Sauce. Makes 8 servings.

SHERRY-ALMOND SNOW

*Frothy sherry gelatin chilled in
layers with toasted almond slivers.*

1 envelope un- flavored gelatin	¼ teaspoon almond extract
¼ cup cold water	3 tablespoons
⅓ cup boiling water	sherry ⅓ cup toasted
3 egg whites	almond slivers
⅛ teaspoon salt	Sherry Custard
½ cup sugar	Sauce, page 292

Soften gelatin in cold water; dissolve
in boiling water. Refrigerate until it
just begins to congeal. Beat until
frothy. Beat egg whites with salt until
stiff; gradually beat in sugar; add almond extract, sherry, and frothy gelatin. Pour into 1½-quart mold, alternating layers of gelatin mixture and almonds. Chill at least 4 hours. Unmold,
and serve with Sauce. Serves 6.

CHOCOLATE NUT PUFFS

They contain candied fruit, too.

2 eggs, separated	2 tablespoons
⅛ teaspoon salt	diced mara-
¼ cup sugar	schino cherries
½ cup semisweet	2 tablespoons
chocolate	diced candied
pieces, melted	lemon peel
½ teaspoon	Unsweetened
vanilla extract	whipped cream
½ cup chopped	Shaved unsweet-
nuts	ened chocolate

Beat egg whites with salt until foam
gradually beat in sugar, and continu
beating until mixture stands in peak
when the beater is lifted. Beat eg
yolks until thick and lemon-colorec
fold into egg whites with cooled choc
late, vanilla, nuts, and fruits. Pile int
4 unbuttered custard cups. Place o
trivet in skillet containing ¾" boilin
water. Cover; put over low heat, an
steam 10 to 12 minutes, or until firm
Serve hot or cold. Garnish with whippe
cream and shaved chocolate. Serves 4

PLUM PUDDING

*You must soak currants and
raisins overnight in brandy.*

½ cup sugar	½ cup chopped
3 cups sifted flour	nuts
1 teaspoon soda	¼ cup each
1½ teaspoons salt	chopped citron
½ teaspoon each	and candied
ginger, cloves,	orange peel
and nutmeg	1 apple, grated
1 teaspoon	1 cup suet,
cinnamon	chopped fine
½ cup dried	1½ cups milk
currants and ½	½ cup molasses
cup raisins,	½ cup brandy
soaked overnight	Brandy Hard
in ⅓ cup brandy	Sauce, page 292

Sift dry ingredients; add currants, raisins, nuts, citron, orange peel, and
apple. Stir in suet, milk, molasses.
Pour into 2 buttered 1½-quart molds.
Cover tightly with a lid or double
thickness of waxed paper or foil; secure with rubber bands or string. Put
on rack in bottom of large kettle; add
boiling water to half-cover mold. Cover,
and steam 3 hours. Unmold. Pour over
½ cup heated and flaming brandy.
Serve with Sauce. Serves 8.

PUMPKIN CUSTARD

It's served with whipped cream,
flavored with sherry and ginger.

cups canned pumpkin	2 tablespoons butter
cup light-brown sugar	1½ cups milk
tablespoon flour	4 eggs, slightly beaten
⅛ teaspoon salt	Sherry-Ginger Cream, page 292
teaspoon each ginger, nutmeg, cinnamon	

n saucepan mix pumpkin, sugar, flour, salt, spices, butter, and milk. Cook, stirring constantly, 5 minutes. Cool slightly; pour over slightly beaten eggs. Pour into well-buttered 1½-quart casserole. Place in pan of hot water. Bake n moderate oven, 350°F., 1 hour, or until pumpkin custard is set. Serve with a daub of Sherry-Ginger Cream. Makes 6 servings.

To use fresh pumpkin: Halve 3-pound pumpkin; remove seeds and stringy part. Pare, and cut in pieces. Cook about 30 minutes; drain well, and mash. Drain again.

ENGLISH TRIFLE

Soft custard chilled on sherried
ladyfingers and macaroons.

1 cup soft custard*	Grated rind ½ lemon
6 ladyfingers	Sherry wine (about ⅓ cup)
Strawberry or raspberry jam	1 cup heavy cream, whipped
12 almond macaroons	Candied cherries, angelica,
18 almonds, blanched and slivered	pistachio nuts

*In the top of a double boiler make a soft custard using 2 egg yolks, 2 tablespoons sugar, and 1 cup scalded milk. Cool slightly.

Split ladyfingers, and spread with jam. Arrange in a serving dish. Cover with whole macaroons; sprinkle with almonds and rind. Pour sherry over to soak. Spoon over the custard, and top with whipped cream. Garnish with cherries, strips of angelica, chopped nuts. Refrigerate several hours, or overnight. Makes 8 servings.

MARMALADE SOUFFLÉ

You mustn't lift the double-boiler
lid while this is cooking.

4 egg whites	¼ cup orange marmalade
¼ cup sugar	Brandy Sauce, page 292
3 tablespoons orange juice	Toasted almond slivers
1 tablespoon brandy	

Beat egg whites until stiff but not dry; gradually beat in sugar and continue beating until mixture stands in peaks when beater is lifted. Fold in orange juice, brandy, marmalade. Butter a 2-quart double boiler, including the cover; sprinkle generously with sugar. Pour in pudding; place over boiling water. Cover, and cook 50 to 60 minutes. Turn out on serving plate. Pour Sauce over; top with nuts. Serves 6.

MACAROON ANGEL PUDDING

Baked graham-cracker crumbs, coconut,
and nuts served with cream.

4 egg whites	1 teaspoon baking powder
¼ teaspoon salt	½ cup flaked coconut
1 cup sugar	½ cup chopped walnuts
1 teaspoon vanilla extract	Whipped cream
1 cup fine graham-cracker crumbs	

Beat egg whites with salt until frothy; gradually beat in the sugar, and continue beating until mixture holds a peak when beater is lifted. Add vanilla. Mix together graham-cracker crumbs, baking powder, coconut, and nuts; fold into egg-white mixture. Pile into well-buttered deep 9" piepan. Bake in moderate oven, 350°F., 30 minutes. Serve warm with cream. Serves 8.

BUTTER SAUCE

Mix together ½ cup butter, 1 cup sugar, and ½ cup cream. Cook until sugar is dissolved, stirring. Serves 6.

"An apple, a plum,
a pear, or a cherry
Any old thing
to make us all merry."
GOURMET'S ALMANAC

HOT BUTTER-CREAM SAUCE

1 tablespoon flour	⅓ cup cream
½ cup sugar	2 tablespoons
½ cup dark corn syrup	butter or margarine
	⅛ teaspoon salt

Mix flour and sugar. Add remaining ingredients, and bring mixture slowly to boiling point. Simmer about 5 minutes. Serve warm. Makes 8 servings.

RASPBERRY SAUCE

Crush 1 box (10 ounces) frozen raspberries, and add 1 teaspoon cornstarch. Cook over low heat, stirring, until sauce is slightly thickened. If desired, add a little sugar. Serves 8.

APRICOT-BRANDY SAUCE

Mix together 1½ cups apricot jam, ½ cup water, 3 tablespoons sugar; simmer 10 minutes; stir often. Add 2 tablespoons apricot brandy. Serves 10 to 12.

SHERRY CUSTARD SAUCE

3 egg yolks, slightly beaten	¼ teaspoon vanilla extract
2 tablespoons sugar	½ cup heavy cream, whipped
½ cup milk	1½ tablespoons sherry wine
Dash of salt	

In top part of double boiler over simmering water, cook, stirring, egg yolks, sugar, milk, and salt until mixture coats a spoon. Cool. Fold in vanilla, whipped cream, and sherry. Serves 6.

SHERRY-GINGER CREAM

Mix 1 cup cream, whipped, ¼ cup confectioners' sugar, 1 tablespoon sherry wine, and ¼ cup chopped preserved ginger. Makes 6 servings.

BRANDY SAUCE

4 egg yolks	2 tablespoons brandy
⅓ cup confectioners' sugar	¾ cup heavy cream, whipped
¼ cup orange juice	

Beat egg yolks and sugar until thick and lemon-colored. Fold in the orange juice, brandy, and cream. Serves 6.

BRANDY HARD SAUCE

Cream 1 cup sweet butter and 2 cups sifted confectioners' sugar; beat in teaspoon vanilla and ¼ cup brandy. Makes 2 cups. (For **Lighted Hard-sauce Stars:** Spread hard sauce in shallow pan. Chill. Cut with a 2″ star cutter. Place small birthday candle in center of each star. Place stars around pudding, and light when served.)

ORANGE SAUCE

1 cup sugar	½ cup orange juice
5 tablespoons flour	3 egg yolks
⅛ teaspoon salt	1 teaspoon butter
Grated rind of 1 orange	1 cup heavy cream, whipped
Juice ½ lemon	

In a heavy saucepan mix together sugar, flour, and salt. Add orange rind, fruit juices, and egg yolks. Cook over low heat, stirring, until thickened and smooth; add butter and cool; fold in whipped cream. Makes 8 servings.

SHERRY SAUCE

2 egg yolks	2 tablespoons sherry wine
⅛ teaspoon salt	1 cup heavy cream, whipped
1 cup confectioners' sugar	

Beat egg yolks and salt until thick; gradually beat in sugar and sherry. At serving time, fold in whipped cream. Makes 6 to 8 servings.

LEMON SAUCE

In saucepan mix ½ cup sugar, ⅛ teaspoon salt, 2 tablespoons cornstarch. Gradually stir in 1 cup boiling water. Cook, stirring, until thickened. Remove from heat; stir in 2 tablespoons butter, juice 1 lemon, and 1 teaspoon grated rind. Serve hot. Makes about 1¾ cups.

CANDY

In the days when transportation was more difficult and cash not so ready, making candy at home was a regular custom. The taffy-pull (with little sister getting it in her hair), making taffy apples, creamy fudge, and snow-white divinity meant fun for the whole family. At holiday time, candy making was as important as baking, and it was the pleasant tradition to give gaily decorated boxes of luscious homemade sweets to friends and neighbors along with Christmas cookies. So here is a good old American custom well worth reviving. The next rainy day, when the cry goes up, "What shall I do?" try a candy-making spree. See what a pleasure it is to produce do-it-yourself caramels, fondants, old-fashioned fudge, and even elegant opera creams. When you make candy, remember that timing and temperature are very important. And do use the best ingredients. There is no substitute for good butter (sweet, not salted), rich cream, corn syrup, honey, and fine nuts.

Fondant-dipped Almonds: Tint Fondant with pink and green food coloring, and flavor, if desired. Melt each color in top part of double boiler over hot water. Dip rounded end of toasted almonds in fondant; put on waxed paper, and let stand until firm.

UNCOOKED FONDANT

Smooth and glossy, with fine flavor.

⅓ cup soft butter or margarine	1 teaspoon vanilla extract
⅓ cup light corn syrup	4½ cups (1 pound) sifted confectioners' sugar
½ teaspoon salt	

Blend all ingredients except sugar; mix in sugar; knead until blended. Makes about 1⅓ pounds.

Almond Diamonds: Substitute almond extract for the vanilla in Uncooked Fondant recipe. Add ½ cup chopped blanched and toasted almonds. Roll to ½" thickness. Cut in diamonds.

COOKED FONDANT

You can shape it into balls, or use it as a dip or stuffing.

3 cups sugar	⅓ cup light corn syrup
1⅓ cups water	
¼ teaspoon salt	1 teaspoon vanilla

Mix first 4 ingredients in large saucepan. Bring to boil, stirring. Cover; boil 3 minutes. Remove cover, and cook until a small amount of mixture forms a soft ball when dropped in cold water (238°F.). Wash down sides of pan several times with a pastry brush dipped in cold water, using up and down motion. Pour out on ungreased platter. Cool to lukewarm (110°F.). Add vanilla, and beat until mixture turns cloudy. Gather into a ball, and knead with lightly buttered hands until smooth and creamy. Put in bowl; cover with damp cloth, and store in cool place until needed. Makes about 2¼ pounds.

Fondant-stuffed Dates: Color Fondant, if desired. Shape in small rolls, and fill pitted dates.

CHOCOLATE FUDGE

An old-fashioned fudge with a slightly grainy texture.

Melt 2½ squares unsweetened chocolate in saucepan. Add 2½ cups sugar, ¼ teaspoon salt, and 1 cup evaporated milk. Cook, stirring, until sugar is dissolved. Continue cooking until a small amount of mixture forms a soft ball when dropped in cold water (234°F.). Remove from heat, and let stand until lukewarm (110°F.). Add 2 tablespoons butter and 1 tablespoon vanilla. Beat until thick and mixture loses its gloss. Turn out on waxed paper, and let stand until lukewarm. Knead in ¼ cup soft butter. Press into buttered 8"x 8"x 2" pan, and when firm, cut in squares. Makes 1¾ pounds.

KNEADED CHOCOLATE FUDGE

It has a creamy texture and a mild chocolate flavor.

2 tablespoons butter	⅛ teaspoon salt
2 squares unsweetened chocolate	1 teaspoon vinegar
	1 teaspoon vanilla extract
1 cup milk	½ cup chopped nuts
3 cups sugar	
¼ cup honey	

Melt butter and chocolate in milk in saucepan. Beat to blend. Add sugar, honey, and salt. Bring to boil; cover, and boil 2 minutes. Uncover, and cook, without stirring, until a small amount of the mixture dropped in cold water forms a soft ball (238°F.). Remove from heat, and add vinegar. Let stand until lukewarm. Then add vanilla, and beat until thick and mixture loses its gloss. Add nuts, and turn out on buttered plate. Let stand until lukewarm. Knead 4 or 5 minutes. Shape into 2 rolls about 2" in diameter. Wrap in waxed paper, and store in cool place until ready to serve. Cut in slices. Makes 1½ pounds.

CHOCOLATE CREAM-CHEESE FUDGE

It has chopped nuts in it.

Beat 1 package (3 ounces) cream cheese and 1 teaspoon heavy cream until smooth. Gradually beat in 2 cups confectioners' sugar. Add 2 squares unsweetened chocolate, melted; blend. Stir in ½ teaspoon vanilla, dash salt, and 1 cup chopped nuts. Press into buttered 8"x 4"x 2" pan, and chill until firm. Cut in squares. Makes 1 pound.

PEANUT-BUTTER FUDGE

There's no cooking involved at all.

Mix well: ¾ cup peanut butter, ½ cup soft butter or margarine, ½ cup light corn syrup, 1 teaspoon vanilla, and ½ teaspoon salt. Gradually stir in 4 cups sifted confectioners' sugar. Knead until smooth. Gradually add ¾ cup chopped peanuts or other nuts. Pack into an 8"x 8"x 2" pan. When firm, cut in squares. Makes about 2 pounds.

WALNUT CREAMS

You can flavor the pink ones peppermint, the green wintergreen.

Mix well ⅔ cup sweetened condensed milk, 4½ cups sifted confectioners' sugar, 1 teaspoon vanilla, ⅛ teaspoon salt. Knead until smooth. Divide; color half pink and half green. Shape in ¾" balls, and press a piece of walnut on each. Let stand until firm. Makes 24.

OPERA CREAMS

You can make these in patties, or in one block, then cut it in squares.

2 cups sugar	⅛ teaspoon salt
2 tablespoons light corn syrup	1 teaspoon vanilla
1 cup light cream	½ cup broken nuts

Mix all ingredients, except last 2, in saucepan. Bring to boil, and cook, without stirring, until a small amount of mixture dropped in cold water forms a soft ball (236°F.). Remove from heat, and let stand until lukewarm (110°F.). Add vanilla and nuts; beat until thick and mixture loses its gloss. Drop by dessert-spoonfuls onto waxed paper, and let stand until firm. Makes about 20.

FRENCH CHOCOLATE BALLS

You roll them in tiny candies, sesame seed, or chopped nuts.

Melt 1 package (8 ounces) of semi-sweet chocolate in top of small double boiler over hot water. Add 2 teaspoons boiling water, and mix well. Shape in ¾" balls, and roll in tiny multicolored candies, sesame seed, or chopped nuts. Store airtight in cool place. Makes 24.

OLD-TIME PENUCHE

It has a rich brown-sugar flavor.

Mix 2 pounds (4½ cups, packed) light-brown sugar, 1 cup evaporated milk, ¼ pound butter, and ¼ teaspoon salt. Cook, stirring, until sugar is dissolved. Continue cooking until a small amount of mixture forms a soft ball in cold water (238°F.). Remove from heat; when lukewarm (110°F.), add 1 teaspoon vanilla and 2 cups chopped walnuts. Beat until thick. Pour into buttered 9"x 9"x 2" pan; when firm, cut in squares. Makes 3 pounds.

WALNUT PENUCHE DROPS

They take half an hour of stirring.

1 cup light-brown sugar, packed	½ cup light cream
	1 tablespoon butter
½ cup granulated sugar	1 teaspoon vanilla extract
¼ cup light corn syrup	1½ cups coarsely chopped walnuts

Mix first 4 ingredients in saucepan. Cook, stirring, until a small amount of mixture forms a soft ball when dropped in cold water (238°F.). (This takes 25 to 30 minutes.) Remove from heat; add butter and vanilla. Beat until blended; add walnuts, and stir until coated. Drop quickly by dessert-spoonfuls onto waxed paper. Makes about 30 pieces.

Store different kinds of candies separately. Brittles soften if stored with creamy candies. Airtight storage in a cool place is best. All the candies given here freeze well except those that require fresh fruits.

PEANUT BRITTLE

A crisp, yet tender brittle.

Cook ½ cup dark corn syrup, ¼ cup each molasses and sugar, and 2 tablespoons butter until blended. Stir in 1 cup salted peanuts, and boil until a small amount of mixture separates into hard threads in cold water (280°F.). Stir in ⅛ teaspoon soda, and pour into a buttered shallow pan. When firm, break in irregular pieces. Makes about 9 ounces peanut brittle.

MARSHMALLOWS

You can roll them in colored sugar instead of cornstarch and sugar.

Soften 1 envelope unflavored gelatin in ⅓ cup cold water, and dissolve over hot water or low heat. Add ½ cup sugar, and stir until dissolved. Put in large mixer bowl with ⅔ cup light corn syrup and ½ teaspoon vanilla. Beat at high speed 15 minutes, or until mixture is very thick and of marshmallow consistency. Cover bottom of 9"x 9"x 2" pan with equal parts sugar and cornstarch. Pour in mixture, and smooth top. Let stand in cool place 1 hour, or until set. Loosen from pan, and turn out on board sprinkled with mixture of equal parts cornstarch and sugar. Cut in squares with knife wet with cold water. Roll in cornstarch and sugar. Makes 1 pound.

Coconut Marshmallows: In above recipe, do not cover pan with cornstarch-sugar mixture. Instead, butter pan, and sprinkle with part of 2 cups flaked coconut, toasted. Pour in mixture; sprinkle with toasted coconut. When firm, cut, and roll in remaining coconut.

Watch candy carefully, especially during last few minutes of cooking, because temperature rises quickly at end.

NUT BRITTLE

This is a tender brittle which even children can make.

Put 2 cups of nuts, such as walnuts or almonds, close together in buttered shallow pan. Heat 2 cups sugar in skillet, stirring constantly until a golden syrup is formed. Remove from heat, and quickly stir in ¼ teaspoon each salt and soda, and 1 teaspoon vanilla. Pour over nuts in pan. When cold, break in irregular pieces. Makes about 1½ pounds nut brittle.

PASTEL POPCORN BALLS

For a children's party, tint the syrup to match the color scheme.

Heat ¼ cup vegetable oil in 4-quart kettle 3 minutes. Add ½ cup popcorn. Cover loosely. Shake frequently over medium heat until popping stops. Mix ½ cup light corn syrup, ½ cup sugar, and ½ teaspoon salt. Add to corn, and stir over medium heat 3 to 5 minutes, or until corn is completely coated. Butter hands, and shape mixture in balls about 1½" in diameter. Wrap in transparent saran. Makes 16.

COCONUT-DATE SLICES

The rolls, stored unsliced in a cool place, keep well.

2 cups sugar	2 tablespoons butter
1 tablespoon light corn syrup	1 cup chopped nuts
¾ cup evaporated milk	½ teaspoon vanilla extract
1 package (6¾ ounces) pitted dates	⅛ teaspoon salt
	1½ cups flaked coconut, toasted

Mix first 3 ingredients in saucepan. Cook, stirring, until a small amount of mixture forms a soft ball when dropped in cold water (232°F.). Add dates; cook, stirring, until mixture returns to 232°F. Remove from heat, and cool to lukewarm (110°F.). Add remaining ingredients, except coconut, and beat until thick. Shape in 2 or 3 rolls 1½" in diameter. Roll in coconut. When firm, cut in ½" slices. Makes about 7 dozen.

APRICOT-COCONUT BALLS

*They have a pleasingly tart flavor
and keep well, too.*

Blend 2 tablespoons soft butter and
½ cup light corn syrup. Stir in 1 tablespoon water, ½ teaspoon vanilla, and
⅔ cup nonfat milk powder. Mix 2 cups
finely chopped dried apricots and 2
cups flaked coconut. Add to first mixture, and knead until blended. Shape
in ¾" balls. Roll in confectioners'
sugar. Makes 42.

COCONUT DREAM ROLL

*You add nuts, cherries, and
marshmallows to coconut fudge.*

Prepare 1 box coconut-fudge mix with
3½ tablespoons water as directed on
the label. Pour out on waxed paper;
let stand until lukewarm. Butter hands;
mix in ½ cup chopped nuts, ¼ cup
chopped candied cherries, and 12
quartered marshmallows or ¾ cup
miniatures. Form into a roll about 12"
long. When firm, slice diagonally. Makes
about 1¼ pounds.

VANILLA CARAMELS

They take time but are worth it.

2 cups sugar	⅓ cup butter
2 cups warm	or margarine
light cream	1 teaspoon vanilla
1 cup corn syrup	extract
½ teaspoon salt	½ cup broken nuts

Mix sugar, 1 cup of the cream, corn
syrup, and salt in large saucepan. Cook,
stirring, about 10 minutes. Add remaining cream very slowly so that mixture does not stop boiling. Cook 5
minutes longer. Stir in butter, 1 teaspoon at a time. Cook slowly, stirring,
until a small amount of mixture forms
a firm ball when dropped in cold water (248°F.). Remove from heat; add
vanilla and nuts; mix gently. Pour into
buttered 8"x 8"x 2" pan, and cool. Turn
out on board, mark off in ¾" squares;
cut with sharp knife. Wrap in waxed
paper. Makes 2 pounds of caramels.

Chocolate Caramels: In above recipe,
add 3 or 4 squares unsweetened chocolate before cooking.

*Allow plenty of time when
making most candies. Many,
such as caramels, take long
period of cooking and stirring.*

BRAZIL-NUT BARK

*You just stir nuts and
raisins into melted chocolate.*

Melt 2 cups (12-ounce package) semisweet chocolate pieces and 1 tablespoon butter over hot water. Remove
from heat, and stir in 1 cup chopped
Brazil nuts, and ½ cup seedless raisins. Spread on cookie sheet lined
with waxed paper. Chill until firm.
Break into pieces. Store in refrigerator.
Makes about 1 pound.

DATE-NUT LOGS

*They look difficult to make, but
you don't even have to cook them.*

1 tablespoon soft butter	¼ teaspoon salt
¼ cup corn syrup	2 cups sifted con-fectioners' sugar
½ teaspoon vanilla extract	1 cup finely cut dates
3 tablespoons nonfat dry milk powder	1 cup chopped nuts

Blend first 3 ingredients. Add nonfat
dry milk, salt, sugar, and dates. Mix
well, .and shape in small rolls. Dip
each roll in nuts. (If nuts don't stick,
moisten rolls with corn syrup.) Makes
about 1¼ pounds.

BUTTERED HONEY NUTS

You can use any unsalted nuts.

Spread 6 ounces shelled, unsalted nuts
on a cookie sheet. Bake in slow oven,
300°F., 15 minutes. Mix 1 tablespoon
each butter and honey; pour over nuts.
Stir until nuts are completely coated.
Store in airtight container. Makes about
1⅓ cups buttered nuts.

DIVINITY

*The two-temperature method reduces
the amount of beating needed.*

½ cup light
  corn syrup
2½ cups sugar
¼ teaspoon salt
½ cup water
	2 egg whites
	1 teaspoon vanilla
	  extract
	1 cup coarsely
	  chopped nuts

In saucepan mix corn syrup, sugar, salt, and water. Cook, stirring, until sugar is dissolved. Continue cooking, without stirring, until a small amount of mixture forms a firm ball when dropped in cold water (248°F.). Beat egg whites until stiff, but not dry. Pour about half the syrup slowly over whites, beating constantly. Cook remainder until a small amount forms hard threads in cold water (272°F.). Add slowly to first mixture, and beat until mixture holds its shape. Add vanilla and nuts; drop by dessert-spoonfuls onto waxed paper; or spread in buttered 9"x 9"x 2" pan, and when firm, cut in squares. Makes about 1½ pounds.

Chocolate Divinity: Follow Divinity recipe, using 1 cup (6-ounce package) semisweet chocolate pieces and 1 cup walnut or pecan halves. Beat until mixture begins to hold its shape; then add vanilla, chocolate, and nuts. Beat until well blended.

Holiday Divinity: Follow Divinity recipe, adding ¼ cup each chopped candied cherries and pineapple with the nuts.

Ginger Divinity: Follow Divinity recipe, using 6 tablespoons water and 2 tablespoons preserved-ginger syrup for the liquid. Add ½ cup finely diced ginger with the chopped nuts.

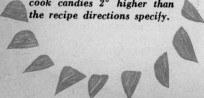

In humid or rainy weather, cook candies 2° higher than the recipe directions specify.

FRESH-COCONUT PATTIES

*A fondantlike mixture,
crunchy with coconut.*

2 cups sugar
1 cup coconut
  milk and water
½ teaspoon
  vanilla extract
	Green and red
	  food coloring
	1 cup grated
	  fresh coconut
	Candied cherries

Mix sugar and coconut milk and water in saucepan. Bring to boil, and cook until a small amount of mixture forms a soft ball when dropped in cold water (240°F.). Pour onto a wet platter, and let stand until lukewarm. Add vanilla, and beat until thick and creamy. Knead until smooth. Divide, and add a few drops of green coloring to half, and red coloring to other half. Sprinkle coconut on a cookie sheet. Dry in slow oven, 250°F., about 15 minutes. Work half of coconut into each mixture. Heat each mixture over boiling water until softened; drop from teaspoon on waxed paper, and flatten slightly. Put a bit of cherry in the center of each. Let harden. Makes 20.

CANDIED GRAPEFRUIT PEEL

*An old-fashioned candy,
inexpensive and a good keeper.*

Peels of 2 large
  or 3 medium
  grapefruit
	Water
	3 cups sugar
	Food coloring

Cover peel with cold water. Bring to boil, and cook until tender, pouring off water and adding fresh cold water several times. Drain. With spoon, remove white inner portion of peel. With knife or tiny star cookie cutter, cut a few stars from peel, if desired. With scissors or sharp knife, cut rest of peel in thin strips. Make syrup by boiling 2 cups sugar with 1 cup water. Add a little red or green food coloring. (A drop or two of yellow coloring with red improves the finished color.) Add peel; cook over low heat until peel has a clear, candied appearance. Remove peel, 2 or 3 pieces at a time, allowing excess syrup to drain back into saucepan. Roll strips separately into remaining 1 cup sugar until well coated. Cool on rack. Store in tightly covered container in cool, dry place. Keeps at least a month. Makes about 1 pound.

COCONUT BURRS

You should use soft, fresh marshmallows to make these.

Melt 1 cup (6 ounces) semisweet chocolate pieces over hot water, and stir until smooth. Cool slightly. Dip 16 marshmallows in chocolate; then roll in toasted flaked coconut.

RAISIN-PEANUT CLUSTERS

Children of every age love these.

Melt 1 cup (6-ounce package) semisweet chocolate pieces in double boiler over hot water. Add 1 can (14 ounces) sweetened condensed milk and dash salt. Cook 10 minutes, or until thickened, stirring constantly. Add 1 cup each seedless raisins and shelled roasted peanuts. Drop from tablespoon onto waxed paper. Refrigerate until firm. Makes 20.

COCONUT POTATO DROPS

A modern version of an old favorite.

Using 2 tablespoons instant mashed potato, 6 tablespoons water, 2 tablespoons milk, and ⅛ teaspoon salt, prepare potato as directed on the package. Add 1 teaspoon butter and ½ teaspoon almond extract. Gradually beat in 1 pound confectioners' sugar, sifted. (Mixture will be thin at first, but thicken later.) Beat until mixture will hold its shape. Add a little more sugar, if necessary. Stir in 1 can flaked coconut, and drop by dessert-spoonfuls on waxed paper. Makes 1¾ pounds.

TWO-TONE TRUFFLES

One layer is smooth, the other crunchy with nuts.

1½ cups finely chopped filberts	2 tablespoons rum
1½ cups sifted confectioners' sugar	1½ cups semisweet chocolate pieces
1 egg white	¾ cup sweetened condensed milk
	1 tablespoon butter

Mix well: filberts, sugar, egg white, and rum. Spread in buttered, waxed-paper-lined 8"x 8"x 2" pan. Melt chocolate in top of double boiler over hot water. Stir in milk and butter; cook until thickened (about 5 minutes). Pour over nut mixture. When firm, cut in squares. Makes about 2 pounds.

CANDIED CRANBERRIES

Colorful and sparkling with sugar.

Wash 2 cups large, firm cranberries; drain well, and spread in bottom of buttered baking dish. Sprinkle with 1½ cups sugar, and cover tightly. Bake in 350°F. oven 1 hour. Stir once to distribute sugar. Let berries cool in the syrup. Lift out onto waxed paper. Sift a little sugar over berries, and let stand until all are dry and firm.

HONEYED ORANGE PEEL

Two flavors that blend deliciously.

Remove peel from 3 oranges. Cover peel with water, and add ½ teaspoon salt. Simmer ½ hour. Drain; cover again with water, and simmer until tender. Drain, and cut in strips. Bring ½ cup sugar, ½ cup honey, and ¼ cup water to boil. Add peel, and simmer until clear. Cool in syrup several hours. Reheat; then drain, and spread out on a sheet of waxed paper to dry.

BURNT ALMONDS

A store treat you can make yourself with just nuts, sugar, and water.

Combine 1 cup sugar and ⅓ cup water in skillet; bring to boil, and cook until mixture spins a thread. Add 6-ounce package almonds; cook 2 minutes, or until syrup begins to sugar. Remove from heat; stir until mixture is dry and sugary. Then, over low heat, cook until sugar is melted and browned, stirring. Remove from heat; stir until nuts are well coated with syrup. Pour onto a buttered platter; separate nuts quickly with 2 forks. Put on another buttered platter; let stand until cold.

Use a heavy saucepan for candies as some (made with milk or cream) burn easily.

INDEX

301

305

315

317